A Handbook of Gods and Goddesses of the Ancient Near East

Three Thousand Deities of Anatolia, Syria, Israel, Sumer, Babylonia, Assyria, and Elam

To W. W. Hallo.

Douglas R. Frayne

To the memory of my father, William Henry Stuckey.

Johanna H. Stuckey

A HANDBOOK OF GODS AND GODDESSES OF THE ANCIENT NEAR EAST

Three Thousand Deities of Anatolia, Syria, Israel, Sumer, Babylonia, Assyria, and Elam

Douglas R. Frayne and *Johanna H. Stuckey*

illustrations by *Stéphane Beaulieu*

EISENBRAUNS | University Park, Pennsylvania

Library of Congress Cataloging-in-Publication Data

Names: Frayne, Douglas, author. | Stuckey, Johanna H., author. | Beaulieu, Stéphane, illustrator.

Title: A handbook of gods and goddesses of the ancient Near East : three thousand deities of Anatolia, Syria, Israel, Sumer, Babylonia, Assyria, and Elam / Douglas R. Frayne and Johanna H. Stuckey ; illustrations by Stéphane Beaulieu.

Description: University Park, Pennsylvania : Eisenbrauns, [2021] | Includes bibliographical references and index.

Summary: "An alphabetical guide to the deities of ancient Eastern Mediterranean civilizations. Discusses each deity's symbolism and imagery its connection to myths, rituals, and festivals described in texts"—Provided by publisher.

Identifiers: LCCN 2020043969 | ISBN 9781575068374 (hardback) | ISBN 9781646021215 (paper)

Subjects: LCSH: Middle East—Religion—Dictionaries.

Classification: LCC BL1060 .F73 2021 | DDC 200.956—dc23

LC record available at https://lccn.loc.gov/2020043969

Printed in the United States of America
Published by The Pennsylvania State University Press,
University Park, PA 16802-1003

Eisenbrauns is an imprint of The Pennsylvania State University Press.

The Pennsylvania State University Press is a member of the Association of University Presses.

It is the policy of The Pennsylvania State University Press to use acid-free paper. Publications on uncoated stock satisfy the minimum requirements of American National Standard for Information Sciences—Permanence of Paper for Printed Library Material, ANSI Z39.48–1992.

TABLE OF CONTENTS

Acknowledgments

We would like to thank the Robarts Library of the University of Toronto and the Scott Library at York University. In addition, York University provided considerable funding for J. Stuckey's research. Shelley Rabinovitch also deserves thanks for having been there for support at the start of the project, and Oana Petrica, Ifrah Ali, and Jenna Danchuk, J. Stuckey's graduate assistants, did sterling work, as did Bill McGrath, D. Frayne's student. There is no way to thank Stéphane Beaulieu for enriching this work with his wonderful drawings; they are a *sine qua non*.

Douglas R. Frayne,
Sessional Lecturer,
Retired Associate Professor,
University of Toronto

Johanna H. Stuckey,
University Professor Emerita,
York University

PREFACE

THE FERTILE CRESCENT, to use the felicitous term coined by Breasted, the zone of relatively fertile, well-watered land that stretched from ancient Susa in the east to Jerusalem in the west, in addition to being the cradle of civilization, was the birth place of the major monotheistic religions of the modern world. As such, its religious traditions are, in an indirect way, of great interest to millions of people today. It is clear that, in a broader view, they were influenced by various earlier polytheistic religions whose homes stretched across the great arc from the Zagros Mountains in Iran in the east to the Mediterranean Sea in the west. This work presents part of that ancient heritage, the deities, both great and small, who were the focus of religious life for four millennia.

Our basic source materials are the ancient texts themselves, written in both cuneiform and alphabetic scripts during the long period beginning with the tablets found in Uruk level IV, ca. 3300–3000 BCE, when divine names first appear in written sources, down to the first century BCE. Since the iconography of deities can be a valuable tool for the better understanding of religion, we have used it as much as possible. We decided to make the terminus of our investigations the late Hellenistic period, the time before the rise of Christianity. In addition to deities named in ritual, literary, and economic texts, we have included many whose names occur only in god lists or in personal names, though this inclusion is far from being exhaustive. This subset has been included to convey a sense of the vastness of deities occurring in the ancient Near East.

This volume is the collaboration of two scholars, an Assyriologist (D. Frayne), and a professor of Women's Studies and Religious Studies, now retired (J. Stuckey). Our original project was to update the Ancient Near Eastern section of an extremely out-of-date dictionary of world religions for a friend's publication. The project was subsequently abandoned because of illness, and we found ourselves with an almost complete manuscript representing some considerable years of work. We were fortunate to have the assistance of Stéphane Beaulieu, an exceptional Canadian artist and ancient Near Eastern scholar, for the images that accompany many of the entries.

THE MESOPOTAMIAN DEITIES

Ancient Mesopotamian science was dominated by the phenomenon of lists, and the Babylonians and Sumerians delighted in compiling seemingly endless catalogues of items of both their material and spiritual worlds. God lists are preserved from ancient Mesopotamia from as early as the Early Dynastic Period, from the sites of Fāra (ca. 2600 BCE) and Abū Ṣalābīkh (ca. 2500 BCE). The framework of the present book relies, to a large degree, on the skeleton provided by the great god list An : *Anum*, known for the most part from tablets from Aššur-banipal's library at Nineveh and its Old Babylonian forerunners. It is available in transliteration in the 1958 Yale dissertation of Richard Litke, which, as a result of the support of William W. Hallo, was published in 1998. Invaluable information on the deities, in addition to that provided in the popular works of Black and Green (2003) and Leick (1998), was found in the various entries of the *Reallexikon der Assyriologie* compiled in recent years in large (but not exclusive) part by W.G. Lambert, M. Krebernik, and A. Cavigneaux. In addition, T. Richter's book on the Mesopotamian pantheon (2004) was indispensable.

THE LEVANTINE DEITIES

While god lists or offering lists are known for other ancient Near Eastern cultures such as at Ugarit, none of these cultural zones has provided us with a god list to match the grand scope of An : *Anum*. The compiling of these other gods and goddesses was a challenging task undertaken by J. Stuckey on the basis of modern dictionaries or specialized regional scholarly studies. Their titles are cited in our bibliography and need not be given here.

THE ELAMITE DEITIES

The framework for the entries on the Elamite pantheon was provided by the index of F. W. König's book on Elamite royal inscriptions (1977) and F. Vallat's article on Elamite religion in the *Encyclopaedia Iranica* VIII (1998).

THE HITTITE AND HURRIAN DEITIES

Deities from the Hittite and Hurrian realms were mainly gathered from the major scholarly works on this area (van Gessel 1998; Haas 1995; Popko 1994).

The names of the deities listed in this work were written using either cuneiform or an alphabetic script. Cuneiform was used to write Sumerian, Akkadian (which includes Babylonian and Assyrian), Eblaic, Amorite, Hurrian, Hittite, Elamite, and sometimes Ugaritic god names. Alphabetic scripts were used to write god names in Ugaritic, Hebrew, and Aramaic. In addition, there are transcriptions of divine names in Greek and Latin sources.

Throughout our work we have adhered to a very broad transcription system for our main entries, one that attempts to convey the approximate sound of the deity's name, rather than one that reflects the writing system. This system has its drawbacks for Sumerian entries. In the Sumerian cuneiform script multiple signs can convey the same sound, yet these homonymous signs have different meanings and so the meaning of the deity's name will differ (and, in fact, may indicate separate deities), depending on which of the homonymous signs is used to write the name. On the other hand, there are occasions when the homonymous signs do not alter the meaning and thus our transcription system enables one unified entry, rather than splitting it into two because of the signs used. Therefore, aware of these pros and cons, we have listed the Sumerian entries according to our general method of transcription, based on sound. However, within the entry, when significant, we have indicated the actual cuneiform signs used to write the name, since this provides the meaning of the name and is vital for differentiating two or more distinct deities whose names may sound the same, but who can be differentiated based on the choice of signs used.

For those unfamiliar with the accepted practices in transliterating cuneiform signs, as we have done for many entries of Sumerian god names, we offer this brief guide. If there are, e.g., several different signs that can convey the sound /ka/, then (based upon sign-numbers established by modern scholars) the first sign is transcribed ka, the second ká, the third kà, the fourth ka_4, the fifth ka_5, and so on. It should be noted that, partly as a result of the evolution of cuneiform writing, one sign may have multiple sounds or values. E.g., the sign ka can represent the sounds /ka/, /gu/, /dug/, /kiri/, /inim/, /zu/, each of which conveys a different meaning. So how one chooses to transcribe a sign reflects a deliberate decision as to the intended meaning of the deity's name. When we are unsure as to which sound is conveyed by a particular sign, we write the sign in capital letters (caps) using any one of its known values, though often the value we think most likely.

Sometimes the ancient scribes have assisted us in how to pronounce a god's name; they have added a gloss. A gloss is one or more cuneiform signs, usually whose reading is obvious, that convey the same sound as the sign or signs in the god's name. In god lists, a gloss that has been added during the transmission or copying of the god list is often raised higher on the line, usually written in a smaller size. We have indicated this type of gloss as a superscript. Other times glosses were added early on in the writing of a deity's name, possibly before the name ever was copied as part of a god list. In these cases the gloss sign appears as part of the name, neither raised higher nor smaller in size than the other cuneiform signs in the deity's name. We have indicated this type of gloss as a superscript within brackets { }.

A thornier issue arises with the transliteration of divine names rendered in alphabetic scripts. While the time frame of Akkadian texts is long, the script gives the false impression of relatively little change, due to the conservatism of the ancient scribes, who preserved "traditional" writings even though the sounds of words, particularly the vowels and case endings, had clearly changed. The documents written in alphabetic scripts come from a much more heterogeneous body of texts, and an attempt to use a unified transliteration system for the various sources proved to be impracticable. Although detailed systems for the transliteration of ancient Ugaritic (minus the unwritten vowels), Biblical Hebrew, and Greek do exist of course, it was decided, after considerable deliberation, not to include these detailed transliterations in our work, a decision based on an appeal to accessibility for the non-specialist reader. Many divine names from the Bible and Greek sources have entered the parlance of educated laypeople: it was decided to render them in forms that might already be known to that audience. For example, the well-known Canaanite goddess Asherah appears with the spelling "sh" for the /sh/ sound, which is rendered in Akkadian names as š (shin). So too, in the main entries we provide alternative systems to a convey the sound /th/, as in the entry: ʻAṯtar, ʻAthtar. In a concession to specificity, it was decided to render the ancient guttural middle consonant found in the name of the Canaanite god Baʻal as *ayin*. It was thought that the sometimes attested form Baal might be misconstrued as representing a long ā vowel.

Because the pantheons we have focused on were polytheistic, it is often very difficult to determine the precise nature of individual deities. This is particularly true of a diachronic study such as this volume, which covers an enormous time span. During the passage of time, deities became identified with one another or, indeed, were assimilated by other deities. In the handbook we have tried to distinguish the various gods and goddesses one from the other as much as is possible, given the sometimes contradictory evidence of the sources. In so doing, we hope that those who consult this book will find it useful, and we take full responsibility for errors that almost inevitably find their way into the best-checked books. Due to the particular evolution of this manuscript, we have tried to reach a happy medium in regard to the needs of two distinct audiences. We have attempted to provide general readers with the information useful for understanding the nature and roles of the many gods of the ancient Near Eastern world. At the same time, we have tried to provide the detail sought by scholars who are steeped in the languages and cultures of the ancient Near East.

Since our inspiration came from ancient texts and images, we follow ancient scribes in giving credit where credit is due.

Praise be to Nisaba!

Douglas Frayne suddenly passed away in December 2017. Few knew that he had been dealing with a debilitating illness, including his slowly increasing blindness, which he bore with amazing courage. It was a cruel affliction for a cuneiform scholar, but he bravely kept on. At the time of his passing, Doug had been reviewing the latest version of the manuscript. Unfortunately, his notes have not been found and so his final thoughts and changes could not be incorporated. Douglas Frayne was a man who loved his work and, for him, it was the focus of his life. Doug will be greatly missed by his fellow scholars, students, and friends.

Abbreviations

Abbreviations of Assyriological publications are according to *The Assyrian Dictionary of the Oriental Institute of the University of Chicago*, vol. 20, U and W, pp. vii–xxix and *The Sumerian Dictionary of the University Museum of the University of Pennsylvania*, vol. 2 B, pp vii–xxv. In addition, almost all the abbreviations used here can be found online at cdli.ox.ac.uk>wiki>abbreviations.

ABD David N. Freedman, ed. *The Anchor Bible Dictionary*. Six volumes. New York: Doubleday, 1992–

Akk. Akkadian

ANEP James B. Pritchard, ed. *The Ancient Near East in Pictures Relating to the Old Testament*. Princeton, N.J.: Princeton University Press, 1969

ANET James B. Pritchard, ed. *Ancient Near Eastern Texts Relating to the Old Testament*. Third Edition with Supplement. Princeton, N.J.: Princeton University Press, 1969

AOAT Alter Orient und Altes Testament

BDTNS Database of Neo-Sumerian Texts. Edited by M. Molina

CAD Martha T. Roth et al. eds. *The Assyrian Dictionary of the Oriental Institute of the University of Chicago*. Twenty volumes. Chicago: The Oriental Institute, 1956–

CDA Jeremy Black, Andrew George, and Nicholas Postgate. *A Concise Dictionary of Akkadian*. Wiesbaden, Germany: Harrassowitz, 2000.

CDLI Cuneiform Digital Library Initiative. Edited by R. Englund

CT Cuneiform Texts from Babylonian Tablets in the British Museum

CUSAS Cornell University Studies in Assyriology and Sumerology. Edited by D. I. Owen

DCPP Edward Lipiński, ed. *Dictionnaire de la civilisation phénicienne et punique*. Turnhout, Belgium: Brepols, 1992

DDDB van der Toorn, Karel, Bob Becking, and Pieter W. van der Horst, eds. *Dictionary of Deities and Demons in the Bible*: Second Extensively Revised Edition. Leiden, Netherlands: Brill / Grand Rapids, Mich.: Eerdmans, 1999

E Elamite

ETCSL The Electronic Text Corpus of Sumerian Literature. Edited by J. Black et al.

H Hittite, also including Hurrian, Luvian, Palaic

IDB G. A. Buttrick et al. *The Interpreter's Dictionary of the Bible: An Illustrated Encyclopedia*. Four volumes and supplementary volume (1992). Nashville, Tenn.: Abingdon, 1991

L Levantine

LAS Jeremy Black, Graham Cunningham, Eleanor Robson, and Gábor Zólyomi, eds./trans. *The Literature of Ancient Sumer*. Oxford: Oxford University Press, 2004

M Mesopotamian

MDP Mémoires de la Délégation en Perse

PSD Åke W. Sjöberg, ed. *The Sumerian Dictionary of the University Museum of the University of Pennsylvania*. Two volumes. Philadelphia: The University Museum, 1992–

PSMFA Pushkin State Museum of Fine Arts tablet number.

RlA E. Ebeling et al., eds. *Reallexikon der Assyriologie*. Berlin: de Gruyter, 1920–

Studies Birot
J.-M. Durand and J.-R. Kupper, eds. *Miscellanea Babylonica: Mélanges offerts à Maurice Birot*. Paris: Editions Recherche sur les Civilizations. 1985.

Studies Levine
R. Chazan et al., eds., *Ki Baruch Hu. Ancient Near Eastern, Biblical, and Judaic Studies in Honor of Baruch A. Levine*. Winona Lake, Ind.: Eisenbrauns, 1999

Sum. Sumerian

— A —

A-al-du (M) Deity attested at third-millennium Ebla. Written ^{d}a/'a$_5$-al$_6$-du. (Fronzaroli 1993: 131)

A-alim-maḫ (M) Deity occurs once in Ur III texts from Umma as the recipient of garments. Name may mean "Strength of a Great Bison." See Alim-maḫ. (Nisaba 24, 34: o ii 30)

A-an-da (M) Deified object(?) associated with Nin-gal at Ur III Ur. Written Á-an-da (*PSD* A/2 41)

Aari (H) Deity associated with the storm god of Šapinuwa. (Giorgieri et al. 2013)

Aasith (L) See ʻAnat(u); Aštarte

Aba (M) Deity associated with leather-workers. (Litke 1998: 110)

Ababšša (M) (1) One of two divine gate-keepers of the E-sag-ila temple at Babylon; the other was Anta-durunu. (2) A name of the goddess Nin-imma, advisor to Enlil at Nippur, personal secretary of the Ekur temple, and wet-nurse of the moon god Nanna/Sîn. Written A-ba$_4$-ba$_4$. (Litke 1998: 57; George 1993: 77 no. 188; Sallaberger 1993: I, 104; Jacobsen 1976: 54)

Ababa-siga (M) Goddess in the circle of the goddess Nin-imma, but may simply have been a form of Ababa, who was identified as Nin-imma (see above). Written A-ba$_4$-ba$_4$-sig$_5$-ga. (Litke 1998: 57)

Abaddon (L) A destructive demon of the netherworld mentioned as a creature in the Bible, in Revelation 9:11, where he is king of the netherworld. His Greek name is given there as Apollyon. In Hebrew, Abaddon means "place of destruction"; almost all instances of the word in the Hebrew Bible carry a meaning like "netherworld." However, in the Book of Job 28:22, the place Abaddon, in the company of Death, is personified as a speaking entity. The situation is similar in Proverbs 27:20. In some later Christian writings Abaddon is another name for Satan or the Devil. (Hutter, *DDDB*: 1; Brownrigg 1993: 1; Brown, Driver, and Briggs 1978: 2)

Abade, Apate (H) Hittite goddess, as well as an attribute of the Hittite goddess Lilluri, tutelary deity of the Hittite city of Mamuziya in Anatolia. Tiyari was her spouse. Probably the same as Apantum. (van Gessel 1998: I, 41–43; Laroche 1976: 33–34)

Aba-Enlilgim (M) Deified standard of Enlil at Nippur attested in Ur III and Old Babylonian texts. Means "Who Is Like Enlil?" (Richter 2004: 30, 48–49, 101; Sallaberger 1993: I, 99; Renger 1967: 162)

Aba-[gal] (M) Sumerian deity named in a probable An : *Anum* fragment that, according to Richter, Edzard thought was part of a tablet dealing with Ištar and her circle of deities. (Richter 2004: 310)

Abara (H) Hurrian epithet of the Hurrian goddess Ša(w)uš(k)a. Originally a local deity of the cult center Šamuḫa in eastern Anatolia. (van Gessel 1998: I, 38–39; Popko 1995: 114, 144; Haas 1994: 579; Ebeling, *RlA* I: 3)

Abara-laḫ (M) See Ebara-laḫ

Ab-ašarid (M). The deity whose name is written áb-[a]ašarid(IGI.[a].DU) is attested in an Early Dynastic god list. Means "Lead (or Foremost) Cow." (Mander 1986: 138)

Aba-šušu (M) See Kilili

Aba-zagmu-ki (M) Old Babylonian deity from the time of Rīm-Sîn for whom there was a *gudu*-priest. (Dalley 2005)

Ab(b)a (M) Deity attested as early as the Early Dynastic period. (Durand 2008: 268; Roberts 1972: 12)

Abba (M) Written Ab-ba_6 and Ab-ba. (1) Doorkeeper of the E-sag-ila in Babylon. (2) Deity of the local cult at Nippur; attested in a seal impression inscription as the father of Damu. (3) In a Neo-Assyrian god list identified with Ninurta. Means "Father" or "Elder." (Litke 1998: 99; Richter 2004: 197; King 1969: pl. 13)

Abbašušu (M) Written Ab-ba-$šu_2$-$šu_2$. See Kilili

Abba-u (M) See Ab-u

Abbūtānītu(m) (M) The goddess's name means "Intercessor." (Watanabe 1990: no. 94)

Ab-enun(n)a / Ab-agrun(n)a (M) Deity mentioned in a Nippur fragment. Means "Cow of the Sanctuary." (Richter 2004: 310)

Ab-etura (M) Deity mentioned in a late ritual for the *akītu* festival at Uruk. Means "Cow of the Cattle Pen." (Cohen 1993: 434)

Abgal-e (M) Deity whose name means "Sage of the House/Temple." Appears in an Early Dynastic god list. (Mander 1986: 37, 51)

Ab-ḫal (M) Sumerian god mentioned in two Ur III texts from Ur dating to the reign of Ibbi-Sîn of Ur. Perhaps the name means "(God of) the Open/Secret Window." (Richter 2004: 414)

Ab-ḫenun (M) Deity attested in a personal name at Ur III Girsu. Written AB-ḫe-nun. (MVN 17, 59: o i 19)

Abī-libluṭ (M) Akkadian god mentioned in a list of offerings to gods of the First Sealand Dynasty. Dalley suggests the name might refer to a deified ancestor. Means "May My Father Live." (Dalley 2009: 81–82)

Abirtu(m), Ebirtu(m), Ḫibirtu(m) (M) God from Mari. Note the goddess Bēlet-Ebirtu at Mari. (Cohen 2015: 320; Durand 2008: 238; Lambert 1985a: 530)

Ab-kar (M) Sumerian god listed in An : *Anum* as a name of Nanna/Sîn at Ur. Appears just before Ab-lulu. Written áb-kár with gloss ab-ka-rum, áb-kar, and áb-TIR. Explained in Anu ša amēli as "The Moon of the Sheepfold (*supūri*)." (Richter 2004: 451, 453; Litke 1998: 117, 231)

Ab-kuga (M) Deity identified with the goddess Nin-kar(r)ak in An : *Anum*. Means "Sacred Cow." (Richter 2004: 215–16; Litke 1998: 182)

AB-kug-maḫ, (M) Sumerian god of the local pantheon of Nippur. Occurs in Old Babylonian texts paired with Lugal-aba, the latter, according to Krebernik, corresponding to the later Lugal-aba "King of the Sea," a netherworld deity. (Richter 2004: 138–39; Krebernik, *RlA* VII: 109)

Ab-lulu (M) Deity identified with the moon god Nanna/Sîn, meaning "(He) who Makes the Cows Multiply." Explained in *Anu ša amēli* as "Moon of the Tax (*igisê*)." (Litke 1998: 117, 231)

Ab-munzer-kiaga (M) Child of Ga'u in An : *Anum*. Note SpTU 1, 126+: o ii 11 ^{d}Ab$_2$-^{ú}munzer-ki-ág$^{ab\ mu-un-zi}$ŠU$^{ir.mi}$. Means either "Cow who Loves the *mun-zer* Plant" or "Beloved Cow of the *munzer* Plant." (Richter 2004: 453; Litke 1998: 127; Civil 1987: 45–46)

Ab-narbu (M) Name of the mother of the moon god Nanna/Sîn. It means "(She) who Nourishes the Cows." The name is apparently a mix of Sumerian and Akkadian. (Litke 1998: 120)

AB-si (M) See EŠ-si

AB-si-sag (M) Sumerian deity attested in a personal name on an Early Dynastic tablet from Nippur. (A. Westenholz 1975b: 18)

Abta-gigi (M) See Kilili

Ab-u (M) Deity worshipped in Ur III times at the small town of Ku'ara, possibly modern Batha on the Euphrates, north of Eridu. One of eight Sumerian deities created by Nin-ḫursag to heal the god Enki. In the Sumerian myth "Enki and Nin-ḫursag," Enki was dying after eating eight different plants that were his own offspring by his daughter Uttu. At the end of the composition Nin-ḫursag declared Ab-u to be ruler of the plant life, a statement based on the meaning of the Sumerian word *u* "plant," "grass." A variant of Ab-u's name (Abba-u) appears in an Ur lament, where he is called son of the goddess Baba. (Sallaberger 1993: II, 134; Attinger 1984: 1–52; Kramer, *ANET*: 40–41; Kramer, *ANET*: 456)

Abublab (M) A god of the Gutians identified with Ninurta. (Litke 1998: 213)

Abūbu(m) (Akk.), **Amaru** (Sum.) The Great Flood personified as a cosmic monster with wings. (Black and Green 2003: 84; Foster 2001: 84–95; Tallqvist 1974: 258; Speiser, *ANET*: 93–97; Oppenheim, *ANET*: 313)

Abul-maḫ (M) Deity attested in an offering list of the Ninurta temple in Nippur. It may be the deified gate of the great courtyard to the south of the ziqqurat at Nippur. It finds a parallel in the Abul-maḫ at Ur in the Old Babylonian period. Means "Lofty Gate." (Richter 2004: 115)

Ab-numun-dudu (M) One of the eight children of Ga'u, who is identified with sheep and grazing animals. Written Áb-$^{ú.nu}$numun$^{mu\text{-}un}$-du$_8$-du$_8$. ^{ú}numun here seems to be a variant for ^{ú}númun "alfalfa-grass," thus "Who Piles Up(?) Alfalfa-grass (for) the Cows" or "The Cow that Piles up(?) Alfalfa-grass." (Litke 1998: 127)

Abzu (M) See Apsû(m)

Abzu-maḫ (M) Deity worshipped in Nippur in Old Babylonian times. Means "Exalted Abzu." (Renger 1967: 162)

Abzuta-e (M) Deity attested in an Early Dynastic god list from Abu Ṣalābīkh. Means "Who Comes Forth from the Abzu." (Mander 1986: 116)

Adabal (M) Deity in the pantheon at Ebla. Possibly a moon god. Spouse was Ba'lat-Adabal, a goddess attested at Ebla in the late third millennium BCE. Written A$_5$(NI)-da-ba-bal(KUL). (Schwemer 2001: 113; Fronzaroli 1997: 288–89; Pomponio and Xella 1997: 256–88; Krebernik, *RlA* IX: 304)

Adad, Addu, Ad(d)a (Akk.), **Iškur** (Sum.) (L, M) Storm and thunder god, and warrior deity. Son of Anu(m). Husband of Šala, who was originally a goddess of the Hurrians. His ministers were Šullat and Ḫaniš. Identified with the Sumerian storm god Iškur, who was the twin brother of Enki and brother of Utu/Šamaš. Depicted standing on a bull or a lion-dragon, holding thunderbolts or a lightening fork, his symbol, and brandishing a weapon.

Adad was responsible for the rain. One Assyrian king prayed to Adad to bring rain in season and water from the earth, so that there would be fertility in the land. Another Assyrian king wrote of descending on the enemy "like Adad when he makes a rainstorm pour down" (Oppenheim, *ANET*: 277). Among his epithets were "Lord of Abundance," "Irrigator," and "Canal Inspector of Heaven and Earth." In the "Epic of Gilgameš," Tablet XI, the Great Flood began when, at dawn, "a black cloud rose above the horizon. Inside it Adad was thundering, while the destroying gods Šullat and Ḫaniš went in front" (Foster 2001: 87). Adad played a prominent role as warrior in the epic of Zimrī-Līm, king of Mari. A number of Assyrian kings used Adad as part of their theophoric throne names: for instance, there were five named Šamšī-Adad and three Adad-nīrārī.

Stele of Adad from Arslan Tash, ancient Ḫadatu. Neo-Assyrian. Basalt. Height 1.36 m. Louvre Museum. After Black and Green 2003: 111.

Adad had many cult centers, including Kurba'il and Zappan (or Zabban), in both of which he was Bēlu(m), "master" or "lord," with the titles Bēl-Kurba'il and Bēl-Zappan respectively. He was worshipped at many other places, among them, Aššur, Babylon, Ebla, Mari, and Sippar. Mention of an annual festival of Adad at Sippar occurs in a letter to the mayor of Šaduppûm, who had promised "one shekel of silver" for the festival, but had not sent it. (Cohen 2015: 255).

In the Levant, especially Syria, his name was usually Had(d)ad. Adad was the chief deity of Aleppo in Syria, where a temple to the god has been excavated. He was often identified with Buriaš, a god of the Kassites. Adad was equated also to Teššub, the storm god of the Hurrians. Name borrowed from Mesopotamia by the Elamites. (Durand 2008: 204–8; Henkelman 2008: 519; Foster 2005: 636–39, 754; Younger 2009: 4; Black and Green 2003: 110–11; Schwemer 2001: 200–10; Leick 1999: 148–49, 181; Leick 1998: 1–2, 95–96; Cohen 1993: 31; George 1993: 66 no. 54, 80 no. 227, 131 no. 861; Michalowski 1988: 265–75; Hinz and Koch 1987: 26; Jacobsen 1976: 233; Speiser, *ANET*: 111; Reiner, *ANET*: 533, 538)

Adad-birqu (M) Form of Adad stressing his connection with lightning bolts. Means "Adad Lightning Bolt." Adad-berqu is attested in lists of gods in rituals associated with the Anu(m)-Adad temple at Aššur. Appears also in the divine address book of Aššur in connection with the Adad temple in Kurba'il. (Schwemer 2001: 60, 597, 602–3 and note 4868).

Adad-ḫalbaḫe (M) Akkadian deity at Nuzi, a form of the storm god Adad, perhaps originating in the cult of the storm god of Aleppo in Syria, in which case *ḫalbaḫe* might be a rendering of "Aleppo." (Schwemer 2001: 464–65)

Adad-nuḫše (M) Manifestation of Adad as the abundance that rain brings. Akkadian *nuḫšu* means "abundance." (Schwemer 2001: 89, 608–9)

A-da-e-ne (E) In a Neo-Assyrian god list identified with Ninurta of Elam. (King 1969: pl. 12)

Adakber (M) One of five gods of fishermen listed in An : *Anum*. Written KÍBIR with gloss a-da-ak-be-er. KÍBIR *kibirru* means "kindling wood," which has nothing to do with fishing. Thus the sign KÍBIR may have been used because of the similarity in sound to the god name and not because of the sign's meaning. (Litke 1998: 113)

Adam(m)a, Adamtera, Adam(m)a-teri, Adamtu(m) (H, M, L) Syrian deity usually treated as female. Wife of the warlike and protective Rešep(h). Well known at Ebla, where she was probably associated with the netherworld and with the storehouse and fertility. A festival in her name was listed in the calendar of Ebla. Associated with the city of Tunip, where the chief god was Rešep(h). Appears in the circle of Kubaba and at times is equated to her. Often forms a triad with Kubaba and Ḫasuntarḫi. Member of the pantheon of the Hurrians. Attested also at Emar and at Ugarit, where she is listed in the Hurrian pantheon and sometimes paired with the goddess Kubaba as Adam(m)a-wa-Kubaba. (Cohen 2015: 19; Lipiński 2009: 51–75; del Olmo Lete 1999: 86; van Koppen and van der Toorn, *DDDB*: 786; Leick 1998: 2; van Gessel 1998: I, 55–56; Pomponio and Xella 1997: 14; Haas 1994: 312, 406–7; Fleming 1992a: 75 and note 20; Laroche 1976: 35)

Adam-kug (M) Attendant of the birth/mother goddess Dingir-maḫ. Means "(God of?) the Sacred Habitation." (Litke 1998: 76)

Adana (M) Associated with the cult of the dead as celebrated in towns near Girsu. At Lagaš he received offerings at a festival devoted to the ancestors. (Selz 1995: 17; Cohen 1993: 55, 471)

Adarim (L) "Noble Ones," beings of more than normal strength or height. Used in the Hebrew Bible to refer to powerful people and kings (Psalms 136:18) and possibly to pagan gods. At Ugarit and elsewhere in the Levant, the term seems to refer to the deified royal ancestors, the Rephaim, and so had netherworld connotations. (Spronk, *DDDB*: 633–34; Smith 1990: 128; Spronk 1986; Brown, Driver, and Briggs 1978: 12)

Adapa (M) Antediluvian sage and protagonist in the tale of humankind's loss of immortality. He eventually was considered divine. Often seen as the prototype of biblical Adam due to the names Adam and Adapa being basically the same (but for the interchange of labials) and because his loss of immortality involved trickery and food. (Beaulieu 2003: 326–27; Black and Green 2003: 27)

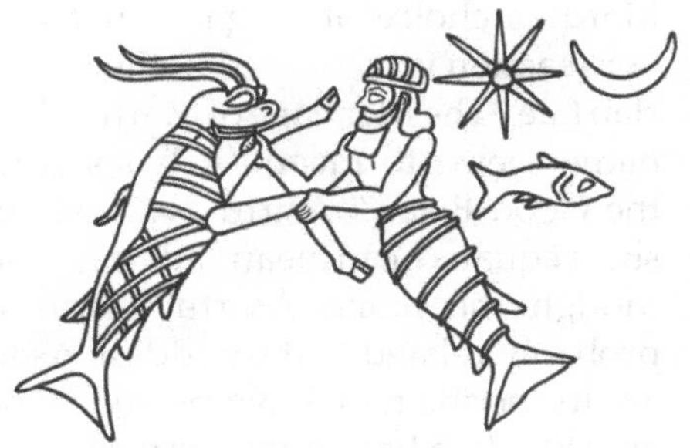

Cylinder seal with Adapa. Neo-Babylonian. Yellow chert. 2.0 x 1.0 cm. Morgan Library no. 788. After Porada 1948: no. 788.

Adat (L) Possibly Asherah, at Ugarit. Also a title of Ba'lat of Byblos, the "Lady of Byblos," and of other goddesses. Female equivalent of the masculine Adon "Lord," Adat means "Lady." (Dukstra, *DDDB*: 6–7)

Ad(d)a, Ad(d)u (M) See Adad

Addirim (L) See Adarim

Ad(d)u (L, M) See Adad

Ad-dug-nuna (M) One of the divine counselors of the goddess Sadar-nuna, wife of Nuska, in the circle of Nippur deities. The name occurs in two versions of An : *Anum*, one with the sign DUG_3, "good," the other with DUG_4, "to speak." Since this deity is a counselor, AD may well mean "voice," thus "(God of) Good Advice (ad-dug_3) Worthy of a Prince" or "(God) Whose Advising (ad-dug_4) Is Worthy of a Prince." There are three other deities with the element DUG_3-nun (Eš$_3$-, Lugal-, Nin-) where a reading ḫe-nun "abundance" seems preferable. (Litke 1998: 52)

Adgar-kidug (M) Wife of Mardu/Amurru(m). Daughter of the god Numušda and his wife Namrat of the city Inab, otherwise unattested. Equated to Ašratu(m)/Aširtu(m). The story of Mardu's choice of Adgar-kidug and her reaction is recounted in the Sumerian tale "The Marriage of Martu." Her name seems to mean "Advisor (of?) the Good Place." Aširtu, with whom she is equated, can mean "advice," and though the name Åsartu/Aširtu is probably related to the goddess Ašerah, the scribe may have played upon an Akkadian homonym for the Sumerian name. (van der Toorn, *DDDB*: 32; Litke 1998: 219; Kramer 1990: 11–27)

Ad-gi (M) Identified with Adad of the Suteans in a Neo-Assyrian god list. Written ad-gi. (King 1969: pl. 16)

Ad-gigi (M) Deity whose name means "Counselor." (1) One of the divinized bull-lyres of the birth/mother goddess Dingir-maḫ. (2) In the circle of the sun god Utu and identified in An : *Anum* as "Whose Gaze Is Favorable." (Litke 1998: 77, 135)

Ad-giri-gidda (M) Deity associated with the handles of the kettledrum. Written ad$_4$-giri$_3$-gíd-da. May mean "Cripple who Drags (his) Leg." (Livingstone 1986: 190)

Ad-giri-ḫaš (M) Considered a daughter of the netherworld god En-me-šara. May mean "Cripple with a Broken Leg." Variant ad$_4$-giri$_3$-ḫuš. Identified with Šuzianna. (Lambert 2013: 213; Litke 1998: 35)

A-diku, A-diku-gal, A-diku-maḫ, A-diku-ušum, (M) All these deities are identified in An : *Anum* as judges, probably alluding to the role of water in the River Ordeal. These names mean "Water Is the Great/Lofty/Only Judge." In a Neo-Assyrian god list the number 50 or 50+50 is inserted. In Litke's copy of YBC 2041 he copies 40. See Id; Il-lu-rugu. (Litke 1998: 225; King 1969: pl. 41; Edzard, *RlA* VI: 375)

A-diriga, Adiri-maḫ (M) Deities identified in An : *Anum* as judges. A-dirig can mean "raft," but here, in light of their identification as judges, a meaning "Flowing (High) Waters," alluding to the role of water in the River Ordeal, seems more likely. See Id; Il-lu-rugu. (Litke 1998: 224–25)

Ad-kug (M) Possibly an epithet of Enki. May mean "Holy Father" or "Clear Voice." God lists of the Early Dynastic period suggest that his cult city was situated in the neighborhood of Umma and Girsu. Ad-kug was part of the name of a chief priestess of Enki. (Krebernik 1986: 178; Mander 1986: 74)

Ad-mu (M) Wife of the netherworld god Nergal. Attested in Sargonic and Mari texts. See NIN-ad-mu. (Milano and Westenholz 2015; Durand 2008: 233–35; Litke 1998: 201)

Ad-mu-saḫara (M) Deity attested in Old Babylonian administrative texts from the temple residence of the high priest(ess) (*gipar*) of Nin-gal at Ur in connection with goddesses Nin-ki-ura and Nin-gal-a-anda. (Richter 2004: 438–39)

Adodos (L) The Greek title of a god equated to the Greek Zeus by Philo of Byblos in *The Phoenician History*. (Attridge and Oden 1981: 55 and 91 note 126)

Adon (L) Semitic/Canaanite title given to a god to denote his authority. At Ugarit it was most often a name of the supreme god El. It might have referred also to the storm god Ba'lu/Had(d)ad. Means "Lord." Adonai is a form of Adon. (Spronk, *DDDB*: 531–33; Brown, Driver, and Briggs 1978: 10–11)

Adonai, Adonay (L) A modified plural form of the Semitic word *adon*, it is usually translated as "My Lord." The word occurs around 450 times in the Hebrew Bible. In the Septuagint, the divine name YHWH was replaced with the Greek word *Kyrios* meaning "Lord." In reading and speaking, Jews normally substitute Adonai for YHWH, the tetragrammaton, the four-letter name of the deity. (Spronk, *DDDB*: 531–33; Zeller, *DDDB*: 494; O'Brien, *ABD* I: 74; Rose, *ABD* IV: 1008; Brown, Driver, and Briggs 1978: 11)

Adonis (L) A disappearing and returning god, a so-called "dying god." Name is the Greek version of the Semitic word *adonai* "My Lord," a title, probably of the storm god Ba'lu, that eventually became the name of a primarily Hellenistic and Greco-Roman god/hero, whose origins were likely Near Eastern, going back eventually to the Egyptian Osiris and the Mesopotamian god Dumuzi. Osiris's cult was certainly known at Phoenician Byblos, and Dumuzi's cult had spread to the Levant by the first millennium BCE (see Ezekiel 8: 14). Adonis was the chief god of Byblos. Usually identified with Ešmun, a god of the Phoenician city of Ṣidōn, and sometimes in the Hellenistic period with the Greek wine god Dionysos. Also a disappearing and returning deity. The myths and cult of Adonis are known from Greek and Roman sources.

The first mention of the god occurs in the poems of Sappho (c. 630–552 BCE). The fullest account comes from Lucian's *De Dea Syria*. Ovid's *Metamorphoses* also tells the story. According to one version of the myth, Adonis was born of an incestuous relationship between Myrrha, the spirit of the myrrh tree, and her father, the mythical king of Cyprus Kinyras or Cinyras. At his birth Aphrodite gave the beautiful child into Persephone's care, but, when Aphrodite asked for him back, Persephone refused. A solution assigned Adonis to Aphrodite for two-thirds of the year, and to Persephone for one-third. Another and more popular version of Adonis's descent to the netherworld had him killed by a boar while hunting and bewailed by his lover Aphrodite (Aštarte?).

The rites of Adonis were noted for lamentations by women. Other aspects varied by time and locality. The celebration of the departure and return of Adonis was "the great Phoenician festival" (Lipiński 1995: 464, our translation). In ancient Greece, the incense-heavy festival of Adonis, the Adonia, was celebrated in July/August and provided a chance for women to break out of their "strictly circumscribed" lives with "unbridled" emotions (Burkert 1985: 177).

Relief of Adonis. Marble. Servais "Adonis," Spada Palace, Rome. After Fondation pour LIMC 1981: 227, no. 40.

In fifth-and-fourth-century BCE Athens, the private festival took place primarily on rooftops, where women, especially prostitutes and concubines, planted clay pots with quickly growing and quickly wilting vegetation like lettuce and fennel. These "Gardens of Adonis" were left on the roofs, in the sun, to die unwatered. At the end of the festival, an effigy of Adonis was laid out on a bier, mourned with loud cries, and then thrown into the sea, along with the little gardens. The Adonia was observed also in Alexandria and throughout the Roman world. The timing of the Adonia during the hot months probably led to the interpretation, starting with Frazer's *The Golden Bough*, of Adonis as a "dying god" associated with the growth and death of vegetation. However, there are no extant ancient descriptions of rituals dealing with Adonis's resurrection from the dead.

Textual evidence of his return from the dead "does not antedate the Christian Era" (Mettinger 2001: 155). Nonetheless, Adonis's annual return was explicit in the myth in which Adonis spent a third of the year in the netherworld with Persephone. Worshipped widely, especially by women, from about 200 BCE to about 400 CE. In the Hebrew Bible, similar rituals were recorded: In Ezekiel 8: 14, women sat at the temple in Jerusalem wailing for "Tammuz" (Dumuzi); in Jeremiah 32: 29, people were performing rituals on rooftops; and Isaiah 17:10 referred to the planting of "disappointing" vegetation. There exist late Greek accounts of the cult of Adonis in the Levant. The most important of these is the work attributed to Lucian, *The Syrian Goddess (De Dea Syria)*. Lucian, who was probably writing in the second century CE, described the festival of Adonis at Byblos. The first day was given over to lamentations for Adonis, and on the next day Adonis was proclaimed to be alive again. Lucian also discussed the river called Adonis, which yearly ran "blood red" to signal the beginning of mourning for the god (Attridge and Oden 1976: 12–15). At the source of the river lay the best-known temple of the Phoenician area, dedicated to the goddess Aštarte and, according to tradition, site of the tomb of Adonis. In the 1930s, a temple to the god was excavated at Dura Europos, now in northeast Syria, where he might have been the consort of the "Syrian Goddess" Atargatis. Adonis was worshipped also in Punic/Phoenician North Africa in Roman times, but the title probably referred to the Carthaginian god Ba'al-Ḥam(m)ōn. According to Herm, writing in 1973, Lebanese women considered the Nahr Ibrahim, the ancient Adonis River, to have healing power and were still making offerings to Adonis, but under the names St. George, if they were Christian, and Al Khadr, if they were Muslim. Likewise, Menen reported in the same year that, on Good Friday, the day of Jesus Christ's death, Christian churches in Rome designated a side chapel loaded with flowers as "the sepulchre," and the faithful made the rounds of the churches to pray at these chapels. On the floors were pots growing new and fragile grass symbolizing Christ's return from Hell. The pots were called "Gardens of Adonis." (Quinn 2018; Peckham 2014: 26–27, 37–38; Leeming 2005: 4–5; Strong 2002: 62–75; Mettinger 2001: 113–54; Ribichini in Xella 2001: 97–114; Smith 2001: 116–18; Markoe 2000: 117; Ribichini, *DDDB*: 7–10; Will 1996; Handy 1994: 59–61; Kraemer 1992: 30–35; Lipiński 1995: 90–105; Lipiński, *DCPP*: 6–7; Turcan 1989; Kraemer 1988: 18–19; Detienne 1986; Burkert 1985: 176–77; Robertson 1982; Ribichini 1981; Soyez 1977; Herm 1975: 115; Menen 1973: 56; Ovid 1967: 241–52; Atallah 1966; Baudisson 1911)

Adrammelech (Adrammelek) and **Anammelech** (Anammelek) (L) Gods venerated by people from Sepharvaim, who were settled in Samaria by the Assyrians (II Kings 17: 24). According to the Hebrew Bible, worship of these deities included burning of children (II Kings 17:31). Adrammelech possibly means "The Glorious (One) Is King" and Anammelech possibly "The King Answers." (Millard, *DDDB*: 10–11; Millard, *DDDB*: 34–35; Comay 1993: 18, 33; J. Day 1989)

Ad-ŠÁR×DIŠ-gi (M) Sumerian deity attested in an Early Dynastic god list from Šuruppak. Perhaps, but not necessarily, to be associated with Ašgi. (Mander 1986: 104)

Aduntarri (H) A primeval prophet deity of the Old Syrian-Hurrian pantheon. (Hoffner 1998: 112; Popko 1995: 99; Archi 1990: 118)

A-du-ru (M) See Ara

A-e-a-sunkir, A-ip-a-sunkir (E) Elamite divinity appearing in a brick inscription of King Untaš-Napiriša from Susa. A variant has the name A-ip-a-sunkir. The element *sunkir* means "king" in Elamite, and the name may be a translation of Akkadian Ea-šarrī, "Ea Is My King." (Hinz and Koch 1987: 29; König 1977: 39, 181, 227)

Aeon (L) See Aion

Aer (L) Along with Aither (Aether) first creator in the Phoenician mythology of Moschus, according to Damascius. Aither occurs also in Hesiod's *Theogony*. (Attridge and Oden 1981: 103, 104 note 5; Albright 1968: 222–24)

Aera and **Aura** (L) Male and female offspring of Pothos and Omicle, the creator deities in the cosmogony of Damascius. Originally a Phoenician myth. (Attridge and Oden 1981: 103, 104 note 5; Albright 1968: 222)

Aeshma (L) See Asmodeus

Aether (L) See Aer

A-e-ya (H) See Aya

A-GA-gig-duga (M) See Ugu-gig-duga

Aga-kug (M) Sixteenth name of Marduk in the *Enūma eliš*. Means "Holy Crown." (Foster 2005: 477; Litke 1998: 91; Foster 1993: I, 393; Speiser, *ANET*: 70; Heidel 1967: 54–55)

Agal-tuku (M) Sumerian deity attested in a Šuruppak-type of tablet said to come from Abu Hatab, ancient Kisura, near Šuruppak. Its provenance is uncertain, and it may actually have come from Šuruppak. Dates to the mid-third millennium BCE. Means "Possessing Strength." (Martin et al. 2001: 99 no. 110)

A-ga-ni (M) Wife of Pa-geštin-du, a wine-steward associated with Nergal. Written á-ga-ni (var. ša/na_5-ne) (Litke 1998: 61)

Agar (M) Deity in an Ur III text: gìr-sè-ga ^{d}A-gàr. (SNAT 453: o ii 4)

A-gi-maḫ (M) See Niggu-maḫ

A-gilima (M) Thirty-second epithet of Marduk in the *Enūma eliš*. (Foster 2005: 480; Litke 1998: 93; Foster 1993: I, 396; Speiser, *ANET*: 71; Heidel 1967: 57)

A-GIM-ma-na-UŠ (M) Son of Nin-marki. (Litke 1998: 125)

A-GIM-SIG-eš (M) Son of Nin-marki. Written a-gim-sig_7-eš. (Litke 1998: 125)

Aglibol (L) See Malakbēl

Agû(m) (M) In the Early Dynastic period, a deity of Ebla. *Agû(m)* is Akkadian for "crown." Possibly a manifestation of the deified crown of the royal dynasty. The deity often appears in the dual form, probably referring to the crowns of the king and the queen. Offerings were made to the two Agû(m)s and to the spirits of the dead at the royal mausoleum of the kings of Ebla in the ancient town of Binaš, northwest of Ebla at modern Binnish. An annual festival for the god was held at Ebla. (Pomponio and Xella 1997: 19–23; Cohen 1993: 33)

Agušaya (M) Name of Ištar. Probably referred to a type of whirling dance. In an Akkadian composition about Ištar as Agušaya, Ea, because Ištar had become unbearable in her ferocity and battle lust, created a goddess Ṣaltu(m) to occupy Ištar by fighting with her. The opening of the composition praises Ištar as goddess of war and describes her as dancing madly on the battlefield. Variants include Gù-ša-ya, Gu-šá-a-[a], and Gu-ša-a-tu. (Foster 2005: 96–106; Litke 1998: 235; Groneberg 1997: 75–93, 93 note to line 8; Cohen 1993: 267; Foster 1977; Tallqvist 1974: 250)

Aḫbita (M) Deity attested in an incantation. (Reiner 1970: 59)

A-ḫe-LUL (M) Son of Nin-šubur. Written á-ḫé-LUL. (Litke 1998: 28)

Aḫlamayītu(m) (M) Means "The Aramaean (Goddess)" or, more precisely "The Aḫlamean (Goddess)," named for an Aramaean tribal group. The deity was worshipped at Uruk and Sippar in the Neo-Babylonian period and may have been involved in the festival of Ištar at Uruk. (Beaulieu 2003: 309)

A-ip-a-sunkir (E) See A-e-a-sunkir

Akka (M) Deity occurring in texts from Emar. (Durand 2008: 634)

Akni (H) Hittite god of fire. Same as the Indo-Aryan fire god Agni. (van Gessel 1998: I, 8; Laroche 1946/47: 119)

Ak-Su'en (M) See Nin-ak-Su'en

Akuṣītum (M) See Inana-Akuz

Ala (H) Protective deity. Associated with Sumerian Alad. Received offerings in a Middle Hittite ritual. Name borrowed from Sumerian/Akkadian. (van Gessel 1998: I, 9–14; Popko 1995: 88, 89; Haas 1994: 449–50)

Ala, Alu (M) Deity attested at Ebla. Also a geographical name. (Archi 1997)

Alad, Alad-lammu, Alad-saga (M) See Šedu; Lama

Ala-edina (M) Sumerian name of the moon god Sîn in an Old Babylonian god list. Said by Richter to be part of the local pantheon of Nippur. Written al-[a-ed]in. (Richter 2004: 104; Green 1975: 85)

Alaga (M) Sumerian name of Šamaš in An : *Anum*, glossed as a^{e}-la-gá. (Richter 2004: 350; Litke: 1998: 132)

Alal (M) Netherworld deity with a temple at Emar. Written A-làl. (Fleming, 2000: 185)

Alala, Alalu (M, H) (1) Akkadian/Babylonian god whose consort was Bēlili. The pair had a "seat" together in the E-sag-ila temple at Babylon. Alala was one of the twenty-one primeval fathers and mothers of An/Anu(m) listed in An : *Anum*. Written A-la-la. The name perhaps is a cry of joy. In one text the god is equated to Enki. Alala occurred also in a myth of the Hurrians, probably associated with Sumerian Alad. (Litke 1998: 22; George 1993: 150 no. 1096; Ebeling, *RlA* I: 67). (2) Primeval and original father god. Occurs in the Kumarbi myths of the Hittites/Hurrians as the first king of the deities. Father of Kumarbi. Deposed by Anu. Name borrowed from the Mesopotamian pantheon. (Hoffner 1998: 41, 42, 53, 109; van Gessel 1998: I, 15–16; Haas 1994: 110; Laroche 1976: 41; Laroche 1946/47: 127; Ebeling, *RlA* I: 67)

A-la-LAB-ki (M) Explained in An : *Anu ša amēli* as "Ištar of Shouting (*yarūrūti*)," perhaps on the basis of a-la designating a sound of joy or even because of the term *a-ḫu-lap*, a sound of woe. (Litke 1998: 235)

Alama (H, L, M) See Ḫalma

A-lam-i (M) Deity appearing in god lists of the Early Dynastic period. (Krebernik 1986: 188; Mander 1986: 102)

Alammuš (M) Vizier or minister of the moon god Nanna/Sîn. His cult was celebrated at Ur and Nippur in Ur III times and at Ur in Old Babylonian times. His wife at Ur and Nippur was Nin-Urima, "Lady of Ur." In the lexical series Diri the deity is written with the logogram TA×ḪI and syllabically rendered as a-la-mu-uš. (Civil 2004; Litke 1998: 121; Richter 1999: 391–92; George 1993: 28; Sallaberger 1993: II, 106)

Alba (M) See Ilba; see Baliḫ (River)

Algarsurra (M) Deified plectrum or drumstick understood as the offspring of Lugalbanda and Nin-sun. (Peterson 2009a: no. 33)

Alḫa (M) See Baliḫ (River)

Alim-banda (M) Deified bison associated with Enki. Means "Wild (or Younger) Bison." (Litke 1998: 84)

Alim-dara (M) Epithet of the Sumerian storm god Iškur. A late hymn refers to

Iškur as alim "bison," but the meaning of dara$_2$, usually "ibex," is unclear as a modifier of "bison" unless a variant for dara$_4$ "red" or "brown." (Schwemer 2001: 63; Litke 1998: 141)

Alim-maḫ (M) Deity occurs once in an Ur III text from Umma as the recipient of garments. Name means "Lofty Bison." See A-alim-maḫ. (SA 54: pl. 77: o 18)

Alim-nuna (M) Deified bison associated with Enki. Means something like "Noble Bison." (Litke 1998: 84)

Alim-siki (M) One of three names of Enki with "bison." Two texts have -sì-ki, one -si-ga. (Litke 1998: 84)

Ālittu(m) (M) Goddess worshipped at Sippar in Neo-Babylonian times. Means "Progenitress." (Bongenaar 1997: 230)

Aliyan, Aleyan, Alein (L) Name or title of the great rain and storm god Ba'lu/Had(d)ad. Normally rendered as "Puissant, Victorious, or Almighty." Wyatt translates it "Valiant." Often used to refer to Ba'lu in the myths of Ugarit. Contrary to earlier views, Aliyan was not a separate divinity. (Wyatt 2002: 39–146; Dukstra, *DDDB*: 18–20)

Aliyan-Ba'lu (L) See Ba'lu/Had(d)ad

Alla (M) (1) Deity associated with the netherworld. According to Jacobsen, the deity may have been a river god, "Owner of the Net" (Jacobsen 1987: 59). (2) Alla written $^{al\text{-}la}$NAGAR occurs in An : *Anum* (Litke 1998: 216). (Jacobsen, 1987: 59). See also Lugal-sapar. (Cohen, 1993: 468)

Alla-gula (M) Sumerian deity whose statue is attested in the "palace" of Atu, the cup-bearer for King Šū-Sîn, in Nippur in the Ur III period. (Sallaberger 1993: I, 106–7)

Alla-pae (M) Deity attested in an Early Dynastic god list. Means "Alla Manifest." (Mander 1986: 138)

Allamu (M) See Umbisag

Allani (H, L M) Hurrian goddess, mistress, and gate-keeper of the netherworld, equated to Babylonian Allatu(m). The Hurrian name Allani means "The Lady." She is also designated "the young woman." Called in Hittite "sun goddess of the Earth [netherworld]" (Hoffner 1998: 67). It was she who ordered the opening of the seven gates of the netherworld to let out deities to attend rituals. Part Three of the Hurrian composition "The Song of Release" describes in some detail a feast given by Allani for the Primeval Deities and the storm god Teššub. She had a temple in Kuwanni in Kizzuwatna, a primarily Hurrian province in the east. God lists and offering texts at Ugarit include Allani. (del Olmo Lete 1999: 86, 210, 212; Hoffner 1998: 72–73, 78 note 26, 112; van Gessel 1998: I, 17–20; Popko 1995: 71, 89, 101, 111, 118, 130; Haas 1994: 130–33; Laroche 1976: 43)

Allanzu (H) Hittite goddess. Daughter of the great goddess Ḫebat. Her sister was Kunzišalli. Allanzu was called "maid of Ḫebat." Often appears in a dyad with her sister or her mother or in a triad with her mother and her sister. Depicted at the rock-carved shrine of Yazılıkaya near Ḫattušas. Mentioned in an offering ritual. Laroche compared her to Mesopotamian Šī-dūri. (Leick 1998: 3; van Gessel 1998: I, 21; Popko 1995: 115, 166; Haas 1994: 387–88, 442; Laroche 1976: 43; Laroche 1946/47: 44–45)

Allašaniša (M) Deity occurring once at Ur III Umma. Written Al-la-ša-ni-ša. May be for ša$_4$-ne-ša$_4$ "prayer." (Santag 6, 349: r 8)

Allatu(m) (M) Akkadian/Babylonian queen of the netherworld. Identified with Sumerian Ereškigal. Another name was Irkala, a designation of the netherworld. One of the seven destiny-decreeing gods of the E-sagil temple in Babylon. At Ugarit, she was identified with Arṣay, daughter of Ba'lu, and also the Hurrian deity Alanni. (George 2004 no. 20; Sharlach 2002: 99–100; del Olmo Lete 1999: 86, 212; Leick 1998: 3; Litke 1998: 188; Tallqvist 1974: 307, 328)

Allu-ḫappu (M) Babylonian netherworld monster. The work "A [Prince's] Vision of the Netherworld" describes it as having the head of a lion and four human hands and feet. The name is a Sumerian loanword meaning "hunting net." (Foster 2005: 832–39; Speiser, *ANET*: 109)

Almanu (M) The husband of Išḫara. *CDA* interprets *almānu* as "widower" (the term occurs also at Mari); however, *CAD* is more cautious of this translation. (Litke 1998: 166; Tallqvist 1974: 259)

Al(la)mu (M) Demon listed in An : *Anum*. (Litke 1998: 210)

Almuš (M) Deity attested in the Mari texts. (Durand 2008: 268–69)

Altâ-ḫulni (M) Deity in the Mari texts (Durand 2008: 261)

Altum (M) Deity in the Mari texts (Durand 2008: 274)

Alu (L) See Ala and see Elyōnna

Alû(m) (Akk.), **Gu-ana** (Sum.) **Bull of Heaven** (M) The Bull of Heaven was a mythical beast of great strength. Appears in the Sumerian "Gilgameš and the Bull of Heaven" and the Babylonian "Epic of Gilgameš," Tablet VI, in which Inana/Ištar demands the creature from the sky god An/Anu(m) in order to punish Gilgameš for disobeying/rejecting her. After the bull causes destruction throughout Uruk and its environs, Gilgameš and Enkidu kill it. Scenes depicting the killing of the bull occur frequently on seals and other small stone carvings.

The Bull of Heaven is the constellation Taurus. (Foster 2001: 46–52; Frayne 2001: 120–27; George 2003: 624–25; Ebeling, *RlA* II: 109)

Plaque displaying the killing of the Bull of Heaven by Gilgameš and Enkidu. Old Babylonian. Clay. Height 13.5 cm. Musées Royaux d'Art et d'Histoire, Brussels. After Black and Green 2003: 90

Al-'Uzza (L) See Atargatis

Am (M) Means "Bull." Explained in *Anu ša amēli* as "The sun when it rises." (Litke 1998, 231)

A-ma (M) Deity identified with the mother goddess Bēlet-ilī. Presumably a syllabic writing for ama "mother." (Litke 1998: 71)

Ama-ab-zi-kura (M) Goddess identified with Ereškigal, queen of the netherworld. Means "Mother, Dependable

Cow of the kur(netherworld)." Perhaps she is being envisioned as the wild bovine inhabiting the far-away mountains, associated with the land of the dead. The Ur III deity Ama-abzu-kár (Studies Levine, 132–8: r ii 24) may be another form of the name. (Litke 1998: 188)

Ama-arazu (M) Goddess associated with Nippur and Umma in the Ur III period; appears in two texts from the reign of Samsu-iluna and one Ur III text. Means "Mother (of) Prayer" (cf. Ama-šude-imin(bi)). The name could refer to three deities, two female and one male. (1) In An : *Anum* Tablet III written Amar-ra-a-zu with variant Amar-ra-zu and identified as one of two daughters of the moon god Nanna/Sîn; (2) In an Old Babylonian god list written Ama-a-ra-zu and identified with the doorkeeper Kalkal; (3) In An : *Anum* Tablet I written Ama-a-ra-zu and identified as the mother of Nin-KIR$_4$-amaš-a in the circle of Enlil. (Richter 2004: 100; Litke 1998: 63, note 352a, 122; Sallaberger 1993: I, 157; Renger 1967: 149)

Ama-arḫuš-su (M) Goddess associated with Gula. Means "The Caring Mother." Occurs also as Nin-ama-arḫuš-sù. (Cavigneaux and Krebernik, *RlA* IX: 327)

Ama-dag-si, Ama-NUN-si (M) Appears in an Old Babylonian god list in the circle of Inana deities. Means "Lady who Occupies the Residence." Corresponds to Ama-NUN-si, who is listed as a messenger of Inana in An : *Anum*. Perhaps NUN is to be understood either as agrun (é-nun), "cella," or as a variant for unu *šubtu(m)*. (Richter 2004: 292; Litke 1998: 159)

Ama-du-bad (M) Deity identified with Bēlet-ilī. Written ama-du$_{10}$$^{du\text{-}ba\text{-}ad}$bad. Explained as *peti'at birki*, literally "who opens the knees (du$_{10}$)," usually a metaphor for "to run quickly." But in view of this being a mother goddess, this may refer to the spreading of the knees at childbirth to enable the baby to come out. (Litke 1998: 71)

Ama-eri (M) Deity in an Ur III personal name at Girsu. Means "Mother of the City." (MVN 7, 225L r 10)

Ama-gan (M) One of the attendants of the healing goddess Gula at Isin. Means "Child-bearing Mother." (Litke 1998: 185)

Ama-gan-ša (M) Written Ama-gan-ša$_4$. See Šakkan

Ama-geštin (M) See Geštin-ana

Ama-gu-ane-si (M) One of the attendants in the circle of the healing goddess Gula at Isin. Means "Mother whose Voice Fills the Heavens." One variant has a gloss tu for gù. See Gu-ane-si. (Litke 1998: 185)

Ama-gula (M) See Gula

Ama-gurušene (M) Deity identified with Nin-Isina/Nin-kar(r)ak attested in An : *Anum*. Means "Mother of the Young Men." Also appears in an Old Babylonian god list. (Richter 2004: 215–16; Litke: 1998: 181)

Amaḫ-ad (M) Identified in a Neo-Assyrian god list with Adad. Written a-maḫ-ad. a-maḫ can mean "flood," which is appropriate for Adad. ad can mean "oarlock," but unclear here. (King 1969: pl. 16)

Amaḫ-tuku (M) The deified harp of Nin-Gublaga, according to An : *Anum*. One of the gods of Ur in the Old Babylonian period and later. Means "Possessing Great Strength." (Richter 2004: 452; Litke 1998: 124)

Ama-izi-la (M) Goddess appearing in an Early Dynastic god list. May mean "Mother/Source Torch." Possibly a name of Inana as the planet Venus. (Krebernik 1986: 175)

Amakandu (M) See Šakkan

Ama-kuta (M) See Men-kuta

Ama-Kul(l)aba (M) Goddess occurring in an Early Dynastic god list. Means "Mother of Kul(l)aba." Probably a form of Inana, who was chief deity of Kul(l)aba in the Early Dynastic period. (Frayne 2001: 100, 101; Krebernik 1986: 183)

Amal (M) See Il-aba

Amal(-gig-dugu) (M) See Ugu-gig-duga

Ama-me-bad (M) Name of Inana/Ištar as Venus. We prefer a reading BAD rather than TIL, since the next entry in An : *Anum* contains -bad. Note the deity Am-mi-ba-da in an Ur III personal name. (BPOA 6, 737: s 1; Litke 1998: 161)

Ama-me-daba (M) Epithet of the Sumerian goddess Nisaba. Means "Mother who Holds the *Me*." (Litke 1998: 55)

Ama-mu-gi (M) The *gudu*-priest of Ama-mu-gi$_4$ is mentioned in an Ur III tablet from Girsu. (*Atiqot* 4, pl. 30, 72: o iii 9)

Ama-muru (M) One of the Sumerian names of Nin-kar(r)ak in An : *Anum* and also in an Old Babylonian god list. Written Ama-GI.KID.MAḪ with gloss a-ma-mu-ru. Means "Mother Reed Mat." (Richter 2004: 215–16; Litke 1998: 182)

Ama-mutin (M) See Geštin-ana

Ama-nir-an(n)a (M) A child of Dingir-maḫ. May mean "The Respected Mother of Heaven." Explained by An : *Anum* as "mother who appears from the inner parts." (Litke 1998: 82)

Amanki (M) See Enki

Ama-(nu)mudib (M) Sumerian deity from at Lagaš. In the Early Dynastic period the name Ama-numudib may mean "The Mother Did Not Pass Me By," that is, "the mother cared for her child." She occurs in texts associated with the Nanše festival at Nimin in the Early Dynastic period. However, in the Ur III period the negative element NU was dropped: the name is attested as Ama-mudib at Girsu, where there is a temple of Ama-mudib. Ama-mudib occurs twice in a personal name. (Selz 1995: 21)

Am-anuna, Anun (M) Names attested in an Early Dynastic god list. Means "Wild Bull with Overpowering Strength (or Horns)." It is unclear whether these two names refer to the same deity or to two distinct gods. (Mander 1986: 47, 116)

Ama-NUN-si (M) See Ama-dag-si

Ama-ra-ba (M) Deity receiving offerings at Ur III Umma. (*Aegyptus* 10, 262, 9: r 8)

Amara-ḫeaga(e), Amara-ḫe'ea (M) Goddess at Šuruppak written Ama-ra-ḫé-ága and in An : *Anum* written Amar-ra-ḫé-ága-e and Amar-ra-ḫé-è-a, where she and Ama-ra-a-zu are identified as daughters of the moon god Nanna/Sîn. Originally the name may have meant "Let Her Measure (It) Out for the Mother." (Litke 1998: 122; Mander 1986: 55)

Amara-ḫesa (M) Deity with *gudu*-priest at Ur III Ur. Written ama-ra-ḫé-sa$_6$. (UET 3, 1105: o 4)

Am-Aral(l)i (M) Occurs as a name of Dumuzi in an Old Babylonian god list. Means "Bull of Aral(l)i," a name for the netherworld. (Richter 2004: 190, 312)

Amar-ba (M) Deity attested in an Early Dynastic personal name. (Westenholz 2014)

Amar-dugud-[...] (M) Sumerian god attested in an Early Dynastic god list from Šuruppak. Means "[...] Weighty (or Important) Bull Calf." (Mander 1986: 102–3)

Amar-ENGURna (M) Deity attested as a tutelary deity of the city of Ašabu, likely in the area of Umma, in the archaic Sumerian zà-mí hymns from Abu Ṣalābīkh and in a god list from Šuruppak. (Mander 1986: 121, 126; Biggs 1974: 52)

Amar-Ezida (M) Deity mentioned in an incantation. (George 2016: no. 1)

Amar-MI.ZA (M) Deity attested in a text from the Early Dynastic period from Šuruppak. (Martin et al. 2001: 99)

Amar-ra-a-zu (M) See Ama-a-ra-zu

Amarra-ḫe'ea (M) Deity written amar-ra-ḫé and amar-ra-ḫé-è-a in a god list from Aššur. May mean "Let (him?) Go Forth for(?) the Bull Calf." (Schroeder 1920: no. 65)

Amarre (M) Sumerian deity mentioned in a god list from Aššur corresponding to the deity Ḫár, "Bull," likely Nin-gublaga. Means "Bull Calf." (Richter 2004: 159)

Amarukkam (M) See Marukka

Amar-Su'en (M) One of the deified bull-harps of the moon god Nanna/Sîn. Means "Bull Calf (of) the Moon." (Litke 1998: 123, 144)

Amar-šuba (M) Son of Nin-marki. May mean "Bright Calf." (Litke 1998: 125)

Ama-sag-nudi (M) Wife of Nin-šubur. Written Ama-ság-nu-di with variant du_7. (Richter 2004: 303; Litke 1998: 27)

Ama-Šakkan (M) See Šakkan

Ama-šude-imin(bi) (M) Sumerian goddess in the circle of Inana deities of Old Babylonian Uruk listed in an Old Babylonian god list. Listed as a messenger of Inana in An : *Anum*. Means "Mother (of) All Prayers" (cf. Ama-ara-zu). (Richter 2004: 292; Litke 1998: 159)

Ama-šu-ḫalbi (M) See Šu-ḫal-bi

Ama-TURma (M) Sister of Nin-geš-zida. Written Ama-TÙR-ma. The following entry is La-bar-TÙR-ma. Note also the deity TÙR-ma, an attendant of Ištarān of Dēr, whose entry in An : *Anum* is glossed tu-ur. Perhaps these three names, all with tùr-ma, reflect a shared value / šilam / for the similar looking TÙR and ŠILAM signs, a reading that had been abandoned and unknown to the scribe of An : *Anum* who added the gloss tu-ur. (Litke 1998: 192, 196)

Ama-ušum-gal-ana (M) Aspect or title of Dumuzi. Originally, Ama-ušum-gal-ana and Dumuzi were separate deities, since both occurred in early god lists. Attested as early as Early Dynastic times as city god of Umma and of Ki-esa, a city in the Lagaš region. Appeared as god of Umma in the Sumerian zà-mí hymns. He was also honored in an Early Dynastic hymn from Ebla. Featured in many of the Sumerian songs devoted to the love between Inana and Dumuzi and probably associated with the "Sacred Marriage" ritual. Inana often addressed her lover as Ama-ušum-gal-ana. Alster translates it: "The Lord Is a Great Dragon of Heaven" (in *DDDB*: 830). Jacobsen suggests "the one great source of the date clusters" and considered the god to be "the power in and behind the date harvest" (1976: 36–37). (Krebernik 2003: 151–80; Sefati 1998: 125, 188)

Ama-utu, Ama-utuda (M) Deity whose name means "Mother (who) Gives Birth." (1) Listed as Ama-ù-tu, one of the attendants of the circle of the healing goddess Gula at Isin; (2) Listed as

Ama-ududa, a name of Bēlet-ilī. (Richter 2004: 215; Litke 1998: 71, 185)

Ama-udu-anki (M) Deity identified with Namma. Means "Mother, Birth-giver of Heaven and Earth." (Litke 1998: 24)

Amaza (M) Deity from Emar, who received offerings during a festival. Paired with the god Alal. (Fleming 2000: 242–43)

Ama-zil-la (M) Goddess appearing in the "Hymn to the Queen of Nippur." Mander suggests a connection to the deity Nin-zil in an Early Dynastic god list from Šuruppak. He compares the latter to Dam-zizzil noted in a god list as a name of the goddess Nanāya in her aspect of "Solicitous Lady."

Am-gal-nuna (M) Means "Noble Great Bull." Appears in a god list of Early Dynastic times and in the Sumerian zà-mí hymns. (Mander 1986: 44; Biggs 1974: 47)

Am-girra (M) Deity attested in a personal name from third-millennium Adab. Means "Raging Bull."

Ami (M) See Āmûm

Amma (M) Deity identified with Allatu(m), queen of the netherworld. Name written KUR and KI in An : *Anum* with gloss amma. May be the name of the seventh month at Mari. (Cohen 2015: 321; Litke 1998: 218)

Amma-bira (M) The temple of this deity is provisioned in a document from Sargonic Adab. Written (^{d}Am-ma-bí-ra). (Pomponio and Visicato 2015: no. 134)

Ammamma, Mamma (H) Hittite netherworld goddess. Associated with mother and earth goddesses such as Allatu(m), Lelwani, and Allani, the grey-haired old ladies. She was called "Great Mother Goddess" and "Evil Goddess." One of her companions was Ḫaḫḫina "Thirst." She was invoked as witness to treaties. Her cult centers were Taḫurpa and Ḫaḫanna Ḫurma, both in Anatolia. (van Gessel 1998: I, 26–28; Popko 1995: 114, 143; Haas 1994: 156, 300; Laroche 1946/47: 20–21)

Amman (M) Deity in the Mari texts. (Durand 2008: 636)

Ammizzadu, Ammezzadu (H) Hurrian primeval god. Mentioned as Ammaza in the cult at Emar, associated with the cult of Allala/u. His name recalls that of King Ammi-ṣaduqa of the First Dynasty of Babylon and also that of a legendary Lycian king. (Hoffner 1998: 41, 42, 53; van Gessel 1998: I, 28–29; Haas 1994: 110, 113; Weissbach, *RlA* I: 98)

Am(m)unki, Am(m)enki (H) Ancient Hurrian netherworld goddess. A "dead" grain deity in the circle of En-me-šara. One of the primeval Old Syrian deities to whom the "Song of Kumarbi" is chanted. Though "dead," she still appears in rituals and receives offerings, especially birds (in the ancient world birds were often associated with the souls of the dead). Often paired with Minki as a female/male dyad. Perhaps the pair might be identified with the Sumerian ancestral deities Enki and Nin-ki. (Hoffner 1998: 41, 42, 112; van Gessel 1998: I, 29–30; Popko 1995: 99; Haas 1994: 112)

ʿAmmu (L) Deity attested in theophoric names from Ugarit. Possibly equivalent to Amorite Ḫammu. One scholar has argued that he was a sun god. (Durand 2008: 228–30; del Olmo Lete 1999: 340 and note 16; van der Toorn, *DDDB*: 383–84)

Amna (M) A name of the sun god Utu/Šamaš. One of the seven destiny-decreeing gods of the E-sagil temple in Babylon. (George 2004: no. 20; Richter 2004: 350; Litke 1998: 128)

Amraru-wa-Qadišu (L) See Qadišu-wa-Amraru

Amri (L) West Semitic deity attested in two names.

Am-ŠE+NÁM (M) Sumerian deity attested in an Early Dynastic god list from Abu Ṣalābīkh. (Mander 1986: 116)

Amu (M) See Āmûm

Āmûm (M) Form of Nergal attested in the Mari texts. The deity Āmûm ša Ḫubšalum is attested. Ami and Amu are attested in personal names in Mari texts and may occur in personal names from the third millennium BCE. (Durand 2005: no. 62; Durand 1993a: nos. 60, 114)

Amurru(m) (Akk.), **Mardu, Martu** (Sum.) A mountain/steppe and shepherd god. Also a warrior storm god of the Adad type. Sometimes identified with Adad. Originally a West Semitic mountain/weather god who was somewhat late in joining the Mesopotamian pantheon. In Mesopotamia, he was the divine personification of the Amorites, whom cuneiform texts call "Amurru(m)." Mardu or Martu was the Sumerian name for the Amorites and their god. In the Sumerian pantheon, Amurru(m)/Mardu was a son of An and Uraš. His usual wife was Akkadian Ašratu(m), Sumerian Gubara. In An : *Anum* his spouse is Ikītum (=*ekkētum* "Scabies," which, if so, would be another instance of the Babylonians slandering the Amorites). George adds that Amurru(m) was sometimes identified with Nin-geš-zida, in the process taking over the latter's wives Geštin-ana and Ekurrītu(m) (1993: 38). In "The Marriage of Martu," the god acquires a wife Adgar-kidu, despite her female friend's opposition. To persuade her to reject Mardu, the friend points out that Mardu's people never stay put and look like monkeys. Further, she says, Mardu is a tent-dweller, dressed in pelts, and eats raw meat. Nevertheless, Adgar-kidu insisted that she would marry him.

At times Amurru(m) took on aspects of Dumuzi, especially in visual material, where he held a shepherd's crook. Amurru(m) was worshipped not only in Mesopotamia proper, but in places such as Emar and Alalaḫ. Explained in An : *Anu ša amēli* as "Sumuqan of the Suteans." (Durand 2008: 188–89; Black and Green 2003: 129–30; Sharlach 2002: 96–98; van der Toorn, *DDDB*: 32–34; Leick 1998: 4; Litke 1998: 218, 236; Klein 1997; Tallqvist 1974: 251; Kramer 1972: 100; Kupper 1961; Edzard, *RlA* VII: 433–40)

An (Sum.), **Anu(m)** (Akk.) Great god of the sky, the heavens. Head of the pantheon. Father and ancestor of all the gods and creator of the universe. An is the Sumerian word for "sky, heaven," borrowed into Akkadian as Anu(m). As befits a supreme deity, his name is listed before all in the great Babylonian god list An : *Anum*. In one tradition, Sumerian An's wife was Uraš, an earth goddess, while, in later ones, she was Ki, "Earth." Akkadian/Babylonian Anu(m)'s wife was Antu(m). One of her other names was Nin-zalle. An/Anu(m)'s offspring were many, including Enlil, Enki/Ea, Utu/Šamaš, Nanna/Sîn, Nin-geš-zida, Baba, the Sibittu, Adad, Amurru(m), Nisaba, Nin-Isina, Šala, Meslamta-e, Aya, and even, in one tradition, Inana/Ištar.

His relationship with Inana/Ištar was complicated. In the "Epic of Gilgameš," Anu(m) and Antu(m) were presented as her parents, and it was from Anu(m) that she begged the Bull of Heaven in order to use him to punish Gilgameš for rejecting her advances. Ištar was also Anu(m)'s "Beloved," and at Uruk they shared a temple complex. Ašratu(m), wife of Amurru(m), was Anu(m)'s daughter-in-law. In Anu(m)'s extensive court of about eighty deities, the gods Il-abrat/Papsukkal and Nin-šubur were his ministers (viziers). An/Anu(m)'s epithets include "Father of the Great Deities" and "King of the Gods."

The deity was rarely depicted on seals and other visual materials, though sometimes the horned crown was his symbol. Although Anu(m) was more remote from human lives than An, both appear in myths and were addressed in prayers and hymns. In "Gilgameš and the Bull of Heaven," An behaved like a reasonable, but indulgent father. At first, he resisted Inana's request for the bull, even though she was weeping copiously. However, after she terrified all the earth with her scream, An gave in to her. In the Babylonian "Epic of Gilgameš," a sensible Anu(m) handled the angry, sobbing Ištar at first by reminding her that she had provoked Gilgameš. Then, when Ištar threatened to bring the dead back to life, to consume the living, he gives her the bull. First, though, he sought her assurance that Uruk had enough food stored to survive seven years of famine. When, in the mythic work "Adapa," the south wind ceased to blow, Anu(m) demanded to know why and took measures to rectify the situation. A Sumerian composition written for a king of Isin, Lipit-Ištar, credited An with highly complicated powers and understood him as king-maker in choosing Lipit-Ištar as monarch.

Detail depicting An/Anu(m) from a relief of a procession of deities from Maltai or Maltaya, Northern Iraq. Carved into the rock face. Neo-Assyrian. After Pritchard 1969b: 181, no. 537. See also Black and Green 2003: 40

Although An/Anu(m) was worshipped throughout Mesopotamia, Uruk was his major cult center. At Uruk, and probably elsewhere, a ritual was held to celebrate the "Sacred Marriage." See discussions of this rite under Dumuzi; Inana. One text refers to an important festival of Anu(m), which was probably held in Uruk. At Dēr he was worshipped as chief deity under the name An-gal, "Great An." See also Antu (H) and Anu (H). (Foster 2005: 525–30, 640; *LAS*: 52–54; Black and Green 2003: 30,102; Foster 2001: 9, 48; Frayne 2001: 124; Leick 1998: 4–6; Litke 1998: 20; Cohen 1993: 335; George 1993: 67 no. 75; Tallqvist 1974: 251–54; Speiser, *ANET*: 85, 101–3, 342–45, 538)

ʻAnaqim, ʻAnakim (L) See Rephaim

A-na madu (M) Goddess at Ebla. Archi suggests a meaning "The Plentiful (or Abundant) Eye(s)" or "The Eye(s) of the Country." (Archi 1997)

Anammelech, Anammelek (L) See Adrammelech

'Anat(u) (Ugarit), **'Anat(h)** (Hebrew Bible), **Antit** (Egypt), **°anat** (Akk.) Young, blood-thirsty warrior goddess, perhaps originally from Mesopotamia or the northwest Semitic area of the Levant. Worshipped from the middle of the second millennium BCE to the Hellenistic period as herself or identified with another goddess. Beautiful 'Anat(u) remained quite popular in the western part of the Near East, including for a time in Egypt. For discussion of the etymology of the name 'Anat(u), see P. Day, *DDDB*: 36. According to mythic material from the Ugarit, 'Anat(u) was probably the daughter of the supreme god El and sister of the weather god Ba'lu/Had-(d)ad, possibly by a different mother. In that material, she was often closely associated with the goddess Aštarte ('Aṯtart).

Detail of warrior 'Anat from an Egyptian plaque. Late Bronze Age, ca. 1550–1200 BCE. Limestone. British Museum. After Cornelius 2004: pl. 5.1

The normal interpretation of 'Anat(u) in Ugaritic texts was and often is to see her as a sexually active "fertility" goddess and consort of the storm god Ba'lu. However, a recent interpretation argues that the goddess was in a transition stage between childhood and adulthood, a fact that explains her usual epithet in the compositions, "Maiden." 'Anat(u) indulged in activities such as the hunt and warfare, "culturally masculine pursuits" (P. Day 1992: 183). Another of 'Anat(u)'s titles was "Destroyer." Her youth, maiden status, and warlike qualities suggest a close connection to the Mesopotamian goddess Inana/Ištar.

As to iconography, an image identified as 'Anat(u) on a now-lost stele perhaps from Ugarit depicts her enthroned, wearing a robe and the royal Egyptian crown; she is carrying a shield and brandishing a weapon. A similar image appears on a "Qudšu plaque" from Egypt. See Cornelius 2004: Pl. 5.1, lower register. In other places, images that may represent 'Anat(u) show her with horns and sometimes with wings. A beautiful ivory furniture panel from Ugarit features a horned and winged goddess suckling two young males (*ANEP*: 352 no. 829).

This image might be 'Anat(u), for, in the Ugaritic mythic text about King Keret or Kirta, the high god El promised that the king that his sons would suckle at the breast of two goddesses, one of whom has been understood to be 'Anat(u). Another text mentioned her as having wings (del Olmo Lete 1999: 188). 'Anat(u) had strong and active roles in several of the Ugaritic mythic compositions. The texts provide a picture of an aggressive and impetuous supporter of the aims and aspirations of the weather god Ba'lu/Had(d)ad. In assisting him to get permission to build a house/temple, 'Anat(u) went as far as threatening to do violence to her "father" El, the venerable king of the cosmos. The texts also make clear that 'Anat(u) had conquered a number of Ba'lu's ferocious enemies for him. When the god of death and sterility, Mōt(u), swallowed Ba'lu, it was 'Anat(u), helped by the sun goddess Šapšu, who searched for Ba'lu and then viciously destroyed Mōt(u). A fragment of Ugaritic poetry demonstrates 'Anat(u)'s prowess in battle, as well as her delight in bloodshed. The story of the semi-divine hero-prince 'Aqhat added to her reputation for ruthlessness. 'Anat(u) coveted a beautiful bow owned by 'Aqhat and, when she asked him to give it to her, he refused her with an insult: "[B]ows (are for) warriors! / Will women hunt now?" (Wyatt 2002: 276). In revenge, 'Anat(u) had 'Aqhat killed.

Cultic texts from Ugarit, such as offering and god lists, make clear that 'Anat(u) was still being worshipped in the Late Bronze Age. Her name appears in god lists, offering lists, and incantations, especially against snakes. In one god list she comes under the deity group "Mountains and Valleys" (del Olmo Lete 1999: 131). 'Anat(u) was known also in Mesopotamia. As Ḫanat (Hanat), she occurs in the eighteenth-century BCE archives of Mari. In the southeast section of Mari's land, 'Anat(u) was worshipped at a city Ana(t)/Ḫanat on the banks of the Euphrates, and which extended onto an island in the river. There she had a temple called "True Hand of Heaven." At Ana(t)/Ḫanat she continued to be revered well into the eighth century BCE. On the island was found a stele dedicated to the goddess dating to that time. 'Anat(u) might be depicted also on a seal found at Ebla. As 'Anat(u)-Aštarte, the goddess had a role in "Elkunirša," the Hittite version of what seems to have been an originally Canaanite composition. Identified as sister of the god Ba'lu, she helped him resist the plotting of the goddess Ashertu (Asherah).

The Hebrew Bible does not mention 'Anat(u) as a goddess, but she certainly formed part of at least one personal name: Šamgar ben 'Anat (Judges 3: 31), and at least one place name: Beth 'Anat (Joshua 19:38 and Judges 1:33). She might appear also in the personal and place name 'Anathoth (Jeremiah 1:1; Nehemiah 10:20, Ezra 2:23). A few scholars have argued that 'Anat(u) was the goddess described in Jeremiah (7:18 and 44:17) as "The Queen of Heaven," but other scholars have made persuasive cases against such an identification. In addition to the Hebrew Bible and the texts from Ugarit, references to 'Anat(u) appear in other Levantine material. An arrowhead dating to about 1100 BCE bears an inscription including a theophoric name with 'Anat(u) as the deity. This object, as well as other evidence, has led some scholars to suggest that "ben 'Anat," as in biblical Šamgar ben 'Anat, was a surname of certain military families or a military title paying tribute to 'Anat(u) as protector deity of warriors. Among Egyptian sources, some military-campaign records mention the Levantine name Ben 'Anat. A thirteenth-century BCE potsherd refers to a festival of 'Anat(u) at Gaza.

Archaeology has shown that 'Anat(u) certainly had one temple in the Land of

Canaan (Rowe 1940: 31). It was unearthed at Beth-shean (Beth-shan), an Egyptian military post situated where the valley of Jezreel meets the Jordan River. A stele depicting the goddess found at the city names her as "queen of heaven, the mistress of all the gods."

However, it was in Egypt itself that 'Anat(u) became a truly important goddess. Evidence points to her having arrived in Egypt with the Hyksos, an Egyptian term meaning "rulers of foreign lands." This "Asiatic" dynasty of Semitic speakers from the Levant lasted from c. 1650 –1550 BCE, but the worship of 'Anat(u) continued in Egypt at least until the Greco-Roman period. 'Anat(u) became well known as war deity of the Ramesside pharaohs. Indeed, the great warrior Ramses II took her as his patron and appealed to her as "Lady of the Heavens" to assist him in battle and validate him as ruler of the world. An Egyptian text describes her as a woman who acts as a man. On an Egyptian plaque of this period there is a representation, with inscription, of an offering rite to 'Anat (Cornelius 2004: Plate 5.1; J. Westenholz 1998: 80 no. 28; *ANEP*: 163 no. 473). In Egyptian material, 'Anat(u) was linked at least once with Aštarte and with another goddess referred to as Qudšu or Qadeš(et), "Holy One" (*ANEP*: 352 no. 830). She was elevated to the position of daughter of the sun god.

The name 'Anat(u) is attested in a quite different source also from Egypt: fifth-century BCE Aramaic texts from an Israelite/Jewish military colony on Elephantine Island at Aswan. Scholars are divided as to whether the references to 'Anat-Bethel ('Anat-bayt'il) and 'Anat-Yahu ('Anat-YHW) were indeed to the goddess 'Anat(u). If they were, then 'Anat(u) was being worshipped there possibly as consort of the Israelite god. A treaty between Assyria and Tyre also mentions 'Anat-Bethel. Several Phoenician inscriptions from Phoenician colonies in Cyprus make clear that 'Anat(u) had been identified with Greek Athena, that she was still associated with Ba'lu, and that she was carrying on her association with war. In Punic (Carthaginian) theophoric names, 'Anat(u) occurs very rarely. Asherah and Aštarte, the other Canaanite great goddesses, possibly survived at least for a time, especially in Carthaginian religion, but 'Anat(u) probably was syncretized with several other goddesses to form part of the later "Syrian Goddess" Atargatis. (Leeming 2005: 17; Lewis 2005: 71–73, 85; Cornelius 2004: 40–42, 92–93; Pardee 2002; Stuckey 2002: 34–35, 43; Wyatt 2002: 39–146, 156, 321, 361–62; Smith 2001: 28, 34–35, 56–57; Bienkowski and Millard 2000: 150–51; J. Day 2000: 134; Parker 2000; P. Day, *DDDB*: 36–43; del Olmo Lete 1999: 51, 57, 60, 71, 188, 363, 373; Leick 1999: 134; Hoffner 1998: 90–92, 109; Leick 1998: 6–7; Pomponio and Xella 1997: 183; Lipiński 1995: 309–13; Handy 1994: 102–5; Lipiński, *DCPP*: 28–29; Redford 1992: 232–33; Maier, *ABD* I: 225–27; Patai 1990: 62; Roaf, Isma'il, and Black 1988: 1–5; Lambert 1985a: 526; Matthiae 1981: 138; Caquot and Sznycer 1980: 14; Hvidberg-Hanson 1979: 133; Bowman 1978: 225–34, 249–58; Oden 1976: 32; Kapelrud 1969: 37; Porten 1969; Porten 1968)

'Anata (L) See 'Anat(u)

'Anat-Aštarte (H) See 'Anat(u)

'Anat-Bethel, **'Anat-bayt'il** (L) See 'Anat(u)

'Anat(u) Ḫablay (L) A manifestation of 'Anat(u) at Ugarit. Perhaps means "'Anat(u) (who Has) Mutilated (Herself in Mourning for Ba'lu(u)." (Pardee 2002: 223, 274)

'Anat-Yahu, 'Anat-YHW (L) See 'Anat(u)

An-dumu-saga (M) According to Mander, a god appearing in a defective writing in an Early Dynastic god list from Abu Ṣalābīkh. Possibly denoting a star. (Mander 1986: 48–50)

An-gal (M) See An/Anu(m)

Angir (M) One of the gate-keepers of the E-babbar temple dedicated to Utu/Šamaš at Sippar and/or Larsa. Written An-gi-ir with variant A-gi-ir. The other gate-keeper was Kigir, thus one gatekeeper was involved with Heaven and one with Earth. (Litke 1998: 136)

A-nir (M) Deity attested in the Early Dynastic period. Name means "Wail." See A-nir-maḫ. (Mander 1986: 137)

A-nir-maḫ (M) Deity identified with the Sumerian goddess Nisaba. Name means "Great Wail." Occurs in a god list as referring to Nisaba and also in a Sumerian myth from Ebla. (Mander 1986: 59)

Ankaldarakar (E) God of Elam. Identified with the moon god Nanna/Sîn. (Litke 1998: 214)

An-ki (M) In An : *Anum* identified as An and Antum and seems to refer to the pair of primordial deities "Heaven" and "Earth." (Litke 1998: 20)

An-kid (M) Deity identified with the sun god Šamaš in An : *Anum*. Variant A-kíd with gloss ki-id and a variant A^{e}-kíd. May mean "Who Breaks Off the Date Cluster." (Richter 2004: 350; Litke: 1998: 130)

An-me-a (M) Explained by An : *Anum* as "Hero who Sits Erectly." It proceeds the homophonous entry Ama-é-a and thus perhaps this unusual name was, at one point, simply a variant. (Litke 1998: 81)

Anna (M) Deity, perhaps identified with Inana, in An : *Anum* with gloss a-nu. Means "The One of An." At Emar a month was named ^{d}An-na and the festival of Anna is mentioned in the Old Assyrian texts. (Fleming 2000: 200; Litke 1998: 164)

Annabītu(m) (M) Akkadian goddess listed in an Old Babylonian god list fragment from Nippur. In the circle of deities associated with the goddess Ištar. (Richter 2004: 295)

An(n)a-ḫiliba (M) Explained in An : *Anum* as one of eight deified lyres of the moon god Nanna/Sîn at Ur. For the possibility that he is the seal-keeper, not the lyre, of Nanna, see our discussion of Nanna-balag-anki. Written an-na-ḫi-li-ba (var. bi). This is probably a syllabic orthography for An-na-ḫilib(IGI.KUR)-ba, "He Is in Heaven and in the Netherworld," referring to the two realms through which the moon travels. (Richter 2004: 452; Litke 1998: 123)

Annedotos (L, M) Greek transcription of the Sumerian name U-an-duga. Among the Apkallū, the Seven Sages who lived before the Great Flood, he was second after Oannes to emerge from the sea and bring civilization to human beings. Attests to the surprisingly long life of a Sumerian mythic tradition. See also Oannes. (van Dijk 1962: 47)

An-NI(-urugal) (M) Deity identified with Bēlet-ilī. Consecutive entries written <d>An^{a}-ni <d>An-ni-uru$_{2}^{ú-ru}$-gal (Litke 1998: 71)

Annunaku(m), Annunakū (H, M) See Anunnaki

Anobret (L) According to Philo of Byblos, the name of a son of the god El/ Kronos. (Attridge and Oden 1981: 62–63, 93–94 note 149)

An-šar and **Ki-šar** (M) Primeval male and female deities who together formed the horizon. In the *Enūma eliš*, they were the third primeval pair, born of Laḫmu(m) and Laḫamu(m), the offspring of Ti'amat and Apsû(m) (Abzu). They, in turn, were parents of Anu(m), the sky god, who was the equal of An-šar. The names can be construed as "Totality of Heaven" and the "Totality of Earth." In "Nergal and Ereškigal," Ki-šar is keeper of the second gate of the netherworld. (Foster 2005: 439; Litke 1998: 21–22; Tallqvist 1974: 263, 342; Speiser, *ANET*: 61; Grayson, *ANET*: 509; Heidel 1967: 18)

An-šar-gal and **Ki-šar-gal** (M) In An : *Anum* identified as An and Antu(m) and seem to be variants for An-šar and Ki-šar. (Litke 1998: 21)

Anta-durunu (M) One of two divine gate-keepers of the E-sagil temple. The other was Abba. (George 1993: 77 no. 188)

Antaeus, 'Anthat, Anthyt, Antit (L) See 'Anat(u)

Antu, A-an-du (H) One of the Hurrian primeval deities. Borrowed from Mesopotamia. Wife of the sky god Anu in Hurrian texts. Appears in An : *Anum*, a trilingual version (Ugaritic, Hurrian, Akkadian) from Ugarit. Equated to Tamatu / Tihāmātu (Ti'amat). She occurs also in treaties. See An. (del Olmo Lete 1999: 137; van Gessel 1998: I, 33–34; Hoffner 1998: 112; Popko 1995: 99; Haas 1994: 107; Laroche 1946/47: 120)

Anu (H) One of the Hurrian primeval deities. Borrowed from Mesopotamia. Second ruler of the gods. Overthrown by Kumarbi. Antu was Anu's spouse. Sire of Teššub, Tašmišu, and the Aranzaḫ River (the Tigris). One of his epithets was "Hero of the Gods." Occurs in treaties, in the Hittite version of the "Epic of Gilgameš," and in texts from Ugarit. See An. (van Gessel 1998: I, 34–35; Hoffner 1998: 41–44, 55, 77, 109; Popko 1995: 99, 123–24; Haas 1994: 108, 112, 114; Laroche 1976: 50; Laroche 1946/47: 120)

Anu(m), Antu(m) (M) See An

Anubu (M) Deity in An : *Anum* identified with Martu. Written A-nu-bu and also KUR with gloss a-nu-bu. Written i-nu-bu-um in an Old Babylonian god list. Just perhaps derives from the Egyptian netherworld god Anubis, particularly since it can be written KUR, which can denote the netherworld. (Litke 1998: 218; Weidner 1924/25)

A-nun (M) See Am-anuna

Anunītu(m), Anu(n)na (M) Patron goddess of the city of Akkad and the Akkadian Dynasty. Considered daughter of Enlil. Identified with Ištar as the Venus star and primarily understood as a war goddess. She was the personal deity of King Narām-Sîn, who called himself her husband, "*mūt* Ištar-Anunītum." A fragment of a limestone mold shows a deified ruler, probably Narām-Sîn, sitting enthroned hand-in-hand with the goddess Ištar. A door-socket inscription from Ur describes the Ur III king Šū-Sîn as spouse of the goddess.

Anunītu(m) was worshipped at Nippur, Ur, and Uruk in Ur III times and in the Old Babylonian period at Nippur, Sippar, and Kisura. At Ur, a festival was held in her honor. At Sippar, she was a principal deity. Indeed, one of the twin cities making up Sippar was called Sippar-Anunītum. A "wailing" ritual was held for her at Uruk. She was worshipped also at Babylon and Mari. (Cohen 2015: 85; Aruz 2003: 206 no. 133; Black and Green 2003: 34–35; Leick 1999: 117, 153–54; Leick 1998: 7; Kienast 1990: 196–203; Tallqvist 1974: 255; Oppenheim, *ANET*: 309)

Anu(m)-rabû(m) (M) Akkadian/Babylonian god who replaced Ištarān as chief deity of Dēr, on the border with Elam. The god's name means "Great Anu(m)." (George 1993: 166 no. 166)

Anunnaki, Anunna, Anunnaku(m), Anunnakū, Ananaki (H, M) A group of Sumerian/Akkadian gods, the seven judges of the netherworld. As early as Early Dynastic times appears as a class of gods in Sumerian and Akkadian myths from Ebla. Later on, the term came to mean deities of Earth and the netherworld, as opposed to the Igigi, the divinities of Heaven. The sky god An/Anu(m) was king of the Anunnaki. Sometimes, as at Eridu, they numbered as many as fifty.

In the myth of Etana, the Anunnaki were said to declare the fates. At the end of the law code of Ḫammu-rāpi of Babylon, they were addressed as "the mighty gods of heaven and earth" and were called upon to carry out curses (Meek, *ANET*: 180). "The Death of Gilgameš" recounts how the hero made offerings before his death to all the main gods, among them "Anuna gods of the Holy Mound," the Du-kug, their primeval home (Frayne 2001: 153). In the Sumerian composition "The Descent of Inana," when Inana appears before them in the throne-room of her netherworld sister, they turn on her the look of death, so that she became a corpse hanging on a peg. A possible meaning of the name Anunnaki is "Princely Seed."

The Anunnaki were worshipped, among other places, at Babylon and Aššur. ANNUNAKI, borrowed from Mesopotamia, was used in Hurrian/Hittite material to refer to deities who lived in the netherworld. Probably the same as the Hittite primeval gods, Karuiles Siunes. (Foster 2005: 535; *LAS*: 70–71; Katz 2003: 402–4; Black and Green 2003: 34; Hoffner 1998: 109; Leick 1998: 7–8; Litke 1998: 221; Popko 1995: 99; George 1993: 77 no. 178; Tallqvist 1974: 255; Speiser, *ANET*: 114)

ANzagar(a) (M) God of dreams and nightmares. Written -gar-, -gàr-, and MAŠ.GI$_6$. The attestation of DINGIR.An-za-gàr suggests a reading An-zag-gar rather than ^{d}Za-gar (unless this is a scribal error). On the other hand, all the other entries in An : *Anum* begin with the theophoric determinative. Moreover, note the deity Za-ga-ri, perhaps syllabic for the god of dreams. Explained in *Anu ša amēli* as Enlil *ša annati* (heavens?). (Litke 1998: 229) (Butler 1998: 83–88; Litke 1998: 137, 229; Tallqvist 1974: 482, 484; *CAD* Z: 60a)

Anziba (M) See Ziba

Anzili (H) Deity involved in the official cult of the Hittite state of Zippalanda and was connected, as were a number of other divinities, to the sacred mountain of the weather god Taḫa, the source of a major river flowing before the city of Zippalanda. (van Gessel 1998: I, 35–36; Haas 1994: 590)

Anzû(m) (M) A huge and powerful eagle-like bird-monster with a lion's head. As described in "Lugalbanda and the Anzû Bird," Anzû(m) had the teeth of a shark and the talons of an eagle. His cry made the earth shake. The Sumerian orthography of the bird's name is IM.DUGUD. The *im* has been interpreted as the Sumerian word for "cloud" and dugud as "heavy"; thus Imdugud was construed to mean "Rain-cloud." So the creature became a storm cloud, thunder-bird, though there is little other evidence. In the "Epic of Gilgameš," Anzû(m) "descend[ed] like a cloud," terrifying in appearance: "His maw was fire, his breath death" (Foster 2001: 34).

Relief plaque of Anzu from Girsu, Mesopotamia. Ca. 2450 BCE. Stone. After Wolkstein and Kramer 1983: 8

Although, in "Lugalbanda and the Anzû Bird," Anzû(m) is indeed ferocious, he does not harm Lugalbanda. On the contrary, he fixes his fate, grants him strength and stamina, and assists him in finding his way back to his troops. However, in "Gilgameš, Enkidu, and the Netherworld," Inana does not welcome Anzû(m) when he establishes his nest in the branches of the *ḫuluppu*-tree that she is carefully growing in her garden. Eventually she has to call on the hero Gilgameš to frighten the bird and his family away. In another composition, the warrior god Ninurta pursues and presumably subdues Anzû(m) when the latter steals the tablets of destiny from Enki (Sumerian version) or Enlil (Akkadian version) and flees with them to the mountains. In other versions of the composition, the heroes are Lugalbanda and Nin-Girsu, and, in a hymn, Marduk.

Anzû(m) was closely associated with Ninurta. Indeed, in a Sumerian hymn-narrative, "Ninurta's Return to Nppur," Ninurta controls the bird, which he conquered and used as a decoration on his chariot. In the city of Girsu, where Nin-Girsu was the local form of Ninurta, Nin-Girsu's temple was called "The Shining Anzû." At Mari, as elsewhere throughout Mesopotamia, a festival involving foot races round the walls of the city commemorated the defeat of Anzû(m) by Ninurta. Images of Anzû(m) with shining eyes, widespread wings, and extended claws were displayed in Mesopotamian temples and other buildings to ward off evil. (Foster 2005: 555–78; *LAS*: 22–31, 164–71, 182–83; J. Westenholz 2004: 32–33; Black and Green 2003: 107–8; Frayne 2001: 130–34; Leick 1998: 9–10; Cohen 1993: 292, 333; Alster 1991: 1–5; Tallqvist 1974: 327; Speiser, *ANET*: 111–13)

A-pa-dun (M) The twenty-fifth name of Marduk in the *Enūma eliš*. Means "Who Digs Watercourses." (Litke 1998: 92)

Apantum, Apate (H) See Abade

Apaštu (H) One of the more obscure Hurrian deities. (Archi 1990: 118)

Apin-Šarada-sua (M) Deified cultic plow. May mean "Plow that Moves along with (the Help of) Šara." An allocation is made to this divinized cultic plow at Ur III Umma, where it is written ᵈApin!-Šara$_2$-dà-su (MVAG 21 22 FH 5). This same cultic plow is attested in a non-divinized form ᵍᵉˢapin-ᵈŠara$_2$-da-sù-a, as receiving oil for the seeding festival (ezem šu-numun) (Cohen 1983: 84).

Aplada(d), Apil-addu (M) Son of the storm god Adad. As Adad-aplad he was a very important god of the Aramaeans. (Lipiński 2000: 636; Leick 1998: 10; Tallqvist 1974: 247, 263)

Apsû(m) (Akk.), **Abzu** (Sum.) Primeval deity of sweet (fresh) subterranean waters, which were the source of springs, lakes, rivers, and well water. His consort was Ti'amat. The *Enūma eliš* told how, in the beginning, the god Apsû(m), sweet waters, mingled with the goddess Ti'amat, salt waters. Another entity, Mummu, Apsû's minister or vizier, might also have been with them. The joining of the primordial pair begat a line of deities starting with Laḫmu(m) and Laḫamu(m) and followed, in sequence, by An-šar and Ki-šar, Anu(m), Ea, and, finally, Marduk. The younger gods were so rowdy and raucous that their parents could not get any sleep. Finally, Apsû(m) persuaded a reluctant Ti'amat that they should rid themselves of their noisy children. When the younger gods got wind of the plan, they quieted down until wise Ea thought of a solution. He put a magical sleeping spell on Apsû(m) and then, while Apsû(m) slept, Ea killed him. On Apsû(m)'s dead body Ea built his house at Eridu and called it "Apsû(m)," the name of Ea's Eridu temple (E-Apsû) from then on. Marduk, Ea's son, was born in the Apsû(m). An Abzu/Apsû(m) tank filled with holy water stood in most temple courtyards. (Foster 2005: 439; Black and Green 2003: 27; Becking, *DDDB*: 300; Leick 1998: 11–12; Jacob-sen 1967: 18–21)

Aqhat(u) (L) Semi-divine hero figure from Ugarit. See 'Anat(u). (del Olmo Lete 1999: 161, 330–33)

Aqtupītu(m) (M) Akkadian goddess attested in a cone inscription of the Isin king Sîn-māgir at Old Babylonian Aqtub. The goddess's temple was rebuilt for Sîn-māgir by the priestess Nuṣṣuptu(m), who was the king's concubine. (George 1993: 148 no. 1079; Renger 1967: 139)

Ara (M) Sumerian name of Usmû(m), the minister of Enki, in a Neo-Assyrian text. Said to be the chief vizier of Ea. Attested also in late hymns. Written ŠA with gloss a-ra. (Litke 1998: 102; Cohen 1988: 90; Mander 1986: 62)

Arazu (M) Artisan god created by Ea to complete the restoration and construction of temples. The account of the making by Ea of a number of minor gods from clay occurs in a short, Hellenistic-period composition at the end of a text in Akkadian, "Ritual for the Repair of a Temple." (Lambert 2013: 380; Thureau-Dangin 1975: 46–47; Sachs, *ANET*: 341)

Arazu-gal, Arazu-maḫ, Arazu-šega, Arazu-šega-gal (M) Divinized attributes of the god Di-ku$_5$ "The Judge" in An : *Anum*. Means "The Great/Lofty One of Prayer" and "He (The Great One) who Listens to/Accepts Prayer." (Litke 1998: 226)

Arda (M) See Arṣay(u)

Ardat-lilî (M) See Lil

Arinnītum (M) See Sun Goddess of Arinna

Arinna (H) See Sun Goddess of Arinna

Arma (H) Luwian moon god adopted by the Hittites. In images his pointed hat was topped by a crescent, and, like the Hurrian moon god Kušuḫ, he had wings. Occurs in many theophoric Luwian names, especially from the first millennium BCE. (Leick 1998: 113; Popko 1995: 92, 168, 173, 177, 184)

Arṣa, Arṣu (L) See Azizos

Arṣay(u), Arṣai (L), **Arda** (M) Earth goddess of Ugarit. Third daughter of the storm god Ba'lu/Had(d)ad or possibly of Mot, the god of death. Perhaps also Ba'lu's wife. Means "Earth(y)." The other two daughters were Piḏray and Ṭallay. A Mesopotamian god list from Ugarit and An : *Anum* (ᵈÁr-da) identify her with the queen of the netherworld, Allatu(m), and the netherworld itself (*erṣetu*). Although not an important goddess, Arṣay(u) did receive offerings in the cult at Ugarit, and she appears in god lists, in one list in the deity group "Mountains and Valleys." (del Olmo Lete 1999: 131). (Wyatt 2002: 77; Smith 2001: 44, 56, 108; del Olmo Lete 1999: 56, 71–73, 79; Litke 1998: 189; Hutter, *DDDB*: 272–73; Smith 1997: 83, 109; Albright 1968: 144–45)

Arṣu-wa-Šamuma (L) A double deity in Ugaritic cultic texts. Means "Earth-and-Heavens." (Pardee 2002: 14, 17, 45, 47, 274)

Aršu (L) Deity at Ugarit. Helper of the sea god Yam. (del Olmo Lete 1999: 56)

Aru(a) (M) Described as the divine queen in a Late-Babylonian ritual. Her two daughters, Ṣilluš-ṭāb and Kaṭuna, resided in the E-sagil in Babylon, where she, too, may have had a residence. See also Aruru; Erua. (Cohen 1993: 319)

Arun(n)aš (H) The Great Sea. He gave his daughter Sertapšuruḫi to Kumarbi and another daughter to Telipinu. Arun(n)a(š) was revered at a Middle Hittite ritual. The sea god was worshipped at the Temple of the Great Sea. He occurs in curse formulae. (Schwemer 2001: 451–54; Hoffner 1998: 26–27, 41, 51, 112; van Gessel 1998: I, 399; Popko 1995: 126; Haas 1994: 86)

Aruru (M) Sumerian/Babylonian goddess of birth and a mother goddess, usually identified with Nin-ḫursag. Sister of Enlil. Patron deity of the city of Šarrāku(m). Attested already in god lists from the Early Dynastic period. In the "Epic of Gilgameš," she was credited with creating human beings, and fashioned Gilgameš's counterpart Enkidu out of clay. Entitled "Water Hastener," she aided the fetus in leaving the womb. Possibly appears under the short form Aru in an Early Dynastic god list. See drawing under Bēlet-ilī. (Foster, 2001: 6; Frayne 2001: 154; Mander 1986: 53; Tallqvist 1974: 256; Krebernik, *RlA* VIII: 504)

Asag, Azag, Asig (Sum.), **Asakku(m)** (Akk.) Hideous monster-demon and the diseases he caused. Agent of death and destruction, especially by plague. Son of An and Ki. The Sumerian narrative "Ninurta's Exploits" describes Asag as a fearless warrior and murderer, supported by an army of stones. After fighting his way to a face-to-face encounter with Asag, Ninurta smashes him to pieces. A different version attributed the killing of Asag to Adad, one of the other warrior gods. In another myth, Ninurta defeated the seven or eight Asakkū, a group of demons, all offspring of Anu(m). Prominent in magical texts, Asag attacked/killed people through illness, particularly fevers in the head. He also attacked cattle. According to Jacobsen, his name means "sling-stone" (1976: 130). See Ninurta for drawing. (*LAS*: 164–71; Black and Green 2003: 35–36; Leick 1998: 13; Tallqvist 1974: 256; Ebeling, *RlA* II: 107–12)

Asar-alim-nuna (M) Sumerian deity identified with Asar-lu-ḫe. Occurs in incantations. Means "Asar, the noble bison." Asar-alim (entry following Asar-lu-ḫe) explained in An : *Anu ša amēli* as "Marduk of life." (George 2016: no. 5; Litke 1998: 236; Cohen 1988: 403, 413)

Asar-lu-ḫe (M) Son of Enki. Known from Early Dynastic times as patron deity of Ku'ara, a town near Enki's city Eridu. From his association with Enki, Asar-lu-ḫe became associated with healing and white magic and was credited with the understanding of magic, one of Enki's special powers. He had a close connection with exorcism rituals. He became important later because of his identification with Marduk, so much so that, eventually, his name and Marduk's became interchangeable. His was the seventh of Marduk's names proclaimed at the end of the *Enūma eliš*. (Foster 2005: 475; Black and Green 2003: 36; Leick 1998: 14; Litke 1998: 224; George 1993: 27 note 233; Biggs 1974: 47; Tallqvist 1974: 264; Speiser, *ANET*: 70; Heidel 1967: 52)

Asarre (M) Deity first attested in an Early Dynastic god list from Šuruppak. Either a variant for or another deity eventually identified with Asar-lu-ḫe. Occurs in incantations where he is clearly identified with Asar-lu-ḫe. See Asaru. (George 2016: no. 46; Litke 1998: 90; Mander 1986: 48)

Asaru (M) Tenth name of Marduk proclaimed at the end of the *Enūma eliš*. Likely a form of Asarre, who is identified with Asarluḫe, the son of Enki. (Foster 2005: 476; Litke 1998: 90; Speiser, *ANET*: 70; Heidel 1967: 53)

Ashdar, Asdar (L) See 'Aṯtar(u)

Asherah, Ašera(h), Athirat, Aṯiratu, Ashirta (L) Canaanite great goddess. Called Aṯirat(u) at Ugarit. Consort of Ugarit's chief god, El or Il(u). Probably for a time also an Israelite goddess and consort of the Israelite god YHWH. The earliest known textual reference to the goddess is from Babylon, where her name was Ašratu(m), and she was consort of Amurru(m). She was entitled Bēlet-Ṣēri "Lady of the Steppe," a name she had at Ugarit, where she was also Ilat(u)/Elat(u), "The Goddess." She might have been introduced into Mesopotamia by the Amorites. See Hadley 2000: 43–53 for a full discussion. At Ugarit she and El "together functioned as the highest authority" in the universe, which they "owned" (Handy 1994: 69, 76–77).

Ugaritic poetry usually calls her "Lady Aṯirat(u) of the Sea" or "One who Treads the Sea." Another title might have been Raḫmay(yu), mentioned in the story of King Kirta and also paired with Aṯirat(u) in another text. Wyatt translates Raḫmay(yu) as "Uterine" or "Womby" (2002: 327 note 16). Raḫmay(yu) could, of course, be a separate goddess. Texts at Ugarit describe Asherah as "creatress (or owner) of the gods." She was understood to have seventy sons. She clearly held the powerful office of "Queen Mother," and as a result she had a role in deciding which deities would succeed to certain responsibilities. For instance, when Ba'lu disappeared into the netherworld, El asked Asherah to nominate one of her sons to take Ba'lu's place. She did not live in El's palace/temple, but had one in her own right. In Ugaritic myth she was presented as doing household chores, such as spinning, washing, and cooking. She functioned as a mediator for El for the other gods. In the group of Ugaritic compositions known as the "Ba'lu Cycle," when Ba'lu and 'Anat(u) needed El's permission for Ba'lu to have his own palace/temple built, they took gifts to Asherah, who then successfully laid their case before El. In another mythic composition, the story of the king Kirta or Keret, Asherah punished the king for breaking a vow he had made to her. In this myth she is specifically named as the main goddess of the Phoenician cities Tyre and Ṣidōn.

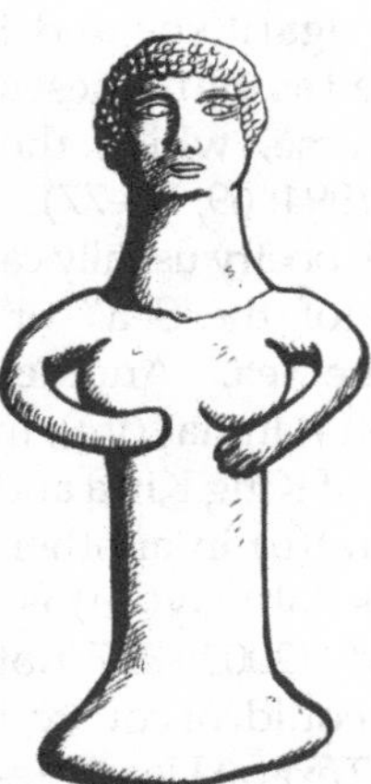

"Pillar" figurine of the type usually identified as Asherah. Ninth century BCE. Clay. Israel. After Patai 1990: pl. 1

Asherah was the most important goddess in the cultic texts of Ugarit: lists of deities and of offerings. She was actively worshipped at Ugarit, as offering lists demonstrate. She appears in one god list in the deity group "Mountains and Valleys" (del Olmo Lete 1999: 131). She was often named in prayers, and a number of theophoric names were constructed with her name.

Divination was also done under her aegis: a tablet found in Israel and dating to the fifteenth century BCE mentioned a diviner, "a wizard of Asherah" (Finegan 1997: 125). Until the discovery and publication of the tablets from Ugarit, most scholars denied that there ever had been a deity Asherah, despite the fact that the Hebrew Bible relates that Jezebel, Ahab's queen and princess of Ṣidōn, fed four hundred prophets of Asherah at her table (I Kings 18; 19). The scholarly problem stemmed from the Hebrew Bible where things termed in Hebrew the *asherim* (masculine plural, with the article "the") were mentioned often, especially in connection with the worship of the Canaanite god Ba'lu. General scholarly opinion was that they were either wooden poles as cult objects or groves of trees. After the Ugaritic finds, most concurred that the objects referred to around forty times in nine books of the Hebrew Bible were both cult objects and a goddess, some even considering the *Asherah* to have been large, carved wooden images. A startling discovery in the northern Sinai both threw light on and complicated this matter. On some sherds of large pots, someone had drawn a few heavily symbolic pictures full of goddess imagery and accompanied them with written blessings that refer to "YHWH of Samaria and his Asherah" and "YHWH of Teman and his/its Asherah." These add support to the work of scholars who argue that, during the period of consolidation of Israelite settlement in Canaan, the goddess Asherah was important to both the official and popular worship of YHWH. Indeed, as the Hebrew Bible makes clear, for around two-thirds of the existence of the Solomonic temple in Jerusalem, as "a legitimate part of the cult ...," it displayed a statue of Asherah (Olyan 1988: 13). Some maintain that Asherah was the consort of the Israelite god.

The goddess continued to be worshipped in the Levant by the Canaanites and Phoenician speakers, especially at Ṣidōn and Tyre. In the "Amarna Letters," one of the Amorite chiefs mentioned bore the name Abdi-Ašerta "Servant (or Slave) of Asherah." Asherah seems to have been an important protector deity of Canaanite and Phoenician sailors. She might later have been subsumed into the chief goddess of Carthage, Tanit, a name that possibly originated as an epithet of Asherah. Asherah's name seemed to have disappeared from inscriptions, personal names, and other Phoenician texts in the first millennium BCE, except, according to Lipiński (1995: 225), when *aširtu* was used to designate a shrine or holy place. However, Asherah probably survived into the Greco-Roman period as part of the "Syrian Goddess" Atargatis. Indeed, the goddess appears in south Arabian inscriptions from the first millennium BCE, and she also had a prominent part in the Hittite "Elkunirsa" myth. Whether she was the "Qudšu" mentioned, along with ʿAnat(u) and Aštarte, on an Egyptian plaque is still unclear. Sometimes the word *asherah* can mean shrine or sanctuary. (Peckham 2014: 9, 83; Dever 2005; Leeming 2005: 32–33; Cornelius 2004: 99–101; Pardee 2002; Stuckey 2002: 30–31, 37–39, 43; Wyatt 2002: 57 note 95, 93, 97–103, 176–243, 206 and note 135, 209, 327, 361–62; Smith 2001: 47–49, 71, 73–74, 172–73; J. Day 2000: 42; Hadley 2000: 4–11, 116–19; del Olmo Lete 1999: 43–55, 56, 57, 119, 340–41; Wyatt, *DDDB*: 99–105; Brody 1998: 26–31; Keel and Uelinger 1998: 236; van der Toorn 1998: 88–89; Binger 1997: 68–69, 89; Finegan 1997: 133–34; Greenstein 1997: 24, 44 note 59; Lewis 1997a: 208; Smith 1997: 122–30, 125, 153–54; Kletter 1996: 79; Schmidt 1996: 137–40, 184, 239–40; Lipiński 1995: 72, 224–26; Handy 1994: 72–75, 84; Hess 1993: 7–9; Hestrin 1991: 50; Patai, 1990: 34–53, 302 note 24; Pettey 1990: 9, 16, 45; Smith 1990: 16; Olyan 1988; Freedman 1987; Betlyon 1985; Dever 1984; Dever 1982; de Tarragon 1980; Coogan 1978: 97, 104, 116; Oden 1976: 32; Yamashita 1963: 126–29; Reed 1949: 33; Danthine 1937: no. 862; Ward 1902–1903: 33)

Ashertu, Asherah (H) See Elkuniřša

Ashima (L) Deity revered by the people of Hamath, Syria after their removal to Samaria by the Assyrians. Referred to in II Kings 17:30. (Cogan, *DDDB*: 105–6; Langdon, 1931: 22)

Ashirta, Ashertu, Ashirtu (L) See Asherah; Ašratu(m)

Ashmodai, Ashmedai (L) See Asmodeus

ʿAshtar-Chemosh (L) See Kamiš **ʿAshtart, ʿAshtereth, ʿAshteroth** (L) See ʿAštart

ʿAshtart-šem-Baʾlu (L) See ʿAštart

Ashura, Asirat (L) See Asherah

Asmodeus, Ashmodai, Ashmedai (L) A demonic figure in the apocryphal book of Tobit written in Greek and generally accepted as dating to the second century BCE. He appears also later in Jewish writings, where he was responsible for causing marital strife. In Tobit 3, it was reported that the demon killed, on their wedding night, seven husbands of Sara, who was then accused of strangling them. With the help of the angel Raphael, Tobit's son Tobias was able to marry Sara and ritually expel the demon. In later Jewish folklore, Asmodeus was the king of the demons. He was often presented as drunken and licentious, but also as sometimes beneficent. Lilith the Younger was his wife. Possibly the demon's name comes from two Persian words meaning "Spirit of Anger." (Hutter, *DDDB*: 106–8; Grether, *ABD* I: 499; Swaim, *IDB* I, 239–40; Patai 1990: 227, 241, 244, 247; "Tobit" in *(The) Apocrypha* [no date]: 68–82)

Asqur (M) See Aškur

As-sig-a (E) In a Neo-Assyrian god list identified with Ninurta of Elam. Written As-sig$_7$-a. (King 1969: pl. 12)

'Astartu, Asteria, Astroarche (L) See 'Aštart

Astronoe, Astrinoe (L) Greek epithet of the goddess Aštarte, especially at Tyre, where she was associated with the god Melqart. In the story of Ešmun, the disappearing and returning god of Ṣidōn, Astronoe revived Ešmun after he had died from self-castration, and she turned him into a deity. The name comes from the Greek word for "star" and probably refers to the planet Venus. (Ribichini, *DDDB*: 307–8; Lipiński 1995: 137, 160; Bonnet, *DCPP*: 48; Redford 1992: 45)

A-su (M) See E-su

Asumûm (M) Deity attested in the Mari texts.

Asu-ziba (M) Identified in a Neo-Assyrian god list with Adad. Means ""Who Sprinkles Water, Giving Life." Written a-sù-zi-ba. (Schwemer 2000: 79, 81; King 1969: pl. 16)

Aša-íl-ana, Abša-íl-ana (M) Deity attested in a god list from Aššur in the circle of Šamaš. Written a-šà-íl-<an>-na and áb-šà-íl-<an>-na. (Schroeder 1920: no. 64)

Aša-nugia (M) See Ige-nugia

Ašar (M) Written ^{d}A-šár. This deity occurs only in personal names during the Sargonic and Ur III periods, from Mari, and in Amorite names. (Roberts 1972: 16–17)

Ašdu (L) Deity attested mainly in Phoenician theophoric names. Probably an epithet. Means "Lion." Arabic form is 'Ašad. (Lipiński 1995: 357–60)

Ašgašepa, Aškašepa (H) Goddess of doors, a genie of doors. Appeared with the horse god Pirwa, especially at Kanesh. One of her epithets was "Queen." Acted as oath goddess in a Hittite state treaty. Also a mountain goddess. (van Gessel 1998: I, 51–52; Popko 1995: 89, 112; Haas 1994: 281)

Ašgi, Ašširgi (M) Son of Dingir-maḫ (Nin-tu(d), the birth goddess. Spouse of Gešḫuranki. Patron god of the city of Šarrāku(m). According to the Sumerian zà-mí hymns, Ašgi was also chief deity of Adab. (Maiocchi 2009: no. 314; Litke 1998: 74; Cohen 1993: 204, 208; Cavigneaux 1992: no. 113; Biggs 1974: 48)

Ašḫara (E) Elamite spelling of the name of the Mesopotamian goddess Išḫara.

Appearing in a list of deities in an Elamite treaty between Narām-Sîn of Akkad and a king of Susa. (Hinz and Koch 1987: 87; König 1977: 29, 184, 227)

Āšib-šamê (M) God mentioned in a tablet from the First Sealand Dynasty. Means "Dweller of Heaven." (Dalley 2009: 78)

Āšibti-Uruk (M) Goddess mentioned in a tablet listing gods honored at the *akītu*. Means "Dweller (in) Uruk." Tablet likely from the capital city of the First Sealand Dynasty. (Dalley 2009: 60)

Ašīyat, Ašiet (H) Luwian/Hittite deity. Appears in rituals at Kanesh. (Popko 1995: 55)

Aškur (L) West-Semitic deity attested only in a personal name Aškur-milki from the "Amarna Letters." Aškur is clearly not to be seen as a writing for the Sumerian weather god Iškur, as Dietrich and Loretz erroneously suggested. Durand reads the name as Asqur. (Schwemer 2001: 30 note 135; Durand 1991: 88; Moran 1987: 574; Dietrich and Loretz 1966: 241)

Ašnan, Ezinu (M) Sumerian goddess of grain (emmer wheat). One of her epithets was "Lady of Abundance." Daughter of Enki and sister of Lahar, goddess of sheep. Appeared in a hymn to Nisaba dating to the Early Dynastic period and found at Ebla. Also occurred in An : *Anum* as part of the circle of deities associated with Enlil's Ekur temple at Nippur. Her name appears in An : *Anum* just before that of another grain goddess, Nisaba. The name Ašnan was borrowed into Akkadian. In images, ears of grain grow from her shoulders. In the Sumerian "Debate between Sheep and Grain," the goddess Grain refers to herself as Ezina-Kusu, Enlil's daughter. In "Enki and the World Order," Enki places agricultural produce under Ezina's aegis. The law code of Lipit-Ištar appealed to Ašnan, along with Šamagan (See Šakkan), the god of the steppe, to withhold abundant produce from anyone who damaged the stele upon which the law code was inscribed.

According to the Sumerian zà-mí hymns, Ašnan's cult center was Apišal, a city north of Umma. Ašnan and Kusu had shrines in the temple of Nin-Ib-gal, "Lady of the Oval" (Inana), at Umma in Ur III times. Offerings were made to her also in Nippur in Old Babylonian times. (*LAS*: 222, 225–29; Cohen 2015: 160; Leick 1998: 14, 108–9; Litke 1998: 53 no. 287; Pomponio and Xella 1997: 62; George 1993: 103 no. 504; Biggs 1974: 49; Tallqvist 1974: 265, 308; Kramer, *ANET*: 161)

Ašnan °ARdaḫi (M) Sumerian goddess. Means "Ašnan of ḪARdaḫi," ḪARdaḫi being a small settlement in the neighborhood of Umma in the Ur III period. (Cohen 1996a: 30)

Ašnan-utu (M) Sumerian deity attested at Ur III Nippur. Means "Ašnan who Gives Birth." (Such-Gutiérrez 2003: 321)

Ašratu(m), Aširtu(m) (Akk.), **Gu-bara** (Sum.) A mountain goddess of abundance, charm, and sexual attractiveness. The fact that she appears often in Akkadian/Babylonian material as wife of Amurru(m) (Sumerian Mardu/Martu) argues for her origin as a goddess of the Amorites. As Amurru(m)'s wife she was daughter-in-law of the head of the pantheon An/Anu(m). Among her epithets were "Lady with Patient Mercy" and "Lady of Voluptuousness and Happiness." Another title was Bēlet-ṣēri, "Lady of the Steppe." She was worshipped in Babylon in a temple called "House of the Luxuriance of the Land." For a possible etymological relationship between Aširtu and Adgar-kidu, Martu's wife in "The Marriage of Martu," see Adgar-kidu. Also a mountain goddess. Same as the Levantine goddess Asherah. (Wyatt, *DDDB*: 100–1; Leick 1998: 14; George 1993: 37–38; Tallqvist 1974: 265)

Ašša (Hurrian) One of the more obscure Hurrian deities. (Archi 1990: 118)

Ašširgi (M) See Ašgi

Aššir-sig (M) Identified in a Neo-Assyrian god list with Adad. Written ^{d}Aš-šir-sig$_7$. (King 1969: pl. 16)

Aššur (M) The great god of the Assyrians and the city god of the Assyrian capital Aššur, the center of his cult. The supreme deity of the Assyrian state and later the empire. God of war who not only supported, but actually ordered the military ambitions of the Assyrians. The Assyrian king was "his chief priest and vicar on earth." As G. Frame points out, "the god, the city, and the land were all known by the same name."

It may be that the god was originally "the personification" of the spirit of the high ground where the city was situated (Frame 1999: 7–9). As the Assyrian version of Enlil, Aššur took over not only Enlil's wife Ninlil (Assyrian Mulliltu(m), Mullissu(m)) as his wife, but also other members of Enlil's family. He was identified with An-sār of the *Enūma eliš* and also with the Babylonian supreme deity, the warrior god Marduk, whose Creation Story role he assumed.

He was the first god listed in Assyrian treaties, with titles such as "King of the Gods," "King of Heaven and Earth," and "Father of the Deities." A number of Assyrian kings took names in which Aššur was an element, for example, Esarhaddon and Aššurbanipal.

Detail showing Aššur from a relief of a procession of deities from Maltai or Maltaya, Northern Iraq. Carved into the rock face. Neo-Assyrian. After Pritchard 1969b: 181, no. 537.

The main temple of Aššur in the city of Aššur was called E-šara, "The House of the Universe." From it, Aššur and other gods visited the royal palace annually. The *akītu* festival was held in his honor, and the king participated in rituals and sacrifices at his temple. (Foster 2005: 318–23, 817–19; Black and Green 2003: 37–39; Leick 1999: 24–26, 57–58; Leick 1998: 15; Livingstone, *DDDB*: 108–9; Becking, *DDDB*: 450; Tallqvist 1974: 265–66; Reiner, *ANET*: 533–34, 538)

Aššurītu(m) (M) Form of Ištar, identified also with Mullissu(m), Enlil's wife, who appears as the consort of the god

Aššur at Neo-Babylonian Uruk. Means "The Assyrian (Woman)." Her cult may have come to the city in the seventh century BCE, and a village and watercourse, likely in the vicinity of Uruk, were named for her. The name may have originally been an epithet of the goddess Šeru'a at Aššur. (Beaulieu 2003: 311–12)

Aštabi(l), Astabi, Aštupinu (H, M) A very ancient warrior god at Ebla. Later attested at Ugarit and in eastern Anatolia. Borrowed from Greater Mesopotamia (Syria) as the Luwian/Hurrian weather and war god. Ally of Teššub in the Kumarbi stories. In Hattic he was Wurunkatte "King of the Land." Depicted at the rock-carved shrine of Yazılıkaya near Ḫattušas. Attested as Aštupinu in a Neo-Assyrian god list. Occurs in theophoric names. Identified with Babylonian Zababa or, sometimes, Ninurta and with Ugaritic ʻAṯtar. (del Olmo Lete 1999: 201; Hoffner 1998: 41, 62, 113; van Gessel 1998: I, 53–54; Pomponio and Xella 1997: 68–77; Popko 1995: 100, 115; Haas 1994: 312, 363; King 1969: pl. 11; Laroche 1946/47: 46)

Aštabi-Il (M) Deity mentioned in the Mari letters. J.-M. Durand has suggested a meaning "Il has taken as Spoil" and links the deity to Ziniyan in the province of Saggaratum. Some have understood this deity to have originally been an ancestor, but Sasson suggests the opposite possibility, that he was originally a god who later was believed to have been a human hero of old. (Durand 2008: 274; Sasson 2001)

Aštakkuwa (M) A second-millennium BCE deity from the area of Ḫana, possibly named for the village of the god's cult. (Durand 1987b: no. 97)

Aštammer (M) Child of Bēlet-bēri. Means "I Shall Give Praise." (Litke 1998: 166)

Aštar (M) See ʻAṯtar

Aštar-ṣarba (M) Goddess who took part in a procession at Emar. Means "The Poplar (Tree) Aštar." Appears earlier at Ebla and Mari in the Early Dynastic period. Local deity of a town north of Mari named "Poplar Town." She was revered as a goddess of plant life, and her rites at Emar took place four months after the crops were planted. (Fleming 2000: 182; Belmonte 1997: 82–83; Durand 1995: 13; Oliva 1993a: 32–34)

Aštar-ṣarbat (M) Goddess attested at Ebla. Means "Aštar of the Town Ṣarbat." (Oliva 1993a: no. 42)

ʻAštart, (Phoenician); **Astarte** (Greek); **ʻAṯtart(u)** (Ugaritic); **ʻAštareth** sg., **ʻAštaroth** pl., **ʻAštoreth** sg., **ʻAšteroth** pl. (Hebrew) (L) The great Levantine goddess of the first millennium BCE. Deity of love and sexuality, of the evening star (Venus), and of war, especially in Greco-Roman times. Equivalent to the Babylonian Ištar. The meaning of the name is obscure, but might have been originally the female form of ʻAṯtar, possibly a male name of the planet Venus, likely as morning star. In Greek material Aštarte certainly represented the evening star. Closely associated with horses and sometimes depicted armed and riding a horse.

Among her epithets were Astronoe/Astrinoe (See Astronoe), Asteria "Starry," Astroarche "Queen of the Stars," and Ourania/Urania "Heavenly," all celestial titles. Her sacred animal was the lion, and her bird the dove. At Ugarit ʻAṯtart(u) was an important goddess. She appears around 46 times in the texts, but more often in the cultic than the mythic material. In one god list she appears in the deity group "Mountains and Valleys" (del Olmo Lete 1999: 131). One of her titles was 'Aṯtart(u)-Šadi "Aštarte of the Steppe," a name that might go back into a nomadic past of the people of Ugarit. The myths associate her closely with Ba'lu /Had(d)ad, calling her 'Aṯtart-šem-Ba'lu "Aštarte-Name-of-Ba'lu," meaning something like "representative of Ba'lu."

Like 'Anat(u), with whom she was often paired, she was Ba'lu's close supporter. 'Aṯtart and 'Anat(u) lived on Mount Inbub, perhaps part of Ba'lu's sacred mountain Ṣapōn. The regular coupling of 'Aṯtart with 'Anat(u) in the texts might indicate that the two goddesses were beginning to meld into one another. The mythic texts present them as models of beauty. 'Aṯtart's name appears often in the cultic material, an indication that she had an important role in Ugaritic worship.

According to an Ugaritic myth about ridding the land of snakes, one of the goddess's cult centers was Mari. A temple dedicated to Aštarte was excavated there. The major temple of Emar belonged to Aštarte and Ba'lu. A fragment of cultic material from Ugarit refers to the goddess as "Aṯtart-of-the-Window" (Wyatt 2002: 387), perhaps identifying the goddess with Mesopotamian Kilili. Many beautiful ivory images of the "Woman at the Window" are extant. They were carved, mostly in Phoenicia, as furniture inlays, especially for beds. The most famous image is the so-called "Mona Lisa of Nimrūd." In most of these images, the goddess was posed full face in a window frame. She usually had heavy, ornately dressed ringlets and often wore a necklace. Kilili has normally been interpreted as a prostitute, for her stance was seen as one of displaying her wares in a window. Some late sources identified temples of Aštarte as sites of "sacred prostitution," a cultic activity whose ancient practice is questioned today.

Figurine, possibly of Aštarte. Found in a Canaanite shrine at Nahariyah, Israel. Dated to Late Bronze Age, ca. 1550-1200 BCE. Ancient steatite (soapstone) mold on left, modern metal cast on right. After Negbi 1976: pl. 39, no. 1532.

The motif of the "Woman in the Window" almost certainly influenced the Hebrew Bible's account of the death of Jezebel, princess of Sidon, the queen of King Ahab of Israel, the northern kingdom (2 Kings 9:30). In the Hebrew Bible, Aštarte appears nine times as 'Aštareth/'Aštaroth. It has been argued that the form resulted from the deliberate substitution of the vowels of the Hebrew word *bošeth* meaning "shame" for the vowels of the goddess's name, but this form might be also a dialectical variant. The often-used plural form means "Aštartes," and it was regularly coupled with the plural *Ba'alim* meaning "Ba'lus," likely indicating that the writers were aware that there were many local versions of these deities. It is also probable that both plurals referred to classes of deities. The repeated connection of Aštarte with Ba'lu in the Hebrew Bible has led some scholars to infer that they were each other's consort, and so to conclude that the goddess was involved with fertility. In this regard, Patai argues that the name originally meant "womb," and he cited passages that referred to "the offspring ['aštaroth] of your flock" coupled with "the increase of your kine." So Aštarte, he thought, was originally a goddess responsible for the fertility of sheep.

In Egypt, Aštarte is mentioned in a number of texts, and she was understood as a daughter of the god Re. In one text, along with 'Anat(u), she is awarded as wife to the god Seth, often identified with Ba'lu. Another Egyptian text describes both her and 'Anat as "the two great goddesses who were pregnant but did not bear" (Quoted by Wyatt, *DDDB*: 111). However, the Egyptians saw Aštarte, like 'Anat(u), as a war deity. Her name also appears, along with those of 'Anat(u) and a goddess called Qudšu, perhaps Asherah, on an Egyptian relief plaque dating to the Late Bronze Age (*ANEP*: 352 no. 830, 379). There was a shrine to her at Memphis in Egypt, and it had its own priest. Interestingly, Budge refers to the introduction into Egypt of a West Asiatic horse-riding war and desert goddess he calls Aasith. It is, of course, possible that Aasith was the name of the deity depicted on a clay plaque from the Nineteenth Dynasty naked on a horse and holding a weapon (1350–1200 BCE) (*ANEP*: 165 plate 479 and 305 no. 479). However, it seems much more likely that Aasith was a version or misreading of 'Anat(u) or Aštarte.

In the Phoenician pantheon, Aštarte was an important deity during the first millennium BCE, but there is extant very little written about her. Her name occurs in about eleven Phoenician texts. A sixth-century BCE sarcophagus from Ṣidōn held the body of a king who was also a priest of the goddess, and another from the same city held the remains of his son, whose mother was a priestess of Aštarte. A long inscription referred to the building of a temple for 'Aštart-šem-Ba'lu "Aštarte-Name-of Ba'lu." The goddess was a patron deity of Ṣidōn, and one of its kings held the theophoric name Abdi-'Aštart "Servant of Aštarte." According to Lucian, she had a huge temple at Ṣidōn. He thought that Aštarte was a moon goddess. The famous Lady of Byblos, whom Lucian called Aphrodite, is thought by some to have been Aštarte. In his *Phoenician History*, Philo of Byblos commented that "Greatest Aštarte" reigned over Phoenicia and consecrated "a star," a meteorite, on the island of Tyre (Attridge and Oden 1981: 54, 55). Her cult at Tyre, where she seemed to have been patron of the royal dynasty, was very old. At the source of the Nahr Ibrahim, the Adonis River, lay the ancient town Aphaca (now Afqa), a day's walk from Byblos. There one of the most famous temples in the area was situated. It was dedicated to Aštarte and, according to legend, was founded by Kinyras, king of Cyprus and father of Adonis, whose tomb was reported to be in the temple. Fourth-century Christian writers, who are hostile sources, condemned the sanctuary as a location of temple prostitution. As a result of her worship by the sea-trading Phoenicians, her cult spread throughout much of the Mediterranean basin.

Attestations to the goddess come from, among other places, Sicily, Carthage, and Malta, where, identified with Hera and then Juno, she had a large temple. On Sicily her main shrine was on Mount Eryx, a location famous for its priestesses and their practice of sacred sexual acts. Another of her major cult centers was Kition on Cyprus. The remains of sacrifices from the Hellenistic period indicate that sheep and goats were her main offerings. Eventually, like Asherah, Aštarte probably became absorbed into the "Syrian Goddess" Atargatis. She might also have been assimilated into the Carthaginian goddess Tanit. The ancient Greeks identified Aštarte with Aphrodite. In Punic North Africa of Roman times, she was worshipped as (Juno) Caelestis. (Quinn 2018: 92, 137–39; Woolmer 2017: 109–15; Aubet 2016; Peckham 2014: 37–38; Betlyon 2005: 9, 14, 29; Leeming 2005: 35; Cornelius 2004: 93–94; Assante 2003: 33; Pardee 2002: 176, 275; Strong 2002: 75–88; Stuckey 2002: 29–30, 35, 43; Wyatt 2002: 40, 56, 62; Smith 2001: 55–57, 74–76; J. Day 2000: 128, 131; Markoe 2000: 20, 180; del Olmo Lete 1999: 56, 71; Moscati 1999: 33–34, 35, 191–94; Seow, *DDDB*: 322–25; Wyatt, *DDDB*: 109–14; Assante 1998: 55, 57, 73–82; Lipiński 1995: 73–75, 105–8, 128–54, 200–5, 281–82, 487–89; Margueron 1995: 130, 132; Röllig, *DCPP*: 46–48; Patai 1990: 54–66; Maier 1986: 119; Attridge and Oden 1981: 51–55; de Tarragon 1980; Attridge and Oden 1976: 12–13; Fitzmyer 1966: 288)

ʽAštarte-abi (M) Form of Aštarte mentioned in a tablet from Emar. (Oliva 1993a: no. 94)

ʽAštarte-Ḫaš(š)i (M) Form of Aštarte mentioned in a tablet from Emar. The element Ḫaš(š)i may be associated with the ancient town of Ḫaššu/Ḫaššuwan. (J. Westenholz 2000: 65)

ʽAštarte-pirikāti (M) Goddess attested at Emar. (Oliva 1993a: no. 98)

ʽAštarte-tāḫazi (M) Goddess attested in tablets from Emar. Name means "ʽAštarte of Battle." (J. Westenholz 2000: 75; Fleming 1996: 90–91; Arnaud 1986: 350)

Aštupinu (M) See Aštabi(l)

A-šumma (M) Sumerian deity attested in an Ur III personal name on tablets from Puzriš-Dagān and Ur. Means "(God Who) Gives Progeny (or Water)." (UET 3, 979: o 5)

Ata (L) See ʽAnat(u)

Ataku (L) Ugaritic god. Helper of the sea god Yam. (del Olmo Lete 1993: 56)

Atargatis, Ataryatis, Attayathe, Atarata/e, Ataryate, Derketo/Derceto (L) Life-giving goddess. Motherly protector of humans and animals. Her name might be a combination of the names of the goddesses ʽAnat(u) and Aštarte. Derketo is a shortened form of the name. Her consort was Dushara, who was supreme deity of the Nabatean capital city Petra. There, Atargatis might have been identified with the Arabian goddess Al-'Uzza, and she had a close association with springs and water. In Syria, where her spouse was usually Ba'lu/Had(d)ad, she was equated to both Greek Aphrodite and Greco-Roman Tyche/Fortuna.

Her cult was wide-spread in Syria and Mesopotamia. Her main cult center was Bambyce, usually called Hieropolis, "Sacred City," in northern Syria. Numerous coins dating to the fourth and early third centuries BCE found at Hieropolis correspond to an early stage of her worship; her name appears on them in a variety of forms. She is depicted riding, or accompanied by, a lion. Sometimes she sits on a throne. Flanked by two sphinxes, she wears a turreted headdress and carries various objects, such as cups or a scepter. On later coins she is almost always enthroned, sometimes wearing a turreted "mural crown" of a tutelary deity of a city. She usually had a lion on either side of her throne. In her hands she held a spindle, a mirror, or a staff. Doves or fish were often depicted beside her. From Hieropolis, the cult of Atargatis disseminated throughout all of Syria, northern Mesopotamia, and the western part of the Greco-Roman world; it even reached Britain. In the West she was called *Dea Syria*, the "Syrian Goddess."

Atargatis arrived in Rome during the first Punic War (264–241 BCE). A splendid statue that might be of her, complete with encircling snake stood on the Janiculum in Rome in the third century CE (Godwin 1981: 158 plate 124). The variations in the iconography of Atargatis resulted from her being identified with local goddesses. In his *De Dea Syria* "About The Syrian Goddess," Lucian of Samosata wrote in the second century CE about his visit to the great temple at Hieropolis. He identified Atargatis with the Greek goddess Hera, but he connected her to several other goddesses, such as Athena, Artemis, and Aphrodite. He also saw her as having aspects of Nemesis and the Fates. Lucian described the temple itself, the cult objects in the temple, the priests, and the rituals celebrated there. In one, young men castrated themselves to become cross-dressing priests at the temple. The goddess he saw was supported by lions and held a scepter and a spindle. She wore on her head "rays and a tower" (Attridge and Oden 1976: 43). She was accompanied by a god sitting on bulls, which Lucian identified as Zeus, likely Ba'lu. The temple at Hieropolis was an asylum, because it was forbidden to kill there. The goddess's shrines always contained a pond filled with sacred fish. Atargatis was associated in some places with dolphins, and Lucian reported that he saw a statue of a Phoenician goddess, whom he called Derketo; she was a mermaid. Atargatis was worshipped in what is now Israel at Ashkelon, the site of her main temple in the southern Levant.

Carving of Atargatis and her consort Ba'al-Hadad. Found in the courtyard of the temple of Atargatis at Duro-Europos. Limestone. Still shows traces of paint. After Binst 2000: 126.

According to the Apocrypha, she also had a temple near Qarnaim (II Maccabees 12: 26). She had a temple at Palmyra and at Dura Europos in northern Syria and seems to have been an important goddess of the Nabateans. At their capital Petra, there was a sanctuary called by archaeologists "Temple of the Winged Lions." It might have been dedicated to her. Atargatis was identified also with the Egyptian goddess Isis. (Encyc. Brit. 2019; Basile 2002: 256; Bedal 2002: 230; Joukowsky 2002: 237, 238; Kanellopoulos 2002: 252–52; Joukowsky and Basile 2001: 53; Wenning 2001: 82, 83, 87; Drijvers, *DDDB*: 114–16; Graf, *ABD* IV: 970–73; Lipiński 1995: 75, 98–99, 108, 280; Lipiński, *DCPP*: 127; Hammond 1990; Kraemer 1988: 367; Meyer 1987: 130–41; Godwin 1981: 38; Attridge and Oden 1976; Oden 1976: 33–36)

Ataryatis, Ataryate, Ataryatis Derketo (L) See Atargatis

'Athirat, 'Aṯirat, 'Athrt, 'Aṯrt (L) See Asherah

'Athtar-Shamayn (L) See 'Aṯtar

'Athtart(u), 'Athtart(u)-Šadi, 'Athtart(u) -šem-Ba'lu (L) See 'Aštart

Attapal, Attapar (L) A variant form of Aštarte, Ugaritic 'Aṯtart(u). Mentioned in offering lists and prayers from Ugarit. (Pardee 2002: 28, 151, 275)

'Aṯtar, 'Athtar, 'Aththar, 'Aṯtar(u), 'Ashtar (L) Male counterpart of Aštarte in the Levant—the morning star to her evening star. Perhaps associated with irrigation and rainfall, especially in desert regions. At Ugarit, member of the family of the chief deities El and Asherah. In the "Ba'lu Cycle" from Ugarit, the god is a son of the chief female deity, Asherah. After Ba'lu's disappearance in the netherworld, Asherah named "Athtar the Brilliant" to succeed Ba'lu as king. However, when he sat on Ba'lu's throne, "... his feet did not reach the footstool," and so he had to give up the role (Wyatt 2002: 132). At the beginning of the Ba'lu collection, 'Aṯtar complained that he did not have a palace and then asked whether he was to be ruler. The answer seemed to be that, because he was not married, he would get neither a palace nor the rule of the land. El favored his son Yam, the sea, instead.

'Aṯtar had a minor role in Ugaritic cult: his name is included in god and offering lists and a divination text. He occurs also as part of Ugaritic theophoric names. At the Semitic-speaking city of Emar, 'Aṯtar was considered "a major warrior deity" (Smith 2001: 65). He was venerated also at Mari. The cult of 'Aṯtar was probably limited to inland sites, where dry or irrigation farming was practiced. In South Arabia 'Aṯtar was venerated as both aspects of Venus. In the seventh century BCE, he might have been worshipped in North Arabia as 'Aṯtar-Šamayn, "'Aṯtar of the Heavens." A Greek text dating to the fifth century CE referred to 'Aṯtar as associated with Bedouin child sacrifice in the Sinai. (Pardee 2002: 14–15, 19, 49, 275; Wyatt 2002: 53–55, 132–33 note 75; Smith 2001: 45, 60. 62, 65; del Olmo Lete 1999: 53 and note 33; Leick 1998: 15; Smith 1997: 96–97; Handy 1997: 84–85; Lipiński 1995: 130; Gelb 1992: 133; Smith 1990: 99; Cross 1973: 7 note 13, 68, 105 note 49; Albright 1968: 228, 231–32)

Attayathe (L) See Atargatis

Atti (M) Deity listed in An : *Anum*. Written At-ti. (Litke 1998: 216)

'Aṯtrt (L) See 'Aštart

A-tu (M) In a lamentation one of the goddesses searching for her lost child. a-tu can designate a temple official. (Cohen 1988: 696)

A-tu-gula (M) One of the sixteen children of Dingir-maḫ. a-tu can designate a cultic functionary. In An : *Anum* explained as "who is revered by those dwelling in heaven" with variant "who is revered by the goddesses." In a god list from Aššur described as "who is revered by the exalted gods" and "who is feared by the goddesses." (Litke 1998: 78; Schroeder 1920: no. 64)

A-tu-ḪURra (M) Goddess associated with Inana/Ištar of Zabala(m) and mentioned in a late cultic lament "The Lowing Cow," in which the name is rendered into Akkadian as [d]Á-dù-a-ḫu. a-tu can designate a cultic functionary. Her temple was called E-siguz "House of Goat Hair." See A-tu-uri. (George 1993: 141 no. 982; Cohen 1988: 613)

A-tu-tu (M) Deity attested in a god list from Aššur. (Schroeder 1920: no. 54)

A-tu-tur (M) One of sixteen children of the birth goddess Dingir-maḫ. Sumerian a-tu can designate a cultic functionary. In An : *Anum*, explained as "Mother with Hair Hanging (Down)." (Litke 1998: 78)

A-tu-uri (M) Demon watchman of the steppe. a-tu can designate a temple official. Thus the name means something like "...-official of Akkad." See A-tu-ḪURra. (Litke 1998: 165)

Aunammu (H) One of the more obscure Hittite deities. (Archi 1990: 118)

Aura (L) See Aer

Awalītum (M) Goddess attested at Old Babylonian Nērebtum. (Greengus 1979)

Aya (Akk.), **Šerda**, **Šarda** (Sum.) (H, M) Goddess of dawn and consort of Akkadian/Babylonian sun god Šamaš, Sumerian Utu. Her Akkadian name is possibly cognate of Greek Eos, "Dawn." Often invoked in prayers and asked to intercede with Šamaš. For instance, in the "Epic of Gilgameš," Nin-sun, Gilgameš's mother, prays to Šamaš for her son's safety on his expedition to the Cedar Forest, which was well guarded by the monster Ḫuwawa (Ḫumbaba): "May Aya, your bride, not fear to remind you" to look after Gilgameš (Foster 2001: 24). "Bride" *kallatu* was one of Aya's epithets, as was "Spouse" *ḫīrtu*.

Usually with Šamaš, she was revered in temples at Larsa, Sippar, Aššur, and certainly elsewhere. A "Sacred Marriage" ritual between statues of Aya and Šamaš took place at Sippar in Neo-Babylonian times. See discussions under Dumuzi; Inana. Also borrowed into Hittite/Hurrian as Aya (variations Aa, A-e-ya) from Mesopotamia's goddess of the dawn. Wife of the sun god Šimege. Associated with the goddess Kubaba as Aya-nikaltu. *Nikaltu* is a Hittite rendering of Akkadian *kallātu(m)* "bride," one of Aya's Mesopotamian epithets. Depicted at the rock-carved shrine of Yazılıkaya near Ḫattušas. She appears in many rituals. Often confused by the Hurrians/Hittites with the god Ea as Eya or even Aya. (Durand 2008: 222–26; Black and Green 2003: 173; Galter, *DDDB*: 125–26; Leick 1998: 16–17; van Gessel 1998: I, 5–6; Popko 1995: 100, 115; Haas 1994: 82, 380; Powell 1989; Laroche 1976: 39–40; Tallqvist 1974: 245; Oppenheim, *ANET*: 557; Forrer, *RlA* I: 2)

Ayya (M) See Aya; Ḫaya

Azag (M) See Asag

'Azazel, 'Azazil (L) Traditionally, the name of a demon of the desert. The name appears in the Hebrew Bible only in the Book of Leviticus (16:8, 10, 26), according to which YHWH instructed Moses to have Aaron acquire from the community two male goats and by lot designate one for the Lord and one "for 'Azazel." The goat for the Lord was to be sacrificed as a "sin offering," and the other, after being ritually laden with the sins of the Israelites, to be sent off free into the wilderness, presumably for 'Azazel. Who or what 'Azazel was is much disputed. The view that 'Azazel was a desert demon to whom the scapegoat was sent has had strong support, and some have argued that the demon took the shape of a goat, whence the idea that the Israelites paid homage to a goat-shaped deity. Others see 'Azazel as the place where the goat was sent or as the ritual title of the goat itself. Explanations of the origin of the ritual do not deal with the identity of 'Azazel. However, he/it might have resulted from a misunderstanding of the name/function of the rite. There is a reference in Leviticus 17: 7 to "goat-demons," but, besides being negative, it is unclear. (Janowsky, *DDDB*: 128–31; Zatelli 1998; Wright, *ABD* I: 536–37; Gaster, *IDB* I, 325–26)

'Azazil (L) See 'Azazel

A-zia (M) Sumerian deity connected in the Ur III period to a town in the environs of Umma. Possibly a short form of A-zia-ibsagan-gar. Means "Life-giving Water." (Cohen 1996a: 30)

A-zia-ibsagan-gar (M) Sumerian deity, connected in Ur III tablets with a town in the environs of Ur III Umma. Means "Life-giving Water that Is Placed in the Middle of the Field." (Cohen 1996a: 30)

Azi(da)-mua, Nin-azi-mua, Nin-izi-mua (M) Sumerian netherworld goddess. In the inscriptions of Gudea of Lagaš Nin-azi-mua and Geštin-ana are names for the same deity; the wife of Nin-geš-zida, the god who stood at the gate between Heaven and the netherworld with Dumuzi. The Old Babylonian god lists, however, differentiate between these two goddesses. In the myth "Enki and Nin-ḫursag," Nin-ḫursag created Azida-mua to heal Enki's arm, basing it perhaps on a meaning "Who Makes the Right Arm Grow." At the end of the composition, Nin-ḫursag declares that the goddess, there called Azi-mua, was to marry Nin-geš-zida. Katz suggests that Nin-azi-mua may occur in the Sumerian zà-mí hymns under the name Nin-a-IZI. Nin-izi-mua means "Lady who Lights the Fire." (Foster 2005: 527; Katz 2003: 397–401; Frayne 2001: 146; Litke 1998: 192; Selz 1997b: no. 36; George 1993: 37; Kramer, *ANET*: 41; Speiser, *ANET*: 101)

Azizu, 'zyz, 'zyzw (Palmyran), **Azizos** (Greek), **Arṣu** (L) Gods of the Venus star, brothers, Azizu being the morning star and Arṣu the evening star. Considered to have been "caravan gods" (Rostovtzeff 1933: 58). Worshipped in Palmyra. A shrine of Arṣu is mentioned in an inscription. In addition, the pair was venerated in pre-Islamic northern Arabia. (Dien 2004; Kaizer 2002; Mulder *DDDB*: 369; Puech *DDDB*: 511 Drijvers 1997; Teixidor 1979: 69–70)

Az(z)uz (L) A Phoenician deity attested in theophoric names. Means "Strong." Probably an epithet. (Lipiński, *DCPP*: 53)

— B —

Ba (M) Deity attested in an Early Dynastic god list. Written ba^{ku_6}, "snail." (Mander 1986: 138)

Ba'lu (masc.) (L), **Ba'lat** (fem.) (L), **Ba'al** (Biblical) (masc.) The West Semitic word for "lord," "master," "owner"; the feminine form means "lady," "mistress," or "owner." Eastern Mesopotamian Semitic equivalents are Bēlu(m) and Bēl and Bēltu, Bēlat, and Bēlet. As applied to deities, the words are actually epithets and occur often as a title of the tutelary deity of a city or state. Since, in an area or time frame, usually one deity received the title more often than another, the epithet could become the name of the deity, as at Ugarit Ba'lu referred to the storm god Had(d)ad, while, at Byblos, Ba'lat was the name of its main goddess, "Lady" of Byblos. In historic times, there were a number of deities that carried the title Ba'lu or Ba'lat. When the Hebrew Bible refers to "the Ba'lus," it may not just be pointing out the polytheism of the Canaanites and surrounding peoples, but recognizing that most towns had their own Ba'lu. Some of the significant Ba'lus and Ba'lats are mentioned below. (van der Toorn, *DDDB*: 171–73; Cohen 2015: 338; Lipiński 1995: 79–81; Tallqvist 1974: 271–72)

Ba'lu/Had(d)a(d) (L) Storm and rain god and warrior deity. Protector against destructive forces such as the sea, and so a deity of sailors. In the Ba'lu temple at Ugarit several votive anchors have been found, evidence of the gratitude of sailors for Ba'lu's protection at sea. Also associated with the netherworld as leader of the Repha-im, especially royal ones. Ba'lu means "Lord" or "Master." The name Had-(d)ad probably means "Thunderer" (Smith 1997: 84). Worshipped from at least the third millennium BCE in northern Mesopotamia and Syria. As main deity of local pantheons, he often became associated with places from which he took his full name, for example, Ba'al-Ṣapōn, Ba'al-Ḥermōn, Ba'al-Lebanon, and Ba'al-Carmel.

The storm god was of particular importance in the Levant, where farming was dependent on rain, which normally returned in late September/early October after a hot summer. Ba'lu manifested himself in the thunder, which was his voice. He was also present in lightening.

Scholars are divided as to whether the god's original name was Ba'lu or Had(d)ad. Some insist that Had(d)ad/Adad was a Mesopotamian deity first, though Had(d)ad and Ba'lu certainly seem identified at Ugarit. However, by the first millennium BCE, they were separate, with Had(d)ad being an Aramaean god and Ba'lu a Canaanite and Phoenician one. As god of Aramaean Damascus he bore the name Rimmōn (Ramānu) meaning "Thunderer." Had(d)ad's wife was Šala.

Ba'lu/Had(d)ad was one of the main deities venerated in the cult of Ugarit, for he was the tutelary god of the city. As such his name consistently appears near the top of offering lists, and a ram and a bull were usually his due.

In Ugaritic poetry Ba'lu was understood to be the son of the grain god Dagān, and as such he was controller of fertile land. Nonetheless he was still considered to be a son of the supreme god El, since El was father of all deities. Thus 'Anat(u), El's daughter, was Ba'lu's sister, but the text termed her, in one translation, Ba'lu's "father's daughter" (Wyatt 2002: 82). Perhaps this meant that Ba'lu's mother was not the same as 'Anat(u)'s. Despite the scholarly prose to the contrary, there is no real evidence that 'Anat(u) was Ba'lu's wife or even lover. In the Ugaritic compositions, however, Ba'lu had at least three wives, who were often also designated as his daughters: Piḍray, Ṭallay, and Arṣay, the "perfect brides" (Wyatt 2002: 84), and possibly seven daughters.

After Pritchard 1973: 348, Fig. 136.
Ba'al on 1.42 m tall limestone stele
in the Louvre

He was regularly called Aliyan Ba'lu "Ba'lu the Victorious." Earlier scholars thought that Aliyan was the son of Ba'lu and so another god. One epithet of Ba'lu was "Rider of the Clouds," and another Ba'al-Ṣapōn "Ba'lu of (Mount) Ṣapōn," which was his earthly home. Ṣapōn or Ṣapānu was the Ugaritic name for the mountain the Greeks called Casius, modern Jebel al-Aqra'. See Ṣapōn. As Ba'al-Ugrt "Ba'lu of Ugarit," the storm god was the divine protector of the land of Ugarit. Above all, he was "king," and his realm was the earth. Thus, he was in charge of its fertility. When Ba'lu was on earth, as the composition said, ""the skies rain[ed] oil" and "the wadis [ran] with honey" (Wyatt 2002: 136–37).

Though clear identification of any visual image as that of Ba'lu is rarely possible, there is general agreement that a stele found at Ugarit (Leick 1998: figure 5) shows the storm god standing on mountains, possibly the range containing Mount Ṣapōn near Ugarit; the sea is below. In warrior stance, he wears a warrior's kilt with a curved dagger in the belt, and he has a high horned helmet on his head. In one hand he wields a mace-like weapon, and in the other he grasps a spear with tip pointed downward. The handle sprouts tree-like leaves. The small figure with him is generally accepted to be the king of Ugarit. Numerous images of the "smiting god" from throughout the Levant are usually understood as representations of Ba'lu (Tubb 1998: 74 figure 14). Ba'lu's sacred animal was a bull calf.

In the "Ba'lu Cycle" of compositions, Ba'lu fought with and conquered the sea god Yam. After Asherah's intervention, El allowed him to have the craftsman god(s) Koṯar-wa-Ḫasis(u) build him a palace / temple. When the god Mōt(u), "Death," demanded that

Ba'lu descend into the netherworld, the storm god obeyed. The supreme deity El mourned Ba'lu's disappearance, and, with the help of Šapaš, the sun goddess, 'Anat(u) found the god's body on the steppe and buried it. The compositions make clear the effect on earth of Ba'lu's descent into the netherworld: "Ba'lu has forsaken the furrows of the ploughland" (Wyatt 2002: 138). He no longer caused the nurturing rains to fall. Thereupon El asks Asherah to appoint one of her sons to replace Ba'lu. She chooses 'Aṯtar, who proves unfit for the position. Later, after Ba'lu returns from the netherworld, there was great rejoicing. In another incident, Ba'lu is challenged by Mōt(u). The two gods fight, but without winner, and the goddess Šapaš has to stop the contest.

Ba'lu's name occurs often in the Hebrew Bible as Ba'al, usually presented negatively. It is clear from the biblical attack that many ordinary Israelites venerated the storm god along with other Canaanite deities. In addition, Ba'al worship was, from time to time, also the official religion. Ahab, king of the northern kingdom Israel, married the princess of Phoenician Ṣidōn, Jezebel, the "bel' of whose name indicated allegiance to Ba'al; Ahab then became a Ba'al worshipper (I Kings 16:31–32). Many scholars argue that the Ba'al Ahab and Jezebel revered was not Ba'al/Had(d)ad, but Melqart, an important Phoenician god. Whichever Ba'al it was, the situation eventually led to the famous trial of divine strength on Mount Carmel between YHWH's prophet Elijah and 450 prophets of Ba'al (I Kings 18), the test being to produce fire (lightening) and rain, two of Ba'lu/Had(d)ad's primary attributes. Often when the Hebrew Bible uses the plural form Ba'alim, it is referring to both Canaanite polytheism and the fact that there were many local Ba'als "Lords or Masters," tutelary deities of towns and cities, many of which were identified with the storm god. Many times the Bible pairs Ba'al(s) with Asherah(s), so much so that earlier scholars thought that Asherah was Ba'al's consort. However, recent scholarship has suggested that this pairing was intended to discredit Asherah, who, for some time, had been associated with the worship of the Israelite god YHWH. Some argue that she was YHWH's consort. Until the time of Elijah, the worship of Ba'al seems to have co-existed with that of YHWH. Biblical accusations that child sacrifice and cult prostitution were part of Ba'al worship are unproven. Though an unfriendly witness, the Hebrew Bible does, however, provide much evidence about Canaanite Ba'lu worship that has been confirmed by archaeology, and, in fact, YHWH assumed many of the traits of Ba'lu. It was common to read or replace the word Ba'al in the Bible with the Hebrew word *boshet* "disgrace" or "ignominy," as in the name Ish-boshet in the book of Samuel.

At Ebla, a city quarter and a gate were named for Ba'al-Hadda, and as Haddu he was worshipped at Mari. The storm god was worshipped also at Emar, and there, with his human high priestess, he was central to the "Sacred Marriage" ritual. At Ba'lubek in Lebanon, there was a magnificent temple of the god, which is still partially standing; the name of the city probably means "Ba'lu of the Beqa'a Valley."

In Israel, at Hazor, a site called by excavators the Orthostat Temple was probably dedicated to Ba'lu. Excavations at Tel Dor in Israel yielded cult objects of the Phoenician period attesting to the worship of Ba'lu.

In Egypt he was worshipped from the middle of the sixteenth century BCE, but became almost totally melded with the Egyptian god Seth. At Memphis in Egypt there was a shrine to Ba'lu in the Phoenician section of the port.

The sea-faring and trading Phoenicians spread the storm god's cult throughout the Mediterranean, but often under another name. Ba'lu was the name of the storm god Haddu in the Hittite "Elkuniša" composition. In the Levant in Greco-Roman times, he was usually understood as the consort of the "Syrian Goddess" Atargatis, and he was identified with Greek Zeus and Roman Jupiter. In the *Phoenician History* of Philo of Byblos, Ba'lu was probably the real name of the deity called Demarous, which might derive from an Ugaritic epithet of Ba'lu *dmrn* "powerful"; Philo also identified Demarous with Adodos, probably a version of Had(d)ad. At Carthage he seems to have been associated with the god Saturn (Ba'al-Ḥamōn) and was understood as the consort of Tanit. He was revered at Palmyra as Bel or Bol. (Peckham 2014: 26–27; Betlyon 2005: 34; Leeming 2005: 42; Black and Green 2003: 35; Pardee 2002: 25–116, 276; Strong 2002: 88–108; Wyatt 2002: 34–146; Smith 2001: 28–30, 56–57, 136–37; Caubet 2000: 216, 218; Hadley 2000: 86–102; Markoe 2000: 20; del Olmo Lete 1999: 71, 74–75; Greenfield, *DDDB*: 377–82; Herrmann, *DDDB*: 132–39; Brody 1998: 10; Hoffner 1998: 109; Finnegan 1997: 125–26, 132–33, 135, 137, 139–46; Smith 1997: 81–180; Schmidt 1996: 81–84; Lipiński 1995: 50–51, 65, 79–90, 122–25, 168–69, 284–88, 306–8; Margueron 1995: 132; Handy 1994: 62, 99–102; Fleming 1993a: 140–41; J. Day, *ABD* I: 545–49; Fleming 1992a; Lipiński, DCPP: 203; Redford 1992: 117; Röllig, DCPP: 55; Olyan 1988; Greenfield 1987: 68; Dever 1984; Dever 1982; Attridge and Oden 1981: 50–55, 88 note 94, 91 note 126; Oden 1976: 33, 36; Albright 1968: 124–28)

Ba'al-addir (L) Name of the storm god Ba'lu meaning "Powerful Lord." Attested at Byblos and often in Phoenician North Africa. Might refer to the Carthaginian god Ba'al-Ḥamōn. (Lipiński 1995: 88–90; Lipiński, *DCPP*: 55–56)

Ba'al-Akka (M) Deity attested in the Mari texts. (Durand 2008: 307)

Ba'al-berith (L) Canaanite deity worshipped by the Israelites instead of their own god (Judges 8:33). Ba'al-berith, "Ba'lu of the Covenant," had a temple at Shechem, where a feasting festival took place (Judges 9:4, 27). Probably the god was a form of Ba'lu. Also note El-berith (Judges 9:46). Cross argues that the epithet was probably El's: El Ba'al-berith "El lord of covenant." (1973: 49 note 23). (Mulder, *DDDB*: 141–44; Lewis, *ABD* I: 550–51; Cross 1973: 51–51)

Ba'al-Carmel (L) See Ba'lu/Had(d)a(d)

Ba'al-Ḥam(m)œn (L) The great god of Carthage and other colonies founded by Phoenicians, for instance, in Malta, Sardinia, and Sicily. Identified with Canaanite El. Though he was not an important deity in the Levant, his name did occur in a ninth-century inscription from the area and in some personal names. At Carthage the god, like Dagān, was associated with farming and the fertility of the land.

Images often show him holding a scepter with ears of grain at its tip. A limestone stele from Hadrumetum in Tunisia probably represents Ba'al-Ḥam(m)ōn enthroned between two sphinxes (Harden 1963: plate 41 and 307). His symbol was "a circle enclosing a cross" (Markoe 2000: 136). In votive inscriptions, he was often paired with Tanit and so was likely her consort at Carthage and elsewhere. By the fifth century BCE, Tanit had supplanted the god as main deity of Carthage, at least in popular religion. A temple excavated in the city's coastal area seems to have been dedicated to Ba'al-Ḥam(m)ōn. There excavators recovered over 3000 clay seals for papyri dating from the seventh to the fourth centuries BCE. The papyri were undoubtedly burned when the Romans razed the city in 146 BCE.

The Greeks, who called him Balamoun, equated him to Kronos/Saturn and the Romans, for whom he was Balamon, identified him with Zeus/Jupiter. Greek writers stated that Carthaginians sacrificed their children to Ba'al-Ḥam(m)ōn, but it seems unlikely that the burnt remains of infants, neonates, and miscarriages that were buried in urns at sacred enclosures were the result of sacrifice (Schwartz 1993: 53–56). The infant graveyards are known as "tophets" from the name used in the Hebrew Bible for places where child sacrifice was supposed to have occurred (2 Kings 23:10; Jeremiah 7:31). Sacred enclosures with urns and steles have been excavated at Carthage, Hadrumetum, and other sites. Human sacrifices, usually of teenagers or adults, did sometimes take place in the Levant and the Phoenician world, but probably only at times of crisis.

Ba'al-Ḥam(m)ōn had a temple at Gades (Cadiz), a Phoenician colony in Spain, and an offering list from the Phoenician colony at Marseilles informs us that incense was especially important in the god's cult. (Quinn 2018: 92–93, 97; Markoe 2000: 39. 107, 118, 130, 132. 136, 183, 189; Moscati 1999: 138,141, 143, 194, 228; Na'aman, *DDDB*: 144; Lipiński 1995: 251–64, 441–47; Warmington 1993: 59, 145, 148; Lipiński, *DCPP*: 57–58; Schmitz, *ABD* I: 551; Smith 1990: 133; J. Day 1989; Herm 1975: 197; Cross 1973: 10, 24–28, 35–36; Clifford 1972: 133–34; Albright 1968: 233; Harden 1963: 87, 120. 200)

Ba'al-Ḥermœn (L) See Ba'lu/Had(d)a(d)

Ba'al-Lebanon, Ba'al-Liban (L) See Ba'lu/Had(d)a(d)

Ba'al-malage (L) Phoenician god mentioned in an Assyrian vassal treaty, but otherwise unknown. One of the many manifestations of the storm god and thus perhaps important to sailors (*malāḥ and malāḫu* meaning "sailor"). (Brody 1998: 11–13; Lipiński 1995: 85, 243–44; Bunnens, *DCPP*: 59; Smith 1990: 25; Albright 1968: 227)

Ba'al-marqod (L) Minor Phoenician god, "Lord of the Dance." Name occurs in three Greek and fifteen Latin inscriptions found at a site near Beirut. Seems to have been a warrior and fertility deity. Identified with Jupiter. His consort was equated to Juno. His cult was taken by Roman soldiers to other parts of the Greco-Roman World. Known in Greek as Balmarkos/Balmarkodes and in Latin as Balmarcodes.

(Tubb 2003: 122; Lipiński 1995: 115–16; Röllig, *DCPP*: 59)

Ba'al-Pe'or (L) Local god of Mount Pe'or in Moab. Probably a netherworld deity, perhaps an aspect of Canaanite Ba'lu, who, in a myth from Ugarit, descended into the netherworld through the mouth of Mōt(u) "Death." Pe'or is possibly associated with the Hebrew word for "open wide," which, in the Hebrew Bible, was used to describe the "mouth" of the netherworld (Isaiah 5: 14). According to the Hebrew Bible, the Israelites practiced the cult of Ba'al-Pe'or, which entailed their participation in what has been interpreted as a licentious banqueting as the direct result of Moabite women enticing the Israelite men with whom they had been "whoring" (Numbers 25). Based on the reference in Psalms 106:28, this "banqueting" was more likely to have been a *marzeaḥ*, a common practice attested as early as at Ebla (c. 2400–2300 BCE). In Jewish tradition the worship of Ba'al-Pe'or was associated with the *marzeaḥ*. Sometimes identified as the Moabite god Kamiš, but this is by no means certain. Later called Beelphegor. (Spronk, *DDDB*: 147–48; Slayton, *ABD* I: 553; Smith 1990: 48, 127–28; Cross 1973: 201–2)

Ba'al-Ṣapōn, Ba'al-Ṣaphōn, Ba'al-Ṣapān, Ba'al-Sapūna/u, Ba'al-Zaphon (L) Canaanite and Phoenician storm god. Revered as protector of mariners. Means "Lord of Ṣapōn," the sacred mountain situated about 40 kms north of Ugarit, today called Jebel al-Aqra'. At 1700 meters high and thus visible from far out at sea, it was an important landmark for sailors. In the Ba'lu temple at Ugarit were found votive offerings of stone anchors and a stele with a dedicatory inscription to Ba'al-Ṣapōn, indicating that sailors in particular worshipped the god.

It has been suggested that he might have been the god on a Syrian seal found in Egypt striding helmeted across two mountain peaks, while brandishing weapons (Brody 1998: 132 fig. 10). At Ugarit, the Lord of Ṣapōn seems to have been an aspect of the storm god Ba'lu/Had(d)ad, whose home was on the mountain. However, based on god and offering lists, it is clear that Ba'al-Ṣapōn had a separate cult. A stele found in the "Baāl temple" at Ugarit depicts the storm god, perhaps as Ba'al-Ṣapōn, standing above a mountain range with the sea below and brandishing a weapon (Leick 1998: fig. 5).

In the thirteenth century BCE the god had a shrine at Memphis in Egypt. Ba'al-Ṣapōn was also a deity of the Phoenicians and Carthaginians. His worship is attested at Tyre, and he had a temple at Carthage. In the Greco-Roman period he was known as Zeus Kasios, a patron deity of sailors. He might have been the source of the Greek storm and chaos-serpent Typhon. In Egypt he was assimilated into the god Horus. (Pardee 2002: 14, 17, 18, 28, 30–31, 33; Wyatt 2002: 353; Markoe 2000: 116, 129; del Olmo Lete 1999: 60; Niehr, *DDDB*: 152–54; Brody 1998: 13–19; Lipiński 1995: 244–51; Bonnet, *DCPP*: 60–61; Raabe, *ABD* I: 554–55; Smith 1990: 25; Albright 1968: 118, 227)

Ba'al-Ṣapunu (L) See Ba'al-Ṣapōn

Ba'al-Ṣidōn (L) See Ba'lu/Had(d)ad

Ba'al-ṣmd (L) Aramaean god attested in a Phoenician inscription. *Ṣmd* may refer to the mace, one of the god's weapons. (Xella, *DCPP*: 62)

Ba'al-šamēm, Ba'al-šamayim (L) Originally a title of the supreme god in Levantine, Sumerian and Akkadian, and Anatolian pantheons. Means "Lord of Sky or Heaven." Worshipped widely from the first millennium BCE to the early Christian period. First mentioned in a fourteenth-century BCE treaty between Ugarit and the Hittites. Probably an aspect or title of the storm god Ba'al-Hadad at Ugarit, where he does not appear to have had a separate cult. His name occurs in an early seventh century BCE treaty between Assyria and Tyre, from which it was clear that he was considered a storm god. At Byblos in the tenth century BCE he was head of the pantheon.

There is also evidence of his veneration at Carthage and other Phoenician colonies. In a commemorative stele from Carthage he is listed first, before the other deities. Sometimes addressed only as Bēl, he was an important god of the Nabateans. Again, often just called Bēl, Ba'al-šamēm was revered by the people of Palmyra. In the *Phoenician History*, Philo of Byblos identified "Beelsamen" with Zeus and suggested that he was a solar divinity. In Latin he was *Dominus Coeli*, "Lord of the Heavens." (Woolmer 2017: 106; Pardee 2002; del Olmo Lete 1999: 49, 56, 60; Röllig, *DDDB*: 149–51; Brody 1998: 11; Lipiński 1995: 84–88; Handy 1994: 30–31; Bonnet, *DCPP*: 61–62; Graf, *ABD* IV: 970–973; Smith 1990: 24–25, 42–44; Attridge and Oden 1981: 40–41, 81 note 49; Albright 1968: 227–32)

Ba'al-Tsaphon (L) See Ba'al-Ṣapōn

Ba'al-Ugarit, Ba'al-ugrt (L) See Ba'lu/Had(d)ad

Ba'al-Zaphōn (L) See Ba'al-Ṣapōn

Ba'al-zebul, Ba'al-zebub (L) Name of the storm god Ba'lu/Had(d)ad occurring frequently in texts from Ugarit. Means "Ba'lu the Prince." In the Ugaritic compositions, the storm god is also entitled "The Prince, Lord of Earth" (Wyatt 2002: 126). In the New Testament (Mark 3: 23), scribes from Jerusalem declare that Jesus was possessed by Bēl-zebul. Ba'al-zebub, now generally accepted to have been a deliberate misspelling for Ba'al-zebul, appears four times in the Hebrew Bible (II Kings 1: 2, 3, 6, and 16). Ba'al-zebub is usually translated "Lord of the Flies," *zebub* signifying "flies." One scholar has considered a possible connection between the Mesopotamian warrior god Zababa and the biblical Ba'al-zebub. Ba'al-zebub is often wrongly rendered as Beelzebub. (Black and Green 2003: 84–85; Herrmann, *DDDB*: 154–56; Handy 1994: 140–41; Brownrigg 1993: 20; Lewis, *ABD* I: 638–40; Maier, *ABD* I: 554; Roberts 1972: 56 and note 473)

Baaltak (L) Goddess of Palmyra. Identified with Ištar. Means "Your Ladyship." (van der Toorn, *DDDB*: 172)

Baaltis (L) See Ba'lat-Gebel

Baau (L) Goddess mentioned in the *Phoenician History* of Philo of Byblos. According to Philo, her name meant "night," and he identified her as wife of the wind god Kolpia and mother of Aion and Protogonos, whose children "settled in Phoenicia." (Attridge and Oden 1981: 40–41, 80–81)

Baba, Ba'u, Bawa (M) Daughter of An/Anu(m). Consort of Nin-Girsu at Girsu and of Zababa at Kiš. As consort of Zababa, Baba was usually equated to Gula and Nin-kar(r)ak and so was concerned with healing. Identified with Gula,who also had the dog as her sacred animal. At Girsu she was the mother of Nin-Girsu's two sons, Šul-šagana and Ig-alima, and seven daughters who were not considered to be Nin-Girsu's offspring. However, all nine were minor deities of the area around Girsu. Later she was identified with Gatum-dug, the chief goddess of the city of Lagaš. Baba was tutelary goddess of the city of Girsu, where she had her main temple.

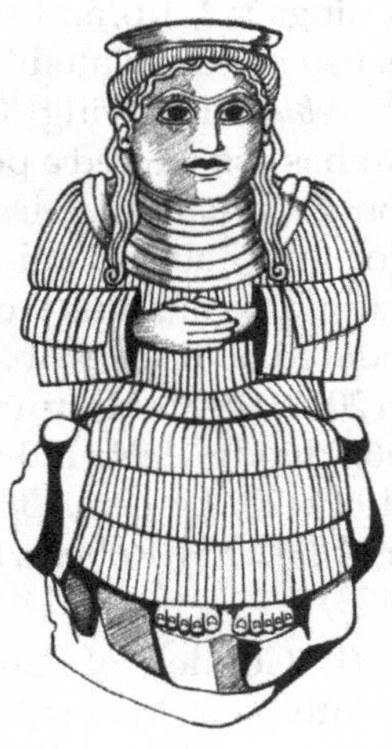

Baba/Ba'u seated on a throne resting on water and supported by water birds. Mesopotamia. Ca. 2060-1955 BCE. Diorite. After Pritchard 1969b: 173, no. 507

One of her shrines in the temple at Girsu was called "House Filled with Counsel." She had chapels at, among other places, Kiš and Dēr. The Festival of Baba at Lagaš was one of the major celebrations of the Lagaš state. It took place in the autumn, and pilgrims from other towns in the area converged on Lagaš, bringing offerings. One aspect of the festival was the making of offerings to the ancestors. At the New Year, there was also a festival of Baba at Girsu, during which a "sacred marriage" rite involving Baba seems to have occurred. (Cohen 2015: 37; Rubio 2010; Black and Green 2003: 39; Leick 1998: 23; Litke 1998: 174; George 1993: 30, 89 no. 333, 148–49 no. 1085 no. 1086, 155 no. 1171; Tallqvist 1974: 268–70; Jacobsen 1976: 156)

Baba-duda (M) Goddess appearing in an Old Babylonian god list in the circle of the healing goddess at Isin. The name contains the divine name Baba, a well-known healing deity, and would seem to mean "Baba of the Mound." Since, in the list, she is followed by Nin-Aral(l)i, Baba-duda may well be a chthonic deity, with the mound having netherworld connotations. (Richter 2004: 216)

Baba-šaga (M) Goddess in a litany of gods in two lamentations to the god Enlil. Means "Good Baba." Likely related to the goddess Baba. (Cohen 1988: 287, 362)

Babay (L) Carthaginian (Punic) epithet of the god Sid. Found in inscriptions. (Lipiński 1995: 333, 338, 350; Roobaert, *DCPP*: 62–63)

Bābu (M) Deified gate, attested in the Mari texts. (Durand 2008: 268)

Baetyl(os), Baityl(os) (L) According to Philo of Byblos, a minor Phoenician god, one of four offspring of Ouranos "Sky" and Ge "Earth." The god Baetylos does not seem to be related to the living baetyls invented by Ouranos later in the text. Some scholars consider Baetylos to be identical to the deity Bethel, "House of God." The first known use of the god's name was in a seventh-century BCE vassal treaty between the Assyrians and Tyre, where he was paired with 'Anat-Baetyl. Documents from the Jewish community at Elephantine Island in Egypt indicate that, in the fifth century BCE, the god Bethel was worshipped there, also along with ʻAnat-Bethel. The Hebrew Bible understands Bethel as a sanctuary of El/ YHWH, except in Jeremiah 48:13, where Bethel seems to be referring to a god. In the third century CE, the name Zeus Baetylos occurred in inscriptions from Syria. The interpretation of the evidence is still contro-versial. Scholars note that the veneration of stones as symbols of various deities was common in the Levant from the second millennium BCE on and continued among the Phoenicians in the Greco-Roman period. The Punic/Carthaginian people of North Africa also followed the tradition, as did the Nabateans. (Ball 2009: 89–90; Smith 2001: 32, 137; Wenning 2001; Ribichini, *DDDB*: 157–59; Lipiński, *DCPP*: 70–71; Graf, *ABD* IV: 970–973; Smith 1990: 25, 144; Attridge and Oden 1981: 48–49, 52–53, 87 note 86; Cross 1973: 74, 198–99; Porten 1969; Albright 1968: 226–27 and note 48; Porten 1968)

Baḫaḫutippe (E) Elamite helping and protective god of heaven and earth, appearing in an inscription of Šilḫak-Inšušinak. (Hinz and Koch 1987: 120; König 1977: 105 note 1, 130, 206, 227)

Baḫakikip (E) Elamite protective deity of heaven, appearing in a treaty of a king of Susa with Narām-Sîn of Akkad. (König 1977: 29, 206, 227)

Baḫaluna (E) Epithet of the Elamite god Ḫumban in an inscription of Attaḫaniti-Inšušinak, a late Elamite king (c. 520). May possibly refer to Ḫumban as a protective shepherd. (König 1977: 175, 207, 227)

Baḫar-e (M) Deity attested in an Early Dynastic god list. Means "Potter of the House." (Mander 1986: 52)

Baḫar-Enunzaku (M) According to an incantation, the god ties the stomachache to the sun and thence it goes to the netherworld. (George 2016: no. 1h)

Ba'iḫ (M) Deity attested in the Mari texts. See Baliḫ (Rivers). (Durand 2008: 240)

Bakur (M) Goddess whose epithet was "Lady of Omens." She was associated with Ninurta and worshipped at Ša-uṣur-adad, a town in southern Babylonia. (George 1993: 149 no. 1087)

Balag (M) Deified harp. Also a logogram for LUM-ḫa, a god of the gala-priests. In An : *Anum* two adjacent entries for the bull-harps of Enki are ^{d}eš-^{qa}gá and $^{d.min-}$balag-gá. Perhaps these two entries originally were one entry: ^{d}eš-balag-gá, although the meaning of eš here would be unclear. Another, but highly speculative, interpretation of this orthography is to read eš as the gloss bà, thus originally $^{d\ bà}$balag-gá, the gloss bà, like other ancient glosses, eventually being written as part of the name and so the term would then originally have denoted just a deified harp. (Litke 1998: 105)

Balag-di (M) Name of the god Enlil. The Sumerian name usually denotes either a harpist or one who recites laments. (Litke 1998: 39)

Balag-e-DIRI (M) Bull-lyre of Nuska. (Litke 1998: 52)

Balag-Enlil (M) A divine musician attached to the court of the god Enlil in Nippur. Means "Harp (of) Enlil." (Litke 1998: 51)

Ba'lat-Adabal (M) Goddess attested at Ebla in the late third millennium BCE. Spouse of Adabal. (Schwemer 2001: 113)

Baʿlat-Bahtim, bʿlt bhtm (L) Akkadian title of a goddess at Ugarit. Means "Lady of the Buildings (or Mansions)." Frequently attested in rituals. Might also have been called Ilatu. Possibly refers to ʿAnat(u) or Asherah. (del Olmo Lete 1999: 34, 118, 120)

Baʿlat-Berytus (L) See Baʿlat-Gebel

Baʿlat-Gebel, Baʿlat-Gubal/Gubla, Bēlet-Gubla (Greek, Baʿltis) (L) "Lady of Byblos." Chief deity of the Canaanite/Phoenician city of Byblos on the coast of the Levant. Tutelary goddess of Byblos, thus concerned with fertility and defense. Baʿlat means "Lady," and so a number of goddesses could hold the title, for instance, Baʿlat-Berytus, the Canaanite/Phoenician tutelary goddess of Berytus, now Beirut. Thus, the ancient name of Byblos's goddess is not known, though she has been explained as both Asherah and Aštarte. The latter's cult is known to have been centered at Byblos.

Worship of the "Lady of Byblos" is attested from the third millennium BCE in inscriptions, and a temple was built for her at that time, which continued in existence until Hellenistic times. In the tenth century BCE her consort was Baʿal-šamem, "Lord of the Heavens."

Baʿlat-Gebel was the dynastic deity of the kings of Byblos. A fifth-century BCE clay plaque shows a shrine in which the king is standing in audience with the enthroned goddess (Markoe 2000: 128 figure 43). Phoenician coins depict the goddess's temple as containing a baetyl or standing stone (Markoe 2000: 99 figure 29k). According to Philo of Byblos in the *Phoenician History*, Kronos (El) gave the city of Byblos to the goddess Baʿltis, who must be the "Lady of Byblos." Philo equated her to the Greek goddess Dione, who, according to Homer, was the mother of Aphrodite. She was identified very early with the Egyptian goddess Hathor and later also with Isis. The Greeks saw her as Aphrodite. (Woolmer 2017: 109; Peckham 2014: 6,8; Strong 2002: 108–13; Markoe 2000: 37, 115, 117–18, 122, 202; Moscati 1999: 31–32, 36; Mullen, *DDDB*: 139–40; Lipiński 1995: 67, 70–76, 96; Lipiński, *DCPP*: 55–56; Redford 1992: 45; Smith 1990: 25, 39 note 112; Moran 1987: 242 and passim; Attridge and Oden 1981: 56–57, 91–92)

Ba'lat-mātim (M) See Baʿlta-māti(m)

Balippiti (E) Elamite helping and protective spirit. (König 1977: 75 note 8, 207, 227)

Balmarcodes, Balmarkos, Balmarkodes (L) See Ba'al-marqod

Baʿlta-māti(m), Ba'lat-mātim (M), **Pel-timāti** (Hurrian) Goddess at Emar and Tuttul and attested at Old Babylonian Mari. Means "Lady of the Land." According to a Mari text, leaders of Emar were summoned to the Euphrates at H'it, a well-known site of the river ordeal, to undergo a trial for misappropriation of funds intended for this goddess. Fleming suggests that Baʿlta-māti(m) is to be equated to Išḫara. (Durand 2008: 261, Durand 2005b: no. 62; Fleming 2000: 94; Trémoiuille 2000: 122)

Balti(s) (L) See Baʿlat-Gebel

Ba'luim (L) See Ba'lu/Had(d)ad

Baluršan (M) See Pasānu(m)

Bandiliša (M) Name written KU_7 with gloss ba-di-li-šá in An : *Anum*. Variant ba-an-dili$_2$-ša. (Litke 1998: 216)

Bani (E) Elamite deity occurring in a treaty between Narām-Sîn of Akkad and a king of Susa. (König 1977: 29 n. 9, 207, 227)

Banītu(m) (M) Goddess appearing in an offering list from Uruk. She occurs also in Neo-Babylonian texts from Uruk, as part of the name Nār-Banītu, a river near Uruk. The Akkadian title means "(Lady) Favor." (Beaulieu 2003: 312)

Ban-kug-la (M) Tutelary deity of the town of Up located on or near the Tigris River. Attested in an Early Dynastic god list from Abu Ṣalābīkh and in the archaic Sumerian zà-mí hymns. Means "One who Draws the Shining Bow," possibly an epithet of the god Ninurta with his drawn bow as the constellation of Canis Major and Sirius as his star. (Mander 1986: 36, 40, 121, 123, 125)

Bāq'atu (L) One of the Kōṯarṯu, seven minor goddesses of fertility at Ugarit. (del Olmo Lete 1999: 57)

Baradu madu (M) Consort of Aštabil. Archi suggests it is the name of a river in the vicinity of Ebla. (Archi 1997)

Bara-Enlil-gara (M) Deity in Old Akkadian tablets, probably from Adab, likely the tutelary deity of a settlement near Adab. Means "Dais Established by (or for) Enlil." (Bartash 2013: no. 167; Maiocchi 2009: no. 84, no. 106, no. 107, no. 141; Visicato and A. Westenholz 2010: no. 149, no. 209, no. 212, no. 213, no. 216, no. 356)

Barama (M) Wife of the Eblaite god Kur(r)a. (Fronzaroli 1993: 131)

Bara-Nigara (M) Goddess equated to Bara-ule-gara in An : *Anum*. The deity was the offspring of the mother goddess Nin-maḫ and the god Šulpa'e. Means "Dais of the Nigara." Her temple at Adab was built during the reign of Rīm-Sîn I of Larsa. See Pa(p)-Nigara. (Richter 2004: 386–87; Litke 1998: 73)

Baraq (M) Akkadian manifestation of the storm god Adad in his connection with thunderbolts. A shortened form of Adad-baraq. Attested in Aramaic personal names. (Schwemer 2001: 60, 602–3 note 4868)

BARA^{ra} (M) Almost certainly a Sumerian writing for the goddess Išḫara. See Išḫara. (Mander 1986: 55)

Barasiga-Nibru (M) Deity listed with Kiri-urur as the two bara$_2$-sig$_5$-ga officials(?) of Ninurta. bara$_2$-sig$_5$-ga is a socle. (Litke 1998: 49)

Bara-ule-gara (M) See Pa(p)-Nigara

Bardad (L) See Ba'lu/Had(d)ad

Barirītu (Akk.) Demoness who serves as a messenger of wrath for Ištar in "The Hymn to the Queen of Nippur." Identified with the goddess Nun-nir-DU.DU, who takes part in the festival of Ištar at Hellenistic Uruk. (Beaulieu 2003: 319–20; Lambert 1982: 209; Reiner 1970: 21, 56)

Bar-PISAN×EN (M) Deity attested in an Early Dynastic god list from Šuruppak. (Mander 1986: 40)

Bar(r)a (M) One of the children of Enki. The following entry in An : *Anum* is Bar-ra-gu-la, listed as a separate child of Enki. (Litke 1998: 101; Galter 1983: 127)

Bar(r)a-gula (M) See Bar(ra)

Barshamin (L) See Ba'al-šamem

Bar-šeg (M) Child of Nin-Girida. Written bar-šèg with gloss še-eg. bar-šèg means "fog," "mist." According to the *PSD* B: 125, bar-šèg is also a variant for bar-sag$_5$ *ṭuplu* "calumny." (Litke 1998: 191)

Basurat (M) Akkadian deity identified with Ištar at Mari. (Archi 1993: 76)

Bašmu(m) (Akk.), **Ušum-gallu, Ušum(gal)** (Sum.) Snake-monster with front legs. Akkadian *bašmu(m)* means "horned serpent." Vizier of Tišpak, chief deity at Ešnunna. Often guarded temple entrances. It was one of eleven creatures to whom Ti'amat gave birth in the *Enūma eliš* to fight on her side against the younger gods. Frequently depicted in Akkadian/Babylonian art. Astrally, represented the constellation Hydra. (Foster 2005: 446; J. Westenholz 2004: 25–26; Litke 1998: 194; Wiggermann 1992: 166–67; Speiser, *ANET*: 65; Heidel 1967: 34; Wiggermann, *RlA* VIII: 258)

Baštum (M) Protective deity whose name means "Dignity." Written [d]LAMA with gloss ba-aš-⸢tum⸣. (Litke 1998: 159)

Ba'ūlu (M) Identified with Adad in a Neo-Assyrian god list. Means "Important One." (King 1969: pl. 17)

Bbt il bt (L) See Ušḫar(ayu)

Beelphegor (L) See Ba'al-Pe'or

Beelshamin (L) See Ba'al-šamem

Beelzebub (L) See Ba'al-zebul

Behemoth (L) A mythological bull-like monster of supernatural size and strength. Described in Book of Job (40: 15–24). The Hebrew word *behemot* is a feminine plural intensive form meaning "beasts, cattle," but in the Book of Job the creature is singular and male. (Frayne 2013; Whitney 2006; Batto, *DDDB*: 165–69)

Bēl, Bēl(u), Bēlu(m) (masc.), **Bēltu(m), Bēlat, Bēlet, Bēlit, Bēltīya** (fem.) (M) The East or Mesopotamian Semitic word for "lord," "master," "owner"; the feminine form *bēltu(m)* means "lady," "mistress," "owner." *Bēlat* is an earlier form of *bēlet*. Bēltīya means "My Lady." The West Semitic equivalents are *ba'l/ba'lat*. As applied to deities, the words are actually epithets and often occur as titles/epithets of the tutelary deity of a city, town, or state. Since, in an area or a time period, usually one deity received the title more often than any other, the epithet could become the name of the deity, as, at Babylon, Bēl(u)/Bēlu(m) signified Marduk and Bēltīya his consort Zarpanītu(m). In a late Babylonian ritual for the *akītu*, the central deities were so named: "the god Bēl and the goddess Bēltīya" (Sachs, *ANET*: 331). The goddess most often bearing the title Bēlet was Ištar. In historic times, there were many deities who carried the titles Bēlu(m) and Bēltu(m); in pre-history there were probably many, many more: local goddesses and gods who eventually were identified with major deities in a ruling pantheon. See also Ba'lu. (van der Toorn, *DDDB*: 171–73; Cohen 2015: 392; Tallqvist 1974: 271–72)

Bēl-Agê (M) Deity accompanying the Assyrian king during observances for the twelfth month in the temple of Anu. Means "Lord of the Crown/Flood."

Bēl-Akka (M) Deity from Emar who received offerings during the new-moon festival in the month of Abi. (Fleming 2000: 177)

Bēl-akussi(m) (M) Akkadian god mentioned in a tablet from the First Sealand Dynasty. According to Dalley, the element *akussi(m)* is Assyrian dialect for *ukultu(m)* probably meaning "plague." See Inana-Akuz, Akuṣītu, a name of Inana, which means "Inana of Akuz." (Dalley 2009: 210–11)

Bēl-ālīya (M) Akkadian term for the divinized mayor especially at Neo-Babylonian

Uruk, where offerings for the god are attested. (Beaulieu 2003: 334)

Bēl-bīni(m), Lugal-šinig (M) Deity identified with Nergal. Means "King of the Tamarisk Tree." Note the god written BE-šinig in an Early Dynastic god list. Tamarisk trees figure prominently in ancient Mesopotamian literature, especially in magical contexts. The deified form of the tree Lugal-šinig (Sum.), Bēl bīni(m) (Akk.), (both meaning "Lord Tamarisk") is in an Old Babylonian forerunner to An : *Anum*, as well as in An : *Anum* itself. The tamarisk appears in some apotropaic incantations in which the speaker identifies various parts of his body with various trees; he indicates that his fingers are "the tamarisk, the bone of the Igigi gods." The importance of the tree is underlined by its appearance in the literary debate composition entitled "The Debate between the Date Palm and the Tamarisk." (Litke 1998: 205; Steinkeller 1992: 270; Vanstiphout 1992: 339–67 commentary; Bottéro 1991: 7–22; Vanstiphout 1991: 23–46 commentary; Vanstiphout 1990a: 271–318; Wilcke 1989: 161–90; Livingstone 1986: 105–6; Mander 1986: 138; Tallqvist 1974: 353; Lambert 1960: 151–64; Lambert, *RlA* VII: 151)

Bēl-Buzqa (M) Tutelary deity of the town of Buzqa located near Emar. One Emar text identifies the lord of Buzqa as Nergal. The place name appears as Buzga in several texts from ancient Ebla. (Belmonte Marin 2001: 61–62; Beckman 1996: 106–7; Bonechi 1993a: 84; Fleming 1992b: 68)

Bēl-dadmē (M) Form of the god Dagān. Means "Lord of Habitations." He received offerings on the twenty-sixth day of the month of Abi in a celebration. Fleming refers to the passage from lunar darkness to light. (Fleming 2000: 177, 195)

Bēl-Ekurri (M) Name of Enlil. Used in hemerologies along with Bēlet-Ekurri.

Bēl-gašer (M) Deity attested at Old Babylonian Šaduppûm, modern Tell Harmal inside modern Baghdad. Means "Lord who Is Strong." At Nērebtum oaths were taken by the deified *sanga* of Bēl-gašer. (Viaggio 2008: no. 40; Renger 1967: 155–56)

Bēl-Ḫalab, Ba'al-Ḫalab (M) Deity with the title "Lord of Aleppo." The title appears as the name of a month in the local calendar at Emar. (Cohen 2015: 339; Beckman 1996: 92: Fleming 2000: 170 and note 138)

Bēl-Ḫarran (M) God of Ḫarran attested in a Neo-Assyrian text. (Radner 1999: 138)

Bēl-illati(m) (M) Form of the god Nergal associated with the city of Isin. Mentioned in an Old Babylonian text from Nippur. Means "Lord of the Troops." (Richter 2004: 206)

Bēl-Ingal (M) God attested in a Neo-Assyrian text. (Radner 1999: 138)

Bēl-Isāna (M) Form of the storm god Adad. Means "Lord of (the City of) Isana." (Schwemer 2001: 578 and note 4665; Radner 1999: 138; Grayson 1987: 204; Postgate, *RlA* V: 173)

Bēl-Kurba'il (M) Epithet of the storm god Adad as chief deity, that is, lord of the town of Kurba'il, northwest of Nine-veh. (George 1993: 113 no. 646)

Bēl-la-maḫar (M) Deity receiving an offering during a festival of Inana of Zabala(m) in the Old Babylonian period. Means "The Lord Is Unrivalled."(Gadotti and Sigrist 2011: 28)

Bēl-mātāti(m) (M) Deity whose name means "Lord of the Lands." See Enlil; Marduk.

Bēl-Mê-Turan (M) Epithet of a local deity, "Lord of (the City of) Mê-Turan." (Nashef 1982a: 195)

Bēl-Rakkab (M) God of Sam'al attested in a Neo-Assyrian text. (Radner 1999: 138)

Bēl-SA-naṣru (M) Likely a consort of the healing goddess Gula in the Neo-Babylonian period, probably at Uruk. (Beaulieu 2003: 274–75)

Bēl-ṣarbi(m) (Akk.), **Lugal-asal** (Sum.) Epithet of a god known in Sumerian as Lugal-asal, "King of the Euphrates Poplar." The deity's title appears in an Old Babylonian forerunner to An : *Anum* and in An : *Anum* itself. Lugal-asal belonged to the circle of Nergal. His cult is documented in northern Babylonia in a Pre-Sargonic Akkadian *kudurru* that records an oath by the dagger of Lugal-asal. Bēl-ṣarbi(m) was a local deity at Baṣ or Šapazzu(m), west of Sippar. Worshipped also in Babylon. Lugal-asal was the deity of a fort town Dūr-Yabušum, in the neighborhood of Kiš, rebuilt by Samsu-iluna. Lugal-asal had a female consort Bēlat-ṣarbi(m). Bēlat-ṣarbi(m) is likely identical with Ištar-ṣarbat, who was venerated in Pre-Sargonic, Old Akkadian, and Ur III periods at Mari and later in Old Babylonian times. (OB Nippur God list: 127)

Bēl-šukurrim / Lugal-^{geš}šukur (M) Deity attested in a personal name at Old Babylonian Mari. Means "Lord of the Lance." See the gods Sappu, Šugur, Šukurrum. (Durand 1987a: no. 14)

Bēl-šulbadda (M) The Akkadian cuneiform form corresponding to Ugaritic male deity ʻAṯtar in a text giving the cuneiform equivalents of Ugaritic deities. Occurs in an Old Babylonian god list written ^{d}Be-el-šul-ba-ad. (Schwemer 2001: 522 and note 4233; Weidner 1924/25)

Bēl-tarbaṣi (M) Deity mentioned in an Assyrian oracle. Means "Lord of the Cattle Pen." (Ivantchik 1993: no. 49)

Bēl-Terqa (M) Name of the god Dagān. Means "Lord of (the Town of) Terqa." Ancient Terqa was located on the Euphrates north of Mari. Schwemer disputes Durand's connecting this god to the storm god Adad as a family member with the name Bēl-māti(m). (Schwemer 2001: 277 note 1911)

Bēl-Tūe (M) God attested in a Neo-Assyrian text. Means "Lord of (the Town of) Tue." (Radner 1999: 138)

Bēlet-Akkad(e), Nin-Uri (M) Name of Ištar meaning "Lady of Akkad." Deity identified with Ištar of Akkad meaning "Lady of the Land of Akkad." Also Bēlet-Akkade "Lady of Akkad." Patron deity of the Old Akkadian period. Her temple at Akkad was called E-ul-maš, whence her Akkadian title Ul-mašītu(m). Her temples in other places often had a similar or the same name. (George 1993: 121 no. 740, 155 nos. 1168–70; Cavigneaux and Krebernik, *RlA* IX: 511)

Bēlet-āli(m) (M) Goddess invoked in an incantation. Had a center at the temple complex of the Elamite deity Šimut. Means "Lady of the City." (Lantos 2013: 142; Reiner 1970 [1958]: 40)

Bēlet-Api(m) (M) Akkadian goddess of the "Land of Apu(m)" in the Ḫabur basin. Attested in texts from Tell Leilān. (Cohen 2015: 269; Schwemer 2001: 272, 274; Charpin 1987a: 129–40)

Bēlet-Aratte (M) See Nin-Aratta

Bēlet-Arba'il (M) Akkadian epithet of Ištar meaning "Lady of Arba'il (Arbela)." (Livingstone 1989: 233)

Bēlet-Ayakki (M) Occurs in Hittite and Assyrian sources as a name for Ištar. (Beaulieu 2002: no. 36)

Bēlet-Bābili(m) (M) Name of Ištar meaning "Lady of Babylon." A calendar recorded processions of the goddess that were celebrated in Assyria, and at Aššur she was the jailor in charge of the *akītu*-house," which was her permanent home. (Cohen 2015: 395; George 1993: 141 no. 991, 151 no. 1117; Tallqvist 1974: 271)

Bēlet-balāṭi(m) (M) See Gula

Bēlet-bīri(m) (M) Deity identified with Išḫara in the god list An : *Anum*. The name, at least in some periods, was understood to mean "Lady of Extispicy." According to *CAD* B 265, Bēlet-bīri is a secondary interpretation of the name Bēlet-Erum. Also occurs as the name of the tenth month at Old Babylonian Mari. (Cohen 2015; Durand 2008: 220–22; Litke 1998: 44)

Bēlet-dalāti(m) (M) Deity whose name means "Lady of the Doors." See Bēlet-ēdilātim, quite likely the same goddess. (Sharlach 2002: 100)

Bēlet-Dēri(m) (M) Tutelary goddess of the city of Dēr, modern Bedreh. Sometimes identified with Ištar. Means "Lady of (the City of) Dēr." (Unger, *RlA* II: 201)

Bēlet-dunāni(m) (M) Akkadian form of the goddess Ištar in her battle aspect. Attested in a text referring to vessels of incense for the goddess in the *akītu*-house. (Schwemer 2001: 604; Cohen 1993: 400–6)

Bēlet-dūri(m) (M) Goddess attested at second-millennium BCE Emar. Also appears in an incantation tablet. Associated with a form of Ištar in An : *Anum*. Based upon a reference to the treasury of Bēlet-dūri in a Neo-Babylonian text from Nippur, she may have had a temple in Nippur. Means "Lady of the Wall." (Litke 1998: 151; Beckman 1996: 20; Beaulieu 1989: no. 64; Reiner 1970: 21)

Bēlet-E-anna (M) Name of Ištar at Babylon, where she had temples in east and west sections of the city. The epithet occurs also at Kiš. Means "Lady of the E-anna (Temple)." (George 1993: 111 no. 621 no. 624, 142 no. 996)

Bēlet-E-anna-Udannu (M) Akkadian form of the goddess Ištar worshipped as late as Hellenistic times, likely as the wife of the tutelary god of the town of Udannu. References to her jewelry occur in Neo-Babylonian texts from Uruk. (Beaulieu 2003: 289–94)

Bēlet-Eanni (M) In the Neo-Babylonian period she is referred to as a daughter of the Eibianna, the temple of Uraš in Dilbat.

Bēlet-Ebirtum(M) Goddess at Mari, whose name may mean "Lady Flood." (Cohen 2015; Cavigneaux and Krebernik *RlA* IX: 342)

Bēlet-ēdilātum (M) Goddess attested at Mari. *ēdilātum* "locking up ones" and *dilātum* "doors" are poetically synonymous, thus likely to be the same deity as Bēlet-dalātim. (Sharlach 2002: 2)

Bēlet-Ekalli(m) (M) See Nin-egal

Bēlet-Ekurri(m) (M) See Ma-nun-gal

Bēlet-Enimma (M) She is the recipient of offerings for the Brazier Festival during the period of the Sealand dynasty. (Dalley 2009: no. 66)

Bēlet-epri(m) (M) Goddess invoked in an incantation. Probably an epithet of Ištar. Means "Lady of the Dust." (Reiner 1970: 40)

Bēlet-Esamitum (M) Deity in an offering list from Mari. (Cavigneaux and Krebernik, *RlA* IX: 350)

Bēlet-Gubla (Akk.) See Ba'lat-Gebel

Bēlet-ḫā/īṣari (M) Deity attested in the Mari texts. Means "Lady of the Sheepfold." (Durand 2008: 264)

Bēlet-Id (M) Deity attested in the Mari texts. Means "Goddess of Hīt." (Durand 2008: 639)

Bēlet-ilī (Akk.), **Dingir-maḫ** (Sum.) Name of the birth/mother goddess, meaning "Lady of the Gods." Her consort was Šul-pa'e. The second tablet of An : *Anum* starts with her Sumerian name, Dingir-Maḫ, an indication of the importance of the birth/mother goddess.

In myth she was often associated with Enki/Ea. In "The Flood Story" with Atra-ḫasīs as the Noah figure, she created not only human beings, but also the god Enki/Ea. She was described in the "Epic of Gilgameš" as having a sweet voice. In the same composition, after the Flood, she stated that she would wear "the great fly-ornaments" (Foster 2001: 90) made by Anu(m), in order not to forget the Flood disaster. A regular festival was celebrated for her in Babylon. She is also associated with the E-meslam in Kutha. (Cohen 2015: 414; Foster 2001: 87, 90, 222; Litke 1998: 66; Tallqvist 1974: 273–75; Krebernik, *RlA* VIII: 504)

Plaque depicting one of the birth/mother goddesses of Mesopotamia. Ca. 2000–1600 BCE. Terracotta. After Black and Green 132.

Bēlet-Kidmūri(m) (M) Deity identified with Ištar. A temple to the goddess that she shared there with Enlil was built by Aššurnaṣirpal II at Kalaḫ just east of the temple of Ninurta, the chief god of Kalaḫ. It was excavated by Rassam in 1878. (Livingstone 1986: 250–51; Grayson 1991: 303–5; Postgate and Reade, *RlA* V: 308–9)

Bēlet-Lagaba, Lagabītu(m) (M) Epithet of Ištar as "Lady of Lagaba." The garments and ornaments that Ištar of Lagaba, a town near Kiš, wore for festivals are known in some detail from a Babylonian tablet. (*LAS*: 66, 69–70; George 1993: 37; Leemans 1952: 19–24)

Bēlet-Larsa (M) Goddess attested in Neo-Babylonian texts from Uruk. Possibly the tutelary deity of the city of Larsa. (Beaulieu 2003: 292)

Bēlet-mātim (M) See Ba'lta-māti

Bēlet-murarat (M) Deity in an offering list at Mari. (Cavigneaux and Krebernik, *RlA* IX: 473)

Bēlet-Nagar (M) Chief goddess of the ancient city of Nagar, almost certainly modern Tell Brak in Syria. Attested in Early Dynastic, Sargonic, Ur III, and Old Babylonian texts. Means "Lady of Nagar." In an Ur III text she is mentioned along with Išḫara, Annunītu(m), and Ulmašītu(m), suggesting that she was a form of Ištar. Archi suggests she might be identified with the goddess Ḫaburītum. (Durand 2008: 311–12; Archi 2004; Sharlach 2002: 100–1; Guichard 1994: 269–72; Sallaberger 1993: I, 46, 205, II, Table 67; Charpin 1987a: 79; Cavigneaux and Krebernik, *RlA* IX: 474–75)

Bēlet-Nanāya (M) Goddess appearing in the "Old Pantheon" at Mari to be associated with Nanāya. (Schwemer 2001: 228 note 1580)

Bēlet-Ninua, Ninua'ītu(m) (M) Name means "Lady of Nineveh." Also called Šarrat-Nin-ua/Nin-a, "Queen of Nineveh." Identified with Ninlil. In addition to Nineveh, she had temples at Babylon and Aššur. (Litke 1998: 150; George 1993: 95 no. 409–10, 121 no. 742, 169 no. 1400; Tallqvist 1974: 416; Cavigneaux and Krebernik, *RlA* IX: 478)

Bēlet-Nippuri(m) (M) See Nin-Nibru

Bēlet-parṣē-ilāni (M) Goddess in a dedication on beads by the Assyrian king Adad-Nirari. Means "Lady of the Rites of the Gods" (Donbaz 1991: no. 107; Farber 1992: no. 20)

Bēlet-qabli(m) (M) Form of the goddess Ištar invoked in an incantation. Means "Lady of Battle." (Reiner 1970: 40)

Bēlet-Qaṭṭarā (M) Form of the goddess Ištar as tutelary deity of the town of Qaṭṭarā in the Ḫabur basin, located at modern Doûgour not far north of Tell Leilān. Means "Lady of Qaṭṭarā." (Schwemer 2001: 269, 274; Dalley, Walker, and Hawkins 1976: no. 154, no. 200)

Bēlet-(ša-)Rēš (M) Tutelary goddess of the Rēš sanctuary in Uruk during the Neo-Babylonian and Seleucid periods. Means "Lady of the Rēš (Sanctuary)." Toward the end of its history, Uruk experienced a renaissance under the Seleucid kings, and one of the new monumental temples was the Bīt Rēš, which included the Anu(m)/Antu(m) temple and the Anu(m) ziqqurat. Bēlet-Rēš participated in the procession with Ištar from the E-anna temple to the Rēš sanctuary. Bongenaar points out that a tablet from Uruk may attest to a small cult center of Bēlet-Rēš also in the neighboring city of Larsa. (Beaulieu 2003: 216–26, 381; Bongenaar 1997: 239–40 note 221)

Bēlet-Sippari(m) (M) Epithet of Ištar meaning "Lady of Sippar." Her temple at Sippar was called "House of the Steppe." During the first month of the calendar, the *akītu* Festival was held for her. (Cohen 2015: 390; George 1993: 81 no. 244)

Bēlet-ṣarbat (M) See Ištar-ṣarbat

Bēlet-ṣēri(m) (M) Scribe and bookkeeper of the netherworld. In some traditions, wife of Amurru(m)/Mardu. Sometimes identified with Geštin-ana or Ašratu(m). Her name means "Lady of the Open Countryside (or the Steppe)." The goddess had shrines at Uruk and elsewhere. A comment in a late text giving instructions for a daily ritual at Uruk states: "Fowl flesh shall never be offered to the goddess Bēlet-ṣēri" (Sachs, *ANET*: 344). (Durand 2008: 253; Foster 2001: 222; Leick 1998: 25; George 1993: 37, 78 no. 192, 99 no. 462, 113 no. 648, 163 no. 1289; Tallqvist 1974: 276; Edzard 1965: 46)

Bēlet-šamê (M) Goddess identified with Ištar. Means "Lady of Heaven."

Bēlet-Šuḫner and **Bēlet-Terrabān** (Akk.), **Nin-Šuḫner** and **Nin-Terrabān** (Sum.) Goddesses foreign to Mesopotamia. Usually paired and worshipped together, Bēlet-Šuḫner means "Lady of (the City of) Suḫner" and Bēlet-Terrabān "Lady of (the City of) Terrabān." Šuḫner and Terrabān were probably non-Babylonian cities in the Diyala region of eastern Mesopotamia. It is likely that the goddesses entered a royal court through diplomatic marriage during the Ur III period and disappeared after that time. Their main cult center was Uruk, where they shared a temple. They were also associated with the cult of Tišpak at Ešnunna, a city east of Babylon in the middle of the Diyala River basin. A "Festival of Chains" was held for the goddess pair in Uruk, possibly based on a belief that the two goddesses were led to the netherworld in chains. Ritual wailing for these two deities is attested at Uruk. (Cohen 2015: 85; Sharlach 2002: 101–3; Sallaberger 1993: I, 19 note 64; Cavigneaux and Krebernik, *RlA* IX: 501)

Bēlet-tarbaṣi(m) (M) Deity attested at Qaṭṭara. (Durand 2008: 264)

Bēlet-Terrabān (M) See Bēlet-Šuḫner and Bēlet-Terrabān

Bēlet-tešmû (M) Goddess attested in a Neo-Assyrian god list explained as *miḫir-tu maḫāru*, "she who listens." (King 1969: pl. 9)

Bēlet-titurri(m) (M) Goddess attested at Uruk, with a chapel at Larsa. Means "Lady of the Bridge (or Causeway)." An Ur III tablet connects this goddess with funerary rites for the Ur III king Šū-Sîn, and it seems to indicate that at Uruk a chapel of this goddess was part of a funerary shrine that housed chapels of Nin-geš-zida, a well-known chthonic deity; the divine (and dead) king Šulgi; the sun god Utu, who had netherworld connections; and Gan-zir, a designation of the gate of the netherworld. Perhaps the symbolism of the name Bēlet-titurri(m) is similar to that found in the later Chinvat Bridge (Avestan Cinvatô Peretûm "Bridge of Judgment" or "Beam-Shaped Bridge") in Zoroastrianism; it separated the world of the living from the world of the dead. According to this tradition, all souls had to cross the bridge upon death. The goddess Bēlet-tu-ur-ri (var. Bēlet-ur-ri), identified in An : *Anum* as associated with outdoor shrines of Inana, may be a corrupted form of Bēlet-titurri. (Litke 1998: 160; Richter 2004: 399; Sigrist 1989: 503 and note 18)

Bēlet-Uruk (M) Akkadian epithet of Ištar meaning "Lady of Uruk." Falkenstein notes a chapel for the goddess in the as-yet-not-located *akītu*-house/temple outside Uruk. The name also occurs as Bēltu-ša-Uruk in the Seleucid period. (Nemet-Nejat 1993: 163–69; Livingstone 1986: 218; Falkenstein 1941: 42)

Bēlet-Zabala(m) (M) Akkadian goddess mentioned in a tablet from the First Sealand Dynasty. Means "Lady of Zabala(m)." (Dalley 2009: 67 and note 6)

Belial (L) In the Hebrew Bible, often personified as a demon of all wickedness (e.g., II Samuel 22: 5). Later the proper name of the devil. After 539 BCE, under Persian influence, the Jews adopted a good deal of folkloric material about spirits and demons: hierarchies of angels and demonic entities such as Asmodeus and Belial. In the Pseudographia, for example, *The Testament of the Twelve Patriarchs*, the devil was called Belial, as he was in one of the Dead Sea scrolls, *The Wars of the Sons of Light against the Sons of Darkness*. In the New Testament, in a list of dualisms, the Apostle Paul asked what Jesus had to do with Belial (II Corinthians 6: 15). Called Beliar in some versions in the New Testament. (Encyclopedia Britannica 2003; Smith 2001: 166; Sperling, *DDDB*: 169- 171; Brownrigg 1993: 20–21; Lewis, *ABD* I: 654–56)

Bēlili (M) A very ancient Sumerian goddess of the netherworld. One of the twenty-one primordial ancestors of the sky god Anu(m). Consort of Alala and, in the Akkadian "Descent of Ištar," sister of Ištar's lover Dumuzi. Bēlili appears in two other mythic tales: the Sumerian "Dumuzi's Dream" and "Inana and Bilulu." It was to the house of Bēlili, represented as an old woman, that Dumuzi escaped when he was being pursued by netherworld demons. They were determined to carry him off to the netherworld as a substitute for Inana. In "Inana and Bilulu," Inana found Dumuzi's body in Bēlili's house. Bilulu, a different person from Bēlili, appears at the end of the story. Bēlili often shared a temple or shrine with Dumuzi. At Babylon, with her consort Alala, she had a seat in the main temple, Marduk's E-sag-ila. She also had temples and shrines of her own, including one at Uruk. Bí-li-li, attested once in a personal name from Ur III Nippur, presumably is a variant for Bēlili. (Foster 2005: 504; *LAS*: 82; Litke 1998: 23; George 1993: 34, 82 no. 253, 150 no. 1096, 157 no. 1202; Tallqvist 1974: 271; Alster 1972: 77; Reiner 1970: 21; Speiser, *ANET*: 109; Jacobsen 1953: 182 and note 49)

Belluki (E) Deity, possibly Elamite, occurring in an Akkadian personal name. Mentioned in a tablet from the First Sealand Dynasty. (Dalley 2009: 83)

Belphegor (L) See Ba'al-phegor

Bēlti(s), Bēltīya (L) See Ba'lat-Gebel

Bēltu-ša-rēš (M) See Bēlet-Rēš

Bēltu-ša-Uruk (M) See Bēlet-Uruk

Belzebub (L) See Ba'al-zebul

Bennu(m) (M) Personification of epilepsy. Identified with the Sumerian god Aga-gig-duga. (Litke 1998: 73; Tallqvist 1974: 250)

Bēr (M) See Wēr

Berial (L) See Belial

Berouth (L) Consort of the god Elioun, the Phoenician equivalent of the Hebrew Elyon, and mother of the sky god Ouranos in the *Phoenician History* of Philo of Byblos. The goddess's name might be an abbreviation of Ba'lat-Beruth "Lady of Beirut," possibly a title of the goddess Asherah. (Attridge and Oden 1981: 46- 47, 86)

BE-šinig (M) See Bēl-bīni(m)

Bethel, Beth-El, Bīt-il (L) Phoenician and Israelite god name. Probably an abbreviated version of El-Beth-El, a god name in the Hebrew Bible, meaning "El of the House of El." Bethel was the name given by Jacob to the sacred place where he had had a dream of angels ascending a ladder into the sky (Genesis 28:10–19). The Hebrew Bible understands Bethel as a sanctuary of El/YHWH, except in Jeremiah 48:13, where Bethel seems to be referring to a god. From the seventh century BCE on, Bethel seems to have replaced the old god El, especially in Aramaic theophoric names. The first known use of the god's name was in a seventh-century BCE vassal treaty between the Assyrians and Phoenician Tyre, where he was paired with 'Anat-Bethel, "'Anat (the consort of ?) Bethel." In Neo-Babylonian tablets West Semites referred to the god as Bīt-il in their names. Documents from the Jewish community at Elephantine Island in Egypt indicate that, in the fifth century BCE, the god Eshem-Bethel "Name of Bethel" was worshipped there along with 'Anat-Bethel. The god Bethel was worshipped also in Carthaginian North Africa. Philo of Byblos names a Phoenician god Baetylos, one of four offspring of Ouranos "Sky" and Ge "Earth." Some scholars consider Baetylos to be identical to the deity Bethel. Texts from Ugarit do not mention the god. (Smith 2001: 32, 137; Ribichini, *DDDB*: 157–59; Röllig, *DDDB*: 173–75; Handy 1994: 57–58; Lipiński, *DCPP*: 71; Xella, *DCPP*: 70; Smith 1990: 25, 145–46; Attridge and Oden 1981: 87 note 86; Cross 1973: 74, 198–99; Porten 1969; Albright 1968: 226–27 note 48; Porten 1968)

Bibbu (M) God who, in the "Epic of Gilgameš," was a butler in the netherworld. (Foster 2001: 222)

Bibra (M) Deified hen-like bird, a *bibru(m)* (Akk.) Also a cult vessel, a rhyton, in the shape of the bird. In a text dating to the reign of Ibbi-Sîn, the rhyton is mentioned in connection with funerary offerings for Ur-Namma. In the lexical series Diri the name is written with the logogram dḪÚL and syllabically rendered bi-ib-ru-um. (Cohen 2015: 97; Civil 2004; Leick 1999: 74–75, 172–73; Litke 1998: 219)

BIL.DAG, NE.DAG (M) Deity first attested in an Early Dynastic god list. Occurs also in an incantation, where he is associated with the é-gùn-na. Andersson suggests reading Dè-pàr, for *dipāru* "torch." See Dipāru. (George 2016: no. 1b; Andersson 2013; Mander 1986: 112)

Bilulu (M) Old woman in the Sumerian myth "Inana and Bilulu." Inana turned her into a water skin because she held Bilulu responsible for the death of Dumuzi. (Jacobsen 1953: 182)

Bindug-baša (M) See Šud-bindug-baša

Binikir (E) See Pirengir

Birdu, Birtu (M) Netherworld god. Son of Enlil. Husband of Manun-gal (Nungal), the goddess of prisons. A canal in Nippur was named for him. (Black and Green 2003: 145; Litke 1998: 185, 197; Tallqvist 1974: 277)

Birqu(m) (M) Attribute of the storm god. Means "Thunderbolt." (Schwemer 2001: 602 note 4868)

Bišašapḫi (H) See Pišaišapḫ(i)

Biti, Piti, Bidu (M) Keeper of the first and main gate of the netherworld. Name probably derives from Akkadian *petû* "to open," thus the name means "Open!" In the Sumerian version of "The Descent of Inana," Biti challenged Inana when she sought to enter the netherworld. In the Akkadian "Descent of Ištar," Ištar addressed him only as "Gatekeeper." The deity appears also in Akkadian composition "Nergal and Ereškigal." A possible expansion of his name is Bi-du-an-ki-šár "Gate-keeper of All Heaven and Earth." Mentioned in "The Death of Gilgameš" as receiving offerings from Gilgameš before the latter died. (Foster 2005: 498–505; Katz 2003: 401; Frayne 2001: 153; *LAS*: 68; Leick 1998: 92; Litke 1998; 189; Tallqvist 1974: 388; Kramer, *ANET*: 54; Speiser, *ANET*: 107, 509)

Bīt-il (L) See Bethel

Bitinḫi (H) See Pidenḫi

Bīt-šemi (M) Babylonian spirit associated with houses. Probably associated with the messenger god Nin-šubur. Means "O House, Hear." (Litke 1998: 29)

Bizaza (M) The Sumerian god in an Old Babylonian text from Nippur. Name means "frog." (Richter 2004: 157)

Bizil-ana, Bizilla (M) Sumerian/Babylonian goddess attested in an Early Dynastic god list from Abu Ṣalābīkh. Perhaps to be associated with Bizilana in a Neo-Assyrian text, listed there as a messenger of Ninlil. In An : *Anum* the adjacent entries Nin-bi-an-na and Bí-zil-lá may refer to this same deity. Associated with Nanaya at Mari. Vizier of Mulliltu(m) (Ninlil) at Ḫursag-kalama, the eastern mounds of Kiš. Bizilla is mentioned in a ritual for the ninth month in Babylon in the Persian period. (Durand 2008: 248–49; Litke 1998: 164; George 1993: 54; Mander 1986: 60; Lambert 1985a: 530)

Bn Aṯrt (L) "The Sons of Asherah." See Asherah

Bn Il/m (L) The "first generation" of deities at Ugarit, "the sons of El/Il," the high god. (del Olmo Lete 1999: 47)

Bnt Ba'lu (L) "Daughters of Ba'lu." See Ba'lu

Bugaš (M) Kassite deity attested only in personal names. (Black and Green 2003: 112; Balkan 1978: 102–4)

Bulala (M) Deity attested in an Old Babylonian god list. Written bu-la-la. (Weidner 1924/25)

Bull of Heaven (M) See Alû(m)

Bunene (M) Charioteer and vizier of Utu/Šamaš. He shared with Šamaš and his consort Aya "the great tripartite cult-center of Sippar" (George 1993: 29). In a brick inscription celebrating the dedication of a new Šamaš temple by a king of Mari, Bunene is called "the great plenipotentiary of Šamaš" (Oppenheim, *ANET*: 557). The god's name, which seems to be Sumerian, appears in both Sumerian and Akkadian. (Litke 1998: 132)

BU-nir (M) Deity identified with the moon god Nanna/Sîn in An : *Anum*. Explained in *Anu ša amēli* as "the rising(*nipḫu*) moon." (Litke 1998: 117)

Bur-ane-suga (M) Goddess, perhaps a protective deity like Lama. She appears in a lamentation, in a litany of goddesses, searching for a child. Although the one attestation of this deity is with the variant sù-ga instead of su_8-ga, the name probably means "Vessel that Stands in Heaven." (Cohen 1988: 695)

Buranun-ta-sá (M) See Burnunta-sa

Burga-lunga (M) See Buru-kaš

Burgul (M) Patron of seal-cutters and other workers in small stone objects. Appears in An : *Anum* in a section dealing with craft gods. Means "Bowl Carver." (Litke 1998: 110)

Buriaš, Ubriaš (M) The storm god of the Kassites. Buriaš was also called Ḫudḫa. He was identified with Iškur/Adad. It has been suggested that there might be a connection between the god's name and that of Boreas, the Greek god of the north wind. (Black and Green 2003: 112; Balkan 1978: 3, 104–5, 107)

Buri-baba (M) Goddess attested in a Neo-Assyrian god list and identified with Aya, the wife of the sun god. Written bu-ri-ba_4-ba_4; following entry šur-ba_4-ba_4 may be a variant. (King 1969: pl. 9)

Burnunta-sa (M) This name of a son of Enki, the god of freshwater, and written bur-nun-ta-sá^{sa}-a may well be a variant for the unattested god name ^{i_7}Buranun-ta sá "The One who Rivals the Euphrates." (Litke 1998: 101; Galter 1983: 127)

Buršu-sikil (M) See Buršu-šal

Buršu-šal (M) Name for Ninlil. Bur-šu presumably is for bur-šu-ma, "matriarch," although it can also denote an official. See Nin-bur-šal with the gloss šá-al. The next entry in An : *Anum* is Buršu-sikil, also a name for Ninlil. (Litke 1998: 40)

Buru (M) Deity attested in an Early Dynastic god list. Written $buru_5^{mušen}$ and designates a flock or swarm. (Mander 1986: 138)

Būru(m) (M) Bull deity associated with the god Teššub. Attested in Old Babylonian, Neo-Assyrian, and Neo-Babylonian documents, especially in personal names. Means "calf." (Schwemer 2001: 487–89)

Buru-kaš, **Burga-lunga** (M) Divine cult officials involved with brewing in the temple precinct of Keš in Šarrākum. These two god names are variants in An : *Anum*. Written bur-u_5-kaš and bur-ga-lunga$^{(ga)}$. Attested also in a god list from Aššur. For the bur-u_5 official (*burrû*) see *PSD* B 186 bur C. Another related cult official, presumably the superior of the bur-u_5, is the bur-u_5-gal. Perhaps bur-ga-lunga is conflated from bur-u_5-gal-lunga. (Litke 1998: 79; Schroeder 1920: no. 64)

Bu-u (M) Sumerian deity forming part of an Ur III theophoric personal name. Written bu-ú "secret" (*pirištu*). (Richter 2004: 118 note 526)

— C —

Cabires, Cabiri (L) See Kabiri

Caelestis (L) Name of the tutelary deity of Roman Carthage, Juno Caelestis. Seems to have been identified with Phoenician Aštarte, especially in North Africa, and also with the Punic (Carthaginian) goddess Tanit. Means "Heavenly One." Also known as Virgo Caelestis "Heavenly Virgin." The realm of this aspect of Juno was both the sky with its astral bodies and the earth, especially its animals. She also was associated with the netherworld. She was particularly associated with the rain and so was concerned with the earth's fertility. As such, she was called Nutrix "Nourisher." Her consort was Saturn, and the two deities were normally worshipped as a pair.

Caelestis was usually depicted veiled, either sitting on a lion or enthroned with lions around her. Her head was surmounted with a crescent, a garland, or snakes. Her cult was observed across North Africa, including the cities Leptis Magna and Sabratha. Her temples were famous for their magnificence. The ruins of one at Dougga, Tunisia, built in the second century CE, are still impressive. Another, not in such good repair, is at Tas Ṣilg on the island of Malta, part of the Roman province of Sicily. As Cicero's oration of 70 BCE "Against Verres" attests, when governor of the province, Verres stripped this great shrine of its treasures. The goddess was popular in Rome in the third century CE. (Ball 2009: 92; Lipiński 1995: 147–49, 435–37; Le Glay, *DCPP*: 86; Cicero. *In Verrem* II. 4)

Chaamu, Chaabou (L) Virgin goddess of the Nabateans. Chaamu was mother of their chief god Dushara (Dusares), according to Christian bishop Epiphanios of Salamis. He reported that the people of Petra sang hymns to her in their temples. (Nehmé 2000: 165; Langdon, 1931: 16–18)

Chemosh (L) See Kamiš

Cherubim (pl.), **Cherub** (sg.) (L) Composite beasts, winged sphinx-like creatures that functioned as guardians either of a throne or of a sacred tree. A sphinx was usually a human-headed lion with wings. The word occurs around ninety times in the Hebrew Bible, and it is probably related to the East Semitic (Akk.) adjective *karibu(m)* or *kuribu(m)*, meaning "blessing" and referring to protective figures that stood at doors and gateways in Mesopotamian iconography and mythology. Interpreted variously as Canaanite or Israelite or a combination of both, the famous cult stand from Taanach in Israel has cherubs on two registers (Hadley 2000: 170 figure 13). Biblical Cherubim, in pairs, one male and one female, were also protective spirits (Ezekiel 28: 14). They guarded the entrance to the Garden of Eden and so the sacred Tree of Life (Genesis 3:24), and they also protected the shrine of Solomon's temple complex in Jerusalem (I Kings 6:23–35). Their most important task, however, was to form or flank the throne that carried the invisible presence of the Israelite deity (I Samuel 4:4, Ezekiel 9–10). Images of thrones supported by sphinxes are attested in a variety of Near Eastern and

Phoenician contexts. (Lewis 2005: 95–97, 104; Stuckey 2002: 47–48; Smith 2001: 171–72; Hadley 2000: 169–76; Mettinger, *DDDB*: 189–92; Meyers, ABD I: 899–900; Patai 1990: 67–95; Smith 1990: 116; Cross 1973: 207, 231)

Chiun (L) See Rephaim

Chousor(os) (L) See Kôṯar-wa-Ḫasīs(u)

Chrysoros (L) See Kôṯar-wa-Ḫasīs(u)

Chusor (L) See Kôṯar-wa-Ḫasīs(u)

Cinyras (L) See Kin(n)ār(u)

Çiravanta (E) See Širumanda

Colpia (L) See Kolpia

— D —

Dabān (M) See Ṭabān

Dabar (M) Deity from Abu Ṣalābīkh. Written Da-bar. (OBO 160/1, 1998, p. 269)

Dabinatu (M) Goddess at Ebla. Archi suggests that the name may mean "Awful Lady." It occurs also as a geographic name. (Archi 1997)

Dada (M) Goddess attested at Nippur in the Ur III period. In An : *Anum* listed as a messenger of Inana. In the Old Babylonian period and onward, Dada is identified with Inana in lamentations and called "The Mother of the House" and "The Beautiful Woman." (Richter 2004: 294; Litke 1998: 159; Sallaberger 1993: I, 102 note 445; Cohen 1988: 533, 561, 651, 711, 714; Black 1985: 50–51)

Dada-gula (M) Sumerian deity whom W. Heimpel suggests may have been a famous harpist who was eventually deified. In Ur III economic texts, a gala-priest Dada receives repaired copper instruments, perhaps cymbals, but whether he is the musician later deified cannot be determined. (Mirelman 2010: no. 33; Heimpel 1997: no. 137)

Dadmiš(u) (H, L) An obscure Hurrian/Hittite goddess officially accepted into the pantheon at Ugarit. In one god list she is grouped with "Assistant Gods of Ba'lu(u)." She is also quite popular in other Ugaritic cultic texts. (del Olmo Lete 1999: 83, 131, 274)

Dadmuštu(m), Dadamušda (M) Daughter of Nergal in the cult of Kutha at the E-meslam. (Litke 1998: 201)

Dagān (L, M) Originally a god of West Semitic speakers from the Levant, but worshipped widely throughout the Near East, including Mesopotamia. Deity of grain, as well as its cultivation and storage. Indeed, the common word for "grain" in Ugaritic and Hebrew is *dagān*. According to one Sumerian tradition and to the much later Philo of Byblos, Dagān invented the plow. In the north, he was sometimes identified with Adad. Thus, he may have had some of the characteristics of a storm god. In one tradition his wife was Išḫara, in another Šalaš, usually wife of Adad. Šalaš was originally a goddess of the Hurrians. Dagān also had netherworld connections. According to an Assyrian composition, he was a judge of the dead in the lower world, serving with Nergal and Mīšaru(m), the god of justice. A tradition going back at least to the fourth century BCE identified Dagān as a fish god, but it is almost certainly incorrect, presumably having been based upon a false etymology that interpreted the element "Dag" in Dagān as deriving from the Hebrew word dag "fish."

The earliest mentions of him come from texts that indicate that, in Early Dynastic times, Dagān was worshipped at Ebla. Dagān was taken into the Sumerian pantheon quite early as a minor god in the circle of Enlil at Nippur. Kings of the Old Akkadian period, including Sargon and Narām-Sîn, credited much of their success as conquerors to Dagān. Sargon recorded that he "prostrated (himself) in prayer before Dagān in Tutul [sic]" (Oppenheim, *ANET*: 268). At the same time, he gave to the god a large area of the country he had just conquered, including Mari, Ebla, and Iarmuti in western Syria. A number of letters from the Mari archives, dated mainly to the reign of Zimrī-Līm, record that Dagān was a source of divine revelation. The letters reported prophetic dreams, a number of which came from Dagān, conveyed by his prophets and ecstatics. In his law code, Ḫammu-rāpi credits Dagān with helping him subdue settlements along the Euphrates. The Assyrian king Šamšī-Adad I commissioned a temple for him at Terqa, upstream from Mari, where funeral rites for the Mari Dynasty took place. In the Old Babylonian period, kings of the Amorites erected temples for Dagān at Isin and Ur.

In the Anzû(m) myth, Dagān was favorably coupled with Anu(m). At Ugarit Dagān was closely associated with, if not equated to, the supreme god El/Il(u). Although he is mentioned in the mythic compositions of Ugarit as the father of the storm god Ba'lu/Had(d)ad, Dagān plays only a very minor role. His popularity is indicated by his importance in offering and god lists, one of which places him third, after the two chief gods and before the active and powerful god Ba'lu/Had(d)ad. Dagān is attested in Ugaritic theophoric names. In Ugaritic texts the god is often referred to as "Dagān of Tuttul." It might also be the case that one of the two major temples of the city of Ugarit was dedicated to him, and he might there have been identified with the chief god Il(u)/El. Festivals for Dagān took place at Terqa and Tuttul, both of which were cult centers of the god. He was certainly worshipped at Ebla and also at Mari. At Mari, in Old Babylonian times, he appears as fourth deity on a god list; that is, he was very important. He was venerated also at Emar. There a "Sacred Marriage" ritual between Dagān and the goddess Nin-kur was celebrated. At the same city, a festival was held in honor of "Dagān-Lord-of-the-Cattle," at which the herds of cattle and probably sheep were blessed.

According to the Hebrew Bible, Dagān was the national god of the Philistines. I Samuel:5–6 tells of the capture of the Ark of the Covenant by the Philistines. It was customary in the Ancient Near East for the conquerors to carry off the deity statues of the conquered to mark the surrender not only of the people, but also of their deities. So the Philistines took the Ark, the symbol of the god of the Israelites, into the temple of Dagān at Ashdod. Since the Israelites had no statues of their deity, the much revered Ark was an obvious substitute. In this way, the Philistines marked the submission of the Israelite god to Dagān. However, on the next day, the people of Ashdod found the statue of Dagān lying face down in front of the Ark. The following day the same thing happened except that the head and hands of Dagān's statue lay broken on the temple threshold. This biblical account seems to be an etiology for a practice of the priests of the temple of Dagān at Ashdod, for it states that for this reason it is the custom of the priests of Dagān not to tread on the threshold as they enter the temple of Dagān. The best-known of the biblical stories that mention Dagān is in Judges 16, the tale of Samson and Delilah. After Delilah arranged for the Philistines of Gaza to capture Samson, they blinded him, shackled him, and made him a slave at a mill. During a festival to Dagān, the Philistines took Samson to be exhibited in Dagān's temple, where thousands of Philistines had gathered for the celebrations. After praying to the Israelite god, the now long-haired Samson got back his old strength. By pushing against two central pillars, he brought the temple crashing down on himself and on more Philistines than he had killed in his whole lifetime of killing Philistines. (Cohen 2015: 15; Lipinski, 2012: 335–44; Durand 2008: 306; Foster 2005: 559; Archi 2004; Feliu 2003; Black and Green 2003: 56; Sharlach 2002: 95–96; Healey, *DDDB*: 216–19; del Olmo Lete 1999: 56, 74; Leick 1999: 65–66; 117–18, 141, 148, 181; Leick 1998: 29; Litke 1998: 42, 43; Pomponio and Xella 1997: 376–77; George 1993: 81 no. 230, 85 no. 285, 110 no. 608; Lambert 1985a: 526; Pettinato 1985: 234–56; Attridge and Oden 1981: 53; Tallqvist 1974: 278–79; Grayson, *ANET*: 515; Meek, *ANET*: 165; Moran, *ANET*: 623–25, 630–32; Speiser, *ANET*: 111)

Dagān bēl buqāri (M) A form of Dagān at Emar, who was the central deity of the *zukru* festival at Emar. Probably means "Dagān Lord of the Cattle," though some read *bēl bukari* "Dagān Lord of the Offspring/Firstborn." (Cohen 2015; Fleming 2000)

Dagān ša ḫarri (M) Deity of the town Terqa on the Middle Euphrates. Gelb proposed "Dagān of the Hurrians." Feliu prefers "Dagān of the ditch/pit." (Feliu 1998: no. 44)

Dagānzipas (H) Earth treated as a Hittite goddess in the "Song of Kumarbi." (Hoffner 1998: 42–47, 110)

Dagōn (L) See Dagān

Daḫ-šešriš, Daḫ-šešra/i (E) Elamite deity appearing in An : *Anum*. (Litke 1998: 213)

Da'in (M) Deity attested at third-millennium Ebla. Written [d]da-i-in.

Dakbak (E) In a Neo-Assyrian god list identified with Ninurta of Elam. (King 1969: pl. 12)

Da-Lagaš (M) See Nin-da-Lagaš

Dalḫamun (M) Deity whose name means "Whirlwind." (1) Horseman of the sun god Utu/Šamaš. Written dal-ḫa-mun. (2) Name of the storm god Adad. (Litke 1998: 134, 232; Tallqvist 1974: 438)

Dam (M) Deity attested in a personal name from Lagaš. Perhaps Dam is a shortened form for Dam-gal-nuna, "Great Spouse of the Prince," the consort of Enki. It is also found outside Lagaš in dedicatory inscriptions of the Šuruppak period. (Selz 1995: 106)

Dam-gal-nuna (M) See Damkina

Damgar (M) Name of Enlil, the last of his names in An : *Anum*. The Sumerian epithet means "Merchant." (Litke 1998: 40)

Dam-ge (M) God attested in the Sumerian zà-mí hymns from Abu Ṣalābīkh of the Early Dynastic period. Tutelary deity of the town EZENxNIMGIR, probably in the Lagaš area. Note Nin-dam-ge6, likely the wife of Damge. The name could mean "Spouse (of) the Night." (Frayne 2009: 75 note 102; Mander 1986: 124)

Dam-ge-DU (M) Deity attested in an Early Dynastic god list. (Mander 1986: 138)

Damiqatu (L) One of the Kōṯarṭu, seven minor goddesses of fertility at Ugarit. (del Olmo Lete 1999: 57)

Damka (M) Identified with Adad in a Neo-Assyrian god list. (King 1969: pl. 16).

Dam-ki-ana (M) Sumerian title probably of Ištar as the planet Venus. Means "Spouse of Earth and Heaven." It occurs in a Babylonian *akītu* ritual from the Hellenistic (Seleucid) period. (Sachs, *ANET*: 333)

Damkina (Akk.), **Dam-gal-nuna** (Sum.) **Damkina(š)**, **Tapkina(š)** (Hittite) (M, H) Wife of Enki/Ea. Mother of the chief Babylonian god Marduk. In the *Enūma eliš*, Damkina lived with Ea in the Apsû, his house/temple at Eridu, where Marduk was born. Her name means "Great Spouse of the Prince." Also known as Nin-dam-gal-nuna. As Damkina(š)/Tapkina(š), borrowed by Hittite from Mesopotamia. Attested outside Lagaš, for example, at Adab, in dedicatory inscriptions of the Šuruppak period. The divine name Dam at Adab may be a shortened form. Dam-gal-nuna, along with Enki, is mentioned in the law code of Ḫammu-rāpi. She appears in Hittite treaties, along with Ea. Labelled Tapkina, she also is depicted in the procession of goddesses in the Hittite rock-cut reliefs at Yazılıkaya near Ḫattušas in Turkey. (Durand 2008: 227–28; Maiocchi 2009: no. 106, no. 141; Foster 2005: 442.; Black and Green 2003: 56–57; Leick 1999: 65–66; Leick 1998: 29–30; Litke 1998: 88; van Gessel 1998: I, 437–39; Popko 1985: 112, 115; Selz 1995: 106; Tallqvist 1974: 279–80; Meek, *ANET*: 165; Speiser, *ANET*: 62; Heidel 1967: 21; Laroche 1946/47: 126; Cavigneaux and Krebernik, *RlA* IX: 338)

Dam-mete-abzu (M) Third name of Enki/Ea's wife Dam-gal-nuna/Damkina in An : *Anum*. Means "Wife, the Befitting One of the Abzu." (Litke 1998: 88)

Damnaššareš (H) Hittite guardian deity (deities), especially protective of the king. In a prayer, Hittite king Muršili II described sphinxes of Damnaššareš standing in the inner section of the temple of the storm god. The god(s) appears in a treaty concerning a border. Also mentioned in a Hurrian/Hittite ritual as watching at a door. Controlled small sphinxes at temple gateways. (van Gessel 1998: I, 439–40; Haas 1994: 335–36, 473)

Damu (M) Sumerian god of healing. Son of the healer goddess Nin-Isina "Lady of Isin" (identified with Nin-kar(r)ak). His father was Enki. In one Sumerian composition Nin-Isina bestows healing powers to her son. Damu seems to have been closely associated with vegetation, for he was an important figure in lamentations dealing with the early grass. In the lament "In the Steppe in the Early Grass," Damu is associated with a cycle of netherworld deities in cities of south Sumer. The lamentation bewailed the fate of Damu as he proceeded to the Land of No Return. In this work, his sister Gunumera and his mother go in search of him. The composition ends with a list of the burial places of kings of the Old Babylonian period. Like his mother, Damu was, then, a deity of healing.

In connection to the cult of Nin-Isina, he was worshipped in Ur III times at Ur, Nippur, and Isin and in Old Babylonian times at Umma with the goddess Nin-Ib-gal. His cult center seems to have been Isin. At Ebla, he occurs frequently in theophoric names; fifty percent or more of the names of personnel in the court, as well as several royal names, were constructed with Damu as an element. He also appears at Emar. Originally Damu was a separate deity and not related to Dumuzi, though some of his attributes and myths seem later to have become attached to Dumuzi. In some Sumerian compositions, Dumuzi was called "My Damu," perhaps a play upon *dumu* "child." (Lapinkivi 2004: 211; Black and Green 2003: 57; Alster, *DDDB*: 828, 832; Leick 1998: 30; Litke 1998: 183; Pomponio and Xella 1997: 387; George 1993: 163 no. 1295; Sallaberger 1993: I, 234; Cohen 1988: II, 678; Tallqvist 1974: 279; Renger 1967: 162)

Damun (M) See Nin-damun

Damusi (E) See Dumuzi

Damu-šaga (M) Probably a form of the god Damu associated with the area of Isin. Means "Beautiful Damu." The deity appears in lamentations as "The Lord of Mersig," Mersig likely being associated with the name Mersig, which refers to a canal in the region of Isin. Some texts render Mersi as Girsu, but the equation is based on similar sounding names, not location. (Cohen 1988: 288, 364)

Dam-zizzil(ZIL.ZIL) (M) Sumerian name of the goddess Nanāya noted in a god list. Means "Lady of Solicitude." (Mander 1986: 95)

Dani (M) Deity in a theophoric name from the Ur III period. (AnOr 7, 249: o 4)

Dannina, Dan-Irnina (M) Goddess associated with the circle of Ereškigal in Old Babylonian god lists. She appears later in An : *Anum* as a name of the Akkadian/Babylonian netherworld goddess Allatu(m). An Old Babylonian lexical list indicates that she was considered to be the gate (also "front") of the netherworld, and she is identified with the goddesses Irkala and Ganzir, who similarly denoted entrances to the netherworld. A variant spelling Dan-Irnina is likely a corruption although there also is a form Irdanni in a late text to compare to it. The corruption may result from the fact that Dannina follows the goddess Irnina in these Old Babylonian god lists. (Richter 2004: 492–93; Litke 1998: 190, 192)

Dapar, Dapan (M) Deity written GUD with gloss da-pár in An : *Anum*. In the lexical series Diri ^{d}GUD is rendered syllabically as da-pa-an, perhaps "The Aggressive One." (Civil 2004; Litke 1998: 215)

Daqītu (L) Deity at Ugarit attested in ritual texts and god lists. (del Olmo Lete 1999: 62, 216)

Dar (M) Along with Dur, a god pair mentioned in an incantation. (George 2016: no. 59)

Darawa (H) See Tarāwa

Dari (M) One of the primeval "fathers and mothers" of An. Paired with her husband Duri. Means "Eternity." (Litke 1998: 22)

Dar-lugal (M) Deity possibly attested in the writing lugal-dar (with reversed word order) in an Early Dynastic god list from Abu Ṣalābīkh. Note the deity Lugal-dar-DU.DU in an Ur III offering list (MVN 3, 228: o 10). The Sumerian term dar-lugal means "rooster." The deity Nuska had the rooster as his symbol. A star associated with the bird is found in the star compendium MUL: Apin beside the twins Lu-lal and La-tarāk, who are identified with the constellation of Gemini. Interestingly, seal impressions from the Old

Akkadian period depict a rooster beside a pair of battling twins likely representing Lu-lal and La-tarāk. The woodpecker that figures in the much later account in Roman sources of the "Battling Brothers" Romulus and Remus may be compared to this bird. (Ehrenberg 2002: 53–62; Mander 1986: 68)

Dašmaš (H) Deity associated with the storm god of Šapinuwa. (Giorgieri et al. 2013)

Datan (M) See Ditānu(m)

d̲bb (L) See Nablu(m)

Dea Syria (L) See Atargatis

Deber (L) Minor nocturnal demon of plague and disease, a cause of widespread death. The ordinary noun, meaning "pestilence," occurs around fifty times in the Hebrew Bible, but was sometimes personified as an evil deity or demon. As a demon Deber was often coupled with Rešep(h), the Canaanite god of destruction. The two sometimes accompanied YHWH as his helpers. On other occasions the deity protected his worshippers from Deber (Psalm 91:6). Demons causing illness were common in Mesopotamia. (del Olmo Lete, *DDDB*: 231–32)

Dedān (M) See Ditānu(m)

Demarous, Demaris (L) See Ba'lu

Dērītu(m) (M) Tutelary goddess of the city of Dēr invoked in an incantation. Means "Lady of Dēr." Her husband was the "Great God." At Mari she seems to have received offerings during Old Babylonian times after the full moon of the eleventh month. (Fleming 2000: 104–5; Oliva 1994: no. 15; Reiter 1992b: no. 74; Reiner 1970: 17)

Derketo, Derceto (L) See Atargatis

Dibar (M) Deity identified with Enlil in *Anu ša amēli*, explained as "Enlil of Decisions." (Litke 1998: 229)

Dido(n) (L) See Elissa Appendix II

Diku (M) Means "Judge." (1) One of the eight judges attached to the god Utu/Šamaš. (2) One of the viziers of Ninegal. (3) Deity occurring a number of times in An : *Anum*, all connected to the god Marduk. (Litke 1998: 97, 135, 155, 224; George 1993: 24 note 111)

Diku-anki (M) One of six counselors of Utu/Šamaš. Means "Judge of Heaven and Earth." (Litke 1998: 134)

Diku-gal (M) Deity listed in An : *Anum* dealing with the names of Marduk. Means "Great Judge." (Litke 1998: 224)

Diku-maḫ(-am) (M) Another name for Pabil-sag, consort of Gula. Means "Lofty Judge." (George 1993: 136 no. 935)

Diku-sisa (M) One of six counselors of Utu/Šamaš. Means "Fair Judge." (Litke 1998: 134)

Dilbat (E, M) The logogram Dil-bat in Babylonian sources refers to a form of the goddess Inana/Ištar. The name occurs in an inscription of a local Elamite ruler named Ḫanni, who had the inscription carved on a rock face at modern Kul-i-Farah not far from Mala-mir in the Bakhtiari Mountains. Possibly a title of the goddess Mašti in the Neo-Elamite period. The king Šilḫak-Inšušinak devoted a temple to Dilbat. (Vallat 1998: 337; König 1977: 160, 222, 227)

Dili-an-ta (M) Doorkeeper of Dingirmaḫ. May mean "The Foremost One from Heaven." (Litke 1998: 83)

Dili-bad (M) This Sumerian goddess's name is translated into Akkadian as "Ištar of the Stars"; the term dili-bad is a name of the planet Venus conceived by the ancients as a star. See Ištar-kakkabī. (Litke 1998: 161; Römer 1965: 169, 174)

DILI-daḫ (M) Attendant at the Ekur of Enlil. (Litke 1998: 65)

Dilim-babbar (M) Another name of Nanna/Sîn, the moon god. Means "White (or Shining) Bowl." Explained in *Anu ša amēli* as "Moon, whose rising is brilliant." (*LAS*: 137; Alster 2004: 1–3; Foster 2001: 63; Cohen 1996b: 7–13; Kramer, *ANET*: 617)

Dili-pap-ḫuš, Dili-pap-dug (M) The bull-lyre of Pa(p)-nigara. The two names are variants in An : *Anum*, perhaps "The Furious (or Good) First, Foremost (Lyre)." (Litke 1998: 78)

Di-meš (M) Deity explained in *Anu ša amēli* as Anu of Women. In a Neo-Assyrian god list explained as Ninurta in Elam. (Litke 1998: 228; King 1968: pl. 12)

Dimgal-abzu (M) Nin-Girsu's herald and constable of the Gu-edina, a steppe area on the border between Umma and Girsu. As guardian of the Gu-edina, he was protector of the birds and other wildlife and their environment. Means "Great Pillar of the Abzu." (Edzard 1997: 95; Selz 1995: 106–8; George 1993: 163 no. 1296; Jacobsen 1976: 83; Falkenstein 1966: 67)

Dimgul, En-dimgal, Nin-dimgul, Nin-dimgal (M) Vizier of Manun-gal/Nungal, the goddess of prisons. Means "Mast" or "Fastening Post," possibly referring to post on which prisoners were tortured. The deities En-te[ti]-gal and Nin-te[ti]-gal in an Early Dynastic god list and in the Sumerian zà-mí hymns from Abu Ṣalābīkh (where En-dimgal is associated with the care of cattle) may correspond to En-dimgal and Nin-dimgal respectively. (Litke 1998: 186; Mander 1986: 93, 121. 126; Cavigneaux and Krebernik, *RlA* IX: 617)

Dimgul-anna (M) In a Neo-Assyrian god list identified with Ninurta. Means "Mast (or Fastening Post) of Heaven." (King 1969: pl. 12)

Dimgul-kalama (M) Identified with Ninurta in An : *Anum*. Means "Mast (or Fastening Post) of the Nation." (Litke 1998: 45)

DIM-me (M) See Kamad-me

Dimmer (M) Name of the sun god Utu/Šamaš. Written DIM$_4$ with gloss dìm (var. di)-me-er. (Litke 1998: 145)

Dim-sa-sa (M) See Gaz-baba

DI mu-un-DUG (M) Deity cited in a Neo-Assyrian tablet that, according to Richter, Edzard thought belonged to a tablet of An : *Anum* dealing with goddesses associated with Inana. Perhaps means "She(?) Decreed My (Legal) Case." (Richter 2004: 310)

Dingir-an-na (M) Deity identified with Nanna/Sîn in a Neo-Assyrian god list. Means "God of Heaven." (King 1969: pl. 12)

Dingir-ba-ti-la (M) Divinized attribute of the god Di-ku$_5$ "The Judge" in An : *Anum*. Means "The God, the Grantor of Life." (Litke 1998: 226)

Dingir-Dilmun (M) Deity explained in *Anu ša amēli* as "Of the temple of Dilmun." Dilmun is normally equated to modern Bahrain. (Litke 1998: 230)

DINGIR. GAL (E) See Ḫumban

Dingirgubbu (M) Deity seated at the left of Ištar in a ritual from Mari. Name means "Deity of the Left." (Durand 2008: 338)

Dingir-ḫuš (Sum.), **Kattillû(m)** (Akk.) Demon associated with Nergal, the lord of the netherworld. Means "Angry God." (Litke 1998: 209)

Dingir-ḫuš-a (M) Name of Marduk. Means "The Furious God." (Litke 1998: 22)

Dingir-kalaga (M) Name of Marduk. Means "The Powerful God." (Litke 1998: 22)

Dingir-maḫ (M) Sumerian great goddess. First and primary designation of forty-four names of birth/mother goddesses appearing in An : *Anum*. Dingir-maḫ's foremost cult center was the city of Šarrākum, where the cultic precinct was called Keš. The goddess was attended by a large number of helpers. Her vizier was Ekigara. Her name means "Exalted Deity." (Stol 2000: 74–83; Litke 1998: 66; Jacobsen 1976: 104; Krebernik, *RlA* VIII: 502–16)

Dingir-maḫ-an-ki (M) Form of the birth goddess Dingir-maḫ attested in a personal name in an Old Babylonian tablet from Nippur. Means "Great Lady of Heaven and Earth." (Richter 2004: 143)

Dingir-sisa (M) Name of Marduk. Means "The God who Makes/Does Things Right." (Litke 1998: 22)

Dingir-šaga (M) Name of Marduk. Means "The Handsome God." (Litke 1998: 22)

Dingir-ušumgal (M) Name of Marduk. Means "The God who Is a Dragon." (Litke 1998: 22)

Dingir-ušum-maḫ (M) Name of Marduk. Means "The God who Is a Lofty Viper" or "The Unique, Mighty God." (Litke 1998: 22)

Dingir-zalag (M) Deity explained in *Anu ša amēli* as "Moon god of Light." Means "Shining God." (Litke 1998: 230)

Dipar (M) See Dapar

Dipāru(m) (M) Deified "Torch." Might be a name of Ištar as Venus. Dipāru(m) had a seat in the temple complex E-šara at Aššur. (George 1993: 125 no. 783)

Dis-dingir (M) Deity attested in Ur III times as being offered a calf. (MVAG 21, 22 FH 5: o i 27)

^{geš}**Dua** (M) See Lugal-^{geš}dua

Ḏū-'Anat (M, L) A name of the god Apladad attested as a deity of the pantheon of Palmyra in Syria. Amorite name means "He of 'Anat." (Schwemer 2001: 80 note 509)

Du-babbara (M) See Nin-tu

Ḍubābu (L) Minor Ugaritic god. Helper of the sea god Yam. (del Olmo Lete 1993: 56)

DUB.ME (M) Deity attested in the Sargonic period, in a text probably from Adab. (Maiocchi 2009: no. 89, no. 106, no. 111)

Dubsag-Unuga (M) See Mes-sanga-Unuga

Dudru (M) See Nindudra

Dudu (M) Deity attested at Early Dynastic Abu Ṣalābīkh and with a cult at Ur III Umma; follows Da-da in an Old Babylonian god list, with variant dù-dù in An : *Anum*, where he is listed as a messenger of Inana, and ^{d}du$_{13}$-du$_{13}$ in an Old Babylonian god list. A deity by the same name occurs in a litany of deities and lamentations. Called "Dimtar with the Beautiful Face." (Richter 2004: 292; Litke 1998: 160; Cohen 1993: 54; Cohen 1988: 502, 507; Mander 1986: 138; Weidner 1924/25)

Dugab-šugigi (M) God attested in a litany of deities in lamentations; he is described as "Great Hero." Means "Speak (and) Reply," possibly referring to an oracle. According to An : *Anum* associated with the E-babbar temple of Utu in Sippar or Larsa. (Gabbay 2019; Litke 1998: 135; Cohen 1988: 135, 157, 162)

Duga-lugalani-šaḫunga (M) Bull-lyre of Nin-Girsu. Means "Whose Sound Soothes His King." (Litke 1998: 177)

Dugana-gati (M) One of six counselors of Utu/Šamaš. Means "Let Me Live According to His Word" (Litke 1998: 134)

Dugani-si (M) Bull-lyre of Nin-Girsu. May mean "His Sound Fills (Everywhere)." (Litke 1998: 178)

Ḏū-Ḫalab (M) Name of the storm god Adad in a Neo-Assyrian god list. Means "He of Aleppo." Written du_6-ḫa-la-ab. (Schwemer 2001: 78; King 1969: pl. 16)

Du-kug (M) (1) Deified cosmic place, the umbilicus of the universe, the creation mound where the gods came into existence. Means "Holy Hill (or Mound)." The Du-kug was where the deities decided all destinies. According to Foster, it served as the throne of Enlil when he presided over the Assembly of the Gods. "The Debate between Sheep and Grain" describes in some detail the beginning of all things in the Holy Mound. The main Du-kug shrine, the earthly counterpart of the heavenly mound, was at Nippur, where, in the third millennium BCE, a "Sacred Mound" Festival was celebrated with offerings to Enlil's ancestors. Offerings were made year round at Du-kug shrines in, among other places, Nippur, Girsu, Lagaš, Umma, Uruk, Babylon, and Eridu. At Ur the corresponding shrine was called Du-ur. The theophoric name of Ur-Dukuga, a king of Isin, means "Servant of the Du-kug." (2) Explained in *Anu ša amēli* as Papsukkal, who performs lustration (*rimki*). (3) Identified with Nabû in a Neo-Assyrian god list. (Cohen 2015: 141; Black, Cunningham, Robson and Zólyomi 2004: 226; Black and Green 2003: 72; Foster 2001: 224; Litke 1998: 233; Sallaberger 1993: I, 129–31; King 1969: pl. 35)

Dulum (M) Child of Manun-gal. It is fitting that the jailor of the netherworld, Manun-gal, has a child Dulum "misery." (Litke 1998: 186)

Dumu-gi (M) (1) Name of the moon god Nanna/Sîn attested in An : *Anum*. Means "Native Prince." Written -gi_7 with gloss gi. (2) Name of Adad in a Neo-Assyrian god list. (Schwemer 2001: 81; Litke 1998: 118; King 1969: pl. 16)

Dumu-nuna (M) Name of the moon god Nanna/Sîn attested in An : *Anum*. Means "Noble Son." See the moon god's name Dumu-gi. (Schwemer 2001: 81; Litke 1998: 118)

Dumuzi (Sum.), **Tammuz** (Akk., Biblical), **Damusi** (Elam.) (M, L, E) Deity whose name means "True (or Faithful) Child." The earliest occurrence of Dumuzi is in a theophoric name around 2500 BCE. The name Dumuzi occurs in the Sumerian King List. In fact, two kings named Dumuzi appear in the list: (1) "the god Dumuzi, the shepherd," an antediluvian king of Bad-tibira, and, after the Flood and just before the semi-divine epic hero Gilgameš; (2) "the god Dumuzi, a ... fisherman—his native city was Ku-ara" near Eridu (Oppenheim, *ANET*: 265–66).

Dumuzi's principal cult center was Bad-tibira, where, with Inana, he was the city's protector and shared a temple. Dumuzi and Inana were worshipped at Inana's city of Uruk and at

Ur, which was closely related to Uruk especially in respect to cult. Dumuzi had temples or shrines at Ur, Isin, Akkad, Babylon, Aššur, and Kissig, a town southeast of Ur. In Early Dynastic times, Dumuzi was worshipped at Šuruppak, Adab, Nippur, Ur, Mari, Girsu, Lagaš, and Kunušir (Kinunir) in the Lagaš region. Dumuzi was equated to the constellation Aries.

Over time, two, and perhaps three, natural phenomena were associated with Dumuzi.

(1) Probably the earliest aspect was Dumuzi as divine shepherd, the provider of milk and dairy products, being associated with the steppe, marginal lands, where sheep grazed. As such he was the son of Enki and Duttur, the divine ewe. One Sumerian work presents a contest-debate between two suitors of Inana, the shepherd Dumuzi and the farmer En-kimdu, a debate won by the shepherd. As shepherd *par excellence,* kings, based on the metaphor of their being the shepherd of their people, identified with Dumuzi. There are a number of Sumerian compositions relating to the love story of Inana and Dumuzi, as well as at least two that deal specifically with the "Sacred Marriage," the ritual that joined kings embodying Dumuzi, with Inana, probably incarnate in a priestess, to confirm the king in his office and to ensure prosperity for the land. Literary evidence comes from the Ur III period and that of Isin, when kings such as Šulgi, Iddin-Dagān, and Išme-Dagān presented themselves as husbands of Inana. Eventually the rite was celebrated symbolically with the deities' statues being brought together. In this aspect Dumuzi's epithets include "Beloved" and "Bridegroom."

(2) Dumuzi was the embodiment of spring vegetation. He may have acquired this aspect independently or it may have resulted from a syncretism with the gods Damu and Nin-geš-zida. It is perhaps in this aspect that Dumuzi was considered to be the brother of Geštin-ana, another deity embodying vegetation, specifically the grape vine. In the story "Inana's Descent to the Netherworld," Dumuzi and his sister alternate six-months a year in the netherworld, serving as Inana's substitute. Just possibly this six-month cycle may reflect the approximate six months between spring vegetation (Dumuzi) and the fall grape harvest (Geštin-ana).

Furniture inlay depicting Dumuzi as shepherd. From Nimrud, Mesopotamia. Ivory, probably carved in Phoenicia. Eighth century BCE. After Mallowan and Herrmann 1974: pl. 66

(3) The third aspect of Dumuzi—and probably latest to develop—was perhaps as the power of the grain. In the first millennium BCE there was a three-

day festival of Dumuzi throughout the cities of Aššur. The first day of the festival was called "the screaming" (*ikkillu*); the second day "the release" (*pašāru*); and the third simply "Dumuzi." One of the rituals performed at that time reflects a ritual performed also at Nippur, in Babylonia. Cohen understands this ritual as marking the clearing away of the remains of the spring grain harvest in preparation for the fall sowing. In this ritual Dumuzi is the embodiment of the grain harvest; it is his remains, his dead body that is being cleared away. This interpretation agrees with Jacobsen, who early on proposed that Dumuzi embodied the power of the grain. This three-day festival of Dumuzi, which originally concerned the removal of any remains from the last harvest, the demise of Dumuzi, "evolved into a time when the entire community confronted the cycle of life and death, with implications far greater than just the Dumuzi narrative.

Cylinder seal showing Dumuzi rising, met by Inana/Ištar. From Girsu, Mesopotamia, Serpentine. Ca. 2320–2150 BCE. Louvre Museum MNB 1351. After Wolkstein and Kramer 1983: 40

It was a time of ghosts, of the spirits of the dead, as well as the appropriate mo-ment for rituals against life-threatening conditions" (Cohen 2011: 258)

Dumuzi was a god of the netherworld, where he stood at the gate between Heaven and the netherworld. "Dumuzi's Dream" dramatically describes the hunting down of Dumuzi by the *galla*-demons of the netherworld and ultimately Dumuzi's death. The fourth month of the standard Mesopotamian calendar was named for Dumuzi; it fell in mid-summer and was understood as the month when the god was bound and taken into captivity. Since Dumuzi was equated to the constellation Aries, the helical setting of Aries occasioned wailing rites for the disappearing god in that month.

The Dumuzi cult survived well into the first millennium BCE and even into the Middle Ages (tenth century CE), when the people of Harrān in Syria were still holding rites for Tammuz, the name used in the Hebrew Bible for the god. The women of Harran in the first millennium CE celebrated a rite called "the rattle," during which they wept for Tammuz, whose master cruelly ground his bones in a mill. The women during this celebration abstained from all milled foods. The cult of Dumuzi had reached Jerusalem by the time of the prophet Ezekiel (late sixth to early seventh centuries BCE). In the Book of Ezekiel 8: 14, the prophet reports a vision in which, at the Jerusalem Temple's north gate, he saw women wailing for Tammuz. The Levantine (Syrian-Canaanite) and Greek god Adonis and, possibly, the Greek figure of Athamas seem to be reflections of Dumuzi.

(Cohen 2015: 14; Durand 2008: 243–47; Foster 2005: 498–505, 641, 950–953,

1025; *LAS*: 66–75, 77–83, 86–88; Lapinkivi 2004: 48–54; Katz 2003: 389; Alster, *DDDB*: 828–833; Leick 1999: 76, 82, 153; Leick 1998: 31–34; Sefati 1998; George 1993: 64 no. 14, 72 no. 121,103 no. 501, 128 no. 822, 129 no. 829, 140 no. 972, 163 no. 1297; Frayne 1985: 6–22; Frazer 1981 (1890): 278, 283–84, 288; König 1977: 227; Jacobsen 1975: 72–76; Alster 1972; Jacobsen 1970: 73–103; Speiser, *ANET*: 107–9)

Dumuzi-abzu (M) Daughter of Enki. Closely associated with water. Appears in An : *Anum* immediately after several river gods. Kinušir (Kuninir) in the Lagaš region was her main cult center. Her name means "Faithful Child of the Abzu." Though her name was sometimes shortened to Dumuzi, she had nothing to do with the god Dumuzi. (Black and Green 2003: 73; Leick 1998: 34–35; Litke 1998: 100; Selz 1995: 114–16)

Dumuzi-da-Lagaš (M) Deity allocated offerings at Ur III Umma directly after Nin-da-Lagaš. May mean "Dumuzi Is at the Side of Lagaš." (*MVAG* 21, 22 FH 5: r ii 2)

Dumuzi-guena (M) Deity in Lagaš in the Early Dynastic period. Offerings were made to this deity at the end of the goddess Nanše's festival in the city of Nimen. Means "Dumuzi of the Throne Room." (Selz 1995: 116)

Dumuzi-Kian (M) Local form of Dumuzi at the city of Kian in the Umma region. (Archi and Pomponio 1995: no. 582)

Dumuzi-Kinušir(KinuNIR) (M) Local form of Dumuzi in the town of KinuNIR in the province of Lagaš in the Ur III period. (Sallaberger 1993: I, notes 284 and 1322)

Dumuzi-Umma (M) Local form of the god Dumuzi at the town of Umma. (Sallaberger 1993: I, 257–64)

Dumuzi-Urua (M) Deity attested at Umma in the Ur III period. The city of Urua was located in western Khuzistan in Iran. (Sallaberger 1993: I, 239–40)

Dunga, Tumga (M) Patron of singers. Dunga means "Musician." His wife's name, Gu-duga-lalbi, means "Sweet Voice, Syrupy." According to another god list, Tumga, a variant spelling, is a name of the great god Enki/Ea. Glossed in Akkadian as "Of Musicians/Singers." Written in the Early Dynastic period as Dun-ga and Dún-ga$^{(ga)}$. Written in An : *Anum* as Dunga$_2$ (NAR) with gloss [du-un]-⌜ga⌝. In the lexical series Diri the logogram ^{d}SANGA$_2$.MAḪ syllabically rendered du-un-ga. (Civil 2004; Litke 1998: 103, 239; Mander 1986: 54)

Dunnān (M) See Tunnan(u)

Dun(n)i (M) In An : *Anum* the name is written with the sign KALAG, meaning "strong," with the gloss du-ni in a section dealing with deities associated with Ninurta. According to An : *Anum*, the goddess Dun(n)i is offspring of the god Nuska and spouse of Inimani-zi, the messenger of Ninurta, who precedes the deity in the list. (Richter 2004: 76; Litke 1998: 48)

Dun-zagin (M) See Zagin-dun

Dur (M) Along with Dar, a god pair mentioned in an incantation. (George 2016: no. 59)

Duraḫ (M) Identified with Adad in a Neo-Assyrian god list. Means "Ibex." (King 1969: pl. 17)

Duraḫ-abzu (M) Name of Enki/Ea in An : *Anum*. Also the name of Enki's deified cult boat. Means "Ibex of the Abzu." (Litke 1998: 84)

Duraḫ-BANDA (M) Name of Enki/Ea in An : *Anum*. Means "Wild (or smaller) Ibex." (Litke 1998: 84)

Duraḫ-DILI-ki (M) Deity identified with Inana in a Neo-Assyrian god list. May mean "Unique Ibex (of) the Earth/netherworld." aš-ki might also be syllabic for aški "rushes," thus "ibex of the rushes" (the duplicate seems to be corrupt). (King 1969: pls. 17 and 44)

Duraḫ-dim, Duraḫ-dim-dim (M) Name of both Enlil and Enki/Ea in An : *Anum*. Means "Creator of the Ibex." (Litke 1998: 39, 84)

Duraḫ-gal (M) Deity whose name means "Great Ibex." Name of Enki/Ea in An : *Anum*. In *Anu ša amēli* explained as "Enlil of kings." (Litke 1998: 38, 229)

Duraḫ-nuna (M) Name of Enki/Ea in An : *Anum*. Means "Noble Ibex." (Litke 1998: 84)

Duranki (M) Name of Enlil. In *Anu ša amēli* explained as "Enlil of decisions." The E-duranki, "Temple of the Bond of Heaven and Earth," was a temple of Ištar at Nippur. (Litke 1998: 39, 229)

Duri (M) See Dari

Durre (M) Deity in a personal name from Ur III Umma. Written Ur-$^{d.anše}$dur$_9$^{ur3}-re. Means "ass." (AnOr 1, 88: r iv 16)

Dushara (Semitic), **Dus(h)ares** (Greek) (L) Supreme god of the Nabateans. Dushara was associated with the sun and with fertility. According to Christian bishop Epiphanios of Salamis, his mother was the virgin goddess Chaamu. Consort of the goddess Al-'Uzza and possibly later Atargatis, the "Syrian Goddess." One explanation of his name is that it means "He of the Shara (Mountain Range)," the east end of which is near Petra. Another is that "Shara" was a nearby wilderness area. The oldest and largest sanctuary at Petra was dedicated to Dushara. At Petra he might have been represented by baetyls or small standing stones. He was worshipped with processions, libations, and animal sacrifices. Identified with Zeus and associated with Dionysus. (Bedal 2002: 230; Joukowsky 2002: 237–38; Kanellopoulos 2002: 251, 253; Wenning 2001: 79. 82–84, 9; Nehmé 2000: 164–66; Langdon, 1931: 16–18)

Duttur (M) Goddess of sheep, the mother of the shepherd Dumuzi, and the spouse of Enki. The name is written Dur$_7$-tur; in the Emesal dialect Zé-ertur. Alster identifies Du$_8$-du$_8$ as a possible orthography for her name. The deity Tur-tur may be an orthography for Duttur. Tur-tur-šu-gi$_4$ "Old Turtur," identified in An : *Anum* as the child of Baba, may be Duttur in the Lagaš pantheon. (Richter 2004: 492; Litke 1998: 174; Alster 1972: 84; Jacobsen 1953: 164 note 14)

Duzagaš (M) Deity who is the recipient of an agate votive shaped like a duck by Ammurapi, the king of Ḫana. (Podany 2002:150).

— E —

Ea (M) See Enki

Ea-diriga (M) Deity identified with Nin-Isina/Nin-kar(r)ak, a Sumerian healing goddess in An : *Anum*. Means "(She) who Is Surpassing in the House/Temple." (Litke 1998: 182)

Ea-šarru, Ea-šarrī (H, M) The names respectively mean "Ea Is King" and "Ea Is My King." Apparently a form of the god Ea mentioned in the letter salutation of an epistle of the Hurrian king Tušratta to Egyptian pharaoh Amenhotep III. Appearing in a section dealing with the major deities of the Hurrian realm, after a mention of the storm god Teššub, Ša(w)uš-(k)a, the deified mountain Ḫam(m)ōn (Amanus), and the Hurrian sun god. Also appears in personal names in tablets from the First Sealand Dynasty and in Hurro-Hittite texts. (Moran 1987: 64, 174; Dalley 2009: 306)

Ebara-laḫ, Abara-laḫ (M) One of the seven children of the netherworld god Enme-šara in the An : *Anum* god list. Identified there as the child of the thirtieth day of the month, that is, the day of the disappearance of the moon. Also occurs as a Sumerian name of Nuska, vizier of Enlil, in a ritual of the Hellenistic period. Deity associated with the handles of the kettledrum and with Nuska. May mean "Who Walks about in the Secret Chamber" or even "Goes about in a Sweat." (Litke 1998: 36; Livingstone 1986: 190, 200; Thureau-Dangin 1975: 17; Tallqvist 1974: 290; Sachs, *ANET*: 335, 337)

Ebirtu(m) (M) See Abirtu(m)

Eblaītu(m) (M) Goddess most likely from a Middle Assyrian original of a ritual from the library of Aššurbanipal. Means "Goddess of Ebla." Mesopotamian sources therefore still retained traces of the ancient divinity even when Ebla was a heap of ruins. The discovery of an inscription in Old Syrian (c. 1900 BCE) indicates that the statue of Eblaītu(m) was devoted specifically to Ištar, who was guardian of the Eblaite Amorite dynasty. Further, a statue fragment was unearthed in the southwest of the acropolis, the same area in which a large basalt stele dating around 1800 BCE, with the four sides sculpted with several registers. The goddess is shown winged, standing inside a small temple, mounted on the back of a bull. (Archi 1993: 71)

E-da (M) Since this deity is listed in An : *Anum* as one of five translators of Inana. Perhaps e here means "to speak," thus "One who Is Speaking." However, the next translator listed is ᵈe-sa-pàr and the meaning of e here is quite unclear. (Richter 2004: 192; Litke 1998: 158)

E-dam (Sum.), **Edammītu(m)** (borrowed into Akkadian) (M) Deity identified with Inana in a section of An : *Anum* that contains the "Inanas" of various towns. Perhaps ᵈé-dam here means "She of the Tavern," a structure with which Inana was often associated. Lagaš texts use the term for a sanctuary of the wife of Nin-Girsu and also for a shrine in a small settlement called Utulgal near Girsu. (Litke 1998: 158; Selz 1995: 220 and note 1045)

Edammītu(m) (M) See E-dam

Edin (M) The deified steppe. (Litke 1998: 164)

Ee (M) Deity at Ur III Umma. Written E_{11}-e. A deity Nin-e_{11}-e is also attested at Umma. (SAT 2, 203: o 2)

E-ga-la-zu (M) Deity receiving offerings at Ur III Umma. Written É-gá-lá-zu. See E-gal-lu-zu. (MVAG 21, 22 FH 5: o i 17)

E-gal-lu(-zu) (M) Likely a divine gate-keeper or guardian of the entrance to a temple. Listed in an Old Babylonian god list after the guardian god Kalkal, the gate-keeper of the Enlil temple. Means "(The One who Knows How to) Open Up the Temple." (Richter 2004: 449: Cavigneaux 1996: 11 note 55; Litke 1998: 53)

Egi/Ereš-anzu (M) Goddess in a Neo-Assyrian god list. Written ^{e}Egí-^{d}anzu$^{an\text{-}zu}$. (King 1969: pl. 27)

Egi/Ereš-edam-kuga (M) Deity whose name means "Lady of the Holy Tavern(?)." In An : *Anum* the sign NIN is glossed ^{e}NIN. (Litke 1998: 181)

Egi/Ereš-egia (M) Deity with a shrine at Ur III Nippur. Means "Lady Bride." (CST 44: r 13)

Egi/Ereš-egula (M) In An : *Anum* identified as the wife of Lugalbanda and thus, perhaps, another name for Ninsun. Means "Lady of the Chapel(?)." See George 1993: 97 for é-gu-la as designating small chapels at Ur III Lagaš (in addition to its designating specific temples elsewhere). Glossed ^{e}NIN. (Litke 1998: 168)

Egi/Ereš-eri (M) Goddess first attested in documents of the Early Dynastic period. In later sources, identified with the healing goddess Gula and with Ninurta's spouse Nin-Nibru. In An : *Anum*, a name of the healing goddess Nin-kar(r)ak. Means "Lady of the City." In An : *Anum* glossed ^{e}NIN. (Richter 2004: 215; Litke 1998: 47, 83, 172, 181; Cavigneaux and Krebernik, *RlA* IX: 527–28)

Egi/Ereš-eri-bara (M) Deity in An : *Anum* identified as a $bara_2$-sig_5-ga official(?) of Nin-Nibru. $bara_2$-sig_5-ga is a socle. Glossed ^{e}NIN. See Lugal-eri-bara. (Litke 1998: 49, 207; Tallqvist 1974: 427; Cavigneaux and Krebernik, *RlA* IX: 528)

Egi/Ereš-eri-BIL (M) Deity identified with the healing goddess Gula. In An : *Anum* glossed ^{e}NIN. The last sign is glossed "bi," possibly for a reading bil or even gibil. (Litke 1998: 181; Cavigneaux and Krebernik, *RlA* IX: 529)

Egi/Ereš-eri-kuga (M) Deity identified with the healing goddess Gula or Nin-kar(r)ak. Means "Lady of the Holy City." In An : *Anum* glossed ^{e}NIN. (Litke 1998: 181; Tallqvist 1974: 427; Cavigneaux and Krebernik, *RlA* IX: 529)

Egi/Ereš-e-uga (M) Sumerian goddess, a name of the healing goddess Nin-kar(r)ak, in An : *Anum* with the variant Egí-gá-ug_5-ga. Nin-ga-uga was the female patron deity of the city of Maš-kan-šāpir and wife of Nergal, who was male patron deity of the same city. A Neo-Assyrian god list has the gloss ^{e}NIN; An : *Anum* does not. Means "Lady of the House of the Dead." (Richter 2004: 215; Litke 1998: 182; King 1969: pl. 29)

Egi/Ereš-Gabura (M) Goddess in the circle of Nin-Isina / Nin-kar(r)ak. Gabura was the name of temples of Nin-Gub-laga in Ur and Ki'abrig, north of Ur. Written $^{d\,e}$Egí-gá^{ga}-bur-ra. (Litke 1998: 182; George 1993: 86 no. 294, no. 295; Cavigneaux and Krebernik, *RlA* IX: 351)

Egi/Ereš/Nin-gagia (M) Sumerian title that could be applied to various goddesses. Often identified as Gula or

Nin-kar(r)ak. Means "Lady of the *Gagû*," usually translated "Cloister." Variant in An : *Anum* ^{e}Egí/Ereš-é-gi$_{4}$-a. However, the Emesal version of the name is Gašan-ma-gi$_{4}$-a, perhaps suggesting a reading Nin-. (Black and Green 2003: 91–93; Litke 1998: 182; Henshaw 1994: 46, 234; George 1993: 153 no. 1137; Harris 1975; Cavigneaux and Krebernik, *RlA* IX: 351–52)

Egi/Ereš-ḫalbi-lib (M) A deity who, according to An : *Anum*, was a form of the healing goddess Gula. Name perhaps means "Lady, Numbing(?) Ice," alluding to ice that was used by healers to ease pain. Glossed ḫal-bi-li-ib. (Richter 2004: 215; Litke 1998: 182; King 1969: pl. 29; Cavigneaux and Krebernik, *RlA* IX: 377)

Egi/Ereš-igi-gunu (M) Deity identified with Inana/Ištar. Means "Lady with Speckled Eyes." In An : *Anum* the beginning of the entry is broken where the gloss e to indicate a reading egí would be. However, an Old Babylonian god list (TCL 15, 10) has the gloss. (Richter 2004: 292; Litke 1998: 150; Tallqvist 1974: 406; Cavigneaux and Krebernik, *RlA* IX: 376)

Egi-la (M) One of the children of birth/mother goddess Nin-maḫ. Said to be an adornment of Nin-maḫ's E-maḫ temple in its precinct Keš, at Šarrākum. In a god list from Aššur written Egí$^{e\text{-}gi}$-lá and described as "who is revered by the exalted gods" and "who is revered and feared (by the goddesses)." (Litke 1998: 79; Schroeder 1920: no. 64)

Egi/Ereš-magura (M) Deity identified with the healing goddess Nin-kar(r)ak. Means "Lady of the Barge." Glossed ^{e}NIN. (Litke 1998: 182; Cavigneaux and Krebernik, *RlA* IX: 462)

Egi/Ereš-Mirsiga (M) Deity identified with Nin-Isina and Nin-kar(r)ak. Means "Lady of Mirsig/Kirsig," the canal that ran through Isin. In An : *Anum* glossed ^{e}NIN. (Litke 1998: 181; Tallqvist 1974: 415; Cavigneaux and Krebernik, *RlA* IX: 449, 471)

Egi/Ereš-Nigara (M) A form of the healing goddess Nin-kar(r)ak/Nin-Isina/Gula, especially at Isin, where the sanctuary of Gula was called "House of Nin-Nigara." Female counterpart of Pa(p)-Nigara at Adab south of Nippur. Also a name of Inana/Ištar at Šuruppak, Akkad, and Zabala(m). Glossed ^{e}NIN. At Šuruppak the temple of Ištar was also named for the title. Means "Lady of the Foetus." The word nigar is written with an element that signifies the unborn or premature foetus, in particular, the aborted foetus. According to one text, the goddess Egi/Ereš-Nigara opened the door of the Nigar and allowed a premature birth to take place. The Nigar has been described as house where "the foetuses are lying down." Jacobsen suggested that the Nigar was a cemetery for stillborn and premature babies (1987: 475 note 1). It is now thought to have been a temple that served in such a way, as well as being a depository for after births. The word nigar is also attested as a metaphor for "the womb." See Nin-pa-Nigara; Pa(p)-Nigara. (Richter 2004: 386–87; Litke 1998: 181; George 1993: 133 no. 885 no. 886; Tallqvist 1974: 416; Krebernik, *RlA* X: 325–26; Cavigneaux and Krebernik, *RlA* IX: 477)

Egi/Ereš-nigbunna, Egi/Ereš-niggunara (M) Deity identified with Nin-kar(r)ak in an Old Babylonian god list and in An : *Anum*. The name is written in an Old Babylonian god list as ^{e}Egí-níg-gù-na-ra. In the later An : *Anum* the writing ^{e}Egí-níg-gù^{gu}-na!-ra occurs. A second copy of An : *Anum* has Egí-níg-bún-⸢na⸣, "Lady Turtle." Perhaps this later níg-bún-na is merely a variant for the earlier-attested but not understood níg-gù-na or it may reflect the true tradition of the name and níg-gù-na merely a syllabic variant. Turtle or tortoise shell was ground for medicinal purposes and this may be the basis of this deity being identified with the healing goddess Gula/Nin-kar(r)ak. (Richter 2004: 215–16; Litke 1998: 180)

Egi/Ereš-tugnigla-šudu (M) Deity in the circle of or identified with Gula. Written in An : *Anum* ^{e}NIN-^{túg}níg-lá-šu-du$_7$ with gloss tu-ni-ig-lal-la-šu-du. šu—du$_7$ "to perfect" does not seem appropriate here with ^{túg}níg-lá "bandage." Since this deity is in the circle of the healing goddess, the name may refer to the use of bandages in the healing process. Perhaps šu—du$_7$ is a variant for šu—dù (*kamû*), which might mean "wrap" or "tie" here. (Litke 1998: 180; Cavigneaux and Krebernik, *RlA* IX: 507)

Egi-Tummal (M) Third name of the goddess Ninlil in An : *Anum*. Patron goddess of the city Tummal, southeast of Nippur. In the Ur III period, Tummal was the location of a "Sacred Marriage" ritual between Enlil and Ninlil. Means "Lady of Tummal." In An : *Anum* the sign NIN is glossed "e-gi." Explained in *Anu ša amēli* as "Ninlil of the People." (Leick 1999: 153; Litke 1998: 40, 230; Tallqvist 1974: 285, 420; Jacobsen 1970: 32)

Egi/Ereš-una (M) Goddess associated with Inana in An : *Anum* and as the wife of Nergal elsewhere in An : *Anum*. Written Egí/Ereš-ùn-na, Egí/Ereš-ùn-ga, and eEgí/Ereš-nun-ùn-na. Means "The Lofty Lady." (Litke 1998: 151, 198)

Egi/Ereš-zu (M) Deity in the circle of Gula in An : *Anum*. Glossed ^{e}NIN. (Litke 1998: 185)

E-gubi-duga (M) Protective spirit, probably of the temple of the god Nin-šubur at Nippur. Means "Temple whose Voice Is Good." See Nin-gubi-duga. (Litke 1998: 27)

Ekaldu, Ekalti, Ikaldu, Ikalti (H) Hurrian/Hittite form of an Akkadian epithet of Aya, *Kallatu(m)*, meaning "Bride." Sometimes occurs as a unified pair Ayyun-ekaldu in offering rituals. See Aya. (van Gessel 1998: I, 60–61; Haas 1994: 380, 469)

Ekigarra (M) Listed in a Middle-Babylonian god list as the vizier of Dingir-maḫ. Written é-ki-gar-ra. (Ashm 1924–855+: o ii 5)

Eku-anna (M) Deity attested in an Ur III text from Lagaš. Written é-ku$_6$-an-na. (courtesy J.-P. Gregoire)

E-kur (M) One of the twenty-one ancestors of An in An : *Anum*. Paired with Gara, likely his wife. (Litke 1998: 17, 22)

Ekur-absa (M) Attested in a god list and written é-kur-ab-sá-a

Ekure-su/si (M) Sumerian equivalent of the Akkadian/Babylonian god Nuska in An : *Anum*. Written é-kur-re-sù with variant -si, in an Old Babylonian god list. si can mean "fill" and sù "adorn." (Litke 1998: 50)

E-kur-eš-diri (M) One of the six counselors of the birth/mother goddess Nin-maḫ in An : *Anum*. Perhaps means "Ekur, the Ultimate Shrine." (Litke 1998: 77)

Ekurrītu(m) (M) Deity whose name means "Lady of the Ekur." (1) Goddess in the circle of Inana/Ištar at Nippur. Appears in An : *Anum* immediately after the goddess Nin-egal. (2) One of two wives of Nin-geš-zida, the other being Azida-mua. As a result of the identification of Amurru(m) with Nin-geš-zida, Ekurrītu(m) became a wife of Amurru(m). (Litke 1998: 155, 192; George 1993: 38; Tallqvist 1974: 291)

El, Il(u) (L) The word *el/il* is the common noun in most Semitic languages for "god," but it also was used as the proper name of a deity, meaning something like "*The* God" (Smith 1997: 83). Thus El was probably the supreme god of the pantheons of the ancient religions of the Semitic-speaking peoples of Syria-Canaan as manifested especially in material from Ugarit, and he was worshipped also by the Israelites.

At Ugarit, El was chief god of the pantheon and head of the assembly of the gods. It was his role to maintain order in the cosmos, and, as such, he was the final judge. His consent was mandatory in all policy matters, such as the question of the storm god Ba'lu's building a house/temple. His consort was the goddess Aṯirat or Asherah, also called Ilat(u) "*The* Goddess." El lived in a palace situated on a mountain at the cosmic source of the rivers and the confluence of the oceans.

His most usual epithet was "Bull," probably a reference to his strength, sexual potency, and responsibility for fertility, particularly that of humans. The "wise" and wily deity also held the titles "Owner of Earth," "Father of the Gods," and "Father of Humanity" (Handy 1994: 76, 78). He was regularly called "Father of the Years."

A stele from Ugarit dated to the thirteenth century BCE very likely depicts El. It shows an elderly bearded god sitting on a lion-footed throne with his feet on a footstool. Horns project from the base of his crown. He holds a cup in one hand and raises his other hand in blessing (Lewis 2005: 82 figure 4.19). A small gold-plated bronze figure from Ugarit probably also represented El (Lewis 2005: 81 figure 4.18). Deity lists from Ugarit normally place Ilu/El near the top after Il-ib, "God of the Father," while El's name occurs near the top in most offering lists.

In the Hebrew Bible, El appears 230 times, most of the uses meaning "god." However, passages in Genesis especially make clear that some instances of the word were naming a god. Thus, as Mark Smith says, the "original god of Israel was El" (1990: 7). Further, the word Israel is theophoric, for it contains El's name. It was he who was the god Elohim (plural of Eloah) of Genesis 1–3. Other names that attest to his worship include El-'Olam "God the Eternal," Elyon "God Most High,' and El-Šaddai "God of the Mountain." Over time, El became identified with YHWH, who then took over most of El's traits and titles, for instance El-berīt(h). He also seems to have taken over El's consort Asherah. By the tenth century BCE, the identification of El and YHWH seems to have been almost complete.

In Phoenician inscriptions El is understood as a creator deity, but is not specifically named as head of the pantheon. Neither did he have an important role in Phoenician/Punic cult, though he seems to have been identified with Ba'al-Ḥamōn. In Aramaic inscriptions he is included in lists of gods. Philo of Byblos identified El, whom he called both El and Elos, with Greek Kronos, and the Greek writer Diodorus Siculus insisted that human sacrifices were limited to the cult of Kronos/El/Ba'al-Ḥamōn. This tradition might be reflected in the biblical view that a first-born son had to be given to the deity.

Bas-relief of enthroned deity El, with worshipper, from Ugarit. Ca. Thirteenth century BCE. Serpentine. National Museum, Aleppo, Syria. After Coogan 1978: Cover.

El features in a Hittite myth from the second millennium BCE as Elkuniršа, a version of one of his titles "El Creator of Earth." In ancient Mesopotamia, a deity Il/El is attested in theophoric names. The plural of *el* in Hebrew and other Semitic languages is *elim*. The feminine form of El, the noun *Elat*, occurs at Ugarit as a title of Asherah/Aṯirat, but, though the word occurs in the Hebrew Bible, translators render it as "terebinth" tree, ignoring the fact that trees and goddesses, especially Asherah, were often identified together in the ancient Eastern Mediterranean. (Woolmer 2017: 106, 108, 114; Durand 2008: 180–88; Leeming 2005: 118; Lewis 2005: 81–82; Black and Green 2003: 35; Pardee 2002: 14–15, 47; Wyatt 2002: 47, 90–102, 330–32; Smith 2001: 55, 135–48; del Olmo Lete 1999: 79, 84–85, 97, 118–19; Herrmann, *DDDB*: 274–80; Nielsen, *DDDB*: 850–51; Röllig, *DDDB*: 280–81; van der Toorn, *DDDB*: 353; Wyatt 1999: 542; Keel and Uelinger 1998: 51; Leick 1998: 38; Finnegan 1997: 138–39; Smith 1997: 86, 116, 124–30; Lipiński 1995: 59–62; Handy 1994: 34–37, 48, 69–72, 75–95; Lipiński, *DCPP*: 147–48; Roberts, *IDB* Suppl.: 255–58; Rose, *ABD* IV: 1004; de Moor 1990: 105–7; Smith 1990: xxiii, 7–12, 50–51; Attridge and Oden 1981: 48–49, 62–63, 86 note 85; Mullen 1980: 111–284; L'Heureux 1979; Brown, Driver, and Briggs 1978: 42; Herm 1975: 108–9; Cross 1973: 13–75; Roberts 1972: 31–35; Oldenburg 1969; Albright 1968: 119–21, 189; Pope 1955; Kapelrud 1952)

Ela'anna (M) Deity written é-lá-an-na. May mean "Canopy of Heaven." (MVN 22, 198: v 5)

Elagu (E) Elamite goddess identified with Zarpanītum in a Neo-Assyrian god list. (King 1969: pl. 35)

Elali (M) Deity attested at Old Babylonian Ur as a witness to a legal proceeding along with Utu and Baba. Elali appears as an element in several theophoric names but sometimes without the divine determinative. (Richter 2004: 496)

Elallu (H) See Enlil

Elamatu(m) (M) Daughter of Allatu(m), queen of the netherworld. Means "The Elamite." (Litke 1998: 190)

Elam-sig (M) Written Elam-sig$_{17}$. See Šala

Elat, Elah (L) See El

El-berīt(h) (L) See Ba'al-berīt(h)

El-Beth-El (L) See Bethel

El'eb (L) See Il-ib

Elegabal(us), Heliogabalos (Greek), **El-Jebel** (L) Possibly a title of the Phoenician/Punic god Ba'al-Ḥamōn, a Latinization of the Semitic El-Jebel "El (or God) of the Mountain." The name adopted by the Syrian who became the Roman emperor Elegabalus or Heliogabalus (203–222 CE). (Ball 2009: 90–93; Smith 2001: 138)

El Elyon (L) See Elyon

Elḫalaḫu (E) Deity appearing in an Elamite female theophoric name, thus likely a goddess. The divine name also appears in a Babylonian god list. (Hinz and Koch 1987: 394; König 1977: 185, 227)

Elim (L) See El

Elkuniřa, (El)quniřa (H, L) God in a Hittite myth that seems to have been derived from a Hurrian forerunner. Means "El-Creator-of-the-Earth." Elkuniřa is likely a transcription of the Ugaritic phrase *il qny arṣ* "the god who created heaven and earth," probably referring to an Enki-like deity located at the "source of the rivers." The composition describes how Elkuniřa's wife, the goddess Ašertu, tried to seduce Ba'lu, who refused her offer. When he related this event to Elkuniřa, the latter told him to humiliate the goddess, which he subsequently did, both sexually and by claiming to have killed her children. Later, Elkuniřa gave Ašertu permission to take revenge on Ba'lu. However, 'Anat-Aštarte overheard and warned Ba'lu. The name Elkuniřa could find a reflex in the figure of the blessed Alkinöos in his home at the "source of the rivers" in the *Odyssey*. See El. (Schwemer 2001: 533 and notes 4297 and 4298 for discussion and previous literature; Hoffner 1998: 90–92, 110; van Gessel 1998: I, 63; Popko 1995: 128; Haas 1994: 172–73)

Ella-buntu (Akk.) One of the attendants of the moon god Nanna/Sîn. Written El/Él-la-bu-un-du/da. Occurs in both an Old Babylonian god list and An : *Anum*. bu-un-du may be an orthography for West Semitic *buntu / bunatu* "daughter." If so, then the name means "The Daughter Is Pure." Moreover, note *CAD* B: 239a for the two references of *bintu* said of goddesses, both of which refer to the daughter of the moon god, as it seems to be here. Note a Neo-Assyrian god list where she is explained as *šá* ᵈD[u-...]. See Ella-mesi for a similarly constructed name. (Richter 2004: 450–52; Litke 1998: 122; King 1969: pl. 19)

Ella-mesi (Akk.) Wife of Sumuqan. Attested in an Old Babylonian god list and in An : *Anum*. Written El-la-me-si. (*CDA:* 70a; Richter 2004: 352; Litke 1998: 138)

Ellil (M) See Enlil

Elluita (H) One of the more obscure Hurrian deities. (Archi 1990: 118)

Elohim, Eloah (L) One of two principal names of the deity of the Hebrew Bible, the other being YHWH. According to the Documentary Hypothesis, the use of the term Elohim for the Israelite god in some contexts distinguishes the northern (Israelite) passages in the first four books of the Bible from the southern (Judean) passages, thus providing the name of the hypothesized biblical source, the "E Document." The word *elohim* "god(s)" is explained as the plural of noun *eloah*, itself an expanded form of *el*, the common Semitic noun for "god." Elohim has a number of meanings, including "gods," but more often than not it refers to a single deity, as in "Chemosh the *elohim* [god] of Moab" (I Kings 11: 33). Since there is no word in the Hebrew Bible for "goddess," Elohim can also indicate a female deity, as in "Ashtoreth the elohim of the Sidonians" (I Kings 11: 33). Scholars explain the form as a plural of majesty, "The God/Goddess." As the word was used to designate "The God of Israel," it gradually became a principal name of the Israelite god.

Elohim could also refer to spirits of the dead, as in the necromancy episode (the "Witch of Endor" incident) in the first book of Samuel. When the spirit of Samuel ascended, the medium called it an *elohim* "divine being" (I Samuel 28:13). The singular Eloah appears around fifty-five times in the Hebrew Bible, mostly in the Book of Job, where it is a name of the deity. (Pardee, *DDDB*: 285–88; van der Toorn, *DDDB*: 352–65; Rose, *ABD* IV: 1006–7)

El-'Olām (L) A name of a deity in many texts in the Ancient Near East expressing totality. Usually translated as "god everlasting." The word *'olām* occurs often in deity epithets in the Near East, for example, at Ugarit of the sun goddess "Šapšu, the Everlasting." Also a title of the god El/YHWH in Genesis (21:33) in the Hebrew Bible, where it means "El/the Lord, the Everlasting." Sometimes 'Olām functions as a proper name. According to Cross, the epithet was associated with the deity's shrine at Beersheba. See Ḫalma. (de Pury, *DDDB*: 288–91; Rose, *ABD* IV: 1004; Cross 1973: 47; Albright 1968: 120)

El-Šaddai, Šaddai (L) The main title of the patriarchal deity (Exodus 6:2–3), who originally may have been a separate deity, but at some point becomes identified with YHWH. El-Šaddai means "God of the Mountain." *šadî* means "of the mountain" in Akkadian and the Israelite god is associated with mountains (Sinai, Seir, Zion). The Greek Septuagint rendered Šaddai as *Pantokrator*, the Latin Vulgate as *omnipotens*, both meaning "Almighty." Šaddai appears as a theophoric element in, among others, Egyptian, Ugaritic, Israelite, and Phoenician names. One of the ritual texts from Ugarit mentions a god Šaddayu as a hunter. (Pardee 2002: 194, 205–6 note 13; Smith 2001: 139, 147; J. Day 2000: 32–34; Knauf, *DDDB*: 749–53; Lipiński 1995: 330; Lillie, *ABD* I: 160; Rose, *ABD* I: 1005; Anderson, *IDB* 1991: II, 412; Smith 1990: 23, 31 note 42; Biale 1982; Cross 1973: 11, 47, 52–60, 322–23; Albright 1935)

Elum (M) Name written E-lum. (OBO 160/1, p. 599)

Elyōn, El Elyōn (L) Name in the Hebrew Bible of Elohim/YHWH, the Israelite god. Means "Most High." According to Cross, Elyōn had its origin at the god's shrine in Jerusalem. The title occurred with the god name El as "El Elyōn" in, for example, Genesis 14:18–20 "God Most High." The epithet was applied also to YHWH. In Psalm 82, the members of the divine assembly, "the divine beings," are called Elyōn's children, "sons of the Most High." Elyōn also occurred as a title of the high god in some extra-biblical sources, such as Ugaritic and Phoenician. However, in the *Phoenician History*, Philo of Byblos assumed that Elioun "Most High" was a separate deity, whose consort was Berouth. They settled around Byblos and became parents of Ouranos (Heaven or Sky) and Ge (Earth). After Elioun was killed by wild animals, he acquired a cult devoted to his worship. The Greek equivalent of Elyōn was Hypsistos, and it was a name of the god Zeus. The title as Hypsistos also appears in the New Testament, especially in the Gospel of Luke. (Smith 2001: 48–49, 71; Elnes and Miller, *DDDB*: 293–99; Lipiński 1995: 60; Handy 1994: 39, 76; Bonnet and Xella, *DCPP*: 150; Rose, *ABD* IV: 1004; Schmidt, *ABD* IV: 922; Anderson, *IDB* III, 451; Attridge and Oden 1981: 46–47, 86 note 80; Cross 1973: 47)

Emeda (M) Child of Nin-marki. Means "Nursemaid." Written Um-me-da with gloss e-me-ed. (Litke 1998: 125)

Emeš (Sum.), **Ummu(m)** (Akk.) Emeš means "Summer." Son of Enlil by Earth. In the Sumerian "Debate between Winter and Summer," En-ten, Winter, starts a quarrel with Summer about who does more work, and they put the issue to Enlil to adjudicate. Enlil finds for Winter because the latter controls the waters that make life possible. (Leick 1998: 51–52; Jacobsen 1976: 103; Landsberger 1949: 248)

En-a (M) Probably a primeval ancestor god. Attested in a god list from Abu Ṣalābīkh. Written En-á. May mean "Lord Strength." (Mander 1986: 109)

En-Abzu (M) One of the names of Enki/Ea in An : *Anum*. Means "Lord Abzu." (Litke 1998: 84)

En-amaš (M) One of the forty-two ancestors of Enlil. Consort Nin-amaš. Means "Lord of the Sheep Fold." (Litke 1998: 33)

En-ana (M) One of the forty-two ancestors of Enlil in An : *Anum*. Consort Ninana. Means "Lord of Heaven." Written en-an in an Early Dynastic god list. (Litke 1998: 33; Mander 1986: 159)

En-anki (M) One of the names of the great god Enki in An : *Anum*. The Sumerian literally means "Lord of Heaven and Earth." May be a conflation of Enki with Amanki, the word for Enki in Emesal. (Litke 1998: 83)

En-a-nun (M) Deity identified with Gula. Means "Lord with Great Strength." See En-na-nun. (Litke 1998: 179; Ebeling, *RlA* II: 370–71)

En-arḫuš-dim (M) One of the names of the Sumerian birth/mother goddess Nin-maḫ in An : *Anum*. Means "Lady(?) who Fashions (in?) the Womb." (Litke 1998: 70)

En-ARA-lu-lu (M) Chief female steward of the goddess Nanše. (Litke 1998: 125)

En-ar-re (M) In An : *Anum* one of a group of four fowlers probably associated with the god Enki/Ea. Written En-ár[ar]-re and the following entry is Nin-ár-re. Both names also written with the sign ÙR. (Litke 1998: 114)

En-banda (M) Identified in a Neo-Assyrian god list as Ninurta, who "acts upon the decisions of the gods." Means "Junior Lord," presumably in relation to Enlil. (King 1969: pl. 11)

En-barage-si (M) In An : *Anum* one of the gate-keepers of the great birth/mother goddess Dingir-maḫ. Means "Lord who Fills the Dais." (Litke 1998: 83)

Enbilulu (M) Sumerian god of irrigation and canals. The divine canal inspector. An Akkadian tradition calls him the son of Ea, but in the myth "Enlil and Ninlil" he is the son of Enlil and Ninlil. In the Sumerian zà-mí hymns, Nin-bilulu, a deity of ditches, may represent another form of the name. When, in "Enki and the World Order," Enki created the waters of the Tigris and the Euphrates by masturbation, he placed the rivers in the charge of En-bilulu. The name En-bilulu is the twenty-fourth and En-bilulu-gugal the twenty-sixth names of Marduk in the *Enūma eliš*. In a god list En-bilulu's name occurs as a name of Marduk. The divine name Ḫegal, "Abundance," follows En-bilulu's entry in An : *Anum* and may be a name of En-bilulu. Explained in An : *Anu ša amēli* as "Marduk of canals (*pattāti*)." (Foster 2005: 479; *LAS*: 106, 221; Leick 1998: 39–40; Litke 1998: 92–93, 237; Foster 1993: I, 395; Biggs 1974: 48; Tallqvist 1974: 292; Jacobsen 1976: 84; Speiser, *ANET*: 71; Heidel 1967: 56)

Enbilulu-gugal (M) Twenty-sixth name of Marduk in the *Enuma eliš*. Means "Enbilulu, the Canal-Inspector."

En-BU-dudu (M) One of the thirteen children of Nin-marki. (Litke 1998: 125; Ebeling, *RlA* II: 371)

En-bulug (M) One of the forty-two ancestors of Enlil in An : *Anum*. Consort Nin-bulug. Written En-bulug$_3$. May mean "The Exalted(?) Lord." (Litke 1998: 32)

Enda (M) One of the forty-two ancestors of Enlil in An : *Anum*. Consort Nin-da. Means "Beside the Lord." (Litke 1998: 31)

En-daga (M) Spouse of Nin-tin-uga. Means "Lord of the Dwelling/Chapel." En-dag-ga is also an epithet of Nergal. (Cohen 2015: 224; Richter 2004: 119–21, 215–16, 534; Litke 1998: 179)

Endagar (M) Deity in a personal name from Ur III Nippur. It is possible that this deity is to be equated to the god En-daga. Alternatively this could be a writing for the deity Indagra. (Richter 2004: 120 note 534)

En-duraḫ-nuna (M) Deity identified with Enki in An : *Anum*. Means "Lord, Noble Ibex." See Duraḫ-nuna. (Litke 1998: 84 note 146)

Enda-šurima (M) Ancestor of Enlil. Wife Nin-da-šurima. In the Sumerian work "The Death of Gilgameš," before dying, Gilgameš made offerings to both god and goddess. In "Nergal and Ereškigal," Enda-šurima was probably the keeper of the third gate to the netherworld. Perhaps šurim "dung heap" reflects the decaying conditions in the netherworld. Written -šùrim with variant -šu-rim-ma. (Foster 2005: 517; Frayne 2001: 153; Litke 1998: 33–34; Tallqvist 1974: 293; Grayson, *ANET*: 509; Cavigneaux and Krebernik, *RlA* IX: 338)

Endib (M) See Gagim

En-dimgal (M) See Dimgul

En-du (M) One of the forty-two ancestors of Enlil. Consort Nin-du. (Litke 1998: 31; Cavigneaux and Krebernik, *RlA* IX: 339)

En-du-amaš (M) Deity attested in two god lists of the Early Dynastic period from Šuruppak. Spouse was Nin-du$_6$-amaš. He was a primeval god. Appearing later in An : *Anum* as En-amaš "Lord Sheepfold," an ancestor of Enlil. Sumerian du$_6$ means "mound" and amaš "sheepfold." See En-amaš. (Mander 1986: 109)

En-Dukuga (M) One of forty-two ancestors of the god Enlil. Consort Nin-Dukuga. Means "Lord of the Holy Mound." In "The Death of Gilgameš," before dying, Gilgameš made offerings to both god and goddess. In "Nergal and Ereškigal," En-Dukuga was the keeper of the fifth gate of the netherworld. (Foster 2005: 517; Frayne 2001: 153; Litke 1998: 34; Tallqvist 1974: 293; Grayson, *ANET*: 510; Cavigneaux and Krebernik, *RlA* IX: 340)

En-Dukugta-ede (M) One of the three cooks of the god An. Means "Lord Coming Out from the Holy Mound." (Litke 1998: 30)

En-du-šuba (M) En-du-šuba may mean "Lord of the Shining Mound" or "Lord of the Mound of *Šuba*(-stones)." In "Nergal and Ereškigal," he was keeper of the sixth gate to the netherworld. If so, the heap of šuba-stones, if that is what the name means, might refer to the beads and other jewelry removed from those about to enter the netherworld, as in the composition "Inana's Descent." (Tallqvist 1974: 293; Grayson, *ANET*: 510)

En-Ekur (M) See Bēl-Ekurri

En-ela (M) God occurring in a school text from Susa with Nin-ela. Written En-e-lá. (Cavigneaux and Krebernik, *RlA* IX: 348)

En-enuru (M) Deity identified with Enki. Means "Lord of Incantation." (Litke 1998: 85)

En-eri-ula (M) One of the twenty-one ancestors of An. Consort Nin-eri-ula. Recognized as keeper of the fourth gate of the netherworld in "Nergal and Ereškigal." Perhaps means "Lord of the Eternal City." (Litke 1998: 23; Tallqvist 1974: 306; Grayson, *ANET*: 510)

En-e-si (M) Deity attested in an Early Dynastic god list from Šuruppak. Means "Lord who Fills the House." (Mander 1986: 45)

En-gal-dudu (M) Deity whose name means "Great Lord who Travels About." In the Akkadian column of An : *Anum* it is glossed as "Herald of the Foreign Land." (Litke 1998: 77)

En-galzu-ešbara (M) Divinity occurring in an incantation against the flooding of fields by the storm god Adad. Means "Lord, Wise One of Decisions." (Schwemer 2001: 679, 681)

En-ga-nu (M) Written en-ga-nú. One text explains the deity as the hairdresser (kinda) of Utu/Šamaš and another as the leader (kingal with gloss *mu'irru*) of Utu/Šamaš. (Litke 1998: 133)

En-gara (M) One of the two cattle herders of the god An. Means "Lord Cream." Written en-gara$_{10}$. (Litke 1998: 30)

En-garaš (M) See Nin-garaš

En-gi(MI)-DUDU (M) A name of Nergal in the Erra Epic. Name means "Lord who Roams the Night." The name may have evolved from the epithet of Nergal en-dagga-DU.DU "lord who walks in the chapel" at third-millennium BCE Uruk. (Cohen 1988, 220; Tinney 1989: no. 3)

En-gidri (M) Deity identified with Nuska in the Emesal god list, which also contains the Emesal form of the name: Umun-muduru, which is the basis of reading En-gidri. However, in an Old Babylonian god list a goddess Nin-PA(-da)(read ḫadda) is listed in Nuska's circle of gods. Means "Lord (of) the Scepter." (Richter 2004: 85)

En-giriš (M) See Nin-giriš

En-gišgal-anna (M) Deified planet Jupiter.

En-gukkal, En-kugal, En-kingal, En-kungal (M) Sumerian deity. Primeval ancestor. Means "Lord Fat-tailed Sheep." Counterpart Nin-gukkal, Nin-kugal, Nin-kingal, Nin-kungal. Name occurs in an Early Dynastic god list from Abu-Ṣalābīkh and in An : *Anum*. (Litke 1998: 33; Mander 1986: 109)

Engura (M) See Nin-engura

En-guru(-guru) (M) Deity attested in an Early Dynastic god list from Šuruppak. Means "Lord of the Grain Silo." (Mander 1986: 101)

En-ḫal (M) In An : *Anum*, one of the forty-two ancestors of the god Enlil. Consort Nin-ḫal. (Litke 1998: 32)

En-ḫun(ga) (M) Sumerian name of the god Nin-šubur, vizier of the god An. En-ḫun(ga) means "Lord who Pacifies." (Litke 1998: 26)

En-idim-an-ki (M) Deity identified with the sun god Utu/Šamaš in An : *Anum*. Variant E_4 instead of EN. Means "Lord, Venerable One of Heaven and Earth." (Richter 2004: 350; Litke 1998: 130)

En-lu-gid (M) See En-nu-gi

Enki (Sum.), **Ea** (Akk.) (H, M) One of the cosmic triumvirate of great Mesopotamian gods, with An/Anu(m) and Enlil. God of the fresh subterranean waters, the Abzu/Apsû(m); of the marshlands; of the fertility of the fields. God of wisdom. Because of the use of water in cultic practices, also god of purification. Deity of healing, medicine, and magic. Organizer of the universe and earth. Bestower of civilization, intelligence, skills, law and order, the arts, and crafts. Patron of gold- and silversmiths, carpenters, and weavers, also of merchants. Male creator *par excellence*. In An : *Anum*, his name follows closely on that of female creator *par excellence* Dingir-maḫ, the birth/mother goddess. As provider of essential water and good counsel, Enki was friend and advocate of human beings. Ea, the name of the Akkadian/Babylonian god who was identified with Enki, had, in general, the same characteristics, genealogy, family, myths, and cult. M. Civil has suggested that the name Ea may be a reflex of the Semitic root *haya* meaning "life."

Son of An/Anu(m) or of Namma, the primordial goddess of the waters of chaos. Twin of Iškur/Adad. Consort of Dam-gal-nun(na)/Damkina. His offspring included Marduk, Asar-lu-ḫe, En-bilulu, Nanše, Dumuzi-Abzu, Gibil/Girru, Nuska, Nin-Girima, and Dumuzi. His vizier was Isimud/Usmû(m), the two-faced god.

Among his epithets were Nu-dim-mud, "He who Engenders," Enlil-banda "Junior Enlil," and Duraḫ-Abzu "Ibex of the Abzu." Other titles included "Lord of Incantation," "Advisor," "Helper," "Father of the Gods," and "Lord of Fate." Enki was often visualized as a huge ibex. On seals he appears seated, bearded, and wearing a many-horned crown. Two rivers, the Tigris and Euphrates (?), often with fish swimming upstream in them, run from his arms. In other images he is enthroned inside the Abzu, a building made of water-filled canals or rivers. Usually Isimud/Usmû is presenting a devotee to him. Among the creatures associated with him were Suḫur-maš, the goat-fish (Capricorn), the fifty giants of Eridu, the fifty Laḫamas of the Abzu, and the seven Apkallū or Sages. The epilogue to the law code of Ḫammurāpi invokes Enki as "the mighty prince whose decrees take precedence..." (Meek, *ANET*: 179).

Enki/Ea had an enormous presence in the myths of Mesopotamia, in which he sometimes seems a rather intellectual trickster figure. The most important of his myths "Enki and the World Order" begins with effusive praise of Enki, to whom Enlil had delegated the power to allot domains and destinies to other deities and to humans. By barge, Enki travelled the land empowering countries and appointing deities to have charge of them. Then turning to the natural world, he assigned specific gods and goddesses to care for each of its elements. Inana, feeling left out, appealed to Enki for a domain, but Enki had not forgotten her. After enumerating her powers: womanliness, female power, warfare, and others, he pinpointed her strongest power, sexuality. Another Sumerian myth, "Enki and Nin-ḫursag," which begins in the Edenic land of Dilmun, recounts one of Enki's adventures as a begetter. First, he impregnates Nin-ḫursag, then the daughter of that union Nin-mu, and thereafter each daughter's daughter in turn, until he gets his come-upance. When Enki impregnates Uttu, she brings forth eight plants, which Enki then eats. Nin-ḫursag curses Enki, and he begins to die. Eventually Nin-ḫursag relents and gives birth to eight gods to heal the eight parts of Enki that the plants were destroying. Another story had the drunken Enki outwitted by a less inebriated Inana, so that, one by one, he gave her the *Me*, which previously had been in his control. Though Enki tried to retrieve the *Me*, Inana succeeded in carrying them off to Uruk. The "Descent of Inana" composition showed Enki's willingness to help those in difficulty, as did the Flood story in the "Epic of Gilgameš," in which, by guile, Ea assisted his devotee Atraḫasīs, and, through him human beings, to escape extinction. On the other hand, in the tale of Adapa, Enki's advice redounded on the hapless Adapa, who had immortality in his grasp, but, on Enki's advice, did not take it. In "Gilgameš and Ḫuwawa B," Gilgameš appealed to "[his] personal god Enki, Nu-dim-mud!" (Frayne 2001: 115).

Enki/Ea's main cult center was the E-Abzu at Eridu, of which city he was patron deity. Archaeological excavations at Eridu have uncovered a series of temples going back to 'Ubaid times; the 'Ubaid level yielded fish bones, probably the remains of offerings. Enki/Ea also had temples in most other Mesopotamian cities, for example, Girsu, Larsa, Uruk, Nippur, Babylon, and Aššur. His precinct at Ur was called "House that Keeps Decisions in Order." In the Ur III period, Enki/Ea received offerings at, among other places, Adab, Girsu, Nippur, Umma, and Eridu. An early calendar from Ebla records a "feast/offerings of Enki 'of the garden'," and at Nippur, during a three-day festival, he was honored with animal sacrifices. At a festival at Emar, a text preserves instructions for a ritual to Ea.

As Ea or I(ya) he was a Hurrian primeval god, in the netherworld and "dead," but still receiving offerings. Appeared also in the Hurrian "Song of Kumarbi" and other compositions. Addressed as "lord, the source of wisdom." See also Eya. Possibly Enki/Ea was equated to the constellation Aquarius and associated with Pisces. Not the same as Enki, "Lord Earth," ancestor of Enlil. (Cohen 2015: 15; Durand 2008: 222–25; Foster 2005: 525–30, 642–51; *LAS*: 72–73, 215–25; Black and Green 2003: 75; Foster 2001: 85; Leick 1999: 65–66; Hoffner 1998: 41–47, 51–53, 60, 63–65, 77–78, 109–10; Leick 1998: 37, 40–41; Litke 1998: 83; Steinkeller 1997: 114 note 16; Popko 1995: 99, 112, 115, 123, 125–27, 132, 165–66; George 1993: 65 no. 30, 77 no. 183, 82 no. 260, 91 no. 359 no. 361, 163 no. 1301, no. 1303, no.

1305; Sallaberger 1993: I, 54, 57, 66, 99, 102, 106–7, 118, 157, 183, 223–24, 238, 246, 254, 296; Mander 1986: 38–39; Attinger 1984; Civil 1983: 44; Biggs 1974: 83; Jacobsen 1976: 85, 112–21; Tallqvist 1974: 287–90, 294; Kramer, *ANET*: 37–41; Speiser, *ANET*: 101–3)

Cylinder seal depicting Enki/Ea enthroned in the Apsû/Abzu. Old Akkadian. Greenstone. 3.9 x 2.55 cm. British Museum no. 89115. After Black and Green 2003: 75.

(2) (M) Sumerian god. In An : *Anum*, one of the forty-two ancestors of Enlil. Consort Nin-ki. Means "Lord Earth." In the Sumerian work "The Death of Gilgameš," before dying, Gilgameš made offerings to both god and goddess. (Frayne 2001: 153; Litke 1998: 30–31)

Enki-Amrimaka (M) Local form of the god Enki at the town of Amrima in the vicinity of Umma. (Cohen 1996a: 30)

Enki-geškinti (M) Sumerian Enki as a smith god in an Ur III text. Means "Enki, the Craftsman," perhaps as patron of craftsmen. Also Enki-geškinti-gula. (AR RIM 1, 27: o 4; MVN 3, 344: o 11)

En-kibir (M) Deity identified with the netherworld god Erra. Means "Lord Firebrand." (Litke 1998: 207)

En-ki-bur-nun (M) Deity allocated offerings at Girsu. ((MVN 6, 412)

Enkidu (M) Legendary Sumerian hero. Servant-companion of Gilgameš in Sumerian Gilgameš compositions and in the Akkadian/Babylonian "Epic of Gilgameš" his friend and equal. A hairy wild man from the steppe, he was created from clay by the birth/mother goddess Aruru to be Gilgameš's equal. In his uncivilized state he helped the wildlife of the steppe and thwarted hunters. He was tamed through sexuality by Šamḫat, usually understood as a temple prostitute, and as a result became "civilized." Enkidu was understood to have netherworld connections, for, in Tablet XII of the "Epic of Gilgameš" and in its Sumerian exemplar, Enkidu died and descended below, but, with the help of Enki, his spirit returned to earth, if only for a brief time. (Frahm 2005: 4–5; Black and Green 2003: 76; Foster 2001: 6, 8–9, 16; Frayne 2001: 104, 138–42; Leick 1998: 44–45; Litke 1998: 220; Tallqvist 1974: 294)

Enki-giguna (M) Written [d]En-ki-gi-gù-na. Presumably "Enki of the Terrace." (OBO 160/1, 1998, p. 599)

Enki-imma (M) Sumerian deity in texts from Nippur. May mean either "Enki of the Clay (of the Abzu)" or "Lord of the Clay(-covered) Earth." Note the goddess Nin-im-ma. (Richter 2004: 30; Sallaberger 1993: I, 103)

En-kimdu (M) Sumerian agricultural god concerned with irrigation and so canals, dikes, ditches. In An : *Anum* he is in the circle of Marduk and is called "the furrow of Nabû[m]." In "Dumuzi and En-kimdu," the shepherd Dumuzi and the farmer En-kimdu were suitors for the hand of Inana, who favored the farmer. Dumuzi challenged the farmer to demonstrate his superiority, but En-kimdu refused to compete. Jacobsen called him "the farmer god" (1976: 85). (*LAS*: 86–88; Lapinkivi 2004: 32; Black and Green 2003: 76; Leick 1998: 45; Kramer, *ANET*: 41–42)

Enki-me-igigal (M) Deity allocated an offering in a text from Ur III Puzriš-Dagan. M. E. Cohen suggests that this name of Enki may be the origin of the name of the twelfth month at Ur, (Ezem)mekigal. (Cohen, 2015: 111; BPOA 7, 214: o 2)

En-kingal (M) See En-gukkal

Enki-nin-ul-guru (M) Sumerian god in Ur III texts from Ur, Umma, and Puzriš-Dagān. A Puzriš-Dagān text refers to the "temple" of the deity. In one text he is allocated offerings immediately after Enki-geškinti. May mean "Enki, the Lord Covered in Glory." (AUCT 1, 209: o 5)

Enki-nirgal (M) Deity mentioned in an Ur III text from Puzriš-Dagān dated to the first year of Ibbi-Sîn. Means "Respected Enki." (AUCT 3, 66: o 2)

En-kug-gal (M) See En-gukkal

Enkum (M) He and his spouse Nin-kum were servants at the temple of Enki and appear most often in conjunction with the Apkallū. Their human equivalents were apparently temple treasurers. (Attinger 1992: 127: Wiggermann 1992: 71; Charpin 1986: 389–91; Sjöberg et al. 1969: 186; Falkenstein 1964: 64; Castellino 1959: 113)

En-kurkur (M) Deity in attested in a Neo-Assyrian god list. Identified with Ninurta. (King 1969: pl. 11)

En-LA-dubur (M) Deity listed among the ancestors of Enlil. Written En-la-dubur$_2$. Spouse was Nin-LA-dubur$_2$. (Lambert 2013: 408)

Enlil, Il-lil, Ellil, Mullil, Ellel, Elallu (H, M) Second in the Sumerian pantheon, after An. Effectively, supreme god and executive of the assembly of the Gods. Understood as creator at Nippur, the religious center of Sumer, where the decisions of the assembly were ratified. Also high god in the Babylonian pantheon and later identified with Marduk, who took over aspects of Enlil's cult. In incantations from Fara, Enlil is the senior god to Ningirima, just as Enki is to Asarluḫe in other incantations. At the city of Aššur, Enlil was equated to the god Aššur, who also acquired some of his cult practices. Enlil's regular titles included King, Lord, Father, Creator, and, among Semitic speakers, Bēlu(m) or Ba'lu. His position as world ruler resulted from his holding the Tablet of Destinies, which, in an Akkadian composition, the Anzû(m) bird stole from him. The Anzû(m) also stole Ellillūtu(m). "Enlilship," Nam-Enlil (Sum.), Ellillūtu(m) (Akk.), which connoted executive power, which other deities, such as Marduk, could be awarded. Scholars have tended to understand the name Enlil to mean "Lord Air," though, properly, Sumerian lil means "spirit," not "air." So they view Enlil as a god of weather and winds. As such, they saw him as both beneficent and destructive, the latter trait manifested in storms. P. Steinkeller has suggested that the name might be of Semitic origin, perhaps originally Il-ili, "God of Gods" (1992: 114 note 16). The form Il-li-lu "God of Gods" is attested from a very early period at Ebla. Mullil is the name of Enlil in the Emesal dialect.

Detail showing Enlil from a relief of a procession of deities from Maltai or Maltaya, Northern Iraq. Carved into the rock face. Neo-Assyrian. After Pritchard 1969b: 181, no. 537. See also Black and Green 2003: 40.

Enlil's most frequent epithets included kur-gal "The Great Mountain," dur-an-ki "Bond of Heaven and Earth," lugal-du$_6$-ku$_3$-ga "Lord of the Dukug," duraḫ-gal "Great Ibex," en-kur-kur "Lord of (Foreign) Lands," and Nu-nam-nir "The One of Lordship." Bēl-mātāti "Lord of the Lands," a name of both Enlil and Marduk at Babylon, was proclaimed in the *Enūma eliš* as the last of Marduk's fifty names. The law code of Ḫammu-rāpi appealed to Enlil as "the determiner of the destinies of the land" (Meek, *ANET*: 179). It enjoined Enlil to expunge completely the name and memory of desecrators of the law code's stele.

Enlil was the son of the sky god An and brother of birth/mother goddess Aruru. His principal wife was Ninlil or Sud, and among his junior wives were Šu-zi-ana and En-zi-kalama. Among his offspring were Ninurta, his eldest son/heir, and Nin-Girsu, often identified with Ninurta; Nanna/Sîn; Utu/Šamaš; Iškur/Adad; and Nergal, as well as Nuska, Pabil-sag, Uraš, En-nugi, and Zababa. One tradition named him Inana's father. His vizier was Nuska.

In "Enlil and Ninlil," Nun-bar-še-gunu warns her virgin daughter Ninlil not to go bathing in the river and to be wary of Enlil. Nonetheless, Ninlil went to the river where Enlil saw and desired her. Overcoming her protestations, he impregnated her with Nanna/Sîn. Then the other deities, declaring Enlil to be polluted, exiled him to the netherworld. However, Ninlil followed him. In order to prevent his son Nanna, the moon god, from being born in the netherworld, Enlil impregnated Ninlil with, in turn, netherworld deities Nergal, Nin-azu, and En-bilulu. The Sumerian "Enlil and Sud" recounts Enlil's courtship of Sud and their marriage, after which Sud received the name Ninlil. Enlil's revenge on Narām-Sîn for plundering the Ekur was lamented in "The Cursing of Agade." In another composition, Išme-Dagān had a chariot, symbol of kingship, made for Enlil. Yet another composition told of a meeting between Nam-zi-tara and Enlil disguised as a crow; it ended with Enlil's appointing the man to permanent service in his temple. A Sumerian hymn, "Enlil in the Ekur (Enlil A)," praises Enlil as the source of life and fertility and lauds his magnificence and power. It also discusses the Ekur "Mountain House," Enlil's temple at Nippur, and refers to its rituals, festivals, and personnel.

The Ekur was Enlil's main cult center, but the god had temples or shrines, often jointly with Ninlil, in most Mesopotamian cities: among them, Uruk, Kiš/Ḫursag-kalama, Ešnunna, and Ur. In the Ur III period, he was worshipped at Ur, Umma, and Girsu, among other places. His "seat" in Marduk's E-sag-ila at Babylon was named "Exalted Abode," and at Aššur Enlil's temple was called "Wild Bull of the Lands." The worship of Enlil as "Lord of the Lands" survived into Hellenistic times.

Ellel/Ellil was the Hurrian/Hittite spelling of the name of Enlil. Ellel was one of the Primeval Deities, the elder gods from the Hurrian/Old Syrian pantheon, whom Teššub and the young divinities exiled to the netherworld. They still received offerings in rituals, though considered as "dead."

(George 2016: 2; Cohen 2015: 105; Wang 2011; Foster 2005: 484, 652–57; *LAS*: 100–25, 320–25; Archi 2004; Edzard 2003: 173–84; Black and Green 2003: 76; Frame 1999: 6, 7, 8; Leick 1999: 65–66, 82, 153; Hoffner 1998: 41–43, 59, 63, 112; Leick 1998: 45–47; Litke 1998: 37; van Gessel 1998: I, 61–62; George 1993: 64 no. 26, 109 no. 584, 116 no. 677, 124 no. 772, 130 no. 849, 138 no. 951, 153 no. 1141, 161 no. 1259; Sallaberger 1993: I, 45–46, 51–57, 88, 97, 98–101, 105–57, 180, 194, 238, 253–54, 257, 305, 308; Selz 1992: 190–93; Civil 1983: 43; Tallqvist 1974: 295–3; Meek, *ANET*: 164, 179; Speiser, *ANET*: 72; Heidel 1967: 59; Laroche 1946/47: 121; *CAD:* I/J, 85)

Enlila-anka (M) Deity whose temple is mentioned in an Ur III text from Girsu. (WMAH 176: r vi 11)

Enlil-adaḫani (M) The deified standard of Enlil appearing in a year name of Lipit-Enlil, king of Isin. Means "Enlil Is His Helper." (Renger 1967: 150)

Enlil-Aššurû(m) (M) The Assyrian god Enlil who resulted from a syncretism of Enlil and Aššur. (Schwemer 2001: 208)

Enlil-banda (M) One of the names of Enki/Ea in An : *Anum*. Means "Junior Enlil." (Litke 1998: 83)

Enlil-kura (M) One of the names of the netherworld god Erra in An : *Anum*. It means "Enlil of the *kur*(netherworld)." (Litke 1998: 201)

Enlil-kur-igigala (M) Form of Enlil associated with the shrine Kur-igigala, which, according to a topographical text from Nippur, lay in the vicinity of the Ekur temple. The shrine was built by the Ur III king Amar-Suen. According to a mythological text, Šu-zi-ana, a daughter of the Sumerian netherworld god En-me-šara, married Enlil in this particular shrine, and offerings to the Kur-igigala and Šu-zi-ana are found together in an Ur III text. Means "Enlil of the Kur-igigala." (Richter 2004: 44)

Enlil-lugal-zi (M) Deity in a Neo-Assyrian god list. Means "Enlil, the True King." (King 1969: pl. 14)

Enlil-meŠA (M) The deified standard of the god Enlil attested in a year name of the Isin king Ur-Ninurta. Written -me-$ša_4$. Note En-meŠA. (Richter 2004: 33)

Enlil-urumaḫ-anki (M) Form of Enlil associated with the Ekur-igigala complex. Written ^{d}En-líl-u_9-ru-maḫ-an-ki "Enlil, the Great Power of Heaven and Earth." (Richter 2004: 44)

Enlila-zi, Enlilza (M) Enlilza occurs as a variant in An : *Anum*. A lieutenant of Enlil's Ekur temple at Nippur. The divine name likely represents a deified historical figure, since it is preceded by Lum(m)a and Ḫataniš, who were almost certainly historical personages.

Records of offerings to him were in texts from Nippur dating to the Early Dynastic and Ur III periods. They were associated with the temple of Enlil's wife Ninlil. (Richter 2004: 57; Litke 1998: 42; Sallaberger 1993: I, 100 note 436)

En-LU (M) One of the forty-two primeval ancestors of the god Enlil in An : *Anum*. Consort Nin-LU. A possible basis for reading En-lu is that this deity immediately follows two deities with somewhat similar sounding names: En-ul and En-mul. (Litke 1998: 31)

En-lulima (M) Deity of the flocks of goats of the temple. His concern was the abundance of milk and butter. Means "Lord Red Deer (or Stag)." (Edzard 1997: 94; Falkenstein 1966: 71)

En-lunga (M) Deity in the OB god list from Nippur. Written En-lu-un-ga. Perhaps syllabic for "Lord Brewer."

En-me-lulu (M) One of the names of Šala, wife of Iškur/Adad, in An : *Anum*. Means "Lord of Numerous *Mes*." (Litke 1998: 143)

En-me-mu (M) In An : *Anum*, one of the children of Nin-Girida, wife of Ninazu. (Litke 1998: 191)

En-men-nun-si-na (M) Deity. One of Lugalbanda's children. The following entry is (En?-)temen-nun-si-na. Although these deities are listed as two of Lugalbanda's ten children, perhaps these two names are simply variants. (Litke 1998: 169; ETCSL 2.4.1.2)

En-meŠA (M) In *Anu ša amēli* explained as "Sin of the Corona (*ša agê*)." Written -me-ša$_4$. Note Enlil-meŠA. (Litke 1998: 230)

En-me-šara (M) Sumerian netherworld god and the model of such deities, a dead god of the previous generation. Primeval ancestor of An and Enlil. Nin-me-šara was his consort. His seven children were the Sibittu(m). Means "Lord of All the *Me*." En-me-šara shared a "seat" with En-bilulu in the E-sag-ila at Babylon and had his own in the main temple at Aššur. Ritual weeping for the capture of En-me-šara by the netherworld (?) is mentioned in a Babylonian cultic calendar. According to tradition En-me-šara rebelled against Marduk and so he was put in chains and consigned to the netherworld and his seven children thrown off a roof. (Cohen 2015: 439; Lambert 2013: 326–29; Foster 2005: 766; Black and Green 2003: 76–77; Foster 2001: 223; George 1993: 77 no. 177, 94 no. 398; Tallqvist 1974: 304; Weidner, *RlA* II: 397–99)

En-mete (M) Deity whose name may mean "The Proper Lord." Attested in Early Dynastic god lists. (Mander 1986: 111)

En-mete-[x]-ušu (M) Deity listed in An : *Anum*. One of the chair-bearers (officials) of the goddess Baba. An : *Anum* has a gloss šu-šu before the sign UŠU. May mean something such as "He Alone Is the Proper Lord." (Litke 1998: 178)

En-me-ur-ana (M) In An : *Anum*, one of the deities attendant on Inana. Means "Lord, Heavenly Gatherer of the *Me*." (Litke 1998: 155)

En-mu(d)la (M) Deity listed among the ancestors of Enlil. En-mu-u$_4$-lá might be a variant for another ancestor of Enlil's, En-mul. (Lambert 2013: 408)

En-mul (M) One of forty-two ancestors of Enlil. In "The Death of Gilgameš," Gilgameš, before dying, makes offerings to him and his wife Nin-mul.

Means "Lord Star." (Frayne 2001: 153; Tallqvist 1974: 304)

En-na-DI (M) See Nun-na-DI

En(n)anun (M) Deity attested at Nippur. In one text listed between Nuska and Ninurta. See En-á-nun. (Sallaberger 1993: I, 103)

En-nigdagala (M) Deity invoked for advice in a Neo-Assyrian "Heart Pacification Prayer." Name might mean something like "Lord of Far and Wide." (Maul 1988: 175)

En-nimgirsi (M) Deity attested at Nippur in the Ur III period after a mention of the warrior god Ninurta. Means "Lord, Best Man of the Bridegroom (*susapinnu*)." In an Old Babylonian god list from Nippur, appears with the gods Dumuzi and Ama-ušum-gal-ana. (Richter 2004: 313; Sallaberger 1993: I, 103, 157)

Ennina (M) Deity attested in a god list from Aššur, perhaps a variant for Innina. (Schroeder 1920: no. 48)

En-nudimmud (M) See Nu-dim-mud

Ennu-gi (M) Canal inspector of the great gods. Son of Enlil or En-me-šara and consort of Nanibgal. Written en-nu-gi. In An : *Anum* he is called chair-bearer (official) of Enlil. He had netherworld associations and might have been the same as Gugal-ana, first husband of Ereškigal. Name might mean "Reliable Watchman (en-nu(-un))," though popularly explained in ancient times as "Lord of (the Land of) No Return." In "Nergal and Ereškigal," he served as keeper of the seventh gate of the netherworld. He had a temple at Nippur and a "seat" at Ur. (Foster 2005: 517; *LAS*: 102–6; Foster 2001: 85; Litke 1998: 58; George 1993: 137 no. 938, 161 no. 1255; Jacobsen 1976: 103–4; Tallqvist 1974: 305; Grayson, *ANET*: 510)

En-nugigi (M) One of two gate-keepers of the goddess of the netherworld Ereškigal, as specified in An : *Anum*. Written en-nu-gi4-gi4. Means "Lord who Allows None to Return," referring to kur-nu-gi4-a, "The Land of No Return." (Litke 1998: 189)

En-nun-dagala (M) In An : *Anum*, one of the bull-lyres of Marduk. (Litke 1998: 98; George 1993: 65 no. 41; Tallqvist 1974: 305)

Ennun-silima (M) God in the service of An/Anu(m). In An : *Anum*, a caretaker or watchman. Means "Sentry of the Peace (or Order)." (Litke 1998: 30; Tallqvist 1974: 305)

En-nutemud (M) See Nudimmud

En-PEŠ-gal (M) See PEŠ-gal

En-saga (M) One of the names of the god Nabû. Means "Chief Lord." (Litke 1998: 96)

Ensi-gal-abzu (M) A form of Mardu. See Amurru(m). Means "Great Governor of the Abzu." (Litke 1998: 101)

Ensi-maḫ (M) A form of Mardu. Means "Lofty Governor." He had a cult at Ku'ara in the Ur III period. (Litke 1998: 102)

En-sig-nun (M) Caretaker of Nin-Girsu's donkeys and chariot. In a variant copy of An : *Anum* the entry may be N[in-sig-nun] and is listed among protective deities in the circle of Nin-Girsu. One Ur III Girsu document refers to the donkeys and asses of the "house" (é) of En-sig-nun. Also the name of a canal dug in Girsu according to Ur-Namma year name 14. (Litke 1998: 176; Edzard 1997: 94; George 1993: 78; Tallqvist 1974: 305; Falkenstein 1966: 71; Cavigneaux and Krebernik, *RlA* IX: 487–88)

En-sudag (M) Deity with a cult at Ur III Umma. Means "Resplendent Lord." (MVAG 21, 22 FH 5: o ii 19)

En-sun (M) The name of the moon god Nanna/Sîn as the half moon. Means "Lord Wild Cow." See Nin-sun. (Jacobsen 1970: 25)

En-šag-dug (M) Deity identified with Nuska. Means "Lord (with) a Good Heart." (Richter 2004: 85)

En-šag (M) See En-zak

En-šara (M) In An : *Anum*, one of the ancestors of both An and Enlil. Means "Lord of All." Wife Nin-šar. (Litke 1998: 22, 32)

En-temen-nun-si-na (M) See En-men-nun-si-na

En-te-na-MAŠ.ḪUM (M) In a Neo-Assyrian god list identified as a constellation. (King 1969: pl. 13)

En-tetigal/me (M) See En-dimgal

En-ti (M) One of the names of Enki/Ea in An : *Anum*. Spouse Nin-ti. TI here might be connected to a meaning "life." (Litke 1998: 87)

En-ti(?)-du (M) Deity attested in personal names in two Early Dynastic tablets from Nippur, one of whom was a governor of Nippur. (A. Westenholz 1987: no. 49, no. 60)

En-TIR-nun (M) Deity attested in an Early Dynastic god list from Abu Ṣalābīkh. Mander suggests that En-TIR-nun might possibly be a writing for En-duraḫ-nuna. (Mander 1986: 54)

En-tur (M) Deity identified with Enki/Ea. Written En-tùr and En-tur. Means "Lord (of) the Cattle Pen." Explained in An : *Anu ša amēli* as "Shepherd of Nanny Goats." (Litke 1998: 240)

En-ug (M) In An : *Anum*, one of forty-two ancestors of Enlil. Wife Nin-ug. Might mean "Lord Lion." (Litke 1998: 33)

En-uḫ (M) Probably a primeval ancestor god. Might mean "Lord Moth" or "Lord Turtle." Attested in a god list from Šuruppak. (Mander 1986: 109)

En-ul (M) In An : *Anum*, one of forty-two ancestors of Enlil. Wife Nin-ul. Means "Ancient Lord." (Litke 1998: 33)

En-urra (M) Deity attested at Ur III Nippur. Written En-ùr-ra. Means "Lord of the Roof/Shelter" (PPAC 5, 331: o ii 12)

En-ur-anna (M) Deity participating in the *akītu* festival in Seleucid Uruk.

En-urta (M) Deity identified with Bennu(m), divinized epilepsy. May mean "Lord (who Causes One to Fall) from a Roof," since epilepsy is known as the falling disease. Another possibility is that ùr here is a variant for ur_4, which can mean to have convulsions or seizures. (Litke 1998: 73)

En-uru, Nin-uru (M) Vizier of Utu. In An : *Anum* the names Nin-$^{ú-ru}uru_3$ and Nin-$^{ú-ru}uru_3$ are juxtaposed, both identified with Enki/Ea. May mean "Lord of Secrets." Jacobsen understands this as meaning "Lord of Reeds," alluding to the making of reed huts. (Richter 2004: 215; Litke 1998: 83; Jacobsen 1970: 22; Cavigneaux and Krebernik, *RlA* IX: 527–28)

En-u-tila (M) One of the forty-two ancestors of Enlil. His spouse was Nin-u-tila. Written En-u_4-ti-la, En-ú-ti-la, and En-ti-la. Might mean "Lord who Grants a Life of (Many) Days" or "Lord who Brings Vegetation to Life." In "The Death of Gilgameš," they both receive offerings from Gilgameš just before he dies. In an Assyrian composition he is a leader of the forces of the first-generation of gods who is slain by Ninurta. (Lambert 2013: 329; Foster 2005: 517; Frayne 2001: 153; Litke 1998: 33)

Ēn-uzun / Īn-uzun (M) Akkadian deity. Doorkeeper of the E-šarra temple in Aššur. Means "Eye and Ear." (Deller 1991: no. 18)

Enza (M) One of the seven destiny-decreeing gods of the E-sagil temple in Babylon. (George 2004 no. 20)

En-zaga (M) Deity identified with Nuska, the god of fire and light. One of the seven destiny-decreeing gods of the E-sagil temple in Babylon. Written En-zà-ga and En-zág(PA), this perhaps somehow related to the writing of Nuska's name, PA+TÚG. (George 2004 no. 20; Litke 1998: 50)

Enzak, Inzak (M) Chief god of Dilmun, modern Baḥrain. He was called "Lord of Dilmun." A later title was "Nabû of Dilmun." Šuluḫiṭu(m) may have been his consort. At Dilmun he shared a temple with Meskilak. En-zak was the last of eight deities created by Ninḫursag to cure Enki's ailments. At the end of the text, En-zak was appointed ruler of Dilmun. He seems also to have had a temple on Failaka Island. A deity In-zak, who may or may not be associated with En-zak, was revered in Elam as part of a trinity with In-šušinak and Enki/Ea. (Black and Green 2003: 66; Litke 1998: 237; Glassner 1984: 48–49; George 1993: 87 no. 314, 107–8 no. 566; Kramer, *ANET*: 41)

En-zida (M) Sumerian deity attested in a god list from Šuruppak. May mean "The Trustworthy Lord." (Mander 1986: 102–3)

En-zi-kalama (M) In An : *Anum*, a secondary wife of Enlil. Means "Trustworthy Lady of the Nation." (Litke 1998: 41)

En-zinise (M) One of five attendants of the healing goddess Gula. Possibly an intercessory goddess. Means "Lord/Lady for His/Her Life." (Richter 2004: 216; Litke 1998: 184)

E-pa (M) Deity associated with the scribe god Nabû. Means "Ditch and Dike." In An : *Anum*, glossed in Akkadian as "Furrow of the God Nabû." Associated with En-kimdu. (Litke 1998: 97; Tallqvist 1974: 286)

E-pa(-gal)-dun (M) Twenty-fifth name of Marduk in the *Enūma eliš*. Means "(Large) Dike (and) Ditch Digger." (George 2016 no. 16; Foster 2005: 479; Litke 1998: 92; Tallqvist 1974: 286; Speiser, *ANET*: 71)

Eraḫ (M) See **Yariḫ(u)**

Eren-kurkura (M) In An : *Anum*, one of the children of the goddess Ninmarki. Means "Yoke of the Lands." Since Ninmarki was involved with cattle, "yoke" is an appropriate name for one of her children. (Litke 1998: 125)

Eren-Utu (M) Goddess attested in a Neo-Assyrian god list and identified with Aya, the wife of the sun god. Means "Troops of the Sun." (King 1969: pl. 9)

Ereškigal (M) Queen of the netherworld and sister of Inana. First husband Gugal-ana, second Nergal. Offspring were the goddess Nungal and the gods Nin-azu and, fathered by Enlil, Namtar "Fate," the latter also being her vizier and messenger. Her scribe was Geštin-ana. Chief administrator (majordomo) Nin-geš-zida, administrator Pabil-sag, chief gate-keeper Biti.

Ereškigal was a major character in the Sumerian composition "Inana's Descent to the Netherworld" and the

unearthed in the goddess's sanctuary at Isin in southern Mesopotamia. Also, according to fifth-century BCE texts from a Phoenician temple at Kition in Cyprus, sacred dogs featured in cult practices there. Ešmun's worship was part of both official and popular cult in Phoenician Cyprus. He was worshipped also in Egypt. Ešmun was a very important god in Punic North Africa. At Utica, where he was identified with Apollo, he had a temple purported to date from the foundation of that city. At Dougga in Tunisia, Ešmun was associated with the goddess Caelestis and shared her sumptuous temple there. At Carthage, his temple crowned the heights of the city. His statue there was of gold, and it sat in a shrine decorated with gold leaf. The temple was completely destroyed in 146 BCE when the Romans conquered Carthage. The city's last defenders were reported to have taken refuge in Ešmun's sanctuary, where they killed themselves rather than surrender. About a hundred years later, Roman Carthage was built on the site; it was populated by Africans speaking Semitic Neo-Punic and worshipping, among other Punic deities, Ešmun, but under the Roman name Asculapius. Ešmun was venerated throughout the Phoenician/Punic area, especially in Sardinia and Spain. On the Spanish island of Ibiza there was a very old cult of the god. Identified by the Greeks with Asclepios and also Apollo in his healing aspect. In the *Phoenician History*, Philo of Byblos designated Asclepios as the eighth son of the god Sydyk and brother of the seven Kabiri.

In a Neo-Assyrian god list it is written ^{d}Eš-mu-úb (entry after Re-ḫa-ab) and identified with Adad. (Woolmer 2017: 110–11, 116; Peckham 2014: 84; Betlyon 2005: 14–15, 20; Pardee 2002: 65; Markoe 2000: 115, 117, 118, 206; del Olmo Lete 1999: 319 and note 90; Moscati 1999: 34–35, 140; Ribichini, *DDDB*: 306–9; Lipiński 1995: 154–68, 289–92; Handy 1994: 59; Bonnet, *DCPP*: 48; Lipiński, *DCPP*: 158–60; Attridge and Oden 1981: 58–59; Pritchard 1978: 26, 42–43; King 1969: pl. 17; Albright 1968: 148–50, 187, 227, 244; Langdon, 1931: 74–75; Baudisson 1911)

Eš-peš (M) Deity attested in god lists and personal names in Old Akkadian texts from Abu Ṣalābīkh and the area of Adab. (Mander 1986: 59, 111; Maiocchi 2009: no. 140; Visicato and A. Westenholz 2010: no. 216 no. 331)

EŠ-si (M) Deity attested in an Early Dynastic god list from Abu Ṣalābīkh. Sumerian name possibly means "God who Fills the Shrine" and may be comparable to En-é-si "Lord who Fills the House" attested at Šuruppak. (Mander 1986: 45)

Eštan, Estan (Hattic), **Ištan(u)** (Hittite, H) Central Anatolian Hattic (pre-Hittite) deity, in the form she/he took when in the netherworld. Paired with Taru, the Hattic storm god. In Hurrian same as Allani, "Sun Deity of Earth." In a Hittite lexical list, called Ištan(u) (a loanword). At Ugarit equated to Allatu(m). Equivalent to Mesopotamian Ereškigal. Eštan actually means "Day." There is some question as to the sex of this deity. While Hoffner states that Eštan was male and identifies him with the Hurrian Šimegi, Popko states that she was female. (Hoffner 1998: 112; Leick 1998: 59–60; van Gessel 1998: I, 67–68, 205–6; Popko 1995: 70, 113; Haas 1994: 132–33; Laroche 1946/47: 25)

Eštar (M) See Inana

Eštutaya-Papaya (H) See Gulša

E-talak (M, E) (1) One of three deities of the bolt or latch listed in An : *Anum*. His "seat" at Uruk was called "Place of the Latch." (2) A god of Elam, entitled "King of Elam." (Litke 1998: 65; Tallqvist 1974: 286; König, *RlA* II: 480)

Etamītu(m) (M) Deity identified with Išḫara, possibly because of her connection with divination. *Tamītu(m)* is the Akkadian word for "oath," as well as for a divinatory text. The name appears in An : Anum right after Bēlet-bēri(m) "Lady of Divination." (Litke 1998: 44, 166; Prechel 1996: 170–71)

Etamu (M) Deity listed in an Old Babylonian god list in the circle of the moon god Nanna/Sîn. (Richter 2004: 453; Hall 1985: 453–54)

Ether (L) See Aer

Ettanam-ilu (M) Deity identified with Inana as Venus. Variant A-ta-nam-AN. Means "God Has Given Me." (Litke 1998: 161)

Eturammi (M) In An : *Anum*, vizier of Birdu. Means "He Returned to Me." (Litke 1998: 187)

Eṭemmu(m) (M) See Gidim

Eya (H, L) Hurrian deity occurring in god lists and ritual texts from Ugarit. Might be the same as Koṯar(u), though Ea also appears in god lists as equated to Koṯar(u). Thus might be a spelling for Ea. (del Olmo Lete 1993: 73, 85, 200)

Ezem-sag (M) One of the names of Enlil in An : *Anum*. Means "Main Festival." (Litke 1998: 39)

Ezem-sag-TUR (M) Sumerian deity attested in the Ur III period. (Sharlach 2002: 92)

Ezinu (M) See Ašnan

—G—

Ga-a-gi (M) See Ka-ka

Gaa'u (M) Sumerian sheep goddess. In An : *Anum*, she appears as shepherd of the god Nanna/Sîn. In the "Lament over the Destruction of Sumer and Ur," the ewe hurls her weapon at her own kind as a symbol of the overturning of normal order in the land. Means "Ewe." Written dGa-a-a-ú and dMIN (=Ga-a-a)-u$_8$. (Black, Cunningham, Robson and Zólyomi 2004: 136; Litke 1998: 126; Tallqvist 1974: 308; Kramer, *ANET*: 617)

Ga-an-gu (M) Deity identified with Ninšubur of the socle in An : *Anum*. (Litke 1998: 233)

GABA-bizbiz (M) Deity identified with Enki/Ea in An : *Anum*. biz-biz means "to drip," which might be appropriate for Enki, a god of water. (Litke 1998: 84)

Gaba-ḫuš-gu-zubi-abzu (M) Counselor of Nin-Girsu. Means something like "Roiling Surface along the Shore of the Watercourse of the Abzu." (Litke 1998: 177)

Gabriel (L) Archangel, a member of the highest level in the hierarchy of angels. One of two archangels to appear in the Hebrew Bible (Daniel 8: 16), the other being Michael. Gabriel was, first and foremost, the one who revealed and interpreted on behalf of the deity. He also interceded with God for humans and punished evildoers. Means "God Is My Warrior." In later Jewish writings Gabriel's position was on the left side of the deity, and he protected the left side of sleeping humans. As warrior he would be the one to fight against the monster Leviathan at the End of Days. In the New Testament, it was Gabriel who revealed to aged Zechariah the coming pregnancy of his wife Elizabeth and the future birth of John the Baptist (Luke 1: 5–24). The archangel later announced to the Virgin Mary that she would bear a son to be called Jesus (Luke 1: 26–56). Along with Michael and other angels, Gabriel was addressed on Aramaic incantation bowls, pottery vessels inscribed with magical invocations to put spells on people; found in Babylonia, they date from after 600 CE. See Lilith for drawing. As Christian saint Gabriel shares his feast day on September 29 with Michael "and All the Angels." In 1929 the pope made him saint of post office, telegraph, and telephone personnel. As Jibril he appears three times in the Qur'ān and is identified as the angel who transmitted the holy text to the Prophet. (Farmer 2003: 210; Collins, *DDDB*: 338–39; van Henten, *DDDB*: 80–82; Bowker 1997: 364; Qur'ān 1996: 11, Sura 2: 97; Brownrigg 1993: 69–70; Newsom, *ABD* II: 863)

Gad, Gadde (L) God of luck or fortune attested in Canaanite, biblical, and Phoenician/Punic texts. Equated to Greek Tyche and Roman Fortuna. Gad occurs in Ugaritic, Amorite, Phoenician, and Punic personal names, as well as in the Hebrew Bible, but it is not always clear that they are theophoric names. Sometimes the word just means "good fortune," for example, in Genesis 30:10–14, when Zilpah bore her first son by Jacob, Leah said "What [good] fortune!" and named the boy Gad. In Isaiah 65: 11, Gad was definitely a deity, for some Israelites were described as forsaking the Lord by venerating Gad "Luck," along with Meni "Destiny." Among the Phoenician colonies, Gad was the god of fortune: inscriptions include dedications to Gad as the deity of luck. In the Greco-Roman period in the Levant, Gad seems to have become a tutelary god of a place, for example, a city or of a tribe. He is attested also in an inscriptions from Palmyra, one of which is bilingual and equates him to Greek Tyche. At Dura Europos in northeastern Syria he had a temple complex. In later Jewish writings Gad was identified with the planet Jupiter. (Joukowsky 2001: 53; Ribichini, *DDDB*: 339–41; Lipiński 1995: 62–64; Bonnet, *DCPP*: 181; Maier, *ABD* II: 863–64; Langdon, 1931: 23)

Gada-bir (M) Deity receiving offerings at Ur III Kutha. The name might mean "Strips Flax (Fibers)." (MVN 13, 99: o 14)

Gadala-abzu (M) Deity identified with Nin-šubur. Means "*Gadala*-priest of the Abzu." gada-lá means "linen-clad" and can refer to cultic personnel. (Litke 1998: 101; Tallqvist 1974: 315)

Gaga (M) See Kaka

Gaggag (M) One of the names of the goddess Išḫara in An : *Anum*. Variant gag-ga. (Litke 1998: 44)

Gagim, Gugim, Endib (M) A male deity whose name is written ᵈZADIM and ᵈḪAR and is glossed gu-qi-im, gu-gim, ga-qi-im, ga-gim, and en-di-ib. Quite possibly the divine lapidary because of the sign ZADIM "lapidary." In one lexical list the name occurs after the divine smith and in another after the divine carpenter, suggesting a profession. (Litke 1998: 108–109, 216)

Gaiu (M) See Gaa'u

GAL (E) See Kiri-rišša; Napi-riša

Gala-gal (M) Appears as an evil god in An : *Anum*. Means "Chief Policeman/ Demon."(Litke 1998: 209)

Galam-ḫar (M) One of four patrons of fowlers in An : *Anum*. Means "Expert in Bird-traps" (*ḫuḫāru*). Name also written MUŠEN.DÙ "fowler." (Litke 1998: 114)

Gal-a-ru-ru (M) Deity attested in a Neo-Assyrian god list. See Aruru. (King 1969: pl. 31)

Gal-enun/agrun (M) Deity attested in an Early Dynastic god list. Means "Great One of the Cella." (Mander 1986: 138)

Gal-ga-eri (M) Deity attested in a tablet said to come from Abu Hatab, ancient Kisura, near Šuruppak, dating from the mid-third millennium BCE. One wonders if the element gal-ga might be a phonetic writing for galga "understanding, foresight, (good) counsel." If so, may mean "(Good) Counsel (of) the City." (Martin et al. 2001: no. 110)

Gal-gal-dumu-an-na (M) Messenger god attested in a god list from Aššur. (Schroeder 1920: no. 64)

Galla (Sum.), **Gallû(m)** (Akk.) netherworld demon. Though usually evil, it can sometimes be beneficial. Responsible for dragging humans, especially sinners, down to the netherworld. In the composition "The Descent of Inana," Galla-demons follow Inana back to earth from the netherworld to claim her substitute, eventually Dumuzi. The Galla might have survived in the ancient Greek demon Gelu. (Black, Cunningham, Robson and Zólyomi 2004: 74–75; Black and Green 2004: 85–89; Leick 1998: 67; Tallqvist 1974: 310; Kramer, *ANET*: 56–57; Ebeling, *RlA* II: 109)

Gal-MU (M) In a Neo-Assyrian god list identified with Ninurta. (King 1969: pl. 13)

Gāmilu(m) (M) Akkadian god occurring in theophoric personal names in tablets from the First Sealand Dynasty. Means "One who Spares." (Dalley 2009: no. 444, no. 447)

Gana (M) In the lexical series Diri the deity is written with the logogram GÁN and explained as *eq-lu-um* "field." (Civil 2004)

Ganana (M) Goddess mentioned in third-millennium BCE texts from Ebla, whose temple was in Binaš; there was a festival for the "opening" of her temple in the fifth month. (Pasquali 2007: no. 44; Archi 2005: no. 42; Pasquali 1998: no. 1)

Gana-si (M) Deity identified with Enki. Means "One who Fills the Field (with water(?))." With gloss ga-na-si. Variant: Gá-si-sá. (Litke 1998: 87)

Gana-šita (M) Sumerian deity attested in god lists of the Early Dynastic period from Šuruppak and Abu Ṣalābīkh. Written ^{d}gana-šita^{gan}. (Mander 1986: 113)

Gana-ur (M) In a Neo-Assyrian god list identified as a constellation. Written gána-ùr, "Harrow" (*maškakātu*). (King 1969: pl. 13)

Gan-dim-kug (M) Daughter of Namtar "Fate." Also a daughter of Enki. In exorcisms, she often follows Namtar and his wife. (Civil 1984: 294; Lambert, *RlA* IV: 244)

Gan-gir (M) Deity attested in an Early Dynastic god list. See Gan-gir-nun, Lugal-gir-nun, Gir-nun. (Mander 1986: 140)

Gan-gir-nun (M) One of the seven daughters of Baba. Attested in Ur III offering lists. She had a temple at Girsu. See Gan-gir, Lugal-gir-nun, Gir-nun. (George 1993: 164 no. 1322; Tallqvist 1974: 322; Falkenstein 1966: 75)

Gangu (M) Deity explained in *Anu ša amēli* as "Papsukkal of the shrine(*aširti*) / morning (*šerti*)." (Richter 2004: 308; Litke 1998: 233)

Ganisura (M) See Kanisura

Gansura (M) A writing of the Sumerian goddess name Kanisura, attested at Uruk in the Ur III period. See Kanisura. (Sallaberger 1993: I, 213, 215, 228)

Gan-tur (M) Worshipped at Girsu and Lagaš. Means "Young Woman (of) the Cattle Pen." (Cohen 2015: 36; Selz 1992: 141–42)

Ganum (M) See Gaa'u

Ganun-ḫedu (M) One of Marduk's two bull harps. Ganun-ḫedu shared a residence with the other harp, Ennun-dagala, in the Eadgigi in Marduk's E-sagil temple at Babylon. Means "Suitable Storehouse." (Litke 1998: 98; George 1993: 65 no. 41; Tallqvist 1974: 310)

Ganzer (M) See Kanisura

Gapan (L) See Gapn(u)

Gapn(u), Gapan, Gepen, Gupan (L) Deity in the mythic texts of Ugarit. Means "Vine." Always accompanied by Ugar(u) "Field." The two were messengers of the storm god Ba'lu/Had(d)ad. Neither deity occurs in the Ugaritic ritual texts. The word for "vine" in Hebrew is *gepen*. See Gapnu-wa-Ugaru; Ugaru. (Wyatt 2002: 79; del Olmo Lete 1999: 52, 56, 340; Smith 1999: 111, 138, 141, 179; Pardee, *DDDB*: 341–42)

Gara, Gari (M) One of the twenty-one ancestors of An. Paired with Ekur, likely her husband. Written Gá-ra and Gá-ri. (Litke 1998: 22)

Gara'inu (M) Deity attested at Ebla.

Gašala (M) In An : *Anum*, one of five gods of fruit. Written GIŠ.Ú with gloss ga-ša-lá. (Litke 1998: 112)

Gašalu (M) Deity attested at Ebla.

Gašam, **Gašmu** (M) Sumerian/Babylonian goddess identified with Zarpanītu(m), wife of Marduk. Means "Wise (One)." (Tallqvist 1974: 311)

Gašan For goddesses beginning with Gašan-, see under Nin-, if it is attested with Nin-. Gašan is the Emesal form of Nin "Lady."

Gašan-ašte (M) Form of the healing goddess Nin-Isina as deity at Larak, a town near Isin. Means "Lady (of) the Throne." (Richter 2004: 265)

Gašan-ibizi-bara (M) See Nin-igizi-bara

Gašan-Larak (M) Deity whose name means "Lady of Larak," a town near Isin. Spouse of the god Pabil-sag, who was the tutelary deity of Larak. (Richter 2004: 196)

Gašan-nam-mu (M) Deity attested in a Neo-Assyrian god list. (King 1969: pl. 43)

Gašan-simar-ana (M) See Nin-sigar-ana

Gašan-til-lu-ba (M) See Nin-tin-uga

Gašan-tur-amaš (M) Deity attested in a text from Tell Rimah. Means "Lady (of) Cattle Pen and Sheepfold." (Dalley 1976: 28)

Gašru(m) (M) See Gaṯar(u)

Gaṯar(u) (L, M), **Gašru(m)** (M) Deity attested in deity lists and other texts from Ugarit, where he was probably a warrior god with netherworld associations. The name means "mighty." As Gašru a name or epithet of the netherworld deity Lugal-irra, a form of Nergal. Mentioned in a text referring to the Neo-Babylonian city of Opis, on the Tigris east of Sippar. Occurs in an offering list from Emar and in theo-phoric names from Ebla and Mari. His identification with Mesopotamian Nin-Girsu and Tišpak also suggests that he was a warlike god. How, if at all, he relates to the Ugaritic palace gods, the Gaṯarūma, is unclear. The name also occurs in Phoenician sources in the first millennium BCE. In the Hebrew Bible (Genesis 10:23), the name Gether likely comes from the same root, but whether it is associated with the deity is unclear. (Beaulieu 2003: 339; Pardee 2002: 19, 49; del Olmo Lete 1999: 187; Pardee, *DDDB*: 342–43)

Gattaḫ(ḫ)a (H) See Kattaḫ(ḫ)a

Gatum-dug (M) Principal deity of the city of Lagaš proper. Daughter of An. Also a Lama or protective deity of Baba. Elsewhere sometimes identified with Baba. She occurs in Early Dynastic god lists and the Sumerian zà-mí hymns, as well as in inscriptions from Lagaš. Her titles included "Mother of Lagaš," "Mother who Founded Lagaš," and "Holy One." Gudea, twenty-second century BCE ruler of Lagaš, revered her as the mother who gave him birth and called himself her "man" in the sense of servant or champion. She had temples at Lagaš and Girsu. Her cult is generally unattested after Old Babylonian times. (Cohen 2015: 34; Black and Green 2003: 86; Leick 1999: 62; Litke 1998: 174; Selz 1995: 134–36; George 1993: 97 no. 430, 164 no. 1314; Steible 1989: 507–13; Tallqvist 1974: 309; Falkenstein 1966: 72)

Gaṭurūma (L) Collective name for the deities of the palace at Ugarit. Probably includes deified royal ancestors. (del Olmo Lete 1999: 32, 245, 306)

Gazbaba, **Gazba**, **Kazba**, **Gazbaya** (M) Daughter of the goddess Nanāya. Her sister was Kanisura. The sisters belonged to the E-zida temple in Borsippa. They were important in a Late Babylonian ritual to adjust the imbalance between daytime and night occurring around the solstices. At or around the solstice, Kaṭuna and Silluš-ṭāb, daughters of Aru'a and by profession divine hairdressers, left the E-sag-ila in Babylon for the E-zida in Borsippa. Then, a little later, the sisters Kanisura and Gazbaba proceeded from the temple in Borsippa to Babylon and the E-sag-ila. In Babylonian potency incantations, Gazbaba was invoked along with Nanāya and Ištar. She was often called "Laughing One." In An : *Anum* Dìm-sa-sa is identified with Gazbaba. (Polvani 2010; Durand 2008: 252; Litke 1998: 165; George 1993: 34, 159 no. 1236; Tallqvist 1974: 311; Zimmern 1918: 172–73; Weidner, *RlA* III: 153)

Gazinbu (M) The entry in An : *Anum* is read $^{d.geš}$Gazinbu(=BU)$^{(ga)}$, "Post." (Litke 1998: 167; Tallqvist 1974: 316)

Ge-AN (M) Deity occurring at Ebla in a ritual and an administrative text. Name written with ge_6. (Catagnoti 2009 no. 42)

Geme-Dukuga (M) Daughter of En-nugi. Means "Young Woman of the Holy Mound." (Litke 1998: 59)

Genos and **Genea** (L) Offspring of Aeon and Protogonos in the *Phoenician History* of Philo of Byblos. They were settlers in the Phoenician area. It is unclear which Phoenician deities/heroes Philo was calling by these names. The children of Genos were Fire, Flame, and Light. (Attridge and Oden 1981: 40–41, 80–81 note 46)

Gepar-si (M) Deity attested at Fara. Written Ge_6-par-si. Perhaps "He who Occupies the gipar"? (SF 5: o iv 2)

Gepen (L) See Gapn(u)

Ge-sa-a, Ge-sa-ana (M) Deity identified with the moon god Nanna/Sîn in An : *Anum*. Means "Jewel of Heaven." Written $^{d}Ge_{16}$-sa-an-na (An : *Anum*) and ^{d}Ge-sa-an-na (SpTU 1 126+: o i 10). Note ^{d}Gilim^{lim}-sá in a god list from Aššur with spouse Ilkātum, presumably the plural of *ilku*. (Richter 2004: 451; Litke 1998: 117–18; Schroeder 1920: no. 64)

Gešbanda-kirzal (M) Deity in the circle of Nin-geš-zida. Nin-geš-zida is associated with the city Gešbanda. Name means "Gešbanda Is Joyous." (Litke 1998: 193)

Gešbara (M) Sumerian Deity identified with Gibil/Girra, "Fire." Emesal form is Mubara. (Richter 2004: 205; Litke 1998: 107; Tallqvist 1974: 315)

Gešbar-ana (M) Sumerian name of Gibil/Girra, the god of fire. He is also called Nunbar-ana. (Litke 1998: 107; Tallqvist 1974: 315; Edzard, *RlA* III: 402)

Gešbar-e (M) A local deity from the Lagaš area. Called "surveyor of Enlil" and "farmer at the edge of the steppe." According to Jacobsen, he was responsible, under Nin-Girsu's direction, for the fertility of the fields by making sure the canals were running with water and also that temple granaries were filled. Jacobsen called him Nin-Girsu's plowman. Attested in a god list from Šuruppak dating to the Early Dynastic period. According to economic texts from the Lagaš region Gešbar-e had his own temple and cult there. (Edzard 1997: 95; Jacobsen 1977: 188; Jacobsen 1976: 83; Tallqvist 1974: 315; Falkenstein 1966: 74–75; Edzard, *RlA* III: 402)

Geš-giri (M) In An : *Anum*, one of the eight messengers of Manun-gal, goddess of prisons. Means "Wooden Leg Restraints," a restraining device for prisoners. (Litke 1998: 187)

Geš-gu (M) In An : *Anum*, one of the eight messengers of Manun-gal, goddess of prisons. Means "Neck-stock," a device for restraining prisoners. (Litke 1998: 187)

Gešḫe-dibdib (M) One of the messengers of the prison goddess, Manun-gal. Means "Who Continually Traverses the Firmament." (Litke 1998: 187)

Gešḫur-an-ki (M) The wife of the god Ašgi of Adab. Means "Design of Heaven and Earth." The name appears in the Emesal form Mu-ḫur-an-ki in a late hymn. (Schwemer 2001: 85; Litke 1998: 75; Cohen 1988: 431)

Gešḫur-maḫ-susu (M) In An : *Anum* a goddess in the circle of Nin-imma, Written -sù-sù. May mean "One who Adorns (with) Great Designs." Since Nin-imma was a mother goddess in some traditions and a scholar in others, perhaps our god name refers either to helping the mother goddess imbue the newborn with positive qualities or to helping the scholar goddess carry out her plans for the world or humankind. (Richter 2004: 93; Litke 1998: 56)

Geškad (M) In the lexical series Diri the logogram ^{d}TUM syllabically rendered mi-eš-ka-ad. (Civil 2004)

Gešnu (M) Sumerian name of the sun god Utu/Šamaš. Means "Light." (Litke 1998: 128; Edzard, *RlA* III: 403)

Gešnugal (M) Sumerian name of the moon god Nanna/Sîn. Means "Alabaster," a reference to the color of the moon. (Litke 1998: 117)

Geš-NUMUN-ab (M) The thirty-fifth name of Marduk at the end of the *Enūma eliš*. (Foster 2005: 481; Tallqvist 1974: 315; Speiser, *ANET*: 71)

Geš-nun (M) Patron of fullers. The name quite likely has something to do with cloth/clothing production, perhaps "Noble Weaving Stool" (for geš, "weaving stool," see Waetzoldt, 1972: 130–31). (Litke 1998: 110)

Gešpa (M) One of the messengers of the prison goddess Nungal. Written geš$^{\text{ge-}}$eš-[x]pa. Perhaps for gešpa, "fist," "strongman," perhaps in the sense of one able to control prisoners. (Litke 1998: 187)

Geš-suga (M) see Lugal-geš-bura

Geš-še (M) In An : *Anum*, one of the eight messengers of Manun-gal, goddess of prisons. Written Geš-^{še}šè (Litke 1998: 187)

Geš-šu (M) In An : *Anum*, one of the eight messengers of Manun-gal, goddess of prisons. Means "Manacles" or the like, a restraining device for prisoners. (Litke 1998: 187)

Geštin-ama-na (M) Deity in a votive inscription on a third-millennium bowl from Uruk. This seems to be a form of Ama-geštin(-ana). (Westenholz 2014: no. 216)

Geštin-ana, Geštin, Nin-Geštin-ana, Ama-geštin, Mutin-ana (Emesal) (M) Though a deity of rural areas and fields, which were often named after her, she had temples in many cities. Scribe of Ereškigal and so scribe of the netherworld. Dream interpreter, poet, and singer. Sister of Dumuzi. Wife of Ningeš-zida and later of Amurru(m), when the latter god was identified with Nin-geš-zida. Her name means "Wine Stock of Heaven (or of An)." Her name was Mutin-ana in Emesal. The goddess Ama-geštin, Ama-mutin

(Emesal) "Mother Geštin," who was envisaged as an old woman expert in dream interpretation, was probably the same divinity. Epithets included "(Wise) Old Woman," "Supreme Scribe of the Netherworld," "Song-Knowing Singer," and "Young One who Knows the Sense of Words." Later equated to Akkadian goddess Bēlet-ṣeṣi(m), "Lady of the Open Countryside." Possibly identified with Nin-seše-gara, at least at Bad-tibira. Mentioned as Nin-Geštin-ana in a unique Babylonian Theogony from Dunnu(m).

In mythic compositions Geštin-ana was entwined in the relationship of her brother Dumuzi with the goddess Inana, and it was she who told him about the goddess's love for him. Geštin-ana's most famous involvement in Sumerian myth, however, was in the composition about Inana's journey to the netherworld, at the end of which Geštin-ana apparently chose to become Dumuzi's substitute in the netherworld for half a year. When Dumuzi had a dream about being pursued by demons, Geštin-ana not only interpreted it for him, but, after it came true, helped him to evade the demons as long as possible. In one version of the tale, she would not reveal her brother's whereabouts even though the demons tortured her.

Geštin-ana was revered throughout Sumer, especially before and during the Old Babylonian period, and had many temples, including those at Lagaš, Girsu, Umma, Adab, Puzriš-Dagān, Bad-tibira, Uruk, and Akkad. She was tutelary deity of Sagub, a small town southwest of Girsu in the Lagaš-Girsu area. She sometimes shared a temple with Dumuzi. Festivals were regularly held in her honor. According to Frayne, she might have been identified astrally with the constellation of Triangulum, which is shaped like a grape-leaf. It lies beside Dumuzi's constellation Aries. (*LAS*: 75, 77–84; Cohen 2015: 138; Black and Green 2003: 88; Leick 1998: 67; Sefati 1998: 153, 156; Selz 1995: 19–21; George 1993: 38, 133 no. 882, 140 no. 975, 146 no. 1044, no. 1315; Jacobsen 1976: 27; Tallqvist 1974: 311; Alster 1972: 55, 89; Falkenstein 1966: 73–73; Edzard 1965: 67–68; Grayson, *ANET*: 518; Edzard, *RlA* III: 299–301)

Detail depicting Geštin-an(a) from cylinder seal made of shell. Jonathan P. Rosen Collection. After Porada 1993: 93.

Geštin-ana-ama-lugala (M) Goddess attested in the Ur III period at Umma and associated with offerings to the queen-mother for the new moon. Means "Geštin-ana, Mother of the King." The name attests to a cult of Geštin-ana associated with the mother of the crown prince. (Sallaberger 1993: I, 44)

Geštin-ana-AN.KU-ti (M) Goddess attested in the Ur III period at Umma. AN.KU-ti is attested otherwise as a personal name, but whether that is its use here is unclear. (UTI 5, 3493: o i 11)

Geštin-ana-Dēritum(m) (M) Means "Geštin-ana, She of Dēr," for whom there is an *elūnum* observance at Ur III Ur. (MVN 15, 162: o 6)

Geštin-ana-Du-Arḫatu(m) (M) Sumerian goddess. Means "Geštin-ana of (the Town) Du-Arḫatu(m)," a settlement in the environs of Ur III Umma. (Cohen 1996a: 35)

Geštin-ana-DU.DU (M) Form of the Sumerian goddess Geštin-ana apparently in one of the towns of suburban Ur III Umma. (Cohen 1996a: 31)

Geštin-ana-e-bar-zagina (M) Form of Geštin-ana in a text of the Ur III period from Umma. See Nin-a-bar-zagin. (UTI 5, 4983: o ii 3)

Geštin-ana-ereš (M) Form of Geštin-ana attested from Ur III Umma. Means "Geštin-ana of the Queen." There were cults of Geštin-ana associated with the king, queen, and queen- mother. (Sallaberger 1993: I, 44, 125–27)

Geštin-ana-Esusu (M) Form of Geštin-ana in a text dealing with a town in the environs of Ur III Umma. Means "Geštin-ana (of?) Esusu." (Cohen 1996a: 31)

Geštin-ana-karBU-ka (M) Form of the Sumerian goddess Geštin-ana in a text from Umma. Kar-BÙ is a location and in one text is written Kar-BÙ[ki]. (UTI 5, 3485+: o i 17)

Geštin-ana-Ki'an (M) Form of Geštin-ana. Means "Geštin-ana of (the Town) Ki'an," a place near Umma in the Ur III period. (Cohen 1996a: 31)

Geštin-ana-lugal (M) Form of Geštin-ana attested from Ur III Umma. Means "Geštin-ana of the King." Apparently there was a cult of Geštin-ana associated with the king, queen, and queen-mother. (Sallaberger 1993: I, 44, 125–27)

Geštin-ana-lugal-bata(-ab)e (M) Form of Geštin-ana mentioned in a tablet dealing with a town in the environs of Ur III Umma. (Cohen 1996a: 31)

Geštin-ana-Maškan (M) Deity whose name means "Geštin-ana of (the Town) Maškan," a small settlement in the Umma district in the Ur III period. (UTI 5, 3495+: r i 8)

Geštin-ana-Nanatu(m) (M) Deity whose name means "Geštin-ana of (the Town? of) Nanatu(m)" in the Umma region in the Ur III period. While the town is not actually attested, a Nana-tu(m) canal is mentioned in the Umma texts. (Cohen 1996a: 31)

Geštin-ana-Pasirra (M) A votive offering (a-ru-a) is presented to her in an Ur III text from Šarrakum. (Nisaba 15/2, 348: r 1)

Geštin-ana sag-UL (M) Form of Geštin-ana, a goddess attested in the environs of Umma in the Ur III period. (Cohen 1996a: 31)

Geštin-ana-sud (M) Her temple is attested in the area of Ur III Umma. (AAICAB 1/1, Ashm/ 1911-229: o iv 27)

Geštug (M) (1) Also Geštugani. One of two ministers or viziers of Dam-gal-nuna, wife of Enki. Probably a title of Isimud, Enki's vizier, who might have served both deities. Means "Wise One"; note the deity Ḫasīsu, the Akkadianized rendering of this name. (Litke 1998: 103); (2) A name of the god Ninurta. Occurs in a section of An : *Anum* dealing with a group of gods of a foreign land (undeterminable). (Litke 1998: 214)

Geštug-abzu (M) One of the names of Sumerian god Enki. Means "Wise One of the Abzu." (Litke 1998: 84)

Geštug-a-diri (M) Deity identified with Enki/Ea in a Neo-Assyrian god list. Means "Wise One with Exceeding Power." Note Šulgi B 262 for geštug á-diri. (King 1969: pl. 125; ETCSL)

Geštug-a-gal (M) Deity identified with Enki/Ea in a Neo-Assyrian god list. Means "Wise One with Great Power." (King 1969: pl. 33)

Geštugani (M) See Geštug

Geštug-gal (M) Name of Marduk in An : *Anum*. Means "Great Wise One." (Litke 1998: 223)

Geštug-la (M) Deity identified with Enki. Means "He who Pays Attention," literally "One who Extends the Ear," Akkadian *uzna tarāṣu*, which is appropriate, since in literature it is usually Enki/Ea who listens to and responds to the problems of humankind. (Litke 1998: 84)

Geštug-šega (M) Name of Marduk in An : *Anum*. Means "He who Listens." (Litke 1998: 223)

Geštug-ušum (M) Name of Marduk in An : *Anum*. Means "Unique Wise One." (Litke 1998: 223)

Geš-zida (M) See Nin-geš-zida

Gibil, Girra (Sum.), **Girru** (Borrowed into Akkadian), **Išātu(m)** (Akk.) God of fire in all its manifestations, including the scorching heat of summer, and god of smiths and other metal-workers. Gibil occurs in god lists from the Early Dynastic period. Semitic form Išatu(m) is attested at Early Dynastic Ebla. In late texts, in particular, Gibil and Girra were interchangeable as fire gods, though probably at one time they were separate deities, since each appears in the same texts from the Old Babylonian period. Gibil and Girra both mean "Fire," but Girra probably originated as the god who caused reed fires. On the one hand, Gibil was feared for his propensity to start fires, but, on the other, he was often invoked in incantations as the destroyer, burner, of evil demons and witches, thus aiding the gods Enki/Ea, Marduk, and Utu/Šamaš in combating them.

In An : *Anum* he belongs to the circle of Enki/Ea and appears just before the artisan deities. The fire god was son of An/Anu(m) or, in some traditions, Enki/Ea and hence called "son of the Abzu," and in an Old Babylonian composition, the son of Enlil. His mother was Šala and his wife Nin-Irigala. He was agent and messenger of Nuska, sometimes even named as his son. Elsewhere he was the vizier of Enlil, presumably identified with Nuska. He had strong connections to Enki/Ea and Eridu, Enki/Ea's cult city, and also to Utu/Šamaš. As a result of his involvement in incantations, he became closely associated with the god Asar-lu-ḫe. His symbol (or counselor according to An : *Anum*) was the torch or brand. In an Old Babylonian composition he is "the purifier par excellence." (Michalowski 1993). His epithets include: "Fighter/Hero of Ea," "Light Bringer," and "Judge." His dwelling was Irigal, a term for the netherworld.

Gibil/Girra did not have a large part to play in mythic material, though, when he appears, he usually assisted another god, normally in doing damage. His name was the forty-sixth title of Marduk proclaimed at the end of the

Enūma eliš. Gibil/Girra was mentioned in prayers and compositions, and he was invoked in treaties to carry out curses: "May Girra, who provides food for young and old, burn your offspring and descendants" (Reiner, *ANET*: 539). Aside from being honored in Enki/Ea's Abzu temple at Eridu, Gibil had a place in Nuska's temple at Nippur. In rituals called "Burning," performed in the month in which festivals for the dead took place and when both benign and malevolent ghosts from the netherworld joined the living, nightly incantations were dedicated to Girra and Nuska with the aim of protecting the living. The fire god is attested sporadically in offering lists from the Early Dynastic, Ur III, and Old Babylonian periods.

(Cohen 2015: 419; Foster 2005: 482, 660–63, 763–65; Black and Green 2003: 88; Leick 1998: 68; Litke 1998: 107; Pomponio and Xella 1997: 185, 201; Michalowski 1993: 156–57; George 1993: 124 no. 767; Tallqvist 1974: 313–15; Kramer, *ANET*: 391, 458, 459, 640; Reiner, *ANET*: 533, 539; Speiser, *ANET*: 72; Edzard 1965: 68–69; Frankena, *RlA* III: 383–85)

Gidim, **Udug** (Sum.), **Eṭemmu(m)**, **Utukku(m)** (Borrowed into Akkadian) (M) Ghost of a dead person who lived in the netherworld. Also a ghost who returned to the earth to wander about and make trouble for the living.

In Mesopotamia, as in many other cultures, not only had the dead to receive correct burial rites, but their spirits had to be regularly cared for after death through funerary rituals and offerings, called *kispu(m)* in Akkadian and *gizbun* in Sumerian. In Mesopotamia the offerings were made primarily by a *pādiqu(m)* or *sāhiru(m)*, a caretaker, normally a family member, whose job was to ensure that the spirits were duly honored by providing them regular food and water and proper recognition through the ritual invoking of their names. Texts dating to the eighteenth century BCE from Mari state that this ritual should be performed four times a month. Such meals shared with the spirits of the ancestors reinforced family solidarity both backward and forward in time: the ancestors, the living, and descendants were linked together in a long line of relationship. These practices maintained social connections making the living and the dead interdependent. By ensuring that the dead received offerings, the living might get favors from the dead. Kings held such ritual meals for dead ancestors in the hope that the ancestor spirits would bless their tenure on the throne. The same cult practices were found at Ebla, Ugarit, and elsewhere. Indeed, the remains of a funerary feast were unearthed at Mešrifeh, ancient Qaṭna. Ancestors could intercede for the living with various gods and with the assembly of the gods.

In Sumer, spirits or shades of dead persons in the netherworld had to be not only propitiated, but venerated to keep them from haunting or hurting the living. This was a primary concern of the concluding section of "The Death of Gilgameš," in which Ur-lugal, Gilgameš's son, was called upon to pour out drink offerings for his father. An angry ghost could become an evil demon. This change might result from its having received a paucity or lack of offerings and rites or having suffered an irregular or violent death, lack of burial or proper burial, and such. If wandering angrily on earth, a ghost might "seize" a living person by entering through the ear and could cause disease, especially psychological.

Magic could be effective against a malevolent ghost. Exorcism was also used to expel such ghosts, who were often associated with demons. In Babylonia, ghosts could be raised to be asked questions about various subjects including the future (necromancy), and a number of necromantic rituals have survived. Healing rituals, incantation and curse collections, magical and medical texts deal with, among other things, the problems caused by malevolent and troublesome ghosts. (Black and Green 2003: 88–89; Frayne 2001: 143–54; Abusch, *DDDB*: 309–12; Lewis, *DDDB*: 225–26; Tropper, *DDDB*: 807–8; Ebeling, *RlA* II: 108)

Gidri-kal(ag) (M) Deity appears in texts from Lagaš in the Early Dynastic period in similar contexts to the god Gidri-palil. He received offerings in the town of Nimen during the great Nanše festival. (Selz 1995: 272; Krebernik, *RlA* X: 190)

Gidri-palil (M) Sumerian god attested in texts from Lagaš in the Early Dynastic period. He received offerings in the town of Nimen during the great Nanše festival held there. (Selz 1995: 271–72; Krebernik, *RlA* X: 190)

Gidri-šudu (M) Deity identified with the sun god Utu/Šamaš as king of righteousness. Means "(He) who Holds the Scepter." Written with gloss gi_6-idra. (Litke 1998: 128 no. 104)

GIG (M) Deity occurring in a personal name from Ur III Umma. (BCT 2, 2: r 28)

GIGIR-gi-zi (M) Deity attested in the Early Dynastic period. (Bartash 2013: no. 8)

Gi-izi-la (M) Bull-lyre of Gibil/Girra. Means "Torch." (Litke 1998: 108)

Gilima (M) Thirty-first name of Marduk proclaimed at the end of the *Enūma eliš*. The thirtieth (Gil) and the thirty-second (Agilima) of the Marduk names are also related to Gilima. They were probably aspects of the same deity, but might originally have represented different gods. Gilima means "Twiner" or "Twister." (Foster 2005: 480; Litke 1998: 93; Tallqvist 1974: 312; Speiser, *ANET*: 71; Lambert, *RlA* III: 374)

Girida (M) See Nin-Girida

GIRI-ena (M) Sumerian deity appearing in an Ur III economic text from Puzriš-Dagān. May mean 'Agent of the *en*-prest." Occurs in connection with the installation of the *en* priestess of Kar-zida, a port city near Ur. The name follows immediately after a reference to the gate of the *gipar* residence of the *en*. (Krebernik, *RlA* X: 572)

GIRI-e-pa (M) Sumerian deity appearing on an Old Akkadian tablet, probably from Adab. Means "... of Dike and Ditch." (Maiocchi 2009: no. 119, no. 156)

Gi-ri-ku (M) Deity associated with the circle of Nin-Isina/Nin-kar(r)ak of Isin. Written Gi-ri-kú in an Old Babylonian god list. In An : *Anum* the corresponding entry is [ ]-ì-kud with gloss me-er-i-ku-ud "cutting knife." (Richter 2004: 216)

Gir-kalama (M) One of the children of Nin-Girida. Written in an Old Babylonian god list Gir_{16}-kalam-ma with variant Gìr- in An : *Anum*. (Richter 2004: 491; Litke 1998: 491; Green 1978: 146)

Gir-nun (M) Deity attested in Early Dynastic school texts from Fara. Written Gír-nun and Gir$_x$(UM)-nun. See Gangir-nun and Lugal-gir-nun, both written -gír. (Cohen 1988: 128)

Girra (M) See Gibil

Girtab-lu-ulu (Sum.), **Girtablulû(m)** (Borrowed into Akkadian from Sumerian) (M) Deity whose name means "Scorpion-man," a human-animal hybrid with the horned headdress of divinity. Human upper body, bird-like lower body, and scorpion tail. In later images winged. Sometimes held a bow and arrow. Associated with other fabulous creatures. Guardians of entrances and doorways. Attendants of Utu/Šamaš, they supported the god in battle. Sometimes Girtab-lu-ulu held up a winged sun disk. By Neo-Assyrian times, they were seen as defenders against demons. They were guardians of the mountain of sunrise and sunset at Mt. Mašu(m). In the Babylonian "Epic of Gilgameš," Gilgameš encounters a scorpion-man and his wife at the gateway of the passage through which the sun traversed the mountain. The scorpion-man was one of the fighters Ti'amat fashioned in the *Enūma eliš* to help her in her battle against the younger deities. A lyre found in the Royal Graves at Ur was decorated with the image of a scorpion-man. (J. Westenholz 2004: 24–25; Black and Green 2003: 161; Foster 2001: 67–69; Wiggermann 1992: 180–81; Heidel 1967: 24; Wiggermann, *RlA* VIII: 242)

Girwa(š) (E) See Kirmaš

Gi-tur (M) Deity attested in an Early Dynastic god list. Written gi$_6$-tùr. (Mander 1986: 140)

Giškim-ti (M) Child of Gaa'u in An : *Anum*. Means "Trustworthy One." (Litke 1998: 126)

Grm-wa-'mqt (L) Deity or pair of deities on the canonical list of gods at Ugarit. (del Olmo Lete 1999: 73, 79)

Gu (M) Deity listed in *Anu ša amēli* as "Enlil of Everything." Written gú. (Litke 1998: 229)

Gu-ana (M) See Alû(m)

Gu-ane-si (M) Reconstruction of a goddess whose name means "(Whose) Voice Fills the Heavens." Two entries in An : *Anum*, both identified with Ereškigal, appear to be variants: Kù-an-né-si and Gu-a-nu-si. (Litke 1998: 188, 196; Tallqvist 1974: 343–44, 353)

Gu-ane-sil (M) Sumerian name of Uraš, god of Dilbat. Means "Whose Voice Splits the Heavens." (Litke 1998: 172)

Gu-an-KA (M) Deity in an Ur III personal name from Umma. Perhaps name related to gú(-an-šè) "everything." (Nisaba 23, 3: o iii 2)

Gu-a-nu-si (M) See Gu-ane-si

Gu-a-nun-gi-a (M) Deity who was in the circle of Nergal deities. Attested in a variety of writings at Old Babylonian Nippur and in an Old Babylonian god list. Name may mean "Bull that Wields Great Strength." The name was later rendered into Akkadian as "The Warrior who Cannot Be Opposed." (Richter 2004: 79; Litke 1998: 200; Selz 1997a: 172; Cohen 1988: 516; Mander 1986: 47)

Gubaba (H) See Kubaba

Gu-bara (M) Sumerian name of Ašratu(m), wife of Mardu/Amurru(m). Her title was "Lady of the Steppe." gú-bar means "outer edge," which seems to agree with her connection to the steppe. See Nin-gú-bar-ra, a name of Inana. (Litke 1998: 218; Tallqvist 1974: 318)

Gubba-gara-e, Tumma-gara-e (M) Deity at Nippur. One of the seven children of netherworld god En-me-šara. Identified with Nin-ka-si, the beer goddess, who was responsible for providing beverages for the temples at Nippur. The name occurs with the variants ga-ra and $gara_{10}$ (GA+NI) "cream." Thus we suggest reading Gub-ba/Tum-ma-gara{ra}-è "Attendant who Brings Out the Cream," which agrees with the deity's involvement with beverages. Said to be an inhabitant of the new city, probably a city quarter of Nippur. Appears in a ritual of Seleucid times that a priest performed when covering a kettledrum. (Litke 1998: 36; Livingstone 1986: 200; Thureau-Dangin 1975: 16–17; Tallqvist 1974: 319; Sachs, *ANET*: 335, 337)

Gubi (M) Deity at Ebla for whom an *izi-gar* observance was performed. Written Gú-bi. (Waetzoldt 2001)

Gubla (M) Along with Igi-tal, a courier of Šerzi-mah-ana, a form of the sun god, in an incantation. George suggests that these may be variant names for the god pair Kardu and Sakardu, also identified as a pair of couriers of the sun god. (George 2016: no. 47)

Gud-alim (M) See Kusarikku(m)

GUD.BALAG (M) May be an orthography for the bull-lyre Adgigi. (Litke 1998: 77)

Gudgud (M) Sumerian netherworld deity. See Qarrādu(m)

Gud-melem (M) Deity identified with Nin-geš-zida. Written Gúd-me-lem_4. Means "Hero, Radiance." (Litke 1998: 192)

Gudnua (M) Sumerian deity attested at Ur III Umma. Means "Bovine (Who Has) Lain Down (or disappeared)." There was a festival at Umma referred to as ezem-gud-nú (SAT 3, 1760: o 9; SAT 3, 2151: o ii 24)

Gudnura (M) Goddess from the pantheon of Isin. Possibly a healing goddess. Daughter of Gula as Nin-Isina and her spouse Pabil-sag. One of her epithets was "Daughter of the House." The earliest evidence of her cult comes from Isin in the Ur III period, where she occurred in theophoric names. Her "seat" in one of the temples in Babylon was called "House of Pure Heaven." In a god list of Old Babylonian times Gunura is given as the second name of Gula. (George 1993: 36; Edzard, *RlA* III: 701–2)

Gud-ti (M) Deity attested in an Early Dynastic god list from Abu Ṣalābīkh. (Mander 1986: 21)

Gu-duga-lalbi (M) Wife of Dunga, patron god of singers. Means "A Sweet Voice like Syrup." (Litke 1998: 104)

Gudu-nun (M) Deity attested in an Early Dynastic god list. Means "Foremost *gudu*-priest." (Mander 1986: 140)

Gu-gal (M) Twenty-sixth name of Marduk at the end of the *Enūma eliš*. Probably occurred in An : *Anum* in a section associated with Marduk and shortly after En-bilulu, but the tablet is broken. Means "Canal Inspector." (Foster 2005: 479; Litke 1998: 93; Speiser, *ANET*: 71; Heidel 1967: 56)

Gugal-ana (M) Ereškigal's first husband, whose recent death, according to "The Descent of Inana," was Inana's excuse for visiting her sister in the netherworld. Means "Canal Inspector of Heaven." An ancient, popular interpretation of the name as "Great Bull of

Heaven" is probably incorrect. (*LAS*: 65–76; Leick 1998: 77; Litke 1998: 188)

Gugalita (M) In the lexical series Diri ^{d}GUD is rendered syllabically as gu-ga-li-ta. (Civil 2004)

Gu-gim (M) See Ga-gim

Gug-gala (M) See Zagul-kala

Gugim, Gagim (M) Patron deity of craftsmen, possibly workers in poor-quality wool or lint resulting from combing wool. Name is written ^{d}MUG-$^{gu\text{-}qi\text{-}im}$ and ḪAR. The name may mean "Like Flax," that is, a substitute for the finer-quality material. His wife is also written MUG or ḪAR with gloss ga-qi-im. The DCCLT reads ^{d}GÍR, which is quite similar to MUG, in the lexical series Diri where ^{d}GÍR is rendered syllabically as qù-qi$_4$-im and qá-qi$_4$-im. (Civil 2004; Litke 1998: 108, 109; Tallqvist 1974: 321)

Gu-guana (M) Deity in an Old Babylonian god list from Mari. gú-an-na might be syllabic for guana "battle" and gu, usually "thread," is attested as "net, web," thus perhaps "Net of Battle." (Studies Birot, 184–85: r ii 26)

Gugumu (M) Deity allocated offerings and an article of clothing at Ur III Umma. Written Gú-gú-mu. (SAT 2, 190: r i 22)

Gu(gu)muktir (E) Elamite deity occurring in a treaty between Narām-Sîn of Akkad and a king of Susa. (König 1977: 29, 197, 227)

Guḫaš, Guḫaš-lala (M) God associated with the sun god Utu/Šamaš as a counselor. Written with gloss ḫa-aš. Means "Nape of the Neck." Appears in An : *Anum* after a list of children and messengers of Utu/Šamaš. In An : *Anum*, the right-side column indicates, in both Sumerian and Akkadian, an epithet meaning "(With) a Beautiful Face" or having a "Shining Face." Guḫaš-lala is a form of Guḫaš in a late text from Uruk. (Richter 2004: 350, 352; Litke 1998: 133)

Gula (M) (1) Sumerian great goddess of healing, medicine, and health, who could also inflict disease. Patron of physicians. Means "The Greatest One," which appears to be the case of an epithet displacing the original divine name. Her titles include: "The Great Mother" and "Mother Gula." In treaties she was referred to as the great physician. She was identified with Nin-kar(r)ak, Nin-tin-uga, Gunura, and Meme, all goddesses in their own right. Bēlat-balāṭi "Lady of Life" was another name of Gula. She was the daughter of An/Anu(m) and consort of Ninurta or Pabil-sag, Lord of Isin. When identified with Baba, she was also the consort of Nin-Girsu. In one tradition she was wife of Ab-u, a god of plants. Two of her seven children were the healing god Damu, who was especially venerated at Isin, and the netherworld god Nin-azu, associated with healing as well. Her vizier was Urmašu.

Gula did not play a prominent part in myth, but she was important in healing rituals and incantations. Those who were deathly ill sought her help by oracles and *šu-ila*, "hand-lifting" incantations. In a literary prayer-letter, King Sîn-iddinam applied to her for healing from his illness. She was sometimes appealed to in law codes and treaties. For instance, the law code of Ḫammurāpi invoked her as Nin-kar(r)ak and asked her to inflict "an evil disease" upon anyone desecrating the stele (Meek, *ANET*: 180).

Gula's main cult center was Isin, where she held the title Nin-Isina "Lady of Isin." Her temple there was the Egalmaḫ "Exalted Palace." She also had temples at most other cities, including Umma, Ur, Borsippa, Sippar, Nippur, Uruk, Larsa, Aššur, and Larak. She had three temples at Babylon. Sometimes she shared a temple with Ninurta. Festivals of Gula are attested as having been held at Umma, Larsa, and Ur. At Umma her statue was carried about in a festival procession. Throughout the land in Assyrian times, during a festival to celebrate Ninurta's victory over the Anzû-bird, foot races were run. According to a record of this festival, a dog running about was "a messenger" from Gula, who had sent it on account of [Ninurta].

Gula with her dog, a detail of from a boundary marker. 978–943 BCE. Stone. After Black and Green 2003: 101.

Gula and Ninurta were protectors of boundaries and boundary stones. Gula's name appears frequently in curse formulas on *kudurrus,* along with her image. She is depicted sitting on a throne, with her sacred dog beside her. The dog was her symbol; models of dogs were dedicated to her in her temples. A large number of dog burials were un-earthed in her precinct at Isin; the dog bones were probably remains of sacrifices made on behalf of sick persons.

(2) Wife of Nergal.

(3) A name of the god Enki/Ea as the constellation Aquarius.

(Cohen 2015: 88; Foster 2005: 583–91, 668–72; Black and Green 2003: 101; Leick 1999: 65–66, 157; Leick 1998: 132–33; Litke 1998: 174, 181; George 1993: 68 no. 92, 88 no. 319–23, 96 no. 424,101 no. 485, 158 no. 1208; Sallaberger 1993: II, 191; Tallqvist 1974: 316–17; Reiner, *ANET*: 534, 538; Frankena and Sollberger, *RlA* III: 695–97)

Gula-Isala (M) The Sumerian goddess Gula at the town of Isala in the Umma region. (UTI 5, 3493)

Gula-Kian (M) The Sumerian healing goddess Gula at the town of Kian near Umma. (BRM 3 45)

Gula-Umma (M) The Sumerian goddess Gula at Umma in the Ur III period. (AnOr 1, 32: r 6)

Gula-zida (M) Form of the healing goddess Gula. Means "Dependable Gula." (Richter 2004: 224)

Gu-la (M) Deity attested at Nippur in the Ur III period. Written gú-lá. Means "embrace," "to put (one's arms) around (somebody's) neck," a sign of affection. (Sallaberger 1993: I, 103)

Guladu (M) Deity coupled with the god Agû(m) in an offering list from Ebla. See Agû(m). (Archi 1993: 74)

Guli-ana (M) Deity identified with Dumuzi. May mean "Dragonfly" or, in light of another name of Dumuzi, Kuli-Enlilla, may mean "Friend of

An." Occurs in the Sumerian love songs as a name of Ama-ušum-gal-ana/ Dumuzi. (Sefati 1998: 187, 282)

Guli-Enlila (M) Deity identified with Dumuzi. Means "Friend of Enlil." Occurs in the Sumerian love songs as a name of Ama-ušum-gal-ana/Dumuzi. (Sefati 1998: 125)

Gulša, Gulza, Gulšeš, Gulašša, Gulzannika, Gulzan(n)ikeš (H) A collection of Hittite netherworld and house goddesses, fate-determining and involved with fertility. Probably originally in the Palaic pantheon. In the composition about the disappearance of Telipinu, the group is consulted on how to find him. Though the reading of the name is somewhat unclear, the *gulš* element means "to mark, carve, split," perhaps emphasizing Gulša's function as recorder or "splitter of fate." The group is depicted at Yazılıkaya and named there as Ḫutena and Ḫutellura (Ḫudena-Ḫudellurra). Generally, in god/offering lists Gulša is associated with Dingir-maḫ or Nin-tu(d), birth/mother goddesses, and in an Akkadian-Hurrian list followed by Dingir-maḫ. These associations suggest that the group was involved with birthing. However, in a Hurrian list of goddesses the collection was adjacent to the love goddess Išḫara. Gulša appears often in incantations as either malevolent or benevolent. In Hattic called Eštutaya-Papaya. (Hoffner 1998: 21, 28; Leick 1998: 77; van Gessel 1998: I. 249–55; Popko 1995: 114; Haas 1994: 398, 372 and note 448, 449, 611; Otten, *RlA*: III: 698)

Gunisura (M) See Kanisura

Gupan (L) See Gapn(u)

Gu-ru (M) Sumerian deity attested in a personal name in tablet from Umma of the Ur III period. (AUCT 2, 259: o 5)

Gu-ru-un (M) Likely a variant spelling for the Sumerian goddess Gunura in a Middle Babylonian inventory text from Isin. See Gunura. (Richter 2004: 208)

Gušaratu(m) (M) Goddess attested in the texts from Ebla who may be identified as Kōṯart(u). (Pasquali 2006: no. 64)

Gušāya (M) See Agušāya

Gu-šudu (M) Deity attested in texts from Lagaš in the Early Dynastic period. The deity occurs only in connection with the ruler Ur-Nanše, who fashioned a statue of the god. Name written gú šu-du$_8$. (Selz 1995: 139; Cooper 1986: 25)

Guza-Enlila (M) Deified throne of Enlil. King Amar-Suen of Ur had the throne of Enlil made for the Ekur in Nippur according to the year formula for his third year. Still given offerings in the Old Babylonian period. (Richter 2004: 57; Sallaberger 1993: I, 99–102, 112)

—H—

Had(d)ad, Hadd(u) (L) See Ba'lu/ Had(d)ad

Harosh (L) See Koṯar

Hawwat (L) See Ḥawwa(h)

Heliogabalus, Heliogabalos (L) See Elegabal(us)

Hiyon (L) See Koṯar

Host of Heaven (L) The divine assembly surrounding the heavenly king YHWH in the Hebrew Bible. In this respect the deity was "Lord of Hosts" (Isaiah 6:3, 5). The origin of the concept was probably the idea that the deity was a warrior and needed the support of warriors and an army (II Kings 6:17, Isaiah 13: 4–5). The Host of Heaven became astral and included the sun, moon, and stars (II Kings 23:5, Psalm 148:2–3). The worship of this astral Host of Heaven was conducted on rooftops (Jeremiah 19:13) and also in the Jerusalem temple (II Kings 23:4). This cult was among the targets of the reforms of King Josiah (II Kings 23). Eventually the title gained the meaning of "divine council." The phrase occurs twice in the New Testament, once in a quotation from the Hebrew Bible (Acts 7: 42) and once probably meaning the assembly of angels (Luke 2: 13). The pattern was likely the Divine Assembly, which usually surrounded the high god(s) of polytheistic traditions. (Smith 2001: 63, 96; Niehr, *DDDB*: 428–30; Handy 1994; Anderson, *IDB* 1991: II, 654–56)

—Ḥ—

Ḥawwa(h), Hawwa(h), Hawwat, Chava, Eve (L) According to the Hebrew Bible, the first woman, created from one of the ribs of the first man, Adam. (Genesis 2:21–22). After their expulsion from Eden, Adam named the woman Eve, Ḥawwa(h), which is probably associated with the Hebrew root *ḥaya* meaning "live" (Genesis 3: 20). Scholars have pointed out that the Arabic word *ḥayya* means "snake" and Eve's name may refer to her disastrous dealings with the serpent in Genesis 3: 1–7. Later Jewish writings called Eve "Adam's snake." One form of the Sumerian birth goddess is Nin-ti, which can mean "Lady Life" but also "Lady Rib (or Arrow)." S. N. Kramer, aware of Mesopotamian influences in the stories of Genesis, suggested that the story of Eve's creation from a rib may have resulted from a word play based on Sumerian ti meaning both "life" and "rib." (Genesis 4:1–2; 5:3–4).

A divine being Hawwat was invoked in a magical text and in an inscription from Carthage. Others have seen Eve as being associated with the Hurrian goddess Ḫebat, consort of the storm god Teššub, but this is unlikely. In the New Testament, Eve was the symbol of all women and responsible for the loss of Paradise (2 Corinthians 11: 3; 1 Timothy 2: 13). In early Christianity and later, the Virgin Mary was understood as the Second Eve, with temptress Eve being balanced by the paragon Mary. (Anderson 2001; Markoe 2000: 131; Kvam 1999; Wyatt, *DDDB*: 316–17; Lipiński 1995: 412–14; Comay 1993: 106; Lipiński, *DCPP*: 212; Phillips 1984; Warner 1983: 50–67)

Ḥokmah, Hokmot (L) Wisdom. Either a minor goddess, an angel-like being, or a literary personification in the Hebrew Bible and the Apocrypha (Proverbs 1–9, Ecclesiasticus or Ben Sirach, Baruch, and Wisdom). As goddess she was patron of scribes, and her realm encompassed intellect, statecraft, knowledge, and shrewdness. Some scholars have argued that, though Wisdom was originally a goddess, over time and with the development of monotheism, she became no more than a figure of speech. "Lady Wisdom" was "begotten" by the Lord before he created anything else, and she watched the process of creation (Proverbs 8:22–31). Later Jewish writings slowly modified this view. Dating around the first century BCE, Ecclesiasticus or Ben Sirach (24: 1–10) identified Wisdom with the Pentateuch, seeing her as the creative word of the deity. In the Book of Baruch, Wisdom became merely a personification, though some elements in the description of wisdom echoed her earlier divine nature (Baruch 3: 29–32). The Book of Wisdom, written in Greek in Alexandria, Egypt, and dating to the first century CE, describes her as "the breath of the power of God," that is, an emanation of the deity spreading throughout creation (Wisdom 7: 22–26). Nonetheless, the text describes her in very personal terms as being like a goddess and pictures her as the king's consort (8: 9). Indeed she sits by the throne of the deity (9: 40). In Gnostic Christianity she had a variety of roles, including mother of God and bride of Jesus. The Greeks called her Sophia. (Leeming 2005: 172,

362; Lang, *DDDB*: 900–5; Patai 1990: 97–99; Long 1988: 21–61)

Ḥoron(u), Ḥoran(u), Horon, Hauran, Haurun, Hawran (L) Levantine netherworld god with power over snakes. Attested in the Levant from the second millennium BCE until about 600 BCE. Name might mean "Deep One" and be related to a Semitic root meaning "depression, cavity, or hole." At Ugarit, Ḥoron(u) appears in the mythic compositions as a deity who could be relied upon to carry out curses: for instance, in *Keret*, King Keret tells his overly ambitious son, "May Horon [sic] crack your head" (Parker 1997a: 42). Ba'lu used this curse during his fight with the sea god Yam. Ḥoron took a major part in the difficult composition "The Mare and Horon [sic]" (Parker 1997c: 219–23), which concerns the mare goddess's attempts to find a spell against snake-bite. After eleven different deities had been asked for help, Ḥoron deals with the problem by rendering the snakes harmless. In another ritual text Ḥoron, helped by the sun goddess Šapaš, banishes snakes from the land.

Ḥoron is featured in theophoric names at Mari. In the Hebrew Bible, Ḥoron appears in the place names Lower and Upper Beth-Ḥoron, two towns near Jerusalem (Joshua 16:3, 5). Meaning "House (or Temple) of Ḥoron," the name probably marked the towns as his cult sites. Ḥoron's cult was practiced by Syro-Canaanites living in Egypt, where, in one source, he aided worshippers against demons. At Giza he was equated to the Great Sphinx. He was sometimes identified with the Egyptian god Horus. In the first millennium BCE, the veneration of Ḥoron made its way through the Mediterranean world. He was mentioned in Phoenician and Punic inscriptions in which he seemed to have been a protective and healing deity. A Greek inscription from Apollo's island of Delos states that he would accept all sacrifices except goats. (Dietrich and Loretz 2003; Pardee 2002: 172–79, 179–84; Wyatt 2002: 56, 241, 384–86; del Olmo Lete 1999: 55, 312–13, 359–70; Rüterswörden, *DDDB*: 425–26; Leick 1998: 80; Finnegan 1997: 147; Parker 1997a: 5, 98, 222–23; Lipiński 1995: 363–66; Xella, *DCPP*: 219–20; Oldenburg, 1969: 43; Albright 1968: 138)

Ḥoṭer Miskar (L) Phoenician-Punic deity attested at Carthage and elsewhere. Means "Scepter of the Herald." (Lipiński 1995: 175–76; Lipiński, *DCPP*: 220)

—Ḫ—

Ḫa'abatu (M) See Ḫalabatu

Ḫa'a'u (M) Goddess whose name is written with the NAGAR sign with gloss Ḫa-a-a-u in An : *Anum*. Explained in An : *Anu ša amēli* as "Nisaba of Prosperity (*mašrê*)." (Litke 1998: 216, 235)

Ḫabatali (H) See Ḫapantali(ya)

Ḫabūr (m.), **Ḫabūru(m)**, **Ḫabūritu(m)** (f.) (L) See Ḫubur

Ḫaḫḫimas (H) A Hittite personification of a mighty and fearsome element in the ritual story "The Disappearance of the Sun God." Hoffner tentatively translates the name "Frost," since the creature can paralyze all nature and all life. (Hoffner 1998: 14–27, 28, 110; Popko 1995: 120)

Ḫaḫḫina (H) See Ammamma

Ḫain (M) Occurs in a unique account of the origin and descent of the deities (Theogony) from the obscure Babylonian city, Dunnu(m) (or the generic name "Fortress"). Ḫain, otherwise unattested, and goddess Earth created the female Sea by plowing. Then they produced the god Šamagan, who killed his father and, with Earth, began an incestuous and murderous line of deities. (Grayson, *ANET*: 517–18)

Ḫala (M) Kassite deity who occurs only in a personal name. (Brinkman 1976: 255)

Ḫa(l)abatu (M) The goddess "She of Ḫalab," wife of Hadda of Ḫalab. Attested in texts from Ebla. (Archi 1994)

Ḫal-an-kug (M) One of the names of both Enki/Ea and his wife Dam-galnunna/Damkina. The é-ḫal-an-kù was a temple of Enki. Note also the é-ḫal-an-ki shrine of Enki/Ea in the E-sagil temple of Marduk in Babylon. George understands ḫal in the name of the shrine to mean "secret." (Litke 1998: 83, 89; George 1993: 98)

Ḫalba (H, L) An obscure Hurrian deity appearing in ritual texts at Ugarit. (del Olmo Lete 1999: 340)

Ḫalbaē, **Ḫarbaḫe** (M) The storm/weather god of Aleppo, mentioned in a handful of texts from Middle Babylonian Nuzi. (Schwemer 2001: 465)

Ḫaldi (M) The chief god of the Urarṭean pantheon. The pantheon was headed by a triad made up of the supreme god Ḫaldi; the god of storms Teišeba, apparently a form of the Hurrian storm god Teššub; and Šiuini, a solar god. (Durand 2008: 314; Schwemer 2001: 446)

Ḫalḫala (M) Deity identified in a Neo-Assyrian god list with Ninurta and explained as "Colleague(?) in (the making of) decisions by Father Enlil." Also a divine river. (George 2016: no. 5; King 1969: pl. 11)

Ḫalib (M) Netherworld deity who is attested in an Ur III text from Puzriš-Dagān. The reading [d]IGI.KUR is in OB Diri 137 in the Personal Name Lists. See Egi/Ereš-ḫalib. (refs. courtesy A. Kleinerman; Civil 2004)

Ḫalipinu (H) Hattic divinity in the circle of the warrior god Aštabi/Zababa. Means "Among the Children." (van Gessel 1998: I, 71–72; Haas 1994: 156, 310–11; Laroche 1946/47: 21)

Ḫalki (H) Hittite deity of grain. Means "Grain." Usually seen as female, but possibly male. One of her titles was "Corn Mother." A Hattic god of grain called Kait was male. In Hurrian texts, equated to Nisaba. She was also identified with Kumarbi. Ḫalki occurred, along with Telipinu and Sumuqan, in festival rituals. Invoked in Hittite treaties. She was an important goddess at Kanesh and at Zippalanda north of Ḫattušas. (Wilhelm 2010; Archi 2004; van Gessel 1998: I, 72–76; Popko 1995: 56, 71, 73–74, 89, 99, 112, 117, 146; Haas 1994: 274–306; von Weiher, *RlA* IV: 60)

Ḫallāba (M) The storm/weather god of Aleppo worshipped in a festival at Emar. (Schwemer 2001: 490)

Ḫalma (H, L, M) Deity of Syrian origin. As a West Semitic deity 'Alma/'Alama means "Eternity." Occurred in Hittite sources. Associated with the cult of Išḫara in one of the Hittite provinces. Also mentioned in an offering list and other texts from Emar, where a month was named for him. Appeared as Alama in texts from Nineveh dated to the first millennium BCE. May be a variant spelling of the ancient name of Aleppo, Ḫalab. Might also be related to the Hebrew Bible's El-'Olām. In the lexical series Diri the god and his spouse's names are written with the logograms dEN.U.KID and dNIN.U.KID and syllabically rendered ḫa-al-mu and ḫa-la-mu respectively. (Cohen 2015: 275; Civil 2004; Pomponio and Xella 1997: 417; van Gessel 1998: I, 77; Haas 1994: 568; Fleming 1992a: 244; Charpin 1987a: 92; van der Toorn, *DDDB*: 312–13)

Ḫalmaš(š)uit, **Ḫanuašuit** (H) Hattic/Hittite deity who protected the king. The divinized throne/throne goddesses at the Hittite capital Ḫattušas. From the Ancient Anatolian/Hattic tradition and borrowed by Hittite from Hattic. As state deity she had a military aspect. Called "Great Princess/Prince" in one city. Had an important role in cult, particularly with kingship. She had a major role in a ritual for building a new palace. Appears in Old Hittite texts, especially those concerning rites of palace purification, and in festival rituals, often associated with Zababa. Also in an offering list from Emar. (Leick 1998: 78; van Gessel 1998: I, 77–79; Popko 1995: 56, 70, 71 and note 161, 76, 80–81; Haas 1994: 11, 188; von Weiher, *RlA* IV: 62)

Ḫalmutum (M) Deity occurring in a personal name at Ur III Umma and Šarrakum. Written ḫal-mu-TÚM. (UTI 3, 1913: o 3)

Ḫalputili (H) Deity, not to be associated with the Syrian city of Aleppo. (van Gessel 1998: I, 79–80; Haas 1994: 299, 701 note 32; von Weiher, *RlA* IV: 63)

Ḫamari (H, M) (1) According to J. Westenholz, the eponymous deity of the city of Emar attested in a few tablets from that city. The name is Semitic and means "Donkey (Town)." It appears as such in an itinerary found at Karnak in Egypt and belonging to Thutmoses III. (2) Deity attested in Hurrian texts from the Hittite capital city of Ḫattušas. (Schwemer 2001: 255–56; J. Westenholz 2000: 50)

Ḫa-MI (M) Deity attested in a personal name in an undated tablet from the Ur III period. (AUCT 1, 586: r 18)

Ḫammu (L) See 'Ammu

Ḫamrišḫara (H) A Luwian/Hurrian form of the goddess Išḫara. Means "Temple of Išḫara" in Hurrian and signifies "The Hurrian Išḫara." Occurs in Hurrian and Luwian incantations and in rituals for the dead. In one text her priestess calls on the spirits of the dead. (van Gessel 1998: I, 81–82; Popko 1995: 94. 98; Haas 1994: 228; Archi 1993: 77, 78 note 45; Laroche 1946/47: 47; Otten, *RlA* IV: 74)

Ḫamun (M) Deity attached to the sun god Utu/Šamaš. Means "Harmony." In An : *Anum*, glossed in Akkadian as "Who Puts the Face in Order." In an incantation, leads the way for Šerzi-maḫ-ana, a form of the sun god. (George 2016: no. 47; Litke 1998: 134)

Ḫamun-ana (M) In An : *Anum*, one of two deified bull-lyres of the goddess Nisaba. Means "Harmony of Heaven." In a god list from Aššur within the circle of Šamaš. (Litke 1998: 55; Schroeder 1920: no. 64)

Ḫamun-šubur (M) Apparently another name for Nin-šubur in an Old Babylonian god list. Occurs with the reversed form Šubur-ḫamun in An : *Anum* also as a name for Nin-šubur. (Richter 2004: 302: Litke 1998: 27)

Ḫamurni (M) Deity identified with Anu and mentioned in the "The Theogony of Dunnu." (Lambert 2013: 395; Lambert 2007: 167f.)

Ḫanat (L) See 'Anat(u)

Ḫanbi (M) See Ḫanpa

Ḫaniš (M) Ḫaniš and Šullat were a pair of gods of destruction. Equated in An : *Anum* with the storm god Adad. In some texts he was associated with lightening. In the account of the Great Flood in the "Epic of Gilgameš," he acted as herald of the coming storm. In general, he controlled very damaging storms. Ur III king Šulgi commissioned a temple for Ḫaniš and Šullat, and the two deities are mentioned in a second-millennium BCE ritual for the *akītu* festival. (Foster 2001: 87, 224; Leick 1999: 153; Litke 1998: 145; Cohen 1993: 307; George 1993: 170 no. 1421; Tallqvist 1974: 321; Speiser, *ANET*: 94; Edzard and Lambert, *RlA* III: 107–8)

Ḫannaḫan(n)a, Hannahan(n)a (H) Hittite goddess appearing in the Old Hittite compositions about the disappearing god Telipinu. She was a protective "mother" and wise helper. However, her anger could be devastating. Occurs in the circle of the storm god. The name probably means "Grandmother" or "Great Mother." One of her epithets was "Great Goddess." It was she whom the other deities consulted when they were faced with a difficult problem, and it was she who finally took decisive action to solve it. She used a bee in her successful search for Telipinu—in many cultures bees are associated with mother goddesses. She had a role in rituals of magic, particularly those concerning pregnancy/birth. She presided over a festival of the herds. Also appears in theophoric names. Same as Kattaḫ-zipuri or Kattaḫziwuri. (Hoffner 1998: 14–15, 18, 21–22, 26–32, 110; van Gessel 1998: I, 82–83; Popko 1995: 55, 82, 87–89, 121; Haas 1994: 259, 271, 300, 304; Otten, *RlA* IV: 108)

Ḫanpa, Ḫanpu (M) Father of Pazuzu, "He Conjures (as of incantations)," or, according to Wiggermann, "The Limping One." (Tallqvist 1974: 320; Saggs 1959–1960: 123–27; Wiggermann *RlA* X: 373)

Ḫantašepa (H) Hittite demon(s) or demonic creature(s). Mentioned in Old Hittite rituals. Had a male body, bloody eyes, and a ferocious face; was fully dressed with a red kilt, and carried a long lance. Name derived from the Hittite word for "face." Occurs in magical rites to banish evil. (van Gessel 1998: I, 84; Popko 1995: 83; Haas 1994: 473, 503; Otten, *RlA* IV: 109)

Ḫantitaššu, Ḫantidaššu (H) Hittite deity of the city of Ḫurma in Anatolia. Probably a mother goddess. Means "Very Strong." Often invoked in treaties, as in the treaty between the Hittite king Šuppiluliuma I and the king of Mittani Šattiwaza. Occurs in theophoric names. One text mentions the deity's priestesses. (van Gessel 1998: I, 84–85; Haas 1994: 280, 309, 776, 777 note 45; Otten, *RlA* IV: 110)

Ḫapantali(ya) (H) Minor Hattic god appearing in Old Hittite mythic material. A very ancient protector divinity. Divine shepherd attending the flock of the sun god. Paired with the Hattic/Hittite goddess Inara. Appears in myths, such as the disappearance of Telipinu. Occurs in later god lists that preserve the earlier tradition. (Hoffner 1998: 16–17, 30, 35–36; van Gessel 1998: I, 88–91; Popko 1995: 55, 71, 113, 121; Haas 1994: 376, 425; Otten, *RlA* IV: 111–12)

Ḫar (M) (1) Deity identified with Nin-Gublaga, the bull god of the city of Ki'abrig (Jacobsen 1976: 25). (2) Deity written ḫár (GUD) with gloss ḫa-ar, in the circle of the moon god. (3) Deity written ḫár (GUD) with glosses ḫa-ar and ḫa-ra, a messenger of Maš-taba, in the circle of Meslamta-ea. (Litke 1998: 121, 197, 215; Lambert, *RlA* VII: 117)

Ḫar, Ḫarru (M) See Gagim; Indagra

Ḫarbaḫe (M) See Ḫalbaē

Ḫarbat (M) A Kassite divine name possibly a variant of Ḫarbe. Ḫarbat occurs also in a personal name in a tablet from the First Sealand Dynasty. (Dalley 2009: 272; Brinkman 1976: 150–51)

Ḫarbe, Ḫarpa/e (M) God of the Kassites. Ḫarbe was identified with Enlil or An/Anu(m). Ḫarbe forms part of the Kassite royal name Kadašman-Ḫarbe. (Black and Green 2003: 112; Rüterswörden, *DDDB*: 424–25)

Ḫarḫab (L) See Ḫiriḫbi

Ḫari (M) Deity attested in a personal name in at Abu Ṣalābīkh in the Early Dynastic period. Possibly corresponds to the mountain god written logographically ḪAR in the Mari texts. See Ḫarim. (Mander 1986: 128: Stol 1979: 75–76)

ḪAR-ib-gi-a (M) Sumerian deity attested in a tablet referring to settlements in the vicinity of Umma. (Cohen 1996a: 33)

Ḫarim (M) Deity attested in a personal name in the Sargonic period in the name Puzur-[d]Ḫa-rí-im. See Ḫari.

Ḫarištaš(š)i (H) Guardian of the storehouse. Mentioned in a Hittite festival text. (van Gessel 1998: I, 95–96; Haas 1994: 261–62; Otten, *RlA* IV: 121)

Ḫasīs(u) (L) See Koṯar-wa-Ḫasīs

Ḫasīsu (M) See Geštug

Ḫašam(m)ili/a, Ḫašammiu, Ḫazamil (H) Hittite god also in the Palaic pantheon. The divine smith. Appears in one of the compositions about the disappearing god Telipinu. Occurs in Hittite texts, for example, in a god list from Ḫattušas from the time of Tutḫalyas IV, included among war deities. Associated with battles against various towns. His statue was placed in the "Holy of Holies" in the storm god's temple at Zippalanda, north of Ḫattušas. Haas suggests that he was a sun god. (Hoffner 1998: 28; van Gessel 1998: I, 98–103; Popko 1995: 55, 72–73, 114, 146; Haas 1994: 245, 363–64; von Weiher, *RlA* IV: 127–28)

Ḫašammiu (H) See Ḫašam(m)ili

Ḫašgala (H) Deity who was protector or talisman of the king. (van Gessel 1998: I, 106; Haas 1994: 450)

Ḫašḫur (M) In An : *Anum*, one of five deities of fruit. Means "Apple." (Litke 1998: 112)

Ḫaššušara (H) Hattic goddess at Kanesh. Means "Queen." (Popko 1995: 89)

Ḫašuntarḫi (H) See Adamma

Ḫatagga (H) See Kattaḫḫa

Ḫataniš (M) Early Dynastic gidim of the Ekur. (Selz 1995: 175)

Ḫatepinu (H) See Telipinu

Ḫatni (H) Hattic deity of Hurrian origin. Belongs to the circle of Teššub. Occurs in Hattic texts and in a god list from Ugarit. (van Gessel 1998: I, 112; Haas 1994: 463; Otten, *RlA* IV: 150)

Ḫaṭṭu(m) (M) The deified scepter, symbol of authority and kingship. It had a temple at Nippur. (George 1993: 164 no. 1320)

Ḫaṭṭu-ša-ṭābti (M) Deity occurs in a variant year name from second-millennium BCE Mari that refers to the statue of this deity. Means "Staff of Peace/ Goodness." (Joannès 1989: no. 75)

Ḫawurni (H) See Eše-Ḫawurni

Ḫaya (M) Steward of Enlil and father of his consort, Ninlil. Husband of Nisaba. There is a hymn to Ḫaya written on behalf of Rim-Sîn I of Larsa. According to Jacobsen, Ḫaya was "the god of stores," probably because of his connection with the grain goddesses Sud, later Ninlil, and Nisaba. Sennacherib built him a temple, and he was made an offering of dates during the *akītu* festival at Ur. (Leick 1999: 135–36, 143–44; Litke 1998: 54; Cohen 1993: 410; George 1993: 23, 164 no. 1321; Civil 1983: 44; Steible 1975: 25; Tallqvist 1974: 320–21; Steible 1967; Reiner 1970: 18)

Ḫayašu (M) Deity identified with Enlil. (Lambert 2007: 167f.)

Ḫazamil (H) See Ḫašam(m)ili

Ḫeam-gina (M) Deity identified with Enlil. Means "Firm Fiat," literally, "A Firm 'Let It Be.'" Refers to Enlil's irrevocable command. (Litke 1998: 40; Tallqvist 1974: 321)

Ḫebat, **Ḫepat(u)**, **Hiputa**, **Kheba(t)**, **Khepa(t)** (H, M) Great Hurrian mother goddess, consort of Teššub and mother of Šarruma, who often accompanies her. Takiti(s) was her minister. She is first mentioned in pre-Sargonic material from Ebla. She was worshipped by the Luwians and equated by the Hittites to the Sun Goddess of Arinna. One of her titles was "Lady (or Queen) of Heaven." At Alalaḫ she formed a triad with Teššub and Ištar. Patron goddess of Ḫalab (Aleppo), where she appears as spouse of the storm god Adad. In the great rock carvings at Yazılıkaya in Turkey, Ḫebat as sun goddess stands with Teššub and their offspring. She wears a long pleated garment and a pill-box hat (*polos*); she stands on a leopard, panther, or lion with the inscription "Hepatu." In a seal depiction she sits on a wild feline. Other images show her enthroned, enveloped in a long dress, and wearing a small pointed hat.

In the Hurrian "Song of Kumarbi," Ḫebat takes sides with her husband Teššub. In "Song of Ḫedammu" she is mentioned as one of the deities who will have to work if human beings are killed off. In the "Song of Ullikummi," the monster blocks off her temple so that she becomes isolated.

In the central display at the outdoor sanctuary of Yazılıkaya in Turkey, Ḫebat as sun goddess stands on a feline and faces her consort Teššub, who stands on the sacred mountains She wears a long pleated garment and a pill-box type of hat (*polos*). Behind her is Šar(r)um-(m)a, her son. The inscription reads "Hepatu." Rock-carved. Hittite. Thirteenth century BCE. Drawing by S. Beaulieu, after Lloyd 1967: 66.

Her cult centers were Kummani in Kizzuwatna in Turkey and Aleppo in Syria, and she had temples at many sites in the Taurus Mountains area. The biggest temple at Ḫattušas from the Middle Hittite period was dedicated to Ḫebat and Teššub. She occurs in a theophoric name at Nuzi as well as elsewhere. Hittite king Muwatalli II mentioned her as Ḫebat of Aleppo (Ḫalab) in one of his prayers and identified her as a deity of Šamuḫa. In the "Amarna Letters," a king of Jerusalem in the Late Bronze Age bears the name Abdi-Ḫepa "Servant/Slave of Ḫebat." She is attested in numerous theophoric names from Ḫattušas and Alalaḫ, where she was also worshipped. Often in god lists and personal names at Ugarit, where she was identified with Piḍray(u). The Hittite queen was understood as embodying Ḫebat. The goddess forms the theophoric part of the biblical name Eliahba, Eli-Heba (II Sam. 23: 32). The goddess's worship may extend back into the Neolithic period at sites such as Çatal Höyök and Haçılar on the Anatolian plain. It certainly continued into Hellenistic times, when she was a Lydian goddess called Hipta. (von Dassow 2008: 293 note 85; del Olmo Lete 1999: 85, 209, 340; van der Toorn, *DDDB*: 391–92; Hoffner 1998: 41, 52, 62, 64, 110; Leick 1998: 80–81; van Gessel 1998: I, 115- 147; Popko 1995: 94, 96–98, 101, 111–12, 114–15, 118, 125, 127, 141, 165–66, 169; Haas 1994: 111, 138, 229, 246; Mellaart 1967; Danmanville, *RlA* IV: 326–29)

Ḫedammu (H) A huge, destructive, and voracious male water dragon or sea serpent in the Hurrian/Hittite "Song of Ḫedammu." Probably the offspring of Kumarbi and his wife Sertapsuriḫi, the daughter of the sea god. The monster strikes fear into both humans and deities. The goddess Ša(w)uš(k)a tries to subdue him by arousing him sexually, but the text breaks off before its conclusion. The monster also occurs in the Kumarbi compositions. (Hoffner 1998: 40, 50–55, 110; Popko 1995: 126–27, 165; Haas 1994: 153, 170, 174, 176, 357, 359, 487, 494; Siegelová, *RlA* IV: 243)

Ḫedu (M) One of the five daughters of Nin-šubur. Name means "Adornment." She is described in An : *Anum* as a gatekeeper of An/Anu(m). (Litke 1998: 27; Lambert, *RlA* IV: 244)

Ḫedu-ana (M) Name of Nanna/Sîn, the moon god. Means "Ornament of Heaven." Part of the priestess name of the famous En-ḫedu-ana, daughter of Sargon, founder of the dynasty of Akkad. (Leick 1999: 141; Tallqvist 1974: 322)

Ḫe-en-ḫe-sa (M) One of the deities of fishermen listed in An : *Anum*. Written with -sa_6. (Litke 1998: 113)

Ḫegal (M) One of the names of the god of dikes and ditches En-kimdu. Also the twenty-seventh name of Marduk at the end of the *Enūma eliš*, as a title of the god En-bilulu, the divine canal-inspector. Means "Abundance." (Foster 2005: 479; Litke 1998: 93; Tallqvist 1974: 322; Speiser, *ANET*: 71; Heidel 1967: 56)

Ḫendur-saga (M) Protector of oaths and guardian of those who travel by night. His consort was Nin-mug. He was vizier of the goddess Nanše. The reading of his name is based on two lexical texts that provide a syllabic writing ḫe-en-du-ur for the sign PA and ḫe-en-du-ur-sag for [d]PA.SAG. In both cases the entry is explained as [(d)]I-šum.

He is first attested in god lists of the Early Dynastic period. Well known in the Lagaš area where he appears in Early Dynastic offering lists and in one Early Dynastic royal inscription as the great herald of the Abzu. Related to Dumuzi-abzu, a daughter of the god Enki. A text of Gudea of Lagaš proclaims him to be herald of the land of Sumer. Connected as early as Ur III times with the god Išum. They had the same wife, Nin-mug. Appears in curse formulas right after the sun god Utu/Šamaš. A hymn from Nippur juxtaposes him with the Pleiades and the fire god Gibil (perhaps the star Aldebaran), and so he might have had astronomical significance. A hymn from Nippur describes him as a lover of justice and hater of evil. A temple to Ḫendur-sag(a) is attested at Girsu. (George 2015; Cohen 2015: 41; Black and Green 2003: 112, 135; Leick 1999: 62; Leick 1998: 82; George 1993: 165 no. 1323; Edzard and Wilcke 1976: 139–76; Edzard, *RlA* IV: 324–25)

Ḫešui (H) Deity associated with the storm god of Šapinuwa. (Giorgieri et al. 2013)

Ḫibirtu(m) (M) See Abirtu(m)

Ḫiliba (M) Deity listed in *Anu ša amēli* explained as "Anu of Everything." Quite likely the same deity as Ḫi-li-BE occurring only once, in a god list where he is equated to a major deity whose name is broken away. (Lambert 2007: 167f.; Litke 1998: 229)

Ḫiriḫbi, Ḫirib(ḫ)i, Ḫarḫabbu, Harhab (L) God (King) of summer in a wedding composition from Ugarit. Either the father of the goddess Nikkal or a divine matchmaker. (Wyatt 2002: 336; del Olmo Lete 1999: 57, 80; Marcus in Parker 1997c: 215)

Ḫišam(ī)tu(m) (M) Goddess of a small town of the same name (Ḫišamta) north of ancient Terqa, the dynastic burial city of Mari king Zimrī-Līm. At a procession in the goddess's honor, she was provided with a diadem(?). (Cohen 2015: 118; Durand 2008: 237–38; Charpin and Ziegler 2003: 178; Lambert 1985a: 526)

Ḫišmidik, Ḫišmitik, Ḫašmitik (E) Elamite god originally a member of the pantheon of Šimaški, located in Elam. Often appearing with Ruḫurater. The deity was originally thought to be female because of his association with a male deity, but apparently this is incorrect. He appears in a brick inscription of the great Middle Elamite king Untaš-Napiriša from Susa and at Choga Zanbil south of Susa, where he had a temple. (Vallat 1998: 339; Hinz and Koch 1987: 664; König 1977: 10, 43, 44, 189, 227; Lambert, *RlA* IV: 426)

Ḫnng (L) Deities mentioned in an offering list from Ugarit. (del Olmo Lete 1999: 84, 85, 209)

Ḫubaḫir (E) Elamite deity occurring in a treaty between Narām-Sîn of Akkad and a king of Susa. (König 1977: 190, 227)

Ḫubiti (H) Deity associated with the storm god of Šapinuwa. (Giorgieri et al. 2013)

Ḫudena-Ḫudellurra (L, H) A pair of Hurrian fate-determining goddesses, included in a list of similar fate-determining and birth goddesses. They are depicted in the great rock carvings at Yazılıkaya near Ḫattušas. In the "Song of Ullikummi," the goddesses assist at the birth of the stone monster. Also in the Hurrian pantheon at Ugarit and attested in a ritual text. They correspond to Hittite Gulša. (del Olmo Lete 1999: 85, 209; Hoffner 1998: 57–58; van Gessel 1998: I, 165–67; Popko 1995: 115, 124; Haas 1994: 372–73; Laroche 1946/47: 49–50)

Ḫudḫa (M) Deity of the Kassites. Ḫudḫa, also known as Buriaš, was identified with Adad/Iškur. (Black and Green 2003: 112; Tallqvist 1974: 322)

Ḫudrudiš (E) Elamite deity who occurs in a personal name. Brinkman suggests this may be a variant for the Elamite deity Ḫutran. (Brinkman 1976: 19, 87, 125)

Ḫul (M) See Bibra

Ḫul-NI-ša (M) Deity perhaps identified with Nergal. Written ḫul-NI-ša$_6$. Occurs directly after the somewhat homophonous entry Ḫul-nu-zu. Variant is Lugal-NI-ša$_6$. (Litke 1998: 207)

Ḫul-nuzu (M) Deity perhaps identified with Nergal. The name means "Knows No Evil." (Litke 1998: 207)

Ḫumana (M) Deity occurring in a god list directly before the god Marduk. (Richter 2004: 141)

Ḫumat (M) Deity in the OB god list from Nippur and in personal names. (Durand 2008: 644)

Ḫumbaba (M) See Ḫuwawa

Ḫu(m)ban, Umban, Humpan (E, M) A sky god. One of Elam's highest-ranked gods. There is evidence of his being worshipped for over two thousand years. Head of the pantheon of the Awan Dynasty that ruled Elam from c. 2400 to 2100 BCE. Awan was a part of Elam, likely near Susa. In the pantheon of the Old Akkadian period, as reflected in a treaty of a king of Susa with Narām-Sîn of Akkad, Ḫumban held the second position, after his spouse, the mother goddess Pinegir. However, in the course of the second millennium BCE, Ḫumban was promoted to the head of the Elamite pantheon, and he remained there virtually unchallenged until the destruction of the Elamite kingdom.

One scholar asserts that the god's name was derived from the root *ḫuba* meaning "to command." Others suggest that the name is related to that of the monster Ḫuwawa/Ḫumbaba. During the second millennium BCE, the writing of the divine name seems to have been taboo. In Middle Elamite inscriptions, for example, the signs used to refer to Ḫumban were the Sumerogram DINGIR.GAL "Great Deity." The reading of this name was Napi-riša, from the words *napir* "deity" and *riša* "great," meaning "The Great God." Some argue that Ḫumban was later called Napi-riša, "Great God," but others see them as separate deities. This taboo was not observed in the writing of various rulers' names such as Kuk-Ḫumban, Simut-Ḫumban, Ḫumban-numena, and Kuter-Ḫumban, and it ended in the eighth century BCE when we find royal and personal names composed with the element Ḫumban written phonetically.

Even with the rise of the god In-šušinak, the tutelary god of Susa, in the thirteenth to twelfth centuries BCE, Ḫumban remained at the head of the pantheon, where he was grouped in a triad with In-šušinak and Kiri-riša. Ḫum-ban almost always led the pantheon, with second and third place alternating between the other two gods.

Evidence of the cult of Ḫumban continued into Achaemenid times with wine and barley offerings to the god described in the Persepolis archive. As in an Assyrian commentary text, the god was from very early times identified with Sumerian Enlil, though there is little evidence that he had any Enlil-like traits. Ḫumban appears in incantation texts from Mesopotamia and occurs, with other Elamite deities in a Late Assyrian literary work as protecting the king. (Tavernier 2013: 482; Henkelman 2008: 521–24; Black and Green 2003: 74, 106; van Koppen and van der Toorn *DDDB*: 432–34; Leick 1998: 84; Vallat 1998: 335–49; Hinz and Koch 1987: 716; Koch 1987: 258–59; König 1977: 190, 227; Reiner 1970: 17; Speiser, *ANET*: 110 and note 17; Meier 1937–1939: 242–43, line 53; Hinz, *RlA* IV: 491–92)

Ḫumban-elu (E) Elamite deity attested in a building inscription of the Elamite king Šilḫak-Inšušinak I. (Hinz and Koch 1987: 678; König 1977: 108, 227)

Ḫumḫum (M) The breast of this deity's statue is to be decorated with gold according to a Neo-Assyrian letter. (Livingstone 1986: 99)

Ḫumkapba-[x] (E) Elamite deity occurring in a limestone inscription of Šilhak-Inšušinak II. (König 1977: 85, 190, 227)

Ḫumkat (E) Elamite deity occurring in a treaty between Narām-Sîn of Akkad and a king of Susa. (Hinz and Koch 1987: 717; König 1977: 29, 190)

ḪUMma (M) One of the *galla*-demons. Attested at Nippur in the Ur III period and in An : *Anum*. May mean "Paralyzer." (Litke 1998: 210; Sallaberger 1993: I, 99; Bauer, *RlA* VII: 170)

Ḫumṣīru (M) Deity identified with Martu. Means "Mouse." In a first-millennium BCE lamentation, described as the "murderer of the mountains" and "he who roams the mountains," perhaps an apt description, from a southern Babylonian point of view, of the despised Amurru-tribesmen at the end of the third millennium BCE. Occurs in An : *Anum* as a name of Ereškigal. (Litke 1998: 188; Cohen 1998: 212)

Ḫumūsu(m) (M) Deity attested in the town of Ṣuprum, near Mari. (Durand 2008: 270)

Ḫumuṭ-tabal (M) Neo-Assyrian demon who ferried the dead across the river boundary of the netherworld. Means "Hurry Up and Take Away." (Foster 2005: 836; Black and Green 2003: 155; Speiser, *ANET*: 109)

Ḫupitam (M) Deity who occurs once, in an Ur III Umma personal name. Written Ḫu-pi$_5$(NE)-tam(UD). (BPOA 2, 1813: o 4)

Ḫurbi (E) Elamite deity occurring in a treaty between Narām-Sîn of Akkad and a king of Susa. The deity could be related to the Elamite word for "fear" or "blood." The deity may appear in the personal name Ḫurpa-tila, but this is uncertain. (Hinz and Koch 1987: 722; König 1977: 29, 191, 227)

Ḫur(r)i, Ḫurriš (H, M) Bull god. Called Tilla / Tella in the east of Anatolia. One of two great bulls who pulled the battle chariot of the storm god Teššub. Ḫurri might mean "Night." The other bull was Šer(r)ri(š) / Šarri, which might mean "Day." Normally mentioned together. Both visually depicted in bull form, as in the rock-cut shrine of Yazılıkaya. Mentioned in the Hurrian mythic story "Song of Ullikummi." Received offerings as member of the circle of Teššub. In state treaties accompanied Teššub. Occurs in theophoric names at Nuzi and in a god list from Aššur. Also known at Ugarit. See Ḫurriš. (Hoffner 1998: 41, 61; Popko 1995: 97, 112; van Gessel 1998: I, 160–62, 396–98; Haas 1994: 319–20, 471–72, 527; Laroche 1977: 227–28; Laroche 1946 / 47: 49, 59; Haas, *RlA* IV: 506–7)

Ḫusa (E) Elamite deity occurring in a treaty between Narām-Sîn of Akkad and a king of Susa. Tavernier suggests he may be a forest god. (Tavernier 2007: no. 19; Hinz and Koch 1987: 702; König 1977: 29, 191, 227)

Ḫussinni (M) Goddess associated in the Neo-Babylonian period with the Edubba temple in Kiš.

Ḫušbi-šag (M) Wife of the netherworld god Namtar. Described as the female steward of the netherworld. According to Langdon, she "kept the tablets of Arallu," the land of darkness, "on which the hour of death of every man is written" (1931: 161). Sometimes known as Namtartu(m). Written with $ša_6$. (Litke 1998: 189; Tallqvist 1974: 323; Lambert, *RlA* IV: 522)

Ḫuš-eri (M) Sumerian form or title of Nergal / Erra. Occurs in An : *Anum* shortly after Erra. Variant is KA_5-ḫuš. (Litke 1998: 207; Tallqvist 1974: 323; Lambert, *RlA* IV: 524)

Ḫuškia (M) Deity identified with Nergal. Attested as deity of a temple at Apiak. Means "Furious one of the netherworld." See also Lugal-ḫuškia. (Litke 1998: 200; George 1993: 165 no. 1324; Tallqvist 1974: 323; Lambert, *RlA* IV: 522–23)

Ḫuš-ušumgal (M) See Ušumgal-ḫuš

Ḫutran (E) Elamite god of middle rank. Originally a member of the pantheon of Awan in Elam. Son of the goddess Kiri-riša "The Great Goddess" and the god Napi-riša. In Old Elamite times the god appears in one theophoric name and in a treaty of a king of Susa with Narām-Sîn of Akkad. In a Middle Elamite inscription of Šilḫak-Inšušinak I from Susa, Ḫutran occurs with eleven other deities, where he is the penultimate god, appearing with the epithet "Strong Lord." In a bronze inscription from Susa the same king invoked Ḫutran to combat any destroyer of his monuments. The king also named Ḫutran as the "beloved mother's son" of Kiri-riša, the great goddess. In a third inscription, from Liyan (modern Bušahr), Ḫutran is mentioned in a broken text along with the god Ḫumban. From Neo-Elamite times there are no attestations of Ḫutran from native Elamite sources. However, the divine name does appear in the form Uduran in an Assyrian account of a campaign of Aššurbanipal directed against Susa in 646 BCE. The victorious king removed the deity's statue from Elam. The divine name also appears in the royal name Kidin-Ḫutrutaš. (Black and

Green 2003: 74; Vallat 1998: 333–38; Hinz and Koch 1987: 728; König 1977: 191, 227; Hinz, *RlA* IV: 526–27)

Ḫuṭāru(m) (M) Deified staff or scepter attested in the Inana temple archive at Uruk in the Neo-Babylonian period. (Beaulieu 2003: 351–33)

Ḫuwašša/inna (H) Goddess of Luwian origin. Tutelary deity of the town Ḫupišna in Anatolia. A deity Tunapi was a member of her circle. Occurs in an oath list in a treaty, in curses, and festival rituals. Identified with Gazbaya, Gazbaba. (Polvani 2010; van Gessel 1998: I, 169–73, 528–29; Popko 1995: 94, 143; Haas 1994: 198 note 104; Laroche 1946/47: 69, 90; Frantz-Szabó, *RlA* IV: 528–29)

Ḫuwattašši (H) Hittite deity. Appears in a treaty next to Zababa. (van Gessel 1998: I, 174; Otten, *RlA* IV: 529)

Ḫuwawa (Sum.), **Ḫumbaba** (Akk.) A ferocious monster, generally depicted as a giant with human body, lion's claws, hideous face, and unkempt hair and whiskers. In the epic Sumerian Gilgameš material and in the Babylonian "Epic of Gilgameš," he was appointed by Enlil as guardian of the Cedar Forest. Gilgameš and Enkidu succeeded in killing him, carrying off his head in a sack.

Faces of Ḫuwawa on clay plaques were hung on walls to ward off evil. Descriptions of his face also appear in instructions for divination. Appears in Hittite/Hurrian versions of the "Epic of Gilgameš."

Ḫuwawa may have survived into the Greco-Roman period as the legendary hero Kumbabos, who appears in *De Dea Syria* attributed to the Greek writer Lucian (c. 115–200 CE), but the association is uncertain. Connected iconographically with the Greek Gorgon. May be a manifestation of the eclipsing binary star Algol "The Ghoul." (Oshima in Westenholz 2004: 39–40; Black and Green 2003: 106, 130–32; Frayne 2001: 104–20; Foster 2001: 18–19, 38–45; van der Toorn, *DDDB*: 431–32; van Gessel 1998: I, 174–75; Haas 1994: 305–6; Carter 1987: 360; Attridge and Oden 1976: 29–37; Tallqvist 1974: 322)

Plaque showing Gilgameš and Enkidu killing Huwawa. Old Babylonian. Burnt clay. Height 8.1, width 13.8 cm. Vorderasiatisches Museum, Berlin. After Black and Green 2003: 90.

— I —

Ialdabaoth (L) See Sabaoth

Iapru (E) Elamite deity invoked as a protector of ghosts. (Tavernier 2013: 482)

Ib (L) See Nikkal

Ibbu (M) In An : *Anum*, vizier of Nin-geš-zida. (Litke 1998: 193)

Ib-Dukuga (M) Deity identified with Išḫara. Written íb. (Litke 1998: 43; Tallqvist 1974: 325)

Ib-gal (M) See Nin-Ib-gal

Ibna (M) Deity attested in a Neo-Assyrian god list. (King 1969: pl. 24)

IIbnaḫašša (E) Deity from Elam, perhaps related to Ibni-ḫaza, a god of another land.

Ibnaḫaza (M) Deity from an unknown land identified with Ea. Perhaps related to Ibni-ḫašša, though our entry is listed after the gods of Elam and Ibniḫašša.

Ibnasasa (E) One of the seven major deities of Elam. Written Ib-na-sá-sá with gloss -sa-sa. In An : *Anum*, ten entries after Ib-na-sá-sá, Ib-na-ḪA-za is a foreign god equated to Ea. Perhaps IbnaḪAza should be read, or was originally, Ib-na-za!-za (Ib-na-sà!-sà), a variant of Ibnasasa. Similarly Ib-na-ḪA-aš-⌜x⌝, the entry immediately above Ib-na-sá-sá, might be understood as a variant, thus originally Ib-na-za!-aš[ ]. (Litke 1998: 213)

Ibnu (M) In An : *Anum* one of a group of deities from an unknown land. (Litke 1998: 214)

Ibrimuša (H) Hurrian deity. *Ibri* is Hurrian for "Lord." In one text, listed before Ḫebat and Šarruma. (van Gessel 1998: I, 192–93; Laroche 1946/47: 50; Otten, *RlA* V: 23)

Id (M) The Divine River and a god of justice. His consort was Ki-ša$_6$ and his son Šà-zi. Arbiter of the River Ordeal, a method of deciding the outcome of a law case when there was no clearly perceivable solution. The law code of Ḫammu-rāpi prescribed the river ordeal in such disputes; for instance, in the case of a sorcery accusation's not being proven, the accused had to "throw himself into the river" to be "overpowered" or "shown ... innocent" by the river (Meek, *ANET*: 166). The god Id is attested very early as part of theophoric names. There are several versions of a Mesopotamian hymn to the Divine River. As a couple Id and Ki-ša had a "seat" or shrine "by the well" in E-šara, the great temple in the city of Aššur. Id was also an important god of justice at Mari. See Il-lu-rugu. (Foster 2005: 726; Black and Green 2003: 156–57; Leick 1999: 65–66; McCarter, *DDDB*: 446; Litke 1998: 99; Frymer-Kensky 1977; Tallqvist 1974: 325)

Ida-ḫedu (M) See Sir-sir

Ida madu (M) Deity at Ebla. (Archi 1997)

Id-gal (M) Another name of the river god. Means "The Great River." Reiter proposes that the name may refer to Nergal. (Litke 1998: 99; Reiter 1992a: no. 73; Tallqvist 1974: 325)

Idim (M) In the lexical series Diri the deity is written with the logogram IDIM and explained as *nagbu* "underground waters." (Civil 2004)

IDIM-ḫuš (M) See MUD-ḫuš

Idrab/p (M) Deity who occurs in a personal name at Old Babylonian Mari. (Durand 2008: 232; Charpin 1987b: no. 119)

Id-silima (M) River god. Means "River of Peace." (Litke 1998: 100)

Ig-alima (M) Second son of Nin-Girsu and Baba and guardian of Nin-Girsu's temple. According to Jacobsen, his duty was "to maintain justice, arrest evildoers, [and] issue ordinances to the city" (1976: 82). His temple at Girsu was called "House of the Great Awesome *Me*s [sic] of Heaven and the Netherworld." At Lagaš and Girsu, Ig-alima received offerings during festivals in honor of his parents. Means "Door of the Bison," which may reflect both the god's role as temple guardian and the actual appearance of the doors leading to (or guarding) the temple. (Edzard 1997: 92; Cohen 1993: 47, 53, 55, 71; Jacobsen 1976: 81–82; Tallqvist 1974: 405; Falkenstein 1966: 76–77)

Ig-ana-gala (M) Wife of Mardu. Means "The One Who Opens the Door of Heaven." See Ig-ana-kešda. (Litke 1998: 102)

Ig-an-gub (M) Name of Nin-šubur explained in *Anu ša amēli* as "Papsukkal of the shrine (aširti)." Means "One who Is Stationed at the Door (of) Heaven." (Litke 1998: 233)

Ig-ana-kešed (M) Wife of Lugal-kisura. Her name means "One Who Locks the Door of Heaven." See Ig-ana-gala. (Litke 1998: 102)

Ige-nugie (M) Deity who occurs in An : *Anum* as one of eighteen messengers of Inana. May mean "Who Cannot Be Turned Away at the Door." The next entry is Za-ra-nu-gi$_4$-a "Who Cannot Be Turned Away at the Door-pivot." An : *Anum* has a variant A-šà-nu-gi$_4$-a. (Richter 2004: 292; Litke 1998: 159)

Ig-gala (M) Name of Nin-šubur as the one at the "door of the twins [(astral) Gemini?]." Explained in *Anu ša amēli* as "Papsukkal of the Double Door (*muterti*)." (Litke 1998: 25; Tallqvist 1974: 325)

Igi-amaše (M) This supposed god is attested only once, at Umma in the personal name Ur-[d]Igi-ama-šè. However, this name is written two other times without the theophoric determinative. So too, the name Lú-igi-ama-šè occurs once, at Umma, also without the theophoric determinative. At Ur III Umma and Girsu also written as [d]Igi-ma-šè. (AAS 187: o 4; BPOA 1, 38: o 2; (Nisaba 11, 19)

Igiana-abdu (M) See Kana-abdu

Igi-anzu (M) Deity attested in a god list from Aššur within the circle of Šamaš. Means "He with the Appearance of the Anzu-bird." (Schroeder 1920: no. 64)

Igi-bar (M) Deity's name occurs in a personal name from Ur III Umma. (AAICAB 1/1, Ashm. 1912–1146: r 9)

Igi-bar-lu-ti (M) One of five translators of Inana. Means "One whose Look Causes People to Live." Mentioned in a late text outlining the order of a procession for the *akītu* festival at the great temple in Uruk. (Litke 1998: 158; Cohen 1993: 437; Thureau-Dangin 1975: 116–17)

Igibiše-namtila (M) One of the eight doorkeepers of Enki according to An : *Anum*. Likely also appears in an Akkadian incantation to protect a field from flooding by the storm god Adad. Means "Before Them (There Is) Life," possibly referring to the life-giving powers controlled by Enki. (Schwemer 2001:

679, 681 note 5599; Litke 1998: 106; Lambert, *RlA* V: 37)

Igibiše-silima (M) One of the eight doorkeepers of Enki according to An : *Anum*. Means "Before Them (There Is) Peace," possibly referring to the beneficial powers controlled by Enki. (Schwemer 2001: 681 note 5599; Litke 1998: 106; Lambert, *RlA* V: 37)

Igi-dada (M) Deity attested in an Old Babylonian god list. (Weidner 1924/25)

Igi-DIB (M) Deity attested in a god list from Aššur. (Schroeder 1920: no. 68)

Igi-gal (M) Deity's name occurs in a personal name from Ur III Umma. Written igi-gál, "The Wise One." (BPOA 2, 2550: r 2)

Igigi, Igigu (M) A class of deities, ten (or seven) great gods, who occur only in epic and hymnic literature, rarely in official religious practices. They were the children of An-šar and Ki-šar, were ruled by Enlil, and served as assistants to An/Anu(m) and the other high deities. Igigi were later referred to the gods of Heaven collectively, while Sumerian Anuna (Akkadian Anunnaki) as a neutral term could designate the pantheon as a whole or specifically the netherworld deities as a group. In "The Death of Gilgameš," the hero, just before his death, made offerings to "the Igigi gods of the Holy Mound" (Frayne 2001: 153). The gods were mentioned in the prologue of the great law code of Ḫammu-rāpi (c. 1792–1750). They were members of the Assembly of the Gods in the *Enūma eliš*, and at its end they joined in proclaiming the fifty names of Marduk. Occasionally the Igigi were mentioned in a ritual, for example, one from Uruk in which they occurred as "the Igigi gods of heaven," along with "the Anunnaki gods of earth" (Sachs, *ANET*: 342). While sometimes seats or daises to them are attested in temples, such as at Babylon and Aššur, no temples are known to have been dedicated solely to the Igigi. (Foster 2005: 471; Black and Green 2003: 106; Leick 1999: 65–66; Leick 1998: 85; Litke 1998: 221; George 1993: 81 no. 234, 96 no. 421, 156 no. 1177; Tallqvist 1974: 323; Speiser, *ANET*: 69; Heidel 1967: 59; Kienast, *RlA* V: 40–44)

Igi-gungun (M) Doorkeeper of the E-galmaḫ of Gula in Isin. Means "(The one with) Multi-colored (or Speckled) Eyes." (Litke 1998: 184)

Igi-ḫegala (M) One of the eight guardian doorkeepers of Enki/Ea. He stood by the lion-faced gate in Eridu. Two lion figures found at or near Eridu probably belonged to this gate. Means "Eye (or Face) of Prosperity." (Litke 1998: 106; Tallqvist 1974: 326; Green 1975: 216; Lambert, *RlA* V: 44)

Igi-labāt (M) Deity attested in an Old Babylonian god list. Written igi la-ba-at. Means "Appearance of a lioness." See Lugal-igi-pirig. (Weidner 1924/25)

Igi-mušḫuš (M) Deity attested in a god list from Aššur within the circle of Šamaš. Means "He with the Appearance of the *mušḫuššu*-dragon." (Schroeder 1920: no. 64)

Igi-muš-ušumgal (M) Deity attested in a god list from Aššur within the circle of Šamaš. Means "He with the Appearance of the Great (Serpentine?) Dragon." (Schroeder 1920: no. 64)

Igi-nun(biše) (M) Deity allocated offerings at Ur III Umma. (Nisaba 27, 217: r 4)

Igi-sasa (M) Deity attested at Old Babylonian Nippur in a pledge text. Means "(With) Beautiful Eyes." (Renger 1967: 150)

Igi-sigsig (M) The gardener of Anu(m) or Enlil who rips out the fronds of the date palm. In a mystical text Igi-sigsig is called *mullilu(m)* "Ritual Sprinkler." Means "Yellow (or Green) Eye (or Face)" and denotes both a type of bird and the medical condition of jaundice. In a second entry in An : *Anum* he is listed among gods of fruit. (Litke 1998: 30, 112; Wiggermann 1992: 69, 115)

Igišṭu(m) (E, M) In An : *Anum*, the name of one of the seven chief deities of Elam. One of the seven brothers of Naḫḫunte, known only from personal names. Also a title of the warrior god Ninurta and elsewhere equated to Nergal. PALIL/*igišṭu* means "Foremost" or "One who is at the Front." In a ritual from Uruk, a kettledrum was played for the deity, who was also named in a late account of the Urukian ritual for the *akītu* festival. An Assyrian treaty appealed to him as "lord of the first rank." In a Neo-Assyrian god list written I-gi-iš-ti. (Reiner, *ANET*: 539). (Litke 1998: 213–14; Vallat 1998: 336; Cohen 1993: 431; Tallqvist 1974: 436; Reiner 1970: 40; King 1969: pl. 34; Krebernik, *RlA* X: 281)

Igi-tal (M) Along with Gubla, a courier of Šerzi-mah-ana, a form of the sun god, in an incantation. Written Igi-ta-al. George suggests that these may be variant names for the god pair Kardu and Sakardu, also identified as a pair of couriers of the sun god. Note the similar-sounding monoculus *i-gi-ti-li*, mentioned in another incantation. (George 2016: nos. 47 and 55)

Igi-zalaga (M) A lord of the netherworld mentioned in a god list from Khorsabad, a capital city of Assyria near the Tigris, and translated in Akkadian as "Judge of Mankind." He is paired with Lugal-dingira. Means "Bright Eyes." (Schwemer 2001: 65)

Igi-zi-bara (M) A divinized harp of Inana. The instrument participated in a festival at Zabala(m) during which statues of goddesses identified with Inana were carried in procession to celebrate the Festival of the Early Grass. Also attested in offering lists from Umma dating from the Ur III period. (Cohen 1993: 164; Sallaberger 1993: II, 142 table 82)

Ig-kuga (M) Deity identified with Ḫaya. Means "Holy Door." (Litke 1998: 54)

Ig-lulima (M) Gatekeeper. Means "Door of the Stag." (Litke 1998: 64)

Ijandu (H) One of the more obscure Hittite deities. (Archi 1990: 118)

Iḫalzi (H) Deity associated with the storm god of Šapinuwa. (Giorgieri et al. 2013)

Ikītum (M) In An : *Anum*, wife of Amurru, god of the Amorites. Written I-ki-tum. Perhaps this is an orthography for *ekkētum* "scabies," in which case this would be another instance of the Babylonians slandering the Amorites. (Litke 1998: 217)

Ikrub-El (M) Deity at Mari. Some have understood this deity to have originally been an ancestor, but Sasson suggests the possibility of the opposite, that he was originally a god who later was believed to have been a human hero of old. Names means "El Has Blessed." (Durand 2008: 239–40; Sasson 2001)

Ikšudu(m) (M) Dog of Marduk. May mean "He Came (when called)." Occurs also in an Old Babylonian text at Terqa. (Durand 2008: 332; Litke 1998: 99)

Ikupi (M) Perhaps for Yikun-pi. (OBO 160/1, 1998, p. 269)

Il (M) Deity identified with the storm god Adad, written EN×EN with gloss il. Presumably means "The God." (Litke 1998: 139)

Il, Ilah (L) See El

Il-aba (E, M) Warrior god who was the personal deity of Sargon of Agade. He is mentioned in inscriptions and seals of Akkadian times. He was worshipped by Narām-Sîn of Akkad and appears near the beginning of a list of gods in an Elamite treaty between the latter king and a king of Susa. A temple of his at Babylon is attested in a year name. (Black and Green 2003: 106–7; Sasson 2001; Leick 1999: 117; George 1993: 75 no. 155, 165 no. 1325; Hinz and Koch 1987: 751; König 1977: 29, 183, 227; Tallqvist 1974: 251; Oppenheim, *ANET*: 268)

Il-abrat, Ili-abrat (M) See Nin-šubur (male)

Il-amurri(m) (M) See Amurru(m)

Ilat(u) (L) See Asherah; El

Ilba (M) Deity identified with Utu/Šamaš in a Neo-Assyrian god list written $^{il\text{-}ba}$GÁN. (King 1969: pl. 27)

Ilba, Alba (M) Deity identified with Martu whose name is written KASKAL.KUR with gloss in An : *Anum*. (Richter 2004: 383–84; Litke 1998: 218)

Il/El bēt, Il bt (L) The title of the tutelary god of the palace at Ugarit. His consort's title was Ilat/Elat Bēt, probably the goddess Ušḫar(ayu) or Ušḫara(tu). (del Olmo Lete 1999: 38, 59, 68)

Il-burka (M) Deity attested in the Mari texts. Means "God of Homage." (Durand 2008: 181)

Ilḫa (M) Deity whose name is written KASKAL.KUR with gloss in An : *Anum*. (Richter 2004: 383–84; Litke 1998: 218)

Il-Ḫalab (M) Identified with Adad in a Neo-Assyrian god list. Written Il-la-ḫa-ab, presumably dittography, and several entries later Il-ḫa-al-la-bu. See Bēl-Ḫalab. (King 1969: pl. 16)

Il-Ḫamazi (M) The god of the city of Ḫamazi located in the eastern Zagros Mountains in the Diyala region. He is attested in a personal name in an Early Dynastic text from Lagaš. (Selz 1995: 139)

Il-ḫanni (M) Deity attested in the Mari texts. Means "God of Mercy." (Durand 2008: 181)

Il-ib, El'eb, Ilu'ibi (L) Probably a primordial ancestral father deity. Primarily attested at Ugarit, where he might have been the divine ancestor of the royal family. Most likely means "god of the fathers" or "divine ancestor," though some have argued for a translation "god the father." Il-ib appears in both mythic compositions and ritual texts from Ugarit. In the ritual texts, his name usually occurs among the top three in a list. In one administrative tablet dealing with the supply of wine for royal sacrifices by towns in the area of the city of Ugarit, the ancestral deity is third on the list. Albright argued that the god was patron of the worship of ancestors and its plural meant ancestor spirits. He connected *eb/ib* with Hebrew *'ob* "ghost." There was probably a connection between Il-ib and Il-aba. (Pardee 2002: 14, 17, 23, 31, 215,

280; Wyatt 2002: 255, 256 note 26, 262; del Olmo Lete 1999: 48, 60, 72, 79; Healey van der Toorn et al. 1999: 447–48; van der Toorn, *DDDB*: 361; Parker 1997b: 53–55; Finegan 1989: 138; Cross 1973: 1–12, 14–15; Albright 1968: 141–42, 168, 204–5)

Ili-Mēr (M) Deity identified with the storm god Iškur/Adad. Written IM with gloss ì-lí-me-er. (Litke 1998: 139)

Ili-mīšaru(m) (M) Vizier of Nizu-ana, the wife of Lugal-Marada. Ilī-mīšaru(m) means "My God Is Justice." (Litke 1998: 171; Tallqvist 1974: 327)

Ili-Wēr (M) See Adad

Ilkātum (M) See Gi(l)-sa-a

Illa (M) (1) Deity whose name is written NAGAR with gloss in An : *Anum*. (Litke 1998: 216) (2) Deity in an Old Akkadian personal name. Written Íl-la. (Such-Gutiérrez: 2005/6)

Illali(y)ant, Illali(y)antikeš, Illali(y)a (H) Divine Hittite group, helpers of the sun god. Also Palaic. Working especially against demons and disease. Member(s) of the pantheon at Kanesh. Appear(s) in a mythic fragment referred to as the sun god's offspring. (van Gessel 1998: I, 182–83; Popko 1995: 55, 89, 113; Haas 1994: 381, 468, 483, 611–12; Otten, *RlA* V: 48–49)

Illil (M) See Enlil

Illuyanka (H) Snake-monster, enemy of the storm god in the Hattic/Hittite "Illuyanka Tales." Depicted in a relief from Melid (Aslantepe) in mid-eastern Turkey. The story introduced the Purulli festival, celebrated in the spring for the protection and prosperity of the land. Hoffner says that the word *illuyanka* is the Hattic/Hittite word for "serpent." The serpent perhaps represents Hydra. Might be related to the Greek myth of Typhon. (Hoffner 1998: 10–14; 111; Leick 1998: 85–86; Otten, *RlA* V: 60–61)

Il-pāda (M) Deity attested in the Mari texts. Means "God of Redemption." (Durand 2008: 181)

Il-simtiša (M) Deity receiving offerings at Ur III Šarrākum. (Nisaba 15/1, p. 556)

Ilšu (L) Ugaritic god. Occurs in several compositions as the herald of the deities and also in ritual texts. Yaṭipanu was his spouse. (del Olmo Lete 1999: 55, 57, 115, 325)

Iltare (H) One of the more obscure Hittite deities. (Archi 1990: 118)

Iltebu (M) Dog of Marduk. May mean "He Was Satisfied." (Litke 1998: 99)

Ilti-āl-Uri(m) (M) One of a group of seven hero gods in An : *Anum*. May mean "(The One) from the city of Ur." Written Il_5-ti- for *išti*. (Litke 1998: 211)

Iltitaddi (M) One of a group of seven hero gods in An : *Anum*. Il_5-ti, as in the god's name Ilti-āl-Uri(m), may be for *išti* "from." (Litke 1998: 211)

Iltum (M) Deity attested in the Mari texts. Means "The Goddess."

Ilu(m)-lemnu(m) (Akk.), **Dingir-ḫul** (Sum.) Demon whose name means "Evil God." Had two shrines at Babylon. (George 1993: 165 no. 1326; Ebeling, *RlA* III: 109)

Ilu(m) (L) See El, Il

Ilu-Mēr, Ilu-Wēr (M) In An : *Anum* a name of the sun god Utu/Šamaš and of the storm god Iškur/Adad. Written with the ASAR and LUL signs for Utu/Šamaš and with IM for Iškur/Adad, all with gloss i-lu-me-er. In the West-Semitic-speaking (Amorite) areas, there was a deity Wēr, Ilu-Wēr, Mēr, or Ilu-Mēr. (Litke 1998: 145)

I-lu-rugu (M) God of the River Ordeal. Means "River that Confronts the Man." One of the ways in which the innocence or guilt of persons involved in a legal dispute could be determined was by the "River Ordeal." Either the accused or the accuser, chosen by lot, plunged into a river to be judged by its god. Emerging unscathed was evidence of innocence; sinking or drowning showed guilt. The deity of the Ordeal is first attested during the time of Gudea. In Ur III times, I-lu-rugu played a role in the cult of Inana at Nippur. According to Heimpel, the town of Ḫīt on the middle Euphrates was a particularly important locale for the performance of the River Ordeal. People travelled considerable distances to be tried there in the choking, hot and sulfurous springs. (Black and Green 2003: 155–56; Leick 1999: 62; Litke 1998: 100; Heimpel 1996: 7–18; Sallaberger 1993: I, 129; Frymer-Kensky 1977; van Soldt, *RlA* X: 126–27)

Imdudu (M) Deity in an Old Babylonian god list. Written im-du-du. (Weidner 1924/25)

Iminbi (M) See Sebettu(m)

Imin-gu (M) Written with gu_7 in An : *Anum*. See Lugal-imin-gi

Immeriya (E) Elamite deity in an inscription of Untaš-Napiriša named as the king's protector. (Paulus 2013: 438)

Impaluri (H) Hurrian/Hittite deity. The sea god's vizier in the Kumarbi stories. In the Hittite version of the "Epic of Gilgameš," mentioned beside Gilgameš. (Hoffner 1998: 41, 57–58, 111; van Gessel 1998: I, 186–87; Popko 1995: 125; Haas 1994: 409; Laroche 1946/47: 50; Frantz-Szabó, *RlA* V: 74)

Imzu-ana (M) See Nizu-ana

IM-?-it-ki (E) Elamite deity occurring in a treaty between Narām-Sîn of Akkad and a king of Susa. (König 1977: 193, 227)

Inana (Sum.), **Ištar** (Akkadian/Babylonian), **Iššar** (Assyrian) One of the seven great deities of the Mesopotamian pantheon. Perhaps the most important goddess in all Mesopotamia. The Sumerian name Inana quite likely comes from the posited form Nin-ana "Lady of Heaven." In a minority view, Jacobsen argues that the name means "Lady of the Date Clusters" (1976: 36) and understands her as the spirit of the storehouse, particularly that of dates.

The Semitic name Ištar is associated with that of the Southern Arabian god ʻAṯtar, who is attested also at Ugarit. In addition, a clearly related female form appears at Ugarit, ʻAṯtart(u). Later she becomes the Levantine goddess Aštarte (Greek), Ashtoreth (biblical). An earlier form of Babylonian Ištar was Eštar. Sumerian Inana was sometimes referred to as Innin(i), which was occasionally applied to other goddesses. Originally Inana and Ištar were two separate goddesses who, particularly in the Old Akkadian period, became equated. In late periods, "Ištar" came to be understood as the normal word for "goddess."

Inana has been characterized as a goddess of "Infinite Variety" (Jacobsen 1976: 135) because of her many aspects, powers, and domains, among them, love and sexuality, war and warfare, and the planet Venus as morning and evening stars. She also had strong netherworld connections. She seems to have been the patron deity of prostitutes, though there has recently been dispute about this designation (Assante 2003; Assante 1998). Cross-dressing was part of her cult, and she had the ability to alter a person's sex, so that a man became a woman and vice versa. In Mesopotamian treaties, the curse on treaty breakers often included lines such as the following from an Assyrian vassal treaty: ... may Ishtar, the goddess of men, the lady of women, take away their 'bow,' cause their steri[lity]..." (Reiner, *ANET*: 533). Like Inana, her Babylonian/Assyrian counterpart Ištar also confused the lines that separated the sexes, the generations, the classes, and the species, human and animal. Ištar was also goddess of love and war, as well as of Venus (see Dilibad; Ištar-kakkabī). Later, as often in earlier periods, Ištar's warlike qualities were emphasized by warrior conquerors such as the Assyrians, for whose kings Ištar was not only "Lady of Battle" but also often a personal deity. She fought beside them and led them to victory. Ištar of Arbela was an especially warlike figure.

In one tradition, closely associated with the southern Sumerian city of Uruk, An/Anu(m) was father of Inana /Ištar. In another, the goddess was daughter of the moon god Nanna/Sîn and sister of the sun god Utu/Šamaš. Still other traditions saw her as daughter of either Enlil or Enki/Ea. Her older sister was goddess of the netherworld, Ereškigal, and her vizier was Ninšubur. Inana/Ištar had no permanent spouse, but her bridegroom was the god Dumuzi. Although motherhood was not an important element in her character, she did have some maternal instincts, and she was, in certain traditions, the mother of the deities Šara, Lu-lal, and Sutītu(m).

Plaque from Mesopotamia, probably depicting Inana/Ištar. Ca. 2000 BCE. Terracotta. British Museum. After Neumann 1970: pl. 126

Inana/Ištar was usually depicted enthroned or standing erect and proud. She wore a high horned crown and a flounced or tiered skirt. Above her shoulders there often protruded a number of what look like carved "rods," which have been interpreted variously as weapons, vegetation, rays of light, symbols of authority, and so on. The sacred animal of Inana/Ištar was the lion, and she was often portrayed standing on the animal. The eight-pointed star was one of her symbols, as, probably, was the rosette, a symbol that goes back into Mesopotamian pre-history. The post with ring and streamers certainly indicated her presence. The sign for her name is a post or standard with a ring at the top and streamers or a scarf flowing down from it, probably a neck or head band like one often called the "sacred knot."

It occurs in the earliest writings and might have been her primary symbol.

Inana/Ištar's role in Mesopotamian myth and literature was enormous. The Sumerian pre-cursor to the Babylonian "Epic of Gilgameš" and the epic itself told of Gilgameš's unsettling encounter with Inana/Ištar, but in very different terms. In "Gilgameš and the Bull of Heaven," Inana forbade Gilgameš to decide legal cases in [her] E-anna temple, but Gilgameš defied the goddess. In the Akkadian/Babylonian epic, on the other hand, Gilgameš refused Ištar's sexual advances in the most insulting terms. Both situations led to the unleashing and killing of the Bull of Heaven. Several hymns to Inana have been attributed to En-ḫedu-ana, "Entu(-priestess) Ornament of Heaven," high priestess of Nanna/Sîn at Ur and daughter of Sargon of Akkad. One of these hymns exalted Inana above the other deities for her powers, her deeds, and her glory. Another Sumerian composition, "Inana and Enki," told how Inana managed to get the drunken god Enki to give her the *Me*.

Two works narrate a tale of Inana/Ištar's descent into the netherworld. The Sumerian tale seems to be based upon Inana's heavenly journey as the planet Venus, whereas the Akkadian tale focuses on Ištar as the cause of fertility. In the Sumerian "Inana's Descent to the Netherworld," the goddess goes to her sister Ereškigal's realm where she is turned into a corpse. With Enki's help she is resuscitated and returns to earth. When she sees how indifferent her bridegroom Dumuzi is in her absence, she consigns him to the netherworld as her substitute. Later, Dumuzi's sister Geštin-ana offers to take Dumuzi's place for part of the year. The composition has been interpreted by some as explaining the cycle of the seasons and, of course, brings to mind the Greek tale of Demeter and Persephone. In the Akkadian/Babylonian version of the story, "Descent of Ištar to the netherworld," when Ištar was in the netherworld, all fertility on earth ceased.

Cylinder seal depicting Inana/Ištar with her foot on a lion. Ca. 2334–2154 BCE. Black stone. After Wolkstein and Kramer 1983: 92.

Perhaps the most important of Inana's mythic and ritual roles was her involvement with the god Dumuzi in the "Sacred Marriage," the ritual that joined Sumerian kings embodying Dumuzi with Inana, probably incarnated in a priestess. A number of sexually explicit songs celebrated the love of Inana and Dumuzi. Some provide information on the ritual and its intent: to confirm the king in his office and bring prosperity to the land. Whether or not the "Sacred Marriage" actually involved human participants is still debated. Literary evidence comes from the Ur III and Isin periods, when kings such as Šulgi, Iddin-Dagān, and Išme-Dagān presented themselves as husbands of Inana. In one case, that of Iddin-Dagān, not only did a composition describe in some detail a "Sacred

Marriage" observance and the king's role in it, but there seems to be some evidence that the king did indeed take part in such a ritual.

Inana's foremost cult center was Uruk, the city of which she was patron deity. Her great temple at Uruk was called E-anna "House of Heaven." In the tenth month at Uruk, Inana's festival of the Boat of Heaven was observed. M. Cohen suggests that the basis of this observance may have been an annual overflow onto some of the streets of Uruk, leading to a "water carnival" atmosphere. He proposes that the tale of Inana's tricking Enki of the *Me*s and escaping with them in the Boat of Heaven, using the flooded streets to float her laden boat right up to the E-anna temple, may have been, among other motifs, an etiological explanation for the annual street flooding. Her temples at Lagaš, Girsu, and Aššur were also called E-anna. She had important sanctuaries at most other towns and cities, among them Nippur, Eridu, and Mari. The sixth month at Nippur was named for a festival of Inana, when a fourteen-day celebration was held at her temple; the major event may have been the performance of an oracle. At Babylon her temple was dedicated to "Ištar of the Star," the goddess as Venus. She was also Bēlet-Akkade, "Lady of Akkade," and Bēlet-Nin-ua, "Lady of Nineveh." As mistress of towns and cities where she had flourishing cults, she held such names as Bēlet-Lagaba (or Lagab-ītu(m)), Bēlet-Sippar, and Supalītu(m) as Ištar of Zabala(m).

At Uruk there were festivals for her as the Morning and Evening Star. At Umma, accompanied by her divinized harp, she took part in the spring festival of the Early Grass. At Emar, an aspect of the goddess, Ištar of the Seas, was offered a sheep at a festival.

Assyrian kings regularly received oracles delivered to them by ecstatics, prophets, and dream interpreters. Many of them were from Ištar, especially Ištar of Arbela: for instance, "I am the goddess Ishtar of Arbela, who will destroy your enemies from before your feet" (Pfeiffer, *ANET*: 449). The goddesses Anunītu(m), Nanāya, and Kilili were closely associated or identified with Inana/Ištar. In addition, Inana/Ištar contributed much of her personality, characteristics, and areas of power to Canaanite, Phoenician, and Carthaginian Aštarte, who was the biblical Ashtoreth, and also to the "Syrian Goddess" Atargatis. All of the latter were worshipped well into Greco-Roman times. (Stuckey 2011: 19–38; Zettler and Sallaberger 2011: 1–71; Nissinen and Uro 2008; Foster 2005: 85–88, 95, 281–85, 327–33, 498–505, 592–610, 673–79, 814, 819–21, 858, 947–48; *LAS*: 66–76, 90–92, 93–99; Lapinkivi 2004: 125; Black and Green 2003: 108–9, 151–52, 154, 156–58, 169–70; Stuckey 2002: 43–44; Frayne 2001: 120–27; Foster 2001: 38, 46–52; Abusch, *DDDB*: 452–56; Leick 1999: 76, 82, 141, 153; Leick 1998: 86–89, 96–97; Litke 1998: 147; Sefati 1998; Charpin 1994: no. 39; Cohen 1993: 129, 164, 186, 209, 235–36, 290, 311–12, 360, 374, 427, 428, 439, 452; George 1993: 30, 37, 45, 68 no. 76 no. 77 no. 80, 67 no. 64, 71 no. 110, 81 no. 244, 83 no. 267, 97 no. 442; Jacobsen 1976: 36, 85, 135, 140; Tallqvist 1974: 328–38; Pfeiffer, *ANET*: 449–51; Speiser, *ANET*: 106–9; Goff 1963: 12, 84)

Inana-Aabba (M) Deity listed in An : *Anum* as Inana-a-ab-ba[ki] with explanation *ayabbītu*, "(Inana) of the Sea." (Litke 1998: 157)

Inana-Agade (M) Inana of the city Akkad, capital of the Sargonic Empire. The goddess was the patron deity of both city and dynasty. (Litke 1998: 157)

Inana-Akuz, Akuṣītu (M) Name of Inana. Means "Inana of Akuz" and rendered Akuṣītu. The city was located near Kiš. Akuṣītu is a goddess of the E-uršabba in Borsippa according to a first-millennium BCE ritual from Babylon. See Bēl-akussi(m). (Litke 1998: 158)

Inana-Anzagara (M) Name of Inana found just after a mention of Inana herself in a fragment of an Old Babylonian god list from Nippur. Means "Inana of the (Fortified) Tower." (Richter 2004: 295)

Inana-da-bada (M) Form of Inana in the Ur III period. Lamentations were made for the goddess at Ur and Nippur in connection with ceremonies related to the moon. Means "Inana (Who Is) by the Side of the Wall." (Sallaberger 1993: I, 47 note 199)

Inana-Dunni-ṣā'idi (M) Name of Inana/Ištar possibly as the tutelary goddess of Dunni-ṣā'idi in the Diyala region. Means "She of (the Fortress) Ṣā'idi." (Litke 1998: 157; Ebeling, *RlA* II: 240)

Inana-E-anna (M) Form of Inana associated with the shrine E-anna. Means "Inana of the E-anna." The shrine name probably refers to her temple in Uruk, but it is separated in the list from her Uruk sanctuary E-unuga by a reference to her temple in Zabala. Whether this indicates one of the E-anna shrines outside Uruk is uncertain. (Richter 2004: 295)

Inana-Edam (M) See E-dam

Inana-eri-silima (M) Name of Inana explained by An : *Anum* as Šulmanītu(m). Name means "Inana who Grants the City Well-being." See Šulmanītu(m). (Litke 1998: 158)

Inana-E-sagrig (M) Form of Inana mentioned in an Old Babylonian god list fragment from Nippur. The shrine is otherwise unattested. Means "Inana of the Temple(?) of the Votary." Perhaps the name is a spelling mistake for Eri-sagrig and so refers to a cult of Inana at the city of Šarrākum, not far from Nippur. (Richter 2004: 295)

Inana-galga-su(d) (M) Form of Inana as consort of the god Amurru(m); also equated to Ištar of Babylon. Means "Inana of Profound Counsel."(Beaulieu 2003: 327–28; Litke 1998: 157)

Inana-gešdal-AŠGAB (M) Name of Inana, explained by An : *Anum* as Tallayaītu(m), presumably "she of the crossbeam(geš-dal, *tallu*)." If the sign SA is to be read AŠGAB, then this might refer to a frame used to stretch or shape the leather by leather-workers. (Litke 1998: 158)

Inana-geš-tir (M) Goddess attested in texts from Mari. Means "Inana of the Forest" (Oliva 1993a: no. 42)

Inana-Ib-gala (M) Form of the goddess Inana attested in a text from Umma. Means "Inana of the Ib-gala," with Ib-gala probably referring to a temple oval. An Ib-gala shrine of Inana at Umma is very well attested in various Ur III texts. (AUCT 1, 182: r 23)

Inana-Ilip (M) Form of the Sumerian goddess Inana associated with the city of Ilip. Means "Inana of (the City of) Ilip." (Frayne 2009: 50–51; Richter 2004: 295)

Inana-ka-giri-Šū-Sîn, Inana-kaskal-Šū-Sîn (M) Variant names written on a deified statue of King Šū-Sîn. The statue, dedicated to the Sumerian goddess Inana in her aspect as the warrior goddess and helper of the king in battle, was set up in Nippur. Means "Inana of the (Military) Campaign of Šū-Sîn." (Frayne 1997b: 292–93; Sallaberger 1993: I, 103)

Inana-KIL.KIL (M) Form of Inana attested in an Old Babylonian god list. Akkadian *kilkillu* is a reed emblem, attested as a symbol of Utu/Šamaš, but not of Inana, and so a relationship with our god name cannot be established. (Weidner 1924/25)

Inana-Kisura (M) Form of the Sumerian goddess Inana at the city of Kisura, located near ancient Šuruppak. (Richter 2004: 292)

Inana-Kiš (M) Form of the Sumerian goddess Inana at the city of Kiš. Inana of Kiš served as patron deity of war for the kings of the Ḫammu-rāpi dynasty. (Richter 2004: 14, 292, 295, 297; Litke 1998: 157)

Inana-kura (M) Form of Inana attested in Pre-Dynastic Uruk. Means "Inana of the netherworld." (Beaulieu 2003: 104; Szarzynaka 1993: 8)

Inana-Larsa (M) Form of Inana attested in an Old Babylonian god list. Means "Inana of Larsa." (Weidner 1924/25)

Inana-Martu (M) Form of Inana attested in an Old Babylonian god list. Means "The Amorite Inana." (Richter 2004: 295)

Inana-Mur (M) Likely a form of Sumerian Inana in the city of Mur, perhaps a shortened form of Muru(m). The goddess is known from a royal inscription of Lipit-Ištar found at Isin. (Frayne 2009: 59; Richter 2004: 248: Frayne 1990: 59)

Inana-Ninua (M) Well-attested Sumerian form of Inana/Ištar of Nineveh. (Richter 2004: 14, 235, 292; Beckman 1998: 1–10)

Inana-nita (M) A masculine Semitic form or aspect of the goddess Inana at Pre-Sargonic Mari (c. 2400 BCE). (Archi 1993: 76)

Inana-NUN (M) Form of Inana in Pre-Dynastic Uruk (c. 3100 BCE). (Beaulieu 2003: 104)

Inana-sig (M) Form of Inana in Pre-Dynastic Uruk (c. 3100 BCE). Means "Inana of the Evening," presumably in her aspect as Venus. (Beaulieu 2003: 104; Szarzynaka 1993: 8)

Inana-Sippar (M) Form of Inana attested in an Old Babylonian god list. Means "Inana of Sippar." (Weidner 1924/25)

Inana-Supal, Supalītum (M) Name of Inana of Zabalam. Powell suggests that the name may be a conflation of the city name Zabala with *supālu*, "juniper." Sugallītum may be another form of this manifestation of Inana (see Sugallītum). (Litke 1998: 158; Michalowski 1986: 169; Powell 1976: 100)

Inana-Suti (M) Means "Inana of the Suteans" and rendered Sutītu(m). (Litke 1998: 158)

Inana-Tintir (M) Form of Inana attested in an Old Babylonian god list. Means "Inana of Babylon." (Weidner 1924/25)

Inana-UD (M) Form of the goddess Inana found already in Pre-Dynastic Uruk. Means "Inana of the Morning," presumably in her aspect as Venus. (Beaulieu 2003: 104; Szarzynaka 1993: 8)

Inana-ugnim (M) Form of Inana attested in an Old Babylonian god list. Means

"Inana (of) the Army." (Weidner 1924/25)

Inana-Unuga (M) Form of Inana in Pre-Dynastic Uruk. (Richter 2004: 295, 297)

Inana-ZA.AN (M) Goddess with a shrine in Ur III Girsu. (UDT 58: r i 6)

Inana-Zabala(m) (M) Name of Ištar as tutelary deity of Zabala(m) near Umma in southeastern Mesopotamia. Means "She of Zabala(m)." (Richter 2004: 365–66; Dalley 2009: no. 66; Litke 1998: 158; George 1993: 67 no. 74, 92 no. 370, 142 no. 1001, 161 no. 1248; Sallaberger 1993: I, 44 note 189, 233–34, 258–63)

Inana-ZA.ZA (M) Akkadian form or aspect of the goddess Inana at Pre-Sargonic Mari (c. 2400 BCE). (Archi 1993: 76)

Inara (H) Hattic/Old Hittite goddess from Central Anatolia. A deity of wild animals and the steppe. City goddess of Ḫattušas in the Old Hittite period. Daughter of the storm god. Her companion was Ḫabatali. Associated or identified with the goddess Tetešḫapi. She has a prominent part in the Hattic/Hittite "Illuyanka Tales" and is central to "Myths of the Goddess Inara." According to Laroche, her cult was Hattic and not Indo-European. In offering lists, she was called "Goddess of the Land." Appears in god lists after Heaven, Earth, the storm god, and the sun god. Associated with the leopard; in one ritual, participants wore leopard masks—this is reminiscent of the centrality of leopards in connection with figurines that might represent goddesses in the excavations at the Neolithic site of Çatal Höyök on the Anatolian plain. (Collins 2005; 38; Hoffner 1998: 10–13, 30–32, 38, 111; Lebick 1998: 93–94; van Gessel 1998: I, 187–90; Popko 1995: 55, 71, 90, 121; Haas 1994: 60, 64, 156–57, 311, 419, 450–53, 619–20; Laroche 1946/47: 82–83; Mellaart 1967; Kammenhubur, *RlA* V: 89–90)

In Ard (H, L) A Hurrian god attested at Ugarit. Perhaps related to Ardn. (del Olmo Lete 1993: 85, 201, 204)

In Atanu (H, L) A Hurrian god attested at Ugarit. Equated to Ilib. (del Olmo Lete 1993: 85)

Inbu(m) (M) Akkadian name of Nanna/Sîn as the waxing moon. It means "The Fruit." (Black and Green 2003: 135)

Indada (M) Deity in an Ur III personal name from Nippur. (NATN 377: r 1)

Indagra (M) Babylonian god of cattle associated with the moon god Sîn. He is mentioned in an *akītu* ritual at Uruk. In a list of offerings from Uruk, bull's meat was taboo as an offering for Indagra. (Cohen 1993: 434; Thureau-Dangin 1975: 79; Tallqvist 1974: 321 (under Khar); Sachs, *ANET*: 344)

Inimani-zi(d) (M) The messenger of Ninurta who precedes his spouse Dunni in An : *Anum*. Means "Whose Word Is True." Also attested at Old Babylonian Nippur and Isin. (Richter 2004: 76; Litke 1998: 48; Renger 1967: 142, 150)

Inim-dug(a) (M) Wife of Ḫasīsu, who was one of two viziers of Damgalnuna. Means "Good Word." (Tallqvist 1974: 321)

INIM.DU-lal-ga (M) Deity in an Old Babylonian god list. May mean "Say the Word and There Is Syrup and Milk." For a similarly constructed name see Qibi-dumqi. (Richter 2004: 205)

Inim-kur-dudu (M) Deity listed in An : *Anum* as a messenger of Inana. Written Inim-kúr-du$_{11}$-du$_{11}$. Means "Who (Keeps) Speaking Inimical Word(s)." (Litke 1998: 159; Richter 2004: 292)

Inimani-zi (M) Vizier of Ninurta. Means "His Word Is True." In The Hymn to the Queen of Nippur Inimani-zi seems to be associated with something that causes rejoicing, perhaps drink. (Lambert 1982: 217)

Inna-saga (M) Doorkeeper of Inana of Uruk. (Litke 1998: 156)

Innin(i) (M) See Inana

In Šalanni (H, L) A Hurrian god attested at Ugarit. (del Olmo Lete 1993: 85)

In-šuš(i)nak, Šušinak (E, M) Tutelary god of the Elamite city of Susa and its surrounding area. Means "Lord of Susa." A netherworld deity, he was important in the cult of the dead as "weigher of souls" and judge of fate. Another epithet was *laḫara* "of Death." Protector of kings. He was one of the deities who designated a person as king. Invoked in oaths. Worshipped in Susa by Awan Dynast Puzur (Kutik-)In-šušinak, when he conquered the city and erected several monuments to the god. Appears in a treaty of Narām-Sîn of Akkad. In a Neo-Assyrian god list name appears as Šušinak. In the Ur III period, the god's temples were restored or new ones built. For a time Inana was his spouse. In the second millennium BCE, he was head of the Elamite pantheon along with the god Napi-riša and the goddess Kiri-riša. The Elamite king Untaš-Napiriša built a small ziqqurat for the deity at the religious center Choga Zanbil south of Susa and later, after its destruction, he erected the great ziqqurat, which he dedicated first to Anšan's Napi-riša and then to Susa's In-šušinak. The statue of this god was removed from Susa by victorious Aššurbanipal. (Vallat 1998: 335–38; Henkelmann 2008; Black and Green 2003: 74; van Koppen and van der Toorn, *DDDB*: 433; Leick 1998: 94; George 1993: 63 no. 2, 110 no. 600; Hinz and Koch 1987: 761; König 1977: 193, 194, 227; King 1969: pl. 12; Hinz, *RlA* V: 117–19)

Inubu(m) (M) See Anubu

In-urta (M) See Ninurta

çn-uzun (M) See Ēn-uzun

In-zak (M) See En-zak

Ipiku (M) Deity attested in an Early Dynastic god list. See Ipuqa. (Mander 1986: 140)

Ipte-bītam (M) Old Babylonian goddess and attested in An : *Anum* as the vizier of Uraš. In the Neo-Babylonian period she is referred to as a daughter of the E-ibianna, the temple of Uraš in Dilbat. Means "He opened the house!" (Nashef 1991: no. 97; Litke 1998: 172)

Ipuḫ (M) Deity attested in a personal name in the Mari texts.

Ipuqa (M) Deity receiving offerings at Ešnunna during a festival of the fourth month. See Ipiku. (Cohen 1988)

Iqalia (M) Deity of the E-uršabba in Borsippa mentioned in a ritual text from Babylon for the eleventh month.

Iqbi-dumqi (M) See Qibi-dumqi

Irb/pitiga, Irwitiga (H) Old Syrian/Hurrian primeval deity. Member of the earliest stratum of divinities regarded as overthrown by younger deities and now inhabiting the netherworld. Entitled "Lord of Earth" and "Lord of Judgment." Appears in Hurrian rituals, translated into Hittite, and recipient of offerings. The "Song of Kumar-bi" is addressed to the primeval deities as a group. (Hoffner 1998: 41, 42, 112; van Gessel 1998: I, 194–95; Popko 1995: 99, Haas 1994: 113–15)

Irda (M) Boatman of the goddess Nin-imma at Nippur. Occurs in An : *Anum* as Irda-malaḫ-gal "Irda, the Great Boatman." He is also attested in a list of temple officials associated with Nippur. (Richter 2004: 93, 95; Litke 1998: 58)

Irdanna, Irdanni (M) See Daninna

Irḫan (M) God of Ur. Later absorbed into the snake god Niraḫ. Possibly he was at one time the god of the Euphrates as a serpentine waterway. Based upon a literary text, Peterson suggests that there may have been a relationship with Nin-ka-si, the goddess of beer. (Peterson 2009b: no. 39; Black and Green 2003: 167; van der Toorn, *DDDB*: 315; Wiggermann, *RlA* IX: 570–74)

Irḫan-gul (M) Son of Lisi. May mean "Irḫan the Destroyer." Written Ir-ḫa-an-gul. (Litke 1998: 75)

Irkala (M) See Allatu(m); Ereškigal

Irnina, Irnini (M) See Inana; Dannina

Irpitiga (H) One of the more obscure Hittite deities. (Archi 1990: 127)

Ir-Qingu (M) The forty-third name of Marduk in the *Enūma eliš*. Means "Ravager of Qingu," referring to Marduk's slaying of Tiamat's spouse Qingu in the *Enūma eliš*. (Litke 1998: 94)

Irra (M) See Erra

Irsirra(s) (H) Group of nurse goddesses. They are helpers of Kumarbi and in the "Song of Ullikummi" they take Ullikummi, the basalt child of Kumarbi, to the netherworld for safety. (Hoffner 1998: 41, 56, 58–59, 111; van Gessel 1998: I, 195–96; Popko 1995: 125; Haas 1994: 309, 372; Laroche 1946/47: 51)

Irša(ppa) (H) See Rešep(h)

Iršu (L) A West-Semitic deity attested in a personal name from the Amarna Letters. (Moran 1987: no. 228)

IR(ARAD)-za(?) (M) Deity with a *gudu*-priest at Ur III Umma. (MVN 4, 250: s 3)

Isadu (M) Deity who was the personification of fire (*išātu*) at Ebla

Isimud (Sum.), **Usmû(m)** (Akk.) Vizier and messenger of Enki/Ea, In "Enki and Nin-ḫursag," Isimud assists Enki in his amorous escapades.

Cylinder seal showing two-faced Isimud with his master Enki/Ea. Old Akkadian. Greenstone. 3.9 x 2.55 cm. British Museum 89115. After Black and Green 2003: 75

In the *Enūma eliš*, Marduk entrusts Usmû(m) with overseeing the Apsû and related shrines. On seals and in other art associated with Enki/Ea, he is depicted as a deity with two faces. A longer form of the name occurs in An : *Anum*, Isimud-abgal, "Isimud, the *abgal*-priest (or 'Sage')"

In the lexical series Diri written with logogram ^{d}ŠA and syllabically rendered uš-mu-ú. See Ara. (Civil 2004; Black and Green 2003: 110; Litke 1998: 102; Grayson, *ANET*: 502; Kramer, *ANET*: 38–41)

Isimud-abgal (M) See Isimud

Išar (M) Deity attested at Mari and allocated offerings destined for Bad-tibira in an Ur III text. Name means "Correctness" (Durand 2008: 241)

Išar-ālišu (M) Attested in a god list from Aššur. Means "The Just One of His City." (Schroeder 1920: no. 65)

Išar-bērišsu (M) In the circle of Nergal gods. The actual form of the name dates back to Old Akkadian times. (Richter 2004: 201, 206; Lambert, *RlA* V: 173)

Išar-kidiššu (M) Deity identified with Nergal. Means "He Is Just to His Countryside." At Lagaba, Ištar was the chief deity, and Išar-kidiššu may have been her consort. The god had a chapel in Nippur in Old Babylonian times. A seal impression calls Išar-kidiššu the seal owner's lord, and the seal bears the name Ikūn-pî-Sîn, probably a ruler of Iščhali, possibly ancient Šadlaš. Likely the god was head of the pantheon of Iščhali and consort of Ištar. (Richter 1999: 68; Litke 1998: 200; George 1993: 37; Greengus 1979: Plate XIII, no. 26; Lambert, *RlA* V: 173)

Išar-mātišu (M) One of a circle of Nergal gods. Attested in Old Babylonian god lists. Means "He Is Just to His Land." The actual form of the name dates back to Old Akkadian times. (Richter 2004: 201, 206; Lambert, *RlA* IV: 173)

Išar-pada(n) (M)(1) Deity attested in a god list from Aššur. (Schroeder 1920: no. 65); 2) Deity attested in a personal name in the Ur III period. (Schroeder 1920: no. 65)

Išartu(m) (Akk.) Wife of Mīšaru(m), god of justice. Her name means "Truth." (Litke 1998: 143; Tallqvist 1974: 324)

Išatu (L) Ugaritic god. Helper of the sea god Yam(m)u. (del Olmo Lete 1993: 56)

Išatu(m) (M) See Gibil

Išḫara (Akk.) (H, L, M) (1) Babylonian goddess of love. Identified with Ištar. Also associated with war. Sometimes a mother goddess. Her consort was Almanu and her vizier Tašme-zikru. She was associated with Dagān in one tradition and might have been his wife. Mother of the Sebettu(m), "The Seven." Her animal was at first the viper and later the scorpion. In the "Epic of Gilgameš," there is mention of a bed's being made probably for Išḫara as "the goddess of lovemaking" (Foster 2001: 16).

One of her cult centers was Kisura in Babylonia. Her temple at Babylon was called "House of the Womb," and a chapel to her in Ištar's temple at Aššur is attested. At Emar she received offerings in three aspects: Išḫara "Lady-of-the-Town," Išḫara "of-the-King," and Išḫara "of-the-Prophetesses" (Cohen 1993: 350). Also at Emar, paired with Ninurta, she was given offerings of bread and barley-beer. At Ugarit, where she was known as a Hurrian deity and called Išḫarayu/Ušḫara, she became part of the official pantheon; she was consort of the tutelary god of the palace *il bt*. She was called "The Snake," and a ritual was dedicated to her. Astrally, she was the Scorpion.

The deity is attested in a god list from Aššur written iš-ḫa-ru and in An : *Anum* as iš-ḫa-ra.

(2) Hurrian/Hittite goddess in the circle of chthonic deities. One of the primeval deities, the eldest stratum of the Old Syrian/Hurrian divinities

regarded as overthrown by younger deities and now inhabiting the netherworld. Sometimes spouse of the moon god Umbu or Kušuḫ. Carries a spindle to spin the destiny of the king. Patron of medicine and guarantor of oaths. One of her epithets was "Queen of Divine Oaths." Important member of the Hurrian pantheon at Alalaḫ and had a temple at ancient Kummani in Kizzuwatna. Appears in the moon god section of the official Hittite god list. She had a role in curse and oath rituals along with Umbu and Šar(r)uma. Invoked in treaties.

(Durand 2008: 263; Richter 2004: 399–400; Black and Green 2003: 110, 160; Becking, *DDDB*: 450; del Olmo Lete 1999: 38, 73, 83, 84, 265, 340, 360 note 89; Hoffner 1998: 41–42, 65, 67, 112; Leick 1998: 94–95; Litke 1998: 43; van Gessel 1998: I, 196–202; Pomponio and Xella 1997: 202–17; Prechel 1996; Haas 1994: 300, 316, 339–40, 349, 357, 362–63, 373–77, 470, 519, 882, 884; Popko 1995: 90, 94, 96, 101, 112; Archi 1993: 72–75; Cohen 1993: 30, 356, 358; George 1993: 165 no. 1330; Tallqvist 1974: 330; Schroeder 1920: no. 48; Laroche 1946/47: 51; Speiser, *ANET*: 78; Frantz-Szabó, *RlA* V: 176–78)

Išḫara-ša-āli(m) (M) Goddess from Emar who is listed as receiving an offering of sheep. Her name means "Išḫara of the City." (Fleming 2000: 94)

Išḫaššara (M) Hittite goddess whose name means "Lady." (Schwemer 2001: 502)

Išib-ENUN (M) Deity attested in an Early Dynastic god list. Sumerian name perhaps means "Incantation Priest (or Exorcist) (of) the Sanctuary." (Mander 1986: 37)

Išimmi-tiklašu (M) Deity invoked in an incantation. Means "I Will Determine (for Him) His Help." (Reiner 1970: 41)

Iškalli (H) Hurrian goddess adopted by the Hittites. Perhaps an epithet of the *Uršui*, a deified cult object or concept. Title "Witness of the Goddesses." Occurs in Hittite and Ugaritic ritual and material associated with Kubaba. (van Gessel 1998: I, 202–4; Haas 1994: 406–7; Laroche 1977: 286; Laroche 1946/47: 52; Otten, *RlA* V: 192)

Iškur (M) See Adad

Išlu (M) See Išru

Iš-ma-gan (M) Occurs in an Ur III text from Šarrākum. Written Iš-má-gán. (Owen 2013: nos. 141, 343)

Išmitik (E) See Ḫišmidik

Išnekarap (E), **Išme-karab** (M) Goddess of the netherworld paired with La-gamāl. A member of the pantheon of Susa and its surrounding area. Along with La-gamāl, considered an assistant of In-šušinak in the cult of the dead. Both deities had strong connections with Susiana. Invoked in the taking of oaths. In the Old Elamite period a temple was built for the god at Susa. The deity had a temple at the religious center Choga Zanbil south of Susa. The Akkadian Išme-karāb may well be a false etymology, "He Listened: A Blessing" based on the sound of the Elamite name. (Black and Green 2003: 74; Litke 1998: 135; Vallat 1998: 335–39; Hinz and Koch 1987: 790; König 1977: 84 note 9, 194, 227; Lambert, *RlA* V: 196–97)

Išpatu(m) (M) The deified quiver; presumably a symbol associated with the goddess Inana (and also elsewhere Ša(w)uš(k)a) in her warrior aspect in the E-anna temple in Neo-Babylonian Uruk. (Beaulieu 2003: 353)

Išru (M) Deity attested at third-millennium Ebla. Written ^{d}iš-ru$_{12}$/lu. (Fronzaroli 1993: 132)

Iššan (E) See Usan

Iššar (M) See Inana

Ištanu (H) Borrowed by Hittite. See Eštan; Sun Goddess of Arinna

Ištar (M) See Inana

Ištar-bēlet-Zabala(m) (M) Akkadian goddess mentioned in a tablet from the First Sealand Dynasty. Means "Ištar, Lady of Zabala(m)." See Inana-Zabala(m). (Dalley 2009: 81)

Ištar-bisrâ (M) Goddess attested at the town Ṣuprum, near Mari. Means "Ištar of Bišri." (Durand 2008: 270)

Ištar-bīti (M) Goddess mentioned in a ritual text from Babylon for the eleventh month. Means "Ištar of the House."

Ištar-Dēritum (M) Goddess in a god list from Mari. Means "Ištar, She of Dēr." (Archi 2004)

Ištar-Irrakal (M) Goddess occurring in Mari texts. Means "netherworld Ištar." (Reiter 1992b: no. 74)

Ištar-kakkabī (M) Akkadian goddess mentioned in a tablet from the First Sealand Dynasty. Means "Ištar of the Stars." See Dili-bad; Inana. (Dalley 2009: 81)

Ištar-Kiti, Kitītu(m) (M) Form of Ištar. Means "Ištar of Kiti." First an epithet related to the obscure city of Kiti and then, more commonly, a name for Inana. One of Kitītu(m)'s prominent Old Babylonian shrines was located at modern Ishchali, possibly ancient Šadlaš near Kiš. She appears in texts from Ešnunna. Her cult is also attested in a text from Uruk dating to the reign of Irdanene of Uruk. (Viaggio 2008: no. 40; Richter 2004: 291, 328; Greengus 1979: 96; Jacobsen in Frankfort et al. 1940: 189)

Ištar-Lagabītum (M) See Lagabītu(m)

Ištar-Ninu'a (M) See Inana-Nin'ua

Ištar-ruru (M) Name of Ištar in a Neo-Assyrian god list. (King 1969: pl. 17)

Ištar-ṣarbat (M) Form of Ištar attested in two Early Dynastic economic texts from Mari. May be identical to Bēlet-ṣarbat. (Durand 2008: 239; Steinkeller 1992: 271; Charpin 1987a: 107, 109)

Ištar-ša-ekallim (M) Goddess attested at Ebla. Means "Ištar of the Palace." (Archi 1993)

Ištar-ša-nubtim (M) Goddess attested at Mari. Means "Ištar of the Bee" (Oliva 1993a: no. 98)

Ištar-tašmê(m) (M) Deity attested at Neo-Babylonian Sippar referring to either a small shrine at Sippar or a visiting deity. Means "Ištar of Obedience." (Bongenaar 1997: 231)

Ištarān (M) Protective god of Dēr. Ištarān was known as negotiator, especially of border disputes, and possessor of justice. His consort was, in some sources, Šarrat-Dēri, "Queen of Dēr," his son was Zizanu, and his vizier was the snake god Niraḫ. He was worshipped from the latter part of the Early Dynastic period. His main cult center was Dēr, where his temple was called "Great Bond of the Land." He had a shrine in the temple of Nin-Girsu at Girsu and also a "seat" in the great temple at Aššur. As Ištarān-ibi-šuba he was associated with the netherworld cults of Dumuzi and Damu. In a first-millennium BCE ritual marking the end of one harvest cycle and the beginning of the next, Ištarān appears to be identified with Inana's spouse, Dumuzi, and embodies the spent harvest. (Black and Green

2003: 111; Novotny 1999: no. 11; Litke 1998: 194–95; Cohen 1993: 468; George 1993: 114 no. 657; Lambert, *RlA* V: 211)

Ištarān-gipar (M) Deity in the Ur III period. (MVN 19, 117: r 3)

Ištarān-ibi-šuba (M) See Ištarān

Ištuštaya (H) Ancient Hattic fate-determining netherworld goddess. Paired with the goddess Papaya, who was also fate determining. In the circle of the goddess Lelwani. Occurs in the tale of the vanishing god Telipinu. Mentioned in a rite for the erection of a palace. (Hoffner 1998: 17; van Gessel 1998: I, 206–7; Haas 1994: 245, 372–73; Laroche 1946/47: 26; Frantz-Szabó, *RlA* V: 175–76)

Išum (M) Deity who often appears in incantations and on boundary stones as a destructive god of pestilence, he was associated with the netherworld and its gods, such as Nergal, Šubula, Lugal-Erra, and Mes-lamta-e. Paradoxically, Išum had a beneficent protective side as herald and night watchman. He was called lord of justice and courier of the street, perhaps because of his role as the firebrand of the night watchman. Son, in one tradition, of Utu/Šamaš and Ninlil. In another, brother of Šamaš. Consort of Nin-mug or Nin-zadim. Vizier of Nergal and companion of Erra. In the late Akkadian composition "A [Prince's] Vision of the Netherworld," an Assyrian prince, in a dream, journeys to the netherworld, but escapes being killed by Nergal when Išum pleads for his life. Išum played a prominent role in the Erra Epic as Erra's messenger, and he counseled Erra to have mercy and give up his destructive rampaging. In the Late period, segments of the Erra Epic were copied onto amulets for protective purposes. He had a sanctuary at Nippur and a shrine at Aššur. His Sumerian name was Ḫendur-saga. (George 2015; Foster 2005: 837, 880–911; Black and Green 2003: 112; Leick 1998: 100; Litke 1998: 201; Cohen 1993: 204; George 1993: 165 no. 1338: Tallqvist 1974: 324; Speiser, *ANET*: 110; Edzard, *RlA* V: 213–14)

Itūr-mātišu (M) Attendant on the god Ištarān. Means "He Has Returned to His Land." (Litke 1998: 196; Edzard, *RlA* V: 222)

Itūr-Mēr (M) God attested in offering lists at Mari. Included in a festival for bringing rain. J. Sasson suggests that his statue was used to solve crimes, such as finding items that were missing, and may have been involved with a ceremony for redeeming or freeing. Some have understood this deity to have originally been an ancestor, but Sasson suggests the possibility of the opposite, that he was originally a god who later was believed to have been a human hero of old. Name means "Mer Has Returned." See Wēr. (Durand 2008: 242–43; Nakata 2011; Sasson 2001; Schwemer 2001: 182–84, 203–4, 298–99; Leick 1998: 100; Cohen 1993: 294; Fleming 1993b: no. 2; Lambert 1985a: 532–35; Langdon, 1931: 81)

Iyarri, Yarri (H) Luwian war god. Origin probably South Anatolian. Epithet "Lord of the Bow." Takes a stance like the weather god, but on a lion. Deemed the source of epidemics. Occurs in oaths and curses in treaties, in rituals, and theophoric names. Associated with the Zababa circle of deities. (van Gessel 1998: I, 178–80; Leick 1998: 113; Popko 1995: 93; Haas 1994: 368–69 and note 407; Laroche 1946/47: 82; Otten, *RlA* V: 267–68)

Iyaya (H) Goddess whose cult places were Lapana and Tiura in Anatolia. A description of her statue in her temple at Lapana is extant. (Collins 2005: 16; Laroche 1946/47: 81)

Izi-gar-dima (M) Deity attested in a text from Šuruppak in the mid-third millennium BCE. Means "Who Fashions the Torch." (Martin et al. 2001: 99)

Izuzu (M) Deity identified with Nabû in a Neo-Assyrian god list. Written i-zu-zu. (King 1969: pl. 35)

Izzariq (M) See Zāriqu

Izzummi (H) Hurrian god. Vizier of the god of freshwater and wisdom Ea. Likely a form of Isimud. Appears in the "Song of the God LAMMA" and in a prayer to Eya/Aya. (Hoffner 1998: 47, 111; van Gessel 1998: I, 209–10; Laroche 1976: 131; Laroche 1946/47: 52)

— J —

Jaldabaoth (L) See Sabaoth
Jehova(h) (L) See YHWH
Juno Caelestis (L) See Caelestis

— K —

Kabani-annake-nukurru (M) Name for Nin-šubur. Means "Whose Utterance Even Those in Heaven Cannot Change." (Litke 1998: 25)

Kabani-namtila (M) One of the eight doorkeepers of Enki. Means "His Utterance Is Life." (Litke 1998: 106)

Kabani-silima (M) One of the eight doorkeepers of Enki. Means "His Utterance Is Well-being." (Litke 1998: 106)

Ka-ba-lu-sa (M) See Qibi-dumqi

Kabiri, Kabeiri, Cabires (L) Group of minor deities originally from Samothrace. According to Philo of Byblos in the *Phoenician History*, they were seven sons or descendents of the Phoenician god Sydyk. They were often confused with the Dioscuri, as they were by Philo. He also seems to have mixed them up with the Korybantes and Samothracians. Philo reported that they invented the boat and were given the city of Beirut by Kronos. The healing god Ešmun, the eighth son of Sydyk and identified with Asculapius, was also of their number. The Kabiri were probably depicted on coins found in the temple of Elagabal (Ba'al-Ḥamōn) at Beirut. They were patron deities of navigation. (Woolmers 2017: 114–15; Lipiński 1992: 86; Attridge and Oden 1981: 46–47, 56–59, 85 notes 74, 76 and 77, 92 note 134)

Kabkabtu(m) (L, M) Deity normally depicted on amulets as a star. In the Neo-Babylonian period, associated with the temple of Marduk. Also mentioned in an offering list from Ugarit. See Uridimmû(m). (del Olmo Lete 1999: 320; Wiggermann 1992: 174)

Kabta (M) Probably male and likely spouse of Inana/Ištar. In seal inscriptions paired with Ninusana, a name of Inana as the planet Venus. According to Tallqvist, he was vizier of Nanna/Sîn. Kabta occurs in theophoric names from Old Babylonian times and the Kassite period. (Black and Green 2003: 109; Litke 1998: 162; George 1993: 34; Tallqvist 1974: 340; Lambert, *RlA* V: 284)

Kadesh (L) See Qadesh

Ka-gal, Ka-maḫ (M) Name of Marduk in An : *Anum*. Means "Great/Lofty Mouth." The reading ka instead of inim "word" is based upon this section of Marduk's names being based upon parts of the body. (Litke 1998: 223)

Kahal (Arabia) Deity from the Rum area in Arabia in the Neo-Babylonian period. (Gentili 2001: no. 90)

Kan-ḫegala (M) Deity in the circle of Enki gods in An : *Anum*. Means "Gate of Abundance." Described in a late text as one of the fifty Laḫamas or servants of the Abzu. Also a gate-keeper of Enki in Eridu. (Richter 2004: 105, 107, 230; Litke 1998: 106; Streck, *RlA* XX: 516–17)

Ka-ḫetila (M) Name of Marduk in An : *Anum*. Means "(His) Mouth (utters) 'Let there be Life'." (Litke 1998: 224)

KA$_5$-ḫuš (M) Sumerian form or title of Nergal/Erra. Occurs in An : *Anum* shortly after Erra. Variant is Ḫuš-eri. Means 'Angry Fox(?)." (Litke 1998: 207)

Kait (H) See Ḫalki

Kaka (Akk.), **Gaga** (Sum.) Vizier and messenger of An/Anu(m) and minister of An-šar. He was equated to the gods Nin-šubur and Pap-sukkal as vizier of An/Anu(m) and An-šar. In the composition "Nergal and Ereškigal," Anu sends Kaka to the netherworld with a message for Ereškigal. In the *Enūma eliš*, faced with the threat from Ti'amat, An-šar sends Kaka (Gaga) to arrange for a meeting of all the younger deities. In An : *Anum* the deity ^{d}Meme, the vizier of Ningal, is glossed gaga, perhaps another role associated with this vizier. (Such-Gutiérrez: 2005/6; Foster 2005: 436–86, 506–24; Litke 1998: 25, 122, 182; Bonechi 1993b: no. 24; Steinkeller 1982; Tallqvist 1974: 308, 340; Grayson, *ANET*: 508, 512; Speiser, *ANET*: 64; Heidel 1967: 33; Edzard, *RlA* V: 288)

Kakala, Kukula, Kakuša (M) Sumerian deity with a temple at the obscure town of Aḫud. In An : *Anum* written with ku_7 and glossed ku-lu-la and ka-ka-la. (Litke 1998: 215; George 1993: 99 no. 467; Lambert, *RlA* V: 288)

Kakanunu wa-Šunama (L) See Takanunu wa-Šunama

Kak-sisa (M) In a Neo-Assyrian god list identified as a constellation. (King 1969: pl. 13)

Kalam-ša-kušu (M) One of six bull-lyres of Utu/Šamaš. Means "(He) who Soothes the Nation." Another lyre of Utu listed in an adjoining entry in An : *Anum* is Ša-kušu-kalam-ma. The two names mean the same thing and so it is possible that originally these two were just variants of the same lyre's name that in time became understood as separate lyres. (Litke 1998: 134; Tallqvist 1974: 341; Lambert, *RlA* V: 289)

Kalbu(m)-Gula (M) The divinized dog as a symbol of Gula, the goddess of healing. Attested at Old Babylonian Larsa. (Renger 1967: 146)

Kalkal (M) Enlil's doorkeeper in the Ekur temple at Nippur. His wife was Nimin-taba. Attested in theophoric names, liturgies, and god lists from Ur III to Old Babylonian times. Appeared in the Old Babylonian flood story. Had a "seat" as a doorkeeper in the main temple at Aššur. (Cohen 2015: 123; Litke 1998: 53; George 1993: 105 no. 535; Lambert, *RlA* V: 323)

Kalkal-Baba (M) In An : *Anum*, Lama of the goddess Baba. (Litke 1998: 174)

Kalkal-ša-Maškan (M) Likely an Ur III form of the Sumerian gate-keeper god Kalkal at ancient Maškan, a settlement in the area of Umma. (Cohen 1996a: 31; Frayne 2007: 10)

Kallat-Ekur (M) Probably a goddess from the city of Opis on the Tigris. Attested with Nergal, perhaps her spouse, in a Neo-Babylonian tablet actually from Sippar. Means "Daughter-in-Law of the Ekur." (Bongenaar 1997: 231 note 206)

Kal(l)u (M) See Galla

KAM (M) Deity, the reading of whose name is uncertain. Occurring in a fragment of an Old Babylonian god list after the goddess Nin-maš. Nin-maš appears, along with the goddess Nin-pirig, as offspring of the god Enlil. In other sources Nin-maš is associated with Nin-ḫursag and Ereškigal. See Nin-maš. (Richter 2004: 159)

Kamad-duru (M) Sumerian demon mentioned in incantations. Written kamad(dìm)-$duru_5$. (George 2016: no. 10a)

Kamadge(n) (M) A Sumerian demon explained in An : *Anu ša amēli* as the demon *lilītu(m)* and mentioned in incantations. (George 2016: no. 28; Litke 1998: 241)

KamadḪAL (M) A Sumerian demon mentioned in an incantation, perhaps for Kamad-tab (see below). (George 2016: no. 10a)

Kamadme (M) Sumerian demon mentioned in incantations. See Lamaštu. (George 2016: no. 9ff.)

Kamad(me)-kug (M) Sumerian netherworld deity in the Sumerian work "The Death of Gilgameš," to whom Gilgameš makes offerings before he dies. In the lexical series Diri [d]Kamad-kù is explained as *ḫallulaya,* a female demon or insect, and *iškarissu,* a rodent. (Civil 2004; Katz 2003: 395–97; Frayne 2001: 153)

Kamad-tab (M) A demon in An : *Anu ša amēli* written ⸢DÌM?⸣-tab and explained as "headache" (*bibītu*). (Litke 1998: 241)

Kamaššuratu(m) (Akk.) Deity identified with Ištar. Occurs in a god list from Mari dating to the Ur III period. Survived in a later god list as a mother goddess. J.-M. Durand suggests the name may be a form of Kotharôt. (Cohen 2015: 320; Durand 1985: 163; Lambert 1985a: 530; Tallqvist 1974: 339)

Kamiš, Kemosh, Chemosh (L) Warrior and patron deity of the Moabite dynasty. Seems to have had netherworld connections. His consort was Sara. Kamiš was worshipped as an important deity at Ebla, where he had a temple and where a month in the calendar was named for him. According to I Kings 11:5–8, Israel's King Solomon had a shrine constructed for the god on a hill close to Jerusalem. On a stele called the Moabite Stone or the Mesha Stele, dating to the ninth century BCE, the Moabite king Mesha boasts of his victory over Israel (this war is recorded also in II Kings 3), and calls himself "son of Kamiš," and refers to a "high place" of the god, whom he names Aštar-Kamiš. This indicates that Kamiš was identified with Aštar, who was, among other things, a male god of war. See ʿAṯtar. The name of the ancient city Carchemish means "Quay of Chemosh." In the Hellenistic period, Kamiš was equated to the Greek war god Ares. (Cohen 2015: 12; Betlyon 2005: 20; Müller, *DDDB*: 186–89; Pomponio and Xella 1997: 175–81; Handy 1994: 126–27; Mattingly, *ABD* I: 895–97; Smith 1990: 24; Finnegan 1989: 135; Albright, *ANET*: 320–21; Albright 1968: 239)

Kammamma (H) Hattic/Palaic/Hittite goddess. A protective mother goddess from the oldest level of Hattic deities. A member of the Hittite state pantheon. In the circle of the sun goddess. Attested in rituals. She was involved with magic. (van Gessel 1998: 215–17; Popko 1995: 113–14; Haas 1994: 246 note 53, 426, 586, 611, 882; Laroche 1946/47: 27)

Kamos (L) See Kamiš

Kamrušepa (Hittite, Luwian), **Kattaḫzipuri, Kattaḫzi(p)wuri** (Hattic, Palaic) Goddess of magic and healing. Patron of herds and, in a Luwian ritual, a birth assistant. One of her epithets was "Mother." Identified with Hattic Kattaḫziwuri in the Old Hittite period, eventually replacing her. Had an active role in the story of the lost god Telipinu and was central in some mythic compositions. Included with Šau(w)uška goddesses in a list of deities from Kültepe and member of the pantheon at Kanesh. Attested in Palaic and Luwian rituals, especially an incantation against disease. In rituals of healing magic, the "Old Woman" who conducted the rite, often brought Kamrušepa into the sacred process by telling a myth that involved her. Associated with the cult of Telipinu. (Soysal 2002: no. 7; Hoffner 1998: 16, 22, 33, 35–36, 111; Leick 1998: 102, 113; van Gessel 1998: I, 217–20, 235–37; Popko 1995: 87–88, 92–93, 105; Haas 1994: 200 note 23, 261, 278–79, 310, 412, 419, 438–41, 466, 613, 620, 882; Laroche 1946/47: 28–29; Frantz-Szabó, *RlA* V: 351–52, 478)

Kamul (E) The deity Kamul and the renovation of the god's temple is the subject on a brick of the Elamite king Šutruk-Naḫḫunte. (Michaud 2000: no. 11)

Kana-abdu (M) One of the eight doorkeepers of Enki. The next entry is Igi-a-na-ab-du$_7$, "In his face (or eyes)...," which suggests that Ka-na here means "in his mouth." (Litke 1998: 106)

Kanab (M) Deity at Mari. Written [d]Ka-na-ab. (Durand 1983: 531)

Kanisura (Sum.), **Uṣur-amassa/u** (Akk.), also written Ganisura. Daughter of Nanāya of Uruk. Sister of Gazbaba. Steinkeller identifies Kanisura with "Venus's invisibility stage, that is, Inana's disappearance in the netherworld." She was known as "Lady of Witches."

The Old Babylonian king Anam of Uruk, who named her as lady of the Iturungal canal, commissioned a temple for her in Uruk. The city of Kanisura was on the Iturungal canal and was probably one of her cult centers. She had a cult in Old Babylonian Kiš, and she also had a temple in the city of Ekallātu(m) on or near the Tigris. In addition, she had sanctuaries in Babylon and Aššur.

She is attested with Gazbaba in a late text in connection with the E-zida temple in Borsippa. The sisters were important in a ritual "to adjust the imbalance between daytime and night occurring around the solstices." At or around the solstice, the divine hairdressers Kaṭuna and Ṣilluš-ṭāb, daughters of Arua, left the E-sag-ila temple in Babylon for the E-zida temple in Borsippa. Then, a little later, the sisters Kanisura and Gazbaba processed from the temple in Borsippa to Babylon to the E-sag-ila. The ritual was intended to cause the days to lengthen. In a lamentation Kanisura is paired with the spider goddess Uttu as searching for their children. (Steinkeller 2013a: 468; Beaulieu 2003: 316–19; Black and Green 2003: 134; Cohen 1993: 318–19; George 1993: 34, 165 no. 1339; Tallqvist 1974: 385; Edzard, *RlA* V: 389)

Kantipuiti (H) A Central Anatolian/Hattic protector goddess(?). Paired with Kappariyamu. Received offerings for fertility. A text from Ḫattušas made note of her priestess and probably her priest. She was keeper of the *kursa*, an important sacred container that was used in rituals. (van Gessel 1998: I, 220–21; Haas 1994: 450, 454; Laroche 1946/47: 83; Otten, *RlA* V: 390)

Kanzura (H) Brother of Teššub. According to the "Song of Kumarbi," he was "produced by Kumarbi when he was inadvertently impregnated by Anu." Holy mountain (see also Deified Mountains). (Hoffner 1998: 41, 44, 111)

Kappariyamu (H) See Kantipuiti

Kara-e (M) Deity identified with Enki/Ea in a Neo-Assyrian god list. (King 1969: pl. 33)

Kar-dug (M) Along with Sakar-dug, courier of Utu. The name is written kar-(du-)ug (Incantation to Utu) and kar-du and [kar^{ka}]$^{-ár-du-ug}$dug$_4$ in An : *Anum*. An incantation refers to the two couriers as Gubla and Igi-tal. George suggests that these may be variant names for the god pair Kardu and Sakardu. Possibly the same deity as occurs at Ur III Umma written Kar-du. (Nik. 2 375). (George 2016: no. 47; Litke 1998: 134; Sallaberger 1993: I, 247, 254; Tallqvist 1974: 341; Lambert, *RlA* V: 423)

Karḫuḫa(s) (H) One of three chief deities of the city of Carchemish. The Hittite/Hurrian triad consisted of Tarḫunzas, Karḫuḫas, and Kubaba. (Schwemer 2001: 622)

Karkar (M) God identified with Dumuzi. May mean "The Kidnapped One," referring to Dumuzi's seizure by the *galla*-demons. Written kar-kar. (Living-stone 1989: 94–95, 102)

Karkara (M) Deity identified with Utu/Šamaš in a Neo-Assyrian god list. Written kár-kár-ra. Means "Shine" or "(Sun)Rise." (King 1969: pl. 27)

Kar-šul (M) Goddess explained in An : *Anu ša amēli* as "Ištar of the Warrior(s)." (Litke 1998: 234)

Karuiles Siunes (H) The oldest layer of Old Syrian-Hurrian deities. Sent to the netherworld by the young group, but still recognized with offerings. They are invoked in the "Song of Kumarbi." Sometimes equated to the Anunnaki. (Hoffner 1998: 42, 112; Leick 1998: 141)

Karzi (H) Hittite or Luwian protective deity. Occurs in treaties. (van Gessel 1998: I, 225; Haas 1994: 450; Laroche 1946/47: 84; Otten, *RlA* V: 459)

Kasios (L) See Ba'al-Ṣapōn

KASKAL.KUR (M) A logographic writing for various deities in An : *Anum*, whose names are glossed: Alba, Ilba, Alḫa, Ilḫa, Baliḫa (Richter 2004: 383–84; Litke 1998: 218)

Kaš-ba (M) Sumerian name of Inana in an Old Babylonian god list. Since Inana was associated with taverns, possibly the name means "She who Distributes Beer."Perhaps even an orthography for Kaš-bar, "Decider." (Richter 2004: 292)

Kaš-bar (M) One of the judges of Utu/Šamaš. Means "Decider." (Litke 1998: 135)

Kaššitu (m) God carried off by Sennache-rib from Uruk. Means "The Kassite." (Beaulieu, 2013: 319)

Kata-e (M) One of five demons listed under the demon category *katillû(m)*. Means "That which Comes Out of the Mouth." (Litke 1998: 209; Tallqvist 1974: 339; Lambert, *RlA* V: 477)

Katar-ana (M) One of seven bull-lyres of An/Anu(m). Means "Praise of An." (Litke 1998: 29; Lambert, *RlA* V: 486)

Kathar (L) See Koṯar-wa-Ḫašis

Katherat (L) See Koṯerat(u)

Katillû(m) (M) See Dingir-ḫuš

Kattaḫ(ḫ)a/i, Gattaḫ(ḫ)a, Ḫatagga (H) Hattic divinity whose name means "Queen." Probably a mother goddess. Tutelary deity of Ankuwa (a town near Ḫattušas), where she had her temple. She was worshipped also in several other cities. Occurs in treaties and rituals. In a treaty from the time of Ḫattušili III, she acted as an oath and curse guarantor. Ḫattušili III offered a city model to her and refrained from setting fire to her city when he could have done so. During the collapse of the Hittite Empire, the goddess was very significant in her cult city. (van Gessel 1998: I, 228–35; Groddek 1997: no. 133; Popko 1995: 72, 113–14, 143; Haas 1994: 310–11; Laroche 1946/47: 28; Ünal, *RlA* V: 477–78)

Kattaḫzip/wuri (H) See Kamrušepa

Kaṭuna (M) One of two divine female hairdressers of Marduk's wife Zarpanītu(m). The other was Kaṭuna's sister Ṣilluš-ṭāb. They were daughters of the birth/mother goddess Arua. Their "seat" in Babylon was called "House of Beautiful Allure." They were important in a late-Babylonian ritual "to adjust the imbalance between daytime and night occurring around the solstices." At or around the solstice, Kaṭuna and Ṣilluš-ṭāb left Babylon for the E-zida temple in Borsippa, and then, a little later, Kanisura and Gazbaba, daughters of Nanāya, processed from the temple in Borsippa to Babylon and the E-sag-ila temple. The ritual was intended to cause the days to lengthen. (Litke 1998: 98; Cohen 1993: 319 note 1; Lambert, *RlA* V: 488)

Kaush (L) See Qaws

Kauthar (L) See Koṯar-wa-Ḫasīs

Kayyāmānu(m) (M) The planet Saturn divinized. Found mainly in astronomical texts. Means "The Steady One." (Stol, *DDDB*: 478; Reiner 1970: 18)

Kazba (M) See Gazbaba

Keldi, Kelti (H, L) Son of Aya according to the one mention of him in Hittite material. Attested at Ugarit in a god list and a ritual text. (del Olmo Lete 1999: 84, 209; van der Toorn, *DDDB*: 479; van Gessel 1998: I, 240; Haas 1994: 380)

Kemosh (L) See Kamiš

Kerub (L) See Cherub

Kettu(m) (M) See Kittu(m)

Kewan (M) See Kayyāmānu(m)

Khosher-et-Ḫašis (L) See Koṯar-wa-Ḫasīs

Ki (M) Sumerian for "earth" and personified as a goddess. Consort and sister of sky god An. Both Ki and An were children of the primordial goddess Namma. Ki was mother of Enlil by An. Together An and Ki produced various plants. Later her role was taken over by various birth/mother goddesses. (Black and Green 2003: 112–13; Leick 1998: 104; Litke 1998: 20, 189; Tallqvist 1974: 341)

Ki-a (M) Sumerian god, the personification of the netherworld. See Erṣetu. (Litke 1998: 221; Lambert, *RlA* V: 586)

Ki-ib (M) Deity attested in a god list from Aššur. (Schroeder 1920: no. 54)

Ki-dur (M) Deity attested in an Early Dynastic god list. According to Lambert the "Bond" is "the cosmic rope holding the parts of the universe together" and perhaps Ki-dur is the point where the rope touches the earth. See Eškita-abzu and Lugal-durmaḫ. (Mander 1986: 141)

Kigir (M) See Angir

Ki-gula (M) (1) A One of seven bull-lyres of the god An/Anu(m). (2) One of the six sons of Enki. (3) Wife of the god Nita, vizier of Uraš. Ki-gula likely means "Greatest Place," perhaps a euphemism for the netherworld. (Litke 1998: 29, 100, 173; Tallqvist 1974: 341; Lambert, *RlA* V: 589)

Kiki (M) A deified bird attested in god lists of the Early Dynastic period from Abu Ṣalābīkh and Šuruppak. His wife appears as Nin-kiki. In the Sumerian zà-mí hymns from Abu Ṣalābīkh, he appears as the tutelary deity of a town in the environs of Umma. The name is likely onomatopoeic. (Mander 1986:

43, 98; Biggs 1974: 49; Cavigneaux and Krebernik, *RlA* IX: 448)

Kiku (M) Deity attested in the Early Dynastic period in the Umma region who participated in the *nesag* festival. Written Ki-ku$_5$. (Bartash 2013 no. 8)

Ki-la (M) See Uttu

Kilaḫ-šupir (E) The Elamite fire god originally from the pantheon of Anšan. King Untaš-Napiriša erected a temple for the deity at Choga Zanbil south of Susa. (Vallat 1998: 337; Black and Green 2003: 75; König 1977: 53–54 and note 12, 227)

Kili-dagala (M) Deity identified with Utu/Šamaš. In An : *Anum* written Kili-dagal with gloss ki-li-da-gal. For the reading of the name with variant gir$_x$(UM)-dagal-la, see Cohen 1993: 127. (Litke 1998: 130; Tallqvist 1974: 342)

Kilili (Akk.) **Abbašušu** (Sum.) Goddess known as the "Woman in the Window." A messenger of Inana/Ištar. Kilili probably means "Garlanded One." The deities Aba-šušu and Abta-gigi are listed in An : *Anum* as messengers of Inana. Aba-šušu "Who Leans in (or Looks out of) the Window" and Abta-gigi, "Who Answers (or Commands) from the Window," are forms of Kilili. Kilili was also a female demon who could cause diseases, as well as cure them. Demon or not, Kilili was considered wise in the sense of skilled or knowing: "You are Kilili, the wisest of the wise, who concerns herself in the matters of people." In this she and Ishtar are one: "at a window of the house sits wise Ištar" (Lapinkivi 2004: 234).

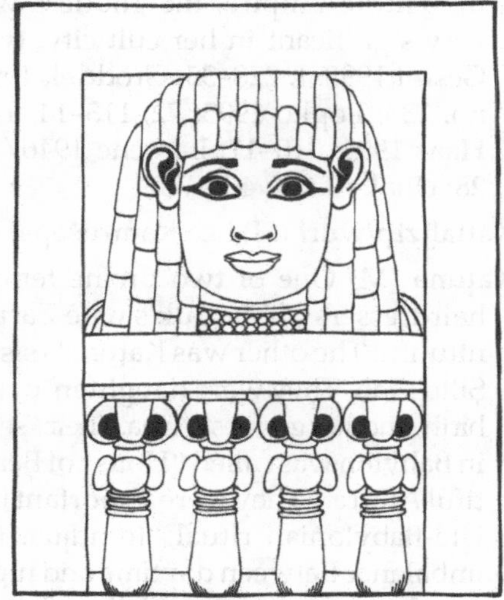

Furniture inlay found in Mesopotamia. Ca. 900 BCE. Ivory, probably carved in Phoenicia. After Shepsut 1993: 115.

Many beautiful ivory images of the "Woman at the Window" are extant. They were carved, mostly in Phoenicia, as furniture inlays, especially for beds. They have been found in three Mesopotamian sites. The most famous image is the so-called "Mona Lisa of Nimrūd." In most of these images, the goddess was posed full face in a window frame, but there are also some ivories in which a goddess, probably Kilili, is depicted in profile seated on throne, accompanied by lily plants, and facing a god who is enthroned opposite her. She usually had heavy, ornately dressed ringlets and often wore a necklace.

Kilili was regularly invoked in incantations and litanies, where she was addressed, for instance, as "Kilili, the queen of the windows, Kilili, who leans into/from the windows" (Lapinkivi 2004: 233 note 1147). Kilili might also have been associated with the *kil-*

ilu(m), "the mural crown," which sported city battlements on top of the wall; the crown was worn by Assyrian queens and by goddesses who protected cities. Kilili has normally been interpreted as a prostitute, or identified with Inana/Ištar as a prostitute, for her stance was seen as one of displaying her wares in a window. Kilili, goddess and demon, was, it seems, much more than a prostitute. The motif of the "Woman in the Window" was likely a factor in the Hebrew Bible's account (in 2 Kings 9:30) of the death of Jezebel, the Phoenician queen of Ahab, king of Israel, the northern kingdom. One of the epithets of Greek goddess Aphrodite, Parakyptousa, "Peeping Out (of a Window/Door)," may have referred to her as the "Woman in the Window." (Beaulieu 2013: 319; Lapinkivi 2004: 232–40; Assante 2003: 33; Assante 1998: 55, 57, 73–82; Litke 1998: 158–59; Lipiński 1995: 140, 488–89; Tallqvist 1974: 342; Zimmern 1928: columns 1–3)

Kinda-zi(d) (M) Goddess particularly associated with the Lagaš area, where she received regular and festival offerings. Wife of Nin-kar-nuna. Jacobsen says that Kinda-zi(d) was the "chamberlain" of Nin-Girsu, preparing his bath "and seeing that there was fresh straw in his bed" (1976: 82). Her name means "Reliable Hairdresser." (Cohen 2015: 44; Litke 1998: 49)

Kingal-uda (M) Demon. Means "Commander of the Storm." (Litke 1998: 209; Tallqvist 1974: 342)

Kingu (M) See Qingu

Kin-la-ŠE (M) Written Kin-la-$ŠE_3$?. Deity attested in a Fara text. (SF 50: iv 10)

Kin-ma (M) Forty-fourth name of Marduk in the *Enūma eliš*, where he is described as "leader' (perhaps for kingal) and "grantor of counsel" (perhaps for kin "oracle" gá). (Foster 2005: 482; Litke 1998: 95; Tallqvist 1974: 343; Speiser, *ANET*: 72; Heidel 1967: 58)

Kin(n)ār(u), Kinnūr (L) Deified lyre. Mentioned in ritual texts from Ugarit and also known in the Phoenician. Perhaps, as Albright suggests, identified with Kinyras, father of Adonis. (Pardee 2002: 15, 18, 48, 49; del Olmo Lete 1999: 131; Wyatt, *DDDB*: 488; Albright 1968: 144, 147)

Kin-nu-šum (M) Deity in the circle of Šala, wife of the storm god. May mean "She who Cannot Be Ordered About" (Akk. *têrta nadānu*). (Schwemer 2001: 400, 402 note 3374; Litke 1998: 143)

Kinyras (L) See Adonis

Kippat-māti (M) Goddess in Aššur attested in a first-millennium ritual for the eleventh month. Means "Circumference of the Land." (Cohen 2015: 442)

Kiri-riša (E) Supreme goddess of Elam since the second millennium BCE, as her name, literally "Great Goddess," makes clear. Spouse of Napi-riša and mother of Ḫutran. Protector of kings. In the third millennium BCE, the name was used as an epithet to refer to the goddess Pinikir; it was apparently taboo to refer to Pinikir by her real name. Kiri-riša is attested for the first time as a separate goddess on an Akkadian alabaster cylinder of the Elamite regent Simut-wartaš of the eighteenth century BCE. The goddess Pinikir appears after Kiri-riša's name in a number of cases during the second millennium BCE, only sporadically at first, but with increasing frequency in Neo-Elamite times. What, then, was originally just an epithet of the goddess Pinikir became later a separate deity in her own right and indeed one of the highest ranked in the Elamite pantheon.

Kiri-riša appears in many theophoric names and in inscriptions from both ancient Liyan (modern Bushehr on the Persian Gulf) and the capital of Elam at Susa. Her titles included "Lady of Heaven," "Mother of the Gods," and "Lady of the Temple." Another one was: "Lady of Life, who has authority over the grove, the gateway, and [the one] who prays." Gateways and groves were prominent in Elamite religion and seem to have had much to do with the cult of the dead. Another epithet was Laḫara "(She) of Death." Even in the third millennium BCE the "Mother of the Gods" stood at the head of the pantheon, unchallenged throughout Elam. In the course of the second millennium BCE, this highest position in the pantheon was turned over to the pair Ḫumban and Kiri-riša. Kiri-riša also was assigned to be the spouse of the god In-šušinak as that god rose in the pantheon in the course of the second half of the second millennium BCE. Then she held the title "Great Spouse."

According to Vallat, Kiri-riša wore a crown with horns on it. There is evidence of the cult of Kiri-riša from early in the second millennium until the Late Elamite period. One of her cult centers was at Liyan, where, in the eighteenth century BCE, the Elamite regent Simut-wartaš made an offering to her. Later, in the thirteenth century BCE, the king of Elam Ḫumban-numena erected a temple for Kiri-riša and Napi-riša at Liyan. Anšan was another important center of her cult and that of her consort Napi-riša. With the political ascent of Anšan in the second millennium BCE, the two deities joined In-šušinak as heads of the state pantheon of Elam. At the ceremonial site at Choga Zanbil there was a temple to the goddess. (Vallat 1998: 337–38; van Koppen and van der Toorn *DDDB*: 489–90; König 1977: 194, 227; Hinz, *RlA* V: 605–6)

Kiri-urur (M) Deity in An : *Anum* who along with Barasiga-Nibru is a bara$_2$-sig$_5$-ga of Ninurta. Kiri-urur occurs after hairdresser and barber gods in the circle of Ninurta gods, raising the possibility that this is a beautifying profession, something like "Who smears / powders(?) the nose." The reading kiri is based on a gloss. See Nin-kiri-ura. (Richter 2004: 75; Cavigneaux and Krebernik, *RlA* IX: 449; Litke 1998: 49, 50)

Kirzal-kalama (M) One of six bull-lyres of the storm god Adad. Means "Joy of the Nation." (Litke 1998: 145; Lambert, *RlA* V: 606)

Kirzal-šu-LIL-du-du (M) One of the six bull-lyres of Dingir-maḫ. (Litke 1998: 77)

Kirmaš, Kirmeš, Girwaš (E) Elamite deity occurring in the royal name Kukkirwaš. Associated with the part of Elam known as Awan. The statue of this god was later taken away from Elam by Aššurbanipal. (Vallat 1998: 337; König 1977: 89 note 4, 227; Hunger, *RlA* V: 607)

Kirmašir (E) Elamite deity occurring in a treaty between Narām-Sîn of Akkad and a king of Susa. Untaš-Napiriša commissioned a temple for the divinity at Susa. The statue of this god was taken away by victorious Aššurbanipal. (Vallat 1998: 335–37; König 1977: 177 note 8, 196, 227

Kirpisir (E) Elamite deity appearing in a treaty between Narām-Sîn of Akkad and a king of Susa. May be a variant spelling of Kirmašir. (König 1977: 29, 196, 227)

Kirwaš (E) See Kirmaš

Kisikil-lila (M) See Lil

Ki-ša (M) Wife of the river god Id. Written ki-ša$_6$ and means "Favorable Place." Equated in one text to the wife of Enki/Ea. Seated, along with Id, near a well in the main temple complex at Aššur. (Litke 1998: 100; George 1993: 104 no. 512; Tallqvist 1974: 342; Lambert, *RlA* V: 620)

Ki-šar, Ki-šar-gal (M) (1) Wife of An-šar and An-šar-gal. Names mean "The Entire Earth" and "The Great, Entire Earth." (2) Wife of An/Anu(m) when he was identified with An-šar. (3) Wife of the star Gudanna, "the Enlil of Šuruppak." (Lambert, *RlA* V: 620)

Kiš-gal (M) The deified city Kiš, "Great Kiš." Attested in an Early Dynastic god list from Abu Ṣalābīkh. Kiš-gal also appears in a theophoric name in the Early Dynastic "Names and Professions List" from Abu Ṣalābīkh and Ebla. (Mander 1986: 41; Biggs 1974: plate 40 no. 73 column iii line 21)

Kiššitum (M) Deity attested in the Mari texts. Means "She of Kiš." (Durand 2008: 260)

Kiš-ursag (M) Deity attested in an Early Dynastic god list. The deity also appears in a theophoric name in the Early Dynastic "Names and Professions List" from both Abu Ṣalābikh and Ebla. Means "Kiš Is a Warrior." (Mander 1986: 41)

Kitītu(m) (M) See Ištar-kiti

Kittu(m) (M) Abstract deity who personified the concept "Truth." Daughter, sometimes son, of Šamaš and Aya. In An : *Anum* Kittu(m) is listed as the son of Utu and Niggina, which is simply the Sumerian equivalent of Kittu(m), and is listed in the previous entry as the daughter of Utu. Often paired with the god Mīšaru(m), "Justice." The goddess appears mainly in prayers and incantations but also in legal documents. She had temples at Bad-tibira and Raḫabu, and was worshipped also at Mari. (Black and Green 2003: 98; Batto, *DDDB*: 930; Litke 1998: 133; George 1993: 165 no. 1340; Tallqvist 1974: 342; Klein, *RlA* IX: 311–12)

Ki-tuš-kirzal (M) See Me-ḫuš(-a)

Ki-tuš-Keši (M) Child of the goddess Lisina. Means "Resident of Keš," the temple precinct of Šarrākum. (Litke 1998: 76; Cohen 1993: 208)

Ki-ud-ug (M) Deity attested in an Early Dynastic god list. Written ki-ud-ug$_5$. (Mander 1986: 141)

Ki-uraš (M) Deity known from a late Assyrian list of gods. (Lambert 2013: 423)

KI.ZA (M) Deity belonging to the Enki temple in Nippur. (Sallaberger 1993: I, 99, 102)

Kizaza (M) One of the seven destiny-decreeing gods of the E-sagil temple in Babylon. (George 2004 no. 20)

Kmṯ-wa-Ẓẓ (L) See Ẓẓ-wa-kmṯ

Kolpia(s), Colpia (L) According to the *Phoenician History* of Philo of Byblos, a wind god whose wife was Baau "Night." Father of Aion and Protogonos. (Attridge and Oden 1981: 40–41, 79 note 42)

Koshar, Kothar (L) See Koṯar-wa-Ḫasīs

Kōṯarṭ(u), Kotherāt(h), Kotharōt(h), Kosharōth, Koshart(u), Katharāt, Kûšarâtum (L, M) Seven goddesses of fertility at Ugarit. Name Koṯarāt(u) means "Skillful Ones." Patrons of marriage and conception. Daughters of El/Il, the head of the Ugaritic pantheon. Most common name for the group was "Radiant Daughters of the [New] Moon." In the 'Aqhat composition, when Danel realized that he was to have a son, he wined and dined the seven goddesses. There is a hymn to them at the end of the composition about the marriage of Yariḫ and Nikkal. The goddesses appear in the god lists at Ugarit, in which they seem to be the equivalent of the group of midwife goddesses who assisted the Mesopotamian mother goddess. Their individual names were Tiluḫahu, Mulughayu, Tātiqatu, Baqr'tu, Taqr'tu, Purubaḫtu, and Damiqatu. In a god list they belonged to the deity group "Earth and Heavens" (del Olmo Lete 1999: 131). (Durand 2008: 218; Pardee 2002: 14, 47, 49; Wyatt 2002: 264–65, 340–41; Smith 2001: 69–70; Stol 2000: 83; del Olmo Lete 1999: 57, 281, 331; Pardee, *DDDB*: 491–92; Finegan 1997: 148; Parker 1997a: 56–57, 249; Albright 1968: 138)

Kôṯar-wa-Ḫasīs(u), Kothar-wa-Ḫasīs, Kothar-u-Ḫasīs, Ktr w Hss, Kauthar, Koṯar(u), Koshar, Kotar, Ḫusor (L) God (or gods) of craftsmanship and skill, as well as wise advisor(s) in texts from Ugarit. General factotum to the deities. He was a talented architect/builder and metal-worker, as well as a musician and diviner. According to Ugaritic mythic texts, he was at home in Memphis in Egypt and Caphtor, probably Crete. The deity Koṯar(u) occurred alone in Ugaritic texts, in addition to forming part of a double name Koṯar-wa-Ḫasīs. Koṯar means "Skillful" and Ḫasīs(u) "Wise," the latter name occurring only in conjunction with Koṯar.

In the group of Ugaritic mythic compositions centered on the storm god Ba'lu/Had(d)ad, Koṯar-wa-Ḫasīs made two invincible weapons for Ba'lu, and with them the storm god subdued Yam, the sea god. When Ba'lu finally was permitted to build his house/temple, Ba'lu sent for Koṯar-wa-Ḫasīs to undertake its construction. The craftsman god disagreed with Ba'lu about construction plans, insisting there should be a window, but gave way to the storm god saying "You will return, O Ba'lu, to my word" (Smith 1997: 133). In the end the window was built.

In the story of the rash young prince 'Aqhat, it was the craftsman god that made the beautiful bow that 'Anat(u) coveted. Ugaritic deity lists and offering lists include only Koṯar, whereas Koṯar-wa-Ḫasīs was invoked in a prayer and in rituals to rid the land of snakes.

Theophoric names found in Phoenician inscriptions indicate that Koṯar/Košar was still worshipped in Phoenician cities and their colonies. In the *Phoenician History*, Philo of Byblos mentioned a god called Chousor(os), who might be the same as Koṯar. Philo said that he was good at spells and prophecies. Called Koshar in the Hebrew Bible. Identified with Greek Hephaestos and Egyptian Ptaḥ. Also has many similarities with the Mesopotamian god Enki/Ea. (Smith 2003: 28, 46, 70–71; Pardee 2002: 14, 15, 17, 21, 124, 151, 177, 194, 280–81; Wyatt 2002: 65–68, 103–5, 268; Smith 2001: 72; del Olmo Lete 1999: 56, 344; Pardee, *DDDB*: 490–91; Leick 1998: 105; Parker 1997b: 58; Smith 1997: 90, 103–4, 132–33; Lipiński 1995: 108–12; Handy 1994: 118, 133–38, 143, 146–47; Smith 1985; Attridge and

Oden 1981: 44–45, 84 note 66; Oldenburg, 1969: 46, 97; Albright 1968: 135–38)

Ku (M) Deity appearing in an Old Babylonian god list. Written Kug. (Richter 2004: 98)

Ku-ad (M) Deity attested in an Early Dynastic god list. Just possibly, particularly in light of the similar name Kù-ad-im-babbar (im-babbar = gypsum), Kù-ad might be the personification of a metal or other substance. (Mander 1986: 43)

Ku-ad-im-babbar (M) See Kug-ad

Ku-ane-si (M) See Gu-ane-si

Kubaba, Kubabat, Kupapuina, Kubebe, Kufada (H, L) Great Hittite/Hurrian mother goddess. Some scholars have suggested that her name may derive from Sumerian kù.Baba "Pure Baba," but this is much disputed. In Old Assyrian she was called Kubabat. At least since the eighteenth century BCE, she was "Queen" of the Hittite city Carchemish, her chief cult center. Her companion there was the young male protective deity Karḫuḫa(s). From there she was adopted as a Hittite deity and included in the circle of Ḫebat. Associated with the storm god and the sun god of Heaven. During the Hittite Empire period, she was known, but mainly as a Syrian deity. In the first millennium BCE, her veneration moved far beyond Carchemish and over the Taurus Mountains well to the west, where her name was changed to Kybebe/Cybele. She was revered by the Luwians and worshipped in Emar, Alalaḫ, Kanesh, Ugarit, Ḫama in Syria, and other Mesopotamian towns. At Alalaḫ she was a protector deity (LAM(M)A), as she was in many Hittite/Hurrian rituals. By the first millennium BCE, she had acquired the consort Sanda/Santa.

In visual material she is associated with the rhombus, usually interpreted as a vagina and thus a birth symbol, and with one or all of the following: bird/dove, mirror, pomegranate, hare, lion, pot or bowl. She was normally enthroned, sometimes on a lion. She is often depicted with a bull god, likely a form of the weather/storm god, or with Karḫuḫa. Her cult center Carchemish has provided a number of inscriptions with her name. She is attested in Luwian inscriptions from Ḫama in Syria. She formed part of theophoric names from Alalaḫ and elsewhere. An Old Assyrian text refers to a priest of Kubaba. Mentioned in a ritual from Emar and a deity list from Ugarit. A name in an Assyrian inscription has been read as Gubaba and presented as another spelling of Kubaba, but this is still disputed. Scholars now agree on the identity of Kubaba with the later Anatolian goddess Cybele/Kybebe. As Cybele she was identified with Greek Aphrodite. (Göhde 2000; Graf, *DDDB*: 67; Hoffner 1998: 111; Leick 1998: 105; van Gessel 1998: I, 264–66; Popko 1995: 55, 100–1, 166–67; Haas 1994: 406–9; del Olmo Lete 1993: 86; Hawkins, *RlA* VI: 257–61)

Kūbu, Kūbi (M) Demon of the netherworld, a deified still-born child (*kūbu* means "foetus"). Held responsible for a variety of illnesses. Had a "seat" in the main temple complex at Aššur, as well as at six shrines in Babylon. Attested in names at Early Dynastic Adab. (George 1993: 64 no. 21, 165 no. 1341; Tallqvist 1974; 344; Reiner 1970: 40; Lambert, *RlA* VI: 265)

Kufada (H) See Kubaba

Kug-nuna (M) See Nin-kug-nuna

Kukkula (M) See Kakkala

Kuksi (M) In the lexical series Diri [d]GUD is rendered syllabically as ku-uk-sí. (Civil 2004)

Ku-ku (M) Deity identified with Nin-kilim in a Neo-Assyrian god list. (King 1969: pl. 11)

Ku-kurum-lam (M) Deity attested in an Early Dynastic god list. (Mander 1986: 141)

Kulitta (H) Hittite/Hurrian goddess. Minister/servant of Ša(w)uš(k)a and always occurs with her companion minister/servant Nin-atta. Maker of music. Seems to have a warlike element to her nature, possibly because of her close connection to Ša(w)uš(k)a/Ištar, particularly of Nineveh and Arbela. Kulitta is depicted with Ša(w)uš(k)a and Nin-atta in the great deity procession carved in stone at Yazılıkaya. In myth, she had a small part in the "Song of Ḫedammu," when, with Nin-atta, she made music during Ša(w)uš(k)a's attempt to seduce Ḫedammu. Kulitta had a role in official curse rituals, the oldest dating to the time of Šuppiluliuma I. Also appears in festival material and rituals. (Hoffner 1998: 51, 54; van Gessel 1998: I, 244–49; Popko 1995: 94, 115; Haas 1994: 347, 470, 474; Laroche 1946/47: 52–53; Frantz-Szabó, *RlA* VI: 303–4)

Kulla (M) Sumerian god in charge of bricks and of brick-making. In the myth "Enki and the World Order," Enki appointed him to the office, and one of his responsibilities was the restoration of temples. He was mentioned in an Akkadian ritual for repairing a temple. Occurs also in a personal name from Ur III Girsu. In Astrolabe B called "Kulla of the Nation." (*LAS*: 222; Jacobsen 1976: 85; Tallqvist 1974: 344; Sachs, *ANET*: 341; Lambert *RlA* 6: 305)

Kulīlu(m), Kulullu(m) (Babylonian/Assyrian) (M) Monster, a merman. A protector associated with Ea/Enki and the Apsû/Abzu. Also one of the monsters created by Ti'amat in the *Enūma eliš* to help her fight the younger deities. Sometimes occurred in magical incantations. Visually he was depicted as a human with the tail of a fish. This image occurs from the Old Babylonian period on. In late art there appears a female version, a mermaid. (Foster 2005: 444; Black and Green 2003: 131–32, 177; Speiser, *ANET*: 62; Heidel 1967: 23–24)

Kulmiš (M) God of the town Kulmiš near ancient Ašnakku(m) in the Ḫabur basin. Priestesses of the god Adad of Kulmiš are mentioned in the Mari texts. (Schwemer 2001: 277)

Kumarbi, Kumarwe, Kuparma (H, M) The chief god of the Hurrians and adopted by the Hittites, who originally assigned him third place in their pantheon. In the first reference to him in Hurrian, he had the name Kumarwe. His Neo-Hittite name was Kuparma. In origin probably a deity of grain and of harvest. In a Hittite inscription he was equated to the grain god(dess) Ḫalki and with the Mesopotamian grain goddess Nisaba. At Tuttul, one of Dagān's cult centers, he was named "The Hurrian Dagān," and in Ugaritic god lists Dagān is his parallel. He was identified by the Hurrians with Sumerian Enlil and by the Ugaritians with El. Associated with the netherworld.

Son of Alalu or, in some sources, Anu, and father of the storm god Teššub. The sea god's daughter Sertapšeruḫi was his wife. He became father of several offspring by various females, divine and human, and the children varied from deity to monster. They include Ḫedammu, Silver, Ullikummi, and perhaps LAM(M)A. Two of his titles were "Father of the Gods" and "King of Heaven." It is likely that he is depicted in the great deity procession carved in stone at Yazılıkaya holding an ear of grain.

Kumarbi is known from a number of mythological Hittite texts, sometimes summarized under the term "Kumarbi Cycle." According to this composition Kumarbi and Teššub battle for dominion over the deities, and the younger Teššub wins.

The source of the Ḫabur River and the area around it was Kumarbi's home. In the third millennium BCE, the center of his cult was Urkiš, and close to Urkiš was Taida, another cult town of the deity. Dagān's city of Tuttul worshipped also Kumarbi as the Hurrian equivalent of its god. At both Emar and Ugarit were found copies of An : *Anum*, Ugarit's version being bilingual; in them Kumarbi is identified with El and Enlil. The god is attested in a Luwian inscription. He also appears in rituals, offering lists, and theophoric names from a variety of places, including Mari, Nuzi, Ugarit, and Ḫattušas. At Ugarit he was accepted into the pantheon and appears in cultic texts. In some texts he was identified with Ba'lu. The ancient Greek narrative of generational conflict among the gods may have been influenced by the "Kumarbi Cycle." Ku-marbi corresponds to Kronos, Anu to Uranos and Teššub to Zeus. (Archi 2004; del Olmo Lete 1999: 84, 85, 200; Hoffner 1998: 4, 9, 40–45, 47–53, 55–59, 63–64, 66–68, 73, 77–78, 111; Leick 1998: 106–7; van Gessel 1998: I, 256–62; Popko 1995; 97, 99–100, 115, 117; Haas 1994: 82–90, 114–15, 123, 125, 142, 167–71, 172–75, 177, 306–9, 332; Laroche 1946/47: 53; Güterbock, *RlA* VI: 324–30)

Kun-šaga (M) Daughter of the nether world deity Nergal. Means "Stairway (or Ladder) of the Interior (of the netherworld?)." (Litke 1998: 202)

Ku-nun-kal (M) Deity attested in an Early Dynastic god list. (Mander 1986: 141)

Kunuš-kadru (M) Deified procession street in Babylon. Means "Bow Down, Proud One." (Livingstone 1989: 158)

Kunzibami (E) Elamite deity identified with Adad in a Neo-Assyrian god list. (Schwemer 2001: 79, 83, 393; King 1969: pl. 16)

Kunzišalli (H) Hittite goddess. Daughter of the goddess Ḫebat and sister of Allanzu. (van Gessel 1998: I, 21; Haas 1994: 387–88)

Kupapuina (H) See Kubaba

Kur (M) One of the Sumerian names for the netherworld. It might be that the Sumerians thought that the entrance to the netherworld was in the mountains. The name of the deity Kur appears in a god list from Mari. (Durand 2008: 219; Black and Green 2003: 114; Tallqvist 1974: 344)

Kur(r)a (M) In the third millennium BCE the most important god of Ebla. Spouse was Barama. The king and queen of Ebla were identified with these two deities, who were closely associated with the cult of dead kings. A mausoleum adjoined Kur(r)a's temple in Ebla. Kur(r)a was commonly attested in Eblaite names. Worshipped also in the first millennium BCE, when he had a temple at Nineveh, and he occurred in

Phoenician inscriptions and personal names. He was probably a storm god. In *Anu ša amēli* explained as "Anu of the land." (Younger 2009: 4, 5, 16; Pasquali 2008: no. 49, 2006: no. 64; Litke 1998: 229; Pomponio and Xella 1997: 245–48)

Kur(r)a-ibba, Kur-ribba, Ku-ribba (M) In the Early Dynastic period a deity Kù-rib-ba ("The Holy Surpassing One") is attested. In an Old Babylonian god list a deity Kur-ra-íb-ba ("Who Is Angry in the Mountain") is listed among deities identified with or in the circle of Gula. In the later An : *Anum* the deity identified with Gula is written Kur-íb-ba with gloss ib and with variant Kur-rib-ba. Lambert suggests a possible connection, based upon similar sounding names, among all these deities. (Richter 2004: 216; Litke 1998: 180; Mander 1986: 42; Tallqvist 1974: 345; Lambert, *RlA* VI: 371)

Kur-ba(-šum) (M) Deity in an Old Babylonian god list from Nippur. (Richter 2004: 310)

Kurdari (M) In a Neo-Assyrian god list identified with Ninurta. (King 1969: pl. 25)

Kur-din-nam (M) Deity in an Old Babylonian god list. The plant [ú]li-li-bi-zi-da is rendered lexically as Akkadian *kurdinnu,* perhaps related to our god name. (Weidner 1924/25)

Kur-e (M) Deity attested in an Early Dynastic god list. Written kur-è. (Mander 1986: 141)

Kurgal (M) Deity whose name means "Great Mountain." Explained in An : *Anu ša amēli* as "Sumuqan of Purification (*tēlilti*)." Also identified with Dagan. (Archi 2004; Litke 1998: 236)

Ku-rib-ba (M) See Kur(r)a-ibba

Kurību(m) (Akk.) Possibly the name for the eagle-headed lion-bodied monster (griffin) that occurs in Mesopotamian art. Not only the monster's name but its associations and function are unclear. If its name was *kurību(m),* it might be associated with the biblical *keruv* "cherub." (J. Westenholz 2004: 33–34)

Kur(r)a-igigal (M) Allocated offerings at Ur III Nippur. The Ekura-igigal may have been located in the Enlil temple complex in Nippur. Note that Enlil and Ninlil have the forms Enlil-kur-igigal and Ninlil-kur-igigal. In a few texts Kur-ra-igi-gál without divine determinative is in a list of deities receiving offerings, suggesting that Kurra-igigal was not an actual god but a deification of the Ekura-igigal. (Richter 2004: 44, 53)

Kur(r)a-ḫušani-nukušu (M) Bull-lyre of Nin-Girsu. Means "In the Land His Fury Does Not Abate." "Fury" here may refer to the sound of the lyre. (Litke 1998: 177)

Kurra-šu-urur (M) In a Neo-Assyrian god list. Written šu-ur_4-ur_4, which means "to gather, assemble." (King 1969: pl. 14)

Kurri (M) Aššurbanipal celebrated a festival of the god Kúr-ri in the seventh month at the city Milkiya while on his Elamite campaign. (Cohen 1993: 323)

Kur-rib-ba (M) See Kur(r)a-ibba

Kur-SA/SIG (M) Deity identified as Anu(m) of creatures/offspring. Written Kur-sa_7/sig_7 and explained by *nabnītu* "creature," possibly on the basis of SIG_7.ALAM = *nabnītu*. (Litke 1998: 228; Lambert, *RlA* VI: 372)

Kurša (H) See Kantipuiti

Kur-šuna-buru-am (M) A general of Nin-Girsu along with with Lugal-kur-duba. Means "The Land Is But a Flock in His Hand." (Edzard 1997: 93)

Kurtae (M) Deity in a Fara text. Written Kur[ki]-ta-è "Came out from the Land/ Mountain." (SF 1: o ix 25)

Kurunta, Runta, Ronda, Ruwat (H) Luwian tutelary deity. A warlike LAM(M)A God. His symbol was the stag. Later called Runta and identified with Greek Hermes. (Popko 1995: 89, 91–92, 168)

Kusarikku(m) (Akk.), **Gud-alim** (Sum.) A bison-man: bovine below the waist, human above. Sometimes stood upright, with bovine horns on his human head. Associated with the sun god and the mountains over which he rose. Often served as a guardian and heard oaths. One of the monsters created by Ti'amat in the *Enūma eliš* to help her fight the younger deities. Ninurta's exploits included the killing of the Kusarikku(m) by the edge of the sea. In lexical texts, it is equated to Ditānu(m). (Foster 2005: 444, 562; *LAS*: 167; J. Westenholz 2004: 26–27; Black and Green 2003: 177; M. Ellis 1989: 122, 126; Grayson, *ANET*: 514 and note 76; Speiser, *ANET*: 62, 63; Heidel 1967: 24)

Kusig-banda (M) God of goldsmiths and other workers in lustrous metals. Possibly associated with Nisaba, the scribe and grain goddess. Kusig means "gold," thus perhaps "Junior Gold(smith)." Kusig-banda is attested in an *akītu* ritual from Uruk. Explained in An : *Anu ša amēli* as "Ea of goldsmiths." (Litke 1998: 56, 57; Cohen 1993: 431; Tallqvist 1974: 320)

Ku-sikil-BU (M) Deity attested in two Early Dynastic cereal texts from Zabalam. One text has [d]kù-BU, the other [d]kù-sikil-BU. Perhaps means "He who Extracts (Pure) Metal." (Monaco 2011)

Kusor (L) See Koṯar-wa-Ḫasīs

Kusu (M) Written kù-sù-ga-PA.SIKIL, a deity attested at third-millennium Lagaš and in a personal name from third-millennium Adab, for which a reading kù-[sù]-su_x(PA.SIKIL)-ga has been proposed. Written kù-sù, Kusu was often evoked in magic and ritual texts, being one of the major deities involved in ritual purification. Her spouse was Nin-inda-gar. She was the purification priest (sanga-maḫ) of Enlil and of the gods and, as such, her symbol was the censer. Cultic documents recorded the carrying of her statue in processions. In the first millennium BCE she is considered to be one of the seven children of En-me-šara. Some texts refer to a Kusu who is identified with the grain goddess Ašnan/Nisaba. However, Kramer and Michalowski assert that this was simply an epithet of Nisaba and not a separate deity. (Cohen 2015: 154; Litke 1998: 55 and note 298, 59; Selz 1995: 157; Michalowski 1993: 158; Kramer 1981: 362)

Kuš (M) A little-known god in a late Babylonian copy of a theogony from Dunnu(m), an obscure Babylonian town. Means "Equerry." Kuš's role was to increase the greenery of the earth and provide pasture for domestic and wild animals. (Jacobsen 1984: 6; Grayson, *ANET*: 517–18)

Kuš-abzu (M) Child of Gaa'u. Written $kuš_7$-abzu with gloss ku!(ŠU?)-uš. Means "Herdsman (or *kizû*-official) of the Abzu," an appropriate name for a child of Gaa'u "The Ewe." (Litke 1998: 127)

Kûšarâtum (M) See Kōṯarṯ(u)

Kuš-baba (M) Deity attested in an Early Dynastic god list. Written kuš$_7$-ba-ba$_6$. (Mander 1986: 141)

Kušgim (M) Deity written GUD with gloss ku-uš-gim in An : *Anum*. (Litke 1998: 215)

Kušu(m) (M) Babylonian demon, often a member of the group of seven to nine demons called the Asakkū. In An : *Anum* written Ku-ú-šum and equated to Lugal-^{geš}nuda. Also written Ku-šú. (Litke 1998: 208; Tallqvist 1974: 343; Lambert, *RlA* VI: 382)

Kušuḫ (Hurrian), **Kašku** (Hattic), **Umbu** (H, L) Hurrian moon god. In Luwian called Arma. Spouses Ningal/Nikkal and Išḫara. Member of the Hittite pantheon from the time of Šuppiluliuma I and worshipped at Ḫattušas. Protector deity and guarantor of the swearing of oaths. In imagery he wore a gown open at the front and a hat with a point decorated with a crescent; he also had wings. In a Hittite treaty his title was "Lord of Oaths." In god lists Kušuḫ follows Šimegi and Aya, and offering lists provide sacrifices of a sheep for each of the eight aspects of the moon. There was a regular festival held for Moon and Thunder. He was revered at Aleppo and elsewhere. At Ugarit he appears in god lists, in one of which he is equated to the Ugaritic moon god Yariḫ(u)/Yarḫu. Kušuḫ also occurred in theophoric names and in ritual/offering texts. (del Olmo Lete 1999: 84, 85, 200, 340; Hoffner 1998: 28, 35, 41, 53, 58, 84; van Gessel 1998: I, 272–74; Popko 1995: 92, 100; Haas 1994: 374–75, 398; Laroche 1976: 156–57; Laroche 1946/47: 53)

Kuš-zi-maḫ-ana (M) God appearing in An : *Anum* as the groom or personal attendant of Šamaš. Written kuš$_7$ with gloss ku. Means "The Trustworthy, Exalted Groom(*kizû*) of Heaven." (Richter 2004: 351; Litke 1998: 134)

Kutta (Hurrian) Deity occurring in a Hurrian personal name. (Pruzsinszky 2003: 235)

Ku-uga (M) Deity attested at third-millennium Lagaš and in a personal name from third-millennium Adab. Written kù-sù-ga-PA.SIKIL, for which a reading kù-^{sù}su$_x$(PA.SIKIL)-ga has been proposed. (Selz 1995: 157)

Kyrios (L) See Adonai

— L —

La (E) Elamite deity named in a stele inscription of Šilḫak-Inšušinak I. (König 1977: 111, 200, 227)

Labā, Lab'um (M) Lion deity attested in personal names in the Mari texts. (Durand 2008: 290)

Laban (M) Deity in an Akkadian personal name in an Old Assyrian text from Kültepe. (Matouš 1962: no. 40. no. 50, no. 70, no. 72, no. 90, no. 104, no. 113, no. 117, no. 130, no. 132, no. 250, no. 339, no. 345)

Labar-TUR-ma (M) Sister of Nin-geš-zida. See Ama-TUR-ma. Both written -tùr-ma. Litke suggests that this may be a mistake for Labar-šilam-ma. (Litke 1998: 192)

Labbat(u) (L) (1) Canaanite lion goddess or her epithet. Means "Lioness." The name of the deity appears in Mesopotamia as Labbatu(m). A goddess form worshipped in the Levant in the second half of the second millennium BCE. It occurred in theophoric names on tablets from Ugarit and on arrowheads found near Bethlehem. A number of artifacts with images of a goddess standing on a lion have been found in excavations in the Levant, and these depictions could represent any one of the three major Levantine goddesses: 'Anat(u), Asherah, or Aštarte. Some scholars have argued that the lion goddess was Asherah, but others infer from the warlike natures of 'Anat(u) and Aštarte that Labbat(u) was a name of one of them. Further evidence comes from plaques from Egypt depicting a goddess standing on a lion. An inscription on one of them labelled the goddess as "'Anat(u)-Aštarte-Qudšu," the latter meaning "Holy One." Qudšu has been interpreted as referring to Asherah, so that some have suggested that Labbat(u) could refer to any or all of the three Canaanite goddesses. It is likely that the town Lebaoth or Beth-lebaoth in the southwest of Judah was a cult center of the goddess (Joshua 15: 32, 19: 6). Possibly related to the warlike Egyptian lion-headed goddess Seḫmet. (2) In An : *Anu ša amēli* explained as "Ištar of Wailing (*lallarāti*)." (Cornelius 2004: pls. 5.1–5.20; Puech, *DDDB*: 524–25; Litke 1998: 164, 235; Albright 1968: 121–22; Lambert, *RlA* VI: 411)

Labbu(m) (M) See Tišpak

Labudu (M) Deity attested at third-millennium Ebla. Written ^{d}la-bù-du, variant ^{d}SI.GAR and La-bu$_{x}$(NI)-tum (Waetzoldt 2001; Fronzaroli 1993: 133)

Lagabītu(m) (Akk.) See Bēlet-Lagaba

La-gamāl, Lagamar, Laqamal (E, M) Netherworld deity of Elam, also known from Mesopotamia. La-gamāl means "No Mercy." In An : *Anum*, offspring of Uraš. The deity was paired with Išnekarap, and they were considered assistants of In-šušinak in the cult of the dead. Both deities had strong connections with Susiana. According to Lambert, La-gamāl was male, but Black and Green treat the deity as female and note that she was a judge in the netherworld. As male, the deity was equated in Akkadian texts to Nergal. Venerated widely during the Neo-Elamite period. A temple at Susa, a capital of Elam, was dedicated to La-gamāl. When Aššurbanipal vanquished Susa, he carried off the god's statue. La-gamāl had a shrine in the main temple of Aššur. Also worshipped at Dilbat,

Mari, and Terqa. (Cohen 2015: 326; Vallat 1998: 335–40; Black and Green 2003: 74; Becking, *DDDB*: 498–99; Litke 1998: 172, 200; George 1993: 105 no. 530; Hinz and Koch 1987: 806; König 1977: 200, 227; Tallqvist 1974: 345; Lambert, *RlA* VI: 418)

Laguda (M) God "associated with Dilmun and the Gulf" (George 1993: 27). Probably a deity of the southern Sumerian town of Nēmed-Laguda, a cult center of Ea. Identified with Marduk. (Tallqvist 1974: 345)

Laḫama (M) (1) Servants of the Sumerian god Enki. Means "Hairy." In "Inana and Enki," the drunken Enki gives the *Me* to Inana. Enki subsequently dispatches fifty of the Laḫama in a vain effort to retrieve the *Me* from Inana. Laḫama was also one of Ti'amat's monsters, whom she created in order to help her fight the younger deities. Appears in iconography as a "naked hero" with long hair (Wiggermann 1992: 165). Might have originated as a river spirit who tended wild and domesticated animals. The water was indicated by his hair, which gave him his name. The word Laḫama also referred to statues that guarded the entrances to major sanctuaries. (2) See Laḫmu(m) and Laḫamu(m). (Foster 2005: 444; Black and Green 2003: 114, 177; Wiggermann 1992: 28, 42, 49, 99–100, 102–3, 128, 139, 143, 148–50, 152, 155–56, 164–66, 186–87; Wiggermann 1983: Jacobsen 1976: 114, 142; Speiser, *ANET*: 62–63; Heidel 1967: 23)

Laḫama-abzu (M) Sumerian/Babylonian god-monster associated with gates. One of two "door-men" of Eridu. (Lambert, *RlA* VI: 431)

Laḫamu(m) (M) See Laḫmu(m) and Laḫama

Laḫamun (M) Goddess of Dilmun, modern Baḥrain. Her title was the Zarpanītu(m) of Dilmun, so identifying her with the wife of the chief god of Babylon, Marduk. (Black and Green 2003: 66; Tallqvist 1974: 346; Lambert, *RlA* VI: 431)

Laḫar (M) Sumerian goddess of the flocks, cattle, and other domestic animals. Sister of the grain goddess Ašnan. In the Sumerian "Debate between Sheep and Grain," the deities create Sheep and Grain in the Holy Mound (Dukug) and send them down to human beings as food. After the debate, Enki judges Grain to be the more important of the two, though he designates them sisters. In a unique Babylonian theogony from the obscure city of Dunnu(m), Laḫar was named as son of "Amakandu" (Šakkan). (Litke 1998: 138; *LAS*: 225–29; Leick 1998: 108–9; Tallqvist 1974: 346; Grayson, *ANET*: 518; Lambert, *RlA* VI: 431)

Laḫmu(m) (M) A friendly, protective deity associated with Enki/Ea and then Marduk. Means "Hairy." Especially in the Neo-Assyrian period, figurines of the god were placed under the foundations of buildings to protect them and their inhabitants from demons and illnesses. In imagery the Kusarikku(m), the Bull-man, often appears with the Laḫmu(m). (Black and Green 2003: 115; Heider, *DDDB*: 502)

Laḫma (male) and **Laḫama** (female) (M) Primeval deities in the *Enūma eliš*. They were the first offspring of Ti'amat and Apsû(m). In some interpretations they were the parents of An-šar and Ki-šar. According to Jacobsen, they represent silt formed in the primordial waters. See Laḫama. (Foster 2005: 439; Black and Green 2003: 115; Heider, *DDDB*: 502; Leick 1998: 109; Litke 1998: 22; Jacobsen 1976: 168; Tallqvist 1974: 346. 347; Speiser, *ANET*: 61; Heidel 1967: 18)

Laḫuratil (E, M) See Ruḫurater

Lakuppītu(m) (M) Akkadian name of a goddess mentioned in a temple list in connection with her sanctuary in Isin. (Richter 2004: 248)

Lal (M) Deity with a cult at Ur III Ur, appearing in an Old Babylonian god list. Means "Sweet" or "Date Syrup." Occurs also in personal names. (Richter 2004: 292)

Lal-an(n)a (M) Son of Lisi. Means "Date Syrup of Heaven." (Litke 1998: 76)

Lala-šaga (M) The divine midwife. Associated with the city Šarrākum, the cult center of the Mother Goddess. (Stol 2000: 76 note 177; George 1993: 25, 166 no. 1343)

Lal-ḫur-galzu (M) Deity identified with Bēlet-ilī. Written Làl-ḫur[ḫu-ur]-gal-zu. Perhaps làl-ḫur here is a variant of ḫur-da-làl "scabies," thus "Expert in (curing) Scabies." (Litke 1998: 71)

Lali (E) Elamite deity. (Basello 2013: 254)

Lama (Sum.), **Lamassu(m)** (Akk.), **LAM(M)A** (H, M) Protector goddess depicted in human form. George calls her "the guardian angel" (1993: 79). Equivalent male protector god was called Alad in Sumerian, Šedu(m) in Akkadian. Her main function was as a go-between and intercessor for humans in relation to deities or, with her male counterpart, as escort in difficult situations. The Lama served as a personal guardian for individuals and protected them from misfortune. Also, they protected not only living monarchs, but deceased monarchs as well, as can be noted by offerings to the Lama of Šulgi after his death and to the Lama of Amar-Su'en(a) during and after his lifetime.

In iconography, she was normally dressed in a layered skirt and sometimes had a single-horned crown. Usually she led a worshipper by the hand into a major deity's presence or faced the deity with arms raised in reverence. The Lama had a connection with entrances. Usually she stood at one side of a temple door, while her male equivalent stood at the other. They also guarded the doors of palaces. The goddess had several temples and shrines, and, according to inscriptions, most major temples had at least one Lama and sometimes more. Indeed, it was only the Lama of Baba who, seemingly, became independent of the deity she served. Lama-e-tar-sir-sir, the Lama of Baba's temple E-tar-sir-sir at Lagaš, was provided with priests and received offerings. Probably Lama originated as a demon. LAM(M)A was a writing used by the Hittites indicating a class of protective deities of either sex starting in the Middle Hittite period. The writing of the name, the actual Hittite value of which is unknown, was borrowed from Sumerian. Some LAM(M)A guarded the king and queen. A LAM(M)A is present on the frieze of deities depicted at Yazılıkaya. One LAM(M)A was probably a Hittite shepherd god, who occurs in the Kumarbi stories as male. He is attested as guardian of Hittite palaces and temples. The god is written in Hittite with the sign KAL. (Black and Green 2003: 115; Hoffner 1998: 41, 111; Leick 1998: 109–10; Litke 1998: 233; van Gessel 1998: II,

681–714; Popko 1995: 58, 88–90, 92, 111, 115; Haas 1994: 97–99, 311, 366, 378–79, 439, 450–59, 582,; Cohen 1993: 47, 49; George 1993: 79 no. 212, 149 no. 1085; Tallqvist 1974: 346; Foxvog, Heimpel, and Kilmer, *RlA* VI: 446–59; Laroche, *RlA* VI: 455–59; McMahon, *RlA* XII: 314–16)

Lama-ama (M) Deity attested in an Early Dynastic god list. (Mander 1986: 140)

Lama-Baba (M) See Lama

Lama-barasig(a) (M) Goddess attested as having a *gudu*-priest in an Ur III text probably from Girsu. Means "Guardian Spirit of the Socle." (*RlA*A, 174: o i 12)

LAMA-da-kara (M) Deity identified with Utu/Šamaš in a Neo-Assyrian god list. (King 1969: pl. 32)

Lama-ea (M) Goddess invoked in a prayer. Means "Guardian Spirit of the House." (Maul 1988: 303)

Lama-E-anna (M) This name of Baba occurs in a prayer to the goddess. Means "Guardian Spirit of the E-anna (Temple)." (Cohen 1981: 139)

Lama-edin (M) (1) The goddess called "Daughter of the E-anna." She had a temple or chapel associated with the E-anna in Uruk during the Seleucid period. Means "Guardian Spirit (of) the Steppe" (Falkenstein 1941: 36, 52). (2) See Šarrabu, an evil netherworld-demon identified with Lama-edin.

Lama-enku-guedina (M) Deity of Early Dynastic Lagaš. Means "Guardian Spirit (of) the Tax-collector of the Guedina." (Selz 1995)

Lama-eri (M) Deity attested in an Early Dynastic god list from Abu Ṣalābīkh. Means "Guardian Spirit of the City." (Mander 1986: 43–44, 98, 126

Lama-E-šaba (M) This name of Baba occurs in a prayer to the goddess. Means "Guardian Spirit of the E-šaba(-temple)." (George 1993: 143, no. 1010; Cohen 1981: 139)

Lama-ḫursaga (M) Sumerian deity from Lagaš in the Ur III period. Means "Guardian Spirit of the Mountain." (Spar 1988: no. 40)

Lama-igi-bar (M) Name of Inana's harp at Early Dynastic Lagaš. (Selz 1995)

Lama-igi-kù (M) Deity at Early Dynastic Lagaš. Means "Guardian Spirit with Bright Eyes." (Selz 1995)

Lama-iši (M) Deity attested as having a *gudu*-priest on an Ur III tablet from Girsu. May mean "Guardian Spirit of the Mountain," thus parallel to Lama-ḫursaga. (*RlA*A, 174: l.e. ii 1)

Lama-irnina (M) Guardian spirit in an Old Babylonian god list. Occurs directly before the goddess Irnina, for which see Inana. (Weidner 1924/25)

Lama-kaka (M) Guardian of Enlil's temple at Nippur. The two names, which are juxtaposed in An : *Anum*, are probably two forms of the same deity, although they counted as two in the total of six UDUG (guardians) in the list. The reading -kà-kà rather than -ga-ga is based on the variant -ka-ka. (Litke 1998: 52–53; Lambert, *RlA* VI: 459)

Lama-lugal (M) Deity attested in the Ur III period. Means "Guardian Spirit (of) the King." In the Ur III texts there are lama identified specifically as the guardian spirit of Šulgi of Apišal, Šulgi of Kian, Šulgi of Umma, Amar-Suen, Šū-Sîn, and Ibbi-Sîn. (AUCT 1, 434: o 11)

Lama-men (M) Deity attested in an Early Dynastic god list. Perhaps "Guardian Spirit of the Crown." (Mander 1986: 140)

LAMA.RA (M) Deity attested in a text from Ur dating to the reign of Warad-Sîn of Larsa. (Richter 2004: 497)

Lama-sag(a), Lama-sig(a) (M) Chief vizier of Baba. Identified with Nin-sun and also Nin-kar(r)ak. Mentioned in the ritual for the *akītu* festival at Uruk. Means "Beautiful Guardian Spirit." See Lam-sag-zagin. (Litke 1998: 52; Cohen 1993: 437; George 1993: 166 no. 1344; Tallqvist 1974: 348; Foxvog, Heimpel, and Kilmer, *RlA* VI: 450, 453)

Lama-sila-sirsir (M) A name of Baba at Early Dynastic Lagaš. (Selz 1995)

Lama-ša-Šamaš (M) Deity attested in an economic text from Larsa dating to the reign of Warad-Sîn. Means "Guardian Spirit of Šamaš." (Richter 2004: 494)

Lama-šazida (M) Deity attested at Old Babylonian Uruk. Means "Trustworthy Guardian Spirit." (Renger 1967: 161)

Lama-Šū-Sîn-tuda (M) Deity attested in the Ur III period. Means "The Guardian Spirit who Has Given Birth to (King) Šū-Sîn." (BPOA 1, 732: r 2)

Lama-u(-e) (M) Ur-Nanše of Lagaš dedicated a statue to Lama-u-e in the Early Dynastic period. Lama-u is a deity in a circle of Inana divinities in an Old Babylonian god list. Written -u_6(-è). May mean "Wondrous Guardian Spirit." (Richter 2004: 292; Cooper 1986: 25)

Lamassu(m) (M) (1) In a Neo-Assyrian god list identified with Adad. (2). See Lama. (King 1969: pl. 16)

Lamaštu(m) (Akk.), **Kamadme** (Sum.) Goddess and monster. "The most dreaded of the demons of Mesopotamia" (J. Westenholz 2004: 30). Daughter of Anu(m) and Antu(m). She was often invoked in incantations, in one of which she was called *qadištu(m)*, "Sacred (or Holy) Female." Unlike ordinary demons she did evil on her own accord without instructions from other deities. She preferred to act at night. Although she killed adult men and women, as well as causing fevers and chills, her particular area of malevolence was the provoking of miscarriages and the killing or kidnapping of newborn babies. She also tore babies from the womb and suckled them with poison. She could be warded off by complicated rituals and magic. Amulets of the head of the male god/demon Pazuzu protected pregnant women against Lamaštu(m). Some plaques show Pazuzu in the process of forcing Lamaštu back to the netherworld.

Fragment of a plaque with image of Lamaštu(m). Ca. 605–562 BCE. Yellow alabaster. After Pritchard 1969b: 215, no. 657

As depicted fully developed in iconography, Lamaštu(m) was a pale, ashen monster with a hairy body covered in blood. A black dog and a pig suckled at her naked, drooping breasts. She dangled snakes from her long clawed fingers and fingernails. Her feet were taloned like those of a bird, and she had a lion or eagle head with the teeth of a dog or a donkey. Her animal was the donkey, and she sailed the river of the netherworld in her own boat. Her equivalent in the Greco-Roman world was the Lamia. (Foster 2005: 173–74, 981–85; J. Westenholz 2004: 30–31; Black and Green 2003: 115–16; Wiggermann in Stol 2000: 217–52; Leick 1998: 110; Litke 1998: 240; Henshaw 1994: 211; Tallqvist 1974: 346; Ebeling, *RlA* II: 109–10)

Lam-sag-zagin (M) Deity attested in an Early Dynastic god list. See Lama-sag. (Mander 1986: 141)

Lānbani (E) Elamite deity occurring in a treaty between Narām-Sîn of Akkad and a king of Susa. (Hinz and Koch 1987: 801; König 1977: 200, 227)

Laqamal (E) See **La-gamāl**

La-qīpu(m) (M) A form of Nergal. Means "Untrustworthy." Explained in *Anu ša amēli* as "Nergal of the Platform." (Litke 1998: 234; Lambert, *RlA* VI: 494)

Larsa-pad(a) (M) One of five deities of fishermen listed in An : *Anum*. Also written ŠU.ḪA. (Litke 1998: 113)

Lāsimu(m) (M) Deity attested in the Mari texts. (Durand 2008: 213)

La-šanān (Akk.) Babylonian netherworld goddess. Means "Unequaled." (Litke 1998: 220; Lambert, *RlA* VI: 507)

La-tarāk (L) See Lu-lal

Latpōn, **Lat(i)pān** (L) Name of the Canaanite/Phoenician supreme god El. Greenstein translates it "Gentle," whereas Wyatt renders it "Wise." (Wyatt 2003: 221; Greenstein 1997: 31)

Laz, **Laṣ**, **Loz** (M) One of Nergal's wives. Possibly also spouse of Erra in some places. Perhaps a form of the healing goddess Gula/Baba. Mentioned with Nergal in an Assyrian treaty. Worshipped with Nergal in his cult city of Kutha and in Assyria. (Black and Green 2003: 136; Litke 1998: 200; Reiner 1970: 18; Reiner, *ANET*: 533; Lambert, *RlA* VI: 506–7)

Lel(u)wani, **Lil(u)wani** (H) Netherworld Hattic/Hittite deity. During the Old Hittite period he was considered male with the epithets "king" and "lord." In mythic material he was sometimes a disappearing or "dying" god. In a text from Ḫattušas, he led netherworld divinities in a ritual of the dead. He also appears in a Hittite treaty. In the thirteenth century BCE, the deity became a goddess identified with Allani, Ereškigal, and Allatu(m). Hittite Queen Pudu-Ḫepa, wife of Ḫattusili I, seems to have been especially devoted to her. Later, the goddess assumed solar attributes. (Leick 1998: 110; van Gessel 1998: I, 280–83; Popko 1995: 72, 90, 106, 112, 118; Haas 1994: 133, 156, 245, 301, 405, 580–81, 618; Laroche 1946/47: 75–76; von Schuler, *RlA* VI: 595–98)

Leviathan (L) Serpentine monster associated with the sea. Usually representative of chaos. Cosmic enemy of Ba'lu/Had(d)ad in the texts from Ugarit and of YHWH in the Hebrew Bible. At Ugarit the monster was called Litān(u), Lōtān(u), or Lôtān(u) and was a helper of the sea god Yam. At least once, 'Anat(u) claimed to have conquered the monster on Ba'lu's behalf. Among its epithets were "Twisting One" and "Encircling One with Seven Heads."

Some Old Syrian seals dating from the eighteenth to the sixteenth centuries BCE show the storm god battling a serpent-monster, almost certainly a depiction of Ba'lu's fight with Litānu. "[W]ith His great, cruel, mighty sword" (Isaiah 27:1), the Hebrew Bible's warrior deity YHWH battled Leviathan, as part, it seems, of destroying chaos and ordering the universe. In the same passage, the monster was called "Elusive Serpent" and "Twisting Serpent" and perhaps also "Dragon of the Sea." In other passages of the Bible, Leviathan was associated with dragon-like creatures such as Raḥab and Tannin. In Psalm 74:14, YHWH was praised for crushing the heads of Leviathan. When the YHWH spoke to Job out of the whirlwind, he asked Job whether he could, as YHWH had done, tame Leviathan (40: 25–31). In rabbinic tradition, Leviathan was understood to be a huge fish that, along with the land monster Behemoth, would serve as food for the righteous at a banquet to take place in the Messianic Age, when the Kingdom of God would be established on earth. In Mesopotamian iconography as early as the third millennium BCE, a hero or god was depicted as attacking a seven-headed serpentine monster, perhaps a forerunner of Leviathan. Probably equivalent to the Greek Ladōn, the serpentine monster-guardian of the golden apples of the Garden of the Hesperides. (Whitney 2006; Wyatt 2002: 115; Schwemer 2001: 235 note 1622; Smith 2001: 17, 36–38, 130; del Olmo Lete 1999: 56; Uelinger, *DDDB*: 511–15; Smith 1997: 141; Lipiński 1995: 250; J. Day, *ABD* IV: 295–96; Smith 1990: 74 note 91; Cross 1973: 118–20, 156)

Liber Pater (L) See Šadrapha

Libittu(m) (Akk.) Deity mentioned in the epilogue of the law code of Ḫammu-rāpi. Presumably the god of brickmaking. (Leick 1999: 65–66; Meek, *ANET*: 178 and note 153)

Libūr-dannu(m) (M) Deity invoked in an incantation. Means "Let the Strong Be Well!" (Reiner 1958: 80; Edzard, *RlA* VII: 15)

Li-el (M) Deity in the circle of Sîn deities attested in an Old Babylonian god list fragment from Uruk. (Richter 2004: 317)

Lil, Lilla, Kisikil-lila (Sum.), **Lilû(m), Lilītu(m), Ardat-lilî** (Akk.) The name derives from Sumerian líl, "air, spirit." The Akkadian Liliu(m) and Lilītu(m) haunted the open spaces and deserts. They posed a threat to pregnant women and infants. They had no spouse and were sexually predatory, rather like incubi and succubi. The Lilītu(m) was incapable of "normal" sexual activity and was very aggressive with young men. She could not give birth or suckle a child. It was a Lilītu(m) that made its home in the trunk of Inana's *ḫaluppu*-tree and refused to leave. Lilītu(m) seems later to have been assimilated with the baby-stealing monster Lamaštu(m). Sumerian Kisikil-lila and Akkadian Ardat-lilî mean "Maiden Air Spirit." The demons, particularly the Ardat-lilî, were often mentioned in magical texts and incantations. The Ardat-lilî were credited with causing sterility in women and impotence in men. (Lapinkivi 2004: 234; Black and Green 2003: 118; Frayne 2001: 132–34; Stuckey 2001; Puech, *DDDB*: 509; Ebeling, *RlA* II: 110–11)

Lilith (L) The Hebrew name Lilith is a form of Akkadian *Lilītu(m)*. There is one possible reference to Lilith in the Hebrew Bible, in Isaiah 34:14, where she inhabited a desolate wasteland. Also an important female evil demon and child stealer in Jewish tradition. Known from writings of the Talmudic period (second-fifth centuries CE) and onwards. Responsible for sterility in women and impotence in men. According to Jewish incantation bowls found at Nippur dated to about 600 CE, three angels with the Aramaic names Senoy, Sansenoy, and Semangelof were sent by God to negotiate with the demon Lilith, whose image was sometimes sketched in the center of the bowls. The angels managed to get her to promise that, wherever she and her associate demons saw the angels' names prominently displayed, they would avoid that place. (Patai 1990: 224–29).

Bowl from Mesopotamia bearing an Aramaic incantation and image of Lilith. Ca. 600 BCE. After Patai 1990: figure 33.

Because of a popular association of her name with the Hebrew word for "night" *layla*, Lilith was pictured as a demon of darkness. Eventually, in the Jewish mystical or Kabalistic tradition, which began in the Middle Ages and still survives, she rose to become "queenly consort at God's side" (Patai 1990: 221).

According to later Jewish legend, Lilith, who had long hair and wings, was Adam's first wife. When the pair quarreled over Adam's wanting superiority over her, Lilith spoke the deity's magic name and flew away to the Red Sea area, where she bore innumerable demon children and started her malevolent career. Against her and other liliths, people needed amulets and used invocations. The Jewish demon Lilith almost certainly originated in ancient Mesopotamia of the third millennium BCE. Called Lamia in Greek. In popular belief of the Middle Ages, Lilith was the devil or his grandmother and also mother of witches and witchcraft. (Black and Green 2003: 118; Patai 1990: 221–54; Hutter, *DDDB*: 520–21; Puech, *DDDB*: 509; Handy, *ABD* IV: 324–25)

Lil, Lil(l)u (M) Child of birth/mother goddess Dingir-maḫ or Bēlet-ilī. In another tradition, offspring of Nin-ḫursag and Šul-pa'e. Sibling of Ašgi and Lisina. The deity had a "seat" in the great sanctuary of Enlil at Babylon. (Black and Green 2003: 173; Litke 1998: 74; George 1993: 104 no. 516, 126, no. 799)

Lili (M) Deity attested in Old Akkadian personal name. Written Li-li. (Such-Gutiérrez: 2005/6)

Lilira (E) Elamite epithet of the god Nuska. (Hinz and Koch 1987: 829; König 1977: 201, 227)

LILla-anna (M) Deity receiving offerings at Ur III Girsu. BDTNS reads é-lá-an-na. (ITT 4, 7310: r i 22)

Lilla-enna (M) Sumerian goddess whose name occurs in a liturgy where she is called "Lady of Sheepfold and Cattle Pen." Identified with (Nin-)Kanisura. (Cohen 1981: 147)

Lilluri (H) Hurrian goddess, probably of the mountains, since *luri* was a Hurrian ending in the names of some mountain deities. Spouse of the weather and mountain god Manuz(z)(i). One of her symbols was an eagle. A lexical list from Emar entitled her "Lady of the Tiara." Her cult was widespread, from the Upper Euphrates to the Orontes River and the Amanus Mountains in the West. See Abade. (van Gessel 1998: I, 284–89; Popko 1995: 101; Haas 1994: 409–10, 849; Laroche 1946/47: 53–54; Frantz-Szabó, *RlA* VI: 594–95)

Li'm, Līmu(m), Lim(m)u (L, M) West Semitic god attested frequently in personal names from Early Dynastic Ebla, Old Babylonian Mari, and Ugarit, including such Mari royal names as Zimrī-Līm and Yaḫdun-Līm. Probably Li'm was not an actual god but rather the divinized "people, clan," which occurs in epithets of the goddess ʻAnat(u). The word means literally "One Thousand" and has cognates in the Hebrew Bible and in Ugaritic, both denoting "people" or "nation." (Seow, *DDDB*: 521–23; Pomponio and Xella 1997: 454; del Olmo Lete 1993: 79, 80, 340; Moran 1987: 273 note 2; Birot et al. 1979: 264; Lipiński 1967: 151–60)

Lipparuma (Hurr.) Vizier of the Hurrian sun god Šimegi. (Franz-Szabó, *RlA* VII: 30)

LIRUM (M) See Šu-kal

Lisi(na) (M) Daughter of Dingir-maḫ. Sibling of Ašgi and Lil/Lillu. Her husband was Nin-sikila. As Mother Lisina, she was identified with Nin-ḫursag. Also sometimes understood as Nin-ḫursag's daughter. At Keš, the mother goddess's sanctuary at Šarrākum, for instance, she and her brother Ašgi were seen as offspring of the city's principal goddess Nin-ḫursag/Nin-maḫ. Quoting from a lament by Lisina, daughter of Nin-ḫursag, for the loss of her foal, Jacobsen identifies her as "a donkey goddess." She was the "weeping mother goddess" par excellence. Kramer calls her a "Sumerian *mater dolorosa*" (1981: 363). Lisina was worshipped, usually with her brother Ašgi, at, among other places, Lagaš, Nippur, Šarrākum, and Adab. At Ur III Umma and Girsu a month was named for her. Because, at one point, scholars misunderstood the name of her husband Nin-sikila as that of a goddess, Lisina was, for a time, understood to be a male. (Cohen 2015: 40; Black and Green 2003: 122; Sefati 1998: 17, 236–46; Litke 1998: 75; George 1993: 157, no. 1197; Kramer 1981: 325–28; Jacobsen 1976: 106; Michalowski, *RlA* VII: 32–33)

Litān(u), Lōtān (L) See Leviathan

Lu-ana (M) One of seven bull-lyres of An. Means "Man of An/Heaven." (Litke 1998: 29; Lambert, *RlA* VII: 106)

Lubadaga, Lubandug, Lupatik (H) See Nubadig

Lu-Enlila (M) Guardian of Enlil's great temple at Nippur. (Litke 1998: 64; Lambert, *RlA* VII: 107)

Lugal (M) Deity identified with the moon god Nanna/Sîn. Means "King." (Litke 1998: 118)

Lugal-aabba (M) Netherworld god in the circle of Nergal. Means "King of the Sea." Considered spouse of the healing goddess Gula. Often mentioned with Lugal-ida, "King of the River." Also associated with Laguda, En-zak, and Meskilak, deities of Dilmun, modern Baḥrain. (Lambert 2013: 240–47; Litke 1998: 198, 202; Tallqvist 1974: 349; Krebernik, *RlA* VII: 109)

Lugal-ab-dubur (M) The thirty-sixth name of Marduk in the *Enūma eliš*. Marduk's spouse, Zarpanītu(m), was entitled Nin-áb-dubur. Written with -áb- and variant -ab-. (Foster 2005: 481; Litke 1998: 94; Tallqvist 1974: 350;

Speiser, *ANET*: 71; Heidel 1967: 57; Lambert, *RlA* VII: 109, 110)

Lugal-AB-KA (M) Deity in an Ur III personal name from Nippur. (NATN 893: o 1)

Lugal-AB-ta-a (M) Sumerian deity attested at Old Babylonian Nippur. May mean "King who Goes out from the Shrine (or Window)." (Renger 1967: 150)

Lugal-abzu (M) Deity identified with Enki/Ea, meaning "King of the Abzu." Attested in god lists of the Early Dynastic period. (Litke 1998: 84; Tallqvist 1974: 350; Krebernik, *RlA* VII: 110)

Lugal-a-dibdib(e) (M) Sumerian netherworld deity associated with Ninurta. Written -á-dib-dib(-bé). á-dib means "foam," but whether it has anything to do with our god name cannot be determined. (Litke 1998: 206; Tallqvist 1974: 350; Krebernik, *RlA* VII: 110)

Lugal-a-dug (M) Sumerian netherworld deity associated with Ninurta. Written -á-dùg in An : *Anum*. In a Neo-Assyrian god list written -á-dug$_4$-ga. The phrase lugal-á-dugud, "king with a heavy arm," and the expression á-dugud by itself are attested (*PSD* A/2: 5). Perhaps our lexical entries are a corruption of an original Lugal-á-dugud. (Litke 1998: 206; Tallqvist 1974: 350; King 1969: pl. 8; Krebernik, *RlA* VII: 110)

Lugal-agidda (M) Deity identified with Ninurta. May mean "King of the Spear," appropriate for Ninurta, a warrior god. (Litke 1998: 46; Krebernik, *RlA* VII: 110)

Lugal-agruna (M) Deity identified with Ninurta. Means "King of the Inner Sanctum." (Litke 1998: 205; Krebernik, *RlA* VII: 110)

Lugal-AKAKeš (M) Sumerian netherworld god. May mean "King of (Ritual) Procedures." Written -ak-ak-eš. (Litke 1998: 210; Krebernik, *RlA* VII: 110)

Lugal-a-ki-a (M) See Lugal-ankia

Lugal-am-Aral(l)i (M) Deity identified with Dumuzi. Means "King, Bull of Aral(l)i (the netherworld)." See Lugal-Aral(l)i. (Richter 2004: 190, 232)

Lugal-amaru (M) Deity perhaps identified with Nergal. Means "King Flood." See Lugal-uru and Lugal-aša-amaru. (Litke 1998: 203; Krebernik, *RlA* VII: 110)

Lugal-AMAŠ-pa'e (M) Netherworld deity. Krebernik suggests a possible reading Lugal-utul$_3$-pa-è. Also a demon of epilepsy. (Tallqvist 1974: 350; Krebernik, *RlA* VII: 111)

Lugal-am-ura (M) Deity identified with Pabil-sag and so spouse of Gula. Written in an Old Babylonian god list with -úr-ra and in the later An : *Anum* with -ur$_5$-ra and -ùr-ra. In a hymn, Nin-geš-zida is called lugal-am-úr(var. ur$_5$)-ùn, which the ETCSL renders as "King, wild bull with tall(?) limbs." (Litke 1998: 179; Tallqvist 1974: 350; ETCSL [c.4.19.1: 8]; Krebernik, *RlA* VII: 110)

Lugal-ana (M) Deity perhaps identified with Nergal. Means "King of Heaven." (Litke 1998: 203; Tallqvist 1974: 35)

Lugal-ane-pada (M) Deity perhaps identified with Nergal. Means "King Called by An/Heaven." (Litke 1998: 206)

Lugal-ankia (M) Deity attested in an Old Babylonian economic text from Uruk. Lugal-a-ki-a in an Early Dynastic god list from Abu Ṣalābīkh may be a variant. Means "King of Heaven and Earth." (Richter 2004: 328; Mander 1986: 69)

Lugal-anzagar (M) an-za-gàr "tower" was often part of geographical names in the Ur III period and so in this god name it might be geographical. Identified with Nergal. (Litke 1998: 204; Tallqvist 1974: 351; Krebernik, *RlA* VII: 115)

Lugal-Api'ak (M) Deity identified with Nergal as "King of Api'ak," Nergal's cult center. (Litke 1998: 204; George 1993: 55; Tallqvist 1974: 350; Stol, *RlA* VII: 115)

Lugal-Apišal (M) Deity perhaps identified with Nergal. Means "King of Apišal," a town near Umma. (Litke 1998: 204)

Lugal-Aral(l)i (M) Deity identified with Dumuzi. Means "King of Aral(l)i [the netherworld]." See Lugal-am-Aral(l)i. (Litke 1998: 203; Krebernik, *RlA* VII: 115)

Lugal-Aratta (M) Attested in a god list. Means "King of Aratta" or "Excellent King." (OIP 99, 82: o ii 18)

Lugal-asal (M) See Bēl-ṣarbi(m)

Lugal-aša-bara (M) Deity identified with Ninurta. Under the entry Šeg-bara-gimgim(e), An : *Anum* explains a-šà-bar-ra-ke$_4$ with variant -mar-ra as *šākin eqli*, "field cultivator," but this reflects the variant -mar-ra. The entry following Lugal-aša-bar-ra is Lugal-a-šà-má-ru, which may simply be a variant, and has nothing to do with a-má-ru flood. (Litke 1998: 46; Richter 2004: 75; Krebernik, *RlA* VII: 115)

Lugal-aša-maru (M) A name of Ninurta in An : *Anum*. Written a-šà-má-ru. Most likely a variant for the preceding entry Lugal-aša-bara and unrelated to a-má-ru "flood." (Litke 1998: 46; Kreber-nik, *RlA* VII: 115)

Lugal-aša-susu (M) Deity identified with the storm god Adad. Written Lugal-aša$_5$-sù-sù Means "The King who Inundates the Field." (Schwemer 2001: 22, 64; Litke 1998: 141; Tallqvist 1974: 352; Lambert, *RlA* VII: 138–39)

Lugal-Awan (M) "King of Awan," chief god of the city Awan in Elam. (Krebernik, *RlA* VII: 116)

Lugal-Bad-tibira (M) Deity identified with Dumuzi as "King of Bad-tibira," his cult center. (Litke 1998: 205; Tallqvist 1974: 351; Krebernik, *RlA* VII: 116)

Lugal-Bagara (M) Deity identified with Nin-Girsu as "King of the Bagara (temple in Lagaš)." (Krebernik, RlA V II: 116)

Lugal-baguba, **Lugal-ibi-guba** (M) Deity identified with Ninurta. May mean "King, Attendant" or "King who Stands at the Front." (Lambert, *RlA* VII: 116–17)

Lugal-baḫar (M) Deity identified with Nin-Gublaga, the bull god of the city of Ki'abrig (Jacobsen 1976: 25). Written Lugal-$^{\text{ba-ḫar}}$GUD. Means "King Bull" or "King (of) the Bull(s)." See Ḫar. (Litke 1998: 121; Lambert, *RlA* VII: 117)

Lugal-Buranuna (M) Deity attested in the Ur III period. Means "King (of the?) Euphrates." (Sallaberger 1993: I, 248)

Lugal-dalḫamun (M) Deity identified with Adad. Means "King Whirlwind." (Lambert, *RlA* VII: 132)

Lugal-dar(-DU.DU) (M) See Dar-lugal

Lugal-Dilmun-aba (M) Deity whose name means "King of Dilmun of the Sea." (Litke 1998: 202, 210; Lambert, *RlA* VII: 153)

Lugal-dimmer-ankia (M) Deity identified with Marduk, the fifth name of the god proclaimed at the end of the *Enūma eliš*. Name is Emesal dialect for Lugal-dingir-ankia. Means "King of the Gods of Heaven and netherworld." Under this name Marduk had a "seat" in his great temple at Babylon. In the first millennium BCE, Marduk's son Nabû also claimed this title. (Foster 2005: 474; Litke 1998: 94; George 1993: 77 no. 180, 160 no. 1237; Tallqvist 1974: 351; Speiser, *ANET*: 69; Grayson, *ANET*: 502 and note 5; Heidel 1967: 52; Lambert, *RlA* VII: 132–33)

Lugal-dingira (M) Deity identified with Adad. Means "King of the God(s)." (Litke 1998: 142; Lambert, *RlA* VII: 133)

Lugal-dubur (M) Sumerian name of Adad. Written with Lugal-dubur$_2$$^{du-bur}$. Perhaps "King of the Foundation." (Litke 1998: 140; Tallqvist 1974: 351; Lambert, *RlA* VII: 133)

Lugal-dubur-ana (M) Perhaps identified with Nergal and if so, foundation of heaven might refer to the netherworld, the bottom-most place under the heavens. Note that Lugal-dubur-ana and Ušum-dubur-ana were names of Adad. (Litke 1998: 202; Lambert, *RlA* VII: 133)

Lugal-dudu-šušua (M) See Lugal-dušua

Lugal-duge-du (M) Deity perhaps identified with Nergal. Means "(When) the King Speaks, It Is Proper." Written Lugal-du$_{11}$-ge-du$_7$. (Litke 1998: 202, Lambert, *RlA* VII: 133)

Lugal-Du-kuga (M) (1) A primordial deity whose name means "King of the Holy Mound." One of the distant ancestors of Enlil. Lamentations were sung for him, and he received offerings for the dead. Lugal-Du-kuga had a "seat" in the great Marduk temple at Babylon. (2) A title of Enki/Ea as lord of the Du-kug, the Holy Mound, in Eridu. (Litke 1998: 37; George 1993: 77 no. 185; Tallqvist 1974: 351; Lambert, *RlA* VII: 133–34)

Lugal-Duluma (M) Patron god of Dulum, a town near Zabala(m). In An : *Anum* the name is glossed il-du, a value attested also in the lexical series Diri for IGI.NAGAR.BU. A deity ^{d}Nin.IGI.NAGAR.BU is attested, once with a syllabic rendering ni-in-du-ru-ma (see Cavigneaux and Krebernik, *RlA* IX: 340). In An : *Anum* there is a variant ^{d}Lugal-nin-IGI.[NAGAR.BU], which may indicate that Lugal-Duluma and Nin-Duluma are names for the same deity (see Nin-duluma). (Litke 1998: 203; Lambert, *RlA* VII: 142)

Lugal-durmaḫ (M) Deity identified with Marduk, the thirty-eighth name of the god proclaimed at the end of the *Enūma eliš*. Means "King of the Exalted Bond." According to Lambert the "Bond" is "the cosmic rope holding the parts of the universe together" (see Eškita-abzu). (Foster 2005: 481; Litke 1998: 94; Tallqvist 1974: 351; Speiser, *ANET*: 71; Heidel 1967: 58; Lambert, *RlA* VII: 134)

Lugal-du-šua, Lugal-ki-du-šua (M) Deity identified with Nergal, written Lugal-dù-šú-a. Means "King who Controls Everything (*ṣābit kiššati*) in the netherworld." Another lexical entry for Nergal in the same god list is Lugal-du-du-šú-šú-a, which is probably just a variant for Lugal-dù-šú-a. (Tallqvist 1974: 351; Lambert, *RlA* VII: 133–34)

Lugal-E-anna (M) Name of An/Anu(m) or, possibly, Dumuzi. Means "King of the E-anna (Temple)." (Litke 1998: 205; Tallqvist 1974: 352; Lambert, *RlA* VII: 136)

Lugal-ea-sag-ra (M) Deity attested in Old Babylonian tablets from Ur. Would seem to mean "King who Bangs(?) (his)

Head in the Temple." In Sumerian Proverbs sag—ra describes the butting of a goat. (Richter 2004: 497; Alster 1997, 414)

Lugal-edin(a) (M) Epithet meaning "King of the Steppe." Shared by deities associated with grazing animals of the steppe or with the netherworld and so a title of both Lu-lal/La-tarāk and Nergal. Sumerian edin, Babylonian *ṣēru(m)*, could mean both "open, uncultivated country" and "netherworld." Lu-lal was a shepherd god, and Nergal was king of the netherworld. A *gudu*-priest of Lugal-edina is mentioned at Šarrākum. (Litke 1998: 205; George 1993: 56; Tallqvist 1974: 352; Lambert, *RlA* VII: 137)

Lugal-eduru-la (M) Deity attested in an Early Dynastic god list from Abu Ṣalābīkh and in an Early Dynastic "riddle text" from Lagaš. Means "The King who Extends over the Settlement." (Mander 1986: 130)

Lugal-ega (M) God in an inscription on an Early Dynastic statue. Means "King of the Dike." (Steinkeller 1990: no. 14)

Lugal-E-gurumma (M) Deity identified with Ninurta. George understands the temple name as "House that Subdues." There is no other attestation of this temple. (Litke 1998: 46; George 1993: 98; Tallqvist 1974: 351; Lambert, *RlA* VII: 137)

Lugal-Elama (E) "King of Elam," the title of a god of Elam. Perhaps referring to Ḫumban, later called Napi-riša, a powerful sky god and, for a considerable time, head of the Elamite pantheon. Ḫumban was identified with Sumerian Enlil. Occurs also at Abu Ṣalābikh. (Black and Green 2003: 74; Mander 1986: 142; van Koppen and van der Toorn, *DDDB*: 432–34; Lambert, *RlA* VII: 137)

Lugal-E-muš (M) Deity identified with Dumuzi in his cult city Bad-tibira. Means "King of the E-muš," Dumuzi's temple at Bad-tibira. He shared the temple with Inana and Lu-lal. During the two-day Barley Festival at Girsu, he was, as Lugal-E-muša, honored with sacrifices of sheep and goats, and he also received offerings at Lagaš and probably Uruk. (Cohen 2015: 37, 213; George 1993: 129 no. 829; Lambert, *RlA* VII: 137)

Lugal-e-na-bu-ul (M) See Lugal-innu-bul

Lugal-ennun-erikuga (M) Deity appearing in texts from Girsu. Means "King, Guard of Erikug." (Lambert, *RlA* VII: 138)

Lugal-ensi (M) Deity occurs in an Ur III text from Šarrākum. ((Owen 2013: 652)

Lugal-e-para (M) Deity in the circle of the netherworld god Nergal. Means "King of Ditch and Dike." (Litke 1998: 202; Lambert, *RlA* VII: 138)

Lugal-eri-bara (M) Deity from Lagaš. Associated with Ninurta/Nin-Girsu. Means "King of the Suburb." Name of Inana's consort at Lagaš and Girsu, and similar to or identified with Dumuzi. Involved with festivals associated with the netherworld. Related to Nergal. See Lugal-eri-saga. (Cohen 2015: 44, 46, 470–71; Litke 1998: 46, 204; Tallqvist 1974: 358; Bauer, *RlA* VII: 152; Lambert, *RlA* VII: 153)

Lugal-Erikuga (M) Deity whose name means "King of Erikug." Erikuga was a name used to denote Lagaš (modern Al-Hibā). (Litke 1998: 204; Lambert, *RlA* VII: 154)

Lugal-eri-pa'e (M) Deity whose name may mean "The King (who is) Manifest (in?) the City" or "King who Makes the City Manifest." (Litke 1998: 204; Lambert, *RlA* VII: 150)

Lugal-eri-saga (M) Deity whose name means "King of the Foremost City." He had a cult at Ku'ara in the Ur III period. (Litke 1998: 203; Lambert, *RlA* VII: 154)

Lugal-eri-šaga (M) Deity whose name means "King of the Inner City." See Lugal-eri-bara. (Litke 1998: 203; Cohen 1993: 55; Tallqvist 1974: 358; Lambert, *RlA* VII: 154)

Lugal-Erra (M) One of the divine twins, the other being Meslamta-e. One Ur III text writes the name as Lugal-ì-ra. Lugal-Erra's wife was Gu-ane-si, and his minister or vizier Zimingi. He was later equated to Nergal. The twins guarded entrances and, in the Neo-Assyrian period, figurines of them were buried under doorways. Visually they were identical, each wearing a horned hat, bearing a mace, and brandishing an axe. Lugal-Erra was worshipped, usually along with his twin, in Ur, Dūru(m), Luḫaya, and Kisiga. Along with Meslamta-e, Lugal-Erra appears in a ritual from Uruk dated to Hellenistic times. Together they represented the astronomical sign Gemini. Name originally read as Lugal-Girra. See Meslamta-e for drawing. (Black and Green 2003: 123–24; George 1993: 72 no. 119, 124 no. 769, 127 no. 804; Tallqvist 1974: 352–53; Sachs, *ANET*: 335; Lambert, *RlA* VII: 143–45)

Lugal-Esa (M) See Lugal-Ki-esa

Lugal-e-saga (M) Deity identified with Nergal. é-sag was a temple of Lugalbanda's in Babylon and a location in the é-šár-ra in Aššur. The next two entries in An : *Anum* are Lugal-eri-sag-gá and Lugal-ki-sag-gá, suggesting the é-sag-gá here simply means "foremost temple" and is not here the name of a particular temple or cella. (George 1993: 138; Litke 1998: 203; Lambert, *RlA* VII: 138)

Lugal-e-susu (M) See Lugal-aša-susu

Lugal-ešbara (M) Deity identified with Adad. Means "King, Decision(-maker)." (Litke 1998: 141; Tallqvist 1974: 352; Lambert, *RlA* VII: 138)

Lugal-ešda (M) Sumerian deity attested in an Old Babylonian god list. Likely associated with Nergal. May mean "The King, the One in Charge." (Richter 2004: 206)

Lugal-Ešnunna (M) Title meaning "King of Ešnunna." Probably refers to Tišpak, whose cult city was Ešnunna. (Black and Green 2003: 178; Lambert, *RlA* VII: 138)

Lugal-gal-abzu An unexpected title of Nergal. Means "Great King of the Abzu." The Abzu and the netherworld were occasionally confused. (Tallqvist 1974: 352; Lambert, *RlA* VII: 138)

Lugal-galama (M) Deity identified with Nergal. Means "The Clever King." (Tallqvist 1974: 352; Lambert, *RlA* VII: 138)

Lugal-gešbur (M) Deity whose name means "King of the Crook." (Litke 1998: 210)

Lugal-geš-bura (M) Deity identified with the demon Muḫra. Means "King who Uproots Trees," with variant Geš-sù-ga, "(King) who Strips Away the Trees" or "who Strips the Trees Bare." See Lugal-geš-dù-a and Lu-geš-suga, Muḫra. (Litke 1998: 208)

Lugal-geš-dù-a (M) Equated to Muḫra, a netherworld demon. Written with and without Lugal-. There are two consecutive entries for the demon, which seem to be opposites. Lugal-geš-bura means to uproot trees and Lugal-geš-dù-a to plant trees. See Lu-geš-bura, Muḫra. (Litke 1998: 47, 208, 210; Tallqvist 1974: 353, 378; Lambert, *RlA* VII: 138–39)

Lugal-gešge-banda (M) Deity in offering lists from Girsu. May mean "King of the Smaller Canebrake." (ITT 4, 7311: o ii 9)

Lugal-gešur (M) see Deified Kings

Lugal-gida (M) Son of the Elamite rainbow goddess Manzi'at. Note also Lugal-á-gíd-da, a name for Ninurta meaning "King of the Spear." (Litke 1998: 167; Lambert, *RlA* VII: 345)

Lugal-GIR-da (M) Sumerian god in a circle of Nergal deities. Perhaps the male form of Nin-Girida, tutelary goddess of a small town near Ur. (Richter 2004: 206)

Lugal-gir-nun (M) Deity in an Ur III offering list at Girsu and in a personal name. See Gir-nun and Gan-gir-nun. (TCTI 1, 946: l.o.2)

Lugal-Girra (M) See Lugal-Erra

Lugal-gir-urra (M) Deity attested in a Neo-Assyrian god list. Written lugal-gír-ùr-ra. The possible interpretations are many. (King 1969: pl. 35)

Lugal-gišimmar (M) Means "King Palm." Venerated in Girsu from the Early Dynastic period until the time of Gudea of Lagaš. This form of the god likely derives from his being a "dead god" defeated by Ninurta in the epic *Lugal-e* and by Nin-Girsu in the Gudea Cylinder inscriptions. A deity "Lord Palm" likely appears with "Lady Palm" in a god list from Abu Ṣalābīkh, but the reading of the two divine names is not entirely certain. (*LAS*: 167; Black and Green 2003: 147; Leick 1999: 62; Litke 1998: 46; Vanstiphout 1992: 339–67; Vanstiphout 1991: 23–46; Vanstiphout 1990a: 271–318; Wilcke 1989: 161–90; Tallqvist 1974: 353; Danthine 1937; Lambert, *RlA* VII: 139–40)

Lugal-gu (M) Deity identified with Enki in An : *Anum*. Means "King Ox." Lugal-gu$_4$-rá occurs in an Ur III offering list from Girsu. (Litke 1998: 84)

Lugal-gu-a-nun-gi (M) Deity attested in a festival at Nippur in the Ur III period. Means "King, Ox that Turns Back the Powerful" or "King, Ox who Wields Noble Horns." (Sallaberger 1993: I, 103)

Lugal-Gudua (M) Name of Nergal, Means "King of (the City of) Kutha." A rendering of the name from Tel ed-Dēr is Šar-Kutê. (George 1993: 167 no. 1364; Richter 1992: no. 25; Litke 1998: 205; Stol, *RlA* VII: 140–41)

Lugal-gu-gu (M) (1) The name of one of the children of Nanna/Sîn in An : *Anum*. Means "King of the Cattle." (Richter 2004: 451; Litke 1998: 121); (2) Deity attested in a Neo-Assyrian god list. (King 1969: pl. 19)

Lugal-gusisu (M) Manifestation of Ninurta when participating in the *Gusisu* festival of the second month at Nippur, a festival that marked the onset of seeding. The name means "King of the *Gusisu* (Festival)." By the Old Babylonian period Sumerian si-sù in gu$_4$-si-sù was replaced with the common verb si-sá "to perform correctly." George suggests that the name is a title of Nergal, under which he was worshipped in a temple at Nippur. (Cohen 2015: 124; George 1993: 166 no. 1346; Tallqvist 1974: 353; Lambert, *RlA* VII: 141)

Lugal-gu-rurugu (M) Deity identified with Adad. Means "The Bellowing King." Written Lugal-gú-ru-ru-gú with variant Lugal-gu$_4$-ru-ru-ga. (Litke 1998: 140; Tallqvist 1974: 353; Lambert, *RlA* VII: 140)

Lugal-ḫar (M) See Lugal-baḫar

Lugal-ḫegala (M) Deity whose name means "King of Abundance." (1) A title of the storm god Adad. (Litke 1998: 142) (2) Vizier of Lugalbanda. (Litke 1998: 169). (Tallqvist 1974: 353; Lambert, *RlA* VII: 141)

Lugal-ḫenuna (M) Deity identified with Adad. Means "King of Plenty." (Litke 1998: 142; Lambert, *RlA* VII: 141)

Lugal-Ḫubura (M) Netherworld god. Means "The King of the Ḫubur (River)." (Tallqvist 1974: 353; Lambert, *RlA* VII: 141)

Lugal-ḫuš-a (M) See Lugal-ḫuš-kia

Lugal-ḫušani-kura-nuila (M) Deity whose name means "The King whose Fury the Mountain(s) Could Not Bear." (Litke 1998: 177; Lambert, *RlA* VII: 141)

Lugal-ḫuš-kia (M) Deity whose name means "King, Furious One of the Netherworld." Identified with Nergal. The following entry in An : *Anum* is Lugal-ḫuš-a, probably a variant of our name. (Litke 1998: 207–8; Tallqvist 1974: 353–54; Lambert, *RlA* VII: 141–42)

Lugal-iba-tum (M) Deity identified with Ninurta in An : *Anum*. May mean "King who Brings Oil Rations(ì-ba)" Note the name Lugal-làl-DU. (Richter 2004: 75; Litke 1998: 46)

Lugal-ibiguba (M) See Lugal-baguba

Lugal-Ida (M) Deity whose name means ""King of the River." Identified with Enki/Ea and perhaps with Nergal. Often paired with Lugal-aaba, "King of the Sea." (Litke 1998: 84, 202; Tallqvist 1974: 354; Lambert, *RlA* VII: 142)

Lugal-igi-alim (M) Divine herald of the city of Adab. Means "King with the Appearance of a Bison." In An : *Anum* he may be identified with Nergal. (Litke 1998: 203; Lambert, *RlA* VII: 142)

Lugal-igi-gungunu (M) Deity identified with Šul-pa'e. Means "King with the Beautiful Face (or Eyes)." (Litke 1998: 72, 203; Tallqvist 1974: 354; Lambert, *RlA* VII: 142)

Lugal-igi-ḫura (M) Deity perhaps identified with Nergal. Lambert suggests that the name may be a variant for Lugal-igi-kur-ra. (Litke 1998: 204; Tallqvist 1974: 354; Lambert, *RlA* VII: 142)

Lugal-igi-ḫuš (M) A divinized harp of Nin-Girsu. Means "King with a Menacing Appearance." (Tallqvist 1974: 354; Lambert, *RlA* VII: 142)

Lugal-igi-kukkua (M) Deity identified with Nergal. May mean "King (with) a Dark Appearance." (Lambert, *RlA* VII: 142)

Lugal-igi-kura (M) Deity whose name means "King, the Eye of the Land." Lambert suggests that this may refer originally to Šamaš and cites the personal name *Šamaš-īn-mātim*. (Litke 1998: 204; Lambert, *RlA* VII: 142)

Lugal-igi-pirig (M) The divine herald of Adab. Means "King (with) the Appearance of a Lion." See IGI-labāt. (Litke 1998: 77; Lambert, *RlA* VII: 142)

Lugal-inim-ge-ana (M) God attested in an Old Babylonian god list. Means "King of the Steadfast Word of An/Heaven." May be a variant of Lugal-inim-gena. (Lambert, *RlA* VII: 143)

Lugal-inim-gena (M) God attested in an Old Babylonian god list and in An :

Anum. Means "King of the Steadfast Word." Perhaps identified with Nergal. May be a variant of Lugal-inim-ge-ana. (Litke 1998: 202; Lambert, *RlA* VII: 143)

Lugal-innu-bul (M) Deity in the circle of Nergal. Means "King who Winnows the Chaff." The deity is attested only in An : *Anum*, where the name is written Lugal-e-na-bu-ul. (Litke 1998: 204; Lambert, *RlA* VII: 138)'

Lugal-inim-gi-a (M) Deity perhaps identified with or in the circle of Nergal in an Old Babylonian god list. Means "The King who Replies." The strange names Lugal-imin-gi and its variant Imin-gu in An : *Anum* may be variants for Lugal-inim-gi(-a). (Richter 2004: 204; Litke 1998: 207; Tallqvist 1974: 354; Lambert, *RlA* VII: 143)

Lugal-Isin (M) Deity identified with Nergal. Means "King (of) Isin." (Litke 1998: 204; Richter 2004: 198, 203)

Lugal-ka (M) Deity attested in a god list from Abu Ṣalābīkh. Means "King of the Gate." (Lambert, *RlA* VII: 145)

Lugal-ka-dudu (M) Written Lugal-ka-dù-dù. Means "King with a Harsh Mouth" (= *pû wašṭu*). The sense of "harsh mouth" is unclear, but see Instructions of Šuruppak, line 104: "He who has a harsh mouth(ka-dù-dù) carries a (litigation) document" (trans. Alster 2005: 139). (Litke 1998: 206; Lambert, *RlA* VII: 145)

Lugal-kalag (M) Deity identified with Nergal. Means "The Mighty King." (Lambert, *RlA* VII: 145)

Lugal-kalama (M) Deity attested in an Early Dynastic god list. Also in the Early Dynastic period a lapis-lazuli bead found at Mari was dedicated to this god by Mes*ANEP*ada, a ruler of Ur. Means "King of the Nation."(Durand 2008: 203; Cooper 1986: 98; Mander 1986: 114)

Lugal-kalama-utu(d) (M) Deity identified with the moon god Nanna/Sîn. Means "King who Begat the Nation." (Lambert, *RlA* VII: 145)

Lugal-Ki-esa, Lugal-Esa (M) Deity whose name means "The King of Ki-esa," a town in the eastern Lagaš area. Allocated offerings at Umma. (Lambert, *RlA* VII: 138)

Lugal-ki-gula (M) Deity identified with Nergal. Means "The King of the Greatest Place," a euphemism for the netherworld. (Litke 1998: 205; Lambert, *RlA* VII: 145–46)

Lugal-kirzala (M) Deity identified with the storm god Adad in An : *Anum*. Means "Joyous King." (Schwemer 2001: 23; Litke 1998: 142)

Lugal-kisa-a, Lugal-kisi-a (M) God usually equated to Ḫaya. Means "The King of the Retaining Wall." (Litke 1998: 54, 206; Tallqvist 1974: 355; Lambert, *RlA* VII: 146)

Lugal-ki-sag, Lugal-ki-sig (M) Deity whose name means "King of the Pleasant Place." (Litke 1998: 206; Lambert, *RlA* VII: 145–46)

Lugal-ki-suna (M) God attested at Old Babylonian Kutalla, a city near Larsa, perhaps Kutalla's city god. According to An : *Anum* a sister! of Nin-geš-zida, despite the masculine lugal. Lambert translates here "pious place." It could also mean "King of the Entrance." (Richter 2004: 205; Litke 1998: 192; Renger 1967: 145; Lambert, *RlA* VII: 146–47)

Lugal-Kisura (M) (1) A name of Ninurta as god of Kisura, on the Euphrates, southeast of Nippur. Means "King of

Kisura." (2) Deity identified with the moon god Nanna/Sîn. Means "King of the Boundary." His wife was Ig-ana-kešda. (Litke 1998: 102, 206; Tallqvist 1974: 355; Lambert, *RlA* VII: 147)

Lugal-kuda (M) Attested in the Early Dynastic period. If kud here is not the verb "to cut," might Mean "King Crocodile." (Mander 1986)

Lugal-kug-nuna (M) Deity identified with Nergal. See (Nin-)kug-nun-na. (Litke 1998: 205; Tallqvist 1974: 355; Lambert, *RlA* VII: 147)

Lugal-Kul(l)aba (M) Deity identified with Lugalbanda. Means "King of Kul(l)aba," a district of Uruk or a town nearby. (Litke 1998: 204; Tallqvist 1974: 355; Lambert, *RlA* VII: 145–46)

Lugal-kur-dub (M) Warrior god associated with Nin-Girsu at Lagaš. Acted as one of two military commanders or generals of Nin-Girsu. Also an emblem of Nin-Girsu. Mentioned in an inscription of Gudea. Means "King who Shatters (or Shakes) the Mountain." (Leick 1999: 62; Tallqvist 1974: 355; Jacobsen 1976: 82; Edzard 1997: 92; Lambert, *RlA* VII: 147)

Lugal-ku-ra (M) Deity identified with Dumuzi. Written Lugal-ku$_4$-ra. (MVN 22, 26: v 12)

Lugal-kuš-la (M) A gate-keeper of the netherworld. Name probably means "Master of the Leather Sash." Lugal-kuš-la appears in the late Assyrian "A [Prince's] Vision of the netherworld." (Foster 2005: 832–39; Lambert, *RlA* VII: 147–48)

Lugal-kuš-susu (M) Deity identified with Adad. Means "King, Devastating Flood." (Lambert, *RlA* VII: 148)

Lugal-lal-DU (M) Deity in Ur III offering lists from Girsu. May mean "King who Brings Syrup." See the name Lugal-iba-DU. (MVN 6, 412: r ii 12)

Lugal-magura (M) Deity identified with Ninurta. Means "King of the Barge." In this same position in an Old Babylonian god list (see Richter 2004: 203) is Lugal-DUG+AB-ra. (Lambert, *RlA* VII: 148)

Lugal-Marada (M) Name of Sumerian war god identified with Ninurta. He was the city god of Marad. Means "King of Marad." His wife was NIN-zu-ana. His minister was Lugal-mea. His temple at Marad was called "Eye of the Land." Identified with Lu-lu in a Neo-Assyrian god list. (Litke 1998: 170; George 1993: 6, 104 no. 520; Tallqvist 1974: 355–56; King 1969: pl. 11; Stol, *RlA* VII: 148)

Lugal-maš(-maš) (M) Deity attested in an Early Dynastic god list. (Mander 1986: 97, 114)

Lugal-me (M) A name for Bennu(m), the god of epilepsy. Since this is a god of illness, the name may mean "King (of) Debility" (me = *lu'tu*). (Litke 1998: 72; Tallqvist 1974: 356; Lambert, *RlA* VII: 149)

Lugal-mea (M) Vizier of Lugal-Marada. It is unclear whether this deity's name is to be associated with Lugal-me, the god of epilepsy. If so, it may mean "King of Debility." Another possibility is "King of the *Mes*." (Litke 1998: 171; Tallqvist 1974: 356; Lambert, *RlA* VII: 149)

Lugal-melema (M) Deity identified with Nergal. Means "The Splendorous King." (Litke 1998: 206; Tallqvist 1974: 356; Lambert, *RlA* VII: 149)

Lugal-Meslama (M) Name of the god Meslamta-e. Equated to Nergal. Means "King of the Meslam (Temple)." (Tallqvist 1974: 356; Lambert, *RlA* VII: 149)

Lugal-me-šudu (M) Deity identified with Nergal. Means "King who Perfectly Performs the *Me*." Nin-me-šudu was Lugal-me-šudu's female counterpart. The preceding entry in An : Anum, Lugal-me-dù, may be a corrupt variant for this name, since the expression me dù is not otherwise attested. (Litke 1998: 206; Tallqvist 1974: 356; Lambert, *RlA* VII: 149)

Lugal-me-urur (M) Deity identified with Nergal. Means "King who Gathers All the *Me*." (Litke 1998: 206; Tallqvist 1974: 356; Lambert, *RlA* VII: 149)

Lugal-mura (M) God associated with the netherworld. Written Lugal-mu-úr-ra with variant Lugal-gír-ra. (Lambert, *RlA* VII: 150)

Lugal-muru (M) Attested in the Early Dynastic period. Means "King (of) Muru." (Mander 2006: 65)

Lugal-mušlaḫ (M) Deity attested in Ur III texts from Ur. Means "Master Snake-charmer." (Richter 2004: 414)

Lugal-namtar (M) Netherworld deity. Means "Master Fate." (Litke 1998: 198, 203; Tallqvist 1974: 356; Lambert, *RlA* VII: 150)

(Lugal-)namuruna (M) Demon of epilepsy. Written nam-uru$_{16}$-na, "overpowering force," thereby alluding to an epileptic seizure. (Litke 1998: 72; *CAD* B: 205a s.v. *bennu*)

Lugal-narua (M) Netherworld deity. Means "King (of the) Stele." (Litke 1998: 203; Lambert, *RlA* VII: 150)

Lugal-NIG.BA (M) Deity identified with Nergal in an Old Babylonian god list.níg-ba, which usually means "gift," is glossed su-qum-bi-⌜x⌝. (Richter 2004: 204).

Lugal-nigsaga (M) Deity perhaps identified with Nergal. Means "Master of Pleasant Things." (Litke 1998: 202; Lambert, *RlA* VII: 150)

Lugal-nimgir (M) See Nimgir(gir)

Lugal-ninda-kaššaga (M) Deity whose name may mean "Master of Food and First-class Beer." (Litke 1998: 206)

Lugal-NI-ra (M) Perhaps an orthography for Lugal-Erra. Occurs in Ur III tablets. (Richter 2004: 282)

Lugal-nir-anna (M) Vizier of Šulpae. Means "King, Respected One of Heaven." (Ashm 1924-855+: o ii 6)

Lugal-nirgal (M) God identified with Nin-Girsu. Means "Respected King." (Litke 1998: 102; Tallqvist 1974: 356; Lambert, *RlA* VII: 150)

Lugal-nita-zi(d) (M) Deity whose name means "King (who is) a Trustworthy Male." He had a cult at Ku'ara in the Ur III period. Note Nin-nita-zi-da, who had a *gudu*-priest at Girsu. (Litke 1998: 202; Lambert, *RlA* VII: 150)

Lugal-nuda (M) Deity attested in the Early Dynastic period. May "Owner of the Bed." In An : *Anum* he is explained as the god Kušum. In the Neo-Assyrian god list written without lugal. (Litke 1998: 208; Mander 1986; Tallqvist 1974: 353; King 1969: pl. 22; Lambert, *RlA* VII: 140)

Lugal-pa'e (M) See Lugal-eri-pa'e

Lugal-pala-mu (M) God possibly identified with Nergal. Means "King Clad in a (Noble) Robe." (Tallqvist 1974: 356; Lambert, *RlA* VII: 150)

Lugal-palil-ana (M) Deity identified with Nergal. Means "King, the Leader of Heaven." (Lambert, *RlA* VII: 142)

Lugal-Pasira (M) Deity in Lagaš in the Early Dynastic period. Means "King of

Pasira," a suburb of Lagaš. (Selz 1995: 162)

Lugal-Rašap (M) Sumerian name of the West Semitic (Canaanite) plague god Rešep(h). Identified with Nergal. Means "King Rešep(h)." (Leick 1998: 143; Tallqvist 1974: 356; Lambert, *RlA* VII: 150)

Lugal-sa-ba-NI (M) See Lugal-zag-ba-KA

Lugal-sa-duku (M) Deity in the circle of Nin-geš-zida. (Litke 1998: 192)

Lugal-sag-ila (M) Deity identified with the storm god Adad. Means "Proud King." (Litke 1998: 142; Tallqvist 1974: 357; Lambert, *RlA* VII: 151)

Lugal-sag-nugia (M) Deity perhaps identified with Nergal. Means "Unopposable King." (Litke 1998: 205; Tallqvist 1974: 357; Lambert, *RlA* VII: 151)

Lugal-Saguba (M) Local title of Dumuzi in the Lagaš area. Means "King of Sagub." (Lambert, *RlA* VII: 154)

Lugal-sapar (M) Possibly a title of the god Alla. Means "King (of the) Net." (Litke 1998: 205; Tallqvist 1974: 356–57; Lambert, *RlA* VII: 151)

Lugal-siga (M) Deity identified with Nergal in three entries in An : *Anum* written with sig "below," sìg "to smite," sig_7 "green," and sì in a Neo-Assyrian god list. In the Early Dynastic period the deity Lugal-sig4 "King of the Brick" is attested (see Nin-sig_4-tu). (Mander 1986: 93; Tallqvist 1974: 357; King 1969: pl. 35; Lambert, RlA VII: 151)

Lugal-silima (M) Deity whose name means "King of Well-Being." (Litke 1998: 203; Lambert, *RlA* VII: 151)

Lugal-sisa (M) Deity whose name means "King who Acts Correctly." Counselor of Nin-Girsu. According to Jacobsen, he acted as deputy ruler when Nin-Girsu was away. Sometimes identified with Nin-Girsu. (Jacobsen 1976: 82; Tallqvist 1974: 357; Lambert, *RlA* VII: 151–52)

Lugal-siskure (M) Deity whose name means "King of Blessings." See Lugal-šud(d)e. (Lambert, *RlA* VII: 152)

Lugal-sud (M) Deity attested in the Early Dynastic period; written -súd. (Mander 1986: 76)

Lugal-sukudra (M) Deity whose name means "Impressive King." Worshipped primarily at Lagaš. See Nin-sukud-da. (Lambert, *RlA* VII: 152)

Lugal-sula (M) Porter in the netherworld. (Livingstone 1989: 158)

Lugal-šenšena (M) Deity identified with the storm god Adad. Means "King of Battle." (Richter 2004: 130; Litke 1998: 140)

Lugal-^{geš}šinig (M) See Bēl-bīni(m)

Lugal-Šuana (M) Forty-first name of Marduk in the *Enūma eliš*. Means "King of Šu-ana." Šu-ana was a district of Babylon and a scholarly name for Babylon. (Foster 2005: 481; Litke 1998: 94; Tallqvist 1974: 357; Speiser, *ANET*: 71; Heidel 1967: 58; Lambert, *RlA* VII: 152)

Lugal-šud(d)e (M) Deity identified with Ninurta, though sometimes equated to Dumuzi or Nergal. Means "King of Prayers." See Lugal-siskure. (Litke 1998: 46, 193, 206; Lambert, *RlA* VII: 152)

Lugal-^{geš}šukur (M) See Bēl-šukurrim

Lugal-šunira (M) Deity whose name means "King of the Standard." (Lambert, *RlA* VII: 152)

Lugal-šu-nugia (M) God associated with La-gamāl. Means "Merciless King." (Litke 1998: 205; Lambert, *RlA* VII: 152)

Lugal-Terqa (M) Main deity of Terqa, probably the god Dagān. Means "King of Terqa." (Lambert, *RlA* VII: 153)

Lugal-tibira (M) Deity whose name means "King of the Fist." (Lambert, *RlA* VII: 153)

Lugal-tilla (M) Deity whose name means "King of the City Square." (Litke 1998: 202; Tallqvist 1974: 357; Lambert, *RlA* VII: 153)

Lugal-uda (M) Deity identified with Šul-pa'e. Means "King of the Storm(-demons?)." In the Early Dynastic period a deity Lugal-UD is attested. Note Lugal-UD (SF 5: o iv 9). (Mander 2006: 60; Litke 1998: 72; Tallqvist 1974: 357; Lambert, *RlA* VII: 153)

Lugal-udeš-duga (M) Deity identified with the storm god Adad. Means "King who Speaks as a Storm." (Litke 1998: 140; Tallqvist 1974: 357; Lambert, *RlA* VII: 153)

Lugal-uga (M) Forty-second name of Marduk proclaimed at the end of the *Enūma eliš*. May mean "King (of) the Dead." (Foster 2005: 482; Tallqvist 1974: 357; Speiser, *ANET*: 71; Heidel 1967: 58; Lambert, *RlA* VII: 153)

Lugal-una (M) Deity perhaps identified with Nergal. Means "The Exalted King." Written Lugal-ùn-na. (Litke 1998: 205)

Lugal-Unuga (M) Deity occurring in an Old Babylonian god list fragment from Isin. The name is broken, and the reading not entirely clear. Means "King of Uruk." (Richter 2004: 200)

Lugal-ura (M) Deity identified with the Sumerian god Šul-pa'e. Means "King of the Roof." (Litke 1998: 72; Tallqvist 1974: 358; Lambert, *RlA* VII: 153)

Lugal-Urima (M) Title probably of the moon god Nanna/Sîn. Means "King of Ur." (Litke 1998: 204; Tallqvist 1974: 358; Lambert, *RlA* VII: 153)

Lugal-ur-tur (M) Deity in Lagaš in the Early Dynastic period. His statue was commissioned by Ur-Nanše of Lagaš. May mean "King, Hero of the Cattle Pen." (Selz 1995: 162–63; Cooper 1986: 25, 27)

Lugal-uru (M) Deity attested in a text from Šuruppak in the mid-third millennium BCE. Name may mean "King Flood." Written URU×UD. See Lugal-amaru. (Martin et al. 2001: no. 110)

Lugal-Uruba (M) Deity identified with Dumuzi. Means "King of Urub," a site near Lagaš. His festival at Lagaš, one of four concerned with the netherworld, featured offerings to ancestors, both royal and common. (Cohen 2015: 37, 45)

Lugal-usu-ša-piriga (M) Deity identified with the warrior god Ninurta. Means "King (with) the Strength and Heart of a Lion." (Litke 1998: 46; Lambert, *RlA* VII: 155)

Lugal-ušim-susu (M) Deity identified with Adad. In light of his being the rain god, it may mean "King who Sprinkles the Vegetation." Lambert suggests "King who Makes the Vegetation Grow Tall." (Litke 1998: 142; Tallqvist 1974: 357; Lambert, *RlA* VII: 154)

Lugal-zag-ba-KA (M) Sumerian deity appearing in an Ur III tablet from Ur. The deity name Lugal-sa-ba-NI may be a variant. (Richter 2004: 203, 414)

Lugal-zag-e, Sa-e (M) Deity identified with Ninurta. Means "Foremost King." Sa-è, probably a variant for zag-è, occurs in an Old Babylonian god list after Lugal-zag-e and Lu-lal and thus is likely equated to them. Possibly Sa-e was a local form of Lu-lal, as several names of the god occur in Old Babylonian god lists from Isin. (Richter 2004: 316; Litke 1998: 46; Lambert, *RlA* VII: 155)

Lugal-za-ru (M) Deity identified with Ninurta. (Litke 1998: 46; Lambert, *RlA* VII: 157)

Lugal-Zimbira (M) God attested in the Ur III period at Umma as having a *gudu*-priest. Means "King of Sippar." (AAICAB 1/2, Ashm. 1937-97: r 7)

Lugal-zulumma (M) Meaning "King (of) Dates." Perhaps a title of Dumuzi. (Lambert, *RlA* VII: 157–58)

Lu-geš-suga (M) Deity identified with Nergal. Means "He who Strips Away the Trees" or "He who Strips the Trees Bare." See Lugal-gešbura for Geš-suga as the demon Muḫra. (Litke 1998: 64)

Lu-gula (M) Name of the mother goddess in an Old Babylonian god list. Means "The Supreme One." (Richter 2004: 144)

Lu-ḫuš, **Luḫušû** (M) In liturgy, a Sumerian epithet of Nergal. This name is also invoked in incantations in which he is the harbinger of plague. Means "The Furious Man." (George 2013: 44; Reiner 1970: 18; *RlA* VII: 159)

Lulaḫ(ḫ)i (H) A little-known god of nomads, but a member of the Hittite pantheon. According to Laroche, a Hurrian transposition of the Sumerian name Lu-lal. His evidence comes from a multilingual god list from Ugarit. (van Gessel 1998: I, 290–91; Laroche 1976: 160–61)

Lu-lal (Sum.), **La-tarāk** (Akk.) He seems to have been a warrior deity and is associated with domesticated animals. George calls Lu-lal "the divine cowherd" (1993: 55). Lu-lal probably means "Man (of the) Date Syrup." His alter ego was La-tarāk. Though they often appear as a closely knit pair, they were probably originally separate deities. In late astrological texts they appear separately, where Lu-lal is identified with the moon god Sîn and La-tarāk with Nergal. In "Inana's Descent to the netherworld," Inana refused to give Lu-lal/La-tarāk of Bad-tibira to the demons of the netherworld as her substitute. He had "a close but unspecified relationship to Inana" (Black and Green 2003: 116). La-tarāk shared with Mīšaru(m) a "seat" at Aššur, and Lu-lal had a temple at Nergal's cult city of Api'ak. He also shared with Dumuzi and Inana the temple at Bad-tibira. (*LAS*: 74; George 1993: 55–56, 129 no. 929, 145 no. 1041, 156 no. 1187; Tallqvist 1974: 346, 349; Lambert, *RlA* VII: 163–64)

Lu-lal-Abzu-Eridu (M) Form of the god Lu-lal associated with the abzu in Eridu. The name appears in a god list from Isin. (Richter 2004: 238)

Lu-lal-ana (M) One of the goddess Lisina's eight sons. Meaning "Man (of the) Date Syrup of An/Heaven." (Lambert, *RlA* VII: 164)

Lu-lal-Maškan-šabra (M) Form of the god Lu-lal associated with the city of Maškan-šabra, a town north of Nippur. The name appears in a god list from Isin. (Richter 2004: 238)

Lu-lal-Unuga (M) Form of the god Lu-lal associated with the city of Uruk. The reading of the name is not entirely certain. It appears in a god list from Isin. (Richter 2004: 238)

Luli (M) Deity attested in Old Babylonian times. (Richter 2004: 237)

Lulu (M) (1) Deity in the pre-Sargonic period and in an Old Babylonian god list. Written lu_5-lu_5 in an Early Dynastic god list. (2) Deity attested in a Neo-Assyrian god list identified with Lugal-Marada and written lu-lu. (Such-Guti-érrez: 2005/6; Richter 2004: 325; Mander 1986: 141; King 1969: pl. 11)

Luluḫe (M) Deity attested in a text from Middle Babylonian Emar. (Beckman 1996: no. 9)

Lumḫa (M) Deity identified with Enki/Ea as god of the *gala/kalû(m)* priests, who were temple singers and musicians. Lumḫa's spouse was Nin-gubiduga. The god is addressed in a ritual for recovering a sacred kettledrum in the Seleucid period. In the lexical series Diri syllabic reading lu-um-ḫa provided, as well as the logogram ᵈEGIR. (Civil 2004; Litke 1998: 104, 239; Tallqvist 1974; 358; Sachs, *ANET*: 334–38)

Lu-Ninlila (M) Guardian of the Kiur in Nippur. (Litke 1998: 64; Lambert, *RlA* VII: 107)

Lu-Ninurta (M) Guardian of the E-šumeša, Ninurta's temple in Nippur. (Litke 1998: 64; Lambert, *RlA* VII: 107)

Lu-Nuska (M) Guardian of the E-melemḫuš Nuska's temple in Nippur. (Litke 1998: 64; Lambert, *RlA* VII: 107)

Lu-sigar(r)a (M) Doorkeeper of Dingirmaḫ. Means "He of the Bolt." (Litke 1998: 83)

Lu-tu (M) Name of Marduk in his capacity as a god of incantations and divination. Means "He of Incantations." Written Lú-tu$_6$. (Litke 1998: 222)

(Lu-)tu-gal (M) Name of Marduk in his capacity as a god of incantations and divination. May mean "Great(?) One of Incantations" or "The One of Major(?) Incantations." Written Lú-tu$_6$-gal. (Litke 1998: 222, 224)

Lu-tu-sisa (M) Name of Marduk in his capacity as a god of incantations and divination. May mean "He who Correctly Performs the Incantation (Ritual)." (Litke 1998: 222)

— M —

Ma (M) Deity identified with the moon god Nanna/Sîn. Means "Boat." The conventional depiction of the crescent moon was with the horns upward, resembling a length-wise, cross-section of a boat. Other similar names for Nanna/Sîn were Ma-gula(-ana) "Greater Boat (of Heaven)" and Ma-gur "Boat of Large Capacity." Also identified with the constellation Sagittarius. (Litke 1998: 119, 231; Lambert, *RlA* VII: 192)

Ma-banda-ana (M) Deity identified with the sun god Utu/Šamaš. Means "Smaller Boat of Heaven." According to Lambert, the name "reflects the theological subordination of Šamaš to Sîn—son to father—rather than anything observed in the sky." (Litke 1998: 129; Lambert, *RlA* VII: 192)

Mādanu, Madanunu (M) As Mādanu chamberlain/throne-bearer of Marduk. In Babylon he had a place in the great Marduk temple and also his own temple as consort of Gula. A shrine to him is attested at Kiš. He is mentioned in an Assyrian treaty. As Madanunu in a Neo-Assyrian god list he is identified as Ninurta and explained as *tizqaru elû*; perhaps plays upon ma-da/maḫ-di and nu-nu/nun. (Litke 1998: 97, 135; George 1993: 24, 80 no. 216,137 no. 936 no. 937; Tallqvist 1974: 359; King 1969: pl. 11; Reiner, *ANET*: 533)

Madi (M) Deity associated with Nergal. Probably attested in a text from Emar. (J. Westenholz 2000: 77–78)

Magala (M) See Ma-nun-gal

Māgiru(m), Magar (Akk.) Name of two different deities. One was a herald of Nin-šubur's temple, the other a bull of Adad. Means "Obedient." (Litke 1998: 29, 144; Tallqvist 1974: 359; Lambert, *RlA* VII: 255)

Magrat-amassu (M) Deity attested in an incantation. Means "His Word Is Favorable." According to An : *Anum*, in the circle of Marduk. (Litke 1998: 97; Reiner 1970: 39)

Ma-gula-ana (M) Deity identified with Nanna/Sîn in An : Anum. Means "Greater Boat of Heaven." (Richter 2004: 451; Litke 1998: 118)

Magur (M) (1) Má-gur$_8$, name of Nanna/Sîn in An : *Anum*. Means "Barge." Explained in *Anu ša amēli* as "Moon of the barge." (2) Deity Ma-gur$_5$ is allocated an offering at Ur III Umma. (Richter 2004: 451: Litke 1998: 119, 231)

Maḫ-di-ana, Maḫ-ti-ana, Maḫ-te-na (M) Deity occurring as Maḫ-ti-an-na in a personal name from Ur III Uruk. Maḫ-di-an-na occurs in a personal name from Ur III Nippur and is a title of the god Kabta in a list of names of Inana/Ištar. Means "Lofty One of Heaven." (Richter 2004: 161; Litke 1998: 162; Tallqvist 1974: 361; Krebernik, *RlA* VII: 255)

Maḫ-di-gal (M) Deity whose name means "The Great Lofty One." In *Anu ša amēli* explained as "Enlil of decisions." (Litke 1998: 229)

Maḫittu, Maḫuttu (sg.), **Maḫittena** (pl.) (H) Hurrian goddess(es) of prophets and prophecy. Attested at Emar and identified with Išḫara. In a Middle Hittite rite for a Hurrian festival, it is an epithet of Nin-gal. (van Gessel 1998: I, 294; Haas 1994: 376 note 481; Frantz-Szabó, *RlA* VII: 259)

Maḫ-te-na, Maḫ-ti-an-na (M) See Maḫ-di-ana

Maḫza (M) One of the seven destiny-decreeing gods of the E-sagil temple in Babylon. (George 2004 no. 20)

Makkal (L) See Mekal

Ma-laḫ (M) The twenty-ninth name of Marduk in the *Enūma eliš*. Means "Sailor." (Foster 2005: 480; Litke 1998: 93, 107; Speiser, *ANET*: 71; Heidel 1967: 57)

Malak (M) Deity likely borrowed from Akkadian by Sumerian. The tenth of Inana/Ištar's eighteen "messengers." Might be related to the Hebrew word for "messenger," *ml'k*. (Litke 1998: 159; Tallqvist 1974: 359; Lambert, *RlA* VII: 275)

Malakbēl (L) The sun god of Palmyra. Malakbēl was brother of Aglibol, the moon god. Palmyra's main deity was Bēl. (Dien 2004; Black and Green 2003: 35; Kaizer 2002; Lust, *DDDB*: 535–37; Röllig, *DDDB*: 150; Drijvers 1997; Lipiński 1995: 255–56; Teixidor 1979; Menen 1973: 202, 221 figure 164; Langdon, 1931: 37)

Mālik (L, M) Semitic divine name, probably originally a title. Means "Counselor" or, in the west, "King." Possibly a netherworld deity since, in some Assyrian writings, he was identified with Nergal. Isaiah 57:9 seems to support the idea of Mālik's netherworld associations. Occurs in Old Akkadian personal names. An important god at Ebla, where he occurs in many theophoric names. Also found in names at Mari, Ugarit, and elsewhere. Appears in Phoenician personal names. In the Qur'ān Mālek was an archangel who was delegated by Allah to rule the damned in Hell (1996, Sura 43: 77). See also Melqart; Molek; Milkom. (Such-Gutiérrez: 2005/6; del Olmo Lete 1999: 340; Müller, *DDDB*: 538–42; Leick 1998: 114; Pomponio and Xella 1997: 458–65; Lipiński 1995: 227–29; Schmidt 1994: 94–97; Tallqvist 1974: 359)

Malikūma (L) The collective name for deified dead kings at Ugarit. (del Olmo Lete 1999: 168, 172)

Maliya (H) Minor Luwian goddess. Appears in texts from Kanesh and had a temple at Kizzuwatna. Later, in Hellenistic Lydia, identified with Greek Athena. (Popko 1995: 73, 88–89, 101, 173)

Malkam (L) See Milkom

Malkandros (L) See Melqart

Malūkatim (M) Goddess in a ritual text from Babylon for the eleventh month.

Mama, Mami (M) Babylonian mother goddess and deity of childbirth in "Creation of Man by the Mother Goddess." Mami the wise was recognized as the divine midwife. Then, as the creator of destiny, she formed seven male/female pairs of humans from clay mixed with the blood of a slain deity. As a result of this deed, she gained the title "Lady of All the Gods." (Durand 2008: 226–27; Speiser, *ANET*: 100). (Black and Green 2003: 133, 136; Foster 2001: 5 note 2; Leick 1998: 114; Litke 1998: 71–72; Tallqvist 1974: 359; Speiser, *ANET*: 99–100; Edzard in Haussig 1965: 95; Krebernik, *RlA* VII: 504–5)

Mamia, Mamie (M) Sister of Marduk listed in An : *Anum*. (Litke 1998: 97)

Mamma (H) See Ammamma

Mammītu(m), Mami, Mamê (M) Originally, the personification of the oath *māmītu(m)* and a deity who punished oath-breakers. Came to be regarded as wife of Nergal/Meslamta-e or sometimes Erra. Often identified with Laz. In the "Epic of Gilgameš," she was called "she who creates destinies" (Foster 2001: 83). She had a month named after her in the Amorite calendars used at Old Babylonian Sippar, Ešnunna, and Šaduppûm. (Cohen 2015: 205; Black and Green 2003: 136; Leick 1998: 114; Litke 1998: 196, 200; Tallqvist 1974: 358–59; Krebernik, *RlA* VIII: 330–31)

Mamu (M) Deity attested in a Sargonic personal name and at Old Babylonian Sippar. Written Ma-mu. (Milano and Westenholz 2015; Renger 1967: 153)

Mamu(d) (M) The personification "Dream." Usually considered female, but sometimes male. As female, she was daughter of Utu/Šamaš. A sanctuary was built for her at Balawat by Aššurnaṣirpal II. Devotees possibly slept in a Mamu(d) sanctuary to receive dream omens. (Black and Green 2003: 128; Butler 1998: 73–78; Litke 1998: 133; George 1993: 166 no. 1352; Tallqvist 1974: 359; Lambert, *RlA* VII: 331)

Ma-mu-un-du (M) Deity identified with the healing goddess Gula/Nin-kar-(r)ak in god lists, wherein the name is written má-mu-un-^{du}dù. (Litke 1998: 182; Lambert, *RlA* VII: 331)

Ma-na-an (M) Deity listed in An : *Anum*. (Litke 1998: 53)

Manawat(u), **Manavat**, **Manathu**, **Manat** (L) Goddess of fate and tutelary deity of Petra, the capital of the Nabateans. Worshipped also at Palmyra. In addition, she was a pre-Islamic Arabian goddess worshipped at Mecca and elsewhere. Mentioned, with two other goddesses, in the Qur'ān (Sura 53: 20). Equated to Greek Tyche, Roman Fortuna. (Dien 2004; Black and Green 2003: 35; Kaizer 2002; Drijvers 1997; Ribichini, *DDDB*: 340; Sperling, *DDDB*: 567–68; Lipiński 1995: 64, 255: Teixidor 1979; Langdon, 1931: 21)

Mannu-šāninšu (Akk.) Daughter of the house of Nin-Gublaga, a cattle god. Means "Who Is His Equal?" (Krebernik, *RlA* VII: 342)

Manun-gal, **Nun-gal**, **Magala**, **Manu-na** (M) Sumerian netherworld goddess. Deity of punishment and prisons. Daughter of Ereškigal. Spouse of Enlil's son Birdu. Supervised the household at the Ekur temple of Enlil at Nippur. One of her titles was Nin-Ekura "Lady of the Ekur." Later identified with Nin-tin-uga, a name of Gula. A few long hymns to her are extant. She was worshipped in many cities. She had at least one temple and also a "seat" in the great sanctuary at Babylon. Variant in the Old Babylonian period is Ma-nun-na and in An : *Anum*: Ma-nu-gal and Ma-nu-kal. In a god list three adjacent entries are ^{d}nun-gal, ^{d}ma-gal-la, ^{d}ma-nun-gal, presumably all for the same goddess. Explained in An : *Anu ša amēli* as "Ea of Prisoners." The writing Ma-nu-gal is attested in an Old Akkadian personal name. (Such-Gutiérrez: 2005/6; Black and Green 2003: 145; Foster 2001: 226; Leick 1998: 138; Litke 1998: 185–86, 240; Civil 1993: 72–78; George 1993: 66 no. 51–52; Tallqvist 1974: 360; Reiner 1970: 21; Krebernik, *RlA* IX: 615–18)

Manzi'at, **Manzât**, **Ma(n)zat**, **Manziat**, **Mazzi'at**, **Mazzât**, **Mazzêt** (Akk., Elamite), **Tir-ana** (Sum.) (E, M) Goddess primarily of Elam and associated with Susiana. Šimut, a netherworld and herald god, seems to have been her spouse, Lugal-gida was her son, and the goddess Sililitu(m) her vizier. Her name was probably borrowed from Akkadian and means "Rainbow," as does the Sumerian Tir-ana, literally "Bow of Heaven." She is first attested in a treaty between Narām-Sîn of Akkad and a king of Susa. In the period 2000–1500 BCE she appears mainly in theophoric personal names. Untaš-Napiriša commissioned a temple for her at Choga Zanbil, and a brick from modern Dhe-e-Nou indicates that Šutruk-Naḫḫunte similarly built a temple for her in that city. A stele of Šilḫak-Inšušinak I refers to a temple of Manzi'at that she shared with Šimut, from which reference it has generally been assumed that she was his wife. In an inscription of Ḫuldelutuš-Inšušinak she is referred to as "great lady," and the same king mentions a joint temple of Manzi'at and Šimut. Manzi'at is likely the same goddess as Mesopotamian Bēlet-āli(m). She had a sanctuary at Nippur and four shrines in Babylon. Manzi'at was also a manifestation of Ištar and part of the constellation Andromeda. (Vallat 1998: 335–36, 340; Black and Green 2003: 75, 153; Litke 1998: 166,167; George 1993: 166 no. 1353–54; Hinz and Koch 1987: 583; König 1977: 202, 227; Tallqvist 1974: 361; Lambert, *RlA* VII: 344–46)

Ma-PEŠ (M) Deity in the Ur III personal name Ur-^{d}Ma-PEŠ$_2$. (OrSP 47-49, 45: r 1)

Ma-ra-li (M) The eleventh of Inana/Ištar's eighteen "messengers." Perhaps this is a conflated orthography for má-a-ra-li "ship of the netherworld," which would be appropriate for a messenger of Inana. (Litke 1998: 159; Lambert, *RlA* VII: 352)

Mārāt-Ani(m) (M) Goddesses in the shrine of the goddess Antu(m). This shrine was part of the Rēš sanctuary in Uruk in the Seleucid period. Means "Daughters of Anu(m)." (Falkenstein 1941: 25)

Mārāt-E-anna (M) Goddesses of the E-anna temple in Uruk in the Seleucid period. Means "Daughters of the E-anna." (Falkenstein 1941: 35 and note 2)

Mārāt-E-babbar (M) Goddesses of the E-babbar temple, both in Larsa and in Sippar. Means "Daughters of the E-babbar." (Beaulieu 2003: 322; Bongenaar 1997: 231, 326, 333. 347, 349, 363, 388)

Mārāt-E-zida (M) Goddesses of the E-zida, the chief temple of Borsippa. Means "Daughters of the E-zida." According to late theology they were related to Gunesura and Gazbaba, the hairdressers of Nanāya, who were originally associated with Uruk. Later, their cult was exported to Borsippa. (Beaulieu 2003: 318)

Mārat-iltim (M) Goddess attested at Terqa and Ḫišamta. Means 'Daughter of a Goddess." (Durand 2008: 271)

Mārāt-Uruk (M) Goddesses in the shrine of the goddess Antu(m). This shrine was part of the Rēš sanctuary. Means "Daughters of Uruk." (Falkenstein 1941: 25, 35)

Mār-bīti(m) (M) God of war and fate. Identified with Nabû. Means "Son of the House/Temple." Worshipped in temples at Borsippa and at Ilip near Kiš. His temple near Babylon or Borsippa was called "Exalted House of Joy." (George 1993: 167 no. 1355–56; Tallqvist 1974: 361–62)

Marduk (Babylonian), **Amar-Utu** (Sum.) Chief god of Babylonian pantheon and, by the Ur III period, tutelary deity of Babylon, the first mention of which occurs c. 2250 BCE. Marduk was understood as a god of justice. These attributes might have resulted from, or explain, his Sumerian name, "bull-calf of the sun," likely "a late, popular etymology" (Black and Green 2003: 128). Marduk had connections with water, the plant world, magic, and wisdom, all of which he probably acquired from identification with Asar-lu-ḫe and the latter's association with Enki/Ea. Like Asar-lu-ḫe, Marduk was deity of exorcism. The spread of his worship was associated with the political fortunes of Babylon as it became an empire. For Babylonians he was Bēl "Lord." In the *Enūma eliš*, Marduk was granted supremacy by all the gods, and, at its end, the names and titles of other deities, especially Ninurta, were recounted as merely aspects of Marduk. His epithets included "King of the Gods of Heaven and the Netherworld," "Lord of Lords," "The Enlil of the Gods," and "Creator of All Humankind." Like Enlil, he was Bēl-mātāti, "Lord of the Lands," the title proclaimed in the Babylonian creation myth as the last of Marduk's fifty names.

Marduk assimilated many attributes of the god Asar-lu-ḫe, and so, like him, became regarded as son of the great god Enki/Ea, indeed as his first-born. In the *Enūma eliš*, Marduk was born of Ea and his wife Damkina. Zarpanītu(m) was his consort, though at times Nanāya took on that role. His son was the divine scribe Nabû, patron god of Borsippa, neighbor of Babylon, and his daughter was Šara. His brother was the sun god Šamaš, and his sister was Ištar, especially the warlike Ištar of Arbela. His chamberlain (chair-bearer) was Mādanu(m). An image of the god shows him arrayed as a Babylonian king, holding in one hand the rod-and-ring symbol of power, in the other a weapon, and accompanied by his animal, the snake-dragon Mušḫuššu(m).

Large cylinder seal showing Marduk standing on one of Ti'amat's monsters. Neo-Babylonian. Lapis lazuli. Height 12.5 cm. Vorderasiatisches Museum, Berlin. After Black and Green 2003: 129.

It was not until the period of Ḫammu-rāpi that Marduk became a really important deity and took over many of the roles and powers of Enlil. The prologue of Ḫammu-rāpi's law code states the change clearly: Enlil determined for Marduk "the Enlil functions over all mankind" (Meek, *ANET*: 164). Since Marduk's ascent to power happened after the composition of most Mesopotamian mythic compositions, he did not usually appear in them. A notable exception was the Erra Epic, in which Erra persuaded Marduk, depicted as incompetent and a bit doddering, to leave the rule of the world to the violent deity. Erra then went on a rampage of destruction. Another was the *Enūma eliš*, in which Marduk was the hero. Its first section told of the struggle of the younger deities against the older ones and ended with Marduk's violent defeat of the primordial goddess Ti'amat. Out of her dead body Marduk made the heaven and the earth. Then the deities created human beings from the blood of Ti'amat's consort Qingu. In the first millennium BCE, with the rise of Assyria, the god Aššur replaced Marduk in the composition. At Babylon, the epic was featured in the twelve-day-long *akītu* festival, much of which took place in Marduk's sanctuary. At this time Marduk determined the destiny of Babylon. Spectacular and opulent processions accompanied the golden and bejeweled barge in which the god rode. Statues of various deities were brought together before Marduk. Rituals were performed and sacrifices made. On day four, the *Enūma eliš* was read aloud in its entirety. On day five, the king was "humbled before Bēl" (Cohen 1993: 438). After stripping the king of the royal regalia and setting them before Marduk, the high priest slapped the king on the cheek. Then he dragged him by his ear into the god's presence. Kneeling, the king swore that he had fulfilled his obligations to Babylon and took an oath to go on doing so. The high priest slapped the king again. If tears came to his eyes, Marduk had favored him, and he received his regalia. No tears meant that Marduk would bring about the king's downfall. On day eleven the marriage of Marduk and Zarpanītu(m), or Bēl and Bēltiya, was celebrated. An psalm served to calm Marduk when he returned to his temple after the *akītu* festival. It listed the main temples at which the god was worshipped.

With Šamaš and Ea, Marduk was often invoked in incantations, for, like them, he was thought of as a deity of compassion and fairness. Although Marduk had shrines and temples in many cities, for instance, Nippur; Sippar-Aruru, a suburb of Sippar; and Borsippa, his cult center was the great temple in Babylon the E-sag-ila. It lay among a group of sanctuary buildings situated in the center of Babylon. Marduk's temple tower (ziqqurat), with his high shrine on its top, was called "Foundation Platform of Heaven and Netherworld." In the E-sag-ila, Marduk had a "seat" called Ti'amat "Sea." Marduk was worshipped also in Assyria, and an *akītu* festival was celebrated for him at the city of Aššur. An Assyrian vassal treaty appealed to Marduk to "determine" for any destroyer of the treaty's tablet "an indissoluble curse as [his] fate" (Reiner, *ANET*: 538). By the middle of the first millennium BCE, the god Aššur had replaced Marduk as Mesopotamia's supreme deity. The Greek historian Herodotus, who possibly, but by no means certainly, travelled to Babylon in the fifth century BCE, reported that Bēl's priests told him that, in the shrine on top of the ziqqurat, there was nothing but "a fine large couch," and that a chosen "Assyrian woman" spent the night there with the god (1983: 114; Book I, 181). (Oshima, 2011; Foster 2005: 611–20, 645–46, 680–94, 821–26, 841–46, 859; Black and Green 2003: 40, 128–29, 157, 168; Abusch, *DDDB*: 543–49; Frame 1999: 6–7, 8; Leick 1999: 65–66; Leick 1998: 115–16; Litke 1998: 89,

221–24, 236; Cohen 1993: 245, 307, 312, 403, 405, 418–20, 438, 439, 446–47, 448; Foster 1993: II, 771–805; George 1993: 83 no. 269, 130 no. 849, 153 no. 1141, 159 no. 1236, 167 no. 1358; Tallqvist 1974: 362–72; Speiser, *ANET*: 62, 66–67, 68, 72; Heidel 1967: 21, 40–43, 47, 59; Sommerfeld, *RlA* VII: 360–70; Rittig, *RlA* VII: 370–74)

Mār-Ḫalab (M) Deity attested in a Neo-Assyrian god list. Perhaps identified with Asarluḫe or Marduk. Written Mar-ḫal-lab. May mean "Citizen of Aleppo." (King 1969: pl. 34)

Ma(r)ru (M) Deity explained in *Anu ša amēli* as "Adad of the Flood (*abūbi*)." Written ma-ru and mar-ru$_4$. (Litke 1998: 232)

Marru(m)-ša-Marduk (M) Deified symbol of Marduk attested from Old Babylonian Kutalla, a town near Ur. Means "The Spade of Marduk," In a legal case, the parties to the dispute would swear by this symbol. (Renger 1967: 145)

Martu, Mardu (M) See Amurru(m)

Martu-edina (M) Form of the god Martu. Means "Martu of the Steppe." (Litke 1998: 217)

Martu-SUR-an-ki (M) See Ḫumṣiru

Martu-ura (M) Deity attested in an Ur III offering list from Puzriš-Dagān. Occurring after a mention of a form of the moon god. Means "Martu of the Roof." (Sallaberger 1993: I, 208)

Marukka (M) The second name of Marduk in the *Enūma eliš*. The name occurs as Amarukkam in the late lamentation. (Foster 2005: 474; Litke 1998: 91; Cohen 1988: 417; Tallqvist 1974: 360; Speiser, *ANET*: 69; Heidel 1967: 52; Krebernik, *RlA* VII: 440)

Mar(u)ru-tukul (M) Name of Marduk. Means "Storm Flood Weapon." (Litke 1998: 91; Krebernik, *RlA* VII: 440)

Maruttaš (M) God of the Kassites identified with Ninurta. (Black and Green 2003: 112; Brinkman, *RlA* VII: 440)

Marutukku (M) The third name of Marduk in the *Enūma eliš*. (Foster 2005: 474; Litke 1998: 91; Tallqvist 1974: 360; Speiser, *ANET*: 69; Heidel 1967: 52)

Maskir, Miskar (L) Deity occurring in Phoenician names from Carthage. Means "Herald." See also Ḥoṭer Miskar. (Lipiński 1995: 174–76)

Massû(m) (M) Deity in a circle of Nergal gods. Invoked in an incantation. Means "Leader." (Reiner 1970: 40)

Maš (M) See Šakkan

Mašdad (M) Deity attested in an Old Babylonian god list. Written maš-da-ad. (Weidner 1924/25)

MašganḪUR (M) See Pasānu

Maš-gi (M) Written maš-gi$_6$. See ANzagar(a)

Maš-gula (M) One of the goddess Nisaba's shepherds. Means "Largest Goat." Occurs in a lamentation, coupled with the goddess Maš-tur, "Little Goat," who is searching for a lost child. (Cohen 1988: 695; Kramer 1981: 363)

Maškim (M) See Rābiṣu(m)

Maškim-ge-lu-ḫarana (M) In An : *Anum* a deity identified as an "evil god" and as a name for the demon Muštabbabbu. Means either "Demon of the Night, Traveller of the Road" or "Demon of the Night (against) the Traveller of the Road." A Sumerian title of the god Šulpa'e. (Litke 1998: 209, 210; Lambert, *RlA* VII: 455–56)

Maš-maš (M), Epithet of both Lugal-Erra and Meslamta-e, who were usually presented together. The word *maš* is Sumerian for "twin." Means "The Twins." Astrally identified as Gemini. (Tallqvist 1974: 372; Lambert, *RlA* VII: 456)

Maš-taba (M) The title of a pair of gods, Lugal-Erra and Meslamta-e. Means "Pair of Twins." Astrally identified as Gemini. (Black and Green 2003: 123–24; Litke 1998: 197; Tallqvist 1974: 372; Hunger, *RlA* VII: 530–31)

Mašti (E) Elamite goddess known in the Neo-Elamite period. Mother and protector of the gods. One of her epithets was "Lady of Tarriša." Worshipped at Susa and a number of other places. (Vallat 1998: 337–40; van Koppen and van der Toorn, *DDDB*: 889)

Maš-tur (M) Deity whose name means "Little Goat." Occurs in a lamentation coupled with the goddess Maš-gula, who is searching for a lost child. (Cohen 1988: 695)

Mati (M) Deity attested in an Early Dynastic god list. Written má-ti. (Mander 1986: 21)

Maṭar (M) Deified rain, attested in the Mari texts. (Durand 2008: 208)

Mazaštum (M) Deity receiving an offering in an Ur III text from Umma. Written Ma-za-aš?-tum. (UTI 6, 3662: o 3)

Ma(?)-zi-x (E) Elamite deity occurring in a treaty between Narām-Sîn of Akkad and a king of Susa. Name perhaps to be read Mazit. (König 1977: 201, 227)

Me-a-ni (M). See Mīnu(m)-anni(m)

Me-abzu (M) A title of the Babylonian goddess Zarpanītu(m), spouse of Marduk. Means "*Me* of the Abzu." (Tallqvist 1974: 373; Krebernik, *RlA* VII: 613)

Medim-ša (M) See Nin-medim-ša

Me-duraḫ (M) Deity explained in *Anu ša amēli* as *ša parṣī*, "An of the *Me*s." However, noting (1) the interchange of Me- and Men- in the god names Men-ku and Me-ku; and (2) the moon god is called Men-duraḫ-an-na and Men-duraḫ-dingir-ra, it is possible that this name is a variant for Men-duraḫ "The Ibex Crown" and, despite the scribe's comment, had nothing to do, at least originally, with the *Me*s. (Litke 1998: 228, 230)

Me-enuna / agruna (M) Deity attested in an Early Dynastic god list. Means "*Me* of the Inner Sanctum." (Mander 1986: 26)

Me-gar (M) Deity attested in an Early Dynastic god list. Means "Silence." (Mander 1986: 142)

Me-ḫursaga (M) The vizier of Nin-Muru(m), "Lord of (the City of) Muru(m)." The name means "*Me* of the Mountain." (Litke 1998: 172; Tallqvist 1974: 373; Krebernik, *RlA* VIII: 31)

Me-ḫuš(-a) (M) (1) One of five offspring of the goddess of strong drink and beer, Nin-kasi. Two of the daughters' names seem appropriate for the child of the goddess of strong drink: Kituš-kirzal, "Merry Residence," perhaps referring to a place to have a drink, and Nusiliga, "Never-ending," presumably referring to a never-ending supply of drink. The term me- in two of the other names: Me-ḫuš and Me-kù (with variant men-kù) might refer to the *Me* of strong drink. The term men occurs in the name of the other daughter, Men-me-te with variant ^{d}Eme$^{e\text{-}me}$-me-te. (2) Also a title of Ištar and possibly of Nergal. (Litke 1998: 62; Tallqvist 1974: 373; Krebernik, *RlA* VIII: 32)

Mekal (L) Canaanite deity about whom little is known. The name was recorded on a stele dated to the fourteenth century BCE and unearthed at Beth-Shean, an ancient city site now in modern Israel. (Lewis 2005: 74, 75; Mazar 1990: 289)

Me-KIN (M) Variant for Me-me, vizier of Ningal. (Litke 1998: 122)

Me-kug (M) See Me-ḫuš(-a)

Melem (M) Deity attested in an Early Dynastic god list. Means "Splendor." (Mander 1986: 142)

Melītum (M) Name of Ištar in a Neo-Assyrian god list. Written me-lí-tùm. Means "Stairway." (King 1969: pl. 17)

Melqart, Melkart(h), Milqart, Melgart (L) Title *Milk-qart* meaning "King of the City," which became the name of an important Phoenician warrior/hero god. As the "Ba'lu (Lord) of Tyre," he was tutelary deity of that city, his cult center, and of its royal dynasty. Attested primarily in the first millennium BCE. Originally he was probably a royal ancestor, a deified hero/king of the city. At Tyre as elsewhere, he was closely associated with the goddess Aštarte, likely her spouse. Associated with the sea and protector deity of sailors and marine voyagers. Many scholars understand him as a disappearing and returning god (a so-called "dying god"), whose "awakening" festival in February/March celebrated his "resurrection ... following his death and ritual cremation" (Markoe 2000: 117). A passage in the Book of Ezekiel (28: 17) in the Hebrew Bible, part of an oracle against the king of Tyre, might contain a reference to this ritual. In another tradition he was killed by the monster Typhon. Thus he had some relationship to the netherworld and was possibly identified with Mesopotamian netherworld god Nergal. Also paralleled to the "dying god" Ešmun of Ṣidōn, with whom he was usually paired in treaties and inscriptions. Often identified with Egyptian Osiris. Depicted as a bearded figure wielding a spear or axe, carrying a shield and sometimes a lotus, and wearing a conical hat. He was often accompanied by a snake.

Melqart had an important role in the ideology of Phoenician maritime trade and commerce and was popular in all Phoenician colonies. Especially worshipped at Carthage ("New City"), which every year sent tribute to Melqart's temple at Tyre, its mother city. The god's cult spread throughout the Mediterranean with shrines and temples in Cyprus, Egypt, Anatolia, and elsewhere. On Cyprus he had an important temple at Kition-Bamboula, shared with Aštarte. An inscription recovered on Cyprus concerned a person who was perhaps a "high cultic functionary of Melqart"; he held the title "raiser/resuscitator of the god" (Mettinger 2001: 180). At Carthage, Melqart was chief god, and he is attested in many Carthaginian theophoric names, for example, that of the Carthaginian general Hamilcar "Servant of Melqart." His great temple at Gadir or Gadeira (now Cadiz) in Phoenician Spain was famous in the Greco-Roman world. In Roman times his cult reached as far as Great Britain. The Greeks and Romans identified him with Herakles/Hercules, though the late writer Lucian, who wrote in Greek, made a clear distinction between the Greek Heracles and the Tyrian one. In the Hellenistic period he was increasingly seen as a sun god. According to Philo of Byblos, Melkarthos was son of Demarous (Ba'lu/Hadad, Zeus) and grandson of Ouranos (Heaven). Some scholars argue that, in the ritual battle on Mount Carmel between the Hebrew prophet of YHWH Elijah and the priests of Ba'lu, the Tyrian Ba'lu/Melqart was the Canaanite god in question (I Kings 18: 16–40). Scholars are in general agreement that Melqart was the "Ba'lu" revered by Jezebel and Ahab in Samaria (I Kings 16–18). (Quinn 2018: 113–14, 121; Woolmer 2017: 105–6, 113, 117, 121–22; Ball 2009: 96–97; Younger 2009: 2; Betlyon 2005: 41. 49; Ruiz Mata in Bierling 2002: 163; Mettinger 2001: 27, 37, 83–111, 180–82; Markoe 2000: 54, 67, 89, 115, 118, 119, 129–30; Smith 2001: 114; Moscati 1999: 26, 34–35, 114, 139, 193; Mulder, *DDDB*: 184; Ribichini, *DDDB*: 563–65; Brody 1998: 25–26, 33–37, 38, 98, 138–40; Leick 1998: 118; Lipiński 1995: 226–43; Bonnet, *DCPP*: 285–87; Lipiński, *DCPP*: 158; Smith 1990: 42–43; Bonnet 1988: 417–33; Attridge and Oden 1981: 53, 54, 90 note 118; Attridge and Oden 1976: 10, 11; Herm 1975: 12, 110, 159, 173–75, 196; Harden 1963: 62, 85–86, Plates 91 and 109 no. n)

Memaḫ (M) Deity identified in a Neo-Assyrian god list with Ninurta and explained as "gatherer of the supreme *Mes*." (King 1969: pl. 11)

Me-me (M) (1) In Tablet III of An : *Anum* name of the vizier of Nin-gal. Gloss ga-ga, which Litke suggests shows a textual variant with Kaka, vizier of An, rather than a pronunciation of me-me. (2) In Tablet IV of An : *Anum* a name of Išḫara. (3) In Tablet V of An : *Anum* a name of Nin-kar(r)ak, followed by Me-me-sa$_6$-ga. Me-me is mentioned in a ritual for the *akītu* festival at Uruk. From Sippar of the Neo-Assyrian period came a figurine of a dog dedicated in Me-me's name, thus the Me-me identified with Gula/Nin-kar(r)ak. (Black and Green 2003: 70, 101; Litke 1998: 122, 166, 181; Cohen 1993: 204, 435; Tallqvist 1974: 316, 373; Krebernik, *RlA* VIII: 56–57)

Me-me-šaga (M) See Me-me

Memešarti (H) Archi suggests the name is from *šarrat māmīti*, "queen of oaths." (Archi 1990: 118)

Men-duraḫ (M) See Me-duraḫ

Men-duraḫ-an-na, Men-duraḫ-dingir-ra (M) Name of the moon god. May mean "Crown (called?) 'Ibex of Heaven'" and "Crown (called?) 'Ibex of the God(s).'" These two names may simply be variants. Men-dàra-AN for the moon god is explained in An : *Anum* as *ša ikribi* "source of blessing." See Me-duraḫ. (Litke 1998: 117, 231; Tallqvist 1974: 374; Krebernik, *RlA* VII: 615)

Men-e-du (M) See Men-šudu

Meni (L) Spirit of fate, fortune, or destiny. Mentioned in the Hebrew Bible paired with Gad "Luck" or "Destiny," both being worshipped by post-exilic Jews (Isaiah 65:11). This passage seems to be referring to ritual banqueting. In the Middle Ages, Jewish scholars considered the possibility that Meni was an astral deity. Translated in the Greek Septuagint as Tyche, who was goddess of fortune, luck, and success. Perhaps equivalent to the pre-Islamic Arabian goddess Man(aw)at, who is named in the Qur'ān (Sura 53: 20). (Ribichini, *DDDB*: 340; Sperling, *DDDB*: 566–68; Lipiński 1995: 63; Maier, *ABD* IV: 695)

Me-nigin-šudu (M) Deity whose name means "Who Perfects All the *Mes*." See Lugal-me-šudu and Nin-me-šudu.

Me-ninnu-ana (M) Deity identified with Papsukkal, vizier of An. Means "The Fifty *Mes* of An." (Litke 1998: 25; Krebernik *RlA* VIII: 58)

Men-kug, Me-kug (M) See Me-ḫuš(-a)

Men-kuta (M) Men-kù-ta is listed in a Neo-Assyrian god list and corresponds in An : *Anum* to Ama-kù-ta, who is in the circle of Nin-geš-zida. (Litke 1998: 193; King 1968: pl. ix 31)

Men-kuta-e (M) One of the fourteen offspring of Nin-šubur, the vizier of An/Anu(m). Men-kuta-e means "Emanating from the Holy Crown." (Litke 1998: 28; Tallqvist 1974: 374; Krebernik, *RlA* VIII: 59)

Men-mete (M) See Me-ḫuš(-a)

Men-šudu (M) Deity identified with Nanna/Sîn. Means "Perfect Crown." Variant is Men-e-du. (Litke 1998: 117; Tallqvist 1974: 375; Krebernik, *RlA* VIII: 62–63)

Men-ud-bur (M) Deity identified with the moon god Nanna/Sîn. May mean "Corona that Spreads Light." (Litke 1998: 117; Tallqvist 1974: 375; Krebernik, *RlA* VIII: 65)

Menune-si (M) One of three daughters of the weather god Iškur/Adad. Variant Mi-. Means "Fulfills the Princely *Mes*." (Litke 1998: 143; Tallqvist 1974: 374; Krebernik, *RlA* VIII: 65)

Mēr (M) See Wēr

Mer-ikud (M) Deity identified with Ninkar(r)ak. The name is written mer-ì-kud with gloss me-er-i-ku-ud in An : *Anum*. (Richter 2004: 215; Litke 1998: 180)

Mermeri (M) Deity identified with the storm god Iškur/Adad. Written IM and EN×EN(DALḪAMUN) "whirlwind," both glossed me-er-me-ri. (Litke 1998: 139)

Merodach (L) Name in the Hebrew Bible for the chief god of Babylon, Marduk, also called B'el (Jeremiah 50:2). His son was biblical Nebo (Babylonian Nabû). (Abusch, *DDDB*: 548–49; Handy, *ABD* IV: 522–23)

Mērtum (M) Deity attested at Mari. (Durand 2008: 243)

Mes (M) A divine title attested in an Early Dynastic god list from Šuruppak. Means "Hero/Young Man." The title was later applied to Marduk. (Mander 1986: 115; Krebernik, *RlA* VIII: 73)

Me-sag-ninnu(50) (M) Explained in Assyrian text as "Great Battle of Enlil."

Me-sag-pirig (M) Deified weapon. May mean "Lion-headed *me*."

Mes-an-GUB (M) Deity of Girsu, likely associated with the netherworld, to whom offerings were made at a barley festival and on other occasions. Spouse in Lagaš was Nin-šubur and elsewhere Ereškigal. Associated with Meslamta-e. Perhaps the name is related to an-gub-ba, *angubbû*, a category of gods. (Cohen 2015: 37, 55–57; Selz 1995: 176, 179–80)

Mes-edin (M) Deity attested in an Early Dynastic god list from Šuruppak. Means "Hero/Young Man (of) the Steppe." (Mander 1986: 115; Krebernik, *RlA* VIII: 73)

Mes-enun/agrunta-e (M) Deity attested in an Early Dynastic god list. See Meslamta-e. (Mander 1986: 143)

Me-sikila (M) Spouse of the goddess Lisina. Means "Pure *Me*." (Richter 2004: 146; Nashef 1986: 340)

Mes-kalam (M) Deity attested in an Early Dynastic god list. Means "Young

Man (of) the Nation." (Mander 1986: 115)

Meskilak (M) The main goddess of the city of Dilmun, modern Baḫrain. Probably either wife or mother of the chief god, En-zak. Possibly related to Nin-sikila, a form of Nin-ḫursag, or Nin-me-sikila. Nin-Dilmun, "Lady of Dilmun," was likely her title. She and En-zak shared "House of the Quay," a temple at Dilmun. (Black and Green 2003: 66; George 1993: 107 no. 566; Nashef 1986: 340)

Meslamta-e (M) Sumerian god of the netherworld. The twin of Lugal-Erra. Son of Ninlil and Enlil. His wife was Mami. His vizier was Zimalarsi. Later he was identified with Nergal and Erra. Means "(He) who Comes Forth from the Meslam," the temple of Nergal at various sites especially Kutha, Nergal's main cult city. The twins guarded entrances and, in the Neo-Assyrian period, figurines of them were buried under doorways. Visually they were identical, each wearing a horned hat, bearing a mace, and brandishing an axe.

Meslamta-e was tutelary deity of both Maškan-Šapir and Dūrum. At a festival held at Uruk, he received an offering of beer, and he was mentioned, along with Lugal-Erra, in a late ritual for covering a temple kettledrum. He had temples at Ur and Girsu and shared, with his twin, a "seat" at Babylon. The Twins represented the astral sign Gemini. (Cohen 2015: 140; Katz 2003: 420–28; Black and Green 2003: 123–24; Litke 1998: 196; George 1993: 124 no. 769 no. 773, 126 no. 802, 127 no. 804, 167 no. 1359; Tallqvist 1974: 375; Sachs, *ANET*: 335; Lambert, *RlA* VII: 143–44)

Amuletic pendant bearing an image of the Divine Twins. Neo-Assyrian. Chalcedony. After Black and Green 2003: 124.

Meslamta-e-lugal-Gudua (M) Netherworld deity attested in the Ur III period. Means "Meslamta-ea, Lord of (the City of) Kutha." (Sallaberger 1993: I, 225–26 note 1078)

Mes-nun-sa-ak (M) Sumerian deity associated with Isin, mentioned along with Damu and Gunura in the Ur III period. Written with -sa$_6$-. May mean something like "Princely Young Man who Acts Favorably." (Richter 2004: 181)

Mes-sanga-Unuga (M) Deity associated with Uruk and possibly the tutelary deity of a town in the region. Attested as early as the Early Dynastic period and as late as Hellenistic (Seleucid) times. Spouse Nin-gu'e-siraka. Might mean "Hero, *Sanga* Priest of Uruk." (Tallqvist 1974: 375; Krebernik, *RlA* VIII: 94–95)

Me-suḫ (M) Son of the snake god Tišpak. Written Me-súḫ, probably a variant for me-sùḫ. If so, the name might mean "The *Me* of Disorientation (or 'Blurred Vision', *ešītu*)," symptoms of snake-bite. (Litke 1998: 194; Krebernik, *RlA* VIII: 96)

Me-šu-nušudu (M) Deity whose name is written Me-šu-nu-šu-du$_7$ in An : *Anum* and Me-nu-šu-du$_7$ in the lexical list Nabnītu. Interestingly, this name, constructed with terrible Sumerian syntax (šu nu-šu-du$_7$), is almost the exact same as a line in the Neo-Babylonian Chronicles: me-bi šu nu-un-šu-du$_7$, "its rites were not performed." Moreover, this negative form makes no sense as the name of a deity, unless it is to be understood as "Has he not perfected the rites?" In An : *Anum* and the lexical list Nabnītu M the name is explained as *ši-lu-tu*. (Litke 1998: 166; Finkel 1982; *CAD* Š/3: 224b)

Mezul(l)a (H) Hittite sun goddess. Daughter of the weather god (Hittite/Luwian Tarḫunta or Tarhunna, Hattic Taru) and the Sun Goddess of Arinna. Mezul(l)a's daughter was called Zintuḫi, also a sun goddess. Originally known in Hattic as Wazulla. Another name of Mezul(l)a was Tappinu. Protector of the Hittite king. Often addressed in Hittite rituals as a dyad with her mother. Regularly asked to mediate between humans and the deities, as well as between the sun goddess and the Hittite queen. Her premier cult site was Arinna, where she had her main temple, but she was venerated also at other sites, including the Hittite capital. Mentioned in god and offering lists from Arinna and elsewhere. (Leick 1998: 118; van Gessel 1998: I, 302–7; Popko 1995: 71–73, 75, 113, 145; Haas 1994: 337, 420, 426–28, 554, 585–86; Laroche 1946/47: 30)

Michael (L) The most prominent of the four archangels and their leader in the final struggle with the armies of evil. Guardian of and warrior fighting for Israel. Heavenly record-keeper. Mediator between the deity and Israel, as well as for all human beings. Especially privileged to stand near to the throne of the deity, normally accompanied by Gabriel and Raphael. The name Michael is usually interpreted to mean "Who Is Like God?" A complicated Jewish hierarchy of angels was elaborated in the Hellenistic period. In the Hebrew Bible, the Book of Daniel, referring to Michael three times, called him "a prince of the first rank" (10: 13) and understood him to be a helper of the people of Israel (10: 21, 12: 1). In later literature he became the main angelic opponent of Satan and "the dragon." In the New Testament, Michael was a warrior (Jude 9; Revelation 12:7), and in Christian imagery he brandished a sword while standing over the fallen dragon. He was also depicted weighing souls. His cult started in the East, where he was associated with healing, and spread widely. A number of sites claim apparitions of the now Saint, the most noted being Monte Gargarino in Italy. His most famous European shrine is Mont-Saint-Michel in Normandy. His feast day is September 29, which in modern times he shares with Gabriel and Raphael as "Saint Michael and All the Angels." (Farmer 2003: 367–68; Mach, *DDDB*: 569–72; van Henten, *DDDB*: 80–82; Comay 1993: 240; Watson, *ABD* IV: 811; Gaster, *IDB* 1991: III, 373)

Mikal, Makkal, Mekel (L) Name of a Canaanite/Phoenician god attested at Beth-shean in the Jordan Valley of Israel and worshipped also on Cyprus. Possibly identified with the plague god Rešep(h). (Mach, *DDDB*: 569; Lipiński, *DCPP*: 292–93)

Milkashtart, Milkastart, Molk-ashtart (L) In the third-second centuries BCE, a minor Phoenician tutelary deity of the city of Hammōn, modern Umm el-Amed, near Tyre. The god's name seems to be a combination of the word for king *mlk* (in feminine, "queen") and the goddess Aštarte. It has been suggested that the combination was intended to locate the deity geographically, that is, Milku at Aštartu. As in two texts dating to the twelfth century BCE from Ugarit that suggested that a deity Milku had his cult center at Aṯtartu, usually understood as Aštaroth-Qarnaim in Israel (Genesis 14:5). Milkashtart was worshipped also at Phoenician colonies, especially Malta, Carthage, and Cadiz. (Pardee 2002: 177, 281; Markoe 2000: 118; Müller, *DDDB*: 540–41; Lipiński 1995: 269–74; Bonnet and Lipiński, *DCPP*: 293; Albright 1968: 241)

Milkom, Milcom, Malkam (L) The supreme god of Ammōn, a small country east of the Jordan River. Name probably derived from *mlk*, the Semitic word for "king." Might have been equated to the Canaanite god El. Although little is known about the deity, the Hebrew Bible tells us that he wore a golden crown adorned with jewels (II Samuel 12:30). In addition, King Solomon, along with many of his people, revered "the abomination" Milkom (I Kings 11:5, 33), and the king built a shrine for him (II Kings 23:13). Worshipped also at Ebla and Mari. Evidence is unclear about whether Milkom and Molek were names of the same god. The Hebrew Bible treats them as separate deities. (Lewis 2005: 92, 101; Müller, *DDDB*: 541; Puech, *DDDB*: 575–76; Leick 1998: 118; *IDB* III, 378; Smith, 1990: 24)

Milku (L) See Milkashtart

Milku (M) Deity identified with Marduk in a Neo-Assyrian god list. (King 1969: pl. 35)

Milqart, Milk-quart (L) See Melqart

Mimijanta (H) Hittite deity. (Wilhelm, *RIA VIII*: 208)

Mimma lemnu(m) (M) A Mesopotamian demon. Means "All that Is Evil." In the late Akkadian composition "A [Prince's] Vision of the netherworld," the demon is said to have two heads, one of which was leonine. (Foster 2005: 836; Black and Green 2003: 98; Speiser, *ANET*: 109)

Mīna-īkul-bēlī (M) Cook in the E-sagil in Babylon. Means "What Did My Lord Eat?" (Litke 1998: 98)

Mīna-išti-bēlī (M) Brewer in the E-sagil in Babylon. Means "What Did My Lord Drink?" (Litke 1998: 98)

Minki, Munki (H) One of the primeval Old Syrian deities to whom the "Song of Kumarbi" is chanted. Though "dead," still appearing in rituals and receiving offerings. Involved in a cultic procession visiting various towns. Invoked in state treaties. Usually paired with Am(m)unki as a male/female dyad in deity lists. The pair might be identified with the Sumerian ancestral deities Enki and Nin-ki, though this is under debate. Hurrian version of the name is Minkišurri. (Hoffner 1998: 41, 112; Leick 1998: 79; van Gessel 1998: I, 309–11;

Popko 1995: 99; Haas 1994: 112, 114–15, 257, 471, 581; Laroche 1977: 170; Laroche 1946/47: 126)

Minkišurri (H) See Minki

Mīnu-amnu (M) Name of Inana. Written *mì-nu-am-nu-ú*. Perhaps means something like "What Did I (Re)count?" (King 1969: pl. 17)

Mīnu-anni(m) (M) Name of Inana in "The Hymn to the Queen of Nippur" and attested in An : *Anu ša amēli* as "Ištar of Wailing." May mean 'What Is This?" See Minû-ulla. Written *mi-nu-ú-an-ni* in the hymn and *mì-nu-an-nim* and *mi*(var. *mi*)*-nu-num* in An : *Anum*. (Litke 1998: 235; Lambert 1982: 199; Krebernik, *RlA* VIII: 652)

Mīnu-a-du/zu (M) Name of Inana. Written *mì-nu-a-du*[ru] with variant *mì-nu-a-zu*. (Krebernik, *RlA* VIII: 65)

Mīnu-ulla (M) Name of Inana in "The Hymn to the Queen of Nippur." May mean "What Is That?" Written *mi-nu-ú-ul-la*. See Mīnû-anni(m). (Lambert 1982: 211–12)

Miqit (M) Nergal's guardian of the door in "Nergal and Ereškigal." Krebernik relates the name, "Falling," to his role, as a servant of Nergal's, in the falling sickness, epilepsy. (Krebernik, *RlA* VIII: 218)

Mirizir (M) Kassite goddess associated with horses. (Krebernik, *RlA* VIII: 220)

Mir-šakuš'u (M) Deity identified with Marduk. Explained in An : *Anum* as *eziz u muštāl* "Angry (yet) Compassionate." (Litke 1998: 90)

Mīšaru(m) (M), **Mīšor, Mīšar(u)** (L) The personified concept of justice. Usually son of Šamaš and brother of the goddess Kittu(m), but in An : *Anum*, he appears as son of Adad and his wife as Išartu(m). Worshipped at Uruk and at Adad's temple at the town of Udada. Also associated with La-tarāk and shared a temple with him at Aššur. At Assyrian Uruk in the second millennium BCE, Mīšaru(m) took part in a procession between temples, and he was mentioned in a late *akītu* ritual for Uruk. (Cohen 2015: 433; Durand 2008: 242; Black and Green 2003: 98; Litke 1998: 143; George 1993: 98 no. 456, 156 no. 1187, 162 no. 1278; Tallqvist 1974: 374)

Minor Canaanite/Phoenician god. The personified concept of justice. In sources from Ugarit and elsewhere, he was paired with Ṣydyk "Rectitude or Righteousness." In the Hebrew Bible the word *mīšor* means "justice" or "equity," but there is no clear evidence that the concept was deified (for example, Psalm 45:7). His Mesopotamian counterpart was Mīšaru(m), whose sister deity was Kittu(m) "Truth." Philo of Byblos credited Misor and Sydyk with the discovery of the use of salt. (Pardee 2002: 151, 281; Batto, *DDDB*: 930–31; Watson, *DDDB*: 577–78; Lipiński 1995: 112–14; Xella, *DCPP*: 431; Attridge and Oden 1981: 44, 45, 85 note 74; Cross 1973: 161, 161 note 74)

Mišini (H) Hittite deity associated with the city Šapinuwa. (Wilhelm, *RlA* VIII: 264)

Mithra (E) See Rašmu; Sraoša

Mitraššil (H) Deity who had an Indian name with a Hurrian ending. Occurs in a treaty and a letter from a king of Mittani to an Egyptian pharaoh. (van Gessel 1998: I, 312; Haas 1994: 543; Laroche 1976: 171; Laroche 1946/47: 118)

Mittununi (H) Hittite deity associated with the city Šapinuwa. (Wilhelm, *RlA* VIII: 316)

Mitum (M) A lyre of the cattle god Nin-Gublaga. The entry in An : *Anum* ([geš] TUKUL.DINGIR.BAD) with gloss mi-ṭu seems to be a conflation of two variants: [geš]mitum(TUKUL.DINGIR) and [geš]mitum$_2$ (TUKUL.BAD). Means "Mace." (Richter 2004: 452; Litke 1998: 124)

Mītūtu(m) (M) Deified personification of "Death." Equated to the deity SaKIN in An : *Anum*. (Litke 1998: 220)

Miyatanzipa (H) Deity with the epithet "King." Occurs in the Old Hittite mythic literature about the disappearing Telipinu and the goddess Inara. (Hoffner 1998: 17, 31; Popko 1995: 73, 82)

MiZi-banītum (M) In a Neo-Assyrian god list identified as a constellation. (King 1969: pl. 13)

Molek, Molech, Moloch, Melech, Melekh (L) Possibly an ancient Semitic god of the netherworld, perhaps associated with ancestor cults, royal or otherwise. According to the Hebrew Bible, a god to whom people, including Israelites, offered human sacrifices, especially of children, at the Tophet(h) in the Valley of Hinnom to the southwest side of Jerusalem (II Kings 23:10, Jeremiah 32: 35). The word *tophet* comes from the Aramaic for "hearth" or "fire." Archaeologists used the biblical word to name sacred areas in many Phoenician/Punic sites where cremated remains of infants and small animals were often found. Molek might be the same as Malik. Indeed it has been suggested that the vowels *o* and *e* were deliberately substituted for those in Malik and were derived from the Hebrew word *bošēt*, "shame." Molek as Molech occurs as a god name eight times in the Hebrew Bible, for example, Leviticus 20:5, which forbids the Israelites from "going astray after Molech." Such texts make it clear that Molek was a Canaanite deity. Leviticus 18:21 and other passages ban a ritual described in the King James translation as passing a child "through the fire to Molech" (Holy Bible 1973). The Jewish Publication Society's *Tanakh* (1988) gives for the same passage: "Do not allow any of your offspring to be offered up to Molech …." Passages such as this gave rise to scholarly controversy about child sacrifice. Some scholars have argued that the biblical phrase "to go for Molech" meant "as a sacrifice," since the Canaanite/Phoenician word for sacrifice was *molk* or *mulk*. Thus they think that there was no such god as Molek. Interestingly, Philo of Byblos explained the practice of child sacrifice as the need to propitiate the deities at times of danger and did not attribute it to the worship of any particular deity. Rabbinical and classical writers borrowed from one another to depict the cult of Molek in horrific terms, and later authors followed suit. John Milton in *Paradise Lost* (I: 392) called him Molech and described him as "horrid king besmeared with blood/Of human sacrifice, and parents' tears…" (1975: 16–17). Gustave Flaubert's novel *Salambo* described him as "Moloch-the-Devourer," a fierce and demanding god to whom the Carthaginians sacrificed their own children (1962: 198–200). See Baāl-Hamōn; Tanit. (Müller, *DDDB*: 538–42; Heider, *DDDB*: 581–85; Schmidt 1994: 183–84; Gómez Bellard, *DCPP*: 461–63; Heider, *ABD* IV: 895–98; Lipiński, *DCPP*: 296–97; Gray, *IDB* 1991: III, 422–23; J. Day 1989; Heider 1985; Attridge and Oden 1981: 62, 63; Herm 1975: 117–20; Menen 1972: 62; Weinfeld 1972)

Molk-aštart (L) See Milkaštart

Moloch (L) See Molek

Mot(u), Mutu, Mut(h), Mawet (L) Canaanite/Phoenician god of sterility, destruction, and death and also of the netherworld. The word literally means "death." In texts from Ugarit, Mot(u) was son of the chief god El, who assigned him to rule as king over the netherworld. The entrance to Earth, his dirty, slimy realm, was beneath two mountains. One of his titles was "Beloved of El," an indication of the status and rights bestowed on him by El. He was also designated "Warrior."

The texts described him as always hungry, especially for human beings. He was a fierce and long-term enemy of Ba'lu/Had(d)ad, the storm god, who represented the fertility brought by the rains of the Autumn. In the first battle between Mot(u) and Ba'lu, Mot(u) forced the rain god to allow himself to be swallowed by Mot(u)'s huge and voracious gullet and so to enter the netherworld for a period of time. To rescue her half-brother, the violent warrior goddess 'Anat(u) ripped Mot(u) apart and scattered his pieces on the fields for the birds to eat. Like Ba'lu, Mot(u) later returned. In the second encounter, the two were evenly matched, so that the contest had to be stopped by the sun goddess Šapaš, who threatened Mot(u) with El's displeasure.

Though the Ugaritians feared Mot(u) and might have given him placatory sacrifices in popular spirituality, he seemed not to have been worshipped in official cult, for his name does not occur in offering lists, nor was his name included in the deity lists, though he was mentioned in what might be a ritual text. The Hebrew Bible often calls the sphere of death *mawet/mōt* and sometimes even personifies death itself. Certain passages in the Bible do appear to refer to a god or demon Death called Mōt (Isaiah 28:15, Jeremiah 9:20). Other biblical texts seem to imply that such a deity existed (e.g., Job 18:13–14). Like Ugaritic Mot(u), he was insatiable (Habakkuk 2:5), and he shepherded the arrogant to Sheol (the netherworld) (Psalm 49:15). However, the lover in the Song of Songs declared that "... love is as fierce as death, / Passion is as mighty as Sheol" (8: 6). According to Philo of Byblos, Mouth (Mot) was offspring of Kronos (Elos) and Rhea, his sister. He added that the Phoenicians considered him to be Death and equated him with Pluto. Mōt occurred in theophoric names from Emar and Ebla, as well as in one or two Hebrew names in the Bible. (Woolmer 2017: 131; Pardee 2002: 211–13, 281–82; Wyatt 2002: 115–31, 133–36, 140–43; Smith 2001: 34, 98–99; del Olmo Lete 1999: 51, 56, 57; Healey, *DDDB*: 598–603; Leick 1998: 119; Smith 1997: 138–52, 155–56, 160–63; Lipiński 1995: 97–98; Handy 1994: 78, 83, 105–6, 111–12; Schmidt 1994; Lewis, *ABD* IV: 922–24; Pope, *IDB* Suppl.: 607–8; Xella, *DCPP*: 300–1; Smith 1990: 53; Attridge and Oden 1981: 56, 57, 91 note 131; Clifford 1972: 79–86; Oldenberg, 1969: 19, 36–38)

Mu'ati (M) God who was absorbed into the cult of Nabû and identified with him. Occurs in the "Love Lyrics" of Abi-ešuḫ, a king of Babylon. He appears as spouse of Nanāya, as was Nabû, and a "Sacred Marriage" rite was celebrated between Mu'ati and Nanāya. (Beaulieu 2003: 186; Millard, *DDDB*: 609; Stol, *DDDB*: 613)

Mu'ati-u-ab-ba (M) One of the small lyres of the storm god Iškur/Adad.

Written PA(with gloss mu-ia-ti)-u_8-ab[!]-ba. (Litke 1998: 144)

Mubara (M) See Gešbara

Mud (M) Deity attested in a god list fragment of the Early Dynastic period from Abu Ṣalābīkh. Means "Creator." (Mander 1986: 129)

MUD-ḫuš (M) Deity identified with the moon god Nanna/Sîn in An : *Anum*. Written BE-ḫuš with gloss dím. The name might then seem to be have been understood as "The Important(=IDIM) Red One," red describing the moon's appearance when the earth comes between the sun and the moon, casting a red shadow on the moon, the red color being caused by the earth's atmosphere. However, the sign BE also has the readings múd and úš, *damu*, "blood," and one of these may well have been the original reading of the name, [d]múd/ûš-ḫuš, the "Blood-Red (Moon)," which is a common term for this atmospheric phenomenon even today throughout the world. A reading úš-ḫuš is also possible. (Richter 2004: 451; Litke 1998: 119)

Mud-keš (M) Deity identified with the mother goddess Bēlet-ilī. May mean "She who Causes the Blood to Coagulate" (cf. *damu kaṣir*, *CAD* K 260). (Litke 1998: 71)

Mudri (H) Deity associated with the storm god of Šapinuwa. (Giorgieri et al. 2013)

Mu-duga-sa (M) Vizier of Marduk. Identified with Nabû. Means "Called by a Good Name." The Emesal dialectal form is Muzebbasa. In a god list from Aššur written in both dialects juxtaposed on two lines: [d]Mu-du_7-sa_4!-a [d]Mu-zib-ba-sa_4!-a. (Litke 1998: 96; Schroeder 1920: no. 68)

Mugurra (M) Deity attested in an Old Babylonian god list. Written mu-gu-ùr-ra. (Weidner 1924/25)

Muḫaldim-zi-Unug (M) Attested in a Fara god list. Means "Trusty Cook of Uruk." (Mander 1986: 123)

Mu-ḫegala (M) Form of Nanna/Sîn in An : *Anum*. Means "Year/Name of Abundance." (Richter 2004: 451; Litke 1998: 118)

Muḫra (M) Sumerian netherworld demon, one of the Asakkū. In "A [Prince's] Vision of the netherworld," the demon had three feet, two bird claws in front, and one of an ox behind. In An : *Anum* equated to Lugal-geš-bura/suga, "King who Uproots Trees (or strips them bare)" and Lugal-geš-dù-a, "King who Plants Trees." This may indicate either the demon having both a benevolent and malevolent aspect or the evolution of the demon's nature. (George 2016: no. 59; Litke 1998: 208)

Mukīl-mê-balāṭi(m) (M) Servant of Marduk, perhaps a divine implement. Means "Keeper of the Water of Life." Mentioned in a first-millennium BCE ritual for the ninth month at the E-sagil temple of Marduk in Babylon. (Wiggermann 1991: 46)

Mukišanu (H) Vizier of Kumarbi. Occurs in the "Song of Ḫedammu" acting as Kumarbi's messenger to the sea god and in the "Song of Ullikummi." (Hoffner 1998: 41, 51–55, 57; van Gessel 1998: I, 313–14; Haas 1994: 151; Laroche 1946/47: 54)

Mu-kug (M) Name of Marduk. Written mú-kù. Explained in An : *Anum* as "Whose Incantation Is Pure." (Litke 1998: 91)

Mul-an-a-diri (M) Deity associated with Inana as Venus. May mean "Star that

Drifts about in the Sky," referring to the movement of Venus. (Litke 1998: 161)

Mul-iku (M) One of seven bull-lyres of An. Written Mul-$^{i\text{-}ku\text{-}u}$AŠ+GÁN. (Litke 1998: 29)

Mulil-du-u(?) (M) Sumerian deity identified in a lexical list of divine names as signifying the goddess Nin-maš. (Richter 2004: 159)

Mulla (M) Name of the sun god Utu. Written Múl-lá with glosses mu-ul-la and mul. May mean "Radiating One." (Litke 1998: 130)

Mullil (M) See Enlil

Mullitu(m), Mulissu(m) (M) The Assyrian name of Ninlil and also, much later, of Ištar. In Assyria, in the later period, she was the spouse of the god Aššur. Herodotus called her Mylitta and identified her as the Assyrian Aphrodite. (Foster 2005: 782–83; Black and Green 2003: 119, 140–41; Stol, *DDDB*: 606; George 1993: 31–32, 53–54; Herodotus 1983: 122 (Book I, 199); Tallqvist 1974: 377)

Mulughayu (L) One of the Kōṯarṯu, seven minor goddesses of fertility at Ugarit. (del Olmo Lete 1999: 57)

Mummu (M) Epithet of various deities, especially Enki/Ea. One of the seven defeated and dead ancestor gods of Enlil. The thirty-fourth name of Marduk in the *Enūma eliš*. Also in the same creation epic, Mummu might be a name of Ti'amat. In addition, Mummu was the vizier of Ti'amat and Apsû. Means "Skilled or Wise." (Lambert 2013: 218–21; Foster 2005: 440, 480; Tallqvist 1974: 378; Speiser, *ANET*: 61; Heidel 1967: 57; Krebernik, *RlA* VIII: 415–16)

Mumu (M) Deity explained in *Anu ša amēli* as "Moon god of the Helical Rising (*nanmurtu*)." Written mú-mú. (Litke 1998: 230)

Mumu-gal, Mumu-ḫuš, Mumu-sisa (M) Names of Marduk in An : *Anum*. Mú-mú may be a variant for mu_7-mu_7 "incantation," particularly since Marduk in earlier and later entries of this section bears names composed of the element tu_6 "incantation." (Litke 1998: 223)

Muntara(-Mutmuntara) (H) One of the primeval Old Syrian/Hurrian netherworld deities to whom the "Song of Kumarbi" is chanted. Paired with Mutmuntara often as Muntara-Mutmuntara. (Hoffner 1998: 41, 112; van Gessel 1998: I, 315; Popko 1995: 99; Haas 1994: 112, 471)

Mu-nun-DU (M) Deity attested in an Early Dynastic god list from Fara. (Mander 1986: 143)

Munus-sa-a (M) Written Munus-sa_{11}(GÙN)-a. See Nunus-sa-a

Munus-saga (M) One of the five daughters of Nin-šubur. Means "Beautiful Woman." (Litke 1998: 28)

Murgu-aški (M) One of the eight sons of Ga'u, the sheep goddess. The entry in An : *Anum* is written Murgu$^{mur\text{-}gu}$-zi.aš.ki, which might be understood as Murgu-$aški_x$(ZI)$^{aš\text{-}ki}$. Sumerian aški means *urbatu* "rushes." The name may mean "Whose Shoulders Are Rushes," which recalls iconography in which grain or plants are pictured sprouting from a figure's shoulders or body. (Litke 1998: 127; Krebernik *RlA* VIII: 433)

Mur-ša (M) Deity who in An : *Anu ša amēli* is explained as "Adad of Roaring." Written ^{d}mur-$ša_4$, "Roar." (Schwemer 2001: 70, 73–74; Litke 1998: 232)

Mur-ša-ni (M) One of six bull-lyres of the storm god Iškur/Adad. Written mur-$ša_4$-ni. Means "His Roar," presumably referring to the sound of the lyre. (Litke 1998: 144)

Murta'īmu(m) (M) Deity identified with Adad in a god list from Nineveh, there associated with the Kassites. Means "Thunderer." (Schwemer 2001: 79, 86)

Murtaṣnu(m) (M) Deity identified with Adad in a god list from Nineveh, connected there with the Kassites. Means "The Roarer." (Schwemer 2001: 79, 86)

Muru (M) Deity identified with the storm god Iškur/Adad. In An : *Anum* written IM with glosses mu-ur, mu-ru, mu-rim. In a Neo-Assyrian god list written niš(=20) with gloss mu-ú-ru-u. (Litke 1998: 139; King 1969: pl. 16)

Muš (M) See Niraḫ

Muš-a-igigal (M) Deity associated with the E-anna temple at Uruk in the Ur III period. After a mention of the gate of the *gipar* residence in Uruk, a year name of a king of Uruk, Irdanene in Old Babylonian times, commemorates the setting up of statues of this deity and of the god Našpartu(m). (Richter 2004: 282, 308–9; Sallaberger 1993: I, 221)

Mušdama (M) Deity of building appointed by Enki in the composition "Enki and the World Order." Described as the chief builder of Enki. Jacobsen called him "the divine architect" (1976: 85). A possible variant for Nin-mušda. In the lexical series Diri the logogram ^{d}DÍM with syllabic rendering mu-uš-da-am. (Civil 2004; *LAS*: 222; Cavigneaux and Krebernik, *RlA* IX: 339; Krebernik, *RlA* VIII: 453)

Muš-ḫuša (Sum.), **Mušḫuššu(m)** (Akk.) Mythical snake-like dragon. Means "Furious Snake." The animal symbol of Marduk and his son Nabû, appropriated from Tišpak, the tutelary deity of Eš-nunna. One of the monsters created by Ti'amat in the *Enūma eliš* to help her fight the young deities. Often functioned as a guarding entity. The creature is depicted on the great Ištar Gate of Babylon. (Foster 2005: 444; J. Westenholz 2004: 25–26; Black and Green 2003: 129, 177; Speiser, *ANET*: 62; Heidel 1967: 23–24; Wiggermann, *RlA* VIII: 455–62)

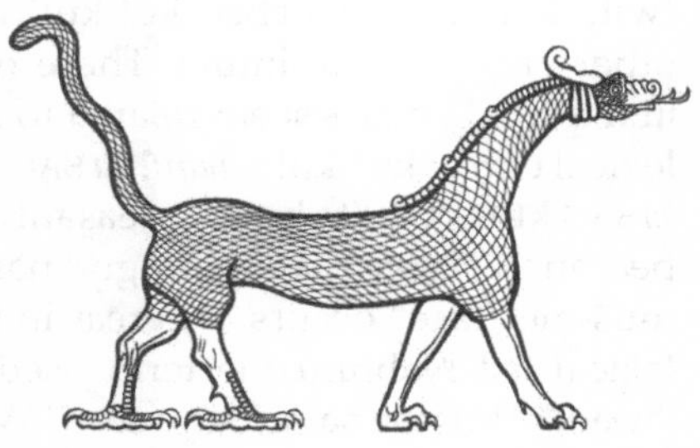

Representation of Muš-ḫuš, a relief from the Ištar Gate of Babylon. Neo-Babylonian. Enameled burnt brick. Iraq Museum. After Orthmann 1975: 327, pl. XXVI.

Mušlaḫ (M) Deity occurring in a personal name from Ur III Umma and Girsu. Written muš-$laḫ_6$(DU). If our interpretation is correct, then it means "snake-charmer." (Nisaba 23, 42: o i 9)

Muš-maḫ (Sum.), **Mušmaḫḫu(m)** (Akk.) A composite figure with leonine forelegs and the taloned hind-legs of a predator bird; its body was reptilian with scales, and its serpentine head had horns. Probably based on a type of horned snake. Means "Lofty Snake." One of the monsters created by Ti'amat in the *Enūma eliš* to help her fight the young deities. In images it often had seven heads on long, serpentine necks. It occurred in incantations. (Foster 2005: 444; Black and Green 2003: 168, 177; Speiser, *ANET*: 62; Heidel 1967: 23–24)

Mušme-ḫuš (M) Deity identified with Šala, wife of the storm god Iškur/Adad. Means "Furious Countenance." (Litke 1998: 143)

Mušme-kulkul (M) Deity identified with Nin-imma. In the Old Babylonian god list the name is written Mùš-me-kul-kul and in An : *Anum* as Múš-me-gul-gul with variant Nin-kul-kul. The next entry in An : *Anum* is Sag-gul-gul (with Emesal variant Šen-kul-kul), another name of Nin-imma. These two juxtaposed entries seem related to the lexical entry: kul-kul = *banû ša* SAG.DU *ša* SAG.KUL.KUL, "to have a pleasant appearance." Note that in our god name mùš-me "face" occurs, whereas in the lexical list Nabnītu the term used is "head." Thus the name may mean "Who Is Pleasant in Appearance." (Richter 2004: 93; Litke 1998: 56; Finkel: 1982)

Muššatur (Sum.), **Bašmu(m)** (Akk.) Horned viper appearing on boundary stones of Kassite times and seals from the Neo-Assyrian period, apparently to ward off evil. One of the monsters created by Ti'amat in the *Enūma eliš* to help her fight the young deities. (Foster 2005: 444; Black and Green 2003: 168, 177; Wiggermann 1992: 168; Speiser, *ANET*: 62; Heidel 1967: 23–24)

Muštabbabbu(m) (M) A name of Lamaštu(m). Means "Blazing One." Equated to the demon pirig-dib-bi-ḫuš, "The furious, angry lion/demon," in An : *Anum*, perhaps on the basis of dib= *kabābu* "to burn, scorch." Described as Maškim-gi$_6$-lú-ḫar-ra-an-na (see above). (Litke 1998: 210; Tallqvist 1974: 379; Lambert, *RlA* VII: 456; Wiggermann, *RlA* VIII: 498)

Muštēšir-ḫabli(m), Multēšir-ḫabli(m), Multēšir (M) Epithet later associated with Marduk as god of justice. He appears in tablets from the First Sealand Dynasty and is referred to simply as Muštēsir in a first-millennium BCE ritual for the ninth month at the E-sagil temple of Marduk in Babylon. He is Marduk's vanguard in the composition "Damkina's Bond." Means "Who Sets Right the Wronged Person." (Lambert 2013: 322; Dalley 2009: no. 67, no. 71, no. 82)

Muš(u)ni (H) Hurrian goddess, a form of Ḫebat. Means "Exalted." Occurs at Ugarit as a compound Ḫebat-Mušuni. (van Gessel 1998: I, 315–18; Haas 1994: 312–13, 387; Laroche 1977: 173; Laroche 1946/47: 54)

Mušunki (H) Deity associated with the storm god of Šapinuwa. (Giorgieri et al. 2013)

MUŠ-zagina (M) Deity associated in An : Anum with an outdoor shrine of Inana. If read MUŠ then "Shining Countenance"; if read SUḪ then "Shining Diadem." See Nin-MUŠ-zagina. (Litke 1998: 160)

Mutu (L) See Mot(u)

Mutmuntara (H) See Muntara

Mūtu(m) (Akk.), **Nam-uš** (Sum.) Personification of "Death." Messenger of the netherworld queen Allatu(m). (Litke 1998: 190)

Myrrha, **Smyrna** (L) Minor Phoenician goddess and mythical figure. Mother of Adonis. Daughter of Kinyras or Theias, who fathered Adonis. She committed incest without her father's being aware of her identity. When he discovered it, he tried to kill her. At her request, the deities turned her into a myrrh tree, as which she gave birth to Adonis. (Capomacchia, *DCPP*: 306)

— N —

Na (M) A writing (nà) for the god Nabû in an Old Babylonian god list. (Richter 2004: 141)

Na-an-na (M) Goddess associated with the mother goddess Nin-ḫursag. (Richter 2004: 364 note 1543; Sallaberger 1993: I, 102)

Nab (M) Goddess identified with Baba in a liturgy called "The First Child of An/ Heaven." Known from Babylon in the Seleucid period with the epithet "Fore-most daughter of An," as are several other goddesses in the liturgy. As an Elamite word for "god," she occurs in god lists. Nab appears in An : *Anum* in connection with the E-ninnu temple in Lagaš, in a circle of goddesses associated with Baba. Explained in *Anu ša amēli* as "Enlil of Heaven." (Litke, 1998: 174, 229; Cohen 1988: 235, 281, 282, 304, 357, 611; Cohen 1981: 139; Krebernik, *RlA* IX: 162)

Nabarbi (H, L, M) A Hittite goddess of north Syrian/Hurrian origin. Best known from Hittite sources. Paired with Šuwāliyat, the Hittite name of Tašmišu, brother of Teššub. The name Nabarbi is similar in structure to that of the great Hurrian god Kumarbi (*kum-ar-we*); in Nabarbi's case the elements are *naw–ar-we*, where *naw-* is the Hurrian root meaning "pasture." The name could therefore be an epithet "She of the Pasture" or, alternately, associated with the place name Nawar located somewhere in the Ḫabur basin of eastern Syria. If the latter, her name would mean "She of Nawar." The coupling of the pair Nabarbi-Šuwāliyat (for example, at the city of Mardaman in the eastern Ḫabur region) favors a place of origin of the goddess in eastern Syria. An image of Nabarbi is present on the frieze of goddesses depicted at Yazılıkaya. Nabarbi appears in oaths in the famous treaty of Šuppiluliumas I and Šattiwaza of Mittani and is named among the gods of Mittani, where she follows a list of the Aryan gods of the Mittani ruling class. From the Middle Hittite Empire on, she appears in Hittite and Hurrian offering lists as part of the pantheon of Ḫattušas and also, at Nineveh, in the offering lists for the goddesses Ḫebat and Ša(w)uš(k)a. She often is associated with the minor goddess Šuwāla in the circle of goddesses of Ištar/Ša(w)uš(k)a of Nineveh and with other similar goddesses. (Schwemer 2001: 410; Hoffner 1998: 113; van Gessel 1998: I, 326–28; Popko 1995: 115; Haas 1994: 309, 332 note 148; Haas, *RlA* IX: 1–2)

Nabītum (L) Goddess in a god list from Nippur. (Krebernik *RlA* IX: 5)

Nablu(m) (L, M) Babylonian deity attested in An : *Anum* as vizier of the Sumerian fire god Gibil/Girra. Nablu(m) means "Flame." His Akkadian name was Išātu(m), but he was also addressed as Girrû(m). A flame goddess ḏbb appears in the Ugaritic texts as "daughter of El." She was one of the deities defeated by the goddess ʻAnat(u). Also in the Ugaritic texts, *Išt* Fire, a very minor goddess, was called the "bitch [that is, dog] of El," and she too was one of the deities defeated by the goddess ʻAnat(u). Both Flame and Fire were possibly minor deities in the Hebrew Bible, servants of the Israelite god (Psalm 104:4). In the *Phoenician*

History, Philo of Byblos identified both Phlos "Flame" and Pyr "Fire" as "mortal" grandsons of the deities Colpia (Kolpia) and Baau. (Wyatt 2002: 80; Watson, *DDDB*: 331–32, 335–36; Litke 1998: 108; Smith 1997: 111; Attridge and Oden 1981: 40–43, 81 note 53)

Nabû (Akk.), **Nebo** (Biblical, M, L) Scribe of the gods and thus patron of scribes and of writing, a role assumed from the goddess Nisaba. He was also a god of wisdom. In some traditions he was an agricultural and irrigation god. As scribe, he recorded the decisions of the deities and held the divine tablets recording the fates. He also kept the accounts of the deities. Eventually Nabû joined Marduk as a supreme deity of Babylon. His name appears early in Akkadian as Nabium. Possibly originally a deity of West Semitic-speaking peoples, Nabû might have been introduced into Mesopotamia by the Amorites, perhaps in association with Marduk. In the first instance he was assigned duty as Marduk's vizier and then became the son of Marduk and Zarpanītu(m). Later he was understood to be the son of the god Aššur. Nabû's earliest spouse was Tašmētu(m), though sometimes Nanāya was so regarded. Later, Nisaba was identified as his wife. Gazbaba and Kanisura, goddesses of the temple at Borsippa, came to be seen as his daughters. His vizier was U-sura. He shared with Marduk as sacred animal the snake-dragon, the Mušḫuššu. In many images, he stood on the animal. He held a wedge-shaped writing implement, his usual symbol, and sometimes a writing tablet.

There are no extant mythic stories in which he appears. However, hymns to Nabû and prayers and incantations asking his help are extant from the early part of the first millennium BCE. Requests for his protection were recorded at the end of tablets from Nineveh and Aššur. He was referred to in the prologue to the law code of Ḫammu-rāpi as "the one who brings joy to Borsippa" (Meek, *ANET*: 165).

Amuletic plaque. Neo-Assyrian. Cast copper or bronze. Provenience unknown. After Black and Green 2003: 134.

Nabû's cult center, Borsippa, was near Babylon to the southwest, and he was its patron deity. The E-zida, "True House," was his temple there. From Borsippa, at the *akītu*, "Nabu, the valiant son," proceeded to Babylon, partly by boat. Nabû had temples and shrines in many places, including Kalaḫ (Nimrūd) with its companion temple for Tašmētu(m), Sippar, Nineveh, and Aššur. In east Babylon the temple of Nabû as god of accounting was called

"House of the Auditor of Heaven and Earth."

Several letters attest to a "Sacred Marriage" ritual involving Nabû and Tašmētu(m) at Borsippa during the Neo-Assyrian period. Mentioned in a ritual from Hellenistic (Seleucid) times, a marriage between the statues of Nabû and Nanāya was celebrated at Borsippa and Babylon. Nabû's worship was particularly strong in the Neo-Assyrian period and by the fourth century BCE reached Anatolia and Egypt.

Nabû was extremely important in the Neo-Babylonian period, as can be noted in the royal names Nabopolassar ("Nabû protect the heir"), Nebuchadnezzar ("Nabû protect the borders"), and Nabonidus ("Nabû be praised!"). Moreover, Nabû had a prominent place in the *akītu* festival at Babylon, during which Marduk granted the king the right to rule another year. Cohen suggests that there were actually two *akītu* celebrations conflated into one: an *akītu* of Marduk and an *akītu* of Nabû.

His name appears in the Hebrew Bible as both Nabû and Nebo (Isaiah 46:1), where he was depicted as a defeated deity. Also known from Levantine inscriptions. His cult was long lived. The Greeks identified him with Apollo. At the time of the early Roman Empire, the god was still being venerated at, among other places, Palmyra and Dura Europos in Syria. Astrally, Nabû represented the planet Mercury. (Cohen 2015: 304, 400, 408, 413, 422; Foster 2005: 621–26, 695–96, 829–30, 846, 849–51, 944–46; Black and Green 2003: 40, 133–34, 153, 157, 166, 185; Leick 1999: 65–66; Leick 1998: 123–24; Millard, *DDDB*: 607–10; Litke 1998: 96, 237; Comay 1993: 260; George 1993: 94 no. 397, 121 no. 734, 159 no. 1236–39; Dalglish, *ABD* IV: 1054–56; Gray, *IDB* 1991: III, 528; Tallqvist 1974: 380–84; Sachs, *ANET*: 331–34; Reiner, *ANET*: 541; Pomponio, *RlA* IX: 16–24; Seidl, *RlA* IX: 24–29)

Na-bur(r)a (M) See Nam-UŠUM

Nadi-lugal-dimmer-ankia (M) Name of Marduk in the *Enūma eliš*. Means "Advisor, King of the Gods of Heaven and Earth."

Nādin-mê-qāti (M) Servant in the E-sagil in Babylon; perhaps a divine implement. Means "The One who Serves Hand-Water." Mentioned in a first-millennium BCE ritual for the ninth month at the E-sagil temple of Marduk in Babylon. (Litke 1998: 99)

NAGAR (M) Logogram with gloss in An : *Anum* for the gods Alla, Illa, Ḫa'a'u. (Litke 1998: 216)

Nagar-namlu'ulu (M) Deity identified with Bēlet-ilī. Means "Carpenter of Humankind." (Litke 1998: 70)

Nagar-pa'e (M) Sumerian deity attested in the Early Dynastic period and in the environs of Ur III Umma specifically at the town of KiAN, near Umma. Means "The Carpenter Manifest," seemingly a craftsman god. (Bartash 2013: no. 8; Cohen 1996a: 31; Sallaberger 1993: I, 238, 256; Heimpel, *RlA* IX: 77)

Nagar-šaga (M) Deity identified with Bēlet-ilī. Perhaps means "Carpenter of the Womb (or Insides)," referring to her role as a mother goddess. Explained as "who makes young girls beautiful." (J. Peterson, *JCS* 72, 2020: 121; Litke 1998: 70, 80)

Nagbu (M) Deity identified with Enki in An : Anum. Means "Underground Spring." (Litke 1998: 87, 145)

Naḫḫu(n)te, Naḫundi (E, M) The sun god and god of justice associated with the part of Elam known as Awan. One of the seven brothers of the goddess Narundi. Name probably means "Creator of the Day" (Leick 1998: 124). Naḫḫu(n)te's name first appears in a variant spelling, Naḫiti, in a treaty between Narām-Sîn of Akkad and a king of Susa. A Middle Elamite inscription of Šilḫak-Inšušinak I from Susa refers to him as being "the god who protects." He appears in various bilingual Middle Elamite royal inscriptions and Neo-Elamite inscriptions in curse formulae. A brick inscription of Untaš-Napiriša refers to the introduction of a golden image of the god into the Siyankuk precinct at Choga Zanbil. His name occurs also in Elamite theophoric names. Naḫḫu(n)te was worshipped throughout the existence of Elam. Considered a moon god in Mesopotamia. (Vallat 1998: 335–37; Black and Green 2003: 74; Becking, *DDDB*: 499; Litke 1998: 213; König 1977: 204, 208, 227; Stolper, *RlA* IX: 82–84)

Na-izi (M) Sumerian deity whose name means "Incense" or "Censer." (Römer 1965: 180)

Nam-abzu (M) Deity attested in an Early Dynastic god list written with nám. May mean "Lord of the Abzu," and, if so, perhaps a name for Enki. (Mander 1986: 116)

Nam-anka (M) Sumerian deity attested in the name Lú-dNám-an-ka at Ur III Umma. (CDLI P235212: r 1)

Nam-bur-ra, Nam-BUR-gal, Nam-BUR-maḫ (M) Deity identified with Marduk in An : *Anum*. Written nám-búr- and na_4-búr-. nám—búr here might mean "to disseminate understanding, thus "The (Great/Lofty) Disseminator of Understanding." (Litke 1998: 222, 223)

Namenna (M) See Lugal-nam-en-na

Nam-gal (M) See Nam-maḫ

Namma (M) Sumerian goddess of the primeval, subterranean ocean. In the lexical series Diri the name has a syllabic rendering na-am-ma. In some traditions she was the mother of the sky god An, the earth goddess Ki, and a number of other deities. Enki/Ea, the god of freshwater and wisdom, was considered her son. In the myth of "Enki and Nin-maḫ," when the other deities began complaining about how hard they had to work, it was Namma who awakened Enki from his sleep to urge him to create more creatures to take on the work of the gods. However, he delegated the task to Namma, who then received the credit for creating human beings. There was a shrine to the goddess in Marduk's great temple at Babylon, and at least one other of her sanctuaries is known. (Lambert 2013: 427–36; Civil 2004; Black and Green 2003: 133; Stolz, *DDDB*: 737–38; Leick 1998: 42–43, 124; Litke 1998: 24; George 1993: 113 no. 641, 167 no. 1360; Tallqvist 1974: 387)

Nam-maḫ (M) Deity whose name means "Greatness." (1) Deity attested at Old Babylonian Nippur. (Renger 1967: 150) (2) Guardian spirit of the E-gal-maḫ temple in Isin. (Litke 1998: 184)

Nam-maḫ, Nam-gal (M) Names of Marduk in the god list An : *Anum*. The reading nám is based on the gloss nam. Name means "Lofty/Great Understanding." (Litke 1998: 223)

Nam-ma-ni (M) Deity allocated offerings at Ur III Umma. (MVAG 21, 22 FH 5: o ii 21)

Nam-me-sud (M) One text of An : *Anum* has Nin-tuk-sud, whose sense is unclear, and the other Nám-me-s[ud], "Lady of the far-reaching(?) *Me*s." Perhaps the variant Nin-tuk-su(d) may be a corrupted form based, in part, upon a scribal reading of nám as túg. (Richter 2004: 351; Litke 1998: 138)

NAM-NAM (M) Deity whose name is written nám-nám, which may mean "Lord of Lord(s)." Equated to Ninkilim and Ninurta. (Litke 1998: 171)

Nam-nam-ena (M) Deity in the circle of Lugal-Marada. May mean "Lord of *En*(-priest)-ship." (Litke 1998: 170)

Nam-nir (M) Deity attested in the Sumerian zà-mí hymns from Abu Ṣalābīkh. Written nám-nir. (Mander 1986: 124, 131)

Namnun (M) Deity in a theophoric name in a tablet of the Early Dynastic period from Nippur and in An : *Anum. Written* nám-nun. May mean "Noble Lord." (Litke 1998: 170; A. Westenholz 1975a: no. 8; Krebernik *RlA* IX: 140–41).

Namra-ṣīt (M) Akkadian equivalent of the moon god Dilim-babbar in An : *Anum*. Means "Who Shines Forth." (Black and Green 2003: 135; Litke 1998: 119; Tallqvist 1974: 387)

Namrat (M) Wife of Numušda, city god of Kazallu in northern Babylonia. Mother of Adgar-kidug, who became the wife of Amurru(m)/Mardu in the Sumerian tale "The Marriage of Martu." Her name means "She Is Shining Bright." (Stol, *RlA* IX: 141)

Namrazunna (H) Goddess who occurs in a hymn to Ištar. (Franz-Szabó *RlA* IX: 141–42)

Namšar(i)a, Napšara (H) One of the primeval Old Syrian/Hurrian netherworld deities to whom the "Song of Kumarbi" is chanted. Paired with Nara and often cited as Nara-Namšara. In the "Song of the God LAMMA," Ea calls Nara-Namšara his "brother," though the pattern with the primeval deities is for the pair to be male (Nara) and female (Namšara). Occurs before Minki in the list of primeval gods. Appealed to in curse and oath incantations. Also appears in treaties. (Hoffner 1998: 41–43, 47, 112; van Gessel 1998: I, 322–24, 329–30; Popko 1995: 99; Haas 1994: 112–15, 284, 471, 581; Laroche 1977: 178–79; Laroche 1946/47: 55, 126; Wilhelm, *RlA* IX: 168–69)

Namšub (M) Name of Marduk. Means "Incantation," as explained in An : *Anum*: *šá šipti* "of the incantation." In the *Enūma eliš* the name is playfully understood as *namru* "shining." (Litke 1998: 90)

Namtagga-burbur, Namtagga-burbur-gal, Namtagga-burbur-ḫuš (M) Divinized attributes of the god Di-ku$_5$ "The Judge." Means "He (Great/Furious One) who Frees One from Sin." (Litke 1998: 225)

Namtar (Sum.), **Namtaru** (Akk.) Deity whose name means "Fate" or "Destiny," the netherworld god of fate or destiny and the ultimate fate, death. Also a netherworld demon, bringer of illnesses and death. The distinction between them was not entirely maintained. Both were associated with plagues and pestilence. In one tradition Namtar's parents were Enlil and Ninlil. In another he was the son of Ereškigal and Enlil. In An : *Anum*, his mother was Martu-LAL-anki. His spouse was Ḫušbišag (or Namtartu), and his daughter Gan-dim(me)-kug. Namtar was minister and messenger of Ereškigal, queen of the netherworld. In the Sumerian "Death of

Gilgameš," Gilgameš, just before his death, makes offerings to Namtar, as does King Ur-Namma, in "The Death of Ur-Namma." It was Namtar who, in the Akkadian "Descent of Ištar to the netherworld," carried out the orders of Ereškigal to afflict Ištar with a myriad of physical miseries, and it was he who led her back to earth. Namtara played a prominent role as messenger of Ereškigal in the Akkadian myth "Nergal and Ereškigal," and he appears as vizier of the netherworld in "A [Prince's] Vision of the Netherworld." (Foster 2005: 506–24; *LAS*: 59; Richter 2004: 491; Black and Green 2003: 134, 180; Katz 2003: 390; Frayne 2001: 153; Leick 1999: 172–73; Lewis, *DDDB*: 333; Litke 1998: 188, 189; Tallqvist 1974: 387–88; Grayson, *ANET*: 507–12; Speiser, *ANET*: 103–4, 108, 109; Ebeling, *RlA* II: 109; Klein, *RlA* IX: 142–45)

Namtartu(m) See Ḫušbišag

Namtar-zu, Namtar-zu-gal, Namtar-zu-maḫ (M) Divinized attributes of the god Di-ku$_5$ "The Judge" in An : *Anum*. Means "The Great/Lofty One who Knows the Fates." (Litke 1998: 226)

Namtila (M) Deity identified with Marduk. Means, "Life." (Litke 1998: 89)

Namudmud (M) Deity identified with Enki/Ea in a Neo-Assyrian god list. Written Na-mu-ud-mu-ud and seems to be a syllabic form related to Enki as Nu-dím-mud. (King 1969: pl. 33)

Namulli (H) Deified bed. (Wilhelm, *RlA* IX: 145)

Nam-urta (M) Deity attested in an Early Dynastic god list. Written nám-urta. See Ninurta. (Mander 1986: 143)

Nam-uš (M) See Mūtu(m)

Namzu, Nigzu (M) Means "Wisdom." In An : *Anum* Namzu identified with Enlil. Nigzu occurs in an Ur III personal name from Nippur, likely a name for Enlil. (Litke 1998: 39; NATN 707: o i 6)

Nanaya, Nanâ (H, M) Sumerian goddess of erotic love and sexual attractiveness and so associated with Inana/Ištar. Also associated with the planet Venus. Usually thought of as the daughter of An/Anu(m), but sometimes of Nanna/Sîn. Sister of Utu/Šamaš and a spouse of Nabû. Her cult center was Uruk, where she was revered along with her daughters Kanisura (Uṣur-amāssa) and Gazbaba. In later times, the city of Kiš became, at least temporarily, another of her cult centers. She was worshipped at Sippar, Ur, Puzriš-Dagān, Borsippa, Umma, Babylon, and Aššur. Nanāya's shrine in the great temple at Uruk was called "House of the Luxuriance of Heaven." At the obscure town of Raqnana she was known as "cleanser of sins, provider of light" (George 1993: 74 no. 139).

Nanay(a), a detail of from a boundary marker from Susa. Kassite. Dark limestone. Louvre Museum SB 23. After Seidl 1989: pl. 11, figure a

At Babylon in Hellenistic times, a "Sacred Marriage" ritual took place between Nanāya and Nabû. Nanāya was mentioned in a few Hittite texts. In later cultic texts she was treated as just another aspect of Inana/Ištar. The Persians equated Nanāya to Anahita. To the Greeks she was Artemis. (Steinkeller 2013b; Streck and Wasserman 2012; Drewnowska-Rymarz 2008: 153–58; Foster 2005: 89–92, 160–64; Black and Green 2003: 134; Stol, *DDDB*: 612–13; Leick 1998: 124–25; van Gessel 1998: I, 324–25; J. Westenholz 1997; Cohen 1993: 137, 311, 452; George 1993: 106 no. 540, 126 no. 794, 143 no. 1015 no. 1018, 157 no. 1195–96; Tallqvist 1974: 385–86; Stol, *RlA* IX: 146–51)

Nani (M) Deity mentioned in a Mari document as the recipient of commodities on the day of the Ḫulili festival. Perhaps to be identified with Nanāya. (Durand 2008: 249–50)

Nanibgal (M) Wife of En-nu-gi, the god of canals and dikes. Nanibgal was often identified with Nisaba, or the name was an epithet of Nisaba, though in later tradition they were usually understood as separate deities. Nanibgal, identified with Nisaba, had a temple at Ereš near Umma, but no evidence exists that Nanibgal had a cult of her own. In the lexical series Diri the name is written [d]AN.ŠE.NAGA and syllabically rendered na-ni-ib-gal. (Civil 2004; Black and Green 2003: 77, 143; George 1993: 159 no. 1221; McEwan, *RlA* IX: 151)

Nanna (Sum.), **Su'en**, **Sîn** (Akk.) The great god of the moon and tutelary deity of the city of Ur. Associated with the fertility of animals, especially bovines. In the astronomical compendium "Enūma Anu Enlil," Nanna measured time, set the seasons, and regulated the tides. Usually called Nanna/Sîn or Nanna/Su'en. First-born son of Enlil and Ninlil, though another tradition names An/Anu(m) as his father. His brothers were Nergal (Meslamta-e), Nin-azu, and En-bilulu. His wife was Nin-gal "Great Lady" or Nin-Urima "Lady of Ur." Nanna's best-known children were Utu/Šamaš, the sun god, and Inana/Ištar, the goddess of love and war, who is identified with the planet Venus. Other offspring include Nin-Gublaga and the goddesses Amara-azu and Amara-ḫe'ea. His vizier was Alammuš. Among his epithets were Dilim-babbar "White or Shining Ladle," Ma-gur "Boat," Inbu "The Fruit," Ḫedu-ana "Ornament of Heaven," and Amar-banda-Enlila "Younger (or Wild) Calf of Enlil."

His symbol was a crescent moon with its horns pointing up, and his sacred beast was the bull. The moon god had an important presence in mythic and hymnic literature. In "Enlil and Ninlil," he was conceived when Enlil raped Ninlil, for which Enlil was banished to the netherworld. In hymns the moon god was lauded as the herder of heaven, because the stars were envisioned as sheep and the moon their shepherd.

Curse formulas often invoked Nanna/Sîn, along with Utu/Šamaš, and he occurred in divination and healing texts. In the composition "Nanna-Su'en's Journey to Nippur," the moon god travelled by boat to bring lavish gifts to his father Enlil in the latter's sacred city and to request that Enlil grant prosperity to Ur.

Nanna's cult center was Ur, where he was venerated from Early Dynastic times. Nanna/Sîn's great temple at Ur was named E-kiš-nugal, "Alabaster

House," also the name of his temple at Babylon. The ziqqurat of the temple precinct at Ur bore the title "Foundation Platform Clad in Terror." Nanna was protector god of the Ur III Dynasty, whose capital was Ur. In the tenth month at Ur the major festival of the city, called the "Great Festival," was held in honor of Nanna. In the first and seventh months, at the equinoxes, Ur celebrated two *akītu* festivals. The *akītu* of the spring equinox marked the beginning of the ascendancy of the sun over the moon in the sky and the *akītu* of the fall equinox the beginning of the ascendancy of the moon over the sun, and thus, for the city of the moon god, the more important of the two *akītus*.

Relief from ancient Til Barsip depicting Nanna/Sîn. Carved stone. Height ca. 55 cm. In two pieces, one in the Aleppo Museum, the other in the Louvre. After Colbow 1997: 31, fig. 16.

The installation of the *entu* or high priestess of Nanna/Sîn at Ur was a ritual marked throughout the land, and was so significant that it was recorded in year names. Seats and shrines to Nanna/Sîn's various aspects were numerous in the temple at Ur, and he had shrines and temples throughout the land, including Larsa, Ga'eš near Ur, Urum near Kiš, Borsippa, Uruk, Aššur, and Akšak in the Tigris-Diyala region. In the Neo-Babylonian period, the temple of the moon god at Harrān in northern Syria became an important cult center and remained so well into the Christian era. Since the Mesopotamians followed a lunar calendar, Nanna/Sîn took theological precedence over the sun, Utu/Šamaš. (Cohen 2015: 85, 88, 214, 248, 409; Foster 2005: 758–62, 863–64; *LAS*: 104, 126–54; Black and Green 2003: 22, 31, 47, 135; Leick 1999: 141; Schmidt, *DDDB*: 585–93; Leick 1998: 125–27; Litke 1998: 116–19, 230; Cohen 1996b: 7–13; George 1993: 64 no. 29, 75 no. 160, 80 no. 214, 99 no. 472, 108 no. 570, 114 no. 653–55, 169 no. 1413; Hall 1985; Tallqvist 1974: 380; Jacobsen 1970: 25, 26; Sjöberg 1960; Krebernik, *RlA* VIII: 360–69)

Nanna-adaḫ (M) Deity attested at Old Babylonian Ur. Means "Nanna Is the Helper." (Renger 1967: 158)

Nanna-balag-anki (M) Deity listed in An : *Anum* as the first seal-keeper of Nanna/Sîn, the moon god. Cohen suggests that something is wrong with this entry in An : *Anum*. The name "Nanna Is the Lyre of Heaven and Earth" seems perfect for one of the lyres of Nanna as in the previous eight entries, but seems to make no sense as a seal-keeper of Nanna as he is identified in An : *Anum*. One of two errors may have occurred. One possibility is that originally there were nine, not eight harps, and for some reason the scribe mislabelled the last lyre as a seal-keeper. However, it is more likely that two entries have been inverted through transmission. The eighth lyre is Nanna-balag-anki and the seal-keeper should be Anna-ḫiliba, now listed as the eighth lyre. (Litke 1998: 123; Krebernik, *RlA* IX: 152)

Nanna-balag-maḫ (M) One of eight bull-lyres of the moon god Nanna/Sîn. Name means "Nanna, Great Harp." Variant is Nanna-búlug-maḫ. (Litke 1998: 123; Krebernik, *RlA* IX: 152)

Nanna-Karzida (M) Form of Nanna at the port city near Ur known as Kar-zi-da. (Sallaberger 1993: I, 170–72)

Nanna-palil (M) Deity attested at Old Babylonian Ur. Means "Nanna Is the Leader/Foremost." (Richter 2004: 432)

Nanni (H) Deity associated with the storm god of Šapinuwa. (Giorgieri et al. 2013)

Nanšak (M) Child of Tišpak. (Litke 1998: 194)

Nanše, Nazi (M) Sumerian goddess associated with fish and birds. A skilled dream interpreter, diviner, and giver of oracles. A goddess who helped those in trouble and the disadvantaged, such as orphans and widows. In addition, associated with boundaries and boundary-stones. Nanše was a highly ranked member of the pantheon of Lagaš. She was tutelary deity of the city of Nimen southeast of Lagaš. Gudea travelled to Nimen to ask Nanše to interpret his dream.

In one tradition, Enki was her father and Nin-ḫursag her mother. She was regarded as sister of Nin-Girsu and, in another tradition, Nisaba. Her spouse was Nin-dara, whose cult city, Ki-eša, was not far from Lagaš. Ninmarki was her child and Ḫendur-saga was her vizier.

In "Enki and the World Order," Enki placed Nanše in charge of the sea, and in "Enki and Nin-ḫursag," the birth goddess bore Nazi (Nanše) to heal one of Enki's hurts. In "Enki and Nin-ḫursag" Nin-ḫursag declares that Na-zi is to marry Nin-dara.

Nanše's cult center was the temple Sirara at Nimen. The Festivals of Barley and of Malt Consumption, both in honor of Nanše, took place mainly at Nimen and were major pilgrimage celebrations of the Lagaš area. Her sanctuary at Lagaš was called "House Chosen in the Heart." It is possible that a "Sacred Marriage" ritual was held for Nanše and Nin-dara at Lagaš. The goddess also had shrines at Nippur, Umma, Kisala near Umma, Gu-aba near Lagaš, Girsu, and Sulum near Lagaš and a "seat" in the great temple in Babylon. (*LAS*: 221–22, 224; Cohen 2015: 34; Black and Green 2003: 123, 135; Leick 1999: 62; Leick 1998: 127; Litke 1998: 124, 125; George 1993: 36, 82 no. 250, 83 no. 266, 142 no. 992; Tallqvist 1974: 388; Kramer, *ANET*: 41; Heimpel, *RlA* IX: 152–60; Braun-Holzinger, *RlA* IX: 160–62)

Nanše-šeše-gara (M) Early Dynastic form of Nanše. (Sallaberger 1993: I 137)

Nap, Napir, Nappi(ya), Napip(e), Nappipira (E) Elamite word for god, a com-ponent of a number of deity names. (König 1977: 205, 227)

Na'para (M) Deity mentioned in an Assyrian ritual text. (Krebernik, *RlA* IX 162–63)

Napešdi (M) Deity identified with Dingir-maḫ/Bēlet-ilī in a section of An : *Anum* listing deities from an unidentified land. Written Na-peš$_4$-di. Litke suggests the possibility that this may correspond to the goddess Naru(n)di, a few entries earlier. The orthography with peš$_4$ "womb" to express the sound peš in this foreign(?) name of a mother goddess would seem intentional. Nor can we totally dismiss the possibility that this foreign(?) name has been somewhat altered to sound like Akkadian *napištu* "life," appropriate for a mother goddess. (Litke 1998: 214)

Napi-riša, Naprušu, Napir (E, M) Deity attested from Old Elamite to Achaemenid times, possibly a moon god. Originally from Anšan, a part of Elam, he is explained as being the "Ea of Elam." As Napir he appears in an inscription of a local ruler named Ḫanni found at Shikāfteh-i-Salman/Kul-e Faran not far from Izeh/Malamir in the Bakhtiari Mountains. Protector of gods and kings. Bears the epithet "Who Weaves (Fate)." His consort was Kiririša. During the second millennium BCE, Napi-riša and Kiri-riša, with Susa's god In-šušinak, were at the head of Elam's pantheon. The god Naprušu is mentioned, along with two other Elamite deities, in "A [Prince's] Vision of the netherworld." Napi-riša means "Great God." (Nap(i) is Elamite for "god"). The name might have been originally used to refer to the god Ḫumban, since in early periods it may have been taboo to utter or inscribe Ḫumban's name. It is clear, however, that very soon the two deities were seen as distinct and Ḫumban was associated with the realm of light, whereas Napi-riša was linked to the realm of the earth. A human-headed snake was the symbol of Napi-riša (Vallat 1998: 338). In a Mesopotamian incantation series, Napi-riša appears after the gods Yabru and Ḫumban. In Old Elamite times the name Napi-riša can be identified in otherwise unintelligible abracadabra incantations from Mesopotamia. The divine name also appears as a theophoric element in personal names, notably in the royal name Untaš-Napiriša. The well-preserved ziqqurat at Choga Zanbil, not far from Susa in Elam, was dedicated to this god. Offerings to Napi-riša are referred to in the Persepolis documents. In a Neo-Assyrian god list written na-ap-riš and na-ap-ri-si. Equated in Akkadian texts with Ea. (Tavernier 2013: 482; Vallat 1998: 337–40; Foster 2005: 838; Black and Green 2003: 75; van Koppen and van der Toorn, *DDDB*: 433; Koch 1987: 258; König 1977: 227; Tallqvist 1974: 388; Reiner 1970: 17; Speiser, *ANET*: 110; King 1969: pl. 7; Koch, *RlA* IX: 163–64)

Nappi (E) Elamite god occurring in a treaty between Narām-Sîn of Akkad and a king of Susa. (König 1977: 29, 227)

Nap-ratep (E) Epithet of a group of eight gods for whom shrines were built at Choga Zanbil by Untaš-Napiriša. Napratep means "Nourishing Gods." (Hinz and Koch 1987: 973; König 1977: 41 note 6, 44, 205, 227)

Naprušu (M) See Napi-riša

Napu (E) Elamite rendering of the Babylonian god Nabû. (König 1977: 60 note 16, 205, 227)

Nara (H) See Namšar(i)a

Nara-Namšara, Nara-Napšara (H) See Namšar(i)a

Narida/e (E) See Narundi

Nār-idaggil, Nār-itakkil (M) Vizier of the river god. Written in An : *Anum* as Ne-e-er-e-tag-mil(var. mi-il). If understood as *idaggil*, it means "He Attends to the River(s) (or 'the River-God)" (though we expect idaggal; however note the form *id-da-gi-il* [*CAD* D: 22e]). Another, possibility is *itakkil* "He Trusts (the River(-God))." (Litke 1998: 190)

Narkabtu(m) (M) Deified "chariot" wor-shipped at Neo-Babylonian Uruk. (Beau-lieu 2003: 295)

Narsina (E) See Niarzina

Nāru(m) (M) Babylonian river god. Means "River." (Durand 2008: 292; Tallqvist 1974: 388, 379; Roberts, 1972: 46)

Narua (M) Attendant of the E-ninnu. Means "Stele." The temple of Narua was in Guabba-gula, where a festival involving a wail was observed around the seventh day of the seventh month. (Cohen 2015: 428; Litke 1998: 177)

Naru(n)di, Narida/e (E, M) A victory goddess of Elam. Sister of the Elamite goddesses Kiri-riša, Siyašum, and Niarzina. Also sister of the Sebettu(m), the Seven, a group of sometimes beneficent and other times malevolent deities. Her seven brothers included Naḫḫunte and Igišti. Was sometimes identified with Inana/Ištar because of her connections to lions and her martial prowess. Also called Nin-ḫursag of Susa. Appeared as Narida in a treaty between Narām-Sîn of Akkad and a king of Susa. Worshipped in Susa by the Awan dynast Puzur(Kutik)-Inšušinak, after he conquered the city. He also erected a statue to her, asked for her help in battle, and invoked her in curses. Ešpum, viceroy of Awan and governor of Susa for Akkadian king Maništusu, dedicated a statue to the goddess inscribed with wishes for the well-being of Maništusu. Attested in personal names, especially female ones. After the second millennium, she does not occur in Elamite sources, but reappears later in Mesopotamian materials. The goddess was mentioned in a late ritual for the *akītu* festival from Uruk. Performers and cult celebrants associated with Ištar donned masks of Naruda and paraded around the assembled statues of the deities. A limestone statue of the goddess is now in the Louvre. (Vallat 1998: 336–37; Garrison 2007; Black and Green 2003: 75, 162; Litke 1998: 213; Cohen 1993: 437; Hinz and Koch 1987: 993; König 1977: 205, 227; Tallqvist 1974: 388; Hinz 1972: 48–49; Reiner 1970: 18)

Narzina (E) See Niarzina

Nassi (M) Deity attested in a personal name in the Mari texts.

Našpartu(m) (M) Deity associated with the E-anna temple at Old Babylonian Uruk. A representation of the deity was set up on a gate in the temple as recorded in a year name of the king of Uruk Irdanene. Deity name means "(Divine) Embassy." (Richter 2004: 309)

Našuḫ (L, M) See Nuska

Natḫi (H) Deified bed. (Wilhelm, *RlA* IX: 145)

Na-ušum, Na-ušum-gal, Na-ušum-maḫ (M) See Nam-ušum

Nawatiyala (H) Deity with cult at Zarwiša. (Wilhelm, *RlA* IX: 190)

Na-zi (M) Deity in a theophoric name in a text from the Old Assyrian period at Kültepe. Perhaps as writing for Nanše. (Matouš 1962: no. 120)

Nazit (E) Elamite day and light god. Attested in an inscription of Untaš-Napiriša from Choga Zanbil. (König 1977: 48 note 11, 205, 227)

Na-zukum-zukum (M) Deity identified with Enki. The following entry in An : *Anum* is MIN-$^{gi-bi-[ir]}$ÉN and the next is

En-é-nu-ru, suggesting that the name is somehow related to Enki's role in incantations and magic. (Litke 1998: 85)

Neanna (M) Name for Ištar in "The Hymn to the Queen of Nippur." Written Nè-an-na. Lambert suggests it is a play on the name Inana, the sign pirig(NÈ), and Ištar's leonine aspect. (Lambert 1992: 212)

Nēberu(m) (M) Name of Marduk. The forty-ninth name of the god proclaimed at the end of the *Enūma eliš*. Means "Ferry Boat." Astrally, the planet Jupiter, the star of Marduk. (Foster 2005: 483; Tallqvist 1974: 396; Speiser, *ANET*: 72; Heidel 1967: 59; Cavigneaux and Krebernik, *RlA* IX: 191–92)

Nebo (L) See Nabû

NE.DAG (M) See BIL.DAG

Nemur (M) See PIRIG.BANDA

Nephilim (L) Genesis 6:4, a passage that reflects Canaanite or early Israelite mythology, relates that once upon a time divine beings cohabited with women. The Bible then states that, at that time, there were Nephilim, "the heroes of old, warriors of renown." In Numbers 13:33 the Nephilim are referenced in an observation on the Anakites, a tribe of Canaanites, as seen by the Israelite spies: "the Anakites come from the Nephilim." Nephilim in this passage is presumably metaphorical, intended to describe the fearsomeness of the Anakites.

Nephilim means "Fallen Ones" and refers to ancient, slain warrior-heroes who, as reward for their valor, were granted life beyond death in some mythical world, a concept common to many peoples. In Norse mythology, for example, as soon as the great warriors fall on the battlefield, they are scooped up on horseback by the Valkyrie and taken to guard the gods' residence, Valhalla.

Immediately thereafter in Genesis occurs the Flood Story, and later Jewish writings played upon the juxtaposition of the two stories to conclude that these Nephilim were the cause of the evil that led to the Flood, though the biblical text makes no such explicit connection. Christian texts understood the Nephilim or "The Fallen" as angels who had rebelled against God (II Peter 2: 4; Jude 6). (Coxon, *DDDB* 9: 618–20; Mussies, *DDDB*: 343–45; Hess, *ABD* IV: 1072–73; Beck, *IDB* 1991: III, 536)

Ne-ra (M) Son of Enki. Written Ne[ni]-ra. ne-ra may mean "brazier," but whether that is intended here cannot be determined. (Litke 1998: 100; Cohen 1993: 127)

Nerariski (H) Deity associated with the storm god of Šapinuwa. (Giorgieri et al. 2013)

Nēr-ē-tagmil (M) In the composition "Damkina's Bond," he is Marduk's rearguard. May mean "Army, Show No Mercy!" (Lambert 2013: 323)

Nergal (M) God of the netherworld and inflictor of death. Responsible for disease and plague, as well as forest fires. Also a warrior deity, whose function, in addition to doing battle in support of war-faring kings, was to guarantee peace. Closely identified with Akkadian Erra, though originally the latter was a separate deity. Nergal was known in god lists and lexical texts as early as the Early Dynastic period. Son of Enlil and Ninlil or of Bēlet-ilī. Sometimes considered son of An/Anu(m). Second husband of Ereškigal. The goddesses Mami/Mamītu(m), Laz, and Nin-šubur are listed among his wives. His son was Šubula and his daughter Dadmuštu(m). His vizier was Uqur, "Destroy," originally the name of the god's sword; later Ḫendur-saga replaced Uqur. In Nergal's retinue was a group of "Day-demons" whose task was to carry out Nergal's commands. His train also included many disease-demons, who caused illnesses such as epilepsy, in addition to spreading plague and pestilence. The Sebettu(m), the "Seven," were found in his court.

One of his many titles was Meslamta-e "Who Comes Forth from the Meslam Temple." Another reflected his role as guarantor of peace: Lugal-silima "King of Peace." Other names included Lugal-Erra, the name of one of the Divine Twins later identified with Nergal, and Gu-anun-gi. He was further likened to a wild ox and a savage lion. In imagery Nergal often appears as a vigorous, young warrior dressed in a long open garment. Often he had one raised leg striding forward to rest on a stool or a conquered soldier. He normally carried a three-headed mace and a double or single axe or a scimitar, or a scepter with lion heads.

Usually in myth and literature, Nergal played a prominent role. It was Nergal as Erra-kal who, when the deities were starting the Great Flood in the "Epic of Gilgameš" version, "tore out the mooring posts (of the world)" (Foster 2001: 87). In the same composition he was called "the plague god" (Foster 2001: 136). The epilogue to the law code of Ḫammu-rāpi appeals to him as a destructive warrior, to smash like a terracotta figurine any desecrator of the code's stele. Nergal was the subject of numerous hymns, prayers, and incantations. In magical texts Nergal protected the house, specifically the bedroom, from evil intruders. Images of him were prominently displayed for this purpose.

Some hymns portray him as an astral deity who took up residence in the netherworld against his will. His becoming king of the netherworld is related in "Nergal and Ereškigal." According to one version, Nergal insults Ereškigal, and so she asks for him to be sent to her so that she can have him killed. On his coming face to face with the goddess, Nergal drags Ereškigal from her throne by her hair, and, when he threatens to cut off her head, she proposes marriage to him. In another version, on Enki/Ea's advice, Nergal behaves contritely with the result that Ereškigal takes him to her bed. After he finally escapes the netherworld, Ereškigal demands him back as her husband.

Nergal was widely venerated in Mesopotamia and had many temples, often called Meslam. His foremost cult center was the Meslam temple at the city of Kutha near Kiš. The temple's name means "Warrior of the netherworld," and a "by-name" of the Kutha cult center was "Fearsome House of the Netherworld" (George 1992: 102). Among his other centers were Api'ak, whence his title Lugal-Api'ak "King of Api'ak"; Marad where his title was Lugal-Marada "King of Marad"; Mê-Turnat (on the Diyala River) with its sanctuary Sirara where he was Lugal-Mê-Turnat "King of Mê-Turnat"; and Maškan-sāpir, where he was the tutelary deity and also had a Meslam temple. Numerous clay plaques showing Nergal in his chariot were found on the surface of Maškan-šapir, indicating that the city was also a Nergal cult center. Appropriately, Nergal had a "seat" in a slaughterhouse at Aššur. He also had at least one in the great temple at Babylon. He was worshipped at, among other places, Larsa, Dūrum, Mari, and Emar. A text from Emar calls him "The-Horned-Lord" and also "Lord-of-the-Marketplace." In addition, he probably had temples at Ur, Isin, and Uruk. In the early second millennium BCE, Nergal was ritually bathed at Larsa, and at Mari in the same period there was a festival for the chariot of Nergal, at which sacrifices were offered. His name and his cult site Kutha are mentioned in the Hebrew Bible in connection with the settlement of people of Kutha in Samaria (2 Kings 17:30). He was equated to Rešep(h) at Ebla. At Ugarit, he was identified with Rešep(h) and later equated to Greek Heracles. Astrally, Nergal represented the planet Mars. (Cohen 2015: 224; Durand 2008: 307; Durand 2005b: no. 62; Foster 2005: 506–24, 706–9; Richter 2004: 78–80, 198–207, 318–20, 392–95; Katz 2003: 404–20; Black and Green 2003: 135–36; Livingstone, *DDDB*: 621–22; Leick 1999: 65–66; Leick 1998: 127–28; Litke 1998: 199–201, 234; George 1993: 90 no. 353, 127 no. 803, 132 no. 876, 144 no. 1019–20, 115 no. 663, 125 no. 782, 167 no. 1364; Reiner 1970: 17; Grayson, *ANET*: 507–12; Meek, *ANET*: 180; Speiser, *ANET*: 103–4; Wiggermann, *RlA* IX: 215–26)

Nergal-Akūṣu(m) (M) Form of Nergal of the city of Akuṣu(m), located not far from Kiš. The name appears in an Old Babylonian god list from Isin. (Richter 2004: 200)

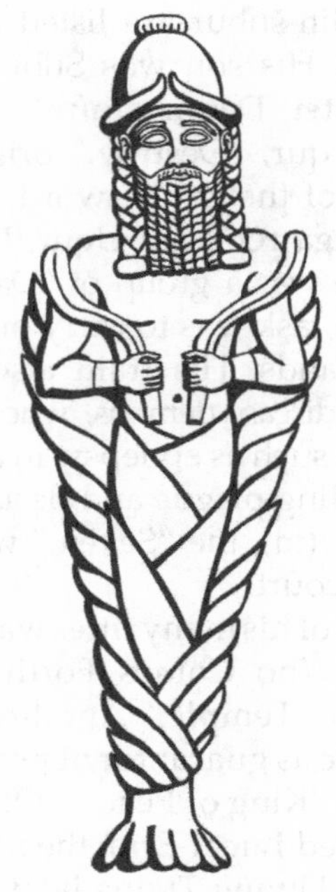

Figurine of Nergal. Old Babylonian. Baked clay. Height 13.6 cm. Louvre Museum. After Black and Green 2003: 136.

Nergal-Aratta (M) Sumerian form of Nergal attested in the environs of Ur III Umma. Means "Nergal of Aratta" or "Superb Nergal." (Cohen 1996a: 31)

Nergal-Azarum-dage (M) Form of the god Nergal at the town of Azarum-dage, near Umma. Attested at Ur III Umma. (Cohen 1996a: 31)

Nergal-Garšana (M) Form of Nergal in the Ur III period at the ancient city of Garšana. (Owen 2009: 711–12; Cohen 1996a: 32)

Nergal-gula (M) Form of Nergal associated with the town of Garšana. (Cohen 1996a: 32)

Nergal-ḪARdaḫi (M) Form of Nergal at the town of ḪAR-daḫi in the vicinity of Umma. (Cohen 1996a: 32)

Nergal-i-Ebla (M) Sumerian deity attested in the environs of Ur III Umma. Means "Nergal of the Ebla Canal." There is clearly no connection here with the Ebla in Syria. (Cohen 1996a: 32)

Nergal-Kiritab (M) Nergal of the city of Kiritab, located not far west of ancient Sippar. He appears in an Old Babylonian god list from Isin. (Richter 2004: 200)

Nergal-ša-abni (M) God of Emar for whom an individual asked a grant from the city to build a shrine. He also requested that he and his progeny serve as priests in perpetuity. Means "Nergal of the Stone(s)." (Fleming 2000: 24)

Nergal-ša-maḫīri(m) (M) Form of Nergal at Emar, where he had a major temple. An individual asked permission to serve as his priest in perpetuity, because he paid a ransom for the king's daughter. Means "Nergal of Commerce." (Fleming 2000: 24)

Nergal-ša-Maškan (M) Form of Nergal at the Ur III town of Maškan in the vicinity of Umma. (Cohen 1996a: 32)

Nergal-Šunamugi (M) Form of Nergal at the Ur III town of Šunamugi in the vicinity of Umma. (Cohen 1996a: 32)

Nergal-Tintir (M) Form of Nergal at the Ur III town of Tintir in the vicinity of Umma. Tintir here is not a reference to a section of Babylon as in Babylonian topographical texts. (Cohen 1996a: 32)

Nergal-Uṣarparā(n) (M) Form of Nergal at the town of Uṣarparā(n) near Uruk. The deity appears in an Old Babylonian god list from Isin. (Richter 2004: 200)

Neti (M) See Biti

Niarzina, Narzina, Narsina (E) Likely female deity, who occurs in a treaty between Narām-Sîn of Akkad and a king of Susa. Sister of Kiri-riša and also of the Sebettu(m), the Seven, a group of both beneficent and malevolent deities. A probable variant Narsina appears in an inscription of a local ruler named Ḫanni found at Shikāfteh-i-Salman/Kul-e Faran not far from Izeh/Malamir in the Bakhtiari Mountains. Identified with Ištar as the planet Venus. (Vallat 1998: 336; Black and Green 2003: 75; König 1977: 227; Stolper, *RlA* IX: 303–4)

Nibas (M) Deity attested in an Old Assyrian text from Kültepe. (Matouš 1962: no. 4)

Nibḫaz (M) See Tartak

Nigal-edina (M) Doorkeeper of Inana of Uruk. Means "Awe-inspiring Radiance (ní-gal) of the Steppe." (Litke 1998: 156)

Nigerim-ḫulgig (M) Watchman of the temple of the sun god Utu/Šamaš. Means "Who Hates Evil." (Litke 1998: 136; Tallqvist 1974: 396; Cavigneaux and Krebernik, *RlA* IX: 310–11)

Nigerim-nudib (M) Deity allocated offerings at Puzriš-Dagān. May mean "Who Does Not Let Evil Pass By." (Studies Levine, 132–38)

Nigerim-šu-tabbe (M) With Níg-erim$_2$-šu-ur$_4$-ur$_4$ two of four doorkeepers of the Dubaragalmaḫ at Ur in a hymn to Rīm-Sîn. Cavigneaux and Krebernik have translated the names based on ur$_4$-ur$_4$ "to gather" and presumably šu—dab$_5$ "to seize." Cf. the deity name Kurra-šu-ur$_4$-ur$_4$. (Cavigneaux and Krebernik, *RlA* IX: 310–11)

Nigerim-šu-urur (M) See Nigerim-šu-tabbe

Nig-ga-na (M) One of the four attendants of the moon god Nanna/Sîn. See Richter 2004 for -ga-na rather than -ga-ba, as Litke reads. (Richter 2004: 450, 452; Litke 1998: 122; Tallqvist 1974: 396; Cavigneaux and Krebernik, *RlA* IX: 311)

Niggena (M) The personification of truth and justice. In An : *Anum*, III 46, Niggina is listed as the daughter of the sun god Utu. In the next entry, Kittum (the Akkadian rendering of Sumerian Niggena) is listed as the son of Utu. Kittum's vizier is listed as Iqbi-damiq. The deity is mentioned in a number of Sumerian literary texts, including collections of proverbs. (Litke 1998: 133; Tallqvist 1974: 396; Klein, *RlA* IX: 311–12)

Niggu-maḫ (M) Son of the birth/mother goddess Dingir-maḫ, identified as the cook of Keš, a temple in the cult city of the goddess. May mean "Great (Provider of) Nourishment," a title fitting for the circle of a birth/mother goddess. Variant is A-gi-maḫ. In a god list from Aššur A-gi-maḫ is called "cook of the exalted gods and great goddesses." (Litke 1998: 79; Schroeder 1920: no. 64; Cavigneaux and Krebernik, *RlA* IX: 312)

NIgKAS-kisikil (M) Herald (nimgir) of the city Kuar. Perhaps means something like "(Keeper of) the Accounts (of) the Pure Place." Cavigneaux and Krebernik raise the possibility of reading uttuku-ki-sikil "abacus of the pure place." (Litke 1998: 107; Cavigneaux and Krebernik, *RlA* IX: 312)

Nig-na (M) Bull-lyre of Gibil/Girra. Means "Censer." (Litke 1998: 108)

NigSAKAR (M) Deity at Early Dynastic Lagaš. níg-sakar, Akkadian *išqarrurtu*, is a tool and a symbol of Inana. But whether this is relevant for early Lagaš is questionable. (Selz 1995)

Nigsisa, Sisa (M) Sumerian Deity identified with Mīšaru(m). Vizier of Utu/Šamaš, the one who stands on the left side. Means "Justice" or "Equity." Nig-zida "Justice" is the vizier on the right side. Appears in a list of viziers of Šamaš in an Akkadian text from Ḫattušas. In an Old Babylonian god list preceded by the deity Si-sá "Who Does Justice." In An : *Anum* Si-sá is listed as one of the eight judges of Utu. (Richter 2004: 348, 350; Litke 1998: 132, 135; Tallqvist 1974: 396; Cavigneaux and Krebernik, *RlA* IX: 313)

Nig-udi-dug (M) Deity appearing in Old Akkadian texts. Name may mean "Good, wondrous thing." (Cavigneaux and Krebernik, *RlA* IX)

Nigzida (M) Sumerian Deity identified with Kittu(m). Vizier of Utu/Šamaš, the one who stands on the right side. Means "Justice." Nig-sisa "Justice" is the vizier on the left side. (Litke 1998: 132; Tallqvist 1974: 397; Cavigneaux and Krebernik, *RlA* IX: 313)

Nigzigal-dima (M) Deity identified with Dingir-maḫ, the birth/mother goddess. Means "(She) who Creates Living Creatures." (Litke 1998: 70; Krebernik, *RlA* VIII: 505)

Nigzu (M) See Namzu

Niḫar (H) Hittite word for "Dowry," sometimes deified, sometimes not. (van Gessel 1998: I, 333; Laroche 1977: 182)

Nikilim (M) See Nin-kilim

Nikkal (M, H) See Nin-gal; Kušuḫ (Hurrian)

Nimgir(gir) (M) Deity identified with the storm god Iškur/Adad. Means "Lightning." Written EN×EN+IM×IM with gloss nim-gi-ig-ri. Nimgir is also a name of Iškur/Adad, written EN×EN with gloss ni-gi-ir. He is also named Lugal-nimgir(EN×EN), "King Lightning." Note that Nim-gír "Lightning" is listed further on in An : *Anum* as the vizier of the storm god. Thus in one tradition Adad is the Lightning and in another lightning is his servant or tool. (Litke 1998: 139–40; Tallqvist 1974: 397; Krebernik, *RlA* IX: 319)

Nimgir-kura (M) Herald of the birth/mother goddess Dingir-maḫ. Means "Herald of the netherworld." (Litke 1998: 77; Krebernik, *RlA* IX: 319)

Nimgir-siga (M) Captain of the barge of the god Enki. Mentioned in "Enki and the World Order." (*LAS*: 218, 219, 226; Krebernik, *RlA* IX: 319)

Nimin-du (M) Deity identified with the warrior god Ninurta and the sun god Utu/Šamaš. The reading du is based upon a gloss. Means "Forty Goes Forth," forty being the number of Ninurta. Note also his name Šu-šanabi "He of Forty Hands." (Litke 1998: 45, 129; Krebernik, *RlA* IX: 319)

Nimin-tab(b)a (M) (1) In An : *Anum* Tablet I, wife of Kalkal, Enlil's doorkeeper in the Ekur temple at Nippur. The goddess probably held a minor office at the court of Utu/Šamaš. Her temple at Ur was built by Šulgi. Written Nimin-^{min}-tab-ba. (2) In An : *Anum* Tablet III identified as an attendant of the moon god Nanna/Sîn (see Richter 2004: 449 for Nimin-tab(b)a in the temple of Nanna). (Leick 1999: 153; Litke 1998: 53, 122; George 1993: 167 no. 1367; Krebernik, *RlA* IX: 319–20)

Nimuš (M) A *gudu*-priest of this deity is mentioned in an Ur III text from Šarrākum. (Nisaba 15, 194:44)

Nin-a (M) Deity attested in an Early Dynastic god list. Written Nin-á. (Mander 1986: 158)

Nin-a-a (M) Deity in a personal name in a third-millennium text from Sippar. (Cavigneaux and Krebernik, *RlA* IX: 325–26)

Nin-a-a-mu (M) Deity allocated offerings at Ur III Puzriš-Dagān. Means "The Lord Is My Father." (Studies Levine, 132–38: r iii 13)

Nin-a-bar-zagin-ka (M) See Nin-é-bar-zagin

Nin-ab-dubur (M) Deity identified with Zarpanītu(m), the spouse of Marduk, who is Lugal-áb-dubur. Cavigneaux and Krebernik suggest that the deity name Nin-áb-U.U should be understand as a variant and be read Nin-áb-dubur$_x$. (Litke 1998: 96; Cavigneaux and Krebernik, *RlA* IX: 324)

Nin-abul (M) Sumerian deity whose name means "Lady (of) the Gate." The goddess is said to be a demon of the Nin-šubur(a) temple. (Gadotti 2015; Richter 2004: 303)

Nin-ab-U.U (M) See Nin-ab-dubur

Nin-abzu (M) Deity identified with Zarpanītu(m), the spouse of Marduk. Means "Lady of the abzu." (Litke 1998: 96; Cavigneaux and Krebernik, *RlA* IX: 325)

Nin-adam-kuga (M) Deity identified with the healing goddess Nin-Isina. Wife of the god Lil. Means "Lady of the Special Settlement." (Litke 1998: 74, 181; Cavigneaux and Krebernik, *RlA* IX: 325)

NIN-ad-mu (M) Deity attested in an offering list from Mari. Cavigneaux and Krebernik suggest a possible identification with the deity Ad-mu. (Cavigneaux and Krebernik, *RlA* IX: 325)

NIN-adqat (M) Deity occurring in an Assyrian ritual text. (Cavigneaux and Krebernik, *RlA* IX: 325)

Nin-a-gal (M) Deity of smiths. His spouse was Nin-imin. Also a name of Enki/Ea as patron of smiths. Means "Lord with Big Arms (or Great Strength)," typical of smiths. He might have had a temple at Girsu. According to An : *Anum* the name could be written with the logogram for smith: SIMUG. Explained in An : *Anu ša amēli* as "Ea of metalworkers." In the lexical series Diri ᵈSIMUG rendered syllabically as ni-na-ga-na. (Civil 2004; Litke 1998: 108, 238; George 1993: 167 no. 1368; Cavigneaux and Krebernik, *RlA* IX: 325–26)

NIN-a-gal-li (M) Deity in an Old Babylonian year formula on a tablet of unknown provenance (courtesy D. I. Owen). Written Nin-a-gal$_5$-li.

Nin-a-gal-zu (M) Goddess attested at Old Babylonian Ur. (Renger 1967: 158)

Nin-aga-sag (M) Deity identified with Gula at Girsu. (Cavigneaux and Krebernik, *RlA* IX: 326)

Nin-aga-šum (M) Goddess attested in an Early Dynastic god list. Means "Lady Given the Crown." (Mander 1986: 143)

Nin-ag-ga (M) Goddess identified with Aya, the wife of the sun god in a Neo-Assyrian god list. Written Nin-ág-gá. (King 1969: pl. 9)

Nin-AGRUN-na (M) Deity attested in the Ur III period and possibly at Mari. (Cavigneaux and Krebernik, *RlA* IX: 350)

Nin-a-izi-mua (M) See Nin-izi-mua

NIN-Akkade (M) Deity identified with Ištar as "Lady of Akkad." (Cavigneaux and Krebernik, *RlA* IX: 326)

Nin-ak-Su'en (M) Sumerian deity attested in the environs of Ur III Umma. A deity Ak-Su'en is also attested. Note also Nin-AK.ḪU(?) attested at Old Babylonian Larsa. (Cohen 1996a: 32; Renger 1967: 147)

NIN-āli (E) Elamite goddess whose name means "Lady of the City." Name borrowed into Elamite from Akkadian. Untaš-Napiriša built a shrine at Choga Zanbil named "Water-sluice" dedicated to NIN-āli and her spouse Šimut, as well as a second building to the same couple. (Hinz and Koch 1987: 1002; König 1977: 41, 43, 206)

Nin-ama (M) Goddess attested in an Early Dynastic god list. Means "Lady-Mother." (Mander 1986: 109)

Nin-ama-arḫuš-su (M) See Ama-arḫuš-su

Nin-ama-kal(l)a (M) Goddess identified with Tašmētum and Nanaya and in one late composition is the sister of Enki. Means "Lady, Precious Mother." (Lambert 2013: 316–17)

Nin-ama-saga (M) Possible reading of the name of a goddess appearing in a seal impression from Ur dating to the reign of Larsa's king Rīm-Sîn I. She may have been the wife of Nin-šubur. Means "Lady, Beautiful Mother." (Richter 2004: 475–76 note 2036)

Nin-amaš (M) See En-amaš

Nin-amaš-kuga (M) One of two goatherds of Enlil. Means "Lord of the Special Pen (or Fold)." His spouse is Nin-kiri-amaš-a. (Litke 1998: 63; Cavigneaux and Krebernik, *RlA* IX: 327)

Nin-a-munGIR (M) See Nin-eri-a-mun-GIR

Nin-a-mutum (M) See Nin-eri-a-mutum

Nin-ana (M) (1) Deity identified with Inana/Ištar as Venus. Female half of a pair of deities, En-ana and Nin-ana, primeval ancestors of Enlil. Means "Lady of Heaven." Occurs as Nin-an in an Early Dynastic god list. (Litke 1998: 33, 148, 161; Cavigneaux and Krebernik, *RlA* IX: 327, 328) (2) Deity whose name is part of the geographical term é-^{d}Nin-á-na^{ki} in an Early Dynastic tablet from Nippur. Ana may be a place in the vicinity of Isin. The geographical name appears thus in the Sumerian zà-mí hymns from Abu Ṣalābīkh, listed between Šuruppak and Isin. (A. Westenholz 1975b: no. 24; Biggs 1974: 51)

Nin-an-ḪAR (M) Sumerian deity attested in texts from Umma as patron of a town in the environs of Ur III Umma. (Cohen 1996a: 32)

Nin-anima (M) See Nin-E-nima

Nin-ansi-ana (M) See Nin-si-ana

Nin-anše-la, Nin-aš$_8$(ḪI×DIŠ)-la (M) Sumerian deity attested in an Ur III tablet from Puzriš-Dagān dealing with expenditures of animals for offerings in the shrine at Tummal. Sallaberger suggests that the deity Nin-anše-lá might be a variant for the attested Nin-an-šè-lá "The Lady who Reaches Heaven." Early Dynastic Nin-aš$_8$(ḪI×DIŠ)-la may be an early form of this deity's name. (Sallaberger 1993: I, 128 note 547)

Nin-anzu (M) The deified bull-lyre of Nin-marki. (Litke 1998: 126 no. 85; Cavigneaux and Krebernik, *RlA* IX: 328)

Nin-apin (M) Goddess attested in an Early Dynastic god list. Means "Lady Plow." (Mander 1986: 64)

Nin-Aral(l)i (M) Sumerian goddess in the Ur III period. Means "Lady of Aral(l)i," a poetic name for the netherworld, as well as an actual place famous for its gold. Written nin-KUR.IDIM. (Richter 2004: 215)

Nin-Aratta (Sum.), Bēlet-Aratte (Akk.) Tutelary goddess of Aratta, a fabled rich city somewhere to the east of Sumer. Famed for its lapis lazuli and gold. Goddess was identified with Inana/Ištar. Means "Lady of Aratta." (Litke 1998: 151; Cavigneaux and Krebernik, *RlA* IX: 328)

Nin-arazu (M) Deity identified with Inana in an Old Babylonian god list. Means "Lady Prayer." (Richter 2004: 292)

Nin-arina-šub (M) Deity attested in god lists from Šuruppak and Abu Ṣalābīkh. (Mander 1986: 113)

Nin-ar-ri (M) See En-ar-ri

Nin-aruru (M) A deified bull-lyre, one of six belonging to Dingir-maḫ, the birth/mother goddess. (Litke 1998: 77; Cavigneaux and Krebernik, *RlA* IX: 329)

Nin-aša (M) Goddess attested in an Early Dynastic god list. Means "Lady (of) the Field." (Mander 1986: 144)

Ninata-e (M) See Sirarata-e

Nin-atta, Nin-itta, Nin-(n)at(t)a (L, H) Hurrian goddess. Maker of music. One of two ministers to the great goddess Ša(w)uš(k)a of Nineveh, paired with the second, Kulitta. The two goddesses appear with their mistress on the frieze of goddesses depicted at Yazılıkaya. In "Song of Ḫedammu," Ša(w)uš(k)a instructs the two to play music while she tries to seduce the sea monster. Attested at Ugarit as Nin-itta. (del Olmo Lete 1999: 86; Hutter, *DDDB*: 759; Hoffner 1998: 51, 54; van Gessel 1998: I, 335–39; Popko 1995: 94, 115; Haas 1994:

312, 347, 470, 474; Laroche 1946/47: 56; Otten, *RlA* VI: 303–4)

Nin-azi-mua (M) See Azida-mua and Nin-izi-mua

Nin-azu (M) Sumerian god of the netherworld, decay (death) and growth (life), and vegetation. In the tradition of the city of Enegir, he was son of Ereškigal and likely her first husband Gugal-ana. In the tradition of the city Ešnunna, where he had warrior attributes, he was the son of Enlil and Ninlil and brother of Nergal, Nanna, En-bilulu, and Nin-mada. His wife was Nin-Girida, though sometimes Ereškigal was named as his consort, rather than as his mother. In "Enki and Nin-ḫursag" Nin-ḫursag decrees that her daughter, Nin-giri-utud, a variant(?) for Nin-girida, is to marry Nin-azu. He and Nin-Girida were occasionally identified with Ninurta and Gula. Nin-azu was father of Nin-geš-zida and of two daughters: Ama-TUR-ma and Labar-TUR-ma. Nin-azu's vizier was Ipaḫu(m), "Viper." His animal was the snake-dragon *mušḫuššu*, a symbol first taken over by Tišpak, then Marduk, and later Nabû.

In "Enlil and Ninlil," Nin-azu, son of Enlil and Ninlil, was engendered to be a netherworld deity and to prevent the moon god Nanna/Sîn from being consigned to the netherworld. In "The Creation of Grain," Nin-azu and Nin-mada provide the then grass-eating Sumerians with both flax and grain. In a lamentation Nin-azu joined Dumuzi and other "dead" deities as recipients of mourning rites. Nin-azu was often invoked in incantations, especially those dealing with snakebite.

His main cult centers were Enegir and Ešnunna, and there were lesser cults at Lagaš and Ur. At Enegir his temple was the E-gida and at Ešnunna it was E-sikila. At Enegir Nin-azu was eventually replaced by Nergal, while Tišpak took his place at Ešnunna. Nin-azu also had a shrine at Nippur, where he received offerings as he did also at Umma, Lagaš, and Girsu. In a month named for Nin-azu, Ur celebrated a major festival for him as a deity who disappeared into the netherworld. Nin-azu's astral identity may have been the planet Mars. (*LAS*: 105; Cohen 2015: 73; Katz 2003: 428–42; Black and Green 2003: 137; Leick 1998: 128–29; Litke 1998: 191; George 1993: 36, 141 no. 987; Jacobsen 1970: 9, 24, 32; Wiggermann, *RlA* IX: 329–35)

Nin-Baba (M) Female chair-bearer of the goddess Baba. Means "Lady (of) Baba." (Litke 1998: 178; Cavigneaux and Krebernik, *RlA* IX: 336)

Nin-bad(-dur-bara) (M) Sumerian title of Inana/Ištar. Nin-bàd is explained in An : *Anum* as Bēlit-dūri "Lady of the Wall." Nin-bàd-dúr-bar-ra is glossed as Bēlet-ibrāti "Lady of the Outside Shrine." Possibly here, bar is a variant for gar, thus dúr gar "to sit" and so the name would mean "Lady who Is Situated by the Wall." (Foster 2005: 678; Richter 2004: 292; Litke 1998: 151; Cavigneaux and Krebernik, *RlA* IX: 335)

Nin-bad-gal-e (M) Goddess attested in an Early Dynastic god list. Means "Lady, Great Wall (of) the House." (Mander 1986: 143)

Nin-baḫar (M) Sumerian title of the birth/mother goddess Dingir-maḫ. Means "Lady Potter." (Litke 1998: 69; Krebernik, *RlA* IX: 335)

Nin-banda (M) Sumerian deity attested in a text from Lagaš in the Early Dynastic period and in an Ur III tablet.

Also appears in a late lament. Name can mean means "Junior/Ferocious Lord/Lady." (Selz 1995: 214–15; Wiggermann, *RlA* IX: 335)

Nin-barag (M) Deity attested at Ur III Girsu and in a personal name. Means "Lady/Lord (of) the Dais." (MVN 6, 314: o i 5)

Nin-barage-si (M) Sumerian title of Zarpanītu(m), the spouse of Marduk. Means "Lady/Lord who Occupies the Dais." (Litke 1998: 95; Cavigneaux and Krebernik, *RlA* IX: 336)

Nin-bara-ge (M) Deity identified with or in the circle of Inana. (Richter 2004: 292; Litke 1998: 152)

Nin-barag-tum (M) Deity at Ur III Umma. Means "Lady/Lord Worthy of the Dais." (Nisaba 11, 22: r iii 13)

Nin-bar-še-gunu (M) See Nun-bar-še-gunu

Nin-bezem (M) See Umbisag

Nin-bi-an-na (M) See Bizil-ana

Nin-bilulu (M) Deity in Early Dynastic god lists. Either a female counterpart to the god of ditches and dikes En-bilulu or another name for him. (Cavigneaux and Krebernik, *RlA* IX: 336)

Nin-biri (M) See Bēlet-bīri(m)

Nin-bulug (M) See En-bulug

Nin-bur-sug (M) Deity attested in an Early Dynastic god list. Means "Lady who Sets up the Stone Bowls." An ancient rite is known that likely dealt with the presentation or manipulation of stone vessels. (Mander 1986: 110)

Nin-bur-šal (M) Deity identified in An : *Anum* with ama-du$_{10}$-bad, "The Fast(?) One." Glossed šá-al. Note the name of Ninlil Bur-šu-ŠAL. If there is a relationship, then bur here may be for bur-šu "old woman(?)." (Litke 1998: 79)

Nin-da (M) Consort of En-da, one of the forty-two ancestors of Enlil in An : *Anum*. Means "Beside the Lady." The goddess occurs in a personal name at Ur III Puzriš-Dagān and once as the recipient of allocations there. (Litke 1998: 31)

Nin-da-galzu (M) One of two deified bull-lyres of the goddess Nin-gal. May mean "Lady who Is at the Side of the Wise." (Litke 1998: 123; Tallqvist 1974: 400; Cavigneaux and Krebernik, *RlA* IX: 337)

Ninda-gu-gal (M) Deity attested in the Early Dynastic period. Written Nínda-gu$_4$-gal. (Mander 1986: 63)

Nin-da-Lagaš (M) Goddess paired with Dumuzi-da-Lagaš. May mean "Lady who is at the Side of Lagaš." ((Cavigneaux and Krebernik, *RlA* IX: 337)

Nin-dam (M) Sumerian goddess attested in an Early Dynastic god list. Means "Lady Spouse." See Nin-dam-ge. (Mander 1986: 113, 115, 143)

Nin-da-maḫdi (M) One of two deified bull-lyres of the goddess Nin-gal. May mean "Beside the Lady (One Is) Exalted." (Litke 1998: 123; Tallqvist 1974: 400; Cavigneaux and Krebernik, *RlA* IX: 338)

Nin-dam-anna (M) Deity for whom offerings were made in the Ur III period. The offerings took place during a cultic voyage made from Uruk to Ur. Means "Lady, Wife of An." (Sallaberger 1993: I, 224 and note 1072)

Nin-Dam-gal-nuna (M) See Damkina

Nin-dam-ge, Nin-ge-dam (M) Tutelary deity of a town near Umma. Attested in an Early Dynastic god list. See Dam-ge. (Frayne 2009: 61; Selz 1995: 261; Mander 1986: 115; Biggs 1974: 52)

Nin-damun, Damun (M) Nin-damun (da-mu-un) is attested in an economic text from the time of Rīm-Sîn I at Old Babylonian Larsa. The god's temple is said to have possessed orchards of date palms. This deity may be identified with Inana, who is identified with Da-mu-un in a Neo-Assyrian god list. (Richter 2004: 400; King 1969: pl. 25)

Nin-dar-a, Umun-dar-a (M) God of Girsu/Lagaš. Husband of Nanše. At the New Year in Lagaš, gifts were presented to Nin-dara and Nanše at the temple. Nin-dara's boat was called "Shrine-Abundance," making a ritual journey from Girsu to Gu-aba. In An : *Anum* he is identified as the moon god Sîn and in an Old Babylonian god list he is listed among the gods in the circle of the moon god.

The reading of the name as Nin-dar-a is based upon a votive inscription in which the name is written Nin-dar-ra and a hymn to Ḫendursaga in which Nin-dar-a is called the dar-bird. Selz suggests that the name may mean "The Lord who Splits," perhaps referring to his warlike nature. At the New Year in Lagaš, gifts were presented to Nin-dar-a and Nanše. In "Enki and Nin-ḫursag" Nin-ḫursag decrees that her daughter, Na-zi (Nanše) is to marry Nindara. (Cohen 2015: 34; Black and Green 2003: 123; Litke 1998: 124; Selz 1995: 315–17; Hallo 1962: 39; Edzard, *RlA* IX: 338)

Ninda-šar (M) Goddess attested in an Early Dynastic god list. Means "Everything Is with the Lady." (Mander 1986: 143)

Nin-dara-ana (M) Deity identified with a mother goddess, probably Bēlet-ilī. Means "Lady, the Ibex of Heaven." (Tallqvist 1974: 400; Krebernik, *RlA* VIII: 505; Cavigneaux and Krebernik, *RlA* IX: 338)

Ninda-šurima (M) See Enda-šurima

NINDA-udi-du (M) One of the cooks of An. Written NINDA-u_6-di-du_{10}^{du}, with variant Nin-ù-[...]. Since this deity is a cook perhaps du is a variant for du_8 "to bake," thus "Who Bakes Wonder Bread." (Litke 1998: 30)

Nin-diba (M) See Nin-riba

Nin-Dilmuna (M) Goddess whose name means "Lady of Dilmun." According to An : *Anum*, it refers to Inana/Ištar, but the "Lady of Dilmun" (modern Baḥrain) was usually Meškilak/Nin-sikila. (Litke 1998: 149; Cavigneaux and Kreber-nik, *RlA* IX: 505)

Nin-dim (M) Deity identified with Bēlet-ilī. Means "Lady Creator." Written nin-$^{di\text{-}im}$dím. (Litke 1998: 68; Tallqvist 1974: 400; Krebernik, *RlA* VIII: 505)

Nin-dim-ana (M) Goddess identified with Dam-gal-nuna, spouse of Enki. (Cavigneaux and Krebernik, *RlA* IX: 339)

Nin-dimgal, Nin-dimgul (M) See Dimgul

Nin-dingirene (M) Deity identified with the Sumerian mother goddess Dingir-maḫ and her Babylonian counterpart Bēlet-ilī. Means "Lady of the Gods." (Litke 1998: 66; Tallqvist 1974: 400; Krebernik, *RlA* VIII: 505)

Nin-diri (M) Deity who in An : *Anum* is identified as a $bara_2$-sig_5-ga (socle) official(?) of Nin-Nibru, wife of Ninurta. Nin-diri appears in an Old Babylonian god list from Isin, likely in a circle of gods associated with Nin-Isina. (Richter 2004: 75, 222; Litke 1998: 49)

Nin-DI-uga (M) Deity attested in an Early Dynastic god list. Likely a variant spelling for Nin-tin-uga. (Mander 1986: 101, 103)

Nin-du (M) (1) Written Nin-du. See En-du. (2) Goddess attested in an Early Dynastic god list. Written Nin-du$_6$. Means "Lady (of) the Mound." See Nin-du-kuga. (Mander 1986: 144). (3) Deity in an Old Babylonian god list from Mari. Written Nin-du$_8$.

Nin-du-amaš (M) Deity attested in two god lists of the Early Dynastic period from Šuruppak. Spouse was En-du$_6$-amaš. (Mander 1986: 109)

Nin-Du-Arḫatum (M) Tutelary deity of the Ur III town of Du-Arḫatum in the vicinity of Umma. (Cohen 1996a: 32)

Nin-duba (M) Deity associated with Nanše and the Lagaš area. Gudea, governor of Lagaš, built him a temple at Uruk. (Leick 1999: 62; George 1993: 167 no. 1372; Cavigneaux and Krebernik, *RlA* IX: 339–40)

Nin-du-babbara (M) See Nin-tu

Nin-dudra (M) *Anu ša amēli* lists a god Du-[ud]-ru with variant Nin-du-ud-ra, who is involved in reed craft. (Litke 1998: 239)

Nin-dug (M) Form given in a god list as the Sumerian equivalent of the goddess Šala(š), wife of Adad. Means "Good Lady." (Schwemer 2001: 13)

Nin-Dugalgal (M) Tutelary deity of the Ur III town of Du$_6$-gal-gal, in the environs of Umma. (Cohen 1996a: 32)

Nin-DuḫulUtu (M) Tutelary deity of the town Du$_6$-ḫul-^{d}Utu, "Mound (where) Utu Rejoices," in the environs of Ur III Umma. (Cohen 1996a: 33)

Nin-DuKAUtu (M) Deity receiving offerings at a location Du$_6$-KA-^{d}Utu in the environs of Ur III Umma. (Nebraska 37: o ii 18)

Nin-Du-kuga (M) See En-Du-kuga

Nin-Duluma (M) The deity of Dulum, a city near Zabala(m). Also a name of Enki/Ea. In the Early Dynastic and Sargonic periods, Nin-Duluma seems to have been the main deity of the cultic calendar of the Umma region, which would include Dulum. In a ritual for the repair of a temple, the god Ea was credited with pinching off a piece of clay to create various deities, among them Nin-Duluma "to be the completers of [the] construction work." For the reading of the name and possible identification with Lugal-duluma, see Lugal-duluma. (Litke 1998: 86; Sachs, *ANET*: 341; Cavigneaux and Krebernik, *RlA* IX: 340–41)

Nin-dumu-sag (M) Goddess identified with Bēlet-ilī. Means "Lady, First-born." Written Nin-dumu^{du}-sag. (Litke 1998: 67)

Nin-dur-ba (M) (1) A doorkeeper of Enki/Ea at Eridu. May mean "Lady/Lord who Opens the Closed (Door)." dur = *markasu*, "closure of a door" (*CAD* M/1: 283b). Called god of the bolt man (dingir lú-si-gar-ra-ke$_4$). (2) One of five fruit gods. Possibly means "Lady/Lord of the Apple," based upon an entry in An : *Anum* indicating the logogram ḪAŠḪUR "apple" as a writing for this deity. (Litke 1998: 107, 112; Cavigneaux and Krebernik, *RlA* IX: 341)

Nin-DušuluḫUtu (M) Tutelary deity receiving offerings at the location Du$_6$-šu-luḫ-^{d}Utu "Mound of the Ritual Cleansing of Utu" in the environs of Ur III Umma. (Nisaba 23, 46: o i 25)

Nin-DuZUM(re)mua (M) Tutelary deity receiving offerings at a location Du$_6$-ZUM(-re)-mú-a in the environs of Umma. Variant is -ZUM-e-mú.

Nin-E-anna (M) Name of Inana/Ištar. Means "Lady of the E-anna (Temple)." The E-anna in Uruk was also associated with An/Anu(m). Temples of Inana/Ištar in other cities were often also called E-anna. (Litke 1998: 149; George 1993: 67–68; Tallqvist 1974: 401; Cavigneaux and Krebernik, *RlA* IX: 341)

Nin-é-bar-zagin (M) Deity attested in the environs of Ur III Umma. Variant is nin-a-bar-za-gìn-ka. See Geštin-ana-e-bar-zagin. (Cohen 1996a: 32)

Nin-Eda (M) Deity from Nippur in the Ur III period. Means "Lady of (the city) Eda." (Sallaberger 1993: I, 104)

NIN-edam-kuga (M) See Egi/Ereš-edam-kuga

Nin-edina (M) Female scribe of the netherworld. Identified with Bēlet-ṣēri(m) and Geštin-ana. Means "Lady of the Steppe." (Cavigneaux and Krebernik, *RlA* IX: 342)

Nin-eduru (M) Deity attested at Fara. Means "Lord of the Village." (Cavigneaux and Krebernik, *RlA* IX: 342)

Nin-ee (M) Deity at Ur III Umma with both a *gudu*-priest and an administrator (sanga). Written Nin-e_{11}-e. A deity E_{11}-e is also attested at Umma. (Aleppo 303: s. 3)

Nin-egal (Sum.), **Bēlet-ekalli(m)** (Akk.) **Pendigalli** (Hurrian) Sumerian/Babylonian goddess. Nin-egal means "Lady of the Palace." Originally a separate deity, but later often equated to Inana/Ištar, so that her name became a name of Inana/Ištar. Nin-egal's spouse was Uraš, the tutelary deity of the city of Dilbat, and her vizier was the judge Diku. In Sumerian love songs in which the lovers compare their pedigrees, Dumuzi calls Inana Nin-egal. In "Gilgameš and the Bull of Heaven," Nin-egal and Inana appear to be interchangeable.

It is also the name of other goddesses. For instance, the patron goddess of prisons, Manun-gal or Nungal, received the epithet on a few occasions, the "Big House" referring to the prison, not to a palace. However, Nin-egal's main function was likely as patron of the royal palace. Her task was to ensure the ruler's position, as well as to guarantee economic well-being. At Mari, Bēlet-ekalli(m) had a shrine inside the palace.

At third-millennium Ebla, SA.ZA was the palatial complex of the royal administration. Archi suggests that the deity Ištar-SA.ZA there is actually to be understood as Ištar-(ša-)ekallim and so it is quite possible that the deity whose name is written NIN.SA.ZA in an Old Babylonian god list and whose name appears in Ur III personal names is Bēlet-ekallim or a writing for Nin-é-gal. In first-millennium An : *Anum* the deity appears as Nin-sa-a and is identified with the sun god. This might represent an error in transmission in which the ZA-sign was misread as A coupled with a loss of knowledge of the original deity's identification. (Litke 1998: 128; Archi 1993; Tallqvist 1974: 416; Cavigneaux and Krebernik, *RlA* IX: 486–87)

An Akkadian treaty appealed to Nin-egal and her husband Uraš to preserve the integrity of the treaty. Bēlet-ekalli(m) was mentioned in two dream revelations sent in letters to Zimrī-Līm, king of Mari.

Nin-egal was worshipped in every major Mesopotamian city. She had a temple at Ur, where her cult was celebrated at least in the Ur III period. At

Umma, also in the third millennium BCE, clothing was provided for Nin-egal for the New Year Festival. At Lagaš in Gudea's time, she was called "Lady of the Scepter" and received offerings in her own temple. Bēlet-ekalli(m) had temples at Ur, Larsa, Aššur, Dilbat, and Qaṭna. She was worshipped also at Nippur, Babylon, Emar, and Elam. At Mari, where she was regularly presented with an offering of oil, she was the patron of the royal family. (Cohen 2015: 71, 76–77, 138, 249; Durand 2008: 209–11; Foster 2001: 225; Frayne 2001: 123; Leick 1999: 153, 181–82; Trémoiuille 1999: 282; Leick 1998: 25; Litke 1998: 155; Sefati 1998: 197; Archi 1993; George 1993: 32, 88 no. 320, 110 no. 604, 138 no. 939, 166 no. 1373; Tallqvist 1974: 401; Kramer, *ANET*: 586, 637; Moran, *ANET*: 630, 631; Reiner, *ANET*: 533; Behrens and Klein, *RlA* IX: 342–47)

NIN.EGAL (E) Elamite goddess whose name means "Lady of the Palace." Name borrowed into Elamite from Akkadian and ultimately from Sumerian. Untaš-Napiriša built a shrine for NIN.E.GAL at Choga Zanbil. (Hinz and Koch 1987: 1002; König 1977: 63, 206)

Nin-egal-edin-ka (M) Deity receiving offerings at Ur III Girsu. Means "Nin-egal of the Steppe." (UNT 16: o iii 28)

Nin-egale-si (M) Divinized harp of the goddess Gula at Umma in the Ur III period. Means "Lady who Occupies the Temple," presumably a reference to the music. (Sallaberger 1993: II, pl. 1)

Nin-e-ge (M) Deity in the personal name Ur-^{d}Nin-é-ge from Ur III Girsu. (CDLI P2100058: o 29)

Nin-egena (M) Goddess in the Neo-Babylonian period associated with the Ebabbar temple of Šamaš at Sippar.

Nin-egia (M) See Egi/Ereš-egia

Nin-Egibile (M) Deity at Ur III Girsu. (CT 5, 17 BM 12231: o v 25)

Nin-egena (M) Goddess in the Neo-Babylonian period associated with the Ebabbar temple of Šamaš at Sippar.

NIN-egula (M) See Egi/Ereš-egula

Nin-eguna (M) Deity identified with Geštin-ana. Means "Lady of the Multi-Colored House." At Mari, E-guna was the sanctuary of Ištar. (George 1993: 97 no. 442; Sallaberger 1993: I, 104; Tallqvist 1974: 401; Renger 1967: 150; Cavigneaux and Krebernik, *RlA* IX: 347–48)

Nin-E-ḫama (M) Likely, spouse of Asar-lu-ḫe, patron deity of Ku'ara. Mentioned in offering lists of the Ur III period. Also identified with Zarpanītu, the spouse of Marduk, and a member of the circle of Inana/Ištar. In both the Old Babylonian god list and in An : Anum the last sign is partially destroyed, but seems to be ⸢ma⸣; however, if so, a meaning for ḫa-ma in this context is unclear. (Richter 2004: 292, 324; Litke 1998: 151; Tallqvist 1974: 401; Cavigneaux and Krebernik, *RlA* IX: 348)

Nin-Eḫubba/Ekabba (M) Name for Inana in an Old Babylonian god list. George notes that Eḫubba occurs as an epithet of the goddess Inana in some late lamentations. The location É-ḫúb/kab^{ki} is attested in Early Dynastic times. George notes a year name of the Old Babylonian king of Marad, Ibni-šadû'i dealing with the construction of the wall of a town named Eḫubba. A place name ḪuPI-um appears in the Ur-Namma cadastre, a monumental text originally carved on stone delineating the borders of the provinces of the Ur III kingdom, and may refer to the same place. (Richter 2004: 47 n. 216; George 1993: 99 no. 468; Zettler 1992: 264; Renger 1963: 150; Kraus 1955: 48)

Nin-e-igara(k) (M) Goddess in charge of the dairy. Wife of the cattle god Nin-Gublaga, whose cult site was Ki'abrig, near Ur. Belonged to the sphere of the moon god Nanna/Sîn. Her name means "Lady of the House of Cream and Cheese." (Litke 1998: 121; George 1993: 28, 85 no. 291, 103 no. 499; Tallqvist 1974: 401; Jacobsen 1970: 7; Cavigneaux and Krebernik, *RlA* IX: 348)

Nin-E-kisal(-libir) (M) Deity with a cult at Ur III Umma. Name means "Lady/Lord of the (Old) Temple Courtyard." (MVAG 21, 22 FH 5: o ii 25, r i 10)

Nin-E-kisiga (M) Deity identified with the goddess Nin-kar(r)ak/Nin-Isina. Possibly means "Lady of the House of the *kisiga*," that is, offerings for the dead. (Tallqvist 1974: 401; Cavigneaux and Krebernik, *RlA* IX: 348)

Nin-e-ku (M) Goddess attested in an Early Dynastic god list and receiving an offering at Ur III Umma. Means "Lady (of) the Holy House." (Mander 1986: 144)

Nin-Ekur(a) (M) See Manun-gal

Nin-ela (M) Goddess occurring in a school text from Susa with En-ela. Written Nin-e-lá. (Cavigneaux and Krebernik, *RlA* IX: 348)

Nin-Emaḫ (M) Deity attested at Ur III Umma. Means "Lady of the Emaḫ." (Nisaba 15/2 1032: o i 8)

Nin-Emaš(-zagin) (M) Tutelary deity of the E-maš temple in Umma, a major shrine in that city. There was a close link in Umma between the goddesses Nin-E-maš and Nin-egal. (Sallaberger 1993: I, 249 and note 1175)

Nin-Emirza (M) Tutelary deity of the field and town named E-mir-za. Attested in tablets from Ur III Umma. (Frayne 2009: 53; Cohen 1996a: 33)

Nin-Emuša (M) Deity identified with Inana/Ištar. Possibly refers to Dumuzi's E-muš temple at Bad-tibira and so might mean "Lady of the E-muš (Temple)." (Cavigneaux and Krebernik, *RlA* IX: 349)

Nin-en-e (M) Sumerian deity attested in an Early Dynastic god list from Šuruppak. May mean "Lady, (in charge of) Incantations (for) the Temple." (Mander 1986: 40)

Nin-en-gal-DU.DU (M) Sumerian deity attested in Ur III texts associated with Nippur. (Richter 2004: 30; Sallaberger 1993: I, 104, 108 note 490)

Nin-Engura (M) One of the protector deities in the circle of Nin-Girsu. Means "Lady of the Underground Waters." The entry directly before is Engur-ra, which may be simply a shortened form of Nin-engur-ra and not really a separate deity. A few entries later Engur-[x-x] with variant Im-kur-ra-NE-in is listed as a protective deity of Baba. (Litke 1998: 176; Cavigneaux and Krebernik, *RlA* IX: 349)

Nin-E-nima (M) Sumerian goddess who perhaps was indigenous to the city of Ur. Means "Lady of the E-nima," the "Upper House." As recorded in the name of his eighth year, Rīm-Sîn I of Larsa built Nin-E-nima's temple in a town in eastern Lagaš province. The shrine E-nima is mentioned in a broken context in an inscription of the *entu* priestess En-ane-du, Rīm-Sîn's sister, possibly referring to a shrine in Ur. In a greeting formula of an Old Babylonian letter, Nin-E-nima is paired with the god Šamaš suggesting that, in at least one town, the two served as tutelary deities. A Neo-Assyrian omen makes reference to a disease(?) called "The Hand of Nin-E-nima," supposedly linked to howling dogs in the house. The goddess occurs in a handful of theophoric names. She is also mentioned in a tablet from the First Sealand Dynasty. Her listing with Inana and Manzi'at ("Rainbow") suggests a connection to the sky. Litke restores An : *Anum* IV 36 as Nin-[a]-nim-ma, an otherwise unattested name, which might mean "Lady of Standing Waters," perhaps to be restored as Nin-[é]-nim-ma. (Dalley 2009: no. 59, no. 66, no. 78, no. 81–84; Cavigneaux and Krebernik, *RlA* IX: 349; Litke 1998: 151)

Nin-en-lil (M) Deity whose name occurs on a lapis-lazuli tablet and an eyestone from Kassite Nippur alongside the royal name Kurigalu. Likely an error in both cases for the goddess Nin-Nibru, spouse of Ninurta. (Brinkman 1976: 223, 227)

Nin-en-lugalene (M) Deity identified with Bēlet-ilī. Perhaps "Lady, *Entu*-priestess of Kings." (Litke 1998: 67)

Nin-ennun-PA (M) In An : *Anum* listed in the circle of Nungal, jailer of the netherworld, where she is explained as herald of the prison of the netherworld. (Litke 1998: 287)

Nin-er (M) Goddess attested in an Early Dynastic god list. Means "Lady Wailing." (Mander 1986: 144)

Nin-(eri-)a-mu(n)GIR (M) Deity identified with Inana/Ištar. Nin-eri-a-mu-un-GIR$_7$(DU) appears in an inscription as patron of merchant sailors. In a lexical list from Isin, written Nin-a-mu-un-GIR$_5$(DU). At Ur III Umma occurs as Nin-a-mu-GIR$_5$(DU) and Nin-eri-a-mu-GIR$_5$(DU). Note Nin-eri-a-mu at Ur III Ur, which might be related. A text from Puzriš-Dagan refers to the šabra of Nin-eri-a-mu-da-ku$_5$-ta. Sumerian a—gir$_5$ seems to refer to the creation of water channels (*PSD* A/1 87) and a-ku$_5$ means "sluice" (*PSD* A/1 98). Thus the name may mean something like "The Lady (who) Has Dug Sluices (for?) the City." (Richter 2004: 222; Litke 1998: 151; Cohen 1996a: 32; Cavigneaux and Krebernik, *RlA* IX: 528)

NIN-eri-bara (M) See Egi/Ereš-eri-bara

NIN-eri-bil (M) See Egi/Ereš-eri-bil

Nin-eri-ki-gara (M) Deity identified with Inana/Ištar. Means "Lady who Established the City." (Litke 1998: 151; Tallqvist 1974: 427; Cavigneaux and Krebernik, *RlA* IX: 529)

NIN-eri-kuga (M) See Egi/Ereš-eri-kuga

Nin-eriniše (M) Goddess allocated hides at Ur III Umma for her journey to Zabala(m). Attested also in a personal name from Umma. May mean "The Lady toward Her City." (TCL 5, 5672: o ii 1)

Nin-eri-saga (M) Deity identified with Nin-Nibru, the wife of Ninurta. Means "Lady of the Capital City." (Litke 1998: 47; Tallqvist 1974: 428; Cavigneaux and Krebernik, *RlA* IX: 529)

Nin-eri-sala (M) Deity identified with Nin-Nibru, the wife of Ninurta. (Litke 1998: 47; Tallqvist 1974: 428; Cavigneaux and Krebernik, *RlA* IX: 529)

Nin-eri-šaga (M) Deity identified with Nin-Nibru, the wife of Ninurta. Means "Lady of the Inner City." (Litke 1998: 47; Tallqvist 1974: 428; Cavigneaux and Krebernik, *RlA* IX: 529)

Nin-eri-ula (M) See En-eri-ula

Nin-Erra (M) Deity identified with the netherworld or a variant of the name Erra, which it directly precedes in An : *Anum*. Written ^{d}Nin-ì-ra. See the variant ^{d}Lugal-ì-ra for ^{d}Lugal-Erra. (Litke 1998: 207)

Nin-E-sag-kala (M) See E-sag-kala

Nin-E-SUM (M) First attested in an Early Dynastic god list and later in an incantation, where the deity is associated with the tùn-ninnu-na, which George suggests might be for é-tùn-ninnu "House of fifty axes/vessels." (George 2016: no. 1b)

Nin-Ešaga (M) Deity attested in an Old Babylonian school text. Cavigneaux and Krebernik suggest a possible identification with the é-šà-ba, the temple of Baba and Sudag. (Cavigneaux and Krebernik, *RlA* IX: 350)

Nin-Ešara (M) Deity identified with Inana/Ištar. Means "Lady of the E-šara" either in Uruk or Nippur. E-šara was the temple complex of the god Aššur in the city Aššur and also part of Enlil's great Ekur temple at Nippur. (George 145 no. 1034). (Litke 1998: 149; George 1993: 145 no. 1035; Cavigneaux and Krebernik, *RlA* IX: 350)

Nin-eš-dar (M) Goddess attested in a god list from Abu Ṣalābīkh. Written - èš-dar. (OIP 99, 82: o ii 9)

Nin-eš-gal (M) Wife of the god of fire, Gibil/Girra, and Nunbarḫuša. Means "Lady (of) the Great Shrine," though it is unclear to what this would refer (for èš-gal, see George 1993: 83–84). (Litke 1998: 108).

Nin-E-šuba(-kalam-ma) (M) Deity identified with Inana. George suggests that É-šuba is an orthography for E-su$_8$-ba, thus "Lady of the House of the Shepherd of the Nation," which would be appropriate for Dumuzi's lover. (Litke 1998: 150; George 1993: 142)

Nin-e-uga (M) See Egi/Ereš-e-uga

Nin-e-umun (M) Deity in an Old Babylonian god list from Mari. Means "Lord/Lady of the Workshop(*bīt mummi*)." (Studies Birot, 184–85: r iv 14)

Nin-ezenna, Nin-ezem (M) Nin-ezem in the Ur III texts. Written in an Old Babylonian god list ^{d}nin-ezen-na. Means "Lady of the Festival." (Weidner 1924/25; MVN 5, 132)

Nin-ezem-ana (M) Name attested only once, at Puzriš-Dagān. It is possible that this is a scribal mistake, confusing the name of the current month on the tablet, ezem-an-na, with the name of the deity Nin-ezem. (SAT 3, 1882: o 16

Nin-ezem-balag (M) One of the four bull-lyres of Enki. May mean "Lord/Lady of the Festival of the Lyre." (Litke 1998: 105)

NIN-Gabura (M) See Egi/Ereš-Gabura

NIN-gagia (M) See Egi/Ereš-gagia

Nin-gal (Sum.), **Nikkal** (Akk.) Goddess whose name means "Great Lady," a title held by several other goddesses, especially birth/mother goddesses. A patron deity of the city of Ur with her spouse Nanna/Sîn, the moon god, and often addressed as Nin-Urima "Lady of Ur" and Ama-Urima "Mother of Ur." A divine dream interpreter. Daughter of Nin-gi-kuga. Jacobsen suggests that, since her mother Nin-ge-kuga was "Lady of the Pure Reed," Nin-gal might originally have been associated with reeds and marshes. Mother of Inana/Ištar and Utu/Šamaš. Other offspring included Nin-Gublaga, Numušda, Amara-ḫe'ake, and, at Harrān in Syria, Nuska. Another of her titles was Ama-dingir-gal-gal "Mother of the Great Gods." Nin-gal was associated with an aquatic bird.

Her role in literature and mythic material was primarily a passive one. She was featured in hymns written at Ur about Nanna/Sîn's courting of the goddess. In one, the god was reported to have married Nin-gal without her father's consent. In two laments over the destruction of Ur (and Sumer), she weeps copiously as she mourns the fall of her city. As mother of Inana, Nin-gal appears in the Sumerian love compositions assigned to the courtship of Inana and Dumuzi and was supportive of the relationship of the two. Nin-gal is mentioned in "Gilgameš and Huwawa A" as mother of Utu, the sun god.

Nin-gal was venerated along with the moon god throughout Mesopotamia. She had sanctuaries at Nippur, Harrān, Urum. and Ilip, and probably elsewhere in temples of her spouse. At Ur the high priestess of the moon god was identified with Nin-gal and was understood as the god's spouse. Part of the residence of the high priestess at Ur housed a shrine of Nin-gal named "Sacred Bedroom."

As Nikkal(u), a relatively minor Canaanite goddess, she was revered at Ugarit. There Nikkal(u) was consort of Yariḫ(u), the Canaanite moon god, and a composition about her betrothal to Yariḫ(u) occurs. In it she might have also been named Nikkal-and-Ib(bu) or Nikkal-Ib, though Wyatt argues that Ib was the bridegroom to be. Nikkal had a shrine at Ugarit where she received offerings, among them cows. Along with the moon god Sîn, she was worshipped at the north Syrian city of Harrān well into the first millennium CE. (Cohen 2015: 51; Durand 2008: 211–12; Black, Cunningham, Robson, and Zólyomi 2004; 127–41; Lapinkivi 2004: 36, 205; Black and Green 2003: 138; Pardee 2002: 55, 64, 90, 92, 95, 282; Wyatt 2002: 336–41; Frayne 2001: 108; Leick 1999: 141; del Olmo Lete 1999: 57, 80, 85; Schmidt, *DDDB*: 587; Sefati 1999: 187–89; Leick 1998: 129–30; Litke 1998: 119, 120, 185, 231; Parker in Parker 1997c: 215–18; George 1993: 74 no. 140, 79 no. 205, 90 no. 345, 93 no. 380; Jacobsen 1976: 124–25; Tallqvist 1974: 403–4; Kramer, *ANET*: 455, 457, 460–63, 617, 619; Zgoll, *RlA* IX: 352–56)

Detail of cylinder seal from the area of the royal tombs, Ur, Mesopotamia, with the goddess Nin-gal enthroned opposite her spouse Nanna/Sîn. Old Akkadian. Dark green. 3.6 x 2.4. After Colbow 1997: 29, fig. 2.

Nin-gal-a-an-da (M) Deity attested at Old Babylonian Ur. In the Nin-gal sanctuary at Ur, there was a cult site devoted to Nin-gal-a-an-da, Nin-ki-ura, and AD-mu-saḫara. (Richter 2004: 383)

Nin-gal-Agruna (M) See Nin-gal-Enuna

Nin-gal-ana (M) Deity identified with Inana/Ištar as the planet Venus. Explained in An : *Anum* as "Queen of Heaven." (Litke 1998: 160; Krebernik, *RlA* IX: 359)

Nin-gal-dudu (M) Sumerian deity attested in variant writings in two god lists as -du_{12}-du_{12} and in a personal name as -du-du from Šarrākum. See Nin-en-gal-DU.DU. (Richter 2004: 255)

Nin-gal-Enuna/Agruna (M) Form of the goddess Nin-gal attested in an Old Babylonian text from Ur. The signs é-nun-na are glossed in some lexical texts as the common noun agrun "inner sanctum." So the divine name here might be read Nin-gal-agruna. (Renger 1967: 159)

Nin-gal-ḫun (M) Bull-lyre of Baba. May mean "Who Calms the Great Lady," referring to the harp's soothing music. (Litke 1998: 178)

Nin-gal-tur (M) Early Dynastic deity. Mander draws attention to gal-tùr (chief herdsman?) in the Early Dynastic professions list, thus perhaps "Lord/Lady, Chief Herdsman(?)" or "Great Lady/Lord of the Cattle Pen." (Mander 1986: 62)

Nin-ganam (M) Goddess in an Assyrian god list. Means "Lady Ewe." (Cavigneaux and Krebernik, *RlA* IX: 360)

Nin-ganuna (M) Deity in an Old Babylonian god list from Mari. Written Nin-gá-nun-na. Means "Lord/Lady of the Storehouse." (Studies Birot, 184–85: r iii 15)

Nin-gara (M) Deity in an Old Babylonian god list from Mari. Written Nin-gá-ra. See Nin-ma-ra.

Nin-garaš (M) (1) In An : *Anum* Tablet I, with En-garaš, listed among the father-mother pairs of ancestors of Enlil. (2) In An : *Anum* Tablet III listed as the wife of Nin-Gublaga with gloss ni-ga-ra. In a Sumerian incantation of the Old Babylonian period, Nin-garaš appears as a child of the abzu. In a late building ritual Nin-garaš appears with Ea's vizier Ara. Krebernik asserts that the Nin-garaš associated with Enki should be kept distinct from the Nin-garaš who appears in An : *Anum*. garaš means "leek" but it is unclear whether that interpretation is appropriate here. See the similar sounding pair of Enlil's ancestors En-giriš and Nin-giriš. (Richter 2004: 451; Litke 1998: 32, 121; Krebernik, *RlA* IX: 360)

NIN-ga-uga (M) See Egi/Ereš-e-uga

Nin-ge (M) Deity attested in a Fara god list. Written Nin-gi: gi_6. (Mander 1986: 81)

Nin-ge(MI)-dam (M) See Nin-dam-gi

Nin-ge-kuga (M) Deity whose name means "Lady of the Pure Reed." (1) Identified with Dam-gal-nuna/Damkina, wife of Enki/Ea. Mother of Nin-gal. (2) A title of Nin-gal. (Litke 1998: 88, 120; Jacobsen 1976: 124; Tallqvist 1974: 404; Cavigneaux and Krebernik, *RlA* IX: 361)

Nin-ge-la(l) (M) First of five deities of fishermen in Tablet II of An : *Anum*. Means "Lady/Lord who Carries Reeds," a task recorded as being performed by workmen in Ur III texts. In Tablet VI of An : *Anum*, the preceding entry is Nin-numun-lá, "Lady/Lord who Carries Seed." (Litke 1998: 113, 220; Cavigneaux and Krebernik, *RlA* IX: 450)

Nin-ge-MI-sar-ra (M) Deity attested in a great offering list from Ur dated to the reign of Ibbi-Sîn. An offering to Nin-ge-MI-sar-ra appears immediately after a mention of a deified statue of Ibbi-Sîn. (Richter 2004: 415; Hall 1985: 327)

Nin-gena (M) Deity identified with Utu/Šamaš attested in an Old Babylonian god list. Means "Steadfast Lord." (Richter 2004: 352)

Nin-gepara (M) Title usually of Inana/Ištar. Means "Lady of the Gipar," the residence of the high priest(ess) in a temple complex. (Black and Green 2003: 91, 93; Cavigneaux and Krebernik, *RlA* IX: 362)

Nin-gešge (M) Sumerian deity attested in an Early Dynastic god list from Abu Ṣalābīkh. Means "Lady of the Reed Thicket." An unknown town Geš-ge is attested at the end of the Early Dynastic Sumerian zà-mí hymns, and this deity might be associated with that town, although, in the Sumerian zà-mí hymns, the link is with the goddess Lisina. (Mander 1986: 112)

Nin-gešḫur-ana (M) Name of the rainbow goddess Manzi'at. Means "Lady, Design of Heaven." (Litke 1998: 167; Cavigneaux and Krebernik, *RlA* IX: 367)

Nin-geš-šaga (M) Deity attested as having a temple and a *gudu*-priest at Ur III Umma. (MVN 1, 34: r 7)

Nin-geš-tete (M) Deity allocated an offering in an Ur III text from Puzriš-Dagan. te-te is "to denigrate, to squeeze." (Studies Levine, 132–38: r ii 23)

Nin-Geštin-ana (M) See Geštin-ana

(Nin-)geš-zida (M) Chief administrator of the netherworld. Associated with the growth and death of vegetation. Concerned with alcoholic beverages, wine and beer. Son of the netherworld god Nin-azu and his wife Nin-Girida. He had two sisters. His wife at Lagaš was Geštin-ana. Elsewhere his wife was (Nin-)azi-mua. In "Enki and Nin-ḫursag" Nin-ḫursag declares that Azi-mua is to marry Ningešzida. Ekur-rītu(m) was yet another spouse. His vizier was Alla.

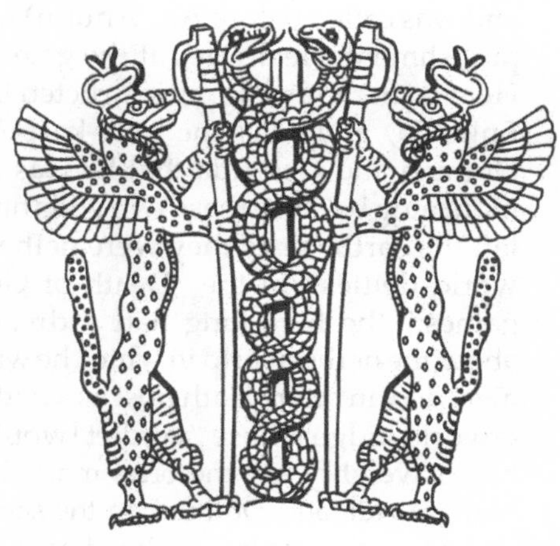

Detail from libation vessel found at Girsu, Mesopotamia. Symbol of Nin-geš-zida. Dated to the time of Gudea, twenty-second century BCE. Steatite (soapstone). Height 23 cm. Louvre Museum. After Orthmann 1975: #119

Like Dumuzi, Nin-geš-zida was a disappearing deity, for whom his sisters mourned during his absence in the netherworld. His most usual epithet was "Chamberlain (literally "chair-bearer") of the netherworld." Another was "Counselor of the Big City," a euphemism for the netherworld. His emblem was the *pāštu(m)*, the scimitar, and his symbolic creatures were the snake-dragon mušḫuššu and the horned viper *bašmu*. In iconography the god was most often depicted with a horned snake protruding from each shoulder. Another of his symbols was a tree with two snakes entwined around it, the prototype of the *caduceus*, now symbol of the medical profession.

Nin-geš-zida had a comparatively small role in Mesopotamian myth and literature, mainly in netherworld contexts. In a composition preserved in both Sumerian and Akkadian, Adapa damages the wings of the south wind and was called before An/Anu(m) for punishment. He arrives at the gate of Heaven in mourning, as instructed by Enki/Ea, and tells the gate-keepers Dumuzi and Geš-zida that he was in mourning because these two gods had left the earth (since they were netherworld deities). In the "Death of Gilgameš," the hero-king had a dream about the netherworld in which he was awarded an after-death post as a netherworld judge whose "verdict [would be] as weighty as" the ones made by Nin-geš-zida and Dumuzi. In the same composition, just before he dies, Gilgameš makes offerings to both deities. Nin-geš-zida is often included in laments for Dumuzi, another disappearing deity, and in both Sumerian and Akkadian there are pieces concerning Nin-geš-zida's journey to the netherworld.

A Sumerian temple hymn described the god's netherworld abode in his cult town near Ur, Geš-banda, perhaps an underground shrine in his temple there, as "a dark cellar, (an) awe-inspiring place" (Leick 1998: 131). In the Babylonian "Epic of Gilgameš," Nin-sun, the hero's mother, prays to the sun god Šamaš to protect Gilgameš on his dangerous journey to confront the guardian of the Cedar Forest, Ḫumbaba. She hopes that, should he die, he will join Nin-geš-zida in the netherworld. Nin-geš-zida was the personal deity of Gudea, the governor of Lagaš, who built a temple for him.

He was widely worshipped and had temples or shrines at Nippur, Uruk, Girsu, possibly Ešnunna, Larsa, Šuruppak, Umma, Ku'ara, Isin, Lagaš, Babylon, and Ur, where his temple was named "House of Truth (or Justice)." At Ur III Girsu, a ritual lament and procession through a silent city marked the god's departure from earth. Nin-geš-zida figured in laments for dead royalty, and later "the all-souls month Abu" was assigned to him (Wiggermann, *RlA* IX: 371). Nin-geš-zida was also an important participant in the Festival of Baba at Lagaš. Typically Nin-geš-zida was worshipped during festivals concerning the netherworld and the dead. Astrally he was associated with the constellation Hydra. (Cohen 2015: 62, 65, 68, 138; Frayne 2009: 59; Foster 2005: 525–30; Katz 2003: 391–95; Black and Green 2003: 86, 138–40, 180; Foster 2001: 25; Frayne 2001: 153; Leick 1999: 62; Leick 1998: 131; Litke 1998: 192, 214; George 1993: 37, 71 no. 102, 95 no. 408, 97 no. 434, 168 no. 1378–80; Tallqvist 1974: 406; Speiser, *ANET*: 101–3; Wiggermann, *RlA* IX: 368–73)

Nin-geštida-E-Geštin-ana (M) Form of Nin-geš-zida who is associated with the "Wine House," apparently a drinking establishment for the royal family at Nippur. (Sallaberger 1993: I, 125–27)

Nin-geštida-ša-Nišbanda (M) Local form of Nin-geš-zida at Gešbanda/Nišbanda. (Frayne 2009: 59; Sallaberger 1993: I, 189 and note 896)

Nin-GIR (M) (1) Goddess attested in god lists of the Early Dynastic period. The name appears in the archaic Sumerian zà-mí hymns in connection with the city of Zabala(m) written Nin-gir$_x$(UM). She may have been a deity from that city. (Mander 1986: 40, 122, 126; Biggs 1974: 47); (2) Deity in an Old Babylonian god list from Mari. Written Nin-GIR$_2$. (Studies Birot, 184–85 r iii 23)

Nin-Girgilu(m) (M) Deity identified with Inana. Means "Lady of Girgilu(m)," a town near Nippur. *Girgilu(m)* was also a type of bird. In a hymn she is call Unga-ibi-mal, "'Wise One of the People,' mother of the right breast," (Litke 1998: 150; Cohen 1993: 63; Tallqvist 1974: 404; Cavigneaux and Krebernik, *RlA* IX: 362)

Nin-Girida, Girida, Nin-giri$_{17}$-ù-tu (M) Likely originally tutelary deity of Girid, a small settlement on the Euphrates just northwest of Ur. A phonetic reading occurs in a personal name in two Ur III tablets. Spouse of Nin-azu. In "Enki and Nin-ḫursag" Nin-ḫursag decrees that her daughter, Nin-giri$_{17}$-ù-tu, a variant(?) for Nin-girida, is to marry Nin-azu. Also an aspect of Gula. In "Nanna/Su'en's Journey to Nippur," the goddess welcomes Nanna's boat to one of Nin-azu's cult centers, Enegir, on the Euphrates between Ur and Uruk, and some temples of Nin-Girida are attested. (Frayne 2009: 56; Richter 2004: 491; *LAS*: 150–51; Litke 1998: 189, 191; George 1993: 36, 167; Tallqvist 1974: 406; Krebernik, *RlA* IX: 162, 362–63)

Nin-girima (M) God of magic, especially efficacious in dealing with snakes. Associated with water and the censer. In incantations from Fara, Ningirima seems to be junior god to Enlil, just as Asar-lu-ḫe is to Enki in other incantations. In one incantation Ningirim is said to release stomach-ache, which was bound to the sun, when it reaches the netherworld. In instructions for the high priest concerning the ritual program for *akītu* festivals at Babylon, Nin-girima was mentioned as casting the spell to rid the temple of evil. Nin-girima's cult center north of Nippur was Muru(m), which was later Nin-kilim's cult center. Sometimes confused or identified with Nin-kilim (Nin-gilim), "Lady Mongoose." (George 2016: no. 1h; Lambert 2013: 427–36; Black and Green 2003: 132; Litke 1998: 63; Cohen 1993: 446; Tallqvist 1974: 397–98; Sachs, *ANET*: 333–34; Krebernik, *RlA* IX: 363–67) (2) A title of Enki/Ea as gardener god. Means "Lord of Fruit." (Litke 1998: 238; Cavigneaux and Krebernik, *RlA* IX: 367)

Nin-giriš (M) Goddess in the circle of Enki. Her spouse was En-giriš. Together they were primeval ancestors of Enlil. Means "Madam Butterfly." Note the similar sounding pair of Enlil's ancestors En-garaš and Nin-garaš. (Volk, *RlA* IX: 367)

Nin-giri-ù-tu (M) See Nin-Girida

Nin-Girsu (M) Sumerian god, the most prominent in the pantheon of the Lagaš area. Tutelary deity of the cities of Lagaš and Girsu. Attested in texts of the Early Dynastic period. Means "Lord of (the City of) Girsu." A warrior god and also concerned with the fertility of nature and the fields and with irrigation, particularly the control of canals, several of which bore his name. Son of Enlil or of An/Anu(m) and the goddess Gatum-dug or sometimes one of the mother goddesses, especially Nin-ḫursag. Brother of the goddesses Nanše and Nisaba. Husband of Baba. His sons were Ig-alima and Šul-šaga. On boundary stones of the Kassite period, a plow was his symbol. He was sometimes associated with the lion.

Tales about Nin-Girsu concentrated on his role as a warrior. In the earlier versions of the Anzû(m) story, Nin-Girsu, not the warrior god Ninurta, pursued and presumably subdued Anzû(m) when the latter stole the tablets of destiny from Enki (Sumerian version) or Enlil (Akkadian version). The Anzû(m) bird then became Nin-Girsu's emblem. There was a group of hero/monsters killed by the god Nin-Girsu. In the Lagaš area at the time of Gudea, these minor deities received offerings in the Nin-Girsu temple. Gudea composed a hymn addressed to Nin-Girsu concerning Gudea's rebuilding of Nin-Girsu's temple at Girsu, the E-ninnu "House Fifty," fifty being Ningirsu's number. In a hymn Gudea recounts how Nin-Girsu as the Anzû(m)-bird came to him in a dream and told him to undertake the work. Nin-Girsu's temple at Lagaš was also rebuilt by Gudea. Though mainly a Lagaš-area deity with a shrine at Dug-ru, near Lagaš, and a temple in the sacred precinct Sirara at Nimen, Nin-Girsu also had a chapel at Ur. One of the major yearly festivals of the Lagaš area was a "Barley and Malt Consumption festival" held in honor of Nin-Girsu, involving a pilgrimage to Girsu. (Cohen 2015: 33). (Foster 2005: 555–78; Black and Green 2003: 40, 43, 123, 138, 149; Leick 1999: 62; Leick 1998: 130–31; Litke 1998: 102, 174; Cohen 1993: 47, 179; George 1993: 69 no. 96, 97 no. 430, 134 no. 894, no. 897; Tallqvist 1974: 404–5; Speiser, *ANET*: 111–13; Streck, *RlA* IX: 512–22; Braun-Holzinger, *RlA* IX: 522–24)

Nin-gir-zida (M) Deity in the circle of Gula. Means "Lady of the Trusty Knife." (Cavigneaux and Krebernik, *RlA* IX: 367)

Nin-giškim-zi (M) Deity allocated offerings at Ur III Šarrākum and occurs as a personal name at Umma. Means "Lady/Lord (of) the True Omen." (courtesy D. I. Owen)

Nin-gu-bara (M) Goddess identified with Inana/Ištar. gú-bar can mean "nape," "enemy," and even "outer edge." See Gú-bar-ra, a name of Ašratu(m), wife of Mardu/Amurru(m). (Litke 1998: 151; Selz 1995: 268 note 1306; Cavigneaux and Krebernik, *RlA* IX: 373–74)

Nin-GUbi-duga (M) Wife of Lumḫa, god of singers and singing. Her name means "Lady, that Voice Is Good." See the possibly homonymous name Nin-INIM-duga. (Litke 1998: 104; Tallqvist 1974: 406; Krebernik, *RlA* IX: 374)

Nin-Gublaga (M) Sumerian god of cattle. Means "Lord of Gublag," possibly a writing for Ki'abrig. Jacobsen calls him "the bull god" (1976: 25). Son of the moon god and his wife Nin-gal. Brother of Alammuš, vizier of Nanna/Sîn. Spouse of Nin-E-i-gara, a dairy goddess. In "Lament for Sumer and Ur," Nin-Gublaga is forced to abandon his devastated city. The god was invoked in magic. One of his epithets, "Lord who Beats Off Evil," speaks to his apotropaic function. At Ki'abrig, his cult center, his temple there, and also at Ur, was called E-ga-bura "Chamber of Jars." Another of his shrines was called "House of the Potter." At Ur, Nin-Gublaga had a high priestess who would have lived in the Gipar. The office was at one time filled by En-nin-sun-zi(d), a daughter of King Lipit-Ištar of Isin, who rebuilt the Gipar for her. Nin-Gublaga was worshipped also at Nippur and Larsa.

(*LAS*: 133; Leick 1999: 97; Litke 1998: 120 no. 30 and note 31; Cohen 2015: 72; George 1993: 28, 93 no. 379; Kramer, *ANET*: 615; Cavigneaux and Krebernik, *RlA* IX: 374–76)

Nin-gu-edina (M) Goddess associated with Inana/Ištar. In one text spouse of Mardu. Means "Lady of the Edge of the Steppe." See Nin-gu-bara. (Cavigneaux and Krebernik, *RlA* IX: 376)

Nin-gu'ena (M) (1) Deity identified with Dingir/Nin-maḫ. (2) Deity in the circle of Baba in the E-ninnu at Lagaš. Whether (1) and (2) refer to the same deity is unclear. Means "Lady of the Assembly," perhaps, at least in (1), referring to Nin-maḫ's high position in the council of the first-rank gods, as reflected in literature. (Litke 1998: 67, 175; Tallqvist 1974: 406; Krebernik, *RlA* VIII: 505)

Nin-gu-esiraka (M) Wife of Mes-sanga-Unuga. See Nin-gú-pa$_4$-sír-ka at Nippur. (Litke 1998: 170; Tallqvist 1974: 406; Cavigneaux and Krebernik, *RlA* IX: 376)

Nin-(gu-)ḫarana (M) Netherworld god. Law enforcer associated with the goddess Manun-gal/Nungal. One of his titles was "Lord of the Pole '(or Mast)," perhaps a whipping post. Might have been identified with Pabil-sag. Means "Lord of the (Side of the) Road." (Litke 1998: 186; Tallqvist 1974: 407; Cavigneaux and Krebernik, *RlA* IX: 376)

Nin-gukkal (M) See En-gukkal

Nin-gula (M) Deity identified with Inana/Ištar. Appears also in the "Lamentation Over the Destruction of Ur," where she is identified as being from Nimen. Means "Greatest Lady." (Litke 1998: 151; Tall-qvist 1974: 406; Kramer, *ANET*: 456; Cavigneaux and Krebernik, *RlA* IX: 376)

Nin-gumada (M) Sumerian Deity of the Ur III period at Girsu(?), written Nin-gu$_2^?$-ma-da. Perhaps "Lady, Tribute of the Land." (PSMFA 698: r 3).

Nin-gumur-ana (M) Deity listed in An : *Anum* identified with or in the circle of Gula; elsewhere in An : *Anum* with Pabilsag or as a demon. Written with variant Níg- for Nin-. Although gú-mur means "throat," in astronomical texts its Akkadian equivalent *ur'udu* also denotes an astral path. If this holds true for the Sumerian term, then the name might mean "Lady, the Astral Path of Heaven." (Richter 2004: 223; Litke 1998: 179, 186)

Nin-gu-pasiraka (M) Deity attested in the Ur III period. Means "Lady of the bank of Pasir." Written pa$_4$-sír. Pa$_5$-sír^{ki} is a location in Lagaš/Girsu texts. (Cavigneaux and Krebernik, *RlA* IX: 377)

Nin-gur, Nin-gurgur (M) Sumerian deity attested in god lists of the Early Dynastic period. Means "Lady of the Silo(s)." (Mander 1986: 113, 130)

Nin-gu-sag (M) Deity attested in an Early Dynastic god list. Means "Lord, Foremost Ox." (Mander 1986: 145)

Nin-ḫadda(PA) (M) In an Old Babylonian god list, goddess listed in the circle of Nuska, who himself, in an Emesal list of gods, is identified with En-gidri (Emesal: umun-muduru). The deity occurs also in the Fara period, where she seems to be related to the palace cult (Nin-ḫadda: é-gal). The reading ḫad-da is based upon the variant Nin-PA-da, which occurs in several Ur III texts in the personal name Ur-^{d}Nin-PA(-da). ḫad-da appears to be a Sumerian loanword from Akkadian *ḫaṭṭum* "scepter." Means "Lady (of) the Scepter." See Nin-ḫadda-unken-na. (Richter 2004: 84; Litke 1998: 187; Selz 1992: 191; Mander 1986: 115; Tallqvist 1974: 416; Cavigneaux and Krebernik, *RlA* IX: 480)

Nin-ḫadda(PA)-unken-gala (M) Deity attested in a tablet and in a god list from Early Dynastic Šuruppak. Means "Lady of the Scepter of the Great Assembly." The may be a longer form of the divine name Nin-ḫadda. For the reading -ḫadda see Nin-ḫadda. (Martin et al. 2001: 111 and no. 105; Selz 1992: 191)

Nin-ḫal (M) See En-ḫal

Nin-ḫalama (M) Deity whose name means "Lady/Lord of Destruction." (Litke 1998: 215)

Nin-ḫalib (M) See Egi/Ereš-ḫalib

Nin-ḫaš-ti (M) Sumerian deity attested in a god list from Early Dynastic Šuruppak. May mean "Lady/Lord who Heals the Broken." (Mander 1986: 110)

Nin-ḫedu(-bi) (M) Gate-keeper of An. One of the five daughters of Nin-šubur. Means "The Lady Is (its) Ornament." (Litke 1998: 27–28; Cavigneaux, *RlA* IX: 360, 378)

Nin-ḫenuna (M) Deity whose name means "Lady/Lord of Abundance." (1) One of eighteen messengers of Inana. (2) One of two deified bull-lyres of Gula. (Richter 2004: 212; Litke 1998: 160, 185; Cavigneaux and Krebernik, *RlA* IX: 378)

Nin-ḫili-su (M) Sumerian deity attested on a tablet referring to towns in the environs of Ur III Umma. Means "Lady/Lord who Exudes Sex Appeal." (Cohen 1996a: 34)

Nin-ḫuluḫa (M) Deity attested in a school text from Susa. Means "Lord/Lady who causes trembling." (Cavigneaux and Krebernik, *RlA* IX: 377)

Nin-ḫursag (M) Mother, birth, and earth deity. Equated to Dingir-maḫ, Nin-maḫ, Nin-tu(d), Aruru, Bēlet-ilī and other mother goddesses. On a par with An/Anu(m), Enlil, and Enki/Ea as one of the most powerful deities in the pantheon. Mentioned in god lists in the Early Dynastic period. The composition Lugal-e, concerning the deeds of Ninurta, explains how Ninurta's mother, the goddess Ninlil, received the name Nin-ḫursag when Ninurta gave her a mountainous area he had conquered, the ḫursag. Among her epithets were ""Mother of the Gods" and "Mother of All Children."

As deity of mountainous regions, she had a special interest in wild animals. She was also "mother" to domesticated herds. Along with An, Enlil, and Enki/Ea, Nin-ḫursag was responsible for decreeing the fates, for instance, of cities, as in the "Lamentation over the Destruction of Sumer and Ur." In texts, such as the Sumerian Deluge story, she was credited, along with An, Enlil, and Enki, with the creation of human beings. As mother of Ninurta she was spouse of Enlil and had eight children by him. Also mother of Lil. Another tradition saw her as the sister of Enlil and spouse of Šul-pa'e, god of wild beasts. Their offspring were Ašgi, Lisina, and Lil. Several kings claimed to have been suckled by the goddess, for instance, E-anatum in his famous Stele of the Vultures. Many kings styled themselves her "beloved."

The symbol often associated with mother goddesses such as Nin-ḫursag was in the shape of the Greek letter omega (Ω) and probably stood for the womb. The "cow-and-calf" motif, common in the Eastern Mediterranean area, might also refer to Nin-ḫursag, as well as to other birth/mother goddesses. A carving with this motif was part of a group of ivories found at Nimrūd. (Mallowan 1978: 56 figure 65)

The composition "Enki and Nin-ḫursag" demonstrates that Nin-ḫursag had life-and-death power even over great deities. Nin-ḫursag saw her daughter, granddaughter, and great-granddaughter all become pregnant by Enki, the father of her daughter. Nin-ḫursag, as retribution, causes Enki to become deathly ill. Eventually Nin-ḫursag relents and gives birth to eight deities to cure Enki's eight afflicted body parts. At the end of "The Death of Gilgameš," the hero presented offerings to Nin-ḫursag, whom the composition coupled with the god Šakkan/Sumuqan, the deity of wild animals.

Nin-ḫursag had shrines and temples or received offerings at Lagaš, Girsu, Umma, Ur, Mari, Adab, and Susa. Šarrākum, whose sacred precinct was Keš, was the cult center of the goddess from the Early Dynastic period to Old Babylonian times. There her temple was called E-Keš "House of Keš." She also had a cult center at Adab, where she was revered in the E-maḫ "Lofty House." Her temples at Girsu and Babylon carried the same name. The site of Tell al-'Ubaid near Ur was also a cult center of the goddess, where she had a famous "temple oval." Many kings declared that they had built temples and shrines for Nin-ḫursag. A tablet from Mari lists Nin-ḫursag among deities receiving oil for ablutions. See drawing under Bēlet-ilī. (Cohen 2015: 76; Black and Green 2003: 53, 133, 140; Frayne 2001: 153; Leick 1999: 50; Leick 1998: 132; Litke 1998: 66; George 1993: 97 no. 430, 108 no. 578, 119 no. 713 no. 716, 168 no. 1381–86; Frankfort 1978: 301; Jacobsen 1976: 104–10, 112, 131; Tallqvist 1974: 407–8; Kramer, *ANET*: 36–41, 43, 613; Krebernik, *RlA* VII: 505; Heimpel, *RlA* IX: 378–81; Braun-Holzinger, *RlA* IX: 381–82)

Nin-ḫursag-A'ebara (M) The local form of Nin-ḫursag at A'ebara in the region of Umma. (Cohen 1996a: 33)

Nin-ḫursag-Aratta (M) The local form of Nin-ḫursag at a town apparently situated near Umma or the name could mean "Great Ninḫursag." This is not a reference to Aratta in Iran. (Cohen 1996a: 33)

Nin-ḫursag-Aša-anše (M) The local form of Nin-ḫursag at the place Aša-anše "Field of the Donkey." (Cohen 1996a: 33)

Nin-ḫursag-Aša-banda-ana (M) The local form of Nin-ḫursag at the ancient town of Aša-banda-ana in the environs of Umma. (Cohen 1996a: 33)

Nin-ḫursag-Aša-GIR (M) The local form of Nin-ḫursag at the ancient town of Aša-GIR in the Umma district. (Cohen 1996a: 33)

Nin-ḫursag-A'u'da (M) The local form of Nin-ḫursag at the ancient town of A'u'da in the environs of Umma. (Cohen 1996a: 33)

Nin-ḫursag-Du-kar-saga (M) The local form of Nin-ḫursag at the ancient town of Du-kar-saga in the environs of Umma. (Cohen 1996a: 33)

Nin-ḫursag-GAR-zida (M) The local form of Nin-ḫursag at the ancient town of GAR-zida in the environs of Umma. (Cohen 1996a: 33)

Nin-ḫursag-ib-sig(?) (M) Goddess attested at Ur III Umma. (ASJ 18, 86 22: o 4)

Nin-ḫursag-kalama (M) Deity identified with Inana/Ištar. (Litke 1998: 151; George 1993: 101 no. 482; Cavigneaux and Krebernik, *RlA* IX: 382)

Nin-ḫursag-Kamari (M) Local form of Nin-ḫursag at the ancient town of Kamari in the environs of Umma. (Cohen 1996a: 33).

Nin-ḫursag-Kubibi (M) Local form of Nin-ḫursag at the ancient town of Kubibi in the environs of Umma. (Cohen 1996a: 33)

Nin-ḫursag-Maškan (M) Local form of Nin-ḫursag at the town of Maškan in the environs of Umma. (Cohen 1996a: 33)

Nin-ḫursag-Nubanda (M) Local form of Nin-ḫursag at the town of Nubanda, in addition to a temple dating to Ur III times, a temple to Nin-ḫursag dating to Early Dynastic times was unearthed. (Sallaberger 1993: I, 59 and note 246, 189 and note 896)

Nin-ḫursag of Susa (E) See Narundi/e

Nin-ḫursag-ša-E-ganu (M) Form of Nin-ḫursag who received regular offerings in her temple "The Ostrich House" (šà é-ga-nu$_{11}$^{mušen}) probably in Ur during the Ur III period. (Sallaberger 1993: I, 59 and note 246, 159)

Nin-ḫursag-Ur-Mami-ša-A'ebara (M) Local form of Nin-ḫursag at A'ebara. (Cohen 1996a: 33)

Nin-ḫursag-zalaga-ša-A'ebara (M) Local form of Nin-ḫursag at A'ebara. Nin-ḫursag-zalaga means "Shining Nin-ḫursag." (Cohen 1996a: 33)

Nin-Ib-gal (M) Deity identified with Inana/Ištar at Umma and elsewhere. Means "Lady of the Ib-gal," her sanctuary at Umma, which may mean "The Great Oval." It was also called E-Ib-gal at both Lagaš proper and Šarrā-kum in its sacred precinct Keš. At Umma the Festival of the Early Grass was celebrated with Nin-Ib-gal and two other goddesses. (Litke 1998: 151; Cohen 1993: 144, 163; George 1993: 103 no. 504–6, no. 1387; Cavigneaux and Krebernik, *RlA* IX: 382)

Nin-igara (M) See Nin-E-i-gara(k)

Nin-igi-abzu (M) Deity identified with Dam-gal-nuna/Damkina, spouse of Enki/Ea. Means "Lady, Eye (or 'One in front') of the Abzu." Also written Nin-[ii]igi-abzu. (Litke 1998: 88; Cohen 1993: 144, 163; Tallqvist: 1974: 408; Cavigneaux and Krebernik, *RlA* IX: 382)

NIN-igi-gunu (M) See Egi/Ereš-igi-gunu

Nin-igi-kug (M) See Niššīku(m)

Nin-igizi-bara, Gašan-ibizi-bara (Emesal) (M) One of two bull-lyres in the service of Inana/Ištar in the name of the twenty-first year of King Ibbi-Sîn. The deified harp in one temple was "plated with 4 pounds of silver and 5 shekels of gold" (Heimpel, *RlA* IX: 382). She was worshipped at Umma, Uruk, Larsa, Isin, and Mari. Also a title of the healing goddess Gula. Means "Lady Looked upon Favorably" or "Chosen Lady." (Litke 1998: 153; Tall-qvist 1974: 408; Heimpel, *RlA* IX: 382–84)

Nin-ildu (M) See Nin-duluma

Nin-imin (M) Wife of Nin-a-gal, the smith god. Means "Lady (of the) Seven" or "Lady of Everything." (Litke 1998: 108; Krebernik, *RlA* IX: 384)

Nin-im-ma (M) It is unclear whether this name, written -im-ma and attested once at Ur III Umma, is a variant for Nin-imma(SIG$_7$) or indicates a separate deity. (Sallaberger 1993: 104; Sigrist 1983: 312)

Nin-imma (M) Enlil's private secretary, the "scholar at Enlil's court" (George 1993: 79). Associated with Nisaba, the scribe of the gods. Also a birth goddess and wet-nurse of Nanna/Sîn. According to Jacobsen, she was "a deification of the female sexual organs" (1976: 113). Mentioned as early as the Early Dynastic period. Daughter of Enlil and sister of Ninurta. Another tradition described her as daughter of Enki and Nin-kura. Her spouse was Kusig-banda. Her main temple was at Nippur, and she had temples or shrines at Ur, Uruk, and Aššur. There is a goddess Nin-ím-ma (Sigrist 1983: no. 312), but whether this is a separate deity or a variant for Nin-imma(SIG_7) is unclear. Note the names Nin-SIG_7-SIG_7 and Nin-SIG_7-gi_4, which might be forms or variants of Nin-imma. A reading Nin-imma_3 for Nin-sig_7 and Nin-imma_x for Nin-sig_7-sig_7 has been proposed. (See Richter 2004: 94–95). (Cohen 2015: 224; Lambert 2013: 427–36; Litke 1998: 56; George 1993: 24, 79 no. 202, 105 no. 525, 123 no. 758, 131 no. 857; Focke, *RlA* IX: 384–86)

Nin-IN (M) See Nin-Isina

Nin-indagar (M) Spouse of the grain goddess Kusu attested in An : *Anum*. The deity may have been associated with cattle and was equated to the god Iškur in some god lists. (Schwemer 2001: 17; Litke 1998: 59; Steinkeller 1989: 228)

Nin-in-dub (M) Sumerian goddess, a form of Nin-kar(r)ak in An : *Anum*. Means "Boundary Lady." (Richter 2004: 215: Litke 1998: 180)

Nin-inim-duga (M) Deity whose name means "Lady/Lord of the Spoken Word." See Nin-GUbi-duga. (Richter 2004: 205)

Nin-inim-gena (M) Deity in an Old Babylonian god list from Mari. Means "Lord/Lady whose Word is Reliable." (Studies Birot, 184–85: r iv 2)

Nin-in-na (M) Deity in a Sargonic text from Nippur by whom an oath was sworn. (Richter 2004: 415)

Nin-intina, Nin-intena (M) Deity identified with Inana of Inana/Ištar. An : *Anum* explains in-te-na as *qurdi*, "heroism." (Litke 1998: 150; Krebernik, *RlA* IX: 386)

Nin-Irigala, Nin-eš-gala (M) Name applied to several goddesses, including Inana/Ištar at Uruk, the healing goddess Gula, and the spouse of the fire god Gibil. Attested in god lists and other material from the Early Dynastic period. Means "Lady of the Irigal (perhaps "Great Shrine"). In the Hellenistic period there was an important Irigal temple in the Kul(l)aba district in the southern part of Uruk. In the Hellenistic *akītu* ritual of Uruk, Nin-Irigal appears with the Gula, Me-me, and Baba. (Litke 1998: 108; George 1993: 83–84 no. 270; Krebernik, *RlA* IX: 386–87)

Nin-Isina (M) Name of the city goddess of Isin, "Lady of Isin" a goddess of healing. Mentioned in god lists and other material from the Early Dynastic period. As "Great Doctor of the Black-Headed(=the Sumerians)," Nin-Isina was all but identical to Gula, with whom she was identified at Larsa and other places. She was also identified with Nin-kar(r)ak. At a later time, she also took over some of Inana/Ištar's warlike traits; she proclaims: "I, woman and hero, I, the mighty warrior, I go against a ['rebellious country']" (Quoted by Jacobsen 1977: 193). She was daughter of the goddess Uraš, commonly understood in ancient times as meaning

"Earth." In some traditions, Uraš was the spouse of the head of the pantheon, the sky god An/Anu(m). Nin-Isina's consort was Pabil-sag, son of Enlil. Their son was the healing god Damu, and their daughters Gunura and Šu-maḫ, messenger of the E-gal-maḫ temple. As with the other healing goddesses, Nin-Isina's sacred animal was the dog.

When in "Enki and the World Order" Inana complains to Enki that she has not been assigned a function, she points out that "[her] illustrious sister" Nin-Isina has been given important jewelry and a function as "An's mistress": "... to stand beside An" and address him when she wants to (*LAS*: 224). Nin-Isina appears as a mourner in Sumerian laments. According to one lament, "She who is of Isin" abandoned her city and "her shrine E-galmah [sic]" (Kramer, *ANET*: 455). In a letter-prayer, Sîn-iddinam, king of Larsa, addresses Nin-Isina as: "Great healer whose incantation is life (health), whose spells restore the sick man, /Mother of the nation, merciful one ..." (Hallo 1976: 215, 217).

Nin-Isina's city Isin was an important pilgrimage destination for the sick, maimed, and dying. The temple also provided midwives. The temple, the E-gal-maḫ "Exalted Palace," and its precinct must have been extremely busy and crowded: patients asking for healing, priests doing rituals and incantations, and dogs barking. Nin-Isina's precinct also housed a sanctuary called "Dog-House," probably a "sacred dog kennel" (George 1993: 156 no. 1182). There the goddess's canine alter ego would have enjoyed a luxurious life, until, perhaps, it became a sacrifice. During excavations about 33 dog burials were unearthed, a discovery that constituted "the first time a ritual burial of animals in a cultic area had been discovered in the Sumerian heartland" (Fuhr 1977: 136). They were probably the remains of votive and ritual sacrifices. Nin-Isina was worshipped throughout Mesopotamia and had temples, usually called E-gal-maḫ, or shrines in most major cities, including Nippur, Ur, Uruk, Lagaš, Girsu, Larsa, Babylon, and Aššur. (Cohen 2015: 62; Black and Green 2003: 140, 182; Leick 1998: 132, 133; Litke 1998: 179; George 1993: 88 no. 318–23,152 no. 1123; Edzard, *RlA* IX: 387–88)

Nin-itta, Nin-(n)at(t)a (H, L) See Nin-atta

Nin-izi-mua (M) See Azi(da)-mua

Nin-kalam-zigala (M) Deity identified with Ḫaya, spouse of Nisaba. Means "Lord who Brings the Nation to Life." (Litke 1998: 54; Cavigneaux and Krebernik, *RlA* IX: 440)

Nin-KA-limmu/imin (M) See NITA-su-limmu

Nin-kalla (M) Deity allocated an offering at Puzriš-Dagan in the Ur III period. Means "The Lady Is Precious."

Nin-kar (M) Deity at third-millennium Ebla. Written Nin-kar. (Waetzoldt 2001)

Nin-kara (M) Goddess identified with Aya, the spouse of Šamaš. Means "Lady who Shines," fitting for the wife of the sun. Attested as early as the Sumerian zà-mí hymns and god lists of the Early Dynastic period. Written Nin-kára. (Litke 1998: 131; Cavigneaux and Krebernik, *RlA* IX: 440–41)

Nin-kar-du (M) See AŠGAB-kar-du

Nin-kar-gal (M) Deity attested in an Early Dynastic god list. (Mander 1986: 159)

Nin-KAR-la (M) Deity attested in a Sargonic personal name. (Milano and Westenholz 2015)

Nin-kar-nuna (M) Deity with a shrine at Nippur and identified in An : *Anum* as the brother of Iminani-zi(d) and the spouse of Kinda-zi, the hairdresser. Explained as the beautician of Ninurta. The name means "Lord of the Noble Quay," though the connection between a quay and the proposed duties of the bar-šu-gál is unclear. (Richter 2004: 75; Litke 1998: 48, 49; George 1993: 168 no. 1389; Tallqvist 1974: 409; Cavigneaux and Krebernik, *RlA* IX: 441)

Nin-kar(r)ak (M) Goddess of health, healing, and medicine. Identified with Baba, Gula, and Nin-Isina. Like other healing goddesses, Nin-kar(r)ak had the dog as a sacred animal and netherworld connections, as one of her titles showed: Nin-E-kisiga "Lady of the House of Offerings for the Dead." The goddess could cause disease, as well as cure it, as seen in the law code of Ḫammu-rāpi, which invokes Nin-kar(r)ak to inflict disease, a never-healing injury, upon those who would deface the stele or refuse to obey its laws.

Nin-kar(r)ak did not have a great presence in myth. However, the Babylonian story of Adapa mentions her near the end of the text: "... what ill he [Adapa] has brought upon mankind, / [And] the diseases that he brought upon the bodies of men, / These Nin-kar(r)ak will allay" (Speiser, *ANET*: 103). There were temples of Nin-kar(r)ak: in Babylon "The Pure Mountain," in Borsippa "House that Gives Life," and in Sippar "House of Rejoicing." Probably centers of healing, as well as sources of divinations and oracles, these temples would have been staffed by personnel trained in healing rituals, dream interpretation, and divination techniques. NIN-karrak was the Elamite form of the goddess borrowed from Babylonian, ultimately from Sumerian. Šilḫak-Inšušinak I invokes the healing goddess at the head of one of his inscriptions. She appears also in a treaty between Narām-Sîn of Akkad and a king of Susa. (Litke 1998: 180; George 1993: 102 no. 488, 150 no. 1095, 155 no. 1167; Hinz and Koch 1987: 1002; König 1977: 29, 119, 206, 227; Tallqvist 1974: 409–10)

Nin-KA-saḫar (M) Deity with a cella at Ur III Umma. (Cavigneaux and Krebernik, *RlA* IX: 441)

Nin-ka-si (M) Sumerian goddess of strong drink, Enlil's brewer, and, sometimes, wine-maker. Responsible for providing beverages, especially beer, for the temples of Nippur. Attested from the earliest periods on. Offspring of Enlil and Nin-ḫursag. In another tradition, child of Nin-ti and Enki. Often cited with her spouse (or brother) Siris or Siraš, a god of fermented beverage. She had nine children representing aspects of "strong drink." Another child was Nin-mada, snake-charmer of An/Anu(m) and Enlil. The name Nin-ka-si possibly means "Lady who Fills the Mouth (with Strong Drink)." It may be just serendipitous that the name seems so close to nin-kaš "Beer Lady." However, note Nin-kaš-si and Nin-kaš in two Ur III texts from Nippur and Umma respectively, which seem to be variants for Nin-ka-si.

"The Hymn to Nin-ka-si," a drinking song dating from the eighteenth century BCE, praises the goddess for producing in beer drinkers "a blissful mood" (Civil 2002a: 3). In the work "Enki and Nin-ḫursag," she was created by Nin-ḫursag to heal Enki's ailing mouth. At the end of the composition,

Nin-ḫursag decreed that the goddess would be "She who sates the desires." Attested sacred sites of Nin-ka-si include a "socle" at Ur and a temple at Nippur. She was worshipped also at Umma and Isin. The deity was sometimes presented as male. (*LAS*: 297–98; Civil 2002a: 2; Civil 2002b; Litke 1998: 61; George 1993: 24, 158 no. 1214, 168 no. 1391; Civil 1991; Katz and Fritz 1991; Tallqvist 1974: 409; Kramer, *ANET*: 40 and note 54, 41; Krebernik, *RlA* IX: 442–44)

Nin-kaskal (M) Goddess attested in an Early Dynastic god list. Means "Lady (of) the Highway." (Mander 1986: 145)

Nin-kaš(-si) (M) See Nin-ka-si

Nin-kašbar (M) Deity identified with Bēlet-ilī. Means "Lady Decision-Maker." Nin-ŠU.UD-aš-bar-re two entries later is probably based upon a miscopying at some point in the transmission. In one lexical text she is the chief herald of a deity whose name is not preserved. (Litke 1998: 67; Krebernik, *RlA* VIII: 506).

Nin-kašbar-an-ki (M) Deity identified with Sadar-nuna, the spouse of Nuska. Means "Lady Decision-Maker of Heaven and Earth." (Litke 1998: 51; Krebernik, *RlA* VIII: 505; Cavigneaux and Krebernik, *RlA* IX: 439)

Nin-KAteš-sisike (M) See Tašmētu(m)

Nin-kešed (M) Deity known from Ur III tablets that associate the deity with the city of Uruk. (Richter 2004: 282)

Nin-ki (M) See Enki (2)

Nin-kiag-nuna (M) Deity identified with Sadar-nuna, spouse of Nuska. Means "Lady Beloved of the Prince." (Litke 1998: 51; Cavigneaux and Krebernik, *RlA* IX: 447)

Nin-kida, Nin-gida, Nin-nigkida (M) Deity identified with Nin-kilim in An : *Anum* and cited directly after Nin-kilim in an Early Dynastic god list. At Šuruppak the form Nin-ki-da is attested. In An : *Anum* the name is written: Nin-[gada]ki-dà and Nin-níg-ki-dà, suggesting the ki-dà might be a rendering for "linen" (gada/*kitû*), thus the "Linen Lady." (Lafont 1997: no. 57; Mander 1986: 94–95 note 28; Litke 1998: 171; Cavigneaux and Krebernik, *RlA* IX: 447)

Nin-kiengiše (M) Deity attested in a Fara god list. (Mander 1986: 145)

Nin-ki-gar (M) Goddess attested in an Early Dynastic god list. (Mander 1986: 145)

Nin-ki-LAGAB×TIL (M) Deity after whom the tenth month was named in third-millennium BCE Mari and who appears in an early Mari god list. (See Cohen 2015: 324)

Nin-kilim/gilim (M) Sumerian deity, usually a goddess, but sometimes male. Associated with the mongoose or palm-rat, whose Sumerian name was synonymous with hers. Kramer says that the deity was "in charge of field mice and vermin" (1981: 364). One of Nin-kilim's cult centers was a city on the Tigris River near Baghdad Diniktum and another in the greater environs of Nippur Muru(m), where Nin-kilim was male and his wife was Nin-Muru(m), "Lady of (the City of) Muru(m)." Possibly was confused with Nin-Girima, a god occurring in magic spells against snakes, whose cult center was also Muru(m). Identified with Ku-ku in a Neo-Assyrian god list. (Black and Green 2003: 132; Veldhuis 2002: 67–69; Litke 1998: 171; George 1993: 30, 43; Tallqvist 1974:

397; King 1969: pl. 11; Heimpel, *RlA* VIII: 423–25)

Nin-k/gilim-kida (M) Deity listed in An : *Anum* between Nin-kilim and Nin-ki-da. Perhaps this was an inadvertent conflation of the two entries that ultimately appeared as a separate deity. (Litke 1998: 171)

Nin-ki-gu (M) Goddess attested in an Early Dynastic god list. Perhaps a variant for Nin-ki-kù. (Mander 1986: 145)

Nin-kiki (M) See Kiki

Nin-ki-ku (M) Goddess attested in an Early Dynastic god list. Means "Lady (of) the Holy Place." (Mander 1986: 145)

Nin-kimdu (M) Perhaps associated with the agricultural god En-kimdu. (Cavigneaux and Krebernik, *RlA* IX: 448)

Nin-kingal (M) See En-gukkal

Nin-kinnir (M) Sumerian deity attested in an Early Dynastic god list. (Mander 1986: 40)

Nin-kiri (M) Sumerian goddess attested in an Ur III tablet from the Inana temple in Nippur.Means "Lady of the Garden." (Richter 2004: 31; Zettler 1992: 271)

Nin-KIR-amaš (M) Wife of Nin-amaš-kug(a) and daughter of Ama-arazu. Allocated offerings at Ur III Nippur. Written nin-kir$_4$(KA)-amaš. Perhaps a variant for or originally kir$_{11}$, thus "The Lady, Lamb of the Sheepfold." (Richter 2004: 69; Litke 1998: 63)

Nin-kir-ura (M) Deity who in An : *Anum* is identified as a bara$_2$-sig$_5$-ga official(?) of Nin-Nibru. Written nin-kiri$_3$-ùr in An : *Anum* and Nin-kir$_4$-ur$_4$-ra with gloss ki-⌜ri?-ur?⌝-ra in an Old Babylonian god list. Note Kir$_4$-ùr-ùr, the similar-sounding bara$_2$-sig$_5$-ga official(?) of Ninurta. kir$_4$ ùr can mean "to smear/rub the nose." If ùr/ur$_4$ here is a variant for ur$_5$, then it might mean "Lady with the Flaring Nostrils." (Richter 2004: 75; Litke 1998: 49, 50; Cavigneaux and Krebernik, *RlA* IX: 449)

Nin-kirzal (M) Means "Lady/Lord Joy." (Litke 1998: 220; Krebernik, *RlA* IX: 367)

Nin-kisura (M) Netherworld deity. Means "Lady/Lord of the Boundary." (Litke 1998: 207; Cavigneaux and Krebernik, *RlA* IX: 449)

Nin-Kiš (M) Goddess attested in an Early Dynastic god list. Means "Lady of Kiš." From later evidence, probably a form of Inana. (Mander 1986: 104)

Nin-kišara (M) Cook of the sky god An/Anu(m). Means "Lord of the Universe." (Litke 1998: 30; Tallqvist 1974: 411; Cavigneaux and Krebernik, *RlA* IX: 449)

Nin-kita (M) Daughter of Nin-šubur. (Litke 1998: 28; Cavigneaux and Krebernik, *RlA* IX: 449)

Nin-kiura (M) Goddess attested at Ur III and Old Babylonian Ur. Her residence was in the temple of Nin-gal. Written nin-ki-ùr-ra, "Lady of the kiur."ki-ùr can mean "foundation" or denote a sacred location. A sector of the E-Kiš-nu-gal temple at Ur was called the Ki-ur. (Richter 2004: 438–39)

Nin-kug-gal (M) See En-gukkal

Nin-kulkul (M) See Mušme-kulkul

Nin-kum (M) Goddess who served with her spouse Enkum at the temple of Enki; they both appear in conjunction with the Apkallū. (Wiggermann 1992: 71, 76)

Nin-kungal (M) See En-kungal

(Nin-)kug-nuna (M) (1) Deity identified with Inana/Ištar at Eridu and especially at Ur. An attested sanctuary to Inana as Nin-kù-nuna was located at Eridu, and archaeologists have excavated a temple at Ur where she was honored in a festival. She also had a sacred garden at Ur. (2) One of the four "attendants" of Nanna/Sîn. (Cohen 2015: 89, 232; Litke 1998: 122; George 1993: 115 no. 667, 165 no. 1328; Tallqvist 1974: 411; Cavigneaux and Krebernik, *RlA* IX: 450–51)

Nin-kura (M) Name of several minor Sumerian deities. Means "Lady/Lord of the Mountain(s)." In An : *Anum*, female Nin-kura was paired with male En-kura, both being primeval ancestors of the god Enlil. In the same god list, Nin-kura was designated as the husband of the goddess of weaving Uttu. In "Enki and Nin-ḫursag," Nin-kura is the daughter of Enki and Nin-NISA and has a daughter Nin-imma or Uttu by Enki. In a text from Šuruppak she has an *išib*-priest. In a Hellenistic ritual for the repair of a temple, the goddess was created by Ea to work on the repairs. At Emar, Nin-kura was the wife of Dagān, with whom she was joined in a "Sacred Marriage" ritual. Also at Emar, a festival was celebrated in Nin-kura's honor. (Litke 1998: 33, 110; Cohen 1993: 344, 356, 358; Jacobsen 1976: 112–13; Tallqvist 1974: 411; Kramer, *ANET*: 39; Sachs, *ANET*: 341; Cavigneaux and Krebernik, *RlA* IX: 451)

Nin-kurušda (M) Deity in an Old Babylonian god list. Means "Lady (animal) Fattener." (Weidner 1924/25)

Nin-kusig, Nim-ku-si (M) Name of Šala(š). In An : *Anum* wife of Dagān; in another, late god list, wife of Adad. Means "Golden Lady." Explained as "Šala of the Mountain." (Schwemer 2001: 74, 401–2; Litke 1998: 43, 232; Tallqvist 1974: 411; Cavigneaux and Krebernik, *RlA* IX: 451)

Nin-KUŠ (M) Deity at Ur III Umma attested as having an exorcist (išib). Possible readings include Nin-iši and Nin-saḫar. (SAT 2, 1144: o 9)

NIN-la (M) See Egi/Ereš-la

Nin-LA-dubur (M) Deity listed among the ancestors of Enlil. Written Nin-la-dubur$_2$. Spouse was En-LA-dubur$_2$. (Lambert 2013: 408)

Nin-Lagaba (M) See Bēlet-Lagaba

Nin-la-ra (M) Sumerian goddess appearing in a god list among various mother deities such as Nin-maḫ and Aruru. (Richter 2004: 145)

Nin-lamma (M) God attested in an Early Dynastic god list. (Mander 1986: 145)

Nin-lamma-edin-ge (M) Deity attested in an Early Dynastic god list. May mean "Lady/Lord who Is the Guardian Spirit (of) the Nighttime Steppe." (Mander 1986: 56)

Ninlil (Sum.), **Mulliltu(m)** (Akk.), **Mullissu(m)** (Assyrian) Her name is the female equivalent of Enlil, her husband. As Mullissu(m), she was wife of Aššur and her sacred animal was the lion. Identified with Nin-ḫursag; Nin-tu(d), a birth goddess; Ašnan, a grain goddess; Šala(š), wife of Dagān; and Šeru'a, wife of Aššur. Later she was equated to Ištar, especially Ištar of Arbela. One account gives her original name as Sud, who was tutelary goddess of Šuruppak. Nin-lil's mother (and Sud's) was Nun-bar-še-gunu, an ancient farming goddess, sometimes equated to Nisaba, the scribe and grain goddess. The god of the storehouse Ḫaya was usually named as her father.

Ninlil was mother of Nanna/Sîn, Ninurta, Nergal/Meslamta-e, Nin-azu, and En-bilulu.

With Enlil, she decreed the fates and managed the *Me*. Ninlil's many titles included "Lady of Heaven and Earth," "Lady of the Lands," "Lady of the Gods," "Mother of the Gods," and "Lordly Wild Cow." The latter title occurs in a Babylonian text in which she is depicted as "butting ... enemies with her mighty horns" (Oppenheim, *ANET*: 300). Often addressed in prayers and hymns as "mother" and "merciful mother," Ninlil originally may have been a birth/mother goddess. She regularly interceded with Enlil on behalf of petitioners. The law code of Ḫammu-rāpi mentions her in this regard.

In myth and literature, Ninlil appears primarily in relation to Enlil. In "Enlil and Ninlil," Enlil rapes the young goddess, who, despite her mother's warning, was wandering by the river. The assembly of deities then exiles Enlil to the netherworld. Ninlil follows and the couple has intercourse several times more. As a result, she bears the moon god Nanna/Sîn and the netherworld gods Nergal/Meslamta-e, Nin-azu, and En-bilulu. When, in "Enlil and Sud," Enlil espouses the goddess Sud, she is renamed Ninlil.

She is identified with Ištar of Arbela, Ninlil gave oracles to warring Assyrian kings. One Assyrian treaty appealed to her as she "who resides in Nineveh" (Reiner, *ANET*: 538). The goddess was worshipped in all the temples of Enlil, particularly at Nippur, where she had several shrines in Enlil's precinct. One of them was entitled "Sacred Bed-Chamber" (George 1993: 106 no. 539). She also had her own temple at Nippur. Her cult center was Tum-(m)al, near Nippur to the south, and so she was Egi-Tummala. As Sud, her cult city was Šuruppak. She also had a sanctuary in the main temple at Aššur. At her temples in Nineveh, Arba'il ("House of the Lady of the Land"), and also at Ḫursag-kalama, a precinct of the greater city of Kiš, she was identified with Ištar. At Dūr-Kurigalzu, just west of modern Baghdad, she had a temple called "House of the Lady on High." She also had temples or shrines at Isin, Kiš, Ur, and Uruk. During the *akītu* at Nippur a festival was held in Ninlil's temple.

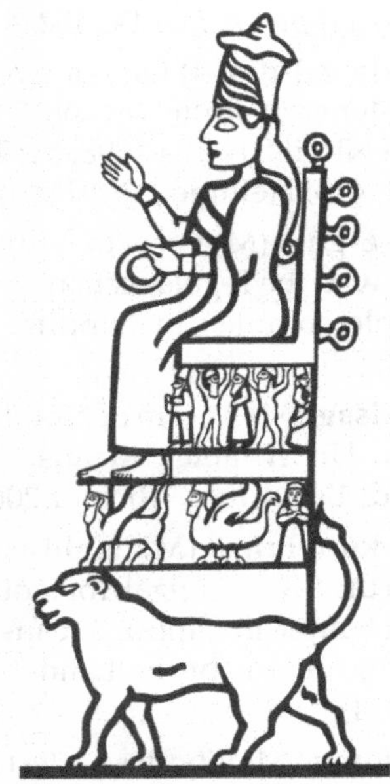

Detail showing Ninlil from a relief of a procession of deities from Maltai or Maltaya, Northern Iraq. Carved into the rock face. Neo-Assyrian. After Pritchard 1969b: 181, no. 537. See also Black and Green 2003: 40.

At Aššur, during the *akītu* festival, among other ritual acts, the king visited the shrine of Ninlil. In the form of her statue, the goddess went in procession to the house erected for the rites, was present at recitations and the playing of kettledrums before the deities, and participated in a ritual feast associated with the event. Her astral manifestation was Ursa Major. (*LAS*: 100–6, 106–11; Black and Green 2003: 40, 140–41; Leick 1999: 65–66; Leick 1998: 133; Litke 1998: 40, 230; Cohen 1993: 16, 81–82, 87–88, 308, 312, 328, 336, 339–41, 424–25; George 1993: 65 no. 38, 86 no. 299, 89 no. 338, 96 no. 425, 112 no. 636–38, 117 no. 683–84 no. 690, 121–22 no. 742, 134 no. 891, 136 no. 925, 151 no. 1113,161 no. 1265; Tallqvist 1974: 411–13; Meek, *ANET*: 179; Pfeiffer, *ANET*: 451; Krebernik, *RlA* IX: 452–61)

Ninlilda-gal-di (M) One of two deified bull-lyres of Enlil. Means "Supreme with Ninlil." (Litke 1998: 51; Tallqvist 1974: 413; Heimpel, *RlA* IX: 461)

Ninlil-E-gula (M) Form of Ninlil associated with the E-gula section of the Ekur temple complex in Nippur. (Richter 2004: 50)

Ninlil-isag (M) A form of Ninlil attested in an Ur III tablet. Means "Ninlil is Good/Beautiful." (Richter 2004: 415)

Ninlil-kura-igigal (M) Ninlil associated with the E-kura-igigal, forecourt of the Enlil temple in Nippur.Means "Ninlil, Insightful One of the Land." (Richter 2004: 44)

Nin-limmu (M) Goddess attested in an Early Dynastic god list. May mean "Lady (of the) four (quarters?)." (Mander 1986: 145)

Nin-LU (M) See En-LU

Nin-mada (M) Sumerian deity appearing in both female and male forms. As female she was snake-charmer to both Enlil and Anu(m). Daughter of Nin-kasi. Means "Lord/Lady of the Land." Name means "Lord of the Land." (Litke 1998: 62; George 1993: 24; Tallqvist 1974: 413; Cavigneaux and Krebernik, *RlA* IX: 462)

Nin-ma-diriga (M) Deity identified with the healing goddess Nin-kar(r)ak. Means "Lady who Floats Downstream by Boat." (Cavigneaux and Krebernik, *RlA* IX: 462)

NIN-magura (M) See Egi/Ereš-magura

Nin-maḫ (M) Birth goddess equated to the mother goddess Dingir-maḫ, but often treated as a deity in her own right. Known already in the Early Dynastic period. Identified with other birth/mother goddesses, such as Nin-ḫursag, Nin-tu(d), and Bēlet-ilī. Means "Exalted Lady." In "Enki and Nin-maḫ," the goddess plays the role of midwife when the goddess Namma brings humans into being. Later in the composition, she and Enki indulge in a drunken contest in which each deity tries to create a deformed or handicapped being for which the other cannot find a suitable role in life. Nin-maḫ appears in the "Lamentation over the Destruction of Ur" having left her cult center Keš in the city of Šarrākum. At the Keš sanctuary she was identified with Nin-ḫursag. She was worshipped in birth/mother goddess temples throughout Mesopotamia. Often the temples were called E-maḫ "Exalted House." Nin-maḫ had temples at Babylon, Adab, Sippar, Dēr, and elsewhere. Explained in An : *Anu ša amēli* as "Ea of Irrigators (*mēkiri*)." (Foster 2005: 847; Zawadzki 2005 no. 8; Black and Green 2003: 133, 141; Litke 1998: 66, 240; George 1993: 119 no. 713–15; Tallqvist 1974: 413; Kramer, *ANET*: 455; Krebernik, *RlA* VIII: 505;

Cavigneaux and Krebernik, *RlA* IX: 462–63)

Nin-MA-lulu (M) see Nin-peš-lulu

Nin-ma-ra (M) Messenger of Enlil. See Nin-marki and Nin-gá-ra. (Litke 1998: 63; Cavigneaux and Krebernik, *RlA* IX: 468)

Nin-marki (M) Goddess of cattle, of oaths, and perhaps of the sea. Tutelary deity of the city Gu-aba in Lagaš province. Known from Early Dynastic times. Written Nin-mar-gi$_4$ in an Early Dynastic god list. Member of the circle of the moon god Nanna/Sîn. Daughter of the Lagaš-area goddess Nanše and her spouse Nin-dara. In another tradition daughter of Enlil. In An : *Anum* thirteen children are listed. Her standard was a bird.

The Sumerian "Lamentation over the Destruction of Ur" lists Nin-marki as one of the deities who abandoned their shrines and cities when the land was devastated. In the "Lamentation over the Destruction of Sumer and Ur," Enlil causes her temple and city to be burned. Her temple at her cult center Gu-aba was called "House that Stretches over the Midst of the Sea," and at Girsu it was "House of the Bejeweled Woman." Nin-marki also had temples or shrines at Lagaš, Nimen, and Ur.

The wife of the governor of Lagaš made offerings to Nin-marki on the first and second days of a festival for the goddess. (Cohen 2015: 34 Richter 2004: 396; Black and Green 2003: 123; Litke 1998: 125; Attinger 1995 no. 33; George 1993: 36; Mander 1986 144; Tallqvist 1974: 414; Kramer, *ANET*: 456, 614; Sallaberger, *RlA* IX: 463–68)

Nin-maš (M) Most often paired with Nin-piriga and known from Early Dynastic times. Invoked in incantations. In the Ur III period occurs only in a personal name. Perhaps to be identified with Nin-amaš. (Cavigneaux and Krebernik, *RlA* IX: 468–69)

Nin-mar-ra (M) Child of Nin-marki. See Nin-ma-ra. (Litke 1998: 125; Cavigneaux and Krebernik, *RlA* IX: 468)

Nin-maš-kuga (M) See Nin-amaš-kuga

Nin-me (M) Deity identified with the goddess Inana/Ištar. Means "Lady of Battle." (Litke 1998: 150 no. 22; Cavigneaux and Krebernik, *RlA* IX: 469)

Nin-me-ana (M) Sumerian deity appearing in offering texts from Ur III Nippur. Means "Lady of the *Me* of Heaven." (Sallaberger 1993: I, 104)

Nin-me-an-ki (M) Name of the standard of Inana at Uruk in Old Babylonian times. Means "Lady of the *Me* of Heaven and Earth." (Renger 1967: 161)

Nin-medim-ana, Nin-medim-anki (M) Deity identified with Damkina/Damgal-nuna, the spouse of Enki/Ea. Means "Lady (who is) the Limbs of Heaven (and Earth)." (Litke 1998: 89; Tallqvist 1974: 414; Cavigneaux and Krebernik, *RlA* IX: 469)

(Nin-)medim-sa (M) Name of Šala, spouse of Adad, the storm god. Means "Lady of Shapely Limbs." (Litke 1998: 142; Tallqvist 1974: 373; Krebernik, *RlA* VII: 617)

Nin-me-gar (M) Goddess attested in an Early Dynastic god list. Means "Lady who Instills Dread Silence." (Mander 1986: 110)

Nin-me-Kiš (M) Deity identified with Inana/Ištar of Kiš. Means "Lady of the *Me*s of Kiš." (Litke 1998: 149; Cavigneaux and Krebernik, *RlA* IX: 470)

Nin-men(a), Nin-men-ana (M) Birth/mother goddess. Identified with

Damkina and Bēlet-ilī. Means "Lady (of?) the Crown (of Heaven)." Nin-men is mentioned in a third-millennium votive inscription from Sippar. (Westenholz 2014: no. 3; Black and Green 2003: 133; Litke 1998: 68; Tallqvist 1974: 414–15; Krebernik, *RlA* VIII: 505–6)

Nin-me-Nibru (M) Deity identified with Inana/Ištar of Nippur. Means "Lady of the *Me* of Nippur." (Litke 1998: 149; Cavigneaux and Krebernik, *RlA* IX: 470)

Nin-men-kal (M) Goddess attested in an Early Dynastic god list. Means "Lady (of) the Precious Crown." (Mander 1986: 145)

Nin-me-sikila (M) See Meskilak

Nin-me-šara (M) Deity whose name means "Lady of All the *Me*s." (1) A title of Inana/Ištar and also of Ninlil. The epithet occurs at the beginning of "The Exaltation of Inana," one of the hymns to Inana/Ištar by the priestess En-ḫedu-ana. (2) Counterpart/wife of the god En-me-šara. They were primeval ancestors of Enlil. (*LAS*: 316; Black and Green 2003: 141; Litke 1998: 34; Tallqvist 1974: 414; Meador 2000: 171; Cavigneaux and Krebernik, *RlA* IX: 470)

Nin-me-šudu (M) Goddess identified with Sadar-nuna, the spouse of the fire god Nuska. Means "Lady who Perfects the *Me*." See Lugal-me-šudu and Me-nigin-šudu. (Litke 1998: 51; Tallqvist 1974: 414; Cavigneaux and Krebernik, *RlA* IX: 470)

Nin-me-tenten (M) Female servant of the moon god. May mean "Lady (of) the *Me*s of Cooling," fitting for a deity associated with the night-time moon. (Litke 1998: 124; Tallqvist 1974: 414; Cavig-neaux and Krebernik, *RlA* IX: 470)

Nin-me-urur (M) Possibly an advisor of Inana/Ištar. Means "Lady who Collects (All) the *Me*." (Cavigneaux and Krebernik, *RlA* IX: 470–71)

Nin-me-zu (M) Name of Damkina / Dam-gal-nuna, spouse of Enki/Ea. Means "Lady who Knows the *Me*." (Litke 1998: 88; Cavigneaux and Krebernik, *RlA* IX: 471)

Nin-min-taba (M) See Nimin-taba

NIN-Mirsiga (M) See Egi/Ereš-Mirsiga

Nin-mu (M) See Nin-NISA

Nin-mug (M) Sumerian goddess, originally male and identified with Enki. Deity of crafts and birth. Wife of Išum and also of Ḫendur-saga. Also a netherworld deity. In "Enki and the World Order," Enki assigns to Nin-mug the art of metal-working in order to make crowns for new-born kings. In "Enki and Nin-maḫ," Nin-mug was one of eight goddesses who helped Nin-maḫ in the creation of human beings. Jacobsen understands the name as "Lady Vulva" (1976: 109). Nin-mug was worshipped at, among other places, Šuruppak; Kisiga, southeast of Ur; Adab; Lagaš; and Umma. (Cohen 2015: 196; Foster 2005: 219; *LAS*: 224; Black and Green 2003: 112; Litke 1998: 201; Jacobsen 1976: 109; Tallqvist 1974: 415; Cavigneaux and Krebernik, *RlA* IX: 471–73)

Nin-mul (M) See En-mul

Nin-mul-gunu (M) Goddess identified with Aya, spouse of the sun god Utu/Šamaš. Means "Lady, Multicolored Star." (Litke 1998: 131; Cavigneaux and Krebernik, *RlA* IX: 473)

Nin-Muru(m) (M) Husband of the mongoose goddess Nin-kilim. Vizier of

Me-ḫursaga. Means "Lord of Muru(m)." Written in An : *Anum* as $^{d.ni-}$Nin-mùr$^{mu.ru.ki}$ with variant mur with the following homonymous entry $^{d.ni}$Nin-^{ur}ur$_5^{ki}$. (Litke 1998: 172; Tallqvist 1974: 415; Cavigneaux and Krebernik, *RlA* IX: 474)

Nin-muš-bara (M) Deity in the Lagaš region in the Early Dynastic period. May mean "Lady/Lord of the Outlying Area(mùš)." (Selz 1995: 262–63)

Nin-mušda (M) See Mušdama

Nin-MUŠ-zagina (M) Deity identified with Šala(š, spouse of Dagān. Name may means "Lady (with a) Shining Countenance." If MUŠ is read SUḪ then could mean "shining diadem." See MUŠ-zagina. (Schwemer 2001: 401–2 and note 337; Litke 1998: 43; Tallqvist 1974: 415; Cavigneaux and Krebernik, *RlA* IX: 474)

NIN-Nagar (M) See Bēlet-Nagar

Nin-Nagsu (M) Deity in an Ur III offering lists from Umma. Means "Lady/Lord of Nagsu." (MVN 13, 192: r 5)

Nin-nam-mu (M) See Gašan-nam-mu

Nin-namri (M) Deity identified as a lapidary or seal-cutter. Possibly a title of Nin-kura, spouse of the weaver goddess Uttu. See Šu-namri. (Litke 1998: 110; Cavigneaux and Krebernik, *RlA* IX: 475)

Nin-nam-tar-tar(e) (M) Birth/mother goddess. Identified with Dingir-maḫ and Bēlet-ilī. Means "Lady who Determines the Fates." (Litke 1998: 67; Tallqvist 1974: 415; Krebernik, *RlA* IX: 475)

Nin-nemur (M) See Nin-PIRIG.TUR

Nin-Nibru (Sum.), **Bēlet-Nippuri(m)** (Akk.) Name of the Sumerian goddess Gula as spouse of Ninurta. Also a name of Inana/Ištar. First appears in documents of the Ur III period. Means "Lady of Nippur." She is mentioned in literary texts concerning Ninurta. As Gula she had a shrine in the Ninurta temple at Nippur, where she received offerings during the gu$_4$-si-sù festival in honor of her spouse. With her Akkadian name she is mentioned in a tablet from the First Sealand Dynasty. She also appears in an incantation tablet. (Cohen 2015: 124; Dalley 2009: 79; Litke 1998: 47 no. 230; George 1993: 106 no. 544; Tallqvist 1974: 416; Reiner 1970: 23; Biggs, *RlA* IX: 476–77)

NIN-nigara (M) See Egi/Ereš-nigara

Nin-NI-garaš (M) Deity in a Neo-Assyrian god list. Written Nin-NI-$^{ga-ra}$ga-raš. (King 1969: pl. 19)

NIN-nigBunna (M) See Egi/Ereš-nig - Bunna

Nin-nigerim(M) Daughter of Ninurta. Means "Lady Evil." Note the daughter of Ninurta Nin-niggina, "Lady Truth," who may be her counterpart. (Litke 1998: 47; Cavigneaux and Krebernik, *RlA* IX: 477–78)

Nin-niggena (M) Daughter of Ninurta. Means "Lady Truth." Note the daughter of Ninurta Nin-nig-erim, "Lady Evil," who may be the counterpart to Nin-niggena. (Litke 1998: 48; Tallqvist 1974: 416; Cavigneaux and Krebernik, *RlA* IX: 477–78)

NIN-niggu-na-ra (M) See Egi/Ereš-nig-Bunna

Nin-nigin (M) Sumerian deity attested in an Early Dynastic god list. May mean "Lady of Everything." (Mander 1986: 108,110)

Nin-nig-kida (M) See Nin-kida

Nin-NISA/SAR (M) The orthography denotes either one deity whose sex was viewed differently over time or two distinct deities—one male and one female—and whose names may even have been read differently. In the Early Dynastic zà-mí hymn called "NAGAR of Heaven and Earth," but it is not clear that "carpenter" is meant here. In An : *Anum* the spouse of Nergal and butcher of the Ekur temple of Enlil at Nippur. In the late ritual for covering a kettledrum, Nin-NISA is a male deity, sharing in offerings and appearing integral to the ritual as one of the deities created by Ea from pieces of clay. In "Enki and Nin-ḫursag," Nin-NISA is the daughter of Enki and Nin-tu, who herself has a daughter Nin-kura by Enki. Nin-NISA had a temple at Nippur called "House Worthy of the Cleansing Ritual." Temples for the deity are attested at Girsu and Ur, and she/he was worshipped at Umma, Lagaš, and Mari. Nin-NISA had a role in the Festival of Baba in the Lagaš state and received offerings on separate days of the celebration.

Various readings of the name have been proposed: Nin-sar, Nin-šar, Nin-mú, Nin-sig$_x$, and Nin-nisig. However, we are unaware of a meaning for any of these readings that is appropriate for the butcher of the Ekur or for the spouse of the chief god of the netherworld, Nergal. In an Ur III text from Umma the occupation lú-nisig-ga occurs after carpenters, leather-workers, and smiths, and before canal inspectors. Note [d]Nin-NISA-sag in an Old Babylonian god list directly after [d]Nin-NISA, which might support understanding the name as an occupation, "Lord/Lady, chief *nisig*." The fact that [d]Nin-NISA was invoked for repair of a kettledrum and may have been called NAGAR "carpenter" (see above) further adds to the likelihood that the sign SAR here denotes an occupation, which, if so, points to the reading nisig based upon the above-cited text from Umma. (Schrakamp: 2015: 197; Litke 1998: 60; Cohen 1993: 53, 55; George 1993: 24, 169 no. 1398–99; Sachs, *ANET*: 335, 341; Cavigneaux and Krebernik, *RlA* IX: 484–86)

Nin-NISA-sag (M) See Nin-NISA

Nin-NITA (M) Deity attested in a personal name at Ur III Girsu. (DAS 129)

Nin-numun-la (M) Netherworld(?) deity. May mean "Lord who Weighs Out (or Supervises) Seed." The following entry in An : *Anum* is Nin-ge-lá, "Lord who Weighs Out (or Supervises) Reeds." (Litke 1998: 220; Cavigneaux and Krebernik, *RlA* IX: 450)

Nin-nuna (M) Deity whose name means "Noble Lady." Deity listed in an Early Dynastic god list and in a personal name from Lagaš in the Early Dynastic period. A goddess Nin-nuna is attested in an Old Babylonian text from Nippur and is identified with Ištar in Neo-Assyrian texts. But whether the Early Dynastic and later deity denote the same deity or two distinct deities cannot be determined. (Selz 1995: 263; Cavigneaux and Krebernik, *RlA* IX: 479)

Nin-nun-kal(ag) (M) Deity attested in an Early Dynastic god list. Means "Lord/Lady, Mighty Prince." (Mander 1986: 146)

Nin-PA (M) See Nin-ḫadda

Nin-PAD-nir (M) Deity in a circle of Nergal deities in an Old Babylonian god list from Nippur. (Richter 2004: 206)

Nin-pa'e (M) Deity whose name means "Lord/Lady who Comes Forth." Had chapels in the temple of Nin-ḫursag at Nippur and the Šara temple at Umma.

Mentioned in connection with the god Šul-pa'e. (Cavigneaux and Krebernik, *RlA* IX: 480)

Nin-pamule-si (M) Goddess whose name means "Lady who Fills the Spreading Branches (or Foliage)." Her spouse was Sag-kud, a form of Ninurta. Possibly one of the stars in the Pleiades. (Litke 1998: 30; Tallqvist 1974: 416; Cavigneaux and Krebernik, *RlA* IX: 481)

Nin-Pa(p)-Nigara (M) See Pa(p)-Nigara

Nin-peš (M) Deity written Nin-peš in an Early Dynastic god list from Šuruppak and written Nin-^{ĝeš}pèš in an Early Dynastic document from the Umma region. Means "Lady/Lord Fig Tree." See Nin-peš-lulu. (Mander 1986: 53)

Nin-peš-lulu (M) The name is written -pèš-lu-lu, which might mean "Lady/Lord who Heaps up Figs." lu = *kamāru*, which is attested as referring to the heaping of dates for sorting. See Nin-peš for Nin-^{ĝeš}pèš. However, in light of this deity being identified as a goatherd of Enlil in An : *Anum*, pèš may be a variant for peš, thus "Lady/Lord who Makes Pregnant (Animals) Abound." (Richter 2004: 99–100; Litke 1998: 63)

Nin-pirig (M) (1) Vizier of the sun god Utu/Šamaš. Means "Lady/Lord Lion." (2) Goddess in Enlil's circle. Most often paired with Nin-maš and known from Early Dynastic times. Invoked in incantations. (Litke 1998: 57, 132; Cavigneaux and Krebernik, *RlA* IX: 481–83)

Nin-PIRIG-AB, **Nin-PIRIG-UG** (M) Two juxtaposed deities associated with outdoor shrines of Inana. May originally have been just variants that became listed as separate deities. (Litke 1998: 160)

Nin-PIRIG.BANDA, **Nin-NEMUR** (M) Deity mentioned in the "Hymn to the Queen of Nippur," possibly as the mother-in-law of Inana at Nippur. Occurs in a god list from Abu Ṣalābīkh. Means "Lady, Lion Cub (or Leopard)." (Lambert 1982: 217; Cavigneaux and Krebernik, *RlA* IX: 483)

Nin-ragaba (M) Deity identified with Inana/Ištar. Means "Lady/Lord Rider." (Richter 2004: 292; Litke 1998: 152; Cavigneaux and Krebernik, *RlA* IX: 483)

Nin-riba (M) Perhaps a name of the goddess Nanāya. The previous entry in An : *Anum* is Nin-dìb-ba, but whether these two names are just variants of a name that contained the d^{r} consonant cannot be determined. (Litke 1998: 164; Cavigneaux and Krebernik, *RlA* IX: 483)

Nin-RIRU (M) Deity attested at Šuruppak. Written Nin-ri$_{8}$-ru. (Pomponio and Visicato 1994)

Nin-saa (M) Deity attested in a god list. Written Nin-sá-a. (OIP 99, 46: o xi 8)

Nin-saga (M) Deity attested in offering lists for Old Babylonian Nippur and Larsa. Means "Beautiful Lady." (Renger 1967: 147, 151)

Nin-sag-mumu (M) Deity identified with the Sumerian birth/mother goddess Dingir-maḫ/Bēlet-ilī. Means "Lady whose Head Shines." (Litke 1998: 67; Tallqvist 1974: 416; Krebernik, *RlA* VIII: 506)

Nin-sag-nita-limmu (M) Deity in an Old Babylonian god list from Mari. May mean "Lord/Lady, (the equal of any) Four Men."

Nin-Saguba (M) Deity identified with the goddess Geštin-ana in the Lagaš area. Means "Lady of Sagub," a town in the

Lagaš region south of Girsu. (Cavigneaux and Krebernik, *RlA* IX: 484)

Nin-SAR, Nin-SAR-sag (M) See [d]Nin-NISA.

Nin-sa-za (M) See Nin-egal

Nin-si-ana (M) The rarely attested Nin-si-an-na should not be confused with the goddess traditionally read as Nin-SI_4-an-na, for which see Nin-usana. (TMHNF 1-2, 83: o 4)

Nin-siga (M) Deity identified with Tašmētu(m), spouse of Nabû. Means "Good Lady." Written Nin-sig_5-ga. (Cavigneaux and Krebernik, *RlA* IX: 487–88)

Nin-sigar (M) Sumerian deity with an išib-priest. (BPOA 1, 1252: r 2)

Nin-sigar-ana, Gašan-simar-ana (Emesal) (M) One of two deified bull-lyres of Inana/Ištar. Means "Lady, Bolt of Heaven." Occurs also in Ur III texts. (Litke 1998: 154; Cavigneaux and Krebernik, *RlA* IX: 488)

Nin-sigar-edin(a) (M) Sumerian deity. Perhaps a form of the goddess Geštin-ana. Name means "Lady/Lord, Bolt of the Steppe." Occurs also in Ur III texts. (Cavigneaux and Krebernik, *RlA* IX: 489)

Nin-sig-nun (M) See En-sig-nun

(Nin-)sig-tu(d) (M) The name means "(Lady of) the Birthing Brick." A woman sat, knelt, or squatted on two bricks while in labor. Attested in an Early Dynastic god list as [d]Sig-tu(d). Also appears in Sumerian literary texts, sometimes associated with the goddess Nin-tu(d) "Lady Birth" at the Keš sanctuary in Šarrākum. (Stol 2000: 120; Mander 1986: 65; Krebernik, *RlA* VIII: 506)

Nin-siki (M) Deity whose name means "Lady/Lord Wool." In An : *Anum* the entry immediately follows the goddess Laḫar "Ewe." (Litke 1998: 138)

Nin-siki-la (M) In "Enki and Nin-ḫursag, "the goddess is created by Nin-ḫursag to treat Enki's diseased jaw and later decreed to be "Patron Deity of Magan," modern Oman. Written nin-siki-lá. (Kramer, *ANET*: 40, 41)

Nin-sikila (M) Goddess whose name means "Faultless Lady." (1) Sumerianized name of Meškilak, the main goddess of the city of Dilmun. Probably either wife or mother of the chief god En-zak. Identified with Nin-ḫursag. The Sumerians understood her as wife of Enki. In "Enki and the World Order," Enki places Nin-sikila in charge of Dilmun, modern Baḥrain. (*LAS*: 220; Black and Green 2003: 66, 140; Litke 1998: 75; Nashef 1986: 343; Tallqvist 1974: 417; Kramer, *ANET*: 38; Cavigneaux and Krebernik, *RlA* IX: 489) (2) At first husband of the goddess Lisina, but when the goddess was later misunderstood as male, Nin-sikila became Lisina's wife. Documents attributed to Gudea, governor of Lagaš make clear that the deity was male. (*LAS*: 220; Black and Green 2003: 122; Leick 1999: 62; Litke 1998: 75; Oppenheim, *ANET*: 268; Cavigneaux and Krebernik, *RlA* IX: 489)

Nin-sila-luḫ (M) Sumerian deity of the Ur III Umma region. May mean "Lady (of?) the Street-sweeper(s)." (SAT 3, 1760: o 12)

Nin-sila-munDU (M) Deity attested in a text from Susa. (Cavigneaux and Krebernik, *RlA* IX: 489)

Nin-sila-ti (M) Deity attested in an Early Dynastic god list. May mean "Lady (of those?) who Live in the Street." (Mander 1986: 110)

Nin-SILA-zi (M) Deity attested in an Early Dynastic god list. Written Nin-sila$_3$-zi. (Mander 1986: 146)

Nin-silig (M) Deity attested in an Early Dynastic god list. May mean "Mighty Lord." (Mander 1986: 146)

Nin-SILIM (M) Deity attested at Šuruppak. May mean "The Lady (of) Well-being(?)." (Mander 1986: 144)

Nin-SILIM-gu-nam-tab-ka (M) Sumerian deity attested in the environs of Ur III Umma. Means "Nin-silim, who Twines the Threads of Fate." The concept of goddesses who twine the threads of fate is common throughout world cultures. (Cohen 1996a: 32)

Nin-simug (M) See Nin-a-gal

Nin-sir-sir (M) See Sir-sir

Nin-su (M) Sumerian deity attested in personal names at Ur III Umma. (UTI 3, 2195: r 10)

Nin-sud (M) Deity appearing in an offering list from Old Babylonian Larsa. Perhaps a connection to the goddess Sud, tutelary deity of Šuruppak. Note a deity in an Old Babylonian god list from Mari written Nin-su$_{13}$-ud. See Lugal-súd. (Richter 2004: 400)

Nin-sudag (M) Deity attested at Fara. Written Nin-sud$_4$-ág. Means "Shining Lady/Lord." (Mander 1986: 146)

Nin-sukkal (M) Deity with a cult at Ur III Umma. Means "Lady/Lord Vizier." (Nisaba 11, 22: r iii 9)

Nin-sukuda (M) Deity attested in a text from Susa. Means "Impressive Lady/ Lord. See Lugal-sukudra. (Cavigneaux and Krebernik, *RlA* IX: 501)

Nin-sun (M) Patron goddess of Kul(l)aba, a section of Uruk. Sometimes identified with the healing goddess Gula, particularly in the Lagaš region. Already known in the Early Dynastic period as wife of the deified king of Uruk, Lugalbanda. Mother of the semi-divine hero Gilgameš. In addition, she was considered to be the divine mother of the kings of the Ur III kingdom. She had ten children by Lugalbanda. One of her titles was Nin-E-gula "Lady of the Great Temple," but it is not clear to which temple this name refers. Nin-sun means "Lady Wild Cow."

When in "Gilgameš and the Bull of Heaven," Gilgameš complains to his mother, Nin-sun, about Inana's refusing him the right to give judgments in her temple, Nin-sun advises him to disobey Inana. When Inana then looses the Bull of Heaven on the city of Uruk, Nin-sun advises her son to kill the bull. In the Babylonian "Epic of Gilgameš," Gilgameš asks his wise and all-knowing mother to interpret his dreams. To his friend Enkidu, he describes her as "the great queen ... who is versed in all knowledge." Acting as the priestess she was, Nin-sun made offerings and prayed to the sun god Šamaš for Gilgameš's safe return from his quest to confront the monster Ḫumbaba of the Cedar Forest. (Foster 2001: 23–24)

One of Nin-sun's cult centers was Ki-kal, a small town between Uruk and Ur. In addition, in Kul(l)aba, she and Lugalbanda had a temple named "Precious Place." A record exists of a five-day festival at Uruk celebrating Inana and Nin-sun. She also had a strong following in the Lagaš area, where she was included in a seven-day festival. She was worshipped also at, Nippur, Ur, Umma, and Ku'ara. (Cohen 2015: 105; Black and Green

2003: 141; Foster 2001: 3–95; Frayne 2001: 99–155; Litke 1998: 168; Leick 1999: 172–73; Leick 1998: 134–35; Cavigneaux and Al-Rawi 1993: 98; George 1993: 88 no. 321, 96 no. 428, 119 no. 717; Tallqvist 1974: 417; Speiser, *ANET*: 76, 77, 81; Wilcke, *RlA* IX: 502–4)

NIN.SUNKIR (E) Elamite deity whose name means "Great King." Appears in an inscription of Untaš-Napiriša. (König 1977: 48, 227)

NIN-ŠA (M) Deity attested in clothing texts at Neo-Babylonian Sippar. (Bongenaar 1997: 231)

Nin-ša-eri (M) Deity attested at Fara. Written Nin-šà-eri. (Martin et al. 2001: 111)

Nin-šage-pada (M) Goddess known in the Gula temple at Ur. As an epithet, the name was applied to a number of goddesses. Means "The Favorite Lady." A temple was built, probably at Ur, to a deity with this title. A deity Šà-pàd who participated in the first-fruits festival is attested in the Early Dynastic period in the Umma region. (George 1993: 169 no. 1397; Tallqvist 1974: 417; Cavigneaux and Krebernik, *RlA* IX: 483)

Nin-ša-gur (M) Deity in a personal name from Susa. Written ša-gur, Cavigneaux and Krebernik suggest it may be for šà-gur$_4$, "Lord/Lady who Feels Wonderful." (Cavigneaux and Krebernik, *RlA* IX: 484)

Nin-šar (M) See En-šar

Nin-šara (M) Deity whose name in An : *Anum* is written Nin-$^{ša-ar}$šara; explained as Antum Ištar, an apparent composite deity. (Litke 1998: 24)

Nin-šar-an-ki (M) Deity occurring at Old Babylonian Larsa. Means "Lady of Everything (in) Heaven and Earth." (Richter 2004: 362)

Nin-še-ḫa-e (M) Deity identified with Zarpanītum in a Neo-Assyrian god list. Written Nin-še-ḫa-è. (Cavigneaux and Krebernik, *RlA* IX: 487)

Nin-šegšeg (M) Deity identified with Bēlet-ilī. Explained as "lady of silence (*šaqummatu*)." Written with šeg$_5$(KA×TU). (Litke 1998: 69; Krebernik, *RlA* VIII: 506)

Nin-šen(šena) (M) Form of Inana/Ištar as goddess of war. She had a cult at Nippur. Identified in An : *Anum* as "Lady of Battle." (Litke 1998: 150; Cavigneaux and Krebernik, *RlA* IX: 487)

Nin-šenšen-kug (M) A birth deity, a form of the birth/mother goddess Dingir-maḫ/Bēlet-ilī. Means "Lady of the Shining Kettles" referring to the provision of water for washing during the birth. (Litke 1998: 67; Tallqvist 1974: 418; Krebernik, *RlA* VIII: 506)

Nin-šešda-edina (M) Deity allocated offerings in an Ur III text from Umma. Means "Lady with the Brother in (or of) the Steppe," which may be a form of Geštin-ana. (Nisaba 11, 22: l.e. ii 1)

Nin-šeše-gara (M) Aspect of Geštin-ana, primarily at Bad-tibira, the cult city of Geštin-ana's brother Dumuzi. Her temple at Bad-tibira was called E-šeše-gara "House Established by the Brother." (George 1993: 146 no. 1044; Cavigneaux and Krebernik, *RlA* IX: 487)

Nin-šitim (M) Deity explained in An : *Anu ša amēli* as "Ea of builders." šitim means "mason." (Litke 1998: 238)

Nin-šuba (M) Deity attested in an Early Dynastic god list. Perhaps means "Glistening Lady." (Mander 1986: 146)

Nin-šubur (M) The name of two Sumerian deities, one female and the other male. According to Wiggermann, when the earliest sources from the third millennium BCE indicate the sex of Nin-šubur, they all treat her as female, for instance, calling her "Mother." Later Akkadian documents consider Nin-šubur as male. Even in bilingual writings, when the Sumerian deity was clearly female, the translation into Akkadian presented her as male. Around the end of the third millennium, the two existed side by side (Wiggermann, *RlA* IX: 491). The sex-gender difficulty resulted in at least one cultic attempt to resolve it by presenting Nin-šubur clothed as a male on the right side and as a female on the left. By the beginning of the second millennium BCE, the situation was seemingly settled, at least at the official level. Early texts of King Rīm-Sîn addressed the deity as female, but in later ones he was male. Nonetheless, popular religion, much of which would have retained early Sumerian traditions, probably continued to understand Nin-šubur as female. In literary material, female Nin-šubur generally served the goddess Inana and male Nin-šubur the god An. (Black and Green 2003: 141–42; Leick 1999: 135–36; Leick 1998: 134; Wiggermann, *RlA* IX: 490–500)

(1) Nin-šubur (M) Sumerian goddess. Vizier of Inana and also, later, of the sky god An. Associated with the vizier Kaka in some sources. One of her titles was Sukkal-ana "Minister of Heaven." There is little known of Nin-šubur's parents and family. A few sources understood her as daughter of An, not surprising given that viziers were often offspring of the deity they served. Another source designated Meslamta-e as her father. Her earliest and only known spouse was a god identified with the netherworld deity Nergal. The nineteen children listed in An : *Anum* as offspring of the male Nin-šubur might originally have been hers. Both goddess and god had courtier-guardians of the same name.

In visual imagery, Nin-šubur, like all viziers, carried the staff of office and it was Nin-šubur who awarded a king his staff of office. The goddess is mentioned in a number of prayers, hymns, royal inscriptions, and dedications, but only rarely in texts of divination and magic. As minister of Inana and An, and so with intimate access to the divine assembly, she was well placed to carry petitions and prayers from humans to the deities. Thus, in devotees' eyes, she was an intercessor and a protective mother.

As Inana's vizier, Nin-šubur played a central part in the Sumerian "The Descent of Inana." It was she to whom Inana left the responsibility for ensuring that Inana could return from the netherworld. In the Akkadian version of the composition, Ištar's vizier was the god Pap-sukkal. Nin-šubur also had a role in Sumerian love songs associated with Inana and Dumuzi. In one of the love compositions she led the king to Inana's bedroom and asked the great goddess to grant him a long reign replete with fame and prosperity.

In the third millennium BCE, Nin-šubur's cult was centered on the town Akkil, near Bad-tibira, where she was Nin-Akkil "Lady of Akkil." Her cult was celebrated at Uruk, the city of Inana, and, among other places, at Nippur, Larsa and Girsu, Adab, Isin, Akkad, and Babylon. Her temple at Ur was called "House Worthy of its Lady." (Cohen 2015: 37;Black, Cunningham,

Robson, and Zólyomi 2005: 66–76; Lapinkivi 2004: 44, 123, 190; Black and Green 2003: 142; Leick 1998: 134; Sefati 1998: 305; George 1993: 105 no. 527, 123 no. 757; Jacobsen 1976: 41–42; Kramer, *ANET*: 52–57, 640–41; Speiser, *ANET*: 108; Wiggermann, *RlA* IX: 490–500)

(2) Nin-šubur (Sum.), Il-abrat (Akk.) Sumerian god. Vizier to the sky god An/Anu(m). Identified with Pap-sukkal, minister to the deities in general. Also equated to the vizier god Kaka. As minister of the god An/Anu(m), Nin-šubur was probably his son. Nin-šubur had two wives, Ama-sag-nudi and Nin-abula. His offspring were many, at least five daughters and fourteen sons. His two counselors were Gidri-sisa, the deified staff, and Ešbar-ana. There were two guardian deities of his temple, E-gubi-duga and Bītu-šemi. Among his titles were Gada-lá-abzu "*gadala*-priest of the Abzu," a name that appears in An : *Anum* as designating a courtier of the god Enki/Ea. Another epithet Ig-gal "Big Door" speaks to his association with entrances.

In visual imagery Nin-šubur/Il-abrat wore a horned crown and a long robe and usually carried the vizier's staff. During the period c. 1000–612 BCE, clay figurines of the deity were often buried under the main platform of temples, perhaps to ensure the proper conducting of rituals. Nin-šubur might also have been symbolized by a shoe, an allusion to his duty as messenger, reminiscent of the winged sandals of Hermes or Mercury. Nin-šubur is mentioned in a late ritual for the repair of a temple as receiving sacrifices, and Il-abrat was present as Anu(m)'s vizier in the Akkadian Adapa story. The popularity of the cult of Nin-šubur is demonstrated by his inclusion in proper names throughout much of Mesopotamian history. He had temples at Akkil near Bad-tibira and at Kiš (and probably others), but it is not always possible to tell whether the deity of that temple was the male or female Nin-šubur. Cults to Il-abrat are attested for Borsippa, Babylon, and Aššur, where he had a "seat" in the main temple. Pap-sukkal, an alternate name of Nin-šubur, was associated with the constellation Orion. (Durand 2008: 247–48; Foster 2005: 502; Black and Green 2003: 141–42; Leick 1998: 134; Litke 1998: 25, 26–29, 101; George 1993: 66 no. 49–50, 148 no. 1084; Deller 1987: no. 54; Tallqvist 1974: 323, 418; Speiser, *ANET*: 101: Wiggermann, *RlA* IX: 490–500)

Nin-šubur-banda (M) Sumerian deity appearing in an Ur III offering list from Ur. Means "Junior Nin-šubur," as opposed to Nin-šubur-gula "Senior Nin-šubur," which precedes this divinity in the list. (Richter 2004: 473)

Nin-šubur-gula (M) Sumerian deity appearing in an Ur III offering list from Ur. Means "Senior Nin-šubur" as opposed to Nin-šubur-banda "Junior Nin-šubur." (Richter 2004: 473)

Nin-šud-ana (M) Deity identified with Zarpanītu(m), the spouse of the god Marduk. Means "Lady, the Blessing of Heaven." (Litke 1998: 98 no. 259; Cavigneaux and Krebernik, *RlA* IX: 500)

Nin-šud-bindu-basag (M) Guardian spirit of the circle of the birth/mother goddess and of Gula. Means "The Lady Uttered a Prayer and It Was Favorable." (Litke 1998: 74, 184; Cavigneaux and Krebernik, *RlA* IX: 500–1)

Nin-šudu (M) Goddess occurring in an Assyrian god list. Identified with Ištar.

Means "Perfect Lady." (Cavigneaux and Krebernik, *RlA* IX: 501)

Nin-šuluḫa (M) Goddess of the netherworld. Member of the court of Ereškigal. She was in charge of ritual washing. Her name means "Lady of Ritual Cleansing," that is, purification. In the Babylonian "Epic of Gilgameš," she was called "housekeeper of the crowded netherworld." (Foster 2001: 63, 226; Cavigneaux and Krebernik, *RlA* IX: 501)

Nin-šunir (M) Deity receiving offerings at Ur III Nippur. Means "Lady Standard." Written ᵈNin-ᵈŠu-nir. (BBVO 11 265 5NT435: r 7)

Nin-šu-suda (M) Deity identified with the healing goddess Gula. Means "Lady who Sprinkles (Water(?) on) the Hands," seemingly referring to a ritual or healing process. (Tallqvist 1974: 418; Cavigneaux and Krebernik, *RlA* IX: 504)

Nin-šušinak (M) Deity attested in an Early Dynastic god list. (Mander 1986: 159)

Nin-ŠU.UD-aš-bara (M) See Nin-kaš-bara

Nin-šušu(ŠEŠ) (M) Goddess identified with the mother goddess Dingir-maḫ/Bēlet-ilī. Explained in An : *Anum* as Bēlet-šūši, "Lady Licorice." (Litke 1998: 69; Tallqvist 1974: 418; Krebernik, *RlA* VIII: 506)

Nin-TAG (M) Deity attested in an Early Dynastic god list. (Mander 1986: 159)

Nin-ᵍᵉˢte-te (M) Deity attested as being allocated offerings at Ur III Puzriš-Dagān. ᵍᵉˢte (and ᵍᵉˢti) is a part of a boat, wagon, or chariot, perhaps the sides or ribbing. But whether this is related to the name of the deity cannot be determined. (Studies Levine, 132–38)

Nin-ti (M) Goddess in texts from the Early Dynastic period. Identified with Damkina/Dam-gal-nuna, the spouse of Enki, one of whose names was En-ti. Daughter of Nin-ḫursag and probably Enlil. Mother by Enki of the goddess of strong drink Nin-ka-si. Means "Lady Life." In "Enki and Nin-ḫursag," Nin-ḫursag gives birth to Nin-ti in order to heal Enki's ailing rib, hence the translation of her name as "Lady Rib" and the speculation, first suggested by Kramer, that the biblical tale of Eve having come from Adam's rib may have been a word play based on the Sumerian word ti. At the end of the piece, Nin-ti is named "Lady of the Month(s)," a wordplay on the homonym iti "month." Nin-ti had a temple at Lagaš and was worshipped at Ur, Nippur, and Mari. (*LAS*: 297; Litke 1998: 87, 88; Tallqvist 1974: 419; Kramer, *ANET*: 41; Cavigneaux and Krebernik, *RlA* IX: 504–5)

Nin-ti-ḫal (M) Guardian deity/spirit of the temple of Manun-gal, goddess of punishment and prisons. May mean "Lady who Allots Life." (Tallqvist 1974: 419; Cavigneaux and Krebernik, *RlA* IX: 505)

Nin-tila (Sum.), **Bēlet-tila** (Akk.) Deity identified with the goddess Gula. Worshipped under this name at Uruk, Dēr, and Babylon. Means "Lady who Grants Life." (Cavigneaux and Krebernik, *RlA* IX: 505)

Nin-ti-mu(d), Nin-ti-mu(d)-kalama (M) Deity identified with the healing goddesses Gula, Nin-Isina, and Nin-tin-uga. Means "Life-creating Lady (of the Nation)." (Litke 1998: 178; Cavigneaux and Krebernik, *RlA* IX: 505)

Nin-Tintir (M) Deity identified with Ištar and perhaps Zarpanītu(m), spouse of Marduk. Means "Lady of Tintir," a poetic name for a district of Babylon. (Cavigneaux and Krebernik, *RlA* IX: 505–6)

Nin-tin-uga, **Gašan-til-lu-ba** (Emesal) (M) Goddess identified with Gula, but originally probably an independent goddess. Her spouse was En-daga. Name probably means "Lady who Causes the Dead to Live." The dog was her sacred animal, and she had shrines at Nippur, Isin, and Ur. (Cohen 2015: 122; Black and Green 2003: 101; Litke 1998: 178, 179; George 1993: 63 no. 11, 131 no. 859, 158 no. 1208; Edzard, *RlA* IX: 506)

Nin-tu(r) (M) Ancient Sumerian mother goddess. Written Nin-tu/tur$_5$, and occurs with Auslaut /r/. She was identified with Dingir-maḫ, Bēlet-ilī, and Aruru. From the Neo-Sumerian period on associated especially with Nin-ḫursag. The meaning of the name is unclear. The obvious meaning for a mother goddess from tu "to give birth" is unlikely since that should be Nin-tud. The ancients also seem unsure. Note AN : *Anum* II 18–20 among deities identified with the mother goddess Dingir-maḫ: ^{d}Nin-^{tur}tùr, ^{d}Nin-tu^{tùr}, ^{d}Nin-dím. Also note AN : *Anum* II 101–2: ^{d}Nin-tùr *šassūru* ^{d}Šà-tùr *šassūru* "womb." And Nin-tu was depicted as an exorcist of the goddesses, as if Nin-tu was a variant for Nin-tu$_6$. Titles of Nin-tu included Nin-tu-babbara (with homophonous entry Nin-du$_6$-babbar) and Nin-tu-maḫ. In An : *Anu ša amēli* (Nin)-du-babbar-ra is explained as "Ea of reed-workers." She was known as Ama-dumu-dumu-ne "Mother of Children." Nin-tu's symbol is in the shape of the Greek letter omega Ω, which some suggest represents the cow uterus. The god Enki assigned to Nin-tu/Aruru the task of being the land's midwife. In "Enki and Nin-ḫursag" Nin-tu is called "the mother of the land." Nin-tu wept for the humans who, in the Sumerian "The Deluge," were going to be destroyed by the Great Flood. In "The Death of Gilgameš," a counselor, after interpreting Gilgameš's dream, reminds him: "The birth goddess Nin-tu has never borne [a man /whom the demon Fate has not] seized." "The Hymn to Enlil" indicates that not only does Nin-tu give birth, but she could also bring death. In a hymn, Šulgi of Ur states that he had been nursed by Nin-tu. It was Nin-tu who, in a fragment of an Akkadian composition, mixed the clay for the making of human beings. She is mentioned also at the beginning and end of the law code of Ḫammu-rāpi. Nin-tu was worshipped in Nin-ḫursag's temple at Šarrākum/Keš; at Adab; and almost certainly at every birth/mother goddess temple in the land. It is likely that the cult personnel of these temples would have included midwives. In a god list from Aššur, For drawing see Bēlet-ilī. (*LAS*: 223–24; Richter 2004: 144; Black and Green 2003: 85, 133, 140; Leick 1999: 65–66, 153; Leick 1998: 135; Litke 1998: 68, 78; George 1993: 25, 108 no. 578, 119 no. 713; Jacobsen 1976: 107; Tallqvist 1974: 419, 420; Schroeder 1920: no. 64; Kramer, *ANET*: 42, 575, 585; Meek, *ANET*: 165, 180; Speiser, *ANET*: 100; Krebernik, *RlA* VIII: 506–7; Cavigneaux and Krebernik, *RlA* IX: 507–8)

Nin-tu-ama-erida-mua (M) Goddess at Lagaš in the Early Dynastic period. Means "Nintu, Mother who Grows Along with the City." (Selz 1995: 267)

Nin-t/du-babbara, Nin-tu-maḫ, Nin-tùr (M) See Nin-tu

NIN-tugnigla-šudu (M) See Egi/Ereš-tugnigla-šudu

Nin-tuk-sud (M) See Nam-me-sud

Nin-tul-gana (M) Deity attested at Ur III Ur. Written Nin-túl-GÍR-na and Nin-túl-ga-na. (UET 3, 72: o 5)

Nin-tulla (M) Deity identified with the spouse of Ninurta. Written Nin-túl-lá. Nin-tul(a) means "Lady of the Well." In "Enki and Nin-ḫursag(a)," she was created by Nin-ḫursag(a) to treat Enki's diseased jaw. At the end of the piece, Nin-ḫursag(a) decreed that Nin-tul(a) would be "Patron of Magan," modern Oman. (Litke 1998: 47; Tallqvist 1974: 420; Volk, *RlA* IX: 506)

Nin-tul-maḫ (M) Deity attested at Ur III Umma. Means "Lord/Lady (of) the Great Well." (TJAMC IOS 46: r 37)

Nin-tul-munna (M) Sumerian deity appearing in offering lists from Ur in the Ur III period. Means "Lord/Lady of the Brackish Well" and may refer to a well in the holy precinct at Ur. (Sallaberger 1993: II, 109 and plate 62b)

Nin-tulsag (M) Deity attested at Ur III Nippur and Umma. Means "Lady of the Pit." The reading túl rather than pú is based on its being directly preceded in a god list from Aššur by ^{d}Nin-^{du}dúl-RA. (Litke 1998: 67; Sallaberger 1993: I, 104; Schroeder 1920: no. 64)

Nin-tu-ma (M) Deity attested at Ur III Umma with a residence in the E-maḫ and with whom a great door (abul-maḫ) was associated. (MVN 13, 775: r 8)

Nin-tu-maḫ (M) See Nin-tu

NIN-Tummala (M) See Egi-Tummal

Nin-tùr (M) See Nin-tu

Nin-tu-zaga (M) Sumerian deity in Lagaš province in the Early Dynastic period. Appears in the Nanše festival at ancient Nimen. Means "Nintu of Zaga," a town not far from ancient Nimen. (Selz 1995: 267)

Nin-UBARA-UBARA (M) Goddess in an Old Babylonian god list from Nippur in a circle of goddesses associated with Nin-ḫursag. Read ubara, the sign means "protection," thus perhaps "Lady who Continually Affords Protection." (Richter 2004: 144)

Nin-UD (M) Deity attested in an Early Dynastic god list. (Mander 1986: 146)

Nin-UD-e-da (M) Deity attested in an Early Dynastic god list. (Mander 1986: 146)

Nin-udi-(ki)šara, Nin-u-kišara (M) Epithet of Šala(š), the wife of Dagān. Means "Lady, Marvel of the Universe." (Litke 1998: 43; Cavigneaux and Krebernik, *RlA* IX: 508)

Nin-UD-KA (M) Deity in an Early Dynastic god list from Šuruppak. (Mander 1986: 96)

Nin-ug (M) See En-ug

Nin-ugnim (M) Deity identified with Inana/Ištar. Means "Lady of the Army." (Litke 1998: 150; Cavigneaux and Krebernik, *RlA* IX: 509)

Nin-ugu-sa (M) deity attested in an Old Babylonian god list from Mari. Written nin-u-gu-sa$_{6}$, perhaps "Lady with a Beautiful Pate(?)."

Nin-ul (M) See En-ul

Nin-ul-šu-taga (M) Deity identified with Aya/Šerda, spouse of the sun god Utu/Šamaš. Means "Lady Adorned with Attractiveness." (Litke 1998: 132; Cavigneaux and Krebernik, *RlA* IX: 510)

Nin-umbisag (M) See Umbisag

Nin-umma-sigga (M) Deity identified with the healing goddess Gula. Means "Lady, the Good-looking Old Woman." Written -sig$_6$- and -sig-. (Litke 1998: 181; Cavigneaux and Krebernik, *RlA* IX: 510)

NIN-una (M) See Egi/Ereš-unna

Nin-Ur (M) See Nin-Muru(m)

Nin-ur (M) Written Nin-úr. Deity in the Offering Bread hemerology.

Nin-ura(-Umma) (M) Goddess known from Early Dynastic times. Wife of Šara, the tutelary deity of Umma. As Šara's wife, she was called "Loving Lady (of Umma)." (George 1993: 152 no. 1126; Cavigneaux and Krebernik, *RlA* IX: 510)

Nin-ur-gena (M) Deity in an Old Babylonian god list from Mari. May mean "Lord/Lady (of?) the Faithful Dog (Fido)." (Studies Birot, 184–85: r iii 22)

Nin-Uri (M) See Bēlet-Akkad(e)

Nin-Uri (M) Goddess identified with Nin-gal, the spouse of the tutelary deity of Ur, the moon god Nanna/Sîn. Mentioned in texts from the Early Dynastic period. Also the name of the spouse of Alammuš, vizier of the moon god Nanna/Sîn. Means "Lady of Ur." (Litke 1998: 122; George 1993: 108 no. 570; Tallqvist 1974: 421; Cavigneaux and Krebernik, *RlA* IX: 511)

Nin-ur-sala (M) Concubine of An/Anu(m). Name possibly means "Lady of the Spread Lap." In An : *Anum* written Nin-úr-sal-la; in an Old Babylonian god list from Mari written Nin-úr-sal$_4$. See Nin-eri-sala and Nin-bur-šal-la. (Litke 1998: 24; Tallqvist 1974: 421; Cavigneaux and Krebernik, *RlA* IX: 511)

Ninurta (M) Sumerian god already mentioned in documents from the Early Dynastic period. A warlike and heroic warrior deity. Ninurta was important as a god of war in Assyria. Also concerned with farming and the weather, especially rain and storm. Thus fertility was perhaps his original domain. Jacobsen characterized him as god of the south wind and of thundershowers. Closely associated with Ninurta was the god Nin-Girsu, who, by historical times, amounted to a local Lagaš-area form of Ninurta. Some of Ninurta's traits/powers were later assumed by the chief god of Babylon Marduk. Son of Enlil and Ninlil/Ninmaḫ or one of the other birth/mother goddesses, especially Nin-ḫursag. In the composition Lugal-e, Ninurta gives his mother Ninlil the name Nin-ḫursag. At Nippur Ninurta was ranked as Enlil's first born. In Assyria he was the son of Aššur. His sister was Nin-uzale. Ninurta's wife was Nin-Nibru "Lady of Nippur," who was equated to the healing goddess Gula. Sometimes Baba, the spouse of Nin-Girsu, was also paired with Ninurta. His daughters were Nin-niggena and Nin-nig-erim. His vizier was Inimani-zi. Among Nin-urta's epithets were: "Helper of His Father," "(He) who Fulfills the Wish of Enlil," and "Right Hand of the Great Mountain [Enlil]."

Ninurta battling Asag from cylinder seal. Neo-Assyrian. Steatite (soapstone). 3.7x1.5. Morgan Library no. 689. After Porada 1948: no. 689E

The meaning of his name remains obscure, though some have suggested translations such as "Lord Earth" (unlikely) or "Lord Plow" (Jacobsen 1976: 127). One of his symbols was the plow, and another a perching bird. The rainbow was described as the crown of Ninurta.

It was as a warrior that Ninurta was most prominent in myth and literature. Ninurta pursued and presumably subdued the anzû-bird when the latter stole the tablets of destiny from Enki (Sumerian version) or Enlil (Akkadian version). The anzû-bird then became Ninurta's emblem, the "thunder bird." In the earlier versions of the anzû story, Nin-Girsu, not Ninurta, was the hero. "Ninurta's Return to Nippur" recounts that Ninurta used the anzû-bird to adorn his chariot.

At Girsu archaeologists discovered fragments of a stele showing Nin-Girsu, the local form of Ninurta, with trophies such as the anzû-bird adorning his chariot (*LAS*: 182 figure 23). In *Lugal-e*, Ninurta vanquishes the monster Asag and his army of stone creatures. After his conquest, Ninurta builds a dike to control the waters of the Tigris River, causing the land to become fertile. At the end of the piece, Ninurta turns the heaping granaries over to the care of the grain goddess Nisaba. This work brought together in harmony both the farming and warrior aspects of the god. Ninurta's concern with farming and fertility was the focus of a hymn to the god and attributed to him all earthly fecundity, including the birth of children. In the Babylonian "Epic of Gilgameš," Ninurta helped bring about the Great Flood by making the dikes overflow. Myths associated with Ninurta were incorporated into the *Enūma eliš*, with Marduk taking over roles originally assigned to Ninurta. An Assyrian treaty called upon the fierce warrior Ninurta to kill those who broke the agreement.

Ninurta's cult center and main temple was at Nippur, the E-šumeša, and a temple of the same name was dedicated to Ninurta at Aššur. As Lugal-Marada "Lord of Marad," he had a major temple at that city northwest of Nippur. He also had temples or chapels in Ur, Larsa, Uruk, and Babylon, and he was venerated at Umma and Emar. Even his divinized maces, such as Šar-ur and Šar-gaz, had shrines. At Nippur, the spring-time gu$_4$-si-sù festival focused on Ninurta as the plowman par excellence. At Isin the king assumed the role of Ninurta in the ceremonies, performing ritual plowing. In Assyria Ninurta was patron deity of the military city of Kalaḫ (Nimrūd) south of Aššur, where he had a large temple with a ziqqurat. He was among the deities honored at the Assyrian *akītu* festival. At another festival, foot races commemorated Ninurta's conquest of the anzû-bird. If during the races a dog came running about, it was considered a messenger from Ninurta's wife Gula. Astrally he was identified with Sirius, as well as the constellation Hercules. The biblical Nimrod is likely a reflex of Ninurta (Genesis 10: 8–12). Some scholars such as Van Dijk have suggested that the deeds of Hercules might be a reflex of the deeds of Ninurta as recounted in "Ninurta's Return to Nippur" and Lugal-e.

The orthography NIN.URTA appears in a broken context in the treaty between Narām-Sîn of Akkad and a king of Susa. Vallat says that five Elamite gods were assimilated to Ninurta, but there is no evidence of any martial epithets. (Cohen 2015: 45, 122, 138, 389; Foster 2005: 555–78, 710–16; *LAS*: 163–87; Black and Green 2003: 42–43, 142–43, 153, 179; Annus 2002; Foster 2001: 87; Uelinger, *DDDB*: 627–30; Leick 1998: 135–37; Litke 1998: 44, 47–48, 212, 233; Vallat 1998: 336; George 1993: 65 no. 32, 102 no. 489, 104 no. 520, 105 no. 524, 120 no. 723–24, 132 no. 874, 147 no. 1065 no. 1067; Hinz and Koch 1987: 1002; König 1977: 29, 227; Jacobsen 1976: 127–34, 167; Tallqvist 1974: 421–27; Jacobsen 1970: 8, 57; Reiner, *ANET*: 538; Speiser, *ANET*: 111–13; Streck, *RlA* IX: 512–22; Braun-Holzinger, *RlA* IX: 522–24)

Nin-uru (M) See En-uru

Nin-Uruba (M) Tutelary deity of the town of Urub near Girsu in the Lagaš region. (Cavigneaux and Krebernik, *RlA* IX: 528)

Nin-uru-lugalene (M) Sumerian birth/mother goddess. Means "Powerful Lady of Kings." (Krebernik, *RlA* VIII: 507)

Nin-usana (M) According to M. Cohen, the deity's name should be read Nin-usan$_4$^{an}-na "Lady of the Evening," (instead of Nin-si$_4$-an-na), referring to the Evening Star, Venus. In a late Assyrian list of gods (Lambert 2013: 423) occurs a goddess ^{d}usan$_2$$^{\{an\}}$-na, quite likely a writing for Nin-usana.

Sumerian androgynous deity with both male and female forms. Together she/he was Inana/Ištar as the planet Venus. In general, the female deity was the evening star and the male deity the morning star. In fact, it was one of the Sumerian names for the planet Venus. Same as Ištar-kakkabī "Ištar of the Stars." By this name the goddess had temples at Ur and Nippur, and she had a role in the *akītu* festival at Uruk. As male the deity was worshipped at Ur, Girsu, Mari, and Sippar-Amnānum, twin city to Sippar. (Cohen 2015: 213)

Nin-us-gidda, Nin-us-gi-da (M) Deity attested as having a *gudu*-priest at Lagaš/Girsu. May mean "Lord/Lady (of) the Long Side." Written Nin-ús-gíd-da, Nin-ús-gi$^?$-da (ITT 3, 5280: r iii 1: o 3; *Atiqot* 4 pl. 30, 72: o iii)

Nin-UŠ-KA-limmu (M) See Nita-su-limmu

Nin-u-tila (M) See En-u-tila

Nin-utula (M) Deity attested in a Sargonic personal name and on a door socket possibly from Ur, which was part of the construction by Ur-Namma of his temple. (Milano and Westenholz 2015; Richter 2004: 415; Frayne 1997b: 29–30)

Nin-uzale (M) Sister of Ninurta. Spouse of Saman. May mean "Lady, the Continuous Light," though ud—zal can mean "to spend time." (Litke 1998: 48; Cavigneaux and Krebernik, *RlA* IX: 514, 531)

Nin-zadima (M) See Nin-muga

Nin-zaga (M) Name of En-zak, one of the gods of Tilmun, modern Baḥrain. Mentioned in an inscription of Gudea. (Leick 1999: 62; Nashef 1986: 343; Oppenheim, *ANET*: 268; Cavigneaux and Krebernik, *RlA* IX: 531)

Nin-zale (M) Deity identified with the goddess Antu(m), Anu(m)'s consort. The goddess had a temple at Uruk. See Nin-uzale. (George 1993: 8 note 28, 84 no. 278)

Nin-zi (M) Deity attested in an Early Dynastic god list. Means "Trustworthy Lady." (Mander 1986: 146)

Nin-zi-ana (M) Aspect of the birth/mother goddess. Name means "Trustworthy Lady of Heaven." Might be related to Nin-zu-ana. (Tallqvist 1974: 428; Cavigneaux and Krebernik, *RlA* IX: 532)

Nin-zil(zil) (M) Deity identified with Nanāya. Means "The Pleasing Lady." (Beaulieu, 2013: 322; George 1993: 34; Cavigneaux and Krebernik, *RlA* IX: 532)

Nin-zizna (M) Deity identified with the birth/mother goddess. May mean "Lady of Children (or 'of the Womb')" (cf. [d]Šassūru). Name written [d]Nin-BÀN.ZA/BÀN.ZA[zi-iz-na]-na and [d]Nin-zaz-na ni-in-za-az-na (OB Nippur Diri: Seg. 11, 23) (Civil 2004; Litke 1998: 69; Krebernik, *RlA* VIII: 507)

NIN-zu (M) See Egi/Ereš-zu

Nin-zu-ana (M) See Nizu-ana

Ni-pa'e (M) Deity whose name means "(She) who By Herself Comes Forth." Had chapels in temples of the deity Lama-šaga, a protective spirit and chief vizier of Baba. (Selz 1995: 212; George 1993: 166 no. 1344)

Nipḫū-ṣalmū (M) Akkadian gods, deified images of sun disks that stood on poles or statues on the heads of servant gods. Means "Sun-disk Images." (Wiggermann 1992: 62)

Niraḫ, Irḫān (Sum.), **Niraḫu(m), Miraḫu(m)** (Akk.) Snake god. Associated with the netherworld and with water. In a hymn for King Gungunum of Larsa, called the twin of Enki. Known from the earliest texts. Divinized snakes were seemingly the only Mesopotamian "fully animal, non-anthropomorphic deities" (Black and Green 2003: 166). Niraḫ was vizier of Ištarān, the tutelary god of the city of Dēr. One of his titles was "Lord of the Earth." Originally a separate god of Ur, Irḫān, who was probably the deified snake-like river Euphrates, was assimilated into Niraḫ by the Ur III period. In An : *Anum*, Irḫān was listed as a child of the goddess Lisina. Images of a god with a serpentine lower body might be images of Niraḫ. He was depicted as a snake on at least one *kudurru* and might be the snake often ap-pearing on others. Images of snakes were regularly used as apotropaic devices to guard doors and were placed under floors to protect houses. He was venerated at Dēr along with Ištarān. He was also a minor presence at Nippur, where he functioned as the sheriff or guardian spirit of Enlil's great temple. At Babylon he was venerated in association with Nin-geš-zida. Irḫān received offerings at Ur at the spring *akītu* festival and had a shrine in Aššur. Astrally Niraḫ was associated with the constellation Hydra. (Cohen, 2017:11–16; Black and Green 2003: 111, 166–68; Hendel, *DDDB*: 744; Litke 1998: 52 no. 275, 75 no. 76; George 1993: 145 no. 1034; Wiggermann, *RlA* IX: 570–74)

Nisaba (M) Goddess of writing, accounting, surveying, scribes and scribal wisdom, and of grain. Often identified with Ašnan, another important grain goddess. In fact, the name Nisaba was used in written material as a word to denote grain. The description of Gilgameš at the beginning of the Babylonian "Epic of Gilgameš" compares the hero's hair with that of Nisaba, that is, like grain growing in a field. As proposed by Selz, the meaning of the name Nisaba might be "Lady of Grain Rations." Her symbol was a sheaf or ear of grain. In the lexical series Diri the name is written with the logogram

^{d}ŠE.NAGA, and syllabically rendered ni-is-sà-ba.

Attested in the Sumerian zà-mí hymns and other literary texts of the Early Dynastic period. Daughter of the sky god An/Anu(m) and of Uraš, an earth goddess. Sister of Nin-Isina, the healing goddess. In the Lagaš region eldest child of Enlil, who in another tradition became her son-in-law; sister of Nin-Girsu and Nanše. Her spouse was Ḫaya, though later she was the wife of Nabû, when he took over as patron of scribes and scribal lore. Her daughter was the goddess Sud, who became Ninlil. Occasionally equated to Nanibgal and Nun-bar-še-gunu. Also had some connection to Ereškigal.

Hymns often saluted her as patron of scribes. In "Enlil and Sud," Nisaba, (also called Nanibgal and Nun-bar-še-gunu) was mother of the potential bride of Enlil.

Many literary pieces concluded with the phrase "Praise (to) Nisaba!"

Cylinder seal possibly showing Nisaba enthroned as grain goddess. Ca. 2350–2150 BCE. After Boehmer 1965: pl. XLVI, no. 541

In the earliest literary materials the goddess was already associated with the city of Ereš. In "En-merkar and En-suḫgir-ana," a sorcerer practices magic at Nisaba's cult city, Ereš. At Ereš Nisaba was worshipped as tutelary deity under the title "Lady of Ereš," and her temple was called "House of Stars." Eventually, the cults of Ereš were transferred to Nippur, and, from then on, her cult was primarily conducted in relation to that of her daughter Ninlil. In the fourth month at Ur III Umma there were special observances for Nisaba. She had shrines at Lagaš, Girsu, Eridu, Uruk, and Babylon. A hymn to Nisaba was regularly recited at Lagaš and at Ur. For the Harvest Festival, according to a composition, her statue was washed and dressed in clean clothes. She was mentioned in an offering list from Mari. (Cohen 2015: 122; Civil 2004; LAS: 3–11, 106–11, 292–94; Black and Green 2003: 143, 182; Lang, *DDDB*: 901; Leick 1999: 135–36; Leick 1998: 137–38; Litke 1998: 54, 55–56, 58; George 1993: 74 no. 140, 79 no. 201, 87 no. 309, 91 no. 355 no. 362 no. 363; Selz 1989: 270; Mander 1986: 40; Jacobsen 1976: 10; Tallqvist 1974: 429–30; Speiser, *ANET*: 74; Michalowski, *RlA* IX: 575–79)

Nisaba-ursag (M) Form of Nisaba in an Old Babylonian god list fragment. Means "Heroic Nisaba." She appears as the wife of Guzala-Enlila "Throne-bearer of Enlil." (Richter 2004: 92)

Nisroch (L) God mentioned in the Hebrew Bible (II Kings 19:37; Isaiah 37: 38). The Bible reported that Sennacherib, king of Assyria, died while worshipping in Nisroch's temple. Sennacherib was assassinated in 681 BCE. Obviously the Bible was referring to an Assyrian deity, but no such deity occurs in Assyrian sources. Almost certainly a Hebrew scribal corruption, probably for the warrior god Ninurta or Nuska. (Black and Green 2003: 143; Uelinger, *DDDB*: 630–32; Comay 1993: 265; Grayson, *ABD* IV: 1122; Gray, *IDB* 1991: III, 554)

Nišpa (M) Deity from the Zagros region. (Durand 2008: 251)

Niššīku(m) (M) Deity identified with Enki/Ea. Mentioned in the *Enūma eliš* and in the "Creation of Man by the Mother Goddess." Explained in An : *Anu ša amēli* as "Ea of Wisdom (*nēmeqi*)" based on reading the name as Sumerian Nin-igi-kù (kù-zu = *emqu*). (Black and Green 2003: 75; Litke 1998: 238; Lambert 1982: 199; Tallqvist 1974: 408; Speiser, *ANET*: 70, 100; Cavigneaux and Krebernik, *RlA* IX: 590)

Nita (M) Vizier of the goddess Uraš. His wife was Ki-gula. Means "Male." In the lexical series Diri the deity is written with the logogram UŠ and syllabically as ni-ta. (Civil 2004; Litke 1998: 173; Cavigneaux and Krebernik, *RlA* IX: 590)

NITA-su-limmu(4), Nin-NITA-su-limmu, Nin-su-limmu/aš(6)/imin(7) (M) Deity whose name is almost always written with a KA-sign. However, one or two Ur III economic texts write su_6(KA×SA). Therefore we read KA as su_{11}. The signs su_6 and su_{11} can denote palm fibers *sû* and, if appropriate here, the god name may indicate the number of fibers either coming out from the god's body or else forming a bundle possibly held by the deity. Another possibility is that su_6 is the original writing and su_{11} is just an abbreviated writing of the sign, in which case su_6 *ziqnu*, "rays of light," might refer to the number of light rays emanating from the deity.

An : *Anum* identifies Nin-su_{11}-àš(6) (with variant Nin-su_{11}-imin(7)) and Nin-su_{11}-limmu(4) with Inana, which makes a reading nita speculative. At Ur III Umma the deity is consistently paired with Enki, where the deity shares a temple with Enki and has a festival. One Umma text refers to the deity's residence in the Emaḫ. (Cohen 2015; Litke 1998: 150; Richter 2004: 292)

Nita-zi(d) (M) Bull harp of Nin-Girsu. Written with gloss ni-ta. Means "Reliable Male." Presumably "male" here refers to the bull that is fashioned in the harp and that this harp is a reliable instrument. (Litke 1998: 177; Cavigneaux and Krebernik, *RlA* IX: 590)

Nitutir (E) Elamite deity appearing in a treaty between Narām-Sîn of Akkad and a king of Susa. (Hinz and Koch 1987: 1004; König 1977: 227)

Nizu-ana (M) (1) Spouse of Lugal-Marada, tutelary deity of Marad. In an Ur III economic tablet in connection to the city Marad, northwest of Nippur, and following a mention of Lugal-Marad(a). Written Ní-zu-an-na with variants Nin-zu-an-na and Ní-zi-an-na. (2) In an Ugaritic lexical text equated to Teššup and Ba'al and would thus seem masculine and so a different god. (Litke 1998: 170–71; Cavigneaux and Krebernik, *RlA* IX: 532)

Nubadig, Nupatik, Lubadaga, Lupatik (H, L) A Hurrian protective and warrior god and member of the pantheon at the Hittite capital Ḫattušas. Its first form was Lubadaga. Identified with Zababa. Depicted on the frieze at Yazılıkaya. Possibly a stag was his emblem. In god lists, included with war/protective deities and followed Aštabi(l). Rituals from Ḫattušas give his name as Nupatik. Attested in god lists and Hurrian ritual texts from Ugarit. (del Olmo Lete 1999: 84–86; van Gessel 1998: I, 341–45; Popko 1995: 89, 94, 100, 115; Haas 1994: 363, 470, 850 note 10; Laroche 1946/47: 56; Wilhelm, *RlA* VII: 173–74)

Nubanda-maḫ (M) Sumerian god from Umma in the Ur III period. Means "Supreme Captain." He apparently supervised festivals at Umma. (Sallaberger 1993: I, 242, 244)

Nudimmud, En-nudimmud (M) Name of the god Enki/Ea. Jacobsen proposes that the name means "Image Fashioner," perhaps a reference to his patronage of craftsmen and artisans (1976: 111). As En-nutemud he is mentioned in the Early Dynastic Sumerian zà-mí hymns, where he is associated with Eridu. In the Sumerian account of the Great Flood, the city of Eridu was given to Enki as Nu-dim-mud, and the *Enūma eliš* also refers to Enki by this epithet. A late ritual for repairing a temple described Nudimmud as creating other gods by shaping them from pinched-off pieces of clay from the abzu. (Foster 2005: 440; *LAS*: 212–15; Foster 2001: 226; Litke 1998: 83, 238; Kramer, *ANET*: 43; Sachs, *ANET*: 341; Speiser, *ANET*: 61, 65; Heidel 1967: 18; Cavigneaux and Krebernik, *RlA* IX: 607)

Nu-gal (M) Deity attested in an Early Dynastic god list. (Mander 1986: 148)

Nu-gig (M) Deity attested in an Old Babylonian god list. (Weidner 1924/25)

Nuha (M) Deity from the Rum area in Arabia in the Neo-Babylonian period. (Gentili 2001: no. 90)

Nu-kiri (M) Deity attested in an Early Dynastic god list. Means "Gardener."(Mander 1986: 148)

Numun-ab-šara (M) Fourth of the ten offspring of the hero/god Lugalbanda and the goddess Nin-sun. May mean "Semen for All the Cows." (Litke 1998: 169; Cavigneaux and Krebernik, *RlA* IX: 611)

Numunki (M) The original name of Nunki, who with Enki formed an early god pair. (George 2016: no. 59)

Numušda (M) Perhaps god of the storm and rain and thus of the fecundity of nature. Attested in documents from the Early Dynastic period. Son of the moon god Nanna/Sîn. His spouse was Namrat and his daughter Adgar-kidug. In the "The Marriage of Martu," Adgar-kidug was determined to marry the nomadic god Martu, despite his being uncouth. Several hymns to Numušda are extant. In a text for the ritual of the *akītu* festival from Babylon, he is described as the one who "brings lasting rain!"

Numušda's cult center was Kazallu northwest of Babylon on the Euphrates River. His temple there was called "Threshold of the Mountain." The god was worshipped also at Nippur, Ur, Umma, Lagaš, and Mari, Kiritab near Kazallu northwest of Babylon on the Euphrates, Inab of unknown location, and Tuttul near the junction of the Balīḫ and the Euphrates.

An orthography ŠITA-muš-da occurs in a theophoric name in an Early Dynastic tablet from Nippur (A. Westenholz 1975b: no. 54), and is, perhaps, a writing for Numušda. (Black and Green 2003: 129–30; Cohen 1993: 139 note 1, 444; Cavigneaux and Krebernik, *RlA* IX: 611–14)

Nu-na (M) Deity, perhaps identified with Inana, in An : *Anum* with broken gloss a-[...]. (Litke 1998: 164)

Nun-abzu (M) Epithet of Enki/Ea. Means "Prince (of the) Abzu." (Litke 1998: 84; Cavigneaux and Krebernik, *RlA* IX: 614)

Nun-a-gal (M) Deity attested in an Early Dynastic god list. Written nun-a-gál. (Mander 1986: 148)

Nuna'itu(m) (M) See Bēlet-Ninua

Nunamnir (M) Common name of Enlil, reflecting his being above all the gods. Means "The One (with) Respect." (*LAS*: 320–25; Black and Green 2003: 76; Leick 1999: 97; George 1993: 116 no. 678; Kramer, *ANET*: 159, 573; Cavigneaux and Krebernik, *RlA* IX: 614)

Nunbar-ana, Nunbar-una (M) Deity identified with the fire god Gibil/Girra. He is also called gešbar-ana, which suggests a connection between the puzzling terms gešbar and nunbar. (Litke 1998: 107; Cavigneaux and Krebernik, *RlA* IX: 614–15)

Nunbar-ḫuša (M) Name of the fire god Gibil/Girra. Spouse was Nin-eš-gal. (Litke 1998: 108; Cavigneaux and Krebernik, *RlA* IX: 615)

Nunbar-še-gunu (M) Name of the grain and scribal goddess Nisaba. In the Sumerian work "Enlil and Ninlil," Nunbar-še-gunu was Ninlil's mother. In "Enlil and Sud" she appears as the mother of Sud/Ninlil. Explained in An : *Anu ša amēli* as "Nisaba of the life of the land." (*LAS*: 102–6, 106–11; Litke 1998: 55, 236; Cavigneaux and Krebernik, *RlA* IX: 615)

Nunbar-uda (M) Name of the fire god Gibil/Girra. (Litke 1998: 108)

Nun-dug (M) Deity identified with Enki/Ea. Means "Goodly Prince." A reading Nun-šár "Perfect Prince" is possible. (Litke 1998: 86; Cavigneaux and Krebernik, *RlA* IX: 619)

Nundum-kuga (M) According to An : *Anum*, the daughter of Kusu. A variant is Šudu$_3$(KA×ŠU)-kuga. Numdum (KA×SA) -kuga means "Holy Lips" or "Holy Utterance"; Šudu$_3$-kuga "Holy Prayer." It is unclear whether one is a scribal error for the other. (Litke 1998: 60)

Nun-gal (M) See Manun-gal

Nun-ki (M) See Numun-ki

Nun-kirzal (M) Deity attested in an Early Dynastic god list. Means "Prince (of) Joy."(Mander 1986: 148)

Nun-na-DI (M) One of three guardian spirits of the goddess Baba. Variant is En-na-DI. (Litke 1998: 176; Cavigneaux and Krebernik, *RlA* IX: 619)

Nu(n)-nir (M) Deity explained in *Anu ša amēli* as "Nergal of battle(*qabli*)," and "Nergal of confrontation(?)(*miḫri*)." May mean "Respected Prince" or "Respected One." (Litke 1998: 234; Cavigneaux and Krebernik, *RlA* IX: 618)

Nun-nir-DUDU (M) See Barirītu

Nun(n)u (M) Demon patrolman of the steppe. (Litke 1998: 165; Cavigneaux and Krebernik, *RlA* IX: 619–20)

Nun-nun (M) Early Dynastic god. Means "Prince of Princes." See Nám-nám for a somewhat similarly constructed name. (Mander 148)

Nun-nu-ru (M) See Nun-ura

Nun-sag-maḫ (M) Deity identified with the sun god Utu/Šamaš. May mean "Proud Prince." See Sag-maḫ. (Litke 1998: 129; Cavigneaux and Krebernik, *RlA* IX: 619)

Nun-si-kur (M) Sumerian deity who appears in a circle of goddesses associated with Kanisura in an An : *Anum* fragment. (Richter 2004: 310)

Nun-ura, Nun-nu-ru (M) Sumerian potter god. Also known for magical skill. Identified with Enki/Ea. Often invoked in incantations. Written -ur$_4$-ra and Nun-nu-ru. Explained in An : *Anu ša amēli* as "Ea of potters." In the lexical series Diri ᵈBAḪAR$_2$ rendered syllabically as ni-in-ur-ra. (Civil 2004; Litke 1998: 86, 238; Cavigneaux and Kreber-nik, *RlA* IX: 620–21)

Nun-ur-DU.DU (M) Female demon associated with Aba-šušu and Kilili. (Cavigneaux and Krebernik, *RlA* IX: 621)

Nunus-aba (M) Seventh of ten children of the god-hero Lugalbanda and the goddess Nin-sun. Means "Woman of the Cow(s)." (Litke 1998: 169; Cavigneaux and Krebernik, *RlA* IX: 621)

Nunus-dili-tummu (M) Fifth of thirteen children of the goddess Nin-marki. (Litke 1998: 125; Cavigneaux and Krebernik, *RlA* IX: 621)

Nunus-dug (M) Goddess at Early Dynastic Šuruppak. Variant is {nu}Nunus-tùr. (Mander 1986: 63)

Nunus-gal (M) Goddess attested in god lists of the Early Dynastic period from Šuruppak and Abu Ṣalābīkh. Means "Great Woman." (Mander 1986: 63, 113)

Nunus-ganam (M) Goddess attested in an Early Dynastic god list. Means "Woman Ewe." (Mander 1986: 98)

Nunus-gunu (M) Goddess at Early Dynastic Šuruppak. Written {nu}Nunus-gú-nu. (Mander 1986: 63)

Nunus-kia (M) Deity attested in Neo-Assyrian god list. Written nu-nus-ki-a "Woman of the Earth/Netherworld." (King 1969: pl. 43)

Nunus-sa-a (M) Deity identified with Nin-imma according to An : *Anum*. Name occurs in the Early Dynastic period and in the Neo-Babylonian period as {nu}Nunus-GÙN-a. Although the name may be read Nunus-gùn-a, the entry Munus-GÙN-a with variant Nin-sa$_4$ in An : *Anum* raises the likelihood of a reading Nunus-sa$_{11}$-a. (Litke 1998: 57; Cavigneaux and Krebernik, *RlA* IX: 622)

Nunus-tur (M) Goddess at Early Dynastic Šuruppak. Written {nu}Nunus-tùr. (Mander 1986: 63)

Nunus-zi(d) (M) Deity appearing in a personal name in an Early Dynastic tablet from Nippur. Meaning "Trustworthy Woman." (A. Westenholz 1975b: no. 46)

Nunuwaḫi (H) A rarely found Hurrian goddess. Probably means "The Ninevite Lady" and refers to Ištar/Ša(w)uš(k)a. (van Gessel 1998: I, 341)

Nūr-ilī (M) Deity associated in An : *Anum* with the sun god Utu/ Šamaš. Means "Light of the Gods." (Schwemer 2001: 27–28, 71–72, 87; Litke 1998: 145–46)

Nūr-Šamaš (M) Second of eight judges of the sun god Utu/Šamaš. Means "Light (of) Šamaš." (Litke 1998: 135; Cavigneaux and Krebernik, *RlA* IX: 623)

Nūru(m) (M) Deity identified with Nuska or of the goddess Aya/Šerda. Means "Light." (Cavigneaux and Krebernik, *RlA* IX: 623–24)

Nu-siliga (M) See Me-ḫuš(-a)

Nuska (M), **Našuḫ** (L) Sumerian and Babylonian god of fire and light. Grand vizier of Enlil. Attested in theophoric names of the Early Dynastic period. Son of Enlil and Ninlil. In another tradition son of En-ul and Nin-ul, primeval ancestors of Enlil. Identified with Girra/Gibil. Sometimes Gibil was named as Nuska's son. At Ḫarrān in northern Mesopotamia considered son of the city's tutelary deity, the moon god Nanna/Sîn. Sadar-nuna was Nuska's spouse. Nuska's symbol, especially on boundary stones, was the lamp. Later, he was identified by the rooster.

As Enlil's vizier Nuska conducted Enlil to his meeting with Ninlil in "Enlil and Ninlil," and he acted as Enlil's ambassador when Enlil wanted to marry Ninlil. The hymn "Enlil in the Ekur" describes Nuska as executor of Enlil's wishes. In magic incantations Nuska was asked to kill sorcerers and witches by fire. Assyrian treaties ap-pealed to Nuska along with other deities.

Nuska's cult center was Nippur, where, as son of Enlil, he had a shrine in Enlil's temple, as well as temples of his own, often sharing them with his wife Sadar-nuna. At the spring gu_4-si-sù festival at Nippur, Nuska and his wife each received offerings. During the Festival of the Dead at Nippur, a ritual called "Burning" was performed to protect the living from demons and witches, and incantations were addressed to Nuska and Girra. Nuska also had a "seat" at Ur and was involved in rites at Uruk. His "seat" in the great temple at Babylon was called "House of the Pure Oven"

In the lexical series Diri the name is written with the logograms ^{d}PA.TÚG and ^{d}PA.LU, both syllabically rendered nu-ús-ka. (Civil 2004; George 1993: 95 no. 402). In later times, as son of Nanna-Sîn, he had his own temple at Harrān. (Cohen 2015: 122; Foster 2005: 717–20; *LAS*: 102–6, 106–11, 320–25; Black and Green 2003: 116, 145; Ehrenberg 2002: 57; Millard, *DDDB*: 609; Leick 1998: 138–39; Litke 1998: 50 no. 252–56; George 1993: 23, 24, 65 no. 42, 85 no. 284, 123 no. 763–64; König 1977: 206, 227; Kramer, *ANET*: 575; Reiner, *ANET*: 533, 534; Cavigneaux and Krebernik, *RlA* IX: 629–33; Streck, *RlA* IX: 187)

— O —

Oannes (Greek), **U'ana** (Babylonian) (M) A mythical monster, half fish and half human. Came from the sea when the world began. Along with other similar monsters, he taught humankind "the arts of civilization" (Black and Green 2003: 41). Associated with the great god Ea. Oannes appears in the *Babyloniaka*, a three-volume work in Greek, now no longer extant. A literary catalogue from Nineveh dating to the first quarter of the first millennium BCE listed the Akkadian name of Oannes, U'ana, as an author. A few otherwise unknown works were attributed to him. Another catalogue, this time of sages and wise men coming from Hellenistic Uruk, included the name U'ana as the first in a series of Seven Sages and said that he lived at the time of mythic monarch Ayyalu(m), the first king in the Sumerian King List. In Mesopotamian iconography, starting at least from the Kassite period, figures dressed in fish skins appears in what look like ritual situations or posted at doorways. They have been explained as exorcist priests or sages who preceded the Great Flood. (Black and Green 2003: 41, 82–83; Van Dijk 1962: 47; Oppenheim, *ANET*: 265; Streck, *RlA* X: 1–3)

'Ob (L) See Rephaim

Odakon (M) A mythical monster, half fish and half man. The last of eight to emerge from the sea in Berossus's account of the beginnings of the world. (Black and Green 2003: 164; van Dijk 1962: 47)

Og (L) See Rephaim

Op (L) According to Albright a Syrian god of the netherworld, whose name was found on two ancient inscriptions. (Albright 1968: 142; Mouterde 1939)

— P —

Pa-a (M) Noting that this is a fowler god, it is quite possible that PA here is based on its common meaning "wing." (Litke 1998: 114; Krebernik, *RlA* X: 160)

Pa'am (L) God known from a Phoenician inscription at Wasta, a grotto near the route from Sidon to Tyre. Means "Foot," according to Lipiński, a euphemism for "Phallus." The inscription states that the author has brought a new servant to the god Pa'am, implying, according to Lipiński, that the shrine was devoted to "sacred prostitution." Nearby walls were decorated with graffiti, most of which seem to depict female genitalia; others represent stylized palm trees. The deity's name occurs in several Phoenician theophoric names. (Lipiński 1995: 215–18, 423; Lipiński, *DCPP*: 497)

Pabil-sag (M) God associated with the netherworld. Tutelary deity of Larag (Larak). Pabil-sag was sometimes identified with Ninurta/Nin-Girsu and so a warrior god. Attested from Early Dynastic times. Son of Enlil and Ninlil or the birth/mother goddess Nin-tu(d). Husband of the healing goddess Gula/Nin-Isina. Father of the healing god Damu and the goddesses Gunura and Šu-maḫ. Administrator to the queen of the netherworld, Ereš-kigal. A Sumerian composition recounts the journey of the warrior god Pabil-sag to Nippur from Larag and describes him as a bull and a scorpion. At the end of the work, his marriage to Nin-Isina occurs.

His main cult center was Larag (Larak). The god was worshipped also at Isin, where he shared the temple complex with Gula/Nin-Isina, and at Nippur as son of Enlil. He was venerated at Ur, Lagaš, Girsu, Umma, Babylon, and Aššur. He and Gula were often worshipped in the same temple. Pabil-sag also had a "seat" in a temple at Babylon. He was possibly associated with the constellation Sagittarius. (*LAS*: 256, Black and Green 2003: 51, 147, 180; Leick 1998: 140; Litke 1998: 179, 201; George 1993: 36, 88 no. 318, 105 no. 534, 136 no. 935; Tallqvist 1974: 435; Oppenheim, *ANET*: 265; Krebernik, *RlA* X: 160–67)

Paḫad Laylah (L) A demon whose name occurs once in the Hebrew Bible. Means "Terror of the Night." In Psalm 91:5, the demon appears in close proximity to the names of other demons. (Malul, *DDDB*: 272–73)

Pairri, Pairra (H) Group of Hurrian deities. A list from Emar indicates that they were seven in number. In a copy of An : *Anum* from Emar, equated to the Akkadian Sibittu(m). Associated with Ša(w)uš(k)a. Involved in war and plague, also associated with Iyarri. The Pairri gods were both good and evil. One offering list specified twelve loaves of bread for the good Pairri and twelve for the evil ones. (van Gessel 1998: I, 346–47; Haas 1994: 309, 475 note 57, 482–83; Laroche 1977: 193; Frantz-Szabó and Gambashidze, *RlA* X: 190)

Pa-lal (M) Deity, perhaps a form of Sîn, who appears in a loan contract from his temple in Old Babylonian Tuttub. (Renger 1967: 156)

Palil (M) See Igišṭu

Palil-ana (M) Deity in a Neo-Assyrian god list. Means "Leader of Heaven." Perhaps identified with Asarluḫe or Marduk. See Lugal-palil-ana. (King 1969: pl. 34)

Palil-dingirene (M) Deity in a Neo-Assyrian god list. Means "Leader of the Gods." Perhaps identified with Asarluḫe or Marduk. (King 1969: pl. 34)

Pane-Ba'lu, Panebal (L) See Tanit

Pa-nun-na (M) See Zarpanītu(m)

Papašarru-wa-Papašarratu (L) A pair of deities at Ugarit. Occurring in an incantation against snakebite. (del Olmo Lete 1999: 377 and note 150)

Papaya (H) Ancient Hattic fate-determining netherworld goddess. Paired with the goddess Ištuštaya, who was also fate determining. The two goddesses use distaff and spindle to spin out the king's years. In the circle of the goddess Lelwani and associated with the Gulša. Occurs in the tale of the vanishing god Telipinu and in rituals involving the dead. (Hoffner 1998: 17; van Gessel 1998: I, 349–50; Popko 1995: 72, 81; Haas 1994: 245, 300, 372–73, 475; Laroche 1946/47: 87; Frantz-Szabó, *RlA* X: 324)

Pa(p)-gal (M) Vizier god Pa(p)-sukkal. Name means "Leader." Explained in *Anu ša amēli* as "Papsukkal of the shrine (*aširti*)." (Litke 1998: 233; Krebernik, *RlA* X: 324)

Pa(p)-gal-gu'ena (M) The thirty-seventh name of Marduk at the end of the *Enūma eliš*. Means "Leader of the Assembly." (Foster 2005: 481; Litke 1998: 94; Tallqvist 1974: 436; Speiser, *ANET*: 71; Heidel 1967: 57; Krebernik, *RlA* X: 324)

Pa(p)-ḫal (M) Deity identified with the scribe god Nabû. Probably here means "secret." (Krebernik, *RlA* X: 324)

Pa(p)-Nigara (M) Deity had a cult center at Adab. Some god lists explain Pa(p)-Nigara as the son of either the mother goddess or of her spouse Šulpa'e. He was, however, father of her son Ašgi, tutelary deity of Adab. According to a hymn, his female counterpart, Nin-Nigara, "The Lady of the Nigar," was another name for the healing goddess Nin-Isina/Nin-kar(r)ak. Jacobsen suggested that the Nigar was a cemetery for stillborn and premature babies (1987: 475 note 1). See Nin-Nigara. The canonical temple list gives the names of various temple sanctuaries of Pa(p)-Nigara in Adab. In addition to the Adab temple, Pa(p)-Nigara had sanctuaries at Šarrākum and elsewhere. Some Old Babylonian god lists identify him with Bara-ulle-gara and Bara-pa(p)-Nigara. (Richter 2004: 386–87; Litke 1998: 74; George 1993: 25, 156 no. 1188; Tallqvist 1974: 436; Cavigneaux and Krebernik, *RlA* IX: 481; Krebernik, *RlA* X: 325)

Pa(p)-NUMUN-DUG (M) Deity identified with the sun god Utu/Šamaš. In An : *Anum* one text contains the gloss x-ad-ki-ga. (Litke 1998: 132; Krebernik, *RlA* X: 327)

Pa(p)-nuna (M) One of the sun god Utu/Šamaš's viziers, often paired in god lists with Bunene, another of the sun god's ministers. Means "Princely Male Progenitor." He had temples in Larsa and Sippar, both cult centers of the sun god. (Litke 1998: 132; George 1993: 29, 106 no. 547; Tallqvist 1974: 436; Krebernik, *RlA* X: 327)

Pa(p)-nun-an-ki (M) See Zarpanītu(m)

Pa(p)-NUNUS.KAD (M) Sumerian name of the sun god Utu/Šamaš in his fertility aspect. Written Pap-[nu]NUNUS.KÀD [mušen]. The NUNUS.KAD bird occurs already in Early Dynastic lexical texts. (Richter 2004: 350; Veldhuis 2004: 277; Litke 1998: 132; Krebernik, *RlA* X: 327)

Pa(p)-pa(p) (M) Sumerian bird goddess. The writing with the determinative for bird implies that Pa(p)-pa(p) also took the form of a bird. According to lexical lists, daughter of Nin-šubur/Pa(p)-sukkal and Nisaba. Name might mean "Nurturer." Appears in female theophoric names from Early Dynastic Lagaš and, as a bird goddess, in a tablet from the First Sealand Dynasty. If correctly read in the later text, this goddess would be the mother of the goddess Nazi (Nanše), who is the patron deity of birds, bird-catchers, fish, and fishermen. (Dalley 2009: no. 78; Litke 1998: 27; Selz 1995: 272–73; Tallqvist 1974: 436; Michalowski, *RlA* IX: 575–77; Krebernik, *RlA* X: 328)

Pap-sig (M) See Isimud

Pa(p)-sukkal (Sum.), **Il-abrat** (Akk.) Messenger god. Vizier of the sky god Anu(m) and the goddess Ištar. Also vizier of the warrior god Zababa of Kiš. Guardian of gates and doors. Usher of visitors into the presence of the deities he served. Intercessor with his masters on behalf of suppliants. Son of Anu(m) or Zababa. His spouses were the same as Nin-šubur's: Ama-sag-nu-di and Nin-abula. Like Nin-šubur he had five daughters and fourteen sons. One of his daughters was called Pa(p)-pa(p). Equated to the god Nin-šubur, with whom Pa(p)-sukkal later assimilated. Name possibly means "Older Brother, Vizier."

In iconography, the god wore a full-length robe and a horned crown and held a staff of office. His symbol on boundary stones from Kassite times was a walking bird (Black and Green 2003: 43). In the Akkadian "Descent of Ištar," it was Pa(p)-sukkal who went to Ea to arrange Ištar's release from the netherworld. He is mentioned in a late temple ritual from Uruk as going with other gods into the courtyard and returning through the "High Gate" (Sachs, *ANET*: 338–39).

Pa(p)-sukkal was worshipped at a town near Uruk Akkil, originally the cult center of Nin-šubur, and at Kiš, the cult city of the god Zababa. He also had cults at Uruk, Babylon, Aššur, Arbela, and Emar. Pa(p)-sukkal was associated with the constellation Orion. (Foster 2005: 502; Black and Green 2003: 141; Litke 1998: 25, 26–27, 173, 232–33; George 1993: 66 no. 49–50, 97 no. 437, 106 no. 550, 139 no. 959; Tallqvist 1974: 436–37; Speiser, *ANET*: 108; Wiggermann, *RlA* IX: 492–94)

Pa(p)-u-e (M) Deified object allocated offerings at Ur III Umma. Also the name of the eleventh month at Umma, which is written both with and without the divine determinative. (Cohen 2015: 166)

Pa(p)-ule-gara (M) A warrior perhaps to be identified with Ninurta. Honored in three hymns of the Old Babylonian period. (Foster 2005: 93–94; Foster 1993: I, 72–73; Krebernik, *RlA* X: 329–30)

Parakara (H) See Piringir

Pardat (M) In An : *Anum* one of a group of hero deities. Means "She Is Frightening." (Litke 1998: 211)

Parka, Parga, Pirka (H) Goddess probably of harvest and fecundity, revered in Asia Minor. Parka belonged to the Anatolian pantheon of the original native population. She was later adopted into the Hittite pantheon in the time of

Tutḫaliya IV. She was widely known in the Hittite period. Often mentioned in material from Kaneš/Kültepe in Turkey, where she might have been a local deity. Occurs at Kanesh in deity lists, a festival ritual, and in an economic text in connection to payments on cultic holidays. Her cult was especially attractive to female slaves. (van Gessel 1998: I, 350–51; Popko 1995: 54; Haas 1994: 613–14, 676; Frantz-Szabó and Gambashidze, *RlA* X: 338–39)

Parti (E) The Elamite goddess of the settlement located in the Zagros Mountains at modern Māl-Amīr, possibly ancient Ayapir. (König 1977: 207, 227; Stolper, *RlA* VII: 276–81)

Pašittu(m) (M) Demon who kills children at birth. (Jacobsen 1976: 120)

Pa-tin-ḪI, Pa-te-en-ḪI, Pa-geštin-ḪI (M) Deity associated with wine. Member of the circle of the goddess of "strong drink" Nin-ka-si. Heimpel reads Pa-ten-ḫi and suggests a translation "wine-conduit mixer." (Litke 1998: 61 no. 334; Heimpel 1994: no. 73; Tallqvist 1974: 435; Krebernik, *RlA* X: 365).

Pazuzu (Sum.; borrowed into Akkadian) (M) Demon god prominent in Babylonia and Assyria. King of the wind demons. Both a welcome guest in the house and a wild inhabitant of deserts and mountains. Usually seen as an evil netherworld creature, he also provided protection against pestilence-bringing winds. He was especially identified with the west wind. Closely associated with the baby-stealing demon Lamaštu(m), he had the power to make her return to the netherworld. Appeared late in the Mesopotamian list of demons, probably to counteract the increasingly powerful Lamaštu(m). His father was Ḫanpa/Ḫanpu, "He Conjures (as of incantations)," or, according to Wiggermann, "The Limping One" (in *RlA* X: 373).

In images he had a canine or dog-like face with human ears and bulging eyes; he was extremely thin, often scaled, and equipped with wings. He had the tail of a scorpion and an erect "snake-headed penis" (Black and Green 2003: 147). His clawed hands and feet with the talons of a bird completed the horrifying picture. Such images were very popular and have been discovered at all the main Mesopotamian sites, including Nippur, Uruk, Ur, Babylon, and Aššur. They were usually made in molds and so produced in large quantity.

Figurine of Pazuzu. Cast bronze. Height 14.6 cm. After Black and Green 2003: 148.

Pazuzu was considered effective not only against Lamaštu(m), but also against Lil and Lilītu(m), male and female wind demons. His ugly head was used as an amulet to ward off other dangerous and destructive demons, sorcery, and diseases caused by evil spells. Pregnant women wore such amulets to protect themselves against Lamaštu(m) and wind demons, and larger images were prominently displayed in residences and other buildings. Pazuzu also had an apotropaic function in exorcism rituals and incantations. Inscribed words from two incantations usually appear on images of the demon. (Foster 2005: 977–78; Westenholz 2004: 29–30; Black and Green 2003: 147–48; Heessel 2002; Saggs 1959–1960; Ebeling, *RlA* II: 111; Wiggermann, *RlA* X: 372–81)

Pelili(t) (E) The Elamite form of the Babylonian goddess Belili as the sister of Damusi (Dumuzi). Appearing in an inscription of Untaš-Napiriša. (König 1977: 56, 208, 227)

Peltimāti (Hurrian) See Ba'lta-māti(m)

Pendigalli (Hurrian) See Nin-egal

Pentaruḫšieš (H) Deity mentioned in a fragment from Ḫattušas. (Groddek 1998: no. 43)

Pessu(m) (M) Perhaps the Assyrian/Babylonian name of the Egyptian dwarf god Bes (Bisu(m)). In the first millennium BCE, amulets very like those of Bes were popular throughout the Near East. (Black and Green 2003: 41–42; te Velde, *DDDB*: 173)

PEŠ-gal (M) Deity identified with Utu/Šamaš. May mean "Large-Fig Tree." Peš is a variant for pèš "fig." An Ur III text from Girsu refers to the figs of the [geš]pèš-gal. See Nin-peš. In the Early Dynastic period from the Umma region a deity En-PEŠ-gal is attested as participating in the first-fruits festival. (Richter 2004: 350; Krebernik, *RlA* X: 436)

Phanebal, Phenebal (L) See Tanit

Phlos (L) See Nablu(m)

Pidenḫi, Pidanḫi, Bitinḫi (H) Hurrian goddess, a form of Šala/Šaluš, spouse of the storm god Adad or of Dagān. Attested in theophoric names at Mari in the Old Babylonian period and also at Alalaḫ. The depiction of the goddess at Yazılıkaya is labelled Šaluš-Pidenḫi. (van Gessel 1998: I, 362–63; Popko 1995: 115; Laroche 1977: 200; Laroche 1946/47: 57)

Piḍray (L) Goddess of Ugarit. First daughter of the storm god Ba'lu/Had(d)ad. Perhaps also Ba'lu's wife. The other two daughters were Aršay and Ṭallay. The meaning of Piḍray is not clear, but some suggestions include "Misty," "Cloudy," and "Fatty." One of her epithets was "Daughter of Light" (Wyatt 2002: 71, 77). At Ugarit she occurs in deity and offering lists; in one god list she appears in the deity group "Earth and Heavens" (del Olmo Lete 1999: 131). A three-day ritual was dedicated to preparing "the bed of Piḍray" (Pardee 2002: 96). This bed preparation was part of the enthronement ceremony of the king and possibly related to a "sacred marriage" rite (del Olmo Lete 1999: 210–12). In treaties between Ugarit and the Hittites, Piḍray was mentioned with Ba'al-Ṣapōn, possibly as his wife. She was identified with the high-ranking Hurrian and Hittite goddess Ḫebat (Ḫepat), consort of the weather/storm god Teššub. Del Olmo Lete considers her to be a netherworld deity (1993: 229). In some places Piḍrāya was a title of Babylonian Ištar. Albright suggested that Peraia, a consort of Kronos (El), in Philo of Byblos's *Phoenician History* was probably Piḍray. (Pardee 2002: 15, 33, 48, 96–116, 282; Wyatt 2002: 71–72,

77; Smith 2001: 56; del Olmo Lete 1999: 73, 81, 83, 225; van der Toorn, *DDDB*: 392; Smith 1997: 106, 109; Attridge and Oden 1981: 52, 53, 89 note 111; Cross 1973: 116; Albright 1968: 128, 148)

Piḫašši (H) Luwian weather god, especially of lightening. Since *piḫaš* means "lightening," Piḫašši may have originally an epithet. Some scholars have suggested that the name of the Greek flying-horse Pegasus comes from this deity name. (Haas 1994: 193, 326, 425, 428, 450, 534, 579–80, 770, 803, 806–7)

P/Binegir, Pirengir, Pinengir, Parikara (E, H, L, M). Name was borrowed from Elamite. An important goddess of Elam, originally from the Šimaški area. She appears in the earliest Elamite historical document, a treaty between Narām-Sîn of Akkad and a king of Susa. She is therefore one of the oldest goddesses of the Elamite pantheon. Her particular position in the pantheon possibly indicates that Elamite succession was matrilinear. Her spouse was Ḫumban. Her name was likely taken over into North Syria and Anatolia in the form Pirengir. The goddess appears as a theophoric element in a small number of personal names. Later she was entitled Kiri-riša, "Great Lady," and became the spouse of Napiriša and mother of Ḫutran. Her usual epithet was "Mother of the Gods."

Her main cult center was on the Liyan peninsula on the Persian Gulf coast. She was worshipped also at Anšan and Susa. At Choga Zanbil, the religious center south of Susa, the Middle Elamite king Untaš-Napiriša built a temple for the goddess, as well as donating a golden statue to her. He also built for her at Choga Zanbil an *āstammu(m)* "tavern," where beer was served; probably it doubled as a brothel. Thus Pinegir may have been associated with love and sexuality like Mesopotamian Inana/Ištar.

She was honored by two late Elamite kings: Šutruk-Naḫḫunte II called her "Lady of heaven, mistress of my divinity," and Tempt(i)-Humban-Inšušinak called her "my deity." Aššurbanipal of Assyria may have mentioned her in his annals, if the divine name Pa-ni-in-TIM-ri indeed refers to her. The goddess's statue was removed from Elam by Aššurbanipal.

As Pirinkar (Pirinkir, Parakara), she was a Hurrian goddess identified with Ša(w)uš(k)a. Associated with horses. She was one of the goddesses called "Lady of the Land" and "Queen of the Gods." Worshipped in Anatolia and northern Syria. Featured in a festival rite in which her horses were central and invoked in a Hurrian text concerning the training of horses. She was the focus of a cult in the Hittite capital and occurs in Akkadian hymns found there. At Carchemish and its surrounding area, she appears in inscriptions and in Luwian texts. At Šamuḫa she was revered as a type of sun disc and venerated in the temple of the Goddess of Night, a little-known Hurrian deity. Also known at Ugarit. In Babylonia Pirengir was understood as a form of Ištar. There she was seen as daughter of the moon god Sîn and his consort Nin-gal and twin sister of Šamaš. Il-abrat was her vizier. Also equated to Nin-usana in the copy of An : *Anum* found at Emar. (Vallat 1998: 335–40; Black and Green 2003: 74; van Koppen and van der Toorn, *DDDB*: 433, 489; Leick 1998: 104–5, 140; van Gessel 1998: I, 354–56; Popko 1995: 114, 165; Haas 1994: 415–16; Laroche 1977:

201; Laroche 1946/47: 57; Koch, *RlA* X: 568; Taracha, *RlA* X: 570–571)

Pirig (M) Deity whose name means "Lion." (1) Deity identified with Di-ku$_5$; (2) Name of Iškur/Adad explained in An : *Anu ša amēli* as "of the cloud." (Litke 1998: 226, 232)

Pirig-ana (M) See Neanna

PIRIG.BANDA, NEMUR (M) Sumerian god appearing in the great god list from Early Dynastic Šuruppak. In later lexical texts listed as a "wandering star," that is, a planet. Pirig-banda can mean "Fierce Lion" or "Lion Cub" or be read nemur "Leopard." See Nin-PIRIG.BANDA. (Mander 1986: 53, 68; Krebernik, *RlA* X: 572)

Pirig-dibe-ḫuš (M) See Muštabbabbu(m)

Pirig-Elam (M) Sumerian and Elamite god E-talak. Means "Lion of Elam." Appears in An : *Anum* in a section dealing with three Elamite doorkeepers. (Litke 1998: 65; Tallqvist 1974: 477)

Pirig-gal (M) Deity identified with Di-ku$_5$ "The Judge." Means "Great Lion." (Litke 1998: 226)

Pirig-gu-duga (M) One of six bull-lyres of the storm god Iškur/Adad. Means "Lion with a Good Voice." (Litke 1998: 144; Krebernik, *RlA* X: 572)

Pirig-ir (M) (1) Sumerian deity attested in an Early Dynastic god list from Šuruppak. Written Pirig-ir$_9$. Means "Mighty Lion." (Mander 1986: 53); (2) In *Anu ša amēli* explained as "Adad of the clouds." (Litke 1998: 232)

Pirig-kalag (M) Deity attested in an Early Dynastic god list. Means "Mighty Lion." (Mander 1986: 53)

Pirig-maḫ (M) Deity identified with Marduk. Means "August Lion." (Litke 1998: 226)

Pirig-meme (M) Sumerian name of Iškur/Adad occurring in An : *Anum*. Might mean "blissful lion" or "gamboling lion." (Schwemer 2001: 22, 63–64; Litke 1998: 141)

Pirig-sagkal (M) Sumerian deity attested in an Early Dynastic god list from Šuruppak. Means "Foremost Lion." (Mander 1986: 53)

Pirka (H) See Parka

Pirwa, Peruwa (H) Well-known god(dess), originally male. Possibly of Hattic origin. Associated with horses. Ruled the pantheon at Kanesh along with the "Queen" and occurs in many theophoric names there. Appeared with Ašgašepa, especially at Kanesh, and associated with Kamrušepa in myths and ritual magic. Prominent in the Luwian religion. His/her cult was disseminated widely from Anatolia to Syria where the deity had several important cult sites. A silver-coated statuette of a man riding a horse, whip in one hand, halter in the other, might be a depiction of Pirwa. (Leick 1998: 140–41; van Gessel 1998: I, 356–59; Popko 1995: 55, 88, 94, 114, 118; Haas 1994: 281, 301, 412–14, 499, 582, 613–14; Laroche 1946/47: 87)

Pisan-unuga (M) See Mes-sanga-unuga

Pistis/Sophia (L) See Sabaoth

Pû(m), Pû-(u)-Lišānu(m) (M) Often appears in third-millennium BCE Akkadian theophoric names as a divine element. Means "Mouth" or "Word." Sometimes occurs later as a composite deity Pû-(u)-Lišānu(m) "Mouth-(and-) Tongue." As divinities both received prayers and presumably offerings and mediated for devotees. (van der Toorn, *DDDB*: 605)

Pumay (L) Probably a pre-Phoenician and pre-Greek deity of Cyprus. Identified with Adonis and Ešmun. Known from the oldest inscription found at Carthage. Also attested in the theophoric name Pumayyatōn (in Greek, Pygmalion); it means "Pumay Has Given." The Greeks assimilated Pumay to Apollo. (Moscati 1999: 109, 228, 241; Lipiński 1995: 297–306; Bisi, *DCPP*: 364; Yon, *DCPP*: 364; Markoe 2000: 129, 177; Cross 1973: 220 note 5; Harden 1963: 119)

Purubaḫṯu (L) One of the Kōṯarṯu, seven minor goddesses of fertility at Ugarit. (del Olmo Lete 1999: 57)

Puzur (M) Deity identified with Utu/Šamaš in a Neo-Assyrian god list and written $^{pu-zu-ur}$20. (King 1969: pl. 27)

Pyr (L) See Nablu(m)

— Q —

Qadištu(m) (L) See Qadeš

Qadišu-wa-Amraru (L) Name of a minor god or pair of gods of Ugarit. Servant(s) of the goddess Asherah. Entitled "Fisherman of Asherah." Other possible readings are Qudiš-wa-Amrar, Qadeš-wa-Amrur, Qudšu-wa-Amruru. Double name might indicate two deities who acted in unison. It might mean "Holy and Blessed." (Wyatt 2002: 89; Hadley 2000: 46–47; del Olmo Lete 1999: 52, 80; Parker 1997a: 251; Smith 1997: 126; Patai 1990: 37; Pettey 1990: 28)

Qarrādu(m) (M) Divinity appearing in a late god list as a form of the obscure Sumerian netherworld deity Gudgud. He also occurs in a tablet from the First Sealand Dynasty. Means "Warrior." (Krebernik, *RlA* XI: 156)

Qassa-ṭābat (M) Deity of the netherworld and servant of its queen, Ereškigal. Supervisor of the rite of sweeping an area prior to the making of offerings. Means "Her Hand Is Good," perhaps referring to her ability to sweep and clean. In the Babylonian "Epic of Gilgameš," Gilgameš makes offerings to her and requests her to welcome the dead Enkidu. (Foster 2001: 63, 226)

Qaštu(m) (M) Deified bow identified with the goddess Inana/Ištar. (Litke 1998: 164)

Qaus(h) (L) See Qôs

Qedeš, Qadeš, Kadeš, Qadoš, Qdš, Qudšu, Qadištu(m), Qedešah, Qedešet (L) Epithet of one or more deities of the Syro-Canaanite area. Means "Holiness" or "Holy One." As Qadoš it was a title of the Israelite god in the Hebrew Bible. The forms Qadeš (masc.) and Qedešah, Qedešet (fem.), also occurring in the Hebrew Bible, were often translated as "sacred prostitute," though they almost certainly referred to a priestess or priest, "Sacred or Set-Apart One." Qodeš indicated a sacred place or shrine.

Egyptian relief plaque of Qadištu. 1198–1166 BCE. Painted limestone. Title reads: "Qedeshet, Astarte, Anat." After Cornelius 2004: pl. 5.16.

In the texts from Ugarit, Qdš was a frequent divine epithet. Even though it is grammatically masculine, many scholars understand it to describe the goddess Asherah. In Egyptian material, 'Anat(u) was linked at least once with Aštarte and with another goddess referred to as Qudšu or Qadeš(et) "Holy One" (*ANEP*: 352 no. 830). Others see it as a name of the god El. (Cornelius 2004: 94–95; Wyatt 2002: 221; J. Day 2000: 48; Hadley 2000: 46, 48, 182–

83, 206; van Koppen and van der Toorn, *DDDB*: 415–18; Binger 1997: 54–61; Greenstein 1997: 31; Lipiński, *DCPP*: 367; Pettey 1990: 28–30; Albright 1968: 241)

Qibi-dumqi, Iqbi-dumqi (Akk.), **Ka-ba-lu-sa** (Sum.) By the Akkadian name he is invoked in an incantation and was the vizier of Nin-gena. By the Sumerian name (ka-ba-lú-sa$_6$) she is one of five translators for Inana, attested in an Old Babylonian god list and in An : *Anum* in the circle of divinities associated with Inana. The Sumerian and Akkadian words may refer to the same deity, but this is uncertain. The deity is referred to as a daughter in the Edubba temple in Kiš. Means "Speak, and There Is Good (or One Is Good)." (Richter 2004: 292; Litke 1998: 158; Reiner 1970: 17)

Qingu (M) In the *Enūma eliš*, Ti'amat creates Qingu to lead her forces against the younger deities and empowers him by giving him "the tablet of destinies" (Heidel 1967: 24). When he is taken prisoner after Marduk's victory, Marduk hands the tablet of destinies to Anu. After Qingu was executed, human beings were made from his blood and given the task of serving the deities. Qingu had a "seat" in Marduk's temple at Babylon. In a Middle Assyrian ritual Qingu and his forty children are thrown down from a roof on the eighteenth of a month, perhaps *Ullūlu*, as part of Bēl's assumption of suzerainty over the gods. (Lambert 2013: 221–24; Foster 2005: 452–55, 459–61; Black and Green 2003: 153; George 1993: 84; Jacobsen 1976: 257 note 337; Speiser, *ANET*: 64–65, 67; Heidel 1967: 26, 41–42)

Qôs, Qaws, Qauš, Kauš (L) National god of Edom. Probably a desert and weather god. Might mean "Bow." He is known from a few inscriptions and several theophoric Edomite names, especially those of Edomite rulers. The form Qôs is unexpected on an etymological basis from its earlier form and may result from it being a loanword from a language in which the Canaanite shift of "s" to "š" had not yet occurred. In a northern Negev-desert shrine dated to the seventh / sixth century BCE, he was worshipped as a "Master of Animals" and was accompanied by a goddess whose name we do not know. He occurs as Qôs in one theophoric name in the Hebrew Bible. Before Edom became a state, Egyptian texts from the thirteenth century BCE recorded several such names as belonging to nomads in the area. Qôs also appears as part of some Nabatean and Arabic names. He was likely identified with the Nabatean god Dušara. (Betlyon 2005: 16, 17; Knauf, *DDDB*: 674–77; Smith 1990: 24)

Qudmu, Qudma, Qudumu, Qadma (M) Name of what seems to be a pair of originally separate Sumerian gods who are predominantly lexically attested. The names are identically or similarly pronounced. They are graphically represented by one of two signs KUD or GUD. KUD in An : *Anum* and in an Old Babylonian god list. KUD appears after Ištarān, the god who settles disputes, and Madānu(m), the god of judgment. In a late incantation, Qudma appears between the deities Manun-gal, the goddess of prisons, and Zizanu, the son of the god Ištarān. The logogram GUD means "bull." In the lexical series Diri ^{d}TAR is rendered syllabically as qù-ud-ma-aš. (Civil 2004; Litke 1998: 215; Krebernik, *RlA* XI: 190–91)

Qudšu See Qedeš

Qul(l)uḫ (M) Deity attested in a text from Tell Sakka. (Durand 2014)

Qurītum (M) Deity having a special observance at Old Babylonian Ešnunna in the sixth month. (Cohen 1988)

Qurnātum (M) Deity attested in the Mari texts. (Durand 2008: 304)

— R —

Rabba-kusbe, Rappan-kusbi (M) God equivalent to Babylonian Šamaš. In An : *Anum* as one of a group of deities from an unknown land, written rab-ba-ku-us-be. In a Neo-Assyrian god list written ra-ap-pa-an-ku-us-bi. (Litke 1998: 214; King 1969: pl. 27)

Rābiṣu(m) (Akk.), **Maškim** (Sum.) Term for a good or bad demon, though in later periods more likely to be evil. In addition, the title of a law-court official: policeman or bailiff. The name Rābi-ṣu(m) means "Who Lies in Wait (or Ambusher)." As a malevolent demon, Rābiṣu(m) was held responsible for several illnesses and was thought to lurk in wait for his victims in toilets/ lavatories, on roofs and roads, and in wastelands. (Black and Green 2003: 63; Barré, *DDDB*: 682–83; Wiggermann 1986: 135–36; Tallqvist 1974: 437; Ebeling, *RlA* III: 109)

Rābiṣ-kussê (M) In a Neo-Assyrian god list identified with Ninurta. Means "Demon of the Chair/Throne." (King 1969: pl. 11)

Rāgimu(m) (M) Deity identified with Adad in a Neo-Assyrian god list. Means "Roarer." (Schwemer 2001: 34, 79, 86; King 1969: pl. 16)

Raḫ (M) See Yariḥ(u)

Rahab(h) (L) Serpentine dragon-monster of chaos in the Hebrew Bible. Often seen as having seven heads. Usually associated with the sea. Traditionally one of the creatures with whom the Israelite deity did battle before creating the heavens and the earth. Its plural Rehabim is understood to refer to similar demons also at enmity with the deity. In the compositions from Ugarit, it was Ba'lu who conquered the god Yam "Sea," and the goddess 'Anat(u) claimed to have defeated both Yam and his monsters.

In a Neo-Assyrian god list dRe-ḫa-ab is identified with Adad and is the entry before Ešmun. (Wyatt 2002: 67–69, 79; Spronk, *DDDB*: 683–84; Smith 1997: 104–5, 111; Smith 1990: 53; Cross 1973: 108, 137, 160–61; King 1969: pl. 17)

Raḫmay(yu), Rahmay (L) Goddess from Ugarit. Mentioned in the story of King Kirta and also paired with Asherah in another text. Some scholars understand Raḫmay(yu) to be an epithet of Asherah. Wyatt translates the name as "Uterine" or "Womby" (2002: 327 note 16). (Wyatt 2002: 57 note 95, 206 and note 135, 209, 327; Smith 2001: 71; del Olmo Lete 1999: 57, 79; Greenstein 1997: 24, 44 note 59; Lewis 1997a: 208; Patai 1990: 302 note 24)

Rakib-El, Rakab-El, Rakkabel, Rakib-'il (L) Little-known god who occurs in Phoenician and Aramaic inscriptions dating to the eighth century BCE found at the ancient city Sam'al, (Zincirli), now in Turkey, but near the border with Syria. It is usually interpreted as meaning "Charioteer of El." The name might have originally been an epithet. The god Ba'lu at Ugarit was entitled *rkb-'rpt* "Rider of the Clouds." Another less-likely suggestion is that Rakib-El was a moon god. (van der Toorn, *DDDB*: 686–87; Handy 1994: 29; Lipiński and Xella, *DCPP*: 369; Cross 1973: 10 and note 32, 67; Albright 1968: 233

Rāma (L) A West-Semitic deity attested in a theophoric name from the Amarna letters. The divine name probably means "Exalted One." (Moran 1987: no. 123)

Rāmimu (M) Deity identified in a Neo-Assyrian god list with Adad. Means "Thunderer." (King 1969: pl. 16)

Rammān(u), Rimmôn, Raman (L) Epithet of the Aramaean storm god Hadad, the tutelary deity of ancient Damascus in Syria. Means "Thunderer." Mentioned as Rimmon in the Hebrew Bible (II Kings 5:18). In Zechariah 12: 11, he is called Hadad-rimmon. Written KUR in An : *Anum* with gloss ra-mu-nu. (Litke 1998: 218; Greenfield, *DDDB*: 379; Comay 1993: 287)

Rapauma (L) See Rephaim

Rapha(h) (L) Legendary, perhaps deified ancestor of Philistine warriors whom, in the Hebrew Bible, Israelite King David had to defeat (I Samuel 21: 15–22). One of the warriors was a six-fingered giant. Some scholars have argued that Rapha was a deity whose cult center was in Gath and see him as associated with the Rephaim. Rapiu, a minor netherworld deity, was known at Ugarit. (Smith 2001: 60, 98; Wyatt 2002: 250 note 5; Becking, *DDDB*: 687–88; Schmidt 1994: 94)

Raphael (L) Archangel, a member of the highest level in the hierarchy of angels, supernatural mediators between the deity and human beings. Name perhaps means "God Healed." Raphael is not named in the Hebrew Bible, but first appears in the apocryphal Book of Tobit (3: 17, 12: 11–15). There he acts as a healer and also one who dispels demons. A complicated Jewish hierarchy of angels was elaborated in the Hellenistic period. Along with Michael, Gabriel, and other angels, Raphael was addressed on Aramaic incantation bowls, pottery vessels inscribed with magical invocations to put spells on people; found in Babylonia, they date from after 600 CE. In later Jewish writings, the archangel continued his healing and demon-fighting activities. To Christians Raphael is a saint. He was patron of a number of healing guilds. In modern times, he shares a feast day, September 29, with Saints Michael and Gabriel and with "All the Angels." (Farmer 2003: 450; Mach, *DDDB*: 688; Bowker 1997: 799)

Rapiu (L) See Rapha(h)

Rapi'u(ma) (L) See Rephaim

Rašapu, Rašpan (L) See Rešep(h)

Rašnu (E) Deity often part of a triad with Mithra and Sraoša. See Zoroastrianism. (Tavernier 2012: 484)

Rašu (M) Deity written KUR in An : *Anum* with gloss ra-šu and follows a list of names of Mardu. (Litke 1998: 218)

Rattaš (M) Kassite god who occurs in a theophoric royal name. (Brinkman 1976: 85–86)

Reḫab (L) See Rahab

Rephaim, Rapauma (L) The meaning of Rephaim is still in dispute, though a likely source is the root *rp'* "to heal." Translations include "Healers" and "Heroes." In texts from Ugarit, they were primarily divinized royal ancestors who could heal and bring fertility. The Rephaim functioned as a group and were said to be healers and sometimes givers of oracles. Ritual banquets were held in their honor. Their patron was the sun goddess Šapšu. Mentioned in Phoenician and Punic inscriptions, in which the Rephaim were deified ancestors who could provide fecundity and act as warriors to protect the living. Might be associated with a little-known god Rapha. The Hebrew Bible calls them Elohim "gods" (I Samuel 28:13). In addition, the Bible refers to what seems to be an ancestral spirit *'ob*, usually in connection with necromancy. In the Hebrew Bible and elsewhere, the term Rephaim also designated the original inhabitants of Syria and Canaan, as well as surrounding areas. A descendant of the Rephaim was Og, king of Bashan (Deuteronomy 3: 11). (Woolmer 2017: 131; Pardee 2002: 85–88, 192–210, 282; Wyatt 2002: 314–23, 430–40; Smith 2001: 123–25; Caquot 2000: 227; Markoe 2000: 120, 137; Schmidt 2000: 238; del Olmo Lete 1999: 57, 166–68, 326, 340; del Olmo Lete, *DDDB*: 638–40; Heider, *DDDB*: 583; Lewis, *DDDB*: 226–31; Mussies, *DDDB*: 343–45; Rouillard, *DDDB*: 692–700; Tropper, *DDDB*: 806–9, 907–8; van der Toorn, *DDDB*: 364; Leick 1998: 143; Lewis in Parker 1997b: 196–205; Schmidt 1996: 71–72, 82–88, 86–93, 100–22, 267–73; Lipiński 1995: 189–90, 229, 273; Xella, *DCPP*: 373; Smith 1990: 26, 128–30; Lewis 1989; Spronk 1986; Pope 1981: 169–72; L'Heureux 1974; Caquot 1960)

Rešep(h), Rašap, Reshef, Rašpu, Rašpan, Irša(ppa) (L, H) At Ugarit and elsewhere in the Levant, a god of the netherworld, a fiery, dangerous, ambiva-lent deity who was usually malevolent, though he could be benevolent, especially with respect to aiding in the cure of diseases. Responsible for plagues and pestilence. A warrior god and wielder of the bow and arrow. The name may be derived from the Semitic root for "burn," thus meaning something like "He who Burns." His iconography is disputed, but many figurines of a warrior in a "smiting" pose have been interpreted as Rešep(h). In Egyptian images he carries a spear and wears a crown fronted by a gazelle head, an emblem of the Mesopotamian god of the netherworld Nergal.

Rešep(h) is attested in northern Mesopotamia, Syria-Canaan, Egypt, and the Phoenician World. He was popular at Mesopotamian Ebla, where his consort was Adamma, and he also appears in theophoric names from Mari. In Hurrian he was Irša(ppa). At Ugarit, he was a plague god, spreading diseases with his arrows. He oversaw battles and seemed to have been the sun goddess's gate-keeper of the netherworld. As god of pestilence, he "gathered" one of the sons of King Kirta or Keret, but was among the deities who attended the wedding banquet later given by the king. In deity lists, he appears in the god group "Helper Gods of Ba'luu" (del Olmo Lete 1999: 131). He appears also in divination and incantation rituals. At Ugarit he was often equated to Nergal and might have been identified with the planet Mars. In Syria-Canaanite royal inscriptions, Rešep(h) was often listed among the deities confirming the king's right to rule.

In Egypt, where he had been introduced by Western Asiatic immigrants, he became very prominent in the sixteenth century BCE both in official religion, as protective war god of the pharaoh, and in popular devotion. He was widely worshipped by the Phoenicians. The "Obelisk" temple at Byblos might have been dedicated to Rešep(h). On Cyprus he was very popular and equated to Greek Apollo. At Carthage he had a temple in the center of the city. He was closely associated with a little-known deity Šed, for there is attested a Phoenician cult dedicated to Rešep(h)-Šed. Tradition named him as father of the Phoenician god Ešmun. In the Hebrew Bible, he was treated as a demon-like figure who served YHWH. Called "Plague," he helped the deity inflict diseases with his arrows (Deuteronomy 32:24). Sometimes the name occurs in the plural. Identified with the Mesopotamian netherworld deity Nergal and with Greek Apollo. See also Rušpan.

Reshep(h). Detail from the upper register of an Egyptian relief plaque. 1550–1200 BCE. Limestone. After Cornelius: 2004; pl. 5.1

(Woolmer 2017: 106, 109–10; Lipiński 2009; Durand 2008: 231–32; Lewis 2005: 74 figure 4.7, 75, 78, 94; Choi 2004; Pruzsinszky 2003: 188; Pardee 2002: 14, 21, 63, 120, 140, 176, 179, 282–83; Wyatt 2002: 181, 206, 350, 362; Smith 2001: 62, 67–68, 149; J. Day 2000: 197–208; Markoe 2000: 116, 118, 124, 129; Pardee 2000: 63–64; Moscati 1999: 37, 110, and Plate 48; del Olmo Lete 1999: 55, 79, 115, 340, 350–51; Xella, *DDDB*: 700–3; Leick 1998: 143; Greenstein 1997: 12, 24, 42 note 4; Lipiński 1995: 179–88; Handy 1994: 29, 55, 62, 109–10; Cornelius 1994; Schmidt 1994: 88 note 203, 95, 96; Handy, *ABD* V: 678–79; Xella, *DCPP*: 373–74; Gray, *IDB* 1991: IV, 36–37; Matthiae 1981: 187; Pope 1981: 173; Bermant and Weitzman 1979: 154–55, 166; Fulco 1976; Oden 1976: 36; Roberts, 1972: 48, 60; Albright 1968: 139–40; Harden 1963: 86)

Ridn (L) Deity from Ugarit. (del Olmo Lete 1993: 119)

Riḫṣu (M) Deity identified with Adad in a Neo-Assyrian god list. Means "Devastation" and written GÌR.BAL-*ú*. (King 1969: pl. 17)

Rimmôn (L) See Rammān(u)

RIN (M) Deity attested in Sargonic personal names. Can be read either as ^{geš}rin$_2$ "scale" or ^{geš}sur$_x$(EREN$_2$) "yoke." (Milano and Westenholz 2015)

Riša (L) Deity attested in a theophoric name in the Amarna Letters. (Moran 1987: no. 363)

Rittu(m)-ša-Dingir-maḫ (M) Deified emblem of the birth goddess Dingir-maḫ. Attested at Old Babylonian Larsa. Means "Wrist of the Goddess Dingir-maḫ." (Renger 1967: 147)

Rkb-ʻrpt (L) Name of the storm god Ba'lu/Had(d)ad at Ugarit. Means "Rider of the Clouds." Also possibly a name of the Israelite god YHWH. (Herrmann, *DDDB*: 703–5)

Ruḫuišna (E) Elamite deity appearing in a treaty between Narām-Sîn of Akkad and a king of Susa. (König 1977: 29, 211, 227)

Ruḫurater, Laḫuratil (E, M) Local Elamite deity whose name may mean "Creator (of) Humans" or, if female, "Who Nourishes the Heir." Originally from the Šimaški area. The deity first appears in an Akkadian royal inscription of the Ur III king Amar-Suen, on a boulder found at Tepe Borme not far from modern Ram Hormuz in Iran. In the period 2000 to 1500 BCE, Ruḫurater accompanied the Mesopotamian sun god Šamaš as divine witness to contracts and as provider of protection. Ruḫarater and Ḫašmitik had a shared temple, built by Untaš-Napiriša, at the religious center Choga Zanbil south of Susa. The sex of both Hišmidik and Ruḫurater is uncertain, so they may have been spouses. (Vallat 1998: 339–40; Black and Green 2003: 75; Hinz and Koch 1987: 1045; König 1977: 211, 227; Reiner 1970: 17; Henkelman, *RlA* XI: 449)

Ruḫusa(k) (E) Deity appearing in the treaty between Narām-Sîn of Akkad and a king of Susa. (Tavernier 2007: no. 19; König 1977: 29, 211, 227)

RU-kalama (M) Sumerian deity in an Early Dynastic tablet, perhaps an epithet of Inana. (A. Westenholz 1975a: 109)

Runta, Ronda, Ruwat (H) See Kurunta

Rušpān, Rušpān-aš-piš, Rušpa-KI-agpuš (E) One of the seven major deities of Elam. The sign GUD is a logogram for a deity Rušpān, but it is unclear whether this is related to the Elamite deity or might even be a variant for the West Semitic god Rešeph. (Durand 2008; 232; Litke 1998: 213, 215)

— S —

Sa, Sa-gal, Sa-maḫ, Sa-ušum, Sa-ušum-gal, Sa-ušum-sisa (M) Names of Marduk with "Net." The name may allude to Marduk's use of a net to ensnare Tiamat, as described in the *Enuma eliš*. (Litke 1998: 222; Tallqvist 1974: 438)

Sabaoth (L) Sabaoth "Hosts" comes from the name/epithet "Lord of Hosts (*Tzevaoth*)," identified with YHWH in the Bible. Also a god of Gnostic Christianity. Ruler of the cosmos. Most important of the sons of the god Ialdabaoth (Yaldabaoth, Jaldabaoth), a creator deity. Ialdabaoth, called Sabbaton or Sabbatum from his connection to the number seven, was made out of chaos by Pistis/Sophia, the primordial creatrix. Alone, Ialdabaoth brought into existence seven androgynous creatures, among them Sabaoth, and put them in charge of the seven heavens. His arrogance led Pistis/Sophia to rename him Samael, "blind god." Sabaoth took the side of Pistis/Sophia against his father and, supported by seven archangels, won the first great cosmic war. Two texts included in the Gnostic material found at Nag Hammadi in Egypt featured the enthronement of Sabaoth and the construction of his throne or chariot. (Choi 2004; Robinson 2000; Baarda, *DDDB*: 717–18; Gordon, *DDDB*: 398; Mettinger, *DDDB*: 924; Riley, *DDDB*: 246; Fallon 1978)

Sabbatōn, Sabbatum (L) See Sabaoth

Sa-BI-an-ka (M) Deity attested in an Ur III Girsu personal name. (PPAC 5, 289: o ii 9)

Sadar-nuna (M) Daughter of An. Consort of Nuska, the vizier of Enlil. Her minister was Ad-dug-nuna. The earliest mention of the goddess is in an offering list from the Ur III period. One of her titles was Nin-me-šudu "Lady who Perfects the *Me*." A hymn to the goddess calls her "the true woman" and "the true counselor." In a memoir, the grandmother or mother of the Babylonian king Nabonidus reported that the king had re-instated the rituals of a number of deities, including those of Sadar-nuna. In addition, Nabonidus's mother, Adda-guppi, a priestess of the moon god Sîn at Harrān in northern Mesopotamia, declared herself on a memorial stele to be a devotee not only of the moon god and his consort, but of Sadar-nuna and her spouse. Her son Nabonidus, who was himself a worshipper of the moon god Sîn, installed Sadar-nuna and other deities in the Sîn temple he had built at Harrān. In the Ur III period and in Old Babylonian times, she seems to have shared, with her spouse Nuska, a chapel in the great temple of Enlil in Nippur. Sadar-nuna took part in the late ritual for the *akītu* at Uruk. (Cohen 2015: 123; Leick 1999: 5, 111–12; Richter 1999: 70–71; Litke 1998: 51; George 1993: 23–24, 85, 99, 146; Tallqvist 1974: 438; Sjöberg 1973: 352–53; Sigrist 1972: 180; Oppenheim, *ANET*: 312, 560–61, 563; Cohen and Krebernik, *RlA* XI: 181–83)

Sa-e (M) See Lugal-zag-e

Sag (M) Deity explained in *Anu ša amēli* as "Sun of the people." (Litke 1998: 231)

Sagbar-šudu (M) Sumerian name of Šamaš in An : *Anum*. Means "Who Has Perfect Hair" or "Who Perfects the Hair." Perhaps a reference to the radiance of the sun, the rays of whom were sometimes conceived in ancient times to be like human hair or beards (cf. NITA-su-limmu). (Richter 2004: 350; Litke 1998: 130)

Sagbiše-ea (M) A title of Nuska. Means "One who Goes Out at the Vanguard." (Litke 1998: 50 no. 255; Krebernik, *RlA* XI: 518)

SAG.GA (M) Sumerian bird deity attested in a god list from Šuruppak. (Krebernik, *RlA* XI: 520)

Sag-gal, Sag-kal, Šur-gal (M) In An : *Anum* one of the *kattillu(m)* demons. Occurs with variant Šúr-gal. Deity attested in theophoric names from the Old Babylonian period. (Litke 1998: 209; Krebernik, *RlA* XI: 520)

Sag-ga-šu-ea (M) Deity identified with Nuska. Perhaps means "He Who Goes Out in Front."(Litke 1998: 50)

Sag-gul-gul (M) See Mušme-kulkul

Sag-il (M) Deity identified with the vizier Nin-šubur/Pa(p)-sukkal. Means "Proud (One)." (Litke 1998: 27)

Sag-kal (M) See Sag-gal

Sag-kara (M) Deity identified with the sun god Utu/Šamaš. May be a variant for sag gar "arrogant" or kár "to glow," thus "glowing head/person," quite fit for the sun. Reading kara based upon gloss. (Litke 1998: 128; Tallqvist 1974: 440)

Sag-ku(d), Sakku(d) (M) A court official of An. Attested from the Early Dynastic period. Might mean "Decapitator." Later equated to Ninurta. According to Selz, he had the title "Tax Collector." Associated with the town of Bubi near the city of Dēr. His spouse was Nin-pa-mula/e-si. (Richter 1999: 439–40; Litke 1998: 30; Selz 1995: 273; Tallqvist 1974: 440; Reiner 1970: 18; Cavigneaux and Krebernik, *RlA* XI: 529–30)

Sag-maḫ (M) Deity allocated offerings at Ur III Girsu. May mean something like "Proud One." See Nun-sag-maḫ, a name of the sun god. (MVN 17, 64: o 2)

Sag-nig-sag (M) Deity attested in a Neo-Assyrian god list. (King 1969: pl. 9)

Sag-sa-KUD-ba (M) Deity, offerings for whom were recorded in a tablet from Larsa dating to the reign of Sumu-el. (Richter 2004: 401; Krebernik, *RlA* XI: 531)

Sag-šen-šen (M) Deity attested in an Old Babylonian god list from Nippur. May mean "Man of War" or perhaps this name somehow derives from šen-šen sag-gi$_4$-a "Unopposed in Battle." (Krebernik, *RlA* XI: 531)

Sag-šu-nuba (M) One of the bull-lyres of the goddess Baba. Occurs in litanies of deities in two lamentations. Perhaps means "Who Never Forgets/Releases Anyone." (Litke 1998: 178; Cohen 1988 229, 446; Krebernik, *RlA* XI: 531)

Sag-šuta-šubšuba (M) One of the bull-lyres of the birth/mother goddess Dingir-maḫ. The name seems to mean "Head (or Front) Falling from the Hand." Being in the circle of the mother goddess, this may refer to the newborn infant coming out of the mother. (Litke 1998: 77; Tallqvist 1974: 440; Krebernik, *RlA* XI: 531)

Sagubba (M) Deity in an Ur III personal name. Means "God of the City Sagubba." (MAOG 4, 191 3: t.r. 16)

Sa-kalama (M) Deity identified with Enki. Means "Advisor of the Nation." Written Sá- with gloss sa. (Litke 1998: 87)

Sakar-dug (M) Along with Kar-dug, courier of Utu. The name is written sakar-du-ug (Incantation to Utu) and sa-kar-du (An : *Anum*). An incantation refers to the two couriers as Gubla and Igi-tal. George suggests that these may be variant names for the god pair Kar-du and Sakardu. (George 2016: no. 47; Litke 1998: 134; Tallqvist 1974: 341; Lambert, *RlA* V: 423)

SaKIN (M) Deity in An : *Anum* equated to the divinized personification of death, Mītūtu(m). Written Sá-KIN with gloss sa-aK. Note the textile *saqqu*, which can denote sackcloth for mourning—appropriate since this deity is identified with death. However, this nuance for *saqqu* is attested only once, in a Neo-Babylonian reference (*CAD* S: 169a s.v.). (Litke 1998: 220)

Sakkukutu (M) Goddess mentioned in the ritual "The Ordeal of Marduk" from Aššur as a wailing woman. (Livingstone 1989: 86)

Sakon, Sikon (L) Phoenician god attested in theophoric names. He was represented by a baetyl, a standing stone that could take various shapes. Sakon had a temple at Carthage. (Lipiński 1995: 176–79; Bonnet and Lipiński, *DCPP*: 385)

Salamanes (L) See Šalmān

Salammbô (L) See Ṣadam-ba'al

Salḫu (L) Deity attested in an offering list from Ugarit. (del Olmo Lete 1999: 90)

Sallimmanu(m) (M) See Šulmānu(m)

Sa-lu-ulu (M) Deity identified with the birth/mother goddess Dingir-maḫ. (Krebernik, *RlA* VIII: 507)

Samael (L) See Sabaoth

Sa-maḫ (M) See Sa-gal

Saman, Saman-ana (Sum.), **Šummanu(m)** (Akk.) Deity attested in god lists of the Early Dynastic period. Son of the sky god An/Anu(m). In one section of An : *Anum* equated to Martu and in another his spouse was Nin-uzale, sister of the god Ninurta. Means "Tethering Rope." Explained in An : *Anu ša amēli* as "Sumuqan of the tethering rope." In the composition Lugal.e, under the name Saman-ana "Tethering Rope of Heaven," he was among those slain by Ninurta. Venerated at Lagaš, where he had a temple, and at a few other Sumerian cities. It is unclear whether the god Saman had any connection to the demon Samana. (*LAS*: 167; Black and Green 2003: 159–60; Litke 1998: 48, 217; Selz 1995: 274; Krebernik 1986: 202; Mander 1986: 113; Tallqvist 1974: 343, under Ku-sir/sir-nun-ku-tu; Cavigneaux and Kre-bernik, *RlA* IX: 531)

Samana (M) Male demon who attacked babies, the young, and prostitutes. A composite creature, he took his features from a number of fierce beasts: from the eagle he got his talons and from the scorpion his tail. His lion mouth was equipped with dragon teeth. The name Samana also has associations with a disease of grain. (Durand 2008: 660; Black and Green 2003: 159–60)

Saman-azu (M) Deity attested in an Early Dynastic god list. Might mean "Tethering Rope of the Physician." Depictions of these restraints show that their purpose was to aid cattle in giving birth. (Mander 1986: 113)

Saman-kas (M) Deity attested in an Early Dynastic god list. Might mean "Tethering Rope of the Courier." (Mander 1986: 58)

Saman-sukkal, Sukkal-saman (M) Deity attested in an Early Dynastic god list. Might mean "Tethering Rope of the Secretary." (Mander: 1986: 113)

Sa-me (M) Deity identified with Ninkar(r)ak in An : *Anum*. The name may be related to zà-mí (*sammû*), "praise" or "song." It could also refer to a lyre or a geometric shape. (Richter 2004: 215; Litke 1998: 183; Krebernik, *RlA* XI: 622)

Sanugara (M) Form of the moon god at Ebla. Said to have two horns. (Fleming 2000: 156–57)

Sanuša (M) Deity mentioned in two texts from the First Sealand Dynasty. (Dalley 2009: no. 77, no. 82)

Sapar-nuna (M) Herald of the sacred precinct Keš at Šarrākum. Means "Noble Net." (Litke 1998: 77; Tallqvist 1974: 439)

Sappum (M) Deity occurring in the Mari texts. Means "Lance." (Catagnoti: 1992 no. 61)

Sarunur (M) Deity known from a late Assyrian list of gods. (Lambert 2013: 423)

Sasma (L) Phoenician deity attested in inscriptions and theophoric names from Cyprus, Ugarit, and elsewhere. (Lipiński 1995: 292–96; Bonnet and Lipiński, *DCPP*: 396)

Sassurrum, Šenšurrum (M) See Šassūru

Satan,Sat(h)anas (L) The "Adversary" in the Hebrew Bible and the Devil in the New Testament and later Christianity. Also called Abaddon, Apollyon, Asmodeus, Bēl-zebub, and Belial. The root of the word *satan* means "obstruct," "oppose." The Greek version of the Hebrew Bible normally translated it *diabolos*, the word that gave us "devil"; it means "slanderer." In the Hebrew Bible, *satan* is not a name but a designation of a function, a common noun probably meaning something like "adversary." Designating a celestial being, it occurs in four passages: Numbers 22:22–35; the first chapter of the Book of Job (1 and 2); the Book of Zechariah 3; and I Chronicles 21, 22: 1. Only in the last reference could the word be a name, but most scholars do not think that likely. In later Jewish writings, Satan began to develop as an enemy of God and human beings. Soon he became warrior king of an army opposing God. In addition, the Serpent in the "Adam and Eve" story (Genesis 2–4) was often identified as Satan in later, Christian sources (II Corinthians 11: 3; Revelation 12:9). In the New Testament, the name Satanas appears thirty-three times, while the title "the Obstructer or Slanderer," the Devil, occurs thirty-two times. Although the personal devils, such as those Jesus cast out of people, were often called Satans. It was the Adversary who tempted Jesus and who, at the Last Judgment, would descend into Everlasting Fire. In other Christian texts Satan controlled the kingdom of Darkness and led a host opposed to God. In Arabic he was called Šaiṭān or El-Šayṭān and, in the Qur'ān, was adversary of Allah and Islam. (Leeming 2005: 347, 351; Breytenbach and P. Day, *DDDB*: 726–32; Qur'ān 1996; Brownrigg 1993: 246–48; Hamilton, *ABD* V: 985–89; Comay 1991: 246–48; Gaster, *IDB* 1991: IV, 224–28)

Sa-ušum, Sa-ušumgal, Sa-ušumsisa (M) See Sa-gal

Selem (L) See Šaḫar and Šalem

Seraphim (L) Winged celestial beings. Known from the Hebrew Bible. Possibly fiery serpents with human elements. Sometimes associated with the

Cherubim. (Mettinger, *DDDB*: 742–44; *IDB* IV, 279)

Siašum (E) Elamite deity attested in a treaty between Narām-Sîn of Akkad and a king of Susa. (Vallat 1998: 336–37; König 1977: 28, 212, 227)

Sibittu(m) (Akk.), **Iminbi** (Sum.) The Divine Heptad, literally "The Seven." Astrally, the group of seven stars known as the Pleiades. The Sumerians called them "the Stars." Their sister was Naruda. The Seven Gods were understood as both helpful and dangerous. Their good aspects could be invoked through incantations against destructive demons. In iconography they wore long robes and tall feathered head-dresses and carried weapons. They were normally symbolized by seven dots or seven stars. They were appealed to in a treaty as "the Seven Gods, the warrior gods" and requested to destroy treaty breakers "with their fierce weapons" (Reiner, *ANET*: 539). There were temples to these gods in the Assyrian cities of Nimrūd, Khorsabad, and Nineveh.

Sibittu(m) referred also to the Seven Demons, who belonged to the category called udug or *utukku*. They were mainly malevolent, though they could also be beneficent. The good ones were all offspring of En-mešara, whereas the bad ones were, like the female demon Lamaštu(m), children of Anu(m) and the earth goddess Uraš. In "Erra and Išum," the malevolent Seven were helpers of the violent and rampaging god Erra. In a work dealing with an eclipse of the moon, the Seven Demons were agents of destruction who were attacking the moon. On Assyrian steles, the Seven Demons commonly stood beside the king to indicate the destructive and warlike nature of the king and the state. Various incantation texts mentioned them. The Sibittu had shrines in Babylon and Nippur, as well as elsewhere. (Foster 2005: 880–911; Black and Green 2003: 162, 190; Foster 2001: 226; Zalcman, *DDDB*: 657–59; Leick 1998: 152; Foster 1993: II, 771–805; George 1993: 96 no. 422, 169 no. 1407–8; Tallqvist 1974: 442; Edzard 1965: 124–25; Hunger, *RlA* X: 592; Wiggermann, *RlA* XII: 459–66)

Si-duri (M) See Šī-dūri

Siga-buluga (M) Deity attested in a seal impression. (Krebernik, *RlA* XII: 479)

SIG.AGA (M) Musical deity occurring in an Old Babylonian forerunner to An : *Anum*. (Krebernik, *RlA* XII: 479)

Sigar-anna (M) Deity at Ur III Umma. In a text from Šarrākum (courtesy D. I. Owen) the name occurs syllabically with his/her temple: é-^{d}si-ma-ra-an-na. Name means "Bolt of Heaven." (ASJ 18, 86, 22: r 11)

Sigga (M) Sumerian Deity identified with Šūlak. Written sìg-ga. Perhaps means "Smiter." (Reiner 1970: 56)

Sig-gul (M) Deity identified with the sun god Utu/Šamaš. Written in An : *Anum* Sig$_7$-gul and Si-gul. (Richter 2004: 350; Litke 1998: 129; Krebernik, *RlA* XII: 480)

Siginna (M) A Neo-Assyrian protective deity. Might refer to a cairn. (Krebernik, *RlA* XII: 479–80)

Sig-nimgir, Nimgir-sig (M) Boatman of Enki in an Old Babylonian god list. Written sig$_7$-nimgir. A city sig$_7$-nimgir occurs in an archaic list of cities. (Richter 2004: 105: Benito 1969: 145)

Sig-sig (M) See Sisig

Sig-tu(d) (M) See Nin-sig-tu(d)

Sig-zagina (M) Deity identified with the birth/mother goddess Dingir-maḫ/Bēlet-ilī. Means "Shining Brick," probably a reference to the bricks upon which women gave birth. See Sig-tu(d). (Stol 2000: 120; Litke 1998: 41; Tallqvist 1974: 442; Krebernik, *RlA* VIII: 507)

SIG-zi-zida (M) Deity identified with Enki/Ea in a Neo-Assyrian god list. Written sig_7-zi-zi-da. (King 1969: pl. 33)

Siki (M) See Šakkan; and Uttu

Silili (M) In the Babylonian "Epic of Gilgameš," mother of the wild horse with which Ištar fell in love and subsequently destroyed. (George 2003: I, 620–23; Foster 2001: 47, 227; Krebernik, *RlA* XII: 496)

Sililitu(m) (M) See Manzi'at

Silir (E) Elamite rain god. Attested in an inscription of Šilḫak-Inšušinak. Means "The Sprinkler." (König 1977: 19, 214, 227)

Simat (M) Deity receiving an offering in an Ur III text from Puzriš-Dagān. Written $^{d}si_4$-ma-at. (TRU 175: o 1)

Simitsararar (E) Elamite deity appearing in a treaty between Narām-Sîn of Akkad and a king of Susa. (König 1977: 28, 214, 227)

Simua, Timua (M) Deity identified with Inana/Ištar as Venus. Perhaps means "Lit Beam of Light." (Litke 1998: 161; Krebernik, *RlA* XII: 508)

SIMUG (M) A writing for the smith god Nin-á-gal. (Litke 1998: 108; Tallqvist 1998: 442; Krebernik, *RlA* XII: 508)

Simut (E) See Šimut

Sîn, Su'en (M) The Babylonian/Assyrian moon god. Deliverer of oracles. Bestower of fecundity on the human, animal, and vegetable worlds. Regulator of time and bringer of justice. Also concerned with healing. In Sumerian called Nanna. In many respects Sîn's character and traits were very much like those of his Sumerian counterpart. Sîn was son of the sky god Anu(m) or, like Nanna, of Enlil and Ninlil. He had several wives, among them Nin-gal and Nin-mena. His sons included Šamaš, Nuska, and Nin-azu, and his daughters Ištar, Nanāya, and Nin-egal. His vizier was Lal.

In iconography Sîn was often depicted standing on a crescent moon and wearing a crescent moon on the top of the horns of his tall headdress. His symbol was a crescent, sometimes enclosed in a disk or arrayed on a post. His animal was a horned bull. Sîn was usually one of the gods invoked in law codes and treaties. In Tablet XII, attached to the Babylonian "Epic of Gilgameš," Gilgameš appeals, in vain, to Sîn to help him when his friend Enkidu becomes caught in the netherworld. Sîn was a very popular deity, as his frequent occurrence in theophoric names and seal inscriptions suggests. He also had many prayers addressed to him, especially ones requesting good omens.

His main cult center was Ur, where there had been from very early times a huge temple precinct to the moon god. The other important sanctuary of his cult was at Harrān in northwestern Mesopotamia. Babylonian king Nabonidus was especially devoted to the moon god Sîn. He installed one of his daughters as *entu(m)* or high priestess of Sîn at Ur, and his mother held a priestly office at Harrān. Sîn had temples in many other cities, for instance, Borsippa, Uruk, Ešnunna, Babylon, and Aššur, as well as being worshipped at Mari and Ebla. At Uruk during a festival, the statues of various deities were paraded to the temple of

Sîn for a consultation with the moon god and his wife Nin-gal. He was also revered in Elam. See Nanna. (Cohen 2015: 13; Durand 2008: 212–14; Foster 2005: 758–62, 863–65; Black and Green 2003: 55–56, 135; Foster 2001: 227; Leick 1999: 111–12; Stol, *DDDB*: 782–83; Leick 1998: 152–53; Litke 1998: 116, 230; Tallqvist 1998: 442–48; George 1993: 75 no. 160, 80 no. 214, 99 no. 470, no. 472, 114 no. 653, no. 654, 138 no. 951; Hall 1985; König 1977: 227; Biggs, *ANET*: 606; Meek, *ANET*: 179; Oppenheim, *ANET*: 560–63; Reiner, *ANET*: 533, 534; Speiser, *ANET*: 98; Stephens, *ANET*: 386; Sjöberg 1960; Krebernik, *RlA* VIII: 360–69)

Sîn-ša-Kamānim (M) Deity in texts from the Diyala region. Means "Moon God of Kamānu." (Viaggio 2008: no. 40)

Sîn-ša-šamê(m) (M) Deity attested in the Neo-Babylonian period at Sippar and in the E-anna temple at Uruk. Occurs in an oath in a text from Tell Leilān. Means "Moon God of Heaven." (Beaulieu 2003: 272, 346–47; Bongenaar 1997: 542)

Sîn-ša-UrAdad (M) Deity in a treaty from the Diyala region. Means "Moon God of (the place) UrAdad." (Viaggio 2008: no. 40)

Sipa-kalamma (M) Presumably a form of Dumuzi, occurring in an Ur III personal name. Means "shepherd of the nation." (Aleppo 40: r 2)

Sirarata-e (M) Deity attested in an Early Dynastic god list. Means "Who Goes Out from Sirara," which was the sacred precinct at Nimen in the state of Lagaš. (Mander 1986: 148)

Sir-e (M) Deity written Sir-è. See Šab-sir

Siris, Siraš (M) Babylonian deity of beer or fermented drink, with which the name was almost synonymous. Sometimes identified with the goddess of "strong drink," Nin-ka-si, and sometimes presented as either her spouse or her brother. Cognate forms are found in Ugaritic, Hebrew, and Phoenician. Siris's "seat" in a temple probably at Babylon was named "House of Liquor." The deity appears in an offering list from Ebla and in an Old Babylonian incantation from Isin. (Litke 1998: 61; Tallqvist 1998: 448–49; George 1993: 118 no. 695; Krebernik, *RlA* IX: 442–44)

[S]irnapir (E) Elamite deity attested in a treaty between Narām-Sîn of Akkad and a king of Susa. (König 1977: 29, 214, 227)

Sir-sir(-e), Nin-sir-sir (M) Boatman of Enki/Ea. Tutelary deity of Kar-adede in the Umma region. Attested as early as the Early Dynastic period in one of the Sumerian zà-mí hymns. Perhaps also one of the gods on seals whose horned heads and torsos constituted the prows of boats and thus indicated the deification of the boat. Probably also the twenty-eighth name of Marduk at the end of the *Enūma eliš*. According to a ritual for the *akītu* festival, Marduk is called Sirsir when he is in his boat. In the lexical series Diri the name is syllabically rendered si-ir-si-re. (Foster 2005: 480; Civil 2004; Black and Green 2003: 45; Litke 1998: 93, 107; Green 1978: 160, note to line 4; Biggs 1974: 49; Speiser, *ANET*: 71; Heidel 1967: 57; Salonen 1942: 12; Lambert, *RlA* VII: 192)

Sisa (M) See Nigsisa

Sisa-kalama (M) In An : *Anum*, one of eight judges of the sun god Utu/Šamaš. Means "Upright (One) of the Nation." Si-sá-ḫa-lam-ma, listed directly after Si-sá-kalam-ma in An : *Anum*, is merely a variant that was listed as a separate deity. (Litke 1998: 135)

Sisig (Sum.), **Zaqīqu(m)** (Akk.) Son of the sun god Utu/Šamaš. Wind demon or spirit in the category of the demon Lil. A god of dreams, listed in An : *Anum* immediately after the dream god Ma-mú. Variant Sìg-sìg. Means "Breeze." (Litke 1998: 133; Butler 1998: 77–78)

Siunes Karuiles (H) See Karuiles Siunes

Siyašum (M) Goddess of Elam. One of the sisters of the great Elamite goddess Kiri-riša. Also referred to as sister of the Sibittu. (Black and Green 2003: 75; Hinz and Koch 1987: II, 1069)

Smyrna (L) See Myrrha

Sophia (L) See Ḫokmah

Sraoša (E) Deity often part of a triad with Mithra and Rašnu. (Tavernier 2012: 484)

Sud (M) Tutelary goddess of Šuruppak. Attested in the Sumerian zà-mí hymns of the Early Dynastic period. Sometimes independent, but usually equated to Ninlil. In "Enlil and Sud," Sud's name was changed to Ninlil when she married Enlil. Her mother was Nunbar-še-gunu, an ancient farming goddess sometimes identified with Nisaba. Her father was the god of the storehouse Ḫaya. (*LAS*: 106–11; Black and Green 2003: 140; Leick 1998: 133; Litke 1998: 40; George 1993: 22 note 63, 75 no. 161, 110 no. 596 no. 609, 141 no. 982, 143 no. 1010; Civil 1984: 44)

Su(d)-ag (M) Deity identified with Aya, the wife of the sun god Utu. Attested in Early Dynastic and Old Babylonian god lists and in An : Anum. Means "Radiating." The previous entry in An : *Anum* (Sù-ud-kam with variant Sù-tuk$_5$-kam) is probably just a variant of the god name in our entry. (Litke 1998: 131; Richter 2004: 352; Powell 1989: 450; Mander 1986: 94)

Su'en (M) See Nanna; Sîn

Sugallītu(m) (M) Recipient of offerings for the Brazier festival during the period of the Sealand dynasty, where the name is written: ^{d}INNIN-NIN-SU.GAL. SU.GAL is a city northeast of Nippur and so in this case the divine name might be read in Akkadian as Sugallītu(m). Sugallītu(m) is the name of Inana of Zabalam. Sugallītu(m) is mentioned in an Old Babylonian literary text dealing with Warad-Sîn, king of Larsa. The name may be related to Supalītum (see Inana-Supal). (Dalley 2009: no. 66; Michalowski 1986: 186)

Suḫ-(gu-)NIGIN, Zaḫ-(gu-)NIGIN (M) The twentieth to twenty-third names of Marduk proclaimed at the end of the *Enūma eliš*. suḫ can mean "crown." za-aḫ "jewelry," thus these similar four names of Marduk may mean "Crown (or Jewelry) of the Assembly (or 'of All')." (Foster 2005: 478; Speiser, *ANET*: 71; Heidel 1967: 55)

Suḫsipa (E) Elamite deity for whom Šutruk-Naḫḫunte I built a limestone basin at Susa. (Tavernier 2013: 474; König 1977: 78, 214, 227)

Suḫurmāšu(m) (Akk.), **Suḫur-maš** (Sum.) The Goat-fish, a sea monster, with the horned-head, neck and front legs of a goat, and fish body and tail. Lived in the subterranean waters of the Apsû. Occurs in the Sumerian version of the story of Adapa. In rituals it had strong protective traits. Astronomically it was Capricorn. (J. Westenholz 2004: 21)

Su-ki-gara (M) One of two gate-keepers of the birth/mother goddess Dingirmaḫ/Bēlet-ilī. A variant may be Sag-su-ki-gar-ra. (Litke 1998: 83; Tallqvist 1974: 449)

Sukkal (M) Name of Pa(p)-sukkal as the vizier of Antu(m), the wife of Anu(m). Means "Messenger" or "Vizier." (Litke 1998: 233; Tallqvist 1974: 450)

Sukkal-anka (M) Sumerian deity attested in two theophoric names in Ur III tablets. (AAS 63: r 16)

Sukkal-maẖam (M) Sumerian deity identified with Ninurta in a late liturgy. Means "He Is a Lofty Messenger."

Sukkal-saman (M) See Saman-sukkal

Sukkulu, Sukkuku (M) One of four deified dogs of Marduk. Sukkulu means "grabbing." The variant Sukkuku means "deaf" and may be an error for Sukkulu. (Litke 1998: 99; Tallqvist 1974: 449)

Sukona (L) Goddess mentioned in a Hellenistic Phoenician text from the island of Delos. (Bonnet and Lipiński, *DCPP*: 385)

Sulumma (M) Deity identified in a Neo-Assyrian god list with Ninurta, Means "dates." (King 1969: pl. 11)

Sulummar (M) Thirty-third name of Marduk in the *Enūma eliš*. Means "tethering rope" or less likely "contenpt." (Foster 2005: 480; Litke 1998: 95; Tallqvist 1974: 485; Speiser, *ANET*: 71; Heidel 1967: 57)

Sumun-ab-šaga (M) Deity in the circle of the sun god Utu/Šamaš. The name may mean "Wild cow, cow of/in the midst (of heaven)," i.e., star, since the mass of stars was frequently pictured as a herd of cattle in the sky. Explained as igi-du$_8$-du$_8$ with variant igi-dugud and Akkadian *amīru* "onlooker." The reading /sumun/ rather than /sun/ is based on ^{d}Numun-ab$_2$-ša$_3$-ga igi du$_8$-du$_8$ (SpTU 1 126+: r i 3). (Litke 1998: 133)

Sumuqan (M) See Šakkan

Sun Deity (H) For the Hittites, the sun took two principal forms: the sun of earth and the sun of heaven. The "Sun Goddess of (Dark) Earth" spent the nights in the Underworld and was chthonic, often invoked in magic rites. The "Sun of Heaven" was male, all seeing, a deity of honor and justice. Other forms of the sun deity were Eštan (Hattic); Tivaz, Tiyat (Palaic); Tiwat (Luwian); Alanni, Šumigi (Hurrian); Ištanu, Sun Goddess of Arinna. In Mesopotamia the deity was Utu or Šamaš. (Hoffner 1998: 17, 24, 26, 58-60, 71, 112; Leick 1998: 155; Popko 1995: 87-89; Beckman in *RlA* XII: 611-613; Giorgieri in *RlA* XII: 614-615)

Sun Goddess of Arinna (H, M), **Arinnītum** Great Hittite goddess. Occurs as Arinnītum in an Old Babylonian god list. Originally an earth and mother goddess. Along with her consort, the storm god of Ḫattušas, she was head of the official Hittite pantheon, as deity lists in treaties attest. In Hattic called Wurunšemu or Urunzima. Always dif-ferentiated from other sun deities by the phrase "of Arinna," for her main cult center near the capital. Also called Arinnīti "The One of Arinna." Identified with Ereškigal and, after the fourteenth century BCE, with Ḫebat, when Ḫebat began to take on solar traits. Her daughter was Mezul(l)a. In incantations her titles included "Queen of the Earth," "Torch," "Queen of Heaven," and "Torch of the Land of Hatti." In a treaty of the Middle Hittite period, she was entitled "Queen of the Land of the Hittites." Visually represented by a winged sun disk, which was also a symbol of kingship.

She does not appear often in mythic material. However, she is mentioned in a story about the disappearance of the storm god of Nerik, whose mother she was said to be, and she is invoked in a ritual at the end of a fragment about a lost deity. In another fragment—of a Hattic-Hittite bilingual work—the sun goddess saw a bleeding (?) apple-tree at a spring and covered it with her elegant robe. By the title "Sun Goddess of Arinna," she first appears in the records of Ḫattušili I, where he entitled himself the goddess's "beloved." He said that she went before him into battle. He led plundering armies into north Syria and was notable for expanding the Hittite Empire. Queen Pudu-Ḫepa, wife of Ḫattušili III, identified the sun goddess with Ḫebat in one of her prayers. Daughter of a Hurrian high priest, Pudu-Ḫepa was, before her marriage, a priestess of Ḫebat and seems to have conceived a plan to reconcile Hurrian and Hittite deities.

The Sun Goddess of Arinna was important to the state cult at Ḫattušas, where she had a major temple. Nonetheless, Arinna was her cult center. There was her principal temple, as well as those of her daughter Mezul(l)a and granddaughter Zintuḫi. Rituals took place in and around the temples, and festivals focused on them. One cultic text contains a short ritual during which the sun goddess's priestess prays to her goddess. Participating in a festival at the town of Taḫurpa, the queen made offerings to eight sun goddesses of Arinna, represented by three statues and five sun disks. (Collins 2005: 28; Hoffner 1998: 24, 38, 112; Leick 1998: 79, 155; van Gessel 1998: II. 882–88; Popko 1995: 72–73, 74, 89–90, 97, 103, 111–13, 118–19, 145; Haas 1994: 26–28, 423, 562–63, 761–63; Weidner 1924/25; Laroche 1946/47: 105–7)

Sun-zi(d) (M) Name of Nin-Gublaga in An : *Anum*. Means "Reliable Wild Cow." Variant sún-si. (Richter 2004: 451, 453; Litke 1998: 121)

Sup/balītu(m) (M) See Inana-Supal

Sur (M) Deity in An : *Anu ša amēli* deity explained as "Adad of Rain(*zunni*)." sur means "to drip, pour." (Litke 1998: 232; Tallqvist 1974: 468)

SUR (M) Deity attested in Sargonic personal names. Can be read either as ^{geš}rin$_2$ "scale" or ^{geš}sur$_x$(EREN$_2$) "yoke." (Milano and Westenholz 2015)

Surru-gal (M) One of the bull-lyres of the storm god Iškur/Adad. Means "Great Lamentation Priest." (Litke 1998: 144)

SUR-SUMAŠ-maḫ (M) Deity attested in an Early Dynastic god list from Šuruppak. (Mander 1986: 100)

Sutītu(m) (M) Inana/Ištar as a goddess of the Sutians, nomadic peoples known to have lived in Syria around 1350 BCE. They were notorious marauders into Mesopotamia. Means "She of the Sutians." She is attested primarily at first-millennium BCE Borsippa. (Frame 2014: 309–11; Litke 1998: 158; Tallqvist 1974: 449)

Suwali(yat)(ti) (H) Hittite god of ancient Anatolian origin. Identified with Hurrian Tašmišu, twin brother of Teššub, and also with Ninurta. Spouse of Nabarbi. Seems to have had some connection to Telipinu. His cult center was Taidu in the Ḫabur region. (van Gessel 1998: I, 417–19; Popko 1995: 97, 117; Haas 1994: 332–33, 443, 473, 613–14; Laroche 1946/47: 60)

Sydyk, Sedek/q, Ṣedek/q, Sadyk, Suduk, Sydycos, Ṣidqu, Zedeq (L) Minor Canaanite and Phoenician god. Personification of Righteousness or Rectitude. In Ugaritic sources and elsewhere, usually paired with Misor, the personified concept of justice. Personal names from Mari, Ugarit, Byblos, Cyprus, and elsewhere attest to the god's worship. In the Hebrew Bible the word *ṣedeq* means "righteousness," but there is no clear evidence that the concept was deified, though it does appear in the names of two kings mentioned in the Old Testament, Melchizedek (Genesis 14: 18) and Adonizedek (Joshua 10:1, 3). Though scholars are unsure whether these names were theophoric, they generally think that the cult of Sydyk was celebrated in pre-Israelite (Jebusite) Jerusalem and that some aspects were transferred into Yahwism. Sydyk's Mesopotamian counterpart was Kittu(m) and, among the Amorites, Īšar, both of whom were attached to the sun god in his function as judge. Philo of Byblos named Sydyk as the father of Asclepius (Asculapius) and the Kabiri. He also credited Misor and Sydyk with the discovery of the use of salt. (Pardee 2002: 151, 284; Batto, *DDDB*: 929–34; del Olmo Lete 1999: 343; Watson, *DDDB*: 577; Lipiński 1995: 112–14; Handy 1994: 137–38; Xella, *DCPP*: 431; Attridge and Oden 1981: 44, 45, 52, 53, 58, 59, 85 note 74, 92 note 140; Cross 1973: 161, 161 note 74, 209; Herm, 1975: 111)

— Ṣ —

Ṣadam Ba'lu (L) Deity mentioned in a Phoenician inscription from Malta. Name Latinized as Salammbô. (Lipiński, *DCPP*: 383)

Ṣā'iditu(m) (M) See Inana-Dunni-ṣā'idi

Ṣalmu(m) (M), **Ṣalm** (Arabia) Assyrian sun god identified with Šamaš and in one text seen as father of Bunene, the minister and charioteer of the sun god. It has been suggested that Ṣalmu(m) was a name for the winged sun disc. The Akkadian word also means "representation" or "image." A deity Ṣalm was worshipped near Tayma in the Arabian peninsula in the Neo-Babylonian period. (Black and Green 2003: 159, 185–86; Gentili 2001 no. 90; Tallqvist 1974: 451–52)

Ṣaltu(m) (M) Babylonian goddess of war and discord. According to "Ea and Ṣaltu(m)" she was created by Ea from the dirt under his fingernails to be an adversary of the goddess of war, Ištar. Ṣaltu(m) is described as huge, hairy, and quite violent. Ištar promises to stop her rampaging in return for Ea removing Ṣaltu. The work is etiological, giving the reason for a ritual whirling dance that people performed yearly in the streets to commemorate the goddess Ištar's behavior as Agušāya and her encounter with Ṣaltu(m). The name Agušāya probably referred to the whirling dance that Ištar did on the battlefield. (Foster 2005: 96–106; Foster 1999: I, 78–90; Groneberg 1997: 75–93, 93 note to line 8; Cohen 1993: 267; Foster 1977: I, 78, 80 and note 13, 87)

Ṣarṣaru (M) Deity explained in An : *Anum* as hero of Keš. Akkadian *ṣarṣaru* denotes a snake or cricket. (Litke 1998: 79)

Ṣe/irbu(m) (M). Deity attested once in a Mari text. (Durand 2008: 269)

Ṣid(u) (L) Minor Phoenician/Punic god, probably of healing. Possibly of Egyptian origin, the name likely being a Semitic rendering of the sacred Egyptian *djed* pillar. Attested in Levantine theophoric names of the seventh-century BCE. Later also in Phoenician names from Egypt, Sardinia, and Carthage. On Sardinia he had a temple, the only one known, where were found numerous inscriptions with his name. One of his epithets was "Powerful," and he was also called Babay, the meaning of which is unclear, though it might have referred to an old Sardinian deity who was assimilated by Ṣid. Babay probably means "Father." At Carthage Ṣid was associated with Tanit and Melqart. A few scholars have suggested that the city of Ṣidōn was named after the god. (van der Toorn, *DDDB*: 777–78; Lipiński 1995: 332–50; Roobaert, *DCPP*: 412–13; Attridge and Oden 1981: 83–84 note 64)

Ṣililītu(m) (M) Minister or vizier of the rainbow goddess Manzi'at. This is also the name of a month in the Elamite calendar, perhaps indicating a festival in Elam for a deity Ṣililītu or the phenomenon he/she embodies, or, conversely, the deification of the phenomenon. (Litke 1998: 167; Lambert *RlA* VII: 345)

Ṣilluš-ṭāb (M) Goddess whose name means "(In) Her Shadow (It) Is Good." With Kaṭuna, she was one of the divine hairdressers of Marduk's wife, Zarpanītu(m). They were daughters of Aru'a. Their "seat" in Babylon was called "House of Beautiful Allure." They were important in a late-Babylonian ritual "to adjust the imbalance between daytime and night occurring around the solstices" (Cohen 1993: 318). At or around the solstice, Kaṭuna and Ṣilluš-ṭāb left Babylon for the E-zida temple in Borsippa. Then, a little later, Kanisura and Gazbaba, daughters of Nanāya, went from the temple in Borsippa to Babylon and the E-sag-ila. The ritual was intended to cause the days to lengthen around the time of the equinox. (Litke 1998: 98; Cohen 1993: 318–19, 319 note 1)

Ṣīt (E) Elamite deity appearing in a treaty between Narām-Sîn of Akkad and a king of Susa. Means "Sunrise" or "East." (König 1977: 214, 227)

— Š —

Šabgal (M) One of two merchants, agents, or assistants in the E-babbar, the temple of the sun god Utu/Šamaš and his spouse Aya in Larsa and/or Sippar. Variant gal-šab. Means "merchant" *tamkāru*. See Šabsir. (Litke 1998: 136; *CAD* Š/1: 291b)

Šabiš (M) Deity from an unidentified foreign country. (Litke 1998: 214)

Šabīkum (M) Deity from an unidentified foreign country. (Litke 1998: 214)

Šabsir (M) One of two merchants, agents, or assistants in the E-babbar, the temple of the sun god Utu/Šamaš and his spouse Aya in Larsa and/or Sippar. Written Šab-sír with gloss si-ir and variant Sir-šab. See Šabgal. (Litke 1998: 136; *CAD* Š/1: 291b)

Šaddai (L) See El-Šaddai

Šadrapha, Shadrafa, Šdrp (L) Phoenician god of healing and fertility. Patron of physicians. Revered as a savior. Associated with the netherworld. Name seems be a compound of the deity Ṣid(u) (Shed) and the word for "repair" or "heal." Mentioned in a number of Phoenician, Punic, Palmyrene, and Greek inscriptions. At Palmyra he was depicted with scorpions and snakes, and elsewhere he was associated with lions. At one Punic site, he was identified with Roman Liber Pater, a type of Bacchus/Dionysos. (Markoe 2000: 124, 129; Moscati 1999: 37; Lipiński 1995: 195–99, 386–87; Lipiński, *DCPP*: 407–8; Pritchard 1978: 97, 101–2; Herm, 1975: 111)

Šadû(m) (M) Akkadian god mentioned in a theophoric name on a tablet from the First Sealand Dynasty. Means "Mountain." (Dalley 2009: no. 374)

Ša-dubur-ru, Ša-dubur-nun (M) Deity identified with Ninurta in an Old Babylonian god list and in An : *Anum*. Written šà-dubur$_2^{\text{du-bur}}$-ru. Variant is šà-dubur-nun. (Richter 2004: 75, 76; Litke 1998: 45; Krebernik, *RlA* XI: 487)

Šaga-duga (M) Deity in a god list from Aššur written šaga(LÚ×KÁR)$^{\text{šá/ša-ga}}$-du$_{10}$-ga. May mean "He Who Rectifies Oppression." (Schroeder 1920: no. 64)

Šaga-dula (M) In An : *Anum*, messenger of the sun god Utu/Šamaš. May mean "Whose Thoughts Are Concealed." (Litke 1998: 134; Krebernik, *RlA* XI: 514–15)

Šagan-gub (M) See Šakkan

Šaganla-lu-karkar (M) Deity in the circle of the sun god Utu. šagan-lá is a trading agent and lú-kar-kar denotes runaways. The name may mean "Dealer (in) Fugitives." Perhaps this alludes to the daylight as being vital for the recapture of fugitives and runaways. (Richter 2004: 351; Litke 1998: 137)

Šagapīru(m) (M) Gloss of the logogram SILIG equated to Adad in a late god list. The name is Akkadian and means "Mighty" or "Majestic," a fitting epithet of the storm god. (Schwemer 2001: 71–72)

Šage-pada (M) Deity attested in the Ur III period and in a Late Babylonian text from Uruk. Means "Favorite." Probably associated with the Old Babylonian goddess (Nin-)šage-pada. Note the Early Dynastic deity Šà-pad. (Bartash 2013: no. 4; Krebernik, *RlA* XI: 514–15)

Šage-pada-ḫursag (M) Sumerian deity attested in the Ur III period. Mentioned in a tablet dealing with the temple of goddess Nin-sun. Means "Favorite (of) the Mountain." (AUCT 1, 488: 11)

Šaggar, Šegar (L) God of the night, probably a lunar deity representing the full moon. Attested in ancient Levantine inscriptions, seals, texts, and theophoric names. Appears also on some Cartha-ginian steles. (Pardee 2002: 283; Schmidt, *DDDB*: 587; Parker 1997a: 251; Lipiński 1995: 195–99, 351–55)

Šagru-wa-Iṯmu (L) Deity or pair of deities from Ugarit in god and offering lists. (del Olmo Lete 1999: 133, 137)

Šaḥar and Šalem, Šaḥru-wa-Šalimu (L) The gods of the morning and evening stars, of dawn and dusk. At Ugarit, Šaḥru, the god of dawn, and Šalimu, the god of dusk, were paired in god lists and normally appear as a double god Šaḥru-wa-Šalimu "Dawn-and-Dusk." Most scholars agree that the Ugaritic composition "The Gracious Gods" tells of their begetting by the supreme god El, their birth, and their establishment as deities. In the Hebrew Bible, *šaḥar* was usually a common noun meaning "dawn," though, in one or two cases, it could refer to a divinity. Scholars generally agree that Šalem is an element in place-names, perhaps including Jerusalem. Šalem possibly formed part of the names of two of King David's sons, Absalom and Solomon. Both gods also appear in Punic theophoric names. (Pardee 2002: 151, 177, 184, 283; Wyatt 2002: 324–35, 362; del Olmo Lete 1999: 57; Huffmon, *DDDB*: 755–57; Parker, *DDDB*: 754–55; Leick 1998: 146–47; Lewis 1997a; Handy 1994: 78; Finegan 1989: 151–52)

Šaḫan (M) Deity identified with Martu in An : *Anum* and an Old Babylonian god list. Written ša-ḫa-an, šaḫ-an, šaḫ-an-na, and KUR with gloss ša-ḫa-an. (Litke 1998: 217; Weidner 1924/25)

Šaḫḫaš (M) Deity in an Old Babylonian god list, written šáḫ-ḫa-aš. See Šiḫḫaš. (Weidner 1924/25)

Šak-ammar-ḫaništa (E) Elamite deity, whose name appears on one inscribed brick. The king Šilḫak-Inšušinak I commissioned a temple for the deity, probably at Susa. (Vallat 1998: 336)

Šakkan (Sum.), **Sumuqan** (Akk.) Deity of the steppe and foothills. From the Early Dynastic period Protector of wild animals and responsible for their fertility. In the lexical series Diri the name is rendered syllabically as ša-am-ka-an. Watched over goats and their herders and so sometimes thought of as a shepherd. Also concerned with cattle. Had netherworld connections. Son of the sun god Utu/Šamaš and his spouse Šerda/Aya. A tradition from an obscure Babylonian city Dunnu(m) records that Šakkan, son of the primeval pair, killed his father, married his mother, and was, in turn, killed by his son. In "Enki and the World Order," Enki appoints Šakkan, who was likened to a lion, as ruler of the hilly areas. The introductory passage of "The Debate between Sheep and Grain" notes that the debate was taking place at a time when Šakkan had not gone to rule the steppe. "The Death of Gilgameš" includes the god among those deities to whom Gilgameš made offerings just before his death. A late ritual text from Uruk specifies that Šakkan should never be presented with an offering of the meat of a ram. At the city of Aššur the god had a "seat" called "Pen of Lions and Wild Beasts" (George 1993: 156 no. 1183); Šakkan shared it with the minor deity Urmaḫ.

In An : *Anum*, eight names glossed sumuqan are listed for Šakkan: Šakkan-dagal-àm (perhaps "Šakkan of the Expansive [Steppe]"); šagan$_x$(AMA)$^{\{gan\}}$-gub(variant DÙ for DU^{gu-ub}), perhaps a play on the homonyms šakkan and šagan$_x$(AMA) "pregnant," thus "Sakkan of the Pregnant Animals (of the Steppe)" referring to the fecundity of the herds; Šakkan-maš ("Šakkan of the Herds"); Šakkan-ú-kú, Šakkan-ú^{ḫá}-KU (Šakkan of Herbivores)"; Šakkan É-a ("Ea [of the Steppe"(?)]); and Šakkan-a ("semen"(?), referring to the fecundity of the herds(?). Also follows an entry SÍK with gloss Sumuqan-siki, perhaps designating shaggy animals of the steppe.

Note also Ama-gan-ša$_4$, the name of a deity of wild cattle, presumably a playful orthography for Ama-šakkan or possibly a phonetic writing for Sumuqan. (Richter 2004: 351; Civil 2004; Richter 2004: 351; Black and Green 2003: 172; Foster 2001: 227; Frayne 2001: 153; Leick 1998: 147; Litke 1998: 137, 217, 236; George 1993: 156 no. 1183; Lambert 1985b: 187; Lambert 1981a; Tallqvist 1974: 450–51; Grayson, *ANET*: 517–18; Sachs, *ANET*: 344; Edzard 1965: 118; *LAS*: 223, 226)

Šakkan-an-na (M) Messenger god attested in a god list from Aššur. Written šakkan$_2$ kán-an-na. (Schroeder 1920: no. 64)

Šakkukutu(m) (M) Goddess in an Akkadian literary text "The Ordeal of Marduk," where she is referred to as "His (Marduk's) Wailing Woman," and described as circumambulating the city. (Krebernik, *RlA* XI: 565)

Ša-kušu-kalama (M) See Kalam-ša-kušu

Šalanni (H, L) Hurrian deity associated with the netherworld. Attribute of Teššub. Attested in god lists, ritual texts, and theophoric names at Ugarit. Perhaps equated to Ṣapōn. (del Olmo Lete 1999: 84, 85, 208 and note 127, 210, 212; van Gessel 1998: I, 367; Haas 1994: 558; Laroche 1977: 312)

Šalaš, Šala, Šaluš (E, H, M) Wife of the storm god Iškur/Adad or, in another tradition, of the grain god Dagān. Her symbol was a stalk of barley, which might indicate her role as a grain goddess. In incantations employed in anti-sorcery rites, Girra/Gibil, god of fire, was invoked as her son. Šalaš often shared shrines with her spouse Iškur/Adad. Šalaš was not native to Mesopotamia, but was probably originally a deity of the Hurrians. In addition, occurs on Babylonian *kudurrus*.

She seems to have also been understood as the spouse of Hurrian/Hittite Kumarbi. Indeed, in some places Kumarbi was identified with Dagān. Laroche thought she was originally Amorite (1977: 213). Identified with the goddess Šer'ua. Appears on the hieroglyphic Hittite rock relief at Yazılıkaya labelled Šaluš-Pidenḫi, the latter name an epithet. Mentioned in a ritual from Hurrian-Luwian Kizzuwatna and represented in astronomical texts as an ear of grain. In offering lists associated with Teššub and invoked in curses and treaties. In a treaty between Hittite king Šuppiluliuma I and Šattiwaza, king of Mittani, she is presented as a vegetation deity, placed after Enlil and Ninlil, and identified as the consort of Kumarbi.

In a ritual at Ugarit she was offered a bowl of soil to promote the fecundity of the land. Often in Syria, she was considered the wife of Dagān and bore the epithet "Daughter of the Hierodule," probably a *nugig*-priestess. Also worshipped in Elam. Šalaš was associated with the constellation Virgo. In *Anu ša amēli* the deity Elam-sig$_{17}$ is explained as "Šala of the mountains" and Šala as "Šala of the dew."(Black and Green 2003: 172–73; Litke 1998: 43, 142, 232; van Gessel 1998: I, 370–71; Popko 1995: 115; Haas 1994: 166–67, 169, 383, 442, 446; George 1993: 81 no. 232, 162 no. 1272 no. 1279; König 1977: 227; Laroche 1977: 213; Tallqvist 1974: 453; Laroche 1946/47: 57; Otto, *RlA* XI: 568–69; Schemer, *RlA* XI: 565–67)

Šalawani, Šalawana, Šaluwanuš, Talawani, Taluwanuš (H) Title "Deity of the Great Doors." Protects city and, particularly, the primary entrance. (van Gessel 1998: I, 367–69; Haas 1994: 282, 473; Laroche 1946/47: 87–88)

Šalim, Šalimtu(m) (M) God of twilight. Female counterpart Šalimtu(m). Equivalent to West Semitic deity Šalem. (Huffmon, *DDDB*: 755–57; Roberts, 1972: 51)

Šalmān, Šalamān (L) Phoenician god mentioned on a stele from Ṣidōn in the first half of the second century BCE. On Cyprus associated with Rešep(h). Attested in Assyria, Egypt, and Ugarit. As Salamanes, explained as the feminine version of the name, the deity survived into the first century CE. (Becking, *DDDB*: 757–58; Lipiński 1995: 174, 187; Lipiński, *DCPP*: 408–9)

Šam (M) Deity listed in An : *Anum* among gods of fruit. Written ^{geš}šam with gloss ša-am. (Litke 1998: 112, 164)

Šamaš (Akk.), **Šemeš** (M, L) Great deity of the sun, a power of national importance. God of justice, truth, and right, since the sunlight could see into every corner. Also a warrior deity and god of divination. Same as Sumerian Utu. Son of the moon god Nanna/Sîn or of Anu(m) or Enlil. His spouse was Aya. Their daughter was Kittu(m) "Truth" and their son Mīšaru(m) "Justice." Šamaš might originally have been female, according to early theophoric names like "My Mother Is Šamaš" (Leick 1998: 147). One of his titles was "Lord of Heaven and Earth." Šamaš means "Sun." He was a very popular god to judge from his occurrence in personal names and on numerous depictions on seals. In iconography a bearded Šamaš was usually shown enthroned and holding court with his saw in one hand. He wore a long, flounced robe and the high horned crown of a great deity. Rays of the sun protruded from his shoulders. Sometimes, as the rising sun, he emerged from between two mountains, having cut his way out with his saw. Sometimes he was engaged in dispensing justice by using a weighing scale. His symbols included the solar disk, a circle containing a four-pointed star with three wavy lines from center to circumference between each star point, and a winged disk, sometimes with the image of the god inside it. The horse was his sacred animal.

In the law code of Ḫammu-rāpi, the king recorded his restoration of Šamaš's temples at Sippar and Larsa and, in the epilogue, appealed to the god to punish anyone damaging the stele. Many hymns and prayers to Šamaš are extant, including the earliest example of literature in a Semitic language.

They usually praised him as bringer of light, fighter against evil, and upholder of justice and the law. In the Babylonian "Epic of Gilgameš," the hero prayed often to Šamaš, who was a god dear to him. Etana, the hero who wanted immortality and was taken up to heaven by an eagle, considered Šamaš his personal deity. Divination rituals and incantations also invoked Šamaš, usually in his capacity as god of justice and warrior against evil. As god of divination, Šamaš was said to write on the entrails of a sacrificial animal the messages he wanted to convey.

Cylinder seal showing the sun god. Old Akkadian. Serpentine. 3.8 x 2.45 cm. British Museum 89110. After Black and Green 2003: 183.

The main cult centers of Šamaš were Sippar, a major city in northern Babylonia, and Larsa in the south, where his temples were both named E-babbar "Shining House," as was his temple at Girsu. At Sippar, there was a three-day festival to initiate a girl as a *nadītu*, a cloistered priestess devoted to Šamaš and his wife Aya. Regular festivals at Sippar also honored the god. Šamaš had shrines at Nippur and Uruk and a temple at Babylon called "House of the Judge of the Land." At Aššur he and the moon god Sîn shared a temple. Šamaš and Aya were also involved in a "Sacred Marriage" ritual.

Šemeš was the Phoenician and Punic sun god. He was worshipped at Tyre, Ṣidōn and elsewhere in the Levant, Cyprus, Egypt, Greece, and Carthage, as well as other places in North Africa. The word *šemeš* in the Hebrew Bible means "sun" and is not a deity name. Nonetheless, several biblical place names, for example, Beth-Shemesh (Joshua 15:10), preserve the deity's name and thus the memory of some of his shrines. He was also included in the "Host of Heaven," a group of deities of whose worship the Deuteronomist writers disapproved (II Kings 21: 3, 23: 5, Ezekiel 8:6). King Josiah claims to have removed from the Jerusalem temple the horses of the sun that were worshipped by the Judeans (II Kings 23: 11). Šemeš might have played a role in funerary rites, as did the sun goddess Šapšu at Ugarit. He had much in common with Šamaš, the sun god of Mesopotamia. At both Ebla, where she was Šamaš, and Ugarit, where she was Šapšu, the deity of the sun was female. (Cohen 2015: 15; Alaura and Bonechi 2012; Durand 2008: 235–37; Foster 2005; 208, 627–35, 645–51, 726–53, 827–28, 860–62; Younger 2009: 4; Black and Green 2003: 40, 42, 98, 103–4, 145, 155, 157, 182–84, 185–86; Foster 2001: 26; J. Day 2000: 156–61; Leick 1999: 65–66; Lipiński, *DDDB*: 764–68; Leick 1998: 147–48; Litke 1998: 145–47, 212, 231; Lipiński 1995: 364–68; Handy 1994: 107; George 1993: 74 no. 140, 99–100 no. 472, 115 no. 672; Bonnet and Lipiński, *DCPP*: 409; Krebernik 1992; Lambert 1989; Tallqvist 1974: 453–60; Meek, *ANET*: 164, 179; Speiser, *ANET*: 80, 115; Stephens, *ANET*: 386–89; Krebernik, *RlA* XII: 599–611; Kurmangaliev, *RlA* XII: 616–20)

Šamnu, Šmn (L) See Ešmun

Šanta, Sanda, Sandes, Sandon (H) War-like Luwian god identified with Marduk. Adopted into the Hittite pantheon. Dispenser of plague and pestilence. Later a protector of grasslands. In the second millennium BCE, regularly formed part of a Luwian/Hittite ritual group. Invoked as "king" in Luwian incantations and appealed to in curses and oaths. Worshipped at Emar and Kanesh. In the first millennium BCE, became consort of Kubaba. In the Hellenistic period, his statues carried a bow, usually of gold, and he was identified with Rešep(h) and Teššub "The Lord of the Bow." Well known in Lydia where he was paired with Kufada (Kubaba). In late times, Tarsus in Cilicia was his cult center. Finally equated to Greek Heracles. He was venerated well into Roman times. (van Gessel 1998: II, 607–8; Leick 1998: 113; Popko 1995: 55, 93, 169, 184–85; Haas 1994: 371, 408, 467–68, 569–70 note 205, 653; Laroche 1946/47: 102)

Šapšu, Šapaš (L) The sun goddess of Ugarit. She seemed to operate under the command of the supreme god El. One of her titles was "Lantern of the Gods." Since she travelled nightly through the netherworld, she had close connections to it and was the patron of dead kings and heroes. As such she was prominent in royal funerary rituals. She was active in the compositions focusing on Ba'lu. For instance, when the god of death and sterility Mōt swallowed Ba'lu, Šapšu helped 'Anat(u) to search for him. In the second fight between Ba'lu and Mōt, the two were evenly matched, and so the sun goddess stopped the contest by threatening Mōt with El's displeasure. In a long, incantatory ritual against horses being bitten by snakes, Šapšu was regularly invoked as a messenger to El and other deities; she was to seek help. In one offering list she appears in the group "Earth and Heavens." (del Olmo Lete 1999: 52–53, 131, 168, 360–70; Lipiński 1995: 268; Krebernik, *RlA* XII: 616)

Šara (M) Tutelary deity of Umma. Son of Inana/Ištar. His wife was Nin-ura. Šara does not appear much in myth and literature, but, when he does, it is usually in association with Inana/Ištar. In "The Descent of Inana," Šara is one of three gods who, wearing mourning garb, greet Inana upon her return from the netherworld. In the work about Lugalbanda and the anzû-bird, Šara is described as a much-loved son of Inana. In one composition, the anzû-bird stole Enlil-ship, which connoted executive power. To get back what the bird had stolen, the deities called upon Ištar's first-born child Šara, but it was Ninurta who finally accomplished the task. Šara's temple at Umma was called E-maḫ, "Lofty House." Šara was mentioned in connection with the gu$_4$-si-sù festival at Nippur. He also had a temple at Babylon. (*LAS*: 25, 74; Cohen 2015: 165; Black and Green 2003: 173; George 1993: 43, 73 no. 126 no. 127, 119 no. 718, 141 no. 983, 143 no. 1017; Tallqvist 1974: 463; Speiser, *ANET*: 111; Huber Vulliet, *RlA* XII: 31–34)

Šara-anzu-babbar (M) Sumerian form of Šara in an Ur III text from Umma. Means "Šara, the Shining Anzû-Bird." (MVN 14, 566)

Šara-Apišal (M) Šara as associated with the town of Apišal in the Umma district. (AAICAB 1/1 Ashm. 1924-0666: o iii 20)

Šara-gešge-gal (M) Deity attested at Ur III Umma. Means "Šara of the Large Reed Thicket." (ASJ 18 86, 22: o 7)

Šara-Kian (M) Šara as associated with the town of Kian in the Umma region. (AAS 39: o 4)

Šara-Nippuri(m) (M) Šara as associated with Nippur. (Richter 2004: 123)

Šara-Umma (M) Šara as associated with his city Umma. (*Aegyptus* 10, 271, 30: r 35)

Šaraḫumma (M) Deity in Ḫibarītum in an Ur III offering list from Umma who is associated with a field at Umma. Written Ša-ra-hum-ma. (CDLB 2007: 3, 3: o 5)

Šár-a-mu-an-na (M) One of the bull-lyres of the moon god Nanna/Sîn in An : *Anum*. Variants are šár-á-gu-an-[na] and šà-an-na[!]. (Richter 2004: 452; Litke 1998: 123)

Šar-gala (M) Deity who in *Anu ša amēli* is explained as "Anu of All the Heavens." (Litke 1998: 229)

Šar-gaz (M) Deified weapon of Ninurta. Means "(He) who Kills Everything." Astrally, Šar-gaz was the pincer of the constellation Scorpio. The second pincer, another of Ninurta's weapons, was Šar-gaz's twin brother Šar-ur "Who Slays Everything." (*LAS*: 164–71)

Šar-gi-a (M) Deity identified with Ninšubur as an advisor. Written šár-gi$_4$(var. gi)-a. (Litke 1998: 26)

Šar-gi-me-ru (M) Deity in a text from Abu Ṣalābīkh. (OBO 160/1, 1998, p. 269)

Šarḫat (M) Akkadian goddess, perhaps of Dilmun, modern Baḥrain. Means "Magnificent." (Litke 1998: 211)

Šar-kin (M) Deity identified with Ninšubur. Explained as director of the temple of An/Anu(m). (Litke 1998: 26; Tallqvist 1974: 462)

Šar-Kutê (M) See Lugal-Gudua

Šarrabu/šarrabtu (M) Evil demon associated with the netherworld. Occurs in Akkadian with and without the divine determinative and with a feminine form Šarrabtu. In An : *Anum* as [d]Lama-edin, "Spirit (of) the Steppe," with glosses ša-ra-ab and šar-ra-bu. (Litke 1998: 197, 198)

Šarraḫītu(m) (M) Goddess identified in an Assyrian text as "Ašrat of the E-sagil, Inana" and is attested in the Seleucid period. Means "The Pre-eminent One." (Livingstone 1986: 61; Weisberg 1991: no. 10)

Šarraḫu(m) (M) Akkadian deity invoked in an incantation. Means "Pre-eminent One." (Reiner 1970: 18)

Šarra-mātim, Šarru-mātim (M) Goddess in an oath in an Old Babylonian treaty from Tell Leilān, the site of the ancient town Šubat-Enlil, in the Ḫabur basin in northeast Syria. Also known from an inscription of Šamšī-Adad I of Assyria. Means "King of the Land."(Schwemer 2001: 238)

Šarrat-Dēri(m) (M) Deity whose name means "Queen of Dēr." (Black and Green 2003: 123)

Šarrat-Kidmuri(m) (M) Akkadian title of the goddess Ištar at Kalaḫ (Nimrūd). Means "Queen of Kidmuri." Under this name, she had a temple at Nineveh. (George 1993: 113 no. 645; Tallqvist 1974: 462)

Šarrat-Kiš (M) Goddess in a ritual text from Babylon for the eleventh month. Her name means "Queen of Kiš."

Šarrat-Kul(l)aba (M) Goddess attested in Neo-Babylonian texts from Uruk.

Means "Queen of Kul(l)aba." (Beaulieu 2003: 323)

Šarrat-Larsa (M) The goddess had a temple, the E-me-kilib-urur, in Babylon during the Neo-Babylonian period. Her name means "Queen of Larsa." (Charpin 1988: no. 32)

Šarrat-nakkamte (M) Goddess whose name means "Queen of the Treasury." She had a "seat" in the main temple at Aššur. (George 1993: 138)

Šarrat-Nin-a (M) Goddess mentioned in a tablet from the First Sealand Dynasty. Her name means "Queen of Nin-a." It is unclear whether the phonetically written place name in the divine name refers to Nineveh, to Nimen, or somewhere else. (Dalley 2009: no. 81)

Šarrat-Nin-u'a (M) See Inana-Nin'ua

Šarrat-nipḫi (M) Akkadian title of Ištar at Aššur, where she had a temple. Under this name, she also had a temple at Kalaḫ (Nimrūd). Means "Queen of Luminous Rising," quite possibly alluding to her manifestation as Venus. (George 1993: 90 no. 348, 152 no. 1120, 170 no. 1417; Tallqvist 1974: 462)

Šarrat-Nippuri(m) (M) See Ungal-Nibru

Šarrat-parakki (M) Goddess participating in the *akītu* festival in Seleucid Uruk. Means "Queen of the Dais."

Šarrat-Sippari(m) (M) Goddess worshipped at Sippar. Her shrine was one of the "minor temples" there. (Bongenaar 1997: 229–30)

Šarrat-šamê (M) Goddess whose name means "Queen of Heaven." Presumably a form of Inana, perhaps as her manifestation in the planet Venus. She is the recipient of offerings for the Brazier Festival during the period of the Sealand dynasty. (Dalley 2009: no. 66)

Šar(r)um(m)a (H, L) Important Hurrian god who does not appear in Hurrian myths or rituals from strongly Hurrian areas, although tied to the Hurrian great goddess Ḫebat. Scholars suggest that Šar(r)um(m)a began as a storm god and the deity of a mountain on the border between Syria and Anatolia and was venerated as a bull. Included in the Hurrian pantheon at first as consort of Ḫebat and then as her son by the storm god Teššub. Title "Calf of Teššub." He was protective god of King Tutḫaliya IV. Appears in the hieroglyphic Hittite rock relief at Yazılıkaya with his parents and sibling. In that part of the relief, he is depicted again as a bull. He also occurs elsewhere in the relief with his arm around King Tutḫaliya IV. Some considered him to be the important storm god of the cult cities of Nerik in northern Anatolia and Zippalanda north of Ḫattušas.

In an oath rite, he occurs with Umbu and Išḫara and was a member of the pantheon at Ḫalab (Aleppo) in Syria. Mentioned in ritual texts and theophoric names from Ugarit. In later times, Šar(r)um(m)a was worshipped in, among other places, north Syria and Commagene and Cilicia now in Modern Turkey. Inscriptions occasionally describe him as a mountain god, and he appears in theophoric names. (Schwemer 2001: 480–81, 484–85, 500, 615; del Olmo Lete 1999: 340; van Gessel 1998: I, 376–82; Leick 1998: 150; Popko 1995: 94, 97–98, 101, 114–15, 133, 165–66, 169; Haas 1994: 318, 337, 374; Gurney 1981: 137; Laroche 1977: 218; Laroche 1946/47: 58)

Šar-ṣarbi(m) (M) See Bēl-ṣarbi(m)

Šar-šar (M) (1) Sumerian title of Enki/Ea. With gloss šá-ar. (Litke 1998: 87;

Tallqvist 1974: 462) (2) Deity described in *Anu ša amēli* as "Sumuqan of the Suteans." (Litke 1998: 236) (3) Deity explained in An : *Anu ša amēli* and a Neo-Assyrian god list as "Ninurta of Destruction (*našpanti*)." Written šár-šár(-ra) and šar-šar-re. (Litke 1998: 233; King 1969: pl. 11)

Šar-ur (M) Deified weapon of the warrior god Ninurta. Means "Flattens Everything." During Ninurta's battle with Asag in Lugal-e, Ninurta and Šar-ur engage in a lively debate about strategy. Astrally, Šar-ur was a pincer of the constellation Scorpio. The second pincer, another of Ninurta's weapons, was Šar-ur's twin brother Šar-gaz. (*LAS*: 164–71; Tallqvist 1974: 462–63)

Šassūru(m), Ša-tura (M) Personification of the womb and identified with the birth/mother goddess Dingir-maḫ/Bēlet-ilī. The plural form Šassūrātu, "Wombs," indicated a group of fourteen birth assistants who, in the "Creation of Man by the Mother Goddess," aided the birth/mother goddess in bringing to life seven female and seven male clay figurines of humans. Associated with the Koṯarātu who appear in texts from the city of Ugarit. A deity Sassurrum, Šenšurrum is attested at Mari, where it may well be a variant of Šassūru. (Durand 2008: 217–18; Pasquali 2006: no. 64; Black and Green 2003: 133; Pardee, *DDDB*: 491–92; Litke 1998: 78; Speiser, *ANET*: 100; Krebernik, *RlA* VIII: 507)

Šaššabtu(m) (M) Goddess at Emar in the Middle Babylonian period. Offerings intended for the Šaššabētū-spirits were given to her. She resided in the temple of the god of the city Il-Emari. (Fleming 2000: 79–80)

Šaššamu (M) Perhaps a demon in An : *Anum*. Written Šà-aš-ša$_4$^{šá}-mu. (Litke 1998: 210)

Šaššaru(m) (M) Deified saw of Šamaš attested at Old Babylonian Sippar. Šamaš used a saw to cut his way out of the eastern mountains each morning. In iconography a bearded Šamaš was usually shown enthroned and holding court with his saw in one hand. (Renger 1967: 155)

Šašum (E) Elamite deity invoked at the end of a royal charter. (Basello 2013: 252)

Šati (E) Elamite goddess often combined with other deities, such as Ḫumban and Napi-riša. (Basello 2012: 254)

Ša'tiqatu (L) Ugaritic demon or genie of magic and healing who cures King Kirta of his illness. (del Olmo Lete 1999: 52, 55, 325, 370)

Šattaḫammu (H) See Teššub

Ša-tura (M) See Šassūru(m)

Ša-tur-nun-ta-e (M) A deified bull-lyre of Ašgi, son of the birth/mother goddess. Means "Who Comes Forth from the Noble Womb." (Litke 1998: 78; Tallqvist 1974: 461)

Ša(w)uš(k)a, Sauska (H, L, M) Great Hurrian goddess, probably of ancient Anatolian origin. Adopted by the Hittites. Identified with Ištar, especially Ištar of Nineveh, and normally written in Hittite texts as ^{d}IŠTAR. Ša(w)uš(k)a, which might mean "The Great One." (Beckman 1998: 2 note 14) She was daughter of the sky god Anu(m) or the moon god Sîn. The Hurrian storm god Teššub was either her spouse or her brother. Tašmišu was her brother. Normally attended by her two female ministers Nin-atta and Kulitta. Also certain demons made part of her train. One of her titles was "Lady of Nineveh," where she was venerated for about 1500 years. King Tušratta of Mittani praised her as "Lady of My Land." She headed the pantheon of Mittani, as well as of Alalaḫ.

Depicted twice in the Hittite rock-cut reliefs at Yazılıkaya: on one side with the goddesses, on the other with the gods. In a representation at Malatya, the very androgynous goddess appears winged. Like Ištar, she was a "Lion Lady," a lion being her sacred animal. She was, also like Ištar, a very ambivalent deity. She could cause discord or unity in a family or a state. She was both belligerent and loving and erotic. She was bisexual, having both female and male attributes, dressing in both female and male clothing and carrying weapons. Dressed in "male" clothes and carrying arms, she was primarily a warrior; as a female, she dealt in the realm of sexuality and love. Indeed, she was known for her control of magic, especially that pertaining to sex and sexuality. According to one ritual, she could take away a man's manliness, remove his weapons and force him to carry distaff and spindle, and dress him in feminine clothing. The goddess was prominent in the Kumarbi stories. In the "Song of Ḫedammu," she perfumes and adorns herself to seduce the dangerous Ḫedammu and, though the text breaks off, probably succeeds. Her similar attempt with the stone Ullikummi, however, resulted in failure. As Ša(w)uš(k)a of Šamuḫa, she became the patron of the Hittite king Ḫattušili I, who credited her with giving him critical help in his acquiring and retaining the throne. She was also patron of Ḫattušili II, and Ḫattušili III took her as his personal protector.

Along with magic, healing was among her powers. Magical incantations invoked her to deal with plague and undo curses. On two occasions, a statue of Ša(w)uš(k)a of Nineveh was sent to Egypt in hopes of curing Amenhotep III of an illness. As a deity concerned with disease and malevolence, she could also cause ills and deaths.

Her cult was most popular in north Syria and south Anatolia. However, during Hittite supremacy, it spread farther, even to the coast of the Mediterranean. A city on the Upper Euphrates, Šamuḫa, "City of Deities," was one of her main cult centers, along with Lawazantiya in Anatolian Kizzuwatna and Nineveh in Mesopotamia. Worshipped as chief deity at various sites in Syria. At Ḫalab (Aleppo), she formed part of a triad with Teššub and Ḫebat. At Nuzi, she was associated with helper spirits, e.g., sphinxes, griffins, and lions. Often witnessed Hittite treaties. Also occurred in god lists and theophoric names at Ugarit, where she was equated to Aštarte. Mentioned in documents from Alalaḫ, Nuzi, and the Hittite capital city Ḫattušas. In Hellenistic times she was associated with Greek Aphrodite. (Sharlach 2002: 105–6; del Olmo Lete 1999: 84, 85, 340; Hutter, *DDDB*: 758–59; Beckman 1998: 8; Hoffner 1998: 41–42, 46, 48–49, 51–56, 58, 60–61, 77, 84–85, 112; Leick 1998: 150–51; van Gessel 1998: I, 385–94; Popko 1995: 94, 96, 98, 101, 112, 114–15, 115–17, 133, 147, 165; Haas 1994: 111, 260, 309–10, 316–18, 337, 346–52, 354–55, 463, 470, 473–75, 482–83, 513, 540–42, 579–82, 881–82; Wegner 1981; Herbordt, *RlA* XII: 103–6; Trémouille, *RlA* XII: 99–103)

Šag-zi(d) (M) Child of the river god Id. (Black and Green 2003: 155; Litke 1998: 100; Tallqvist 1974: 461; Krebernik, *RlA* XII: 110)

Šag-zu (M) Eighteenth name of Marduk at the end of the *Enūma eliš*, where Šag-zu is explained as "the one who knows the thoughts(heart) of the gods." Šag-zu can mean "midwife," and is explained in An : *Anu ša amēli* as "Marduk of the womb." (Foster 2005: 477; Litke 1998: 91, 237; Tallqvist 1974: 461; Speiser, *ANET*: 70; Heidel 1967: 55; Krebernik, *RlA* XII: 110)

Šagzu-dingirene (M) Sumerian title of the birth/mother goddess Dingir-maḫ/Bēlet-ilī. Means "Midwife of the Gods." (Litke 1998: 70; Tallqvist 1974: 461; Krebernik, *RlA* VIII: 507)

Šagzu-maḫ (M) Daughter of the birth/mother goddess Dingir-maḫ/Bēlet-ilī. Means "Exalted Midwife." Akkadian gloss explains the name as "female metal-worker of the land." (Litke 1998: 80; Tallqvist 1974: 461; Krebernik, *RlA* VIII: 507)

Šb'm bn Aṯrt (L) "The Seventy Sons of Asherah." See Asherah

Še-ba (M) One of two gate-keepers of Eridu. (Litke 1998: 107; Tallqvist 1974: 463; Krebernik, *RlA* XII: 140)

Šēdu(m) (Akk.), **Alad** (Sum.) Protector god, the male equivalent of the female Lama. See Lama. (Black and Green 2003: 115; Leick 1998: 109–10; Litke 1998: 159; Tallqvist 1974: 464; Foxvog, Heimpel, and Kilmer, *RlA* VI: 446–59, on Lama; Löhnert and Zgoll, *RlA* XII: 311–14)

Šegbara-gimgim(e) (M) Deity identified as the canal-inspector god Ennugi. Also one of the seven children of En-mešara. With the variant spelling Sa-bara-gim$_4$-gim$_4$-e in a ritual from Seleucid Uruk for re-covering a kettle-drum. Name may mean "Running Mountain Goat." An : *Anum* explains as a-šà-bar-ra-ke$_4$ with variant -mar-ra and translation *šākin eqli*, "field cultivator." Also associated with the handles of the kettle-drum. (Litke 1998: 35; Livingstone 1986: 190, 200; Tallqvist 1974: 464; Kreber-nik, *RlA* XII: 345; Thureau-Dangin 1975: 16–17; Sachs, *ANET*: 335)

Še-guna (M) Deity attested in an Early Dynastic god list. Written še-gu-na. May mean "Motley Grain." (Mander 1986: 149)

Šeg-mungigi (M) Deity identified with Adad in An : *Anum*. Means "He Roared." (Schwemer 2001: 26, 71; Litke 1998: 144; Krebernik, *RlA* XII: 389)

Šembi-zi(d) (M) Deity identified with Inana/Ištar. Means "Kohl/Antimony Paste (that is, Eye-shadow)." (Litke 1998: 25)

Šemītu(m) (M) Goddess attested in a text from Old Babylonian Uruk, where she is said to have had a temple and a garden, and in an Old Babylonian offering list associated with Irnina (Inana) in Larsa. Means "One who Hears." (Richter 2004: 329–30, 401; Krebernik, *RlA* XII: 388)

Šenā-ilāna (M) Deity identified with the divine duo Šullat and Ḫaniš. (Litke 1998: 146; Tallqvist 1974: 463)

Še-nir (M) Deity attested in an Early Dynastic god list. Written šè-nir. (Mander 1986: 149)

Šen-mu-mu (M) Deity attested in a Neo-Assyrian god list. (King 1969: pl. 43)

Šen-nu-imin(-na) (M) Deity identified with Inana/Ištar, explained in An : *Anu ša amēli* as "(Ištar) of the (beautiful) appearance" (*ša bunnannî*). šen-nu might well be syllabic for šennu, "high priest(ess)," thus "High-priestess of All," which would be apt for Ištar. (Litke 1998: 235; Krebernik, *RlA* XII: 391)

Šen-nukuš(u) (M) God identified with Adad. This name seems to be Sumerian, meaning "Does Not Tire of Battle." Appears in An : *Anum* as a deity of an unknown land. (Litke 1998: 214)

Šerda, Šarda, Šerida (M) Sumerian goddess of dawn. Also concerned with sexual love and fertility. Consort of sun god Utu. Venerated in Early Dynastic to Ur III times in Umma and Nippur and in Old Babylonian times at Sippar and Larsa. Same as Akkadian goddess Aya. Explained in *Anu ša amēli* as "Aya of the cella(*maštaki*)." (Black and Green 2003: 173; Litke 1998: 131, 231; Powell 1989; Tallqvist 1974: 464; Krebernik, *RlA* XII: 394–95)

Šeriš, Šerri, Šarri (H, M) One of the bulls of the storm god, originally, one of the bulls pulling the chariot of the Hurrian storm god Teššub. Also appears in An : *Anum*. See Ḫurri. (Litke 1998: 144; Wilhelm 1989: 50; Beal, *RlA* XII: 398–99)

Šertapšuruḫi (H) A huge sea creature. Daughter of the sea god. Kumarbi's wife and mother of Ḫedammu. Attested in texts from Ḫattušas. (Schwemer 2001: 450; Hoffner 1998: 51; van Gessel 1998: I, 399; Popko 1995: 126; Haas 1994: 86; Wilhelm, *RlA* XII: 399)

Šēru(m) (M) Personification of Dawn. Occurs in the circle of Nisaba, where she is placed between Tir-ana "Rainbow" and Maḫ-di-ana "Morning Star." Attested in theophoric names, including that of a river at Larsa. Known during the First Sealand Dynasty. Corresponds to Ugaritic deity Šaḥar. (Dalley 2009: no. 243; Durand 2008: 263; Renger 1967: 146; Krebernik, *RlA* XII: 400)

Šer'ua, Šeruya (M) Assyrian goddess. Same as the Babylonian goddess Eru'a. Family member of the god Aššur, at first his daughter and later his wife, along with Ninlil. In an Assyrian treaty, Šer'ua was listed between two birth/mother goddesses. In the city of Aššur, she shared a temple with Aššur. (Frame 1999: 8; Livingstone, *DDDB*: 109; W.G. Lambert 1987 no. 115; George 124 no. 779; Tallqvist 1974: 463; Reiner, *ANET*: 534; Krebernik, *RlA* XII: 399–400)

Šerzi-maḫ-ana (M) A form of the sun god invoked in an incantation. Means "Exalted Radiance of Heaven." His two couriers were Gubla and Igi-tal. (George 2016: no. 47)

Šešda-edina (M) Deity attested in the environs of Ur III Umma. Means "With the Brother in the Steppe" and may be a name of Geštin-ana, who, according to literature, found her brother Dumuzi in the steppe. (Cohen 1996a: 34; Krebernik, *RlA* XII: 405)

Šībum (M) Deity attested in Old Babylonian personal names. Means "Elder" or "Witness." (Jursa 1994: no. 65)

Šī-Dada (M) Goddess associated with a suburb of the city of Sippar in Babylonia. The suburb was equated in a later text with the Babylonian town of Dūr-Šarru-kīn, where, according to George, a temple named "House that Gleans Barley" was dedicated to the deity (1993: 145 no. 1042). Means "She Is Luxuriant." (Radner 1999: 138; George 1993: 43, 83 no. 269; Krebernik, *RlA* XII: 452)

Šiddu-kišara (M) A minister or vizier of the chief Babylonian god Marduk.

Means "Accountant of the Universe." (Litke 1998: 96; Tallqvist 1974: 465)

Šī-dūri, Si-dūri (M) Akkadian title of the goddess Inana/Ištar. Also the name of the divine innkeeper (*sabītu*) whom Gilgameš met at the end of the earth. Before the hero left her, Šī-dūri advised him to enjoy the life he had been given, instead of seeking immortality. Name possibly means "She Is My (Protective) Wall." It is not certain if there is a connection to the Hurrian word *šiduri* glossed in Akkadian as "maiden." Šī-dūri is a figure like Calypso in Homer's *Odyssey*. (Black and Green 2003: 164; George 2003: I, 148–49; Foster 2001: 72–76; Litke 1998: 148; Tallqvist 1974: 441, 464; Krebernik, *RlA* XII: 459)

Šiḫḫaš (E, M) An obscure god named in a late god list that identifies him as a form of the storm god Adad in Elam. See Šaḫḫaš. (Schwemer 2001: 79, 86, 393)

Šiḫṭu(m) (M) The deified planet Mercury. Sometimes equated to Sumerian Mēr-mēr(i) "Storm" as a name of Adad. Means "Attack" or "Raid." (Schwemer 2001: 59)

Šipak (M) Kassite god who occurs in a royal theophoric name. Equated to Sîn in a god list. Occurs in other theophoric names. (Brinkman 1976: 253; Balkan 1954: 4; Krebernik, RlA XII: 480)

Šikagu (M) Enki/Ea as the god of leather workers. (Litke 1998: 240; Krebernik, *RlA* XII: 482)

Šī-labbat (M) One of five translators of Inana/Ištar. Means "She Is a Lion." (Litke 1998: 158 and note 142; Krebernik, *RlA* XII: 483)

Šilam-kura (M) First of ten children of Nin-sun. Occurs in An : *Anum* and in an *akītu* ritual from Seleucid Uruk. Means "Cow of the Mountain/Land." (Litke 1998: 168; Krebernik, *RlA* XII: 485)

Šilanu (M) Deity attested during the Kassite period in a theophoric geographical name Kar-Šilanu, "Quay of Šilanu." (Brinkman 1976: 46 note 100)

Šilir-qatru (E) Deity, originally from Anšan, a part of Elam. Protector of kings. (Vallat 1998: 335. 340)

Šimegi (H, L) A Hurrian sun god. One of the most important deities of Mittani. In many ways like the Mesopotamian Šamaš. Concerned with justice. Sees all; favors the good and punishes the bad. Adopted into the Hittite pantheon. His consort was Aya. Often invoked in treaties. Concerned with divination and oracles. Called "King of Heaven" and "Shepherd of Mankind. "His visual appearance was influenced by that of Utu/Šamaš. Depicted in the Hittite rock-cut reliefs at Yazılıkaya. Ally of Teššub in the Kumarbi stories. Invoked in treaties in the Middle Hittite period.

His cult was widespread, extending from Anatolia to the Levant. Worshipped at Ḫattušas and Nuzi, as well as at other places. Occurring in god lists, ritual texts, and theophoric names at Ugarit. In a multilingual text, he was equated to Sumerian Utu and the Ugaritian sun goddess Šapšu. (del Olmo Lete 1999: 84, 85, 340; van der Toorn, *DDDB*: 773–74; Hoffner 1998: 60, 112; van Gessel 1998: I, 400–3; Popko 1995: 89, 100, 112; Haas 1994: 379–81, 581; Laroche 1977: 232; Laroche 1946/47: 59; Beckman, *RlA* XII: 611–13; Giorgieri, *RlA* XII: 614–15; Herbordt, *RlA* XII: 620–23)

Šim-gig (M) Deity in a text from Fara. (Martin et al. 2001: 113)

Šimmišu (H) Deity attested in the Mari texts. (Durand 2008: 664)

Šīmtu(m) (M) See Nam-tara

Šimu(m) (M) Deity in a personal name mentioned in a text from the First Sealand Dynasty. (Dalley 2009: no. 432)

Šimut, Šimutta, Simut (E) Major deity of Elam. Called "The God of Elam." Herald of the gods and associated with the netherworld. His wife was the rainbow goddess Manzi'at, and the couple often had a joint temple or shrine. Deity originally from Anšan, a city and an area of Elam. Appears first in a treaty between Narām-Sîn of Akkad and a king of Susa. Attested in Old and Middle Elamite texts. Often occurs in juridical and economic texts as a divine witness. The Elamite king Untaš-Napiriša commissioned a temple for him at the religious center Choga Zanbil south of Susa. Later Šilḫak-Inšušinak I built a temple for Šimut and Manzi'at at Susa, as commemorated in a stone stele found there. In a second stele of the same king also from Susa, Šimut is called "Mighty Herald of the Gods." The statue of this god was removed from Elam by Aššurbanipal. (Potts 2013: 130; Black and Green 2003: 75; Vallat 1998: 336–39; Hinz and Koch 1987: II, 1084; König 1977: 218, 227; Henkelman, *RlA* XII: 511–12)

Šī-šarrat (M) Wife of Uqur, the vizier or minister of the god Nergal. Means "She Is Queen." (Litke 1998: 174; Tallqvist 1974: 464; Krebernik, *RlA* XII: 555)

Šitame-karabu (M) Deity whose name means "Listen to Prayer." (Deller 1991: no. 18)

Šitame-pîšunu (M) One of eight judges of the sun god Utu/Šamaš. Means "Listen to Their Speech." (Litke 1998: 135; Tallqvist 1974: 465; Krebernik, *RlA* XI: 358)

Šī-tarruru, Šī-ul-tarruru (M) Daughter of Mūtu(m), "Death." In a Neo-Assyrian god list followed by the negative: ši-NU-tàr-ru-ru, and both seem to be a name of Ištar. An : *Anum* has ši-ta-tar-ru. Particularly in light of her being the daughter of Death, perhaps related to *arāru* "to rot," referring to Ištar's rotting corpse in the netherworld. The positive and negative forms may refer to her corpse, which at first was rotting, but then was resuscitated. (Litke 1998: 190; King 1969: pls. 17 and 44; Krebernik, *RlA* XII: 558)

Šiuini (M) Urarṭean solar god. The Urarṭean pantheon was headed by a triad made up of the supreme god Ḫaldi, the god of storms Teišeba, apparently a form of the Hurrian storm god Teššub, and Šiuini. (Schwemer 2001: 446)

Šiuš, Šiu(n), Šiuš(um)mi (H) Etymologically it seems that Šiuš is associated with the Indo-European root for light and sky and so is related, etymologically and otherwise, to the Greek Zeus. However, the exact nature of the deity is not clear from Hittite sources. The argument that he was originally a sun god has been rejected. He might have been both protective of and equated to the Hittite king. Later, the storm god and the Sun Goddess of Arinna took Šiuš's place. Finally, Šiuš came to be the common noun for "deity." Šiuš(um)mi might mean "Our/My/Their God." The god Šiuš does occur in a late ritual, part of a group of mostly netherworld deities led by Lelwani. (van Gessel 1998: I, 407; Popko 1995: 56; Haas 1994: 188–89; Gilan, *RlA* XII: 559–60)

Šiwat (H) Deity whose name means "Day." Occurs often in Hittite funerary rituals. Appears in a ritual involving the "dead temple," perhaps a charnel house, in the company of nine chthonic deities led by Lelwani. Also occurs in a text from Kanesh. Thought to refer to the "favorable day," which some scholars suggest refers to the day of death. (van Gessel 1998: I, 408; Popko 1995: 67, 72, 89; Haas 1994: 245; Gilan, *RlA* XII: 560–61)

Šiyašum (E) Elamite deity occurring in a treaty between Narām-Sîn of Akkad and a king of Susa. Also named in an inscription of Untaš-Napiriša from the religious center Choga Zanbil south of Susa. (König 1977: 217, 227)

Šu-a-la (M) Deity attested in the Ur III period with Annunītu(m) and Allatu(m). (Richter 2004: 416; Loding 1976: no. 111)

Šuba (M) (1) Deity attested in an Early Dynastic god list written MÙŠ.ZA. (2) Identified with Utu/Šamaš in a Neo-Assyrian god list and written ZA.MÚŠ with gloss šu-ba. (3) In an Old Babylonian god list written ZA.MÙŠ, where it is a name for either Damu or Dumuzi. (Mander 1986: 149; King 1969: pl. 27; Weidner 1924/25)

Šuba-nuna (M) One of three daughters of the storm god Iškur/Adad. The tenth month at Adab was named for her. (Litke 1998: 143; Tallqvist 1974: 467)

Šubi-gar, Šu-gaga (M) Deity identified with the Sumerian god Di-ku$_5$, "Judge" and was the chamberlain/chair-bearer of Marduk. šu—gar means "to carry out (a task)," perhaps referring to the execution of justice or punishment if required. (Litke 1998: 224)

Šubirbi (H, L) Hurrian god. (del Olmo Lete 1999: 208 note 128)

Šubur-azida (M) One of two chief herdsmen of An/Anu(m). Name possibly means "Servant at the Right Side." (Litke 1998: 30)

Šubur-ḫamun (M) See Ḫamun-Šubur

Šudanni (M) Deity forming part of a theophoric name in a tablet from the First Sealand Dynasty. (Dalley 2009: no. 442)

Šud[anu] (E) Elamite deity appearing in an inscription of Tempt(i)-Ḫumban-Inšušinak (c. 664–663). (König 1977: 172, 216, 227)

Šud-bindug-basag (M) Guardian of the E-maḫ temple in Isin. Means "He Uttered a Prayer and It Was Favorable." The following entry in An : *Anum*, Bindug-baša, may be an abbreviated form of this same name and not a separate deity despite the total count of guardian spirits. Note Tu-bindug-bašag. (Richter 2004: 215; Litke 1998: 184)

Šud-kuga (M) See Nundum-kuga

Šudšud (M) Deity in a god list from Aššur. Spouse is Šudšud-balag. (Schroeder 1920: no. 64)

Šudšud-balag (M) Deity in a god list from Aššur. Spouse is Šudšud. (Schroeder 1920: no. 64)

Šu-ereš (M) Deity identified with the Sumerian birth/mother goddess Dingirmaḫ/Bēlet-ilī. Written šu-GAL.AN.ZU. Means "Skillful Hand." (Litke 1998: 70; Tallqvist 1974: 465; Krebernik, *RlA* VIII: 507)

Šugab (M) A Kassite chthonic deity in the theophoric name Šindi-Šugab. Šindi-Šugab was a messenger referred to in an Amarna period letter of Burnaburiaš II, Kassite king of Babylon, to Pharaoh Akhenaten. (Moran 1992: 20)

Šu-gaga (M) See Šubi-gar

Šu-gal (M) Deity identified with Marduk in An : *Anum*. Means "Great Hand (i.e., strength, ability)." Occurs also in an Early Dynastic god list. (Litke 1998: 223; Mander 1986: 149)

Šugar-durun (M) Deity in an Old Babylonian god list. (Weidner 1924/25)

ŠuGIDla (M) Son of Nergal/Erra. Worshipped at Lagaba, just east of Kiš. Mentioned in a late *akītu* ritual from Uruk. The name is written šu-gid$_2$-lá and šu-gid$_2$-la. (Cohen 2015: 228; Litke 1998: 201; George 1993: 37, 170 no. 1419; Tallqvist 1974: 465; Reiner 1970: 40)

Šugu (E) Elamite deity from Awan, a city and state of Elam. Divinity brought to Susa by Puzur(Kutik)-Inšušinak when he conquered the city. (Vallat 1998: 336–37)

ŠuGUR (M) Deity appearing in a late god list. If the gur sign is a scribal mistake for kur and the name was read Šukur, it would signify the divinized lance šukur, *šukurru*. (See the gods Sappu, "Lance," Bēl-šukurrim, "Lord of the Lance," Šukurrum.) The sign kur could also be read *-lat*, in which case the name would be Šullat, vizier of the storm god Adad. (Schwemer 2001: 79–80)

Šu-ḫal-bi (M) One of five guardian spirits of the E-gal-maḫ, the name of several temples of the healing goddess Gula/Nin-Isina. Also called Ama-šu-ḫal-bi. Variant Šu-ḫal-ḫal-bi. (Litke 1998: 184; George 1993: 88–89 no. 318–23; Tallqvist 1974: 465)

Šu-i (M) Spouse of Nin-kar-nuna. Means "Barber." (Richter 2004: 75: Litke 1998: 49)

Šū-illat (M) Akkadian deity attested Nippur, Umma, and Uruk in the Ur III period. See Šullat. (Sallaberger 1993: I, 105, II, pls. 7, 70a)

Šū-kal (M) Deity attested at Ur III Umma. The reading Šu-kal rather than Lirum (=ŠU.KAL) is based on the orthography Ur-^{d}Šu-kal-la. ^{d}Šu-kal is attested also at nearby Lagaš in the Early Dynastic period and often appears in curse formulas. (Selz 1995: 276–77)

Šu-kešed (M) Divinized attribute of Marduk in An : *Anum*. Means "He who Binds the Hands." (Litke 1998: 223)

šuku (M) Deity attested at Ebla. Perhaps means "Fisherman." (Waetzoldt 2001)

Šuku-BANDA-abzu (M) One of the children of Nin-Girida. Means "Junior Fisherman of the Apsû." (Litke 1998: 191)

Šukur-gallu (M) Deity with a seat in the great temple complex at Aššur. (George 1993: 79 no. 208)

Šukurrum (M) Deity attested at Old Babylonian Nērebtum. Means 'Lance." See Bēl-šukurrim. See ŠuGUR. (Greengus 1979)

Šul-a-gub(u) (M) One of seven offspring of Nin-Girida, wife of the netherworld god Nin-azu. Means "Young Man on the Left Side." See Šul-a-zida. (Litke 1998: 191)

Šūlak (M) Lion-monster of the netherworld, mentioned in "A Prince's Vision of the netherworld," a text dated to the mid-seventh century BCE. (Foster 2005: 836; Speiser, *ANET*: 109)

Šul-a-zida (M) One of seven offspring of Nin-Girida, wife of the netherworld god Nin-azu. Means "Young Man on the Right Side." See Šul-a-gub(u). (Litke 1998: 191)

Šul-edin (M) Deity attested in an Early Dynastic god list. Means "Young Man (of) the Steppe." (Mander 1986: 149)

Šul-ge (M) Deity attested in a god list from Aššur. Means "Steadfast Young Man." (Schroeder 1920: no. 63)

Šuli(n)katte (H) Hattic god of plague and warfare. Personified Fate. Identified with Nergal and Uqur. Related to Wur(r)unkatte. The word *katte* means "king"; the meaning of Šuli(n) is not known. The local storm god of Nerik (Šar(r)uma?) was considered son of Šuli(n)katte. Worshipped by the Luwians and the Hittites. Member of a list of war gods. Had a cult center at ancient Tamarmara in Anatolia. (van Gessel 1998: I, 411–13; Popko 1995: 94, 100, 117, 146; Haas 1994: 300, 310–11, 363, 367; Laroche 1946/47: 31)

Šul-lala (M) Deity identified with Enki/Ea in a Neo-Assyrian god list. Written šu-ul-la-la. Perhaps syllabic for šul-la-la "Young Man of Happiness." (King 1969: pl. 33)

Šullat (Akk.) With Ḫaniš, a pair of gods of destruction. Šullat was equated in An : *Anum* to the sun god Šamaš. Along with Ḫaniš, he was minister of the storm god Adad. In the account of the Great Flood in the Babylonian Gilgameš epic, he acted as herald of the coming storm. King Šulgi commissioned a temple for Ḫaniš and Šullat, and the two deities are mentioned in a second-millennium BCE ritual for the *akītu* festival. (Black and Green 2003: 110; Foster 2001: 87; Litke 1998: 145; Cohen 1993: 307; George 1993: 170 no. 1421; Tallqvist 1974 467; Speiser, *ANET*: 94; Grayson, *ANET*: 513; Edzard and Lambert, *RlA* IV: 107–8)

Šulmanītu(m) (M). Assyrian name of the goddess Inana/Ištar. Means "She of the Peace Offering." Some biblical scholars have connected her to the Šulamite of Song of Songs. See Inana-erisilima. (Cogan, *DDDB*: 775–76; Litke 1998: 158; Tallqvist 1974: 467)

Šulmānu(m) (M) Assyrian god occurring only in theophoric names, for example, that of the Assyrian kings named Shalmaneser. Deity name means "Official Gift" or "Peace Offering." (Radner 1998; Cogan, *DDDB*: 774–75; Leick 1999: 145–47)

Šul-pa'e (M) Deity attested in god lists of the Early Dynastic period. Husband of the birth/mother goddess Nin-ḫursag/Bēlet-ilī. Vizier was Lugal-nir-ana. Associated with the steppe and its wild animals. In a later tradition, Šul-pa'e seems to be the name of a demon. Offspring by Nin-ḫursag were Ašgi, Lisina, and Lil. Šul-pa'e means "Young Man who Is Manifest." In "The Death of Gilgameš," Šul-pa'e was one of the deities to whom the dying Gilgameš sacrificed. The god was honored in a number of temples. Offering lists from Girsu recorded gifts to Šul-pa'e, and the god's statue was present during the *akītu* celebration at Uruk. Astrally, Šul-pa'e was one of the names of the planet Jupiter. (Cohen 2015: 62; Black and Green 2003: 173; Frayne 2001: 153; Leick 1998: 153; Litke 1998: 41, 72, 165; George 1993: 24, 170 no. 1422; Jacobsen 1976: 105; Tallqvist 1974: 467–68)

Šulpa'e-amaš (M) One of three attendants of the E-maḫ temple of the goddess

Gula. Means "Šul-pa'e of the Sheepfold." (Litke 1998: 73; Tallqvist 1974: 467)

Šulpa'e-barbara (M) Form of Šul-pa'e worshipped at Girsu in the Ur III period. Means "Shining Šul-pa'e." (Sallaberger 1993: I, 93, 283)

Šulpa'e-egala (M) Form of Šul-pa'e worshipped at Girsu. Means "Šul-pa'e of the Palace." The name stresses the links of this god with the ruling family of governors at Girsu in the Ur III period. (Sallaberger 1993: I, 93)

Šulpa'e-gunu-a (M) One of three attendants of the E-maḫ temple of Gula. Perhaps "Resplendent Šulpa'e" or "Blessed Šulpae." (Litke 1998: 73)

Šul-pa'e-kiri (M) Sumerian form of Šul-pa'e worshipped at Girsu. Means "Šul-pa'e of the Garden." (Sallaberger 1993: I, 93)

Šulpa'eta-ria (M) Sumerian name of the demon Bennu(m) "Epilepsy." May mean "Cast down from Šulpa'e," perhaps referring to an epileptic fit. (Litke 1998: 73; Tallqvist 1974: 468)

Šulpa'e-utula (M) Sumerian form of Šul-pa'e attested in an Old Babylonian god list. Means "Šul-pa'e of the Herdsman." (Richter 2004: 158, 219, 312)

Šul-pirig (M) Deity attested in an Early Dynastic god list. (Mander 1986: 150)

Šul-šagana (M) Known from the Early Dynastic period. Often mentioned with his sibling Ig-alima. Son of Baba and Nin-Girsu. As the eldest son, he "supervised the meals and carried the pitcher of water for washing the hands before and after eating" (Jacobsen 1976: 82). Means "Young Man after His Own [Nin-Girsu's] Heart." He had a shrine in Girsu and a "seat" in the main temple at Aššur. (Black and Green 2003: 39, 123; Selz 1995: 277–79; George 1993: 64 no. 22, 111 no. 618; Tallqvist 1974: 468)

Šuluḫītu(m) (M) Goddess referred to in a Babylonian hymn as consort of En-zak, chief god of Dilmun (Baḥrain). (Black and Green 2003: 66)

Šul-UDUL (M) Personal god of rulers of Lagaš, of the Ur-Nanše Dynasty (c. 2600 BCE onward). May mean "Young Man, the Shepherd." The god had a shrine in Girsu, statues were dedicated to him, and he occurred in offering lists. (Leick 1999: 173; Selz 1995: 279–81; George 1993: 120 no. 719; Kramer 1981: 365)

Šul-UDUL-Emaḫ (M) Sumerian form of Šul-UDUL worshipped at a shrine called E-maḫ, which lay in the province of Girsu in Early Dynastic times. Offerings to the god were made at the city of Nimen in the eastern part of Lagaš province. (Selz 1995: 281)

Šul-UDUL-eš (M) Sumerian form of Šul-UDUL meaning "Šul-UDUL (of) the Shrine." He always appears with Šul-UDUL-Emaḫ in offerings associated with the town of Nimen in the eastern part of Lagaš province. (Selz 1995: 281–82)

Šulzi-maḫ-ana, Šurzi-maḫ-ana (M) Deity attested in a god list from Aššur in the circle of Šamaš. Written šul-zi-maḫ-<an>-na and šúr-zi-maḫ-<an>-na. (Schroeder 1920: no. 64)

Šum (M) Deity attested in an Early Dynastic god list. Perhaps means "Slaughterer." (Mander 1986: 150)

Šu-maḫ (M) (1) Deity attested at Isin and Nippur in the Ur III period and at Old Babylonian Nippur. Served as guardian spirit of the Nin-Isina temple at Isin, the E-maḫ. (2) Divinized attribute of Marduk in An : *Anum*. Means "The

Mighty One." (Richter 2004: 213–14; Litke 1998: 184, 223; Sallaberger 1993: I, 100, 102, 153)

Šumalia (M) Goddess of the Kassites. With her husband Šuqamuna, she was tutelary deity of the king. One of her titles was "Lady of the Pure Mountains." Shared temples with her spouse Šuqamuna, who was identified with Nergal and associated with Nuska. It has been suggested that her name might be associated with the Old Iranian word *zima* meaning "snow" and also that it might have an association with the name for the Himalayan mountains "Abode of Snow." (Black and Green 2003: 112; Becking, *DDDB*: 776; George 1993: 170 no. 1423; Balkan 1978: 116–18; Tallqvist 1974: 466)

Šumeša (M) Deity attested in a theophoric name in an Early Dynastic or possibly Sargonic tablet from Nippur. E-Šumeša was the name of the temple of Ninurta at Nippur, suggesting a connection between the temple and the deity. (A. Westenholz 1975: no. 127)

ŠUMku (M) Deity attested in a god list from Aššur. Written ŠUM-ku. Might also be read Takku. (Schroeder 1920: no. 63)

Šummānu(m) (M) See Saman

Šunama (L) See Ṯakamuna-wa-Šunama

Šu-namri (M) Deity identified with the great god Enki/Ea. Explained in An : *Anu ša amēli* as "Ea of the coppersmiths." Note ᵈNin-namri, identified as a lapidary or seal cutter. (Litke 1998: 239; Tallqvist 1974: 466)

Šuni-dug (M) One of eight children of Gaa'u. The "Lamentation over the Destruction of Sumer and Ur" bewailed the fact that Šu-ni-dug no longer piled up cheese and other dairy products. Means "Her/His Hand Is Good." Also written with the sign GANAM$_4$. Occurs also in an incantation. (George 2016: no. 6; *LAS*: 136; Litke 1998: 127; Tallqvist 1974: 466; Kramer, *ANET*: 617)

Šuni-dugud (M) One of two bull-lyres of the god Lugal-Marada. Means "Her/His Hand Is Weighty." (Litke 1998: 171; Tallqvist 1974: 466)

Šu-nir (M) See Šurinnu(m)

Šu-pa-su (M) Deity identified with the storm god Iškur/Adad. (Litke 1998: 145)

Šuqamuna (M) Major god of the Kassites who almost always occurs with his wife Šumalia. Had a special association with the royal family, and, along with his wife, was protective deity of the king. Identified with Nergal and associated with Nuska. Equated to Marduk as "Marduk of the container (*pisannu*)." He and his wife Šumalia were called the twin deities of battle. They usually shared a temple. (Lambert 2013: 264; Black and Green 2003: 112; George 1993: 170 no. 1423; Balkan 1978: 118–22; Tallqvist 1974: 466; Reiner 1970: 17)

Šur-baba (M) Goddess attested in a Neo-Assyrian god list and identified with Aya, the wife of the sun god. Written šur-ba$_4$-ba$_4$; preceding entry Bur-ri-ba$_4$-ba$_4$ may be a variant. (King 1969: pl. 9)

Šur-gal (M) See Sag-gal

Šuriaš (M) Well-known god of the Kassites. Identified with Utu/Šamaš. An equation with the Hindu sun god Surya has been suggested, but has been disputed. (Black and Green 2003: 112; Balkan 1978: 122–23; Tallqvist 1974: 466)

Šūriḫḫa (H, M) Deity attested in a Middle Assyrian tablet possibly from Šura/Šuri, in the kingdom of Mittani. The Hurrian name means "He of

Šura/Šuri." Theophoric names containing this god are also attested at Nuzi. (Schwemer 2001: 578)

Šurinnu(m) (Akk.) **Šu-nir** (Sum.) Deified standard, attested at Šuruppak in the third millennium BCE and at Old Babylonian Sippar and Babylon. The moon god's emblem occurred in the writing of the name of the city of Ur and in the god's name. Deity standards were used to head divine processions and are attested for various deities, including the moon god Nanna/Sîn, Ninurta, Marduk, and Aššur. (Martin et al. 2001: no. 110; Litke 1998: 220; Tallqvist 1974: 466; Renger 1967: 140, 155; Sjöberg 1967: 205–7 note 9; Pongratz-Leisten, *RlA* XIII: 107–8)

Šurinnu-ša-Sîn (M) The Akkadian deified standard of the moon god appearing in a trial document from Old Babylonian Kutalla near Ur. (Renger 1967: 145)

Šurinnu-ša-Šamaš (M) The Akkadian deified standard of the god Šamaš attested at Old Babylonian Sippar. (Renger 1967: 155)

Šu-šanabi (M) Deity identified in a Neo-Assyrian god list with Ninurta with gloss šu-šá-na-bi and explained as "War-like Ninurta." Means. "He with Forty Hands." Forty is the number of Ninurta, who is also called Nimin-DU "Forty Goes Forth." (King 1969: pl. 11)

Šušin (M) Deity listed in An : *Anum* after the sons of Tišpak, the chief god of Ešnunna, and preceding Ištarān, god of Dēr. Written MÙŠ.ŠÉŠ, one of the attested orthographies for Šusin (Susa), usually written MÙŠ.EREN. The name may mean "(God of) Susa." (Litke 1998: 194)

Šušinak (E) See Inšušinak

Šušum (M) Deity in an Ur III personal name from Šarrākum. (Nisaba 152: 1031: r ii 26)

Šu-tila (M) Deity identified with Marduk. Means "Hand that Causes Life." (Litke 1998: 223; Tallqvist 1974: 467)

Šuš-urugala (M) Deity attested in god lists of the Early Dynastic period. May mean "Net of the Netherworld." (Mander 1986: 100, 113, 115)

Šuwāla (M) An originally Syrian/Upper Mesopotamian goddess. Her spouse was Šuwaliyaz. Appears in personal names and equated in a bilingual Akkadian-Aramaic inscription to the storm god's wife Šala. She was apparently imported into the Mesopotamian pantheon as early as the Ur III period. She occurs in Hurrian-Hittite texts in the circle of the goddess Ḫebat. Earlier, in the Ur III period, she was associated with the goddesses Anunnītu(m) and Allatu(m). See Nabarbi. (Schwemer 2001: 408–10)

Šuwaliyaz (H) Anatolian god, spouse of Šuwāla, and brother of Teššub. (Schwemer 2001: 410, 418, 500 and note 3710)

Šu-zabar-kug (M) Goddess identified with Šala, wife of the storm god Iškur/Adad. May mean "Clear Reflecting Mirror." In a Neo-Assyrian god list called "Šala of the Valley." (Litke 1998: 143; Tallqvist 1974: 467; King 1969: pl. 10)

Šu-zi-ana (M) Enlil's junior wife. Means "Reliable Hand of Heaven." The *gagû* in Enlil's Nippur temple was dedicated to her, and she had a temple there. "Perfect Beloved House" was probably a temple to the goddess and maybe the bed chamber of Šu-zi-ana and Enlil (George 1993: 109 no. 582). Apparently Enlil and Šu-zi-ana were celebrants in the ritual of the "Sacred Marriage." Šu-zi-ana also had a "seat" at Ur. (Cohen 2015: 135; Litke 1998: 41; Tallqvist 1974: 467; George 1993: 23, 78 no. 191, 83 no. 265, 86 no. 296–97, 117 no. 683)

— T —

Taautos (L) According to Philo of Byblos, the Phoenician god who invented writing and record-keeping. A metal smith, he created the emblems of the deities. His father was Misor. Equated to Egyptian Thoth and Greek Hermes. (Handy 1994: 135 note 12, 138–39; Attridge and Oden 1981: 28, 29, 38, 39, 46, 47, 56, 57, 62, 63, 72 note 6)

Tab (M) Deity attested at Fara. (Martin et al. 2001: 113)

Tab-ana (M) Deity identified with the rainbow goddess, Manzi'at/Tir-anna. Perhaps the name means "Companion of An(or Heaven)." (Litke 1998: 167)

Tabub, **Tabbu** (M) Deity attested in a personal name in the Mari texts. (Durand 2008: 665)

Tadmuštu(m) (M) Akkadian goddess in an Ur III text from Garšana, which refers to the textiles of Tadmuštu(m). Possibly appears in an Old Babylonian text from Uruk. (Owen and Mayr 2007: no. 617; Richter 2004: 327, note 1396)

Tag-nun (M) Sumerian deity attested in an Early Dynastic god list. (Mander 1986: 60–61)

Taḫâra-pî-nīši (M) Goddess in the temple of Nabû in Babylon during the first millennium BCE. According to *CAD* Ḫ: 119 sub *ḫâru* A "The idiom *pī nišī ḫâru* may mean 'to bind the mouth magically to compel people to speak the truth in preparation for judgment'." (Watanabe: 1990 no. 94)

Taḫat(t)anuiti(š) (H) Ancient Anatolian goddess. A mother and earth deity and a form of the goddess Inara. Consort of the Hattic storm god of an unnamed town. The storm god's concubine was Tašimmet(i). Wattarašanaš, one of Taḫat(t)anuiti's Hittite titles, means "Mother of the Springs." She is mentioned in a Hittite story about Telipinu, the disappearing god. From Hittite documents concerned with the prince's ritual trip to a state in the north, we learn that the goddess had two names, the one humans addressed her by—Taḫat(t)anuiti—and the one she held among the deities—"Mother of the Spring [Water], Queen," that is, of the deities. (Leick 1998: 79; van Gessel 1998: I, 426–27; Popko 1995: 72–73; Haas 1994: 156, 311–12; Laroche 1946/47: 31)

Taištara (H) One of the more obscure Hittite deities. (Archi 1990: 118)

Takiti(s), **Takidu** (H) Hurrian goddess. Maidservant of Ḫebat. Companion of goddess Taru/Daru, together often forming a dyad Daru-Takitti. Depicted together in the procession of goddesses in the Hittite rock-cut reliefs at Yazılıkaya. Mentioned in the Hurrian mythic story "Song of Ullikummi." Attested at Kizzuwatna and at Ugarit. (Hoffner 1998: 41, 62; van Gessel 1998: I, 433–35; Popko 1995: 63, 115; Haas 1994: 388, 447, 471, 581; Laroche 1976: 70; Laroche 1946/47: 60)

TaKUna (M) One of two gate-keepers of the E-sagil, Marduk's temple at Babylon. (Richter 1999: 174 note 712; Litke 1998: 99)

Tališu-Damgayu (L) Deity (or pair of deities) in Ugaritic texts. Enemies of the god Ba'al-Hadad. (del Olmo Lete 1999: 57)

Tamar(u) (H) Deity attested in personal names. (Durand 2008: 665)

Tammuz (L, M) See Dumuzi

Tanit(h), Tannit, Tennit, Tinnit(h), (Phoenician) **Tenneith** (Greek) The tutelary goddess of Carthage, originally a Phoenician colony in North Africa. Worshipped in other Phoenician colonies and also in Phoenicia proper. Closely associated with Aštarte. An ivory plaque found in an eighth-century BCE temple at Ṣarepta in the Levant was dedicated to "Tanit-Aštarte." Further, a Carthaginian inscription read "To the Ladies Ashtart and Tannit in Lebanon" (Cross 1973: 30). On the other hand, some scholars see her as having closer connections to Asherah, while Albright argued that she was identified with 'Anat(u). One scholar equated her with all three Canaanite great goddesses. The meaning of her name is disputed. One explanation is that the word comes from a Semitic root "to lament" and so signifies "She who Weeps," perhaps for a disappearing god like Adonis. Another suggestion, "Dragon or Serpent Lady," sees her name as derived from the same root as Tannin, the snake-dragon. Yet another scholar explains it as coming from the word for "fig."

The details of her personality and powers are not really clear. She is often seen as a goddess of the moon, of fertility, and of the heavens. Like Asherah, she had maritime connections and might have been a patron of sailors. At Carthage she seems to have been a deity of good fortune. Reminiscent of "Name of Ba'lu," one of Aštarte's titles at Ugarit and in Phoenicia, was the early Tanit epithet *pene Ba'lu* "Face of Ba'lu." A later title, *rabat* "Chief," indicated her supreme status. Attested on a large number of Carthaginian carved stones (steles), in which she was normally paired with the god Baāl-Ḥamōn, in all likelihood her consort at Carthage and elsewhere. By the fifth century BCE, Tanit had supplanted him as main deity of Carthage, at least in popular religion.

Bust of Tanit, half life-size, found in a Punic graveyard on Ibiza, Spain. Fifth-fourth century BCE. Terracotta. Archaeological Museum, Barcelona.

In images she was often accompanied by dolphins, fish, pomegranates, palm trees, an open hand, and doves. She was depicted in winged form in a cult cave on the Spanish island of Ibiza. Many steles featured the "Sign of Tanit," perhaps a stylized human body, formed by a triangle topped with a circle, the two shapes being separated by a horizontal line with upturned ends. Sometimes it also included a crescent (moon?). Since the circle occasionally had a human face sketched on it, the "Sign of Tanit" is generally accepted as representing the goddess, though some think the circle to be the disk of the full moon.

Tanit's huge sanctuary was a central feature of the city of Carthage. Its oldest level dated to the eighth century BCE It was destroyed by the then-Christian Romans in 421 CE. From the evidence of archaeology, Tanit was a very popular goddess in Sardinia, as well as other Phoenician settlements in the West. She had a temple at Tas Ṣilg on the main island of the Maltese archipelago. According to Greek and later Christian writers, the Carthaginians sacrificed their children to Ba'al-Ḥamōn. Originally, the god was the primary recipient of such sacrifices, but later they were also made to his consort Tanit. The cremated remains were buried in urns and other containers at sacred enclosures associated with the sanctuaries of the deities; the enclosures are known as "tophets" from the name used in the Hebrew Bible for a place of child sacrifice (2 Kings 23:10; Jeremiah 7:31). At Carthage and elsewhere, "tophets" contained cremated remains of very young humans and animals and were accompanied by inscribed markers often naming the contents as *molk* offerings to Ba'al-Ḥamon and Tanit. Such sacred enclosures with urns and steles have been excavated at Hadrumetum, and other sites. Whether these urns held babies who had been sacrificed is much disputed. Under what conditions these "sacrifices" were offered to the deities is also in question. As elsewhere in the Ancient Near East, human sacrifice seems to have been practiced in the Phoenician world in times of crisis, but normally the person sacrificed was a teenager or an adult. Tenneith or Tinnith was the Greek version of Tanit's name. The Greeks identified her with Hera, while the Romans named her Juno Caelestis. The Syrian who became Roman emperor (203–222 CE) under the name Elegabalus ("God of the Mountain" Ba'lu Ḥamōn?) took a statue of Tanit to Rome and identified his wife with the goddess. From then on, Tanit was worshipped in Rome. (Quinn 2018: 97–98, 103–4; Woolmer 2017: 115; Betlyon 2005: 16, 29, 40; Bierling 2002: 158; Markoe 2000: 107, 118, 130, 132, 134–36, 199; Moscati 1999: 124, 137, 138–39, 155, 160, 193–94, 228, 241; Ribichini, *DDDB*: 340; Seow, *DDDB*: 322; Brody 1998: 30–33, figures 13–20: Lipiński 1995: 62–64, 199–215, 423–26, 440–46; Schwartz 1993: 28; Warmington 1993: 145–46; Frendo and Inglott 1992; Lipiński, *DCPP*: 438–39; Smith 1990: 138; J. Day 1989; Betlyon 1985: 54–55; Hvidberg-Hansen 1979: 115–42; Pritchard 1978: 20, 105–8; Oden 1976: 32; Cross 1973: 28–34; Albright 1968: 130, 234–37; Harden 1963: 75, 87–89, 120)

Tannin (L) See Tunnan(u)

Tapkina(š) (H, M) See Damkina

Tappinu (H) See Mezul(l)a

Taqi'atu (L) One of the Kōṯarṯu, seven minor goddesses of fertility at Ugarit. (del Olmo Lete 1999: 57)

Tar'am-Mēr (M) Akkadian goddess attested in the old pantheon of Mari. Means "Beloved of Mēr." Some have understood this deity to have originally been an ancestor, but Sasson suggests the possibility of the opposite, that he was originally a god who later was believed to have been a human hero of old. See Wēr. (Sasson 2001; Schwemer 2001: 203 note 1400)

Taramuya (M) Akkadian deity associated with the Anu(m)-Adad temple in Aššur and apparently the Adad temple at Kurba'il, a city northwest of Nineveh. (Schwemer 2001: 580, 597, 602)

Tarāwa, Darawa (H) Luwian deity. Haas describes Darawa as a "netherworld monster of some sort." (van Gessel 1998: I, 444. 445; Popko 1995: 55, 89; Haas 1994: 133)

Tarḫunta, Tarḫuant, Tarḫunda, Tarḫunza Tarḫu(na), Tarḫun(n) (H) Luwian/Hittite weather/storm god. The word *tarḫu* means "heroic." Rarely attested in material of the Old Hittite period, during which time Tarḫunta began to be identified with the Hattic storm god Taru. As Tarḫu(na), he appears in texts from ancient Kaneš. Originally a typical storm god, but gradually acquired traits of an agricultural and vegetation deity. An eighth-century BCE relief represents him as holding what seem to be grain and grapes. Usually, however, he carried an ax, wore his hair in a pigtail, and was associated with the trident. According to one magical rite, he rode in a wagon/chariot drawn by horses. During the Hittite Empire, he received the title *piḫaššašši* "The One of Lightening." His cult city Tarḫuntašša was for a time the Hittite capital. He was patron god of King Muwattali II. Found in Hurrian inscriptions written in Hittite and attested in Hittite and Luwian theophoric names. In north Syria Tarḫunta was equated to the Semitic storm god Ba'lu. Tarḫunza was widely known as a name of the storm god of Aleppo. As Tarḫunza, the god was companion of Kubaba. He had a temple in Carchemish. His veneration persisted into Hellenistic and Roman times. Cognate with the Celtic god of thunder Taranis. (Schwemer 2001: 6, 234, 244, 486, 612–13; Greenfield, *DDDB*: 379, 381; Leick 1998: 113; van Gessel 1998: I, 446; Popko 1995: 69, 91, 110, 166–68, 173; Haas 1994: 308–9; Laroche 1946/47: 89)

Tartak, Tarhak (L) According to the Hebrew Bible, one of a pair of deities worshipped by a group of people from Avva or Awwah. After the Assyrians conquered the area, they settled these people in Samaria (II Kings 17: 24, 31). The other deity was Nibhaz, who might have been the same as a little-known Elamite god Ibnaḫaza. The latter was equated in a god list to the Babylonian god Ea. Tartak has also been explained as Elamite. An alternate view sees the deity as being a reference to Atargatis. (Cogan, *DDDB*: 836–37; Millard, *DDDB*: 623; Fulco, *ABD* IV: 1104; Handy, *ABD* VI: 334–35)

Taru (H) Hattic form of Tarḫunta. Hattic storm god, the weather god of Nerik, a sacred Hattic city. Along with Eštan, the sun goddess, he was head of the Hattic pantheon. Considered son of the Sun Goddess of Arinna or, sometimes, of Lelwani. Like Telipinu, he occasionally disappeared, and there were rites to bring him back. Patron deity of Ḫattušili III. Appears in texts from ancient Kanesh. (Schwemer 2001: 126 note 871, 234; Hoffner 1998: 21–26; Leick 1998: 164; van Gessel 1998: I, 448–49; Popko 1995: 55, 69, 91, 113, 115, 117; Haas 1994: 438, 471, 597; Laroche 1976: 70; Laroche 1946/47: 61)

Taru, Daru (H) Hurrian goddess, often forming the dyad Daru-Takitti. Depicted with Takitti in the procession of goddesses in the Hittite rock-cut reliefs at Yazılıkaya. (Popko 1995: 115)

Tašila (M) Deity attested in an Old Babylonian god list. Written ta-ši-la. (Weidner 1924/25)

Tašimmet(i), Tašimet(iš), Tašammat(ta), Tašamet, Tašimmez (H) Hattic goddess. In an unidentified town, she was concubine of the local storm god. She, like the storm god's wife, was associated with springs. From Hittite documents concerned with the prince's ritual trip to a state in the north, we learn that the goddess had two names, the one humans addressed her by—Tašimmet(i)—and the one she held among the deities—"Queen Ištar." In a text about Lelwani and the "dead" temple from Ḫattušas, Tašamat and Tašimmez constituted a dyad. See Taḫat(t)anuiti(š). (Leick 1998: 164; van Gessel 1998: I, 454–58; Popko 1995: 72–73; Haas 1994: 245, 446–47)

Tašmētu(m) (M) Daughter of Uraš. Wife of the scribe god Nabû, tutelary god of Borsippa. One of her titles was Šarrat-Barsip "Queen of Borsippa." Name associated with the Akkadian word *šemû* and possibly means "Listening (to Prayers)." Often invoked in Babylonian and Assyrian ritual texts and prayers as an intercessor and protector, as well as a deity able to help with love and sexual potency. In a hymn the writer appeals to the goddess to intercede with her father-in-law Marduk. Aššurbanipal praises the goddess in a hymn.

Tašmētu(m) often shared temples with Nabû, her husband, as she did at Borsippa, Nabû's cult center. At Babylon she had shrines in the temples of Nabû and Marduk. In Assyria a procession of the goddess occurred on the fifth day of every month. At Kalaḫ (Nimrūd) and also at Babylon, a "Sacred Marriage" rite was celebrated for Nabû and Tašmētu, probably at the *akītu* festival. Astrally, Tašmētu was associated with Capricorn. (Foster 2005: 944–46; Lapinkivi 2004: 83–86; Black and Green 2003: 133; Leick 1999: 24–26; Leick 1998: 156; Cohen 1993: 247, 311–12, 337, 427, 453; George 1993: 132–33 no. 878, 156 no. 1176; Livingstone 1989: 17–18; Matsushima 1987; Litke 1974: 96; Tallqvist 1974: 470–71; Stephens, *ANET*: 390)

Tašme-zikri (M) Minister of Bēlet-bēri(m)/Išḫara. Means "She Has Listened to My Command." (Litke 1998: 44, 166; Tallqvist 1974: 471)

Tašmidiršu (E) Elamite deity for whom Šilḫak-Inšušinak I commissioned a temple in Susa. (König 1977: 86, 220, 227)

Tašmišu, Tasmisu (H) Hurrian god in the circle of Teššub. The word *tašmi* means "strong." Twin brother of Teššub and his companion and vizier. Also a warlike deity, as attested by his inclusion in a list of warrior gods. The Hittites called him Suwaliyat. Regularly equated to Ninurta and, in a lexical text from Emar, identified with Pa(p)-sukkal. Depicted in the procession of gods in the Hittite rock-cut reliefs at Yazılıkaya. In the "Song of Kumarbi," born, along with Teššub and the Aranzaḫ River, as a result of the castration of Anu by Kumarbi, who then became pregnant with the brothers. In the "Song of Ullikummi," Tašmišu advises Teššub and acts as his messenger. Worshipped widely in Anatolia. (Schwemer 2001: 448 note 3719, 451, 480, 553 note 4415; Hoffner 1998: 41, 43, 49–50, 56, 58–64, 72–73, 77, 113; Leick 1998: 106; van Gessel 1998: I, 458–60; Popko 1995: 97, 115, 117, 125, 165; Haas 1994: 309, 332, 363, 473, 494, 581, 634; Laroche 1977: 259)

Tašqi-Mama (M) Deity at Mari. Some have understood this deity to have originally been an ancestor, but Sasson suggests the possibility of the opposite, that he was originally a god who later was believed to have been a human hero of old. Name means "Mama Irrigates." (Sasson 2001)

Tauri(t) (H) Deity mentioned in the "Song of Kumarbi." According to offering lists, Tauri(t) once preceded the Sun Goddess of Arinna in the pantheon of Ḫattušas. Occurs in rituals and might have been associated with the town Taurіša. (Hoffner 198: 45; van Gessel 1998: I, 462–63; Popko 1995: 113; Laroche 1946/47: 33)

Tazzuwaši (H) Hattic(?) concubine of the mountain god Zaliyanu, storm deity of the state of Kaštama in central Anatolia. Worshipped in the state cult of Kaštama as part of a triad made up of Zaliyanu, his wife Za(š)ḫapuna, and Tazzuwaši. (van Gessel 1998: I, 463–65; Popko 1995: 114; Haas 1994: 446, 463; Laroche 1946/47: 33–34)

Tega (M) Sumerian deity appearing in an Old Babylonian god list from Nippur. Corresponding to En-nimgir-si; the latter appearing with the gods Dumuzi and Ama-ušum-gal-ana. Means "Approach!" (Richter 2004: 313)

Teišeba (M) The Urarṭean god of storms, apparently a form of the Hurrian storm god Teššub. The Urarṭean pantheon was headed by a triad made up of the supreme god Ḫaldi, the sun god Šiuini, and Teišeba. (Schwemer 2001: 446)

Telam (M) Deity identified with Zarpanītum in a Neo-Assyrian god list. Written Te-la-am. (King 1969: pl. 35)

Telipinu, Talapinu, Dalapinu (H) Agricultural and vegetation god, likely originally Hattic. Had a number of traits of a storm god. Son of the storm god and the Sun Goddess of Arinna. Means "Strong Child." One of his epithets was "Fruitful." According to Haas, he was worshipped as the branch of an oak tree, the oak being a symbol of kingship. In hieroglyphic writing, he was represented by a tree. Equated by Hittite priests to Dumuzi. Telipinu was a disappearing god central to several myths. These myths are closely associated with rituals designed to bring the missing god back. According to the myth, after an angry Telipinu goes into hiding, everything begins to dry up, resulting in famine throughout the land. The divinities started to look for Telipinu, but he was not to be found. Then the goddess Ḫannaḫanna sent a bee to locate him. The bee stung the sleeping god, who eventually returned. In another disappearing god story, it was the sun god who was missing. The storm god sent Telipinu to bring him back from the Great Sea; Telipinu did so, but, in addition, brought back the daughter of the Sea, Ḫatepinu, as his wife.

In the Old Hittite period he was a member of the Hittite pantheon at Ḫattušas and continued to be an important deity. Muršili II worshipped him as his guardian god. Attested in theophoric names. Hittite King Telipinu bore the name, as did Prince Telipinu, whom his father Šuppiliuma I installed as high priest at Kummani, Telipinu's sacred city and capital of Kizzuwatna. Telipinu was routinely mentioned in god lists, offering lists, and official documents, such as treaties. In addition to Kummani, his cult centers were

Ḫanḫana and nearby Kašḫa to the north of Ḫattušas. Laroche mentions a theory that Telepinu and the Mysian hero Telephos, founder of Pergamon, are connected. (Wilhelm 2010; Leick 1998: 156–57; van Gessel 1998: I, 466–78; Popko 1995: 63–64, 71, 80, 83–84, 87–88, 97, 106, 110–14, 120, 143–44; Haas 1994: 193, 305, 310, 312, 332, 442–45; Laroche 1946/47: 34–35)

Telītu(m) (Akk.), **Zibba** (Sum.) Name of Ištar. Means "The Capable One." The prologue to the law code of Ḫammurāpi mentioned the goddess by this name. An attested "seat" of Ištar as Telītu(m) was probably part of the great temple of Marduk at Babylon. (Leick 1999: 65–66; George 1993: 85 no. 290; Meek, *ANET*: 165)

Temen-kug (M) Deity attested in an Early Dynastic god list. Means "Holy Foundation." (Mander 1986: 150)

Temen-nun-si-na (M) See En-men-nun-si-na

Tempt(i), Tepti (E) Middle and Neo-Elamite god whose name means "(Gracious) Lord." Appears in inscriptions of King Untaš-Napiriša and Ḫanni, an Elamite vassal king. Also occurs as a component in various royal names. (Hinz and Koch 1987: 313; König 1977: 166, 227)

Tenu (M) Deity attested at Emar. (J. Westenholz 2000: 78)

Tešmēt-māti(m) (M) Akkadian deity mentioned in a tablet from the First Sealand Dynasty. The name may be a variant of Tašmētu(m) in Nuzi texts and mean "Reconciliation of the Land." She may, perhaps, be the deified wife of King Gulkišar of the First Sealand Dynasty, who appears in the next line of the tablet. (Dalley 2009: no. 83)

Teššub, Teššup (H, L) Hurrian storm god, ruler of the deities. He was identified / syncretized with the storm god of Ḫatti / the Heavens. His realm was the skies, the storm, thunder, lightening, and rain. He resided on mountain peaks. Adopted into the Hittite pantheon and, after the fourteenth century BCE, held a top position in it. Son of Anu. His brother Tašmišu was his vizier. Other brothers were the Aranzaḫ River and Šattaḫammu. His sister was Ša(w)uš(k)a. He was spouse of Ḫebat (Sun Goddess of Arinna). Their son was Šarruma, who was syncretized with the storm god of Nerik. His two divine bulls were Ḫurri and Šeriš, which pulled his chariot. His epithets included "God of Gods" and "King of the Gods." He was called Teššub of Life, Teššub of Salvation, and Teššub of the Battlefield. Visually he often stands on two mountain tops, usually brandishing a club. In this pose he is depicted in the Hittite rock-cut reliefs at Yazılıkaya. In the mythic Kumarbi cycle, Teššub defeated Kumarbi for sovereignty over the deities.

He was head of the pantheon of Mittani and protector of the country and its king. A prayer of Muwatalli II treats Teššub and Ḫebat of Ḫalab as deities of Šamuḫa. Worshipped at Malatya, along with Ša(w)uš(k)a, in the twelfth and eleventh centuries BCE. A Hittite rite appealed to both the weather god of Kumme / Kummiya and Teššub of Kumme / Kummiya. Mentioned in a Hurrian text from Old Babylonian Mari and also on a Mari cult vessel. He is first on a Neo-Hittite official list from Aleppo. Occurs in god lists, ritual texts, and theophoric names at Ugarit, where he was equated to the storm god Ba'lu and sometimes Dagān. He occurred in personal names from, among other places, Ḫattušas, Mari, Alalaḫ, Carchemish, Nuzi, and Aleppo. The largest temple, the ruins of which remain in Ḫattušas, was dedicated to Teššub and Ḫebat. His main cult center was Kummiya or Kumme in the north of Mesopotamia. The battle for supremacy among the gods is echoed in ancient Greek myth, with Uranos corresponding to Anu, Kronos to Kumarbi, and Zeus to Teššub. In a Neo-Assyrian god list written [d]te-eš-su-ub and identified with Adad of the Suteans. (del Olmo Lete 1999: 84, 85, 200, 340; Hoffner 1998: 40–65, 69–70, 72–77, 83–84, 113; Leick 1998: 157; van Gessel 1998: I, 482–508; Popko 1995: 70, 94, 96–98, 100, 112, 114–15, 123–27, 141, 165–66, 169; Haas 1994: 322–39; King 1969: pl. 16)

Teššub-piḫaimu (H, M) Form of the storm god attested at Middle Babylonian Emar. The name contains the Luwian epithet *piḫaimi* "powerful/radiant." (J. Westenholz 2000: 77; Haas 1994: 569–70; Lebrun 1988: 147–55)

Tetišḫapi, Tetešḫawi (H) Goddess of wild animals and the hunt. Probably of Hattic origin. Hattic name means "The Great Divinity." Connected or equated to Inara. Tetišḫapi occurred in Hattic and Hittite cultic texts, one of which mentions an antelope and a kid as being associated with her. She had a shrine at the source of a spring. Seems to have been important in the Hittite *Purulli* festival, a spring ritual in which she appears as a hunter. Devotees wore wolf and leopard masks in her honor and two celebrants in wolf masks circled around the goddess (her statue?). This description is reminiscent of the finds in the excavations at the Neolithic site of Çatal Höyök on the Anatolian plain, where leopards were associated with figurines that might represent goddesses. (Hoffner 1998: 10–11, 13, 112; van Gessel 1998: I, 509–12; Popko 1995: 72, 149; Haas 1994: 311, 438; Laroche 1977: 35; Mellaart 1967; Laroche 1946/47: 35)

Ti'amat, Tâmtum (M) Primeval goddess, personification of the sea, in the *Enūma eliš*. Attested as early as the Ur III period in a theophoric name of one of the wives of Šū-Sîn. The goddess's name means "Sea" *ti'amtu(m)*. At first, according to the *Enūma eliš*, Ti'amat's salt waters were co-mingled with those of her husband Apsû, the fresh waters, and together they engendered various deities, including the sky god Anu. Eventually, Ea, Anu's son, slew Apsû. Then, in a heroic battle, Ea's son, Marduk, slew Ti'amat, splitting her body in half. Marduk made one part into the vault of the heavens and the other into the surface of the earth. He made the clouds from her spittle, the mountains from her head, and the Tigris and Euphrates Rivers from her tears. She had bestowed the Tablet of Destiny on Qingu, but when Marduk defeated Qingu, he gave the tablet to Anu. There was a "seat" of Ti'amat in the temple of Marduk in Babylon, and Marduk's "seat" there was named Ti'amat. An Ugaritic lexical text equates Ti'amatu to the Mesopotamian goddess Antu(m). She occurs in an Ugaritic god list as Tihāmātu/Tamatu. (Lambert 2013: 236–40; Foster 2005: 439–65; Black and Green 2003: 153, 173, 177; Alster, *DDDB*: 867–69; del Olmo Lete 1999: 137; Leick 1999: 153–54; Leick 1998: 52–55; Cohen 1993: 420; George 1993: 113 no. 640, 149 no. 1094; Frankfort 1978: 325–33; Tallqvist 1974: 471–72;

Grayson, *ANET*: 501–2; Speiser, *ANET*: 60–67; Heidel 1967: 18–43)

Ti'arra (H) Deity associated with the storm god of Šapinuwa. (Giorgieri et al. 2013)

Ti-ba-nima (M) Deity whose name may mean "One Above who Grants Life." Explained in An : *Anu ša amēli* as "Ištar of the Fates(*isqāti*)." (Litke 1998: 235; Tallqvist 1974: 472)

Tibira-dingirene (M) Deity identified with the birth/mother goddess Dingir-maḫ/Bēlet-ilī. Means "Metal-worker of the Gods." (Litke 1998: 70; Waetzoldt: 1997 no. 96; Tallqvist 1974: 472; Krebernik, *RlA* VIII: 507)

Tibira-kalama (M) Deity identified with the birth/mother goddess Dingir-maḫ/Bēlet-ilī. Means "Metal Worker of the Nation." (Litke 1998: 70; Tallqvist 1974: 472; Krebernik, *RlA* VIII: 507)

TiDU (M) Deity attested at Ebla. (Waetzoldt 2001)

Tila (M) Deity occurring only once, in a god list where he is equated to a major deity whose name is broken away. (Lambert 2007: 167f.)

Ti-mu-a (M) See Si-mu-a

Ti-mu-du/Ti-mu-ud (M) Deity for whose festival supplies are given at Ebla. (Waetzoldt 2001)

Ti-nigba (M) Deity in an offering list from Ur III Girsu, whose cult perhaps was in the temple of Nin-Girsu. Possibly means "Life Is a Gift." Note Ti-ba-nima. (Amherst 17: o ii 10)

Tipanītum (M) Deity attested in an Old Babylonian god list. (Weidner 1924/25)

Tir-ana (M) See Manzi'at

Tirāṯu (L) Deity mentioned in an offering list relating to the funerary cult of the palace of Ugarit. (del Olmo Lete 1999: 57, 216)

Tirum (M) Deity in the Ur III personal name za-^{d}ti-ru-um from Umma. Note, however, that the same name occurs in another Ur III text without the divine determinative. (TCS 1, 140: o 4)

Tirumithir (E) Elamite deity named in a sandstone stele fragment found on the acropolis of Susa. In it Šilḫak-Inšušinak I describes his military campaign in the Zagros Mountains northwest of the Diyala River. (König 1977: 119, 132, 222. 227)

Ti-RU-RU (M) Deity explained in An : *Anu ša amēli* as Ištar *šá pišaḫti*, "of soothing." (Litke 1998: 235)

Tirutur (E) Elamite deity invoked in a rock-relief inscription of a local ruler named Ḫanni. He had the inscription carved at modern Kul-i-Faraḥ not far from Malamir in the Bakhtiari Mountains. (König 1977: 155–60, 222, 227)

Tišamme-pî-mukarribi (M) Deity whose name means "She Listens to Those who Give Homage." (Deller 1991: no. 18)

Tišalītum (M) Deity attested in an Old Babylonian god list. (Weidner 1924/25)

Tišpak (M) Babylonian warrior and storm god. One of his epithets was "Lord of Armies." Identified with the warrior god Nin-azu and later with Ninurta. His wife was Ugula. Among his offspring was Nanšak. His vizier was Bašmu(m), the viper. His animal was the snake-dragon. In an Akkadian mythic composition called "The Lion-Serpent" the gods ordered Tišpak to kill the lion-serpent, which was devastating the land. Tišpak is mentioned in the prologue to the law code of Ḫammu-rāpi. Tišpak was also a guarantor of oaths. He replaced the god Nin-azu as tutelary deity of the city of Ešnunna, where Tišpak received offerings during the *akītu* festival. He had festivals at Šaduppû(m) and Nērebtu(m) in the Diyala region. He was associated also with the city of Dēr. (Foster 2005: 581–82; Black and Green 2003: 178; Sommerfeld 2002: 701–6; Leick 1999: 65; Leick 1998: 157; Wiggermann 1997: 37–39; Cohen 1993: 251–52, 255, 267, 396; George 1993: 35; Litke 1998: 193–94, 234; Tallqvist 1974: 472; Roberts, 1972: 54; Jacobsen 1970: 34; Meek, *ANET*: 165)

Titiuti (H) Hattic maiden goddess. A metal statue of her, coated with silver, was found with a collection of cult objects. (van Gessel 1998: I, 521; Haas 1994: 503 note 100; Laroche 1946/47: 35)

Tiūk (E) Elamite deity attested in a treaty between Narām-Sîn of Akkad and a king of Susa. (König 1977: 29, 222)

Tiwat (H) Luwian sun god, spouse of Kamrušepa. Their son was protective deity of the city Taurиša. The name comes from the Indo-European word *šiuš*, originally the name of the god of the light of heaven. Also referred to in Palaic material. He held a high place in the Luwian pantheon and was widely worshipped. He occurs in mythic material that forms part of magical incantations. Often accompanies the goddess Kubaba and the storm god. (van Gessel 1998: I, 523; Popko 1995: 55–56, 68, 91–92, 167, 168; Haas 1994: 378 note 500, 439, 611–12)

Ti(ya)banti, Ti(ya)benti, Ti(ya)pinti (H) Deity, probably female. Means "Who Speaks Well." Member of the circle of Ḫebat. Appears as vizier of Ḫebat in some rituals from Kizzuwatna. Another ritual carries an offer to adorn her statue with jewelry from Ḫebat's temple. A prayer to her in Hurrian is extant. (van Gessel 1998: I, 512–15; Haas 1994: 309–10, 389, 470; Laroche 1977: 265; Laroche 1946/47: 62)

Tiyat (H) Palaic sun god. Third in the pantheon, following the storm god and Kattaḫzipuri, the goddess of healing and magic. Like Tiwat, the name derives from the Indo-European word *šiuš*, originally the name of the god of the light of heaven. (van Gessel 1998: I, 519; Popko 1995: 56, 68, 113)

Tu(-da) (M) Goddess occurring in an Early Dynastic personal name. (Such-Gutiérrez: 2005/6; Krebernik *RlA* XIV,: 152–54)

Tubaka (M) Deity appearing in an Old Babylonian forerunner of An : *Anum*. Listed after netherworld goddesses such as Ereškigal and Allatu(m). Occurs also in a god list from Aššur. (Richter 2004: 492, 493; Schroeder 1920: no. 63)

Tu-bindug-basag (M) Sumerian divinity appearing in an Old Babylonian god list in a circle of healing deities associated with Isin. Means "He uttered an Incantation and It Was Favorable." Note Šud-bindug-basag. (Richter 2004: 216)

Tud-uga (M) One of three attendants associated with Šul-pa'e. Perhaps means "(Deity of) Birth and Death." (Litke 1998: 73)

Tu-gal (M) See Lu-tu-gal

Tugur (M) Deity identified with the sun god Utu/Šamaš. Means "Dove." (Litke 1998: 129; Tallqvist 1974: 472)

Tuḫuši (H) One of the more obscure Hittite deities. (Archi 1990: 127)

Tuku (M) The seventeenth name of the Babylonian chief god Marduk in the *Enūma eliš*. Means "Pure Incantation." (Foster 2005: 477; Litke 1998: 91; Speiser, *ANET*: 70; Heidel 1967: 55)

Tukul-sag-ninnu(50) (M) Deified weapon. Means "Fifty-headed Weapon."

Tukul-sag-pirig (M) Deified weapon. Means "Lion-headed Weapon."

Tullat (E) Elamite deity attested in a treaty between Narām-Sîn of Akkad and a king of Susa. (Hinz and Koch 1987: 356; König 1977: 29, 223, 227)

Tu-(lu-)tila (M) Deity identified with Marduk. Means "Incantation that Makes People Live." (Litke 1998: 224)

Tu-maḫ (M) Deity identified with Marduk. Means "Lofty Incantation." (Litke 1998: 224)

Tummal (M) Deity who occurs in a personal name from Ur III Umma and Puzriš-Dagān; probably an epithet of Ninlil, mistress of the Tummal complex in Nippur. (TCL 2, 5546: o 8)

Tumtum (M) Deity in an Old Babylonian god list. Written tum-tum, where it occurs directly before ^{d}tu-tu. (Weidner 1924/25)

Tunapi (H) See Ḫuwaššanna

Tu-ni-ir-an (M) Deity identified with Marduk. Written tu_6-ni-ir-an. (Litke 1998: 224)

Tunnan(u), Tannin, Dunnān (L, M) Snake-like dragon-monster from the sea. As Dunnān, it is attested in two incantations from Early Dynastic Ebla. The deity-monster appears in the texts before a reference to the storm god Adad and is said to have seven choppers or hackers, literally "hoes." Schwemer notes that Fronzaroli takes these incantations to refer to the earliest attestation of the myth of the storm god attacking a primordial serpentine creature living in the sea. In texts from Ugarit, Tunnan(u) appears eight times as a helper of the sea god Yam. In the mythic works dealing with the deeds of Ba'lu, he was among the monsters defeated by 'Anat(u) or Ba'lu. One suggestion connects the snake-dragon name to that of the Punic (Carthaginian) goddess Tanit. It suggests that an epithet of Asherah, Tanit (meaning "Dragon" or "Serpent Lady"), became the name of a separate deity (Cross 1973: 32–33). In the Hebrew Bible, Tannin was usually a serpentine cosmic monster defeated by YHWH (Isaiah 51: 9). See also 'Anat(u); Ba'lu/Had(d)ad; Leviathan; Tanit. (Wyatt 2002: 79, 368–69; Schwemer 2001: 117–18; Smith 2001: 33, 168; del Olmo Lete 1993: 56, 80; Heider, *DDDB*: 834–36; Parker 1997a: 251–52; Smith 1997: 111; Lipiński 1995: 201; Finegan 1989: 142; Albright 1968: 185)

Turān (M) See Turul

Turgu (M) God of the Kassites. (Black and Green 2003: 112; Balkan 1978: 123)

TURma (M) See Ama-TURma

Tu-tila (M) See Tu-(lu-)tila

Tutu (M) The thirteenth name of the Marduk in the *Enūma eliš*. Tutu was also a name of Nabû. A late text suggests that he was associated with birth-giving. There was a temple at Borsippa dedicated to this aspect of Marduk. Written as both tu-tu and tu_6-tu_6 "incantations." Explained in An : *Anu ša amēli* as "Marduk of sickness beyond(?) prayer." (Such-Gutiérrez: 2005/6; Foster 2005: 476; Litke 1998: 91, 237; George 1993: 159 no. 1236; Tallqvist 1974: 472, 473; Speiser, *ANET*: 70; Heidel 1967: 54)

Tu-ušumgal (M) Name of Marduk, who, with his father Enki, was often invoked in rituals involving incantations. Means "Incantation (of) the Dragon." (Litke 1998: 224)

Tu-zi (M) See Tu-zi-ba

Tu-zi-ba (M) Deity attested at Old Babylonian Mari. Perhaps the same deity as Tu-zi attested in an Old Babylonian god list fragment from Nippur. (Richter 2004: 85)

— Ṭ —

Ṭaban (M) Deity occurs at second-millennium BCE Tuttub. (Charpin 2004: no. 78)

Ṭallay(u), Tallai, Ṭalliya (L) Goddess of Ugarit. Second daughter of the storm god Ba'lu/Hadad. Perhaps also his wife (the other two were Arṣay and Piḍray). Ṭallay means "Dew(y)." One of her epithet was "Daughter of Fine Rain or Mist." Clearly not an important goddess, Ṭallay did not appear in Ugaritic god lists. (Wyatt 2002: 72 note 13, 77, 105; Smith 2001: 44, 56, 108; Healey, *DDDB*: 249–50; del Olmo Lete 1999: 71–73; Parker 1997a: 251; Smith 1997: 106, 109, 115; Albright 1968: 145)

— Ṯ —

Ṯakamuna wa-Šunama (L) Pair of deities or a single deity at Ugarit. Attested often in literary texts and in god and offering lists. Important in the palace cult. Son(s) of the supreme god El/Il(u), probably his gate-keeper(s) and messenger(s). In one composition, the god(s) did a son's duty and carried the drunken El home after a feast. Probably associated with the netherworld. (Pardee 2002: 22, 63, 285; Becking, *DDDB*: 776–77, 866–67; del Olmo Lete 1999: 65, 67, 68, 71, 115, 215, 216, 341, 342, 343; Parker 1997a: 195)

Ṯamaqu (L) Deity or deified hero, one of the Rephaim (Rapi'uma) in the Ugaritic netherworld. A helper close to El/Il(u). (del Olmo Lete 1999: 57, 166)

Ṯatiqatu (L) One of the Koṯarṭu, seven minor goddesses of fertility at Ugarit. (del Olmo Lete 1999: 57)

Ṯiluḫahu (L) One of the Kōṯarṭu, seven minor goddesses of fertility at Ugarit. (del Olmo Lete 1999: 57)

— U —

U (M) Written u. (1) Deity identified as "Adad of Lightning"; (2) Deity identified with Aya explained as *ša kunê*. (Litke 1998: 232)

U (M) Deity identified with Enlil, whose name is written u_5 "Rider." (Litke 1998: 38)

U-an-duga (M) See Annedotos

Ubda-DU.DU (M) Deity listed in An : *Anum* as two messengers of Inana. Probably just originally variants and not two separate deities. In the Old Babylonian god list written Ub-da-a-DU.DU and Da-a-DU.DU; in An : *Anum* Ub-da-DU.DU and Da-LU-DU.DU. Means "Who Lurks(?) in the Corners."(Richter 2004: 292; Litke 1998: 159)

Ub/pelluri (H) Hurrian god of the netherworld who supports earth and heaven. In the "Song of Ullikummi," the god Kumarbi sires Ullikummi by copulating with a great rock. He plans for his son to defeat Teššub, so, from birth, the child has to be hidden from the storm god until he is grown. So the netherworld goddesses, the Irširra, attach the child to Ubelluri's right shoulder. The weight of the quickly growing stone god hurt Ubelluri's right shoulder until deities allied with Teššub cut Ullikummi away. Ubelluri is similar to the Greek Atlas, who holds up the world. (Hoffner 1998: 41, 56, 58–59, 64, 113; van Gessel 1998: I, 539–40; Popko 1995: 125, 129; Haas 1994: 136, 409; Laroche 1946/47: 63)

Ub-kalama (M) One of eight deities associated with outdoor niche shrines of Inana/Ištar. Possibly means "Corner of the Nation." (Litke 1998: 160)

Ublila, Ub-li-a (M) Two names juxtaposed of deities associated with outdoor niche shrines of Inana/Ištar. ub-líl-lá means "outdoor shrine." These two entries may just be variants. (Litke 1998: 160)

Ub-saḫara (M) One of eight deities associated with outdoor niche shrines of Inana/Ištar. Means "Shrine of the Dust/Soil" or "Dusty Corner." (Richter: 2004: 292; Litke 1998: 160)

U-dag-gur-si (M) The divinity is attested on a tablet from Old Babylonian Nippur. May possibly mean "Who Fills the Circumference (gúr) of the Entire (U) Inhabited World (dag)." See Kippat-māti. (Richter 2004: 161; Renger 1967: 152)

Ud (Sum.), **ēmu(m)** (Akk.) Demon who often appears as a leonine monster. (Wiggermann 1992: 146, 164, 170)

U(d)-al-KUD (M) Deity identified with Šul-pa'e mentioned in An : *Anum* and appearing in a text from Lagaš from the Ur III period. Means "Storm that Cuts Down." The word combination (but not the divine name itself) appears a number of times in the Sumerian "Hymn to the Hoe" because of punning on the element al, "hoe." (Lafont and Yıldız 1989: no. 833; Litke 1998 72; Tallqvist 1974: 475)

U(d)-an-edina-guba (M) Deity identified with Adad/Iškur in a Neo-Assyrian text. It is also attested in texts from Nippur. Means "Storm Located in the High Steppe." (Schwemer 2001: 62, 88, 91; Tallqvist 1974: 475)

U(d)-aššakam (M) Deity identified with the sun god Utu/Šamaš in An : *Anu ša* *amēli*. Written ud-aš-ša-kam. May mean "He Is the One of Perfect Light." Explained as "of the experts." (Litke 1998: 231)

U(d)ba-nuila(mu) (M) Deified weapon of Ninurta. (Tallqvist 1974: 475)

U(d)-bubul (M) Deity identified with the netherworld god Nergal. Means "The Day of the Disappearance of the Moon," the last day of the month, an unlucky day. (Litke 1998: 200; Tallqvist 1974: 474)

U(d)-e (M) Deity identified with Utu/Šamaš. Means "Emanating Light." (Litke 1998: 130; Tallqvist 1974: 476)

U(d)-ezi-ana (M) One of eight bull-lyres of the moon god Nanna/Sîn. Means "Light, True House of Heaven." (Litke 1998: 123)

U(d)-gal-gal (M) Deity identified with the storm god Adad/Iškur. Means "Great Storms." A temple of Adad in Karkar was called E-u(d)-gal-gal "House of Great Storms." (George 1993: 152 no. 1130; Tallqvist 1974: 476)

U(d)-gu-de (M) Deity identified with the storm god Adad/Iškur. Means "Roaring Storm." (Tallqvist 1974: 476)

U(d)-gu-nun-di (M) One of the bull-lyres of Ninurta. Means "Storm that Rumbles Loudly." (Litke 1998: 52)

U(d)-gur (M) Deity attested in an Early Dynastic god list. (Mander 1986: 150)

U(d)-gu-rara (M) Deity identified with the storm god Adad/Iškur. Means "Howling Storm." (Tallqvist 1974: 476)

U(d)-ḫegala (M) Deity identified with the netherworld god Nergal. Means "Storm Aplenty." (Tallqvist 1974: 476)

U(d)-kašbar-daba (M) Identified in a Neo-Assyrian god list with Adad. May mean "Storm that Seizes Upon Decisions." (King 1969: pl. 16)

U(d)-kirzal-ana (M) One of eight bull-lyres of the moon god Nanna/Sîn. Means "Light, Joy of Heaven." (Litke 1998: 123)

U(d)-men-ana (M) Bull-lyre of Nanna/Sîn. Perhaps means "Light that Is the Corona (or Crown) of Heaven." (Litke 1998: 123)

U(d)-men-šu-gala (M) Bull-lyre of Baba. The word u(d)-men, as early as the Early Dynastic period, occurs in terms indicating professions and cardinal points. See U(d)-men-ana. (Litke 1998: 178)

U(d)-NAM-edin-na (M) One of the ten children of Lugalbanda. May mean "Storm, Fate of the Steppe" or even bir_5-edin-na "Storm, Locust of the Steppe." (Litke 1998: 169)

U(d)-namgimeašmu (M) One of the ten children of Lugalbanda. Written $U(d)^{ud}$-nam-gi_6^{gi}-me-mu. This may be an unusual variant for nam-gi_4-me-a-aš "collegium," "collegiality," thus perhaps "The Storm Is My Associate." (Litke 1998: 169; Alster 1997)

U(d)-sagkal-ana (M) Deity attested in god lists of the Early Dynastic period from Šuruppak and Abu Ṣalābīkh. A later list identifies the god as "the storm (or lion) of heaven." He is also called "the yoke of Šamaš." Sumerian name likely means "Foremost Storm of Heaven." (Mander 1986: 52–53; Tallqvist 1974: 476)

U(d)-sakar (M) Deity identified with the moon god Nanna/Sîn. Means "New Moon." (Tallqvist 1974: 476)

U(d)-zala (M) Deity identified with the storm god Ištar/Adad. Means "Daybreak." (Tallqvist 1974: 476, under Udzalma)

Ude-ana, Ude-anta (M) Deity identified with the storm god Adad/Iškur. It may simply mean "Storm of/from Heaven." Note that in an incantation-hymn, Ninurta is called ud an-ta ra-ra "Storm that beats down from Heaven." (Litke 1998: 141)

Ude-guba (M) Deity identified with the sun god Utu/Šamaš. The name may mean "Stands at the Light." (Litke 1998: 130; Tallqvist 1974: 475)

Ude-kita (M) Deity identified with the storm god Adad/Iškur. Means "Storm (that roars(?)) from Below(?)." See Ude-anta. (Litke 1998: 141; Tallqvist 1974: 475)

Ude-ra-ra (M) Deity identified with the storm god Adad/Iškur. Means "Inundating Storm." See Ude-anta. (Litke 1998: 141; Tallqvist 1974: 475)

Udug (Sum.), **Utukku(m)**, **Utukkū** (Akk.) A category of demon, either good or evil, and also the general word for "demon." Basically spirits of the dead and agents of Fate, Nam-tara, minister or vizier of the netherworld god Nergal. Offspring of An/Anu(m) and Earth. They reside in graveyards, wasteland, and deserts. In incantations Udug denotes a specific demon as well as the entire group. In "A [Prince's] Vision of the Netherworld," the Utukkū appears as a composite monster. The Sibittu were members of this category of demon. In addition, good Udug often functioned as guardian spirits of the temples of deities. The Sumerian word udug means "bailiff" or "policeman." (Foster 2005: 835; Black and Green 2003: 162, 179; Leick 1998: 30–31; Litke 1998: 210; Geller 1985: Wiggermann 1992: 36 note 5, 58; Wiggermann 1986: 135–36; Speiser, *ANET*: 109; Ebeling, *RlA* II: 107–8)

Ud-ug (Sum.), **ëmu** (Akk.) The weather-beast demon. (Litke 1998: 208)

(Ud-)ug-eri (M) Demon whose name means "Demon/Storm of the City." (Litke 1998: 208)

(Ud-)ug-eri-tab-ba (M) This entry may be a mistake, a conflation of the previous entry Ud-ug-eri and the following Ud-ug-ka-tab-ba. (Litke 1998: 208)

Ud-ug-IN (M) Deity attested in an Old Babylonian god list. Written ^{d}Ud-ug-In^{ki}, "Demon of Isin." (Weidner 1924/25)

(Ud-)ug-ka-duḫa (M) An animal-demon, *kattillu(m).* Literally "Raging Weather-beast." Occurs with both -duḫ and -dù. Variant Ur-ka-duḫ-a *kattillu* occurs in the lexical list Ḫḫ XIV. (Litke 1998: 208; Wiggermann 1992: 147–48, 150, 160, 171, 184–87; Tallqvist 1974: 477)

(Ud-)ug-ka-taba (M) An animal-demon, *kattillu*. Variant Ur-ka-tab-ba *kattillu* occurs in Ḫḫ XIV. ^{kuš}ka-tab is a bridle, but whether this somehow relates to this name is unclear. (Litke 1998: 209; Tallqvist 1974: 477)

Udu-idim (M) Deity in a Neo-Assyrian god list identified with Ninurta. Means "planet" (literally "wild sheep"). (King 1969: pl. 13)

U-en-ša (M) Son of Nin-šubur. Written ^{d}ù-èn^{nu}-ša$_4$^{šá}. May mean "he who provides a solution." Litke suggests that glosses may have evolved erroneously from two names, thus Ù-èn-ša$_4$ and Ù-nu-ša$_4$. (Litke 1998: 28)

Uga-e (M) Deity identified with the netherworld god Nergal. Means "Death." (Tallqvist 1974: 477)

Ugallu(m) (M) A composite lion-headed dragon monster, a beneficent demon that afforded protection against diseases and evil demons. In the *Enūma eliš* one of the monsters created by Ti'amat to help her fight the younger deities. May mean "Great Weather-Beast." (Foster 2005: 444; Black and Green 2003: 121, 177; Wiggermann 1992: 169–71, 186; Tallqvist 1974: 474–75; Speiser, *ANET*: 64; Heidel 1967: 31)

Ugar(u) (L) See Gapnu

U-gu-de (M) Deity whose name is written U_4-gù-dé with gloss -gu-di. Variants with Ù and U. Means "Roaring Storm." Explained in An : *Anu ša amēli* as "Adad of destruction (*riḫṣi*)." (Litke 1998: 140, 232)

Ugu-gig-duga (M) Deity identified with the Bennu(m), a personification of a type of epilepsy. Written a-gá-gig-du_{11}-ga. Perhaps A.GÁ here should be understood as an unexpected variant for A.KA /ugu/ "head," thus meaning something such as "headache," describing one effect of epilepsy. (Litke 1998: 73; Tallqvist 1974: 250)

Ugula (M) Wife of Tišpak, the tutelary god of Ešnunna. Written Ú-gù-lá, Ú-kul-lá, and Ú-kul-ÁB. (Cohen 2015: 289; Litke 1998: 193)

UGULA.URUGAL/UNU (M) Deity attested in an Early Dynastic god list from Šuruppak. Could mean "Overseer of the Netherworld" or "Overseer of the Dining Hall," though many readings and meanings are possible. (Mander 1986: 97)

UGUR (M) (1) Deity written sig_7, in *Anu ša amēli* explained as "Enlil of the Universe." (Litke 1998: 229; Krebernik, *RlA* XII: 479) (2) A bird deity appearing in the great god list from Šuruppak. (Krebernik, *RlA* XII: 479)

Uḫ (Sum.), **Uplu(m)** (Akk.) One of two bull-lyres of the prison goddess Manun-gal. The name "(Head-)Lice" is fitting for a deity in the circle of the goddess of prisons. (Litke 1998: 187)

U-ḫal-e-si (M) Deity in an Old Akkadian tablets probably from Adab. Written U-ḫal-é-si. (Maiocchi 2009: no. 118, no. 119)

Ukgabna (E) Elamite deity attested in a treaty between Narām-Sîn of Akkad and a king of Susa. (König 1977: 117, 225)

Ukkumu (M) One of the four dogs of Marduk. His dais is mentioned in ritual instructions for an *akītu f*estival. May mean "Predator." (Litke 1998: 99)

U-ku (M) Written Ú-kú and $Ú^{ḫá}$-KU; see Šakkan

Uli (E) Elamite deity occurring in feminine personal names in Middle Elamite texts. Means "Manliness." (Hinz and Koch 1987: 7, 121; König 1977: 225)

Uliša (M)Son of Ninšubur. Written ^{d}Ù-li^{nu}-$ša_4^{šá}$. May be for ^{geš}ù-lú-$ša_4$ *inu*, thus a deified string instument. (Litke 1998: 28)

U-li-u(d) (M) See Utud

Ullānum (M) Deity attested at Old Babylonian Mari. (Durand 2008: 270)

Ullikummi (H) Huge Hurrian stone monster. Fathered by Kumarbi, birthed by a Great Rock. In the "Song of Ullikummi," the god Kumarbi plans for his son to defeat Teššub. To hide him from the storm god until he is grown, the netherworld goddesses, the Irširra, attach the new-born child to the Hurrian Atlas's right shoulder. Ullikummi grows quickly and becomes a real threat. The goddess Ša(w)uš(k)a gets ready to seduce him, but is told he is deaf and blind and lacking in compassion. Finally, deities allied with Teššub cut him away from Ubelluri and, presumably, manage to defeat him. (Schwemer 2001: 230, 450–51, 457–58; Hoffner 1998: 40–42, 55–65, 113; Popko 1995: 124–25, 129; Haas 1994: 86, 88–96, 123, 136–37, 140, 174, 307–8, 329, 372, 527)

Ulmaš (M) One of two attendants of the Ekur temple of Enlil at Nippur. (Litke 1998: 65; Tallqvist 1974: 477)

Ulmašītu(m) (M) Aspect of Ištar worshipped especially in the city of Akkad. Ištar was patron deity of the Old Akkadian period. Her temple at Akkad was called E-ulmaš, whence her title Ulmašītu(m). Her temples in other places often had a similar or the same name. She had an temple in Malgium. Records show her as having often been paired in cultic texts with the goddess Annunītu(m). Her cult was celebrated at Ur and at Uruk. (Cohen 2015: 85; Black and Green 2003: 34; George 1993: 121 no. 740, 155 no. 1168; Sallaberger 1993: I, 198)

Ulme (H) Deified arm attested in the text from Mari. (Durand 2008: 667)

Ul-siga (M) Deity identified with Inana/Ištar. Written -sig$_7$-ga and -si-ga, the latter being explained in An : *Anum* as "of heaven and earth." Perhaps these are variants for sig as in Inana-sig, the Morning Star, Venus, thus possibly the name means "Joy of the Morning(-star)." ul is attested as "star" in an Emesal vocabulary list and in another lexical list. So just possibly this entry actually means Morning Star, Venus. Explained in An : *Anu ša amēli* as "Ištar of heaven and earth/netherworld." (Litke 1998: 148, 235; Cohen 1993: 209; George 1993: 99 no. 462; Tallqvist 1974: 477)

Ul-šara (M) Deity identified with the goddess Nisaba. Means "Universal Joy" (*rīštu*). (Litke 1998: 55)

Ulul (M) Son of Bilulu in "The Myth of Inana and Bilulu." Written ul$_4$-ul$_4$ with gloss ul in An : *Anum*. In "The Myth of Inana and Bilulu" there is a play on his name with the verbal form ul$_4$-ul$_4$-e, meaning "hurrying." (Jacobsen 1970: 58; Jacobsen 1953: 175)

Umani-sasa (M) One of three bull-lyres of the god Ninurta. Means "He Achieves His Victory." (Litke 1998: 52)

Umbisag, Allamu, Almu, Nin-umbisag, Nin-bezem (M) A deity Umbisag is attested in the Early Dynastic period and in An : *Anum*. But whether the god is the same in both periods cannot be determined. The name means "Scholar."

Nin-umbisag means "Lady Scholar." Although the adjacent entry Nin-bezem simply means "Lady (of) the Basket," it may have been intended by the scribe to convey the meaning "she of the (tablet-)basket," i.e., bisag-dubba, "archivist," which is more in keeping with the sign ŠID×A denoting "scholar" when used in the name of a god.

ŠID×A with glosses al-mu and al-lamu may also mean "scholar," "expert." It may be connected to a West Semitic /al(a)mu/ "scholar," which occurs in the lexical entry Malku VIII 110, in which the Akkadian entry *almû* occurs directly before the entry *itpušu* "expert." (*CAD* A: 364a s.v.). (Mander 1986: 97; Steinkeller 1981: 247)

Umbu (H) Moon god of the western Hurrians. Spouse of Nikkal. Beginning in the reign of Šuppiluliuma I, Umbu had a connection to the military and occurred in oaths. As a pair,

Umbu and Nikkal were worshipped in north Syria and southern Anatolia. Appears as Ibbu at Ugarit. See Kušuḫ. (van Gessel 1998: I, 536–37; Popko 1995: 100; Haas 1994: 312, 374–75, 491; Laroche 1946/47: 63)

Um(m)egala-zi (M) Deity identified with the healing goddess Nin-Isina/Nin-kar(r)ak. Means "Trustworthy Wet Nurse." (Litke 1998: 182)

ūmu(m) (M) Deity identified with the storm god Iškur/Adad. Means "Storm." (George 1993: 170 no. 1428; Vallat 1988: no. 14; Tallqvist 1974: 478)

ūmu-dabrūtū (M) Babylonian demons/deities. Name is Babylonian for "Violent Storms." One of the eleven demon-monsters created by Ti'amat to fight against the younger deities. (Foster 2005: 444; Black and Green 2003: 177, 179–80; Wiggermann 1992: 145, 163, 172; Speiser, *ANET*: 64; Heidel 1967: 26)

Umun (M) Deity identified with the moon god Nanna/Sîn. umun is Emesal for en "Lord." The reading umun in An : *Anum* for the U-sign is supported by the previous entry "lugal." The reading umun for U is late and cannot reflect an Old Babylonian or earlier tradition, when /umun/ is always written ù-mu-un. (Litke 1998: 118)

ūmu-nā'iru(m) (M) Composite beast sacred to the weather god Iškur/Adad. A kind of lion-bird with a gaping mouth. Means "Raging Storm." See Ud-ug-ka-duḫa (Black and Green 2003: 121; Wiggermann 1992: 147–48, 150)

Umuš-a (M) Deity attested in a Neo-Assyrian god list and possibly identified with Asarluḫe or Marduk. May mean "He of Wisdom." (King 1969: pl. 34)

Undurupa (H) One of the more obscure Hittite deities. (Archi 1990: 118)

Unga-ibimal (M) Emesal name of Nin-Girgilu(m) in a hymn in which she is described as the "mother of the right breast." Means "The Wise One among the People." (Cohen 1981: 64)

Ungal-Nibru (M) Name or title of the goddess Inana/Ištar at Nippur. Means "Queen of Nippur." Her temple at Nippur was called "Dais of the Throne," which Esarhaddon rebuilt. There is a lengthy hymn in Akkadian addressed to Un-gal-Nibru as Queen of Nippur, possibly composed for this event. (Leick 1999: 57–58; George 1993: 71 no. 110; Lambert 1982)

UNga-saga (M) One of two bull-lyres of the goddess Nisaba. Written UN-ga-sa$_6$-ga. (Litke 1998: 55)

Un-il (M) Deity identified with the goddess Ninlil. The standard meaning "menial" seems inappropriate here. Perhaps this is just some type of homophonous variant for the name Ninlil, the entry that precedes this or to be understood literally, as "She who Raises up the People." (Litke 1998: 40)

Unir-sisa (M) One of two bull-lyres of the god Lugal-Marada. May mean "Who Keeps the Ziqqurat in Order/Upright." (Litke 1998: 171)

Unkin(-uru) (M) Deity identified with the moon god Nanna/Sîn. Written -u$_x$ (EN)-ru. May mean "Effective Assembly." (Litke 1998: 119)

Unneḫum (M) Deity in an Old Babylonian text from Isin in connection with textiles. (Richter 2004: 252)

U-nudiba (M) One of eight messengers of the prison goddess Manun-gal. Means "Who Never Sleeps," an appropriate name for one tasked to oversee prisoners. (Litke 1998: 187)

Unu-dudu (M) One of the butchers of the Ekur. Written unú-du$_{10}$-du$_{10}$ and unú-dù-dù. It is unclear which variant reflects the original meaning. Since the deity is a butcher, it might mean something like "(Who makes) Good Meals." (Litke 1998: 60; Tallqvist 1974: 479)

Un-un-ta-ba-ba (M) One of four guardian spirits, probably of Nin-Girsu. (Litke 1998: 176; Tallqvist 1974: 479; Krebernik and Cavigneaux, *RlA* IX: 489)

U-PAD-nir-nir (M) Deity attested in an Old Babylonian god list. Written ù-PAD-nir-nir. See Nin-PAD-nir. (Weidner 1924/25)

Upillu (H) Deity occurring in a text from Ḫattušas. (von Soden 1992: no. 53)

Uplu(m) (M) See Uḫ

Upur-kupak (E) Elamite goddess originally from the Elamite city and area of Anšan, associated with the netherworld. An epithet is *laḫara* "of Death." Untaš-Napiriša commissioned a temple for this goddess at Susa. (Tavernier 2013: 471; Vallat 1998: 337, 340)

Uqur (Akk.), **Ugur**, **Ukur** (Sum.) Deity identified with both the netherworld god Nergal and of one of his ministers or viziers. Means "Destroy!" Uqur had temples in Girsu and Isin. (Litke 1998: 64, 173, 234; George 1993: 38, 127 no. 807, 142 no. 997, 170 no. 1430; Tallqvist 1974: 474)

Ur (M) Deity attested in an Early Dynastic god list. Written úr. (Mander 1986: 150)

Ur-ala (M) Deity in the circle of the sun god Utu. Written Úr-á-lá. Means "Base of the Drum." Explained in An : *Anum* as *supalu*, "juniper wood," likely a mistake for *šupālu*, "base." (Richter 2004: 351: Litke 1998: 136)

Ur-ana (M) Goddess attested in a Neo-Assyrian god list. Written úr-an-na, perhaps "Foundation of Heaven." Wife of Enki. (King 1969: pl. 9)

Ur-aru (M) Bull-lyre of Dam-gal-nuna in An : *Anum*. Written úr-a-ru$_6$. Name would seem to mean "Lap of the sister-in-law," which would make little sense here. (Litke 1998: 106)

Ur-Asar (M) Deity allocated offerings in Ur III Urub, a city near Girsu, and occurs in a personal name at Girsu. (UNT 916: o ii 22)

Uraš (M) (1) A god of Dilbat. Possibly a grain god. Name might mean "Earth." According to one tradition, he was an ancestor of An/Anu(m). Later he was identified with An/Anu(m) or Ninurta. Possibly Babylon's Uraš Gate was named for him. At Dilbat, an *akītu* festival was held for him. He was worshipped in the city of Aššur, where he had a "seat" in the great temple. Uraš also had attested shrines at Nippur and Isin. Appears in a Neo-Assyrian god list with gloss ú-ra-aš, and explained as "Ninurta of the Calendar Date (*uddazallû*)." (2) A Sumerian earth and birth/mother goddess. Sometimes understood as the consort of An/Anu(m); she was mother of Nin-Isina and Nisaba. According to tradition, Uraš meant "earth," and since An's wife was Ki, "Earth." Uraš was identified with Ki. In the lexical series Diri the name is written with the logogram ^{d}IB and explained as *an-tum*. (Civil 2004; Black and Green 2003: 182; Litke 1998: 172, 229, 233; Cohen 1993: 427; George 1993: 35, 76 no. 172, 102 no. 493, 170 no. 1431–32; Tallqvist 1974: 480; King 1969: pl. 11)

Ur-bada (M) Deity identified with the goddess Nisaba as Ku-su. Also a title of Marduk as Tutu. Means "High Roof." See Urbada-gubgubbu. (Lambert 2013, 213; Tallqvist 1974: 480)

Urbada-gubgubbu/gungunnu/ gumgum (M) One of seven children of En-me-šara. ùr-bàd-da means "high roof." Var.: ur- and ùr-; -gub-gub-bu, -gùn-gùn-nu, -gúm-gúm. The sons of En-me-šara were executed by being thrown off a roof and so ùr-bàd-da may refer to this event. Astrally perhaps one of the Pleiades. Identified also with Ninnisig. (Lambert 2013, 213; Litke 1998: 36; Tallqvist 1974: 479)

Ur-bad-dumu (M) One of seven children of En-me-šara. dumu is read according to a gloss. See Urbada-gubgubbu. Astrally perhaps one of the Pleiades. (Litke 1998: 36; Tallqvist 1974: 479)

Ur-bar-tab (M) Sumerian deity attested in the environs of Ur III Umma. bar-tab means "inferior," which hardly seems approprite here. If read maš[!]-tab, then "twin." (Cohen 1996a: 34; Sjöberg 1984: 130)

Urbatu(m) (M) Wife of Mardu/Martu. Akkadian *urbatu* may denote "rushes" here. (Litke 1998: 217)

Urda (M) Deity after whom a month is named in a colophon from a literary text from Emar. May be a variant for the writing NIN.URTA, which Fleming suggests may be an orthography for Il-Emari. (Fleming 2000: 78)

Ur-gula (M) Demon associated with the god Enlil and also the god La-tarāk. Means "Greatest Lion/Dog." (Litke 1998: 209; Tallqvist 1974: 479)

Ur-gu-ru (M) Deity whose name is glossed in Sumerian and Akkadian as "suitable for the rites." Variant is Ur-gu-la, a lion/dog demon. (Litke 1998: 81; Tallqvist 1974: 479)

Uri-bara (M) A deified protective standard situated not at a gate but in an outside position. It is mentioned in a temple inventory from Old Babylonian Ur. (Wiggermann 1992: 70)

Ur-idim (Sum.), **Uridimmu(m)** (Akk.) Babylonian/Assyrian composite monster, human above the waist, two-legged lion below. One type of monster created by Ti'amat to help her fight the younger deities. Means "Mad Dog." Possibly to be associated with the ancient Greek canine Cerberus and the constellation Lupus. (Foster 2005: 444; Black and Green 2003: 122, 177; Wiggermann 1992: 172–74, 186; Speiser, *ANET*: 64; Heidel 1967: 26)

Uri-gal (M) Deity identified with the sun god Utu. Means "Standard" (*urigallu*). (Litke 1998: 130; Wiggermann 1992: 70)

Uri-kirzala (M) Sumerian divinized harp of Nanna-Sîn in An : *Anum*. Means "Ur Is Joy." (Richter 2004: 452: Litke: 1998: 123)

Uri-maš (M) Divinized twin protective standards. (Wiggermann 1992: 70)

Urkīt(t)u(m), Urukā'ītu(m) (M) Deity whose name means "The Urukean." Attested at Old Babylonian Sippar. Appears in Neo-Assyrian texts. The deity is to be identified with Ištar of Uruk. Known by the name Urukā-'ītu(m) in the Seleucid period and equated to Aškā'ītu(m). (Richter 2004: 492; Renger 1967: 155; Falkenstein 1941: 42)

Urmaḫ-lulu (Sum.), **Urmaḫlilu(m)** (Akk.) Babylonian/Assyrian composite monster, a lion-centaur. Human above the waist, lion complete with four legs below. (Black and Green 2003: 119, 132; Wiggermann 1992: 52, 86, 98, 99–100, 102–3, 128, 141, 143, 181–82, 186–87)

Ur-maš (Sum.), **Ur-mašu(m)** (Akk.) (1) Deity identified with the warrior god Zababa, possibly as a form of Nergal. (2) Vizier of Gula, whose symbol was the dog. The name may mean "Twin Dog(s)." (Litke 1998: 184; George 1993: 82 no. 247; Tallqvist 1974: 479)

Ur-mašum (M) Vizier of Nin-Isina. Attested at Old Babylonian Isin. A prebendary text refers to a gate of Isin that was named for this god. (Richter 2004: 211)

Ur-me-šum (M) Deity in a god list from Aššur (VS 24 20).

Urnunta-ea (M) According to An : *Anum*, one of eight children of Lisina. In another tradition one of seven children of Baba. Means "Who Comes Forth from the Lap of the Prince (Nin-Girsu)." The deity had a chapel in a temple of Lama-saga at Girsu. (George 1993: 166 no. 1344; Litke 1998: 76; Tallqvist 1974: 480; Falkenstein 1966: 112–13)

Urra (M) One of sixteen children of the birth/mother goddess Dingir-maḫ/Bēlet-ilī. The explanation of Urra in An : *Anum* states "... that is born in the lap," indicating that the scribe apparently understood ur-ra here as a variant for úr-ra, "lap." (Litke 1998: 82)

Ur-sa (M) In An : *Anum*, one of five gods of fishermen. Written ur_5-sa_6 with gloss ur-sa. Also written ŠU.ḪA. (Litke 1998: 113)

Ursag-ana (M) Deity associated with Nippur in the Ur III period. Means "Hero of Heaven." (Sallaberger 1993: II, 19)

Ursag-iminbi (M) Collective name of seven heroic deities probably associated with the Pleiades. (Litke 1998: 211)

Ursag-pa'e (M) Sumerian god from Lagaš during the Ur III period. Means "Resplendent Hero." (Lafont and Yıldız 1989: no. 695)

Ur-Su'ena (M) A deified historical figure whose statue was placed in the Ninlil temple at Nippur in the Ur III period. Means "Man of Sîn," the moon god. (Richter 1999: 42; Litke 1998: 42; Sallaberger 1993: I, 100; Tallqvist 1974: 479, read as Ur-^{d}En-zu-(na)

Ur-šabi-duga (M) One of three ministers or viziers of Gula. Means "The Good-hearted Dog," referring to the dog, which is the symbol of the healing goddess Gula. (Litke 1998: 184)

Ur-Šanabi, **Sur-Sunabu(m)** (M) Servant and boatman of the Flood hero Ut-napišti(m) in the Babylonian *Epic of Gilgameš*. He ferried Gilgameš over the waters of death and, later, back to Uruk. The meaning of the name is uncertain, but it probably was associated with a mystical interpretation of the name of Ea. (Black and Green 2003: 44; 90, 155; George 2003: I, 149–51; Foster 2001: 77–80, 93–95)

Uršui (H) Hurrian deified idea/concept or cult object, associated with witnessing. Occurs in the Kizzuwatna pantheon as an epithet of Iškalli. See Iškalli. (van Gessel 1998: I, 541–42; Haas 1994: 407; Laroche 1977: 286; Laroche 1946/47: 63)

Ur-teš (M) Deity in an Ur III personal name from Umma. Perhaps means "Proud Man." (Nisaba 11, 22: r iii 19)

Ur-TUR (M) Deity in Lagaš in the Early Dynastic period. Perhaps means "Youthful (or Little) Man." (Selz 1995: 284–85)

Uru (M) Deity identified with Ninurta, a deity of farmers. Means "Plowman," in which capacity Ninurta was the central figure of the gu_4-si-sù festival at Nippur each spring. Written uru_4. In a Neo-Assyrian god list glossed ú-rum and explained as "Ninurta of the Hoe (*allu*)," Ninurta's symbol. (Litke 1998: 47 no. 229 and note 229; Tallqvist 1974: 481; King 1969: pl. 11; Cavigneaux and Krebernik, *RlA* IX: 528)

Uru-gal (M) Minister or vizier of Alammuš. Written uru_{16}(EN)-gal with gloss ú-ru and variant ùru. (Litke 1998: 122)

Uru-maš (M) Deity identified with Ennugi. Explained as the great herald of the mother goddess Dingir-maḫ. Written $^{d}uru_3{}^{ú-ru-ma-áš}$-maš. (Richter 2004: 447–48; Litke 1998: 58, 77).

Urunzimu (H) See Wurunšemu; Sun Goddess of Arinna

Uru-tab (M) Deity identified with the storm god Iškur/Adad. Written $^{d}uru_2{}^{ú-ru}$-tab. Means "Flood that Flattens." (Litke 1998: 77, 141; Tallqvist 1974: 480)

U-sakar (Sum.), **Uskarû(m)** borrowed into Akkadian (M). The new moon listed in *Anu ša amēli*. (Litke 1998: 119, 231)

Usan (M) Personification of "Evening." See Nin-usana

Usan / Iššan (E) Deity whose name might mean "lord" and is sometimes written ^{d}U. (Vallat 1987: no. 89)

Usan-an-na (M) See Nin-usana

Usan-da (M) Deity in a personal name at Ur III Umma. Written $^{d}Usan_4$-da and $^{d}Usan_4{}^{\{ú\}}$-da. Means "With the Evening Star." (Cohen 2015)

Usandu-kugzu (M) One of seven children of Nin-Girida, wife of Nin-azu. Means "Skilled Bird-Catcher." (Litke 1998: 191; Krebernik, *RlA* VIII: 453)

Usan-pa-sikila (M) Deity identified with Inana/Ištar as the planet Venus. May mean "Pristine Winged Evening." The Greek goddess Eos, Dawn, was described as winged. (Foster 2005: 217; Black and Green 2003: 109; Litke 1998: 160, 161; Cohen 1993: 434; George 1993: 34, 83 no. 261, 169 no. 1396; Cavigneaux and Krebernik, *RlA* IX: 487–88)

Usmītu(m) (M) The female counterpart of Usmû(m), the two-faced god and the vizier of Ea. See Isimud. (Falkenstein 1941: 11)

Usmû (M) See Isimud

Usu-maḫ (M) Deity identified in a Neo-Assyrian god list with Ninurta. Means "Great Strength." (King 1969: pl. 11)

U-sura (M) Minister or vizier of the scribe god Nabû. Written ^{d}ú-sur-ra. (Tallqvist 1974: 381, 474; Pomponio, *RlA* IX: 16–24)

Uṣur-amassu (M) (1) A form of Kanisura. She played an important role in Neo-Babylonian Uruk. Numerous texts describe the cult paraphernalia of the goddess and offerings to her. See Kanisura. (2) Son of the storm god Iškur/Adad. Occurs in Old Babylonian personal names and in incantations in the circle of Adad gods. In a god list she appears with the gods of justice Mīšaru(m) and Išartu(m). The Babylonian name means "Protect His Word." (Beaulieu 2003: 226–55, 268, 353–54, 381; Schwemer 2001: 14–15, 25, 68–69, 414; Litke 1998: 143; Tallqvist 1974: 481)

Ušbar (M) Deity identified with the moon god Nanna/Sîn. Also an orthography for Uttu, the weaver goddess. Means "Weaver." Explained in *Anu ša amēli* as "Moon god of the Vanguard (*meḫertu*)." (Litke 1998: 110, 230)

UŠ-da-ša (M) Deity attested in a personal name from Ur III Girsu. (HLC 2 22: o i 4)

Uš-du (M) Deity attested in a personal name from Ur III Girsu. Written uš-dù. May mean "Sets the Foundation." (MLC 3, 238: r ii 3)

Ušḫar(ayu), Ušḫara(tu) (L) Minor Ugaritic goddess. As *bbt il bt*, consort of the god of the palace. Together they seem to be protective deities of the palace, although they are not members of the official pantheon. In cultic texts Ušḫar(ayu) is called "The Snake" and is associated with serpents. Del Olmo Lete understands her to be a fertility goddess. In Ugaritic god lists she appears under the heading "Mountains and Valleys" and is equated to Babylonian Išḫara. (del Olmo Lete 1999: 38, 73, 131, 141, 216, 265, 267, 269, 360, 365)

UŠ-ḫuš (M) See MUD-ḫuš

UŠ-KA-limmu (M) See NITA-su-limmu

Ušum-bar-gešbu-E-ninnu (M) One of seven bull-lyres of Nin-Girsu. Gloss ú-šum-ba-ra-ge-eš-bu. (Litke 1998: 177; George 1993: 134; Tallqvist 1974: 481)

Ušum-dua (M) Deity identified with the chief Babylonian god Marduk. Means "Dragon of All." (Litke 1998: 221)

Ušum-dubur-ana (M) Deity identified with Adad. Note that Lugal-dubur-ana was identified with Nergal. (Schwemer 2000: 20, 61 note 20 line 220)

Ušumgal (M) Deity whose name means "Great Dragon." (1) Minister or vizier of Nin-kilim. Also identified with Marduk. (2) A Sumerian serpentine monster. Akkadian name Ušumgallu(m). One of the kinds of demon-monster created by Ti'amat to fight on her side against the younger deities. Ušumgal had a "seat" in the great temple at Babylon. (Foster 2005: 444; Black and Green 2003: 71, 168, 177; Litke 1998: 172, 221; George 1993: 80 no. 223; Tallqvist 1974: 481; Speiser, *ANET*: 64; Heidel 1967: 26)

Ušumgal-ana (M) Deity identified with both Dumuzi and Nanna/Sîn. Means "Dragon of Heaven." Also appears in the form Ama-ušum-gal-ana. (Tallqvist 1974: 482)

Ušumgal-ḫuš (M) Deity identified with Marduk. Means "Furious Dragon." Occurs also as Ḫuš-ušumgal. (Litke 1998: 221; Tallqvist 1974: 482)

Ušumgal-kalama (M) Deified harp of Nin-Girsu. Means "Dragon of the Nation." The fashioning of this harp is referred to in a year name of Gudea of Lagaš and is mentioned in the Gudea cylinders containing a hymn for the building of Nin-Girsu's E-ninnu temple at Girsu. (Litke 1998: 177; Jacobsen 1976: 82; Falkenstein 1966: 113 and note 5)

Ušum-maḫ (M) Deity identified with Marduk. Means "Lofty Dragon." (Litke 1998: 221; Tallqvist 1974: 482)

Ušum-mašgan-°UR (M) See Pasānu

Ušum-šag-su(d) (M) Daughter of the birth/mother goddess Nin-tu(d). Means "Unfathomable Dragon." (Litke 1998: 80)

Ušum-ursag, Ušum-ur-ša-an (M) Bull-lyre of Tišpak. (Litke 1998: 194)

Ušum-ursag(-kura-dibdibe) (M) One of seven bull-lyres of Nin-Girsu. Means "Heroic Dragon that Traipses through the Land." (Litke 1998: 177, 194; Tallqvist 1974: 482)

Uta-ulu (M) (1) Form of Ninurta in An : *Anum*. Several of his temples are attested, and he appears in various Sumerian literary texts. The name U-GIŠGAL-lu of Ninurta in An : *Anum*, glossed as "first son of Enlil," is likely a variant of the name Uta-ulu. (2) One of the seven destiny-decreeing gods of the E-sagil temple in Babylon. See Utu-lu-alim. (George 2004 no. 20; Richter 2004: 75–77; Annus 2002: 4, 28, 56, 87, 144; Litke 1998: 44; George 1993: 25, 96 no. 423, 158 no. 1212; Cohen 1981: 113, 143, 145, 147)

Uttu (M) Goddess of weaving and patron of clothiers. Daughter of Enki and Nin-kura or Enki and Nin-imma. According to An : *Anum*, her husband was Nin-kura. Since the sign for Uttu was used to write "spider," Uttu might originally have been a spider goddess, who, as Black and Green note, might be associated with weaving because of a spider's spinning of webs. In "Enki and Nin-ḫursag," Enki impregnated his great-granddaughter Uttu, and she bore eight plants. Uttu had a "seat" in the Marduk temple in Babylon and at least in one other temple. Orthographies listed in An : *Anum* for Uttu are Uttu, TAG(.TÚG), UŠ.BAR, NUN.TÚG, KI.LÁ, and SIKI. (Black and Green 2003: 182; Litke 1998: 109–10, 211; George 1993: 83 no. 263, 170 no. 1425; Vanstiphout 1990b: no. 57; Jacobsen 1976: 112–13; Kramer, *ANET*: 39–40)

Utu (M) Sumerian god of the sun. Deity of justice, equity, and truth; guardian of right and assailer of evil; also a warrior. Same as Akkadian Šamaš. Attested from Early Dynastic times. Son of Nanna, the moon god, and his wife Nin-gal. Twin brother of the goddess Inana and the netherworld goddess Ereškigal. Utu's consort was Šerda (Akkadian Aya). His son and main minister, Bunene, guided the sun's chariot through the day- and night-time skies. Utu's symbol was the sun disk, and he usually held a saw, with which he daily cut his way out of the mountains/earth. At dusk he entered the mountains/earth through a gate held open by two gate-keepers. In iconography, he was depicted as wearing a tall horned crown, having a long beard, clothed in long flounced robe, and holding his signature saw. A hymn celebrates the sun god as a youthful bringer of fertility to the flocks and herds. In "Enki and the World Order" Enki gives Judge Utu responsibility for the universe. Utu was known for being an aid to human beings. When in "Dumuzi's Dream" and "The Descent of Inana," Dumuzi was trying to evade the *gallu*-demons who wanted to take him to the netherworld, it was Utu who aided him in his escape. Utu's attempt to influence his sister Inana's choice of a mate led to the debate between the shepherd and the farmer, "Dumuzi and En-kimdu." In "The Deluge," the gods granted Utu the city of Sippar and, once the waters began to subside, it was Utu who greeted Zi-usudra with his rays and to whom Zi-usudra then paid homage.

Theophoric names often included Utu or his most common epithet, Babbar "White" or "Shining." Utu's major cult centers were Larsa and Sippar, and at both cities his great temple was the E-babbar, "White (or Shining) House." He also had a lavish temple at Eridu. See Šamaš. (Steinkeller 2005; *LAS*: 75, 81–83, 86–88, 223, 261–62; Richter 2004: 246–47, 325–26, 338–46, 493–95; Black and Green 2003.: 52, 86, 182–84; Leick 1998: 161–62; Litke 1998: 132, 231; George 1993: 98 no. 457, 135 no. 915, 170 no. 1433; Jacobsen 1976: 7, 134; Tallqvist 1974: 270, 453–60, 482; Kramer, *ANET*: 41–42, 42–44)

U-tu-di-muš (M) Deity identified with Utu in a Neo-Assyrian god list. Written ù-tu-di-muš. (King 1969: pl. 27)

Utu-e (M) Deity attested in a Neo-Assyrian god list, presumably the god Utu as "Sunrise." (King 1969: pl. 27)

Utu-ḫegal (M) Deity attested in a god list from Aššur within the circle of Šamaš. There is no reason to associate him with the third-millennium ruler of Uruk, although possible. Means "Utu Is Abundance." (Schroeder 1920: no. 64)

Utu-ḫegal-ana (M) Deity attested in a god list from Aššur within the circle of Šamaš. Means "Utu Is the Abundance of Heaven." (Schroeder 1920: no. 64)

Utu-inim-kal(?)-ana (M) Deity attested in a god list from Aššur within the circle of Šamaš. Means "Utu, the Precious(?) Word of Heaven." (Schroeder 1920: no. 64)

Utu-inimzi-ana (M) Deity attested in a god list from Aššur within the circle of Šamaš. Means "Utu, the Steadfast Word of Heaven." (Schroeder 1920: no. 64)

Utu-ka-Ningala (M) Sumerian deity attested at Old Babylonian Ur. Means "Utu (at?) the Gate of Nin-gal." (Renger 1967: 160)

Utu-kirzal-ana (M) Deity attested in a god list from Aššur within the circle of Šamaš. Means "Utu, Joy of Heaven." (Schroeder 1920: no. 64)

Utu-men-ana (M) Deity attested in a god list from Aššur within the circle of Šamaš. Means "Utu, the Crown of Heaven." (Schroeder 1920: no. 64)

Utud, Uliud (M) One of seven bull-lyres of the sky god An/Anu(m). Written Ù-tu-ud and Ù-li-ud. Ù-li can mean "lamentation." (Litke 1998: 29)

Utulu-alim (M) Deity whose name is written ut-ùlu-a-lim. This deity is different from or another form of Uta-ulu (ut-u_{18}-lu). Both gods are listed in a ritual text for the eleventh month as going to the Edubba in Kiš.

Utu-zalag (M) Goddess attested in a Neo-Assyrian god list glossed: min *ú-tu* min *na-bi* ("shining one"?) and identified with Aya, the wife of the sun god. (King 1969: pl. 10)

Uwwi(na) (H) Deity associated with the storm god of Šapinuwa. (Giorgieri et al. 2013)

Uz (M) Deity probably to be identified with a constellation near Lyra. Means "Nanny Goat." (Tallqvist 1974: 482)

— W —

Waḫiši (H) Deity in the Hittite pantheon of Ḫattušas, originally Hattic. Also god of Zippalanda, not far from Ḫattušas to the north. Attested in many rituals. (van Gessel 1998: I, 547–48; Popko 1995: 72; Laroche 1946/47: 36)

Wardat-lili (M) See Lilītu(m)

Wašizzil, Wašalli, Wašezzili (H) Hattic god, companion of the storm god. Called "Lion" or "Lion King." Four Hittite prayers are addressed to him, and other texts mention him. In his incantations, a prince declares that humans call the god Wašizzil, but among deities he is "lion-owning god." (Leick 1998: 79; van Gessel 1998: I, 554–56; Popko 1995: 71, 73; Haas 1994: 312, 445, 589 note 339, 620; Laroche 1946/47: 37)

Waškuwatašši (H) Luwian deity. (van Gessel 1998: I, 558–59; Popko 1995: 73)

Wazul(l)a (H) See Mazul(l)a

Wê (M) Deity whose name is written We-e. (Krebernik 2002: 289–98)

Weda (M) Semitic deity attested at Emar, perhaps cognate of Akkadian *wēdu(m)* "singular," "unique." As a theophoric element occurs in Old Babylonian personal names. (J. Westenholz 2000: 62)

Weda'anu (M) Deity at Ebla. (Waetzoldt 2001)

Wēr, Ilu(m)-Wēr, Mēr, Ili-Mēr, Bēr (M) Deity identified with the weather god Adad/Iškur in West-Semitic-speaking (Amorite) areas. The form Mēr is attested in the Early Dynastic period. In the "Epic of Gilgameš" Wēr is a protective deity of the Cedar Forest. At Mari, a city gate was called the Gate of Mēr. As Bēr, the god was revered from Middle Assyrian times in the Ištar temple at Aššur and in the Aššur temple at Nineveh. At Nērebtum, near Ešnunna, oaths were taken by the deified lance of Wēr. P. Steinkeller suggests that the name derives from the ethnic group War(i). (Viaggio 2007: no. 40; Schwemer 2001: 200–10; George 1999: 109; Litke 1998: 139; Bonechi 1997; Tallqvist 1974: 375, 482; Krebernik, *RlA* VIII: 66)

Wišaišapḫe (H) Deity associated with the storm god of Šapinuwa. (Giorgieri et al. 2013)

Wišuriyant (H) Netherworld goddess or a group of goddesses. Associated with the demonic. Known as "The Evil Goddess." Described by the Hittites as "Mighty" or "Esteemed." Paired with Ammamma. (van Gessel 1998: I, 562; Haas 1994: 156, 312)

Wur(r)unkatte (H) Hattic war god. In the circle of Hurrian gods often equated to Nergal and Rešep(h). Regularly identified with Zababa. Name consists of Hattic words *katte* "king" and *wurun* "land." Worshipped widely. (Leick 1998: 79; van Gessel 1998: I, 563–64; Popko 1995: 113; Haas 1994: 310, 363, 438, 600; Laroche 1946/47: 37–38)

Wurunšemu, Wuruntemu (H) Great Hattic sun goddess, also called Urunzimu. The Hattic word *wurun* means "land." Identified with the Sun Goddess of Arinna. In the circle of the sun goddess of Earth. In a ritual she was equated to Ereškigal, queen of the netherworld. Mother of the storm god. At Ḫattušas a temple to Urunzimu was near the storm god's temple. (van Gessel 1998: I, 565; Popko 1995: 70; Haas 1994: 421–22 and notes 13, 14, 599–600, 619; Laroche 1946/47: 38)

—Y—

Ya (M) Deity attested in the personal name Ya-ramu at Ebla. See YHWH

Yabnu, Yabna (M) Deity identified with Enlil. One of a group of deities from an unknown land. (Litke 1998: 214)

Yabru (E, M) An Elamite deity invoked in an incantation along with the Elamite gods Ḫumban and Napi-riša. Equated to Anu(m). (Frayne 2009: 69; Vallat 1998: 340; Reiner 1970: 17)

Yah(u) (L) See YHWH

Yaḫipānu (L) A deified dead hero. One of the Rephaim in the Ugaritic netherworld. A helper close to El/Il(u). (del Olmo Lete 1999: 80, 81, 166)

Yakrub-El (M) See Ikrub-El

Yam, Yamm(u) (L) God of the sea in texts from Ugarit. Also the destructive power of rivers. In the Ugaritic texts, Yam, son of the high god El, was a chaotic force and the enemy of the storm god Ba'lu. His titles included "Prince Sea," "Judge (or Ruler) River," and "Beloved of El." He was associated with several monsters, such as Leviathan and Tunnan(u). The fight between Yam and Ba'lu began with the decision of El to turn Ba'lu over to Yam, but Ba'lu refused to go. A very vivid exchange between Yam and El followed, after which a fierce battle ensued. With weapons fashioned for him by the craftsman god Koṯar, Ba'lu defeated Yam. Yam was actively worshipped at Ugarit. He occurred in god lists, and in one offering list he was to receive a ram as sacrifice. His name also figured in magical texts, where he appears at least once in the form of a fish-like dragon. In the Hebrew Bible, YHWH battles and defeats the Sea and monsters associated with Sea, for instance, Leviathan. The fullest accounts can be found in various psalms (for example, Psalms 74:13–14 and 89:10). One scholar identified Yam with Greek sea god Poseidon, though Philo of Byblos seemed to equate Greek Pontus, "Sea," with Yam. (Durand 2008: 293–94; Pardee 2002: 15, 16, 19, 48, 85, 285; Wyatt 2002: 48–69; del Olmo Lete 1999: 48–49, 50, 56; Stolz, *DDDB*: 708, 737–42; Brody 1998: 22 note 63; Leick 1998: 166; Smith 1997: 87–105; Lipiński 1995: 122; Handy 1994: 110, 112–13, 125–29; Xella, *DCPP*: 499; J. Day 1985; Attridge and Oden 1981: 52, 53, 90 note 119)

Yandi (H) Deity at Aleppo. (Durand 2008: 207)

Yarhibol (L) A prominent god of Palmyra. Yarhibol was the deity of the source or spring, and his name meant "Lord of the Source." Although he has been described as a sun god, another god Malakbel represented the sun. Identified with Gad, the god of good luck. (Dien 2004; Black and Green 2003: 35; Kaizer 2002; Ribichini, *DDDB*: 340; Stolz, *DDDB*: 805; van der Toorn, *DDDB*: 914; Teixidor 1979: 29–34)

Yariḫ(u), Yarḫu, Yarah, Yareaḫ, Eraḫ, Raḫ (L) God of the moon. Yariḫ(u) was moon god at Ugarit, where his titles included "Prince" and "Luminary of Heaven." Because he travelled through the netherworld during the day, he had strong associations with the netherworld. One of the extant works from Ugarit celebrated the betrothal and wedding of Yariḫ(u) to Nikkal, the

West-Semitic name of the Mesopotamian goddess Nin-gal, spouse of the Mesopotamian moon god Nanna-Sîn. Yariḫ(u) had a place in Ugaritic god lists, in one of which he appears in the deity group "Earth and Heavens" (del Olmo Lete 1999: 131). He is described as preparing El's goblet at a ritual banquet. His name appears in incantations and in theophoric names.

As Yareaḥ in the Hebrew Bible, he was one of "the Host of Heaven" (II Kings 23:5, Psalm 148:2–3). The worship of this astral Host was conducted on rooftops (Jeremiah 19:13) and also in the Jerusalem temple (II Kings 23:4). The cult was among the targets of the reforms of King Josiah (II Kings:23). The time of the new moon seems to have called for ritual activity in New Moon festivals. The Hebrew word for "moon" or "moon deity" was *yareaḥ*. The Hebrew Bible attests to several theophoric names featuring Yareaḥ. In addition, a number of Phoenician theophoric names contained the element *yhr*, indicating the god's worship. Yariḫ(u) is to be associated with the name of the ancient city Jericho. (Durand 2008: 214–15; Pardee 2002: 15, 33, 47, 168, 282, 285; Wyatt 2002: 336–41; Lipiński, *DDDB*: 505; Schmidt, *DDDB*: 585–93; Spronk, *DDDB*: 532; Marcus 1997: 215–18; Handy 1994: 110, 113 note 100)

Yarri (H) See Iyarri

Yaṭipān(u) (L) Wife of the Ugaritic herald god Ilšu. (del Olmo Lete 1999: 55. 57, 80, 331)

YHWH (L) The tetragrammaton, the four-letter name of the official Israelite deity, both in Judah, the southern kingdom, and in the northern kingdom, Israel. The god of the Covenant, who entered into agreements with Noah, Moses, and David. Deity of the earliest texts of the Hebrew Bible: "YHWH, god of Israel" (Judges 5:5). He was a storm and mountain god, both a fertility deity who controlled life and death and a warrior god who battled and conquered huge monsters such as Leviathan. For a period of time, YHWH seems to have had a consort, the Canaanite goddess Asherah. In addition, at the Jewish colony on the island of Elephantine in Egypt, YHWH was paired with the Canaanite goddess ʿAnat(u).

Variant, seemingly regional renderings of the name, are Yah(u), Yaw, Yau, Yo, Yeho, Ya, and Iah. The later version "Jehovah" resulted from a combination of the consonants of the tetragrammaton with the vowels of Adonai (a substitute for saying YHWH's name). Translated in the Greek Septuagint as *kyrios* "Lord," and the Latin Vulgate as *Dominus* "Lord." Also "God the Father" of the Christian Trinity, translated into the English of the King James version as "Lord" (Genesis 2:4).

YHWH might be derived from the Hebrew root "be, exist." When Moses met YHWH through the Burning Bush and asked for his name, YHWH replied, "Ehyeh-Ašēr-Ehyeh," (among the possible translations is "I Am That I Am" [Genesis 3:14]) and instructed Moses to tell the Israelites to call him Ehyeh.

Evidence points to Edom and Midian as lands that revered YHWH before he began to be worshipped by Israelites in Canaan, probably around 1000 BCE. He may have been introduced into the Israelite tribal areas by nomads immigrating from those areas. He became the national Israelite god under David and Solomon. Outside the Bible, the earliest mention of YHWH is on a Moabite stele of the ninth century BCE, which considered him to be Israel's primary deity.

He had several local manifestations, for instance, YHWH of Samaria and YHWH of Teman. YHWH became identified with other, early Israelite deities, such as El-šadai, so that these separate deities eventually became merely attributes or other names of YHWH. As can be seen in a fragment from the Dead Sea Scrolls (see Hendel 1993) and in the Septuagint, Deuteronomy 32:8–9 originally reflected an early Israelite belief that YHWH was but one of the lesser gods under the supreme Canaanite deity El, under whom each god was assigned a nation, YHWH being apportioned Israel.

His titles included "Rider upon the Clouds," which he shared with Ba'lu, and "Ancient of Days," which is reminiscent of El's Ugaritic epithet "Father of the Years." He was YHWH Ṣabaōth or Zebaōth "YHWH of the Host," a title that also connects him to the Canaanite El. According to Philo of Byblos, the Phoenician Elos (Kronos) was supported by "allies," that is, a Host. YHWH Ṣabaōth occurs 284 times in the Hebrew Bible and refers to his assembly and his army. The epithet was associated with Jerusalem, and Mount Zion was named as his dwelling-place. He was also conceived as an invisible king seated on a lofty Cherubim throne in the Solomonic temple. (Leeming 2005: 153–54, 170–74; Choi 2004; Smith 2001: 140–43; Mettinger, *DDDB*: 920–24; van der Toorn, *DDDB*: 910–19; Handy 1994: throughout; Rose, *ABD* IV: 1002–3; Thompson, *ABD* VI: 1011–12; Anderson, *IDB* II, 409–11, 417–30; Moule, *IDB* II, 430–36; Patai 1990: 226; Smith 1990: 7–26; Cross 1973: 61; Attridge and Oden 1981: 50, 51; Albright 1986: 33–34, 168–72)

— Z —

Zababa (H, M) A warrior god identified with Ninurta or Nin-Girsu. Tutelary deity of the city of Kiš in northern Babylonia. In a god list he was called "Marduk of Battle." At Kiš his wife was Inana/Ištar. His symbol was a griffon- or lion-headed staff. A seal from the Old Babylonian period excavated at Kiš shows a deity, presumably Zababa, holding a mace and standing beside a bird, a snake, and a fly. The god was honored already in hymns of the Early Dynastic period, in one of which he has the epithet "Dragon." In the prologue to his law code, Ḫammurāpi mentions that he had decorated Zababa's temple and restored the temple of Inana/Ištar at Kiš. In the epilogue to the code, the king appeals to Zababa the great warrior to deal harshly with anyone ignoring the laws or damaging the stele on which they are inscribed.

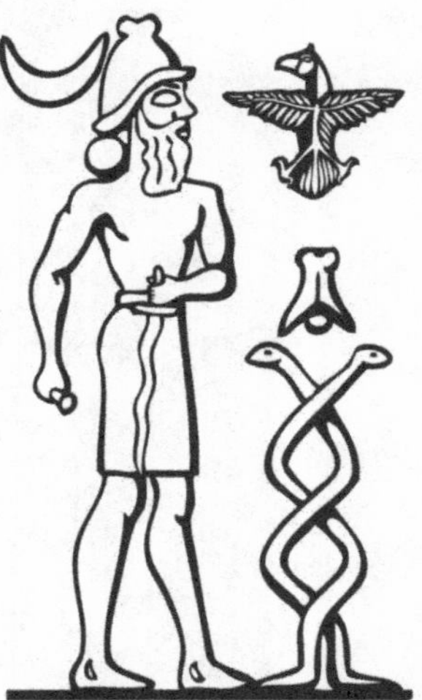

Cylinder seal from Kiš, with warrior Zababa. Old Babylonian. Basalt. 3.1 x 1.5 cm. Ashmolean Museum 1928.469. After Buchanan 1966: no. 517.

In his sanctuary at Kiš, Zababa's ziqqurat was "House Worthy of the Hero." At Lagaš he might have been the consort of Baba. He had a temple at Ur and a "seat" at Aššur.

"Zababa" was a Sumerian writing for the Hittite war god. His Hattic name was Wurunkatte, "King of the Land," and he was called Aštabi(l) in Hurrian. Lists of war gods from the time of Tutḫalia IV contain several Zababas: of Kizzuwatna, of Hatti, and so on. (Black and Green 2003: 39, 169, 187; Leick 1999: 65; Hoffner 1998: 113; Leick 1998: 167; Litke 1998: 173; van Gessel 1998: II, 961–69; Haas 1994: 363–66, 597, 600, 619–20; George 1993: 30, 65 no. 37; 77 no. 186, 78 no. 200, 105 no. 533, 112 no. 633, 116 no. 673, 148 no. 1075, 154 no. 1151; Tallqvist 1974: 483; Roberts 1972: 56 and note 473; Meek, *ANET*: 164, 179; Laroche 1946/47: 107–8)

Zabaḫundi (E) See Zammaḫundi

Zabar-daba (M) Deity identified with Adad in a Neo-Assyrian god list. The term designate a high military official. (Schwemer 2001: 79, 80)

Zag(-an)-gala (M) Deity identified with Nin-šubur and an adviser of An/Anu(m). May mean "(At) the Side of the Great One (or: of Great An)." (Litke 1998: 26; Tallqvist 1974: 484)

Zagar (M) See ANzagar

Za-ga-ri (M) Deity in an Ur III personal name from Ishān Mizyad, a town near Kiš. If this is syllabic for the god of dreams, then it indicates a reading ^{d}Zagar instead of reading anzagar. See ANzagar.

Zagin (M) Deity in a text from Fara. (Martin, 2001: 114)

Zagin-birbir (M) Deity attested in a Neo-Assyrian god list. May mean "Who Strips away(?) the Lapis-lazuli," possibly referring to a process involving the stone. (King 1969: pl. 9)

Zagin-dun, Dun-zagin (M) Deity attested in a Neo-Assyrian god list. May mean "Who Digs out the Lapis-lazuli." (King 1969: pl. 9)

Zagin-Elamma (M) Deity attested in a Neo-Assyrian god list. May mean "Lapis-lazuli of Elam." (King 1969: pl. 9)

Zagin-gaz (M) Deity attested in a Neo-Assyrian god list. May mean "Who Grinds the Lapis-lazuli." (King 1969: pl. 9)

Zagmu (M) Deity allocated offerings at Šarrākum. Means "(God of) the New Year." ((Owen 2013: no. 885)

Zagul-kala (M) Deity identified with Inana/Ištar as Venus. Means "Precious Carnelian." The deity name Gug-gá-la (gug "carnelian") may be just a variant of Zagul-kala. (Richter 2004: 294; Litke 1998: 161)

Za-ḫum (M) Deity in an Ur III personal name from Girsu. za-ḫum is a metal basin, but whether this is related to this deity name is unclear. (ITT 5, 6854: o ii 2)

Zalam (M) Deity identified with Utu/Šamaš. Written $^{\text{za-lam}}$DÙL in An : *Anum*. Sumerian zalam means "tent." (Litke 1998)

Zalmi (H) A deified statue. Loanword into Hittite and Hurrian from Akkadian *ṣalmu(m)* meaning "statue" or "image." Epithet of Nubadig. Occurs in an offering list associated with Nin-egal. (van Gessel 1998: I, 574; Haas 1994: 383; Laroche 1977: 301; Laroche 1946/47: 63)

Zammaḫundi, Zabaḫundi (E) Probably variants of the same Elamite deity, juxtaposed in Tablet VI of An : *Anum*. (Litke 1998; 213-14)

Zana (E) Epithet of the Elamite deity Parti. Means "Divine Lady." (König 1977: 212, 227)

Zannaru (M) Name of Ištar. In "The Hymn to the Queen of Nippur" Ea assigned the name to Ištar. There was a "seat" of Zannaru in the temple complex at Uruk. Explained in An : *Anu ša amēli* as "Ištar of the lands." Some posit a possible etymology with *zannaru*, a lyre. (Litke 1998: 234; George 1993: 112 no. 628; Lambert 1992: 213; Krispijn 1990: 12)

Zaqīqu(m) (M) See Mamu(d); Sisig

Zara(-e)-nugia (M) See Ige-nugia

Zāriqu (M) Deity mentioned in a first-millennium BCE ritual for the ninth month at the E-sag-ila temple of Marduk in Babylon in which the god strews palm fronds from a boat. Name means "The Strewer," alluding to this ritual strewing of palm fronds. In an Old Babylonian god list occurs directly after ^{d}Iz-za-riq, possibly a variant name for this god. (Weidner 1924/25)

Zarium (M) See Zurme

Zarpanītu(m), (M) Wife of Marduk, the chief god of Babylon, and thus the chief female deity of Babylon. As such, she assumed the roles of many other goddesses, for example, acting as intercessor and protector of the land. Worshipped also as Eru'a, a minor Babylonian goddess of pregnancy and birth, who finally merged with Zarpanītu(m). A popular interpretation of the name was that it meant "the creatress of seed/offspring" (Cogan, *DDDB*: 822). The epilogue to the law code of Ḫammu-rāpi mentions Zarpanītu(m) with Marduk. A text of the Babylonian king Nabonidus praises Zarpanītu(m) as a steady base for the throne. During the *akītu* festival at Babylon, a priest recited a hymn to Zarpanītu(m) as Bēltīya. Zarpanītu(m) had a shrine in the great temple of Marduk at Babylon. A "Sacred Marriage" between Marduk and Zarpanītu(m) took place in Babylon during the *akītu* festival. (Black and Green 2003: 160; Leick 1999: 65, 111; Leick 1998: 149–50; Litke 1998: 95, 96; Cohen 1993: 439; George 1993: 74 no. 145, 98 no. 448, 99 no. 461; Tallqvist 1974: 452–53; Meek, *ANET*: 178; Oppenheim, *ANET*: 310; Sachs, *ANET*: 332)

Zawal(li) (H) Group of Hittite deities that appear in magical oracles. The cities of Zitḫara and Ankuwa near Zippalanda were home to their cult. (van Gessel 1998: I, 577–80; Laroche 1946/47: 92)

Za-zagin (M) Deity in a text from Fara. May mean "Lapis lazuli stone" or "Gleaming stone." (Martin, 2001: 114)

Zazaru (M) Daughter of Baba and Ninurta. (Selz 1995: 268–69; George 1993: 166 no. 1344; Tallqvist 1974: 483; Falkenstein 1966: 114)

Zazin (M) Deity identified with Enki/Ea as a maker of bows and arrows (*sasinnu*). (Litke 1998: 240)

Zedek, Zedeq (L) See Sydyk

Zeus Casios (L) See Ba'al-Ṣapōn

Zi(-kala), Zi-gal, Zi(-kala)-maḫ, Zi-ušum, Zi-kal-la-ba (M). Divinized attributes of the god Di-ku$_5$ "The Judge" in An : *Anum*. Means "He (the Great/Lofty One) of (Precious) Life," "The Foremost One of Life," "The Grantor of Precious Life." (Litke 1998: 226–27)

Zib(b)a (M) See Telītu(m)

Zi-ba-an (M) Divinized attributes of the god Di-ku$_5$ "The Judge" in An : *Anum*. Zi-ba-an probably here denotes "scales (of justice)," Akk. *zibānītu*. The names occurs as Zi-ba-an-maḫ, -silim, -tur, -maḫ, -gu, -gal, -ušumgal, -šu-ḫuš-a, -engur, -engur-gal, and -engur-maḫ. (Litke 1998: 226)

Zibzib (M) Deity in a god list from Aššur. (Schroeder 1920: no. 64)

Zi-gara, Zi-gar-si (M) Vizier of the netherworld deity Meslamta-e. Written Zi-gar-ra with variant Zi-gá-ar-si. This name might contain a syllabic spelling of Sumerian /zigar/ "top part." (Litke 1998: 197)

Zi-gula (M) Deity identified with the birth/mother goddess Dingir-maḫ/Bēlet-ilī. Name might mean "(Who Makes) the Greatest Life." (Litke 1998: 70; Tallqvist 1974: 484; Krebernik, *RlA* VIII: 507)

Zi-kala (M) See Zi

Zikkanzipa (H) Deity whose name possibly means "Genie of Zikkan." (Durand 1988 no. 8)

Zi-kug (M) Fifteenth name of Marduk in the *Enūma eliš*. Means "Pure Life." (Foster 2005: 477; Litke 1998: 91; Tallqvist 1974: 484; Speiser, *ANET*: 70; Heidel 1967: 54)

Zilašu (M) Deity attested at Ebla. (Waetzoldt 2001)

Zilipura/i, Zalipura/i (H) Hattic god worshipped by the Hittites and the Luwians. In a mythic tale, he constructs the cult throne, and is personified by the goddess Ḫalmaš(š)uit. One text recounts offerings to the Hattic house god Zilipuri. In the "dead house" cult of Lelwani on the central mound at

Ḫattušas, the god was honored with other netherworld deities and paired with Ḫašam(m)ili/a. (van Gessel 1998: I, 581–83; Popko 1995: 71–72, 94; Haas 1994: 245, 263; Laroche 1946/47: 39)

Zimingi (M) See Zimu

Zimu (M) Minister or vizier of the god Lugal-Erra. Variant Zi-mi-in-gi. (Litke 1998: 197)

Zinkuruwa (H) In Hattic texts, a vegetation deity. Equated to Ḫalki, the Hittite grain god(dess). Also identified with Kumarbi and Nisaba. In a rite celebrating the weather god of Zippalanda, Zinkuruwa is a vegetation deity. (van Gessel 1998: I, 584–85; Haas 1994: 306)

Zintuḫi (H) Sun goddess. Hattic name means "Little Daughter" or "Granddaughter." Daughter of Mezul(l)a. Granddaughter of Wurunšemu and Taru or, in Hittite terms, the Sun Goddess of Arinna and the storm god. Muwatalli II invoked the weather god Piḫašši and connected Zintuḫi to him. She occurs in a list of deities from Zippalanda and in the prayer of Queen Pudu-Ḫepa. She had her own cult. She had a temple at Arinna, where she was a member of the pantheon. See Mezul(l)a. (van Gessel 1998: I, 585–87; Popko 1995: 72, 75, 145; Haas 1994: 428–29, 447, 585–86; Laroche 1946/47: 40)

Ziparwa, Zaparwa (H) Palaic storm god. In addition, was concerned with vegetation. According to an Old Hittite god list, he was chief deity of the Palaic pantheon. His spouse was Kattaḫzipuri. Also member of the state pantheon at Ḫattušas where he had a temple. Occurs with Kattaḫzipuri in a Palaic rite. The eleventh and twelfth days of a festival (?) ritual focused on him. (van Gessel 1998: I, 575–76, 588–92; Popko 1995: 73–74, 87–88, 113; Haas 1994: 438, 611, 619; Laroche 1946/47: 92)

Ziplanti(l) (H) Storm god revered at Zippalanda. Queen Pudu-Ḫepa prayed to the Sun Goddess of Arinna and the storm god of Zippalanda together. (van Gessel 1998: I, 592–93; Popko 1995: 72, 113; Haas 1994: 589)

Ziqqurrat (M) Deity in the Ebabbar temple in Sippar. (Zawadski 2006 no. 39)

ZIRQI (M) Deity identified with Ninurta. (Litke 1998: 45)

Zi-si, Zi-su (M) Nineteenth name of Marduk in the *Enūma eliš*. (Foster 2005: 478; Litke 1998: 92; Tallqvist 1974: 485; Speiser, *ANET*: 70; Heidel 1967: 55)

Zi-šage-diri (M) One of thirteen children of Nin-marki. (Litke 1998: 125)

Zi-šumma (M) First of seven children of En-me-šara. Also a title of Gula as Lady of Nippur. Means "Who Grants Life." In one tradition, associated with Nin-imma. (Litke 1998: 34; Livingstone 1986: 200; Tallqvist 1974: 485)

Zit(ta)ḫariya (H) City deity of Zitara and of the land of the Kaška people. Witness in Middle Hittite treaties with the Kaška. Worshipped as a cult object that was carried along on military campaigns and ritually reinstalled in his temple upon return. (van Gessel 1998: I, 593–97; Popko 1995: 86–87, 89–90; Haas 1994: 281, 306, 450, 454–56, 458–59, 589; Laroche 1946/47: 40)

Zi-unkina (M) Fourteenth name of Marduk in the *Enūma eliš*. Means "Life of the Assembly." dZi-unkin-na has a gloss *napišti ummanišu*. (Talon 2005: 70; Foster 2005: 476; Litke 1998: 91–92; Tallqvist 1974: 485; Speiser, *ANET*: 70; Heidel 1967: 54)

Ziza (M) Deity with a cult at Ur III Umma. (MVAG 21 22 FH 5: o i 18)

Zizanu(m) (M) Son of the god Ištarān. Written $^{zi\text{-}za\text{-}nu}$KUR in An : *Anum*. In a Neo-Assyrian god list identified with Ninurta of the Suteans and written ^{d}zi-za-nu. See Qudmu. (Litke 1998: 218; Reiner 1970: 40; King 1969: pl. 11)

Zi-zida (M) Deity identified with both Ninurta and Enki. Means "True Life." (Litke 1998: 45, 87; Tallqvist 1974: 485)

Zizzil (M) Daughter of Nin-marki. Written zíl-zíl with gloss zi-iz-zil. Might mean "Membrane of the Womb" or "Pleasing." (Litke 1998: 125)

Zoroastrianism, **Zoroaster**. Religion based on the teachings of the spiritual leader Zoroaster (Zarathustra) and still practiced today in Iran, India, and elsewhere. (Bowker 1997: 2070)

Zulki (H) Primeval goddess, seer, and interpreter of dreams. Appears in a treaty, in texts concerning extispicy, and in personal names. Means "The Ancient One." (Hoffner 1998: 112; van Gessel 1998: I, 602; Popko 1995: 99; Haas 1994: 113, 115; Laroche 1976: 307; Laroche 1946/47: 64)

Zulum-mar(a) (M) Thirty-third name of Marduk proclaimed at the end of the *Enuma eliš*. (Foster 2005: 480; Litke 1998: 95; Tallqvist 1974: 485; Speiser *ANET*: 71; Heidel 1967: 57)

Zunkir-rišarra (E) Elamite netherworld deity attested on brick inscriptions of Untaš-Napiriša from the religious center Choga Zanbil, south of Susa. (König 1977: 53, 215, 227)

Zurme (M) Deity rendered by Akkadian Zarium. The name is written zu-úr-me. (Litke 1998: 79)

Zurmuzarmu (M) Deity identified as the child of the E-šaba, the temple of Baba. The name is written zu-ur-mu-zar-mu. Litke suggests that either zu-ur-mu or zar-mu in the name may represent an original gloss. (Litke 1998: 79; George 1993: 143 no. 1010)

Ẓẓ-wa-kmṯ (L) Pair of deities appearing at Ugarit in god lists and in an incantation against snakebite. (del Olmo Lete 1999: 64, 80, 373)

APPENDIX

I. Deified Rivers

In the Ancient Near East, where rivers and their waters usually meant life, it is not surprising that many rivers were sacred, if not deified. Mesopotamian examples include the Tigris and the Euphrates, the Turul/Diyala, and the Ṭaban.

Much of the Elamite domain was mountainous, and numerous rivers crisscrossed the landscape. Our basic source for our knowledge of Elamite sacred rivers is the Persepolis Fortification Tablets, which date to Achaemenid times. Only five rivers for which offerings were made by various Achaemenid officials are known from this archive. The rivers lay in a fairly restricted area near the modern Iranian city Kazerun on the road from Susa to Persepolis (Henkelman 2008: 539–40).

In the Levant, as elsewhere, life-giving rivers were often sacred or deified, for example, the Balīḫ River in what is now Syria. In the Hebrew Bible, rivers were often treated as primordial, divinized forms of nature when, along with elements such as heaven and earth, they became witnesses to treaties or oaths. The four cosmic rivers flowing out of Eden, Pishon, Gihon, Tigris, and Euphrates, correlated with the four corners of the earth (Genesis 2:8–14). In Christian imagery, the River Jordan was often anthropomorphized.

Alba (M) Deity invoked in an incantation as a brook in the high mountains. Ety-mology uncertain. The reading of the logogram KASKAL+KUR used to write the name comes from an Old Babylonian lexical text. Terms rendered KASKAL +KUR can designate underground rivers or springs. (Reiner 1970: 41)

Aranzaḫ(i), Aranzi (H) Deified Hittite river. Hurrian/Hittite name of the deified Tigris River. Offspring of the gods Anu and Kumarbi, and brother of Tasmisu and of the storm god Teššub. Aranzaḫi was the divine river that Kumarbi spat out of his mouth onto Mount Kanzura. Later Aranzaḫi conspired with Anu and Teššub to destroy Kumarbi. (Alster, *DDDB*: 870; Hoffner 1998: 41; del Monte and Tischler. 1978: 524–25)

Arziya (H) Sacred river associated with the ancient town of Arziya located near ancient Šamuḫa, likely modern Osmancik. Offerings to the mountains and rivers of Arziya are attested in Hittite texts. (del Monte and Tischler. 1978: 45)

Ayanḫarišda (E) Elamite sacred river to be located in modern Iran beside the road to Persepolis in the vicinity of Kazerun, specifically at the modern village of Imamzadeh on the west side of the modern Shapur River. (Henkelman 2008: 539–40)

Balīḫa, Balīḫu(m), Alba, Alḫa (L, M) The deified Balīḫ River in Syria. It may be related to the royal name Balīḫ, which in the Sumerian King List appears as that of a king of Kiš after the Flood, but this is uncertain. Attested in an Early Dynastic god list from Abu Ṣalābīkh and an incantation from Ebla. Also appears in Early Dynastic administrative texts from Ebla in connection, in some cases, to the chief god of Ebla, Kur(r)a. Interestingly, it is mentioned in a text in connection with sacred Mount Arduwan, probably located just northwest of modern Aleppo. Balīḫu(m) may have been a cosmic river. Arduwan may, in turn, be associated with the Greek mythology figure Rhadamanthys, a wise king, who appears as one of the judges of the netherworld. The god Balīḫ occurs in theophoric names in Sargonic texts and, possibly, in the form Walīḫ in Ur III texts from Lagaš. Balīḫu(m) referring to the Balīḫ River appears in personal names from Neo-Babylonian Sippar. Is found rarely in theophoric names from Old Babylonian Mari and also similarly from Middle Bronze Emar.

The divine names Alba, Alḫa, and Baliḫa are all written KASKAL.KUR in the lexical series Diri and in An : *Anum* with the syllabic renderings al-ba/il-ba, al-ḫa/il-ḫa, and ba-li-ḫa respectively. Thus all three divine names would appear to be a variants of the deified Baliḫ River. (Durand 2008: 291; Richter 2004: 383–84; Civil 2004; Litke 1998: 218; Bongenaar 1997: 464; Pomponio and Xella 1997: 78–79; Mander 1986: 68–69; Roberts 1972: 17–18)

Diyala (M) Deified river, often mentioned with the Taban River. The Diyala is a major tributary of the Tigris, in eastern Iraq. Joins the Tigris southeast of Baghdad. Known in ancient texts as the Turul, with its major tributary the Turan (the modern Sirwan). One of the last kings of the Old Akkadian period, Šū-Turul, included the river god as part of his theophoric name. (Nashef 1982a and b)

Euphrates (M) See Tigris

Ḫalḫala (M) A divine river mentioned in incantations. (George 2016: no. 5)

Ḫallasua (H) Hurrian deity who is the deified source of the Tigris (Deller 1987 no. 101)

Ḫubur (M), **Ḫabūr** (m.), **Ḫabūru(m)**, **Ḫabūrītu(m)** (f.) (L) Deified river of the netherworld, the Ḫabur River, which those who died had to cross in order to reach the Land of the Dead. In some texts, Ḫubur designated the netherworld as a whole. A brick inscription by a governor of Mari, Ilum-išar, in the Ur III period was written for a statue called King Ḫubur; the statue was situated at one of the gates of the city. The netherworld river Id-kura, which was a "man-eating river," and its ferry-boatman Silu-igi(?) figured in the Sumerian mythic composition "Enlil and Ninlil." Ḫubur was also a name or title of Ti'amat, who, in the *Enūma eliš*, is called "Mother Ḫubur." A goddess in the form Ḫabūrītum appears in the pantheon in Ur III times. Archi suggest that she might be identified with Bēlet-Nagar. The name may possibly find a reflex in ancient Greek Charybdis. (Foster 2005: 444; Archi 2004; Black and Green 2003: 155–56; Sharlach 2002: 103–5; Galter, *DDDB*: 430–31; Menzel 1981: 64; Frayne 1997b: 443; Frymer-Kensky 1977; Tallqvist 1974: 322; Heidel 1967: 23; Matouš 1962: 17; Frankena 1954: 124; Speiser, *ANET*: 63; Edzard, *RlA* IV: 29)

Ḫuburše-igidu (M) Demon patrolman of the steppe. Means "(He) Looks at the Ḫubur," which is the river that must be crossed to arrive at the Land of the Dead. See Ḫubur. (Litke 1998: 165)

Ḫubutiš (E) Elamite sacred river possibly marked by the modern Āb-i-Bīdu ("Bīdu River") just west of the modern Shapur River in the Kazerun district. (Henkelman 2008: 539–40)

Mala (H) Important sacred river on the eastern frontier of the Hittite kingdom. The Luwians celebrated a cult of the Mala and the Hurrian god Nubadig. As a result of an oracle indicating how to remove a plague that had beset the land of Ḫatti, king Muršiliš II travelled to make offerings at the "Festival of the River Mala." The towns mentioned elsewhere in campaigns of the Hittites reveal that the river flowed near modern Ortaköy, likely ancient Hittite Taḫara, located north east of modern Kayseri in Turkey. Lexical texts equate the River Mala with the Puratti, the Hittite name for the Euphrates. (Popko 1995: 94; del Monte and Tischler 1978: 423–24; Garstang and Gurney 1959: 46–47)

Maraššant/da, Maraššantiya (H) A major Hittite sacred river, corresponding to the ancient Greek Halys and modern Turkish Kızılırmak. Offerings of sheep were made to the river in a ritual dealing with the ancient gods. The name may be associated with the ancient Hittite town of Maraštiya, which texts indicate was located near the ancient town of Šamuḫa, likely modern Turkish Osmanacik, near the source of the modern Kızılırmak River. Maraštiya, in turn, may have been situated at modern town of Mezre not far from modern Osmanacik. The Hittite river was sometimes written with the logogram denoting the color red, and it is of interest that the modern name Kızılırmak means "Red River." (del Monte and Tischler 1978: 538–39)

Marriš (E) Elamite sacred river possibly marked by the modern Ab-i-Baryo ("Baryo River") located just west of the modern Shapur River east of modern Kazerun in Iran. (Henkelman 2008: 539–40)

Nahar(u), Nahr (L) Minor Syro-Canaanite god closely associated with the sea god Yam or perhaps a name of, or another name for, Yam. Means "River." Texts from Ugarit regularly identify Sea and River in parallel lines: "… build a house for Prince Yam,/[constr]uct a palace for Ruler Nahar" (Wyatt 2002: 52–53). As the house and the palace were understood to be the same building, so were Yam and Nahar(u) likely the same deity. In the "Ba'lu Cycle" of compositions, the supreme deity El appointed Yam as Lord and designated him "Beloved of El" (Wyatt 2002: 49) and thus by-passed the storm god Ba'lu/Hadad. Ba'lu won the resulting battle between the two over who should rule. In a later passage, however, the goddess 'Anat(u) claimed to have "exterminated" Yam/Nahar(u) on behalf of Ba'lu (Wyatt 2002: 79). Though Yam's name occurs in deity or offering lists, Nahar(u)'s does not. In the Hebrew Bible, the word for "river" was also *nahar*, and rivers were often treated as primordial, divinized forms of nature when, along with elements like heaven and earth, they became witnesses to treaties or oaths (Genesis 2:8–14). Naru(m) was the Babylonian name of the Divine River, and Id his Sumerian name. (Pardee 2002: 15, 212; Wyatt 2002: 39–69; Stolz, *DDDB*: 707–9; Smith 1997: 87–111; Finnegan 1989: 140–41)

Rannakarra (E) Elamite sacred river possibly located in Iran near the modern village of Gauhar just west of the modern Shapur River a short distance east of modern Kazerun. (Henkelman 2008: 539–40)

Šanah/ḫuita (H) Sacred Hittite river and mountain near the Hittite town of the same name. The town made offerings to both mountain and river. (del Monte and Tischler 1978: 342)

Šaušanuš (E) Elamite sacred river possibly located at the modern village of Dashtas just west of the modern Shapur River and just east of modern Kazerun in Iran. (Henkelman 2008: 539–40)

Tigris and Euphrates (M) Although we would expect that both the Tigris and Euphrates Rivers were divinized, the actual evidence for this is not overwhelming. Both rivers occurred in theophoric names in the Old Babylonian period and in North Syria. However, neither the Tigris nor the Euphrates is included in An : *Anum,* although the generic term for river, Id, does appear. In an Old Babylonian forerunner to the An : *Anum* list, there is a reference to a god whose name could refer to either the "Tigris" or "The Shining River." In a study of the gods of Ebla no reference to either the Tigris or Euphrates is given. A perusal of all the Ur III administrative documents yields no evidence for cult offerings to either the Tigris or Euphrates, nor do references to the two rivers appear in Sallaberger's study of the Ur III cultic calendar. Literary texts give us snippets of mythology associated with the Tigris and Euphrates. In an Akkadian hymn to the goddess Nisaba, the Euphrates River was addressed as father of the gods. "Enki and the World Order" seemingly took it for granted that the Euphrates preceded the Tigris in existence. When Enki masturbated to fill the Tigris with water, he was standing looking across the Euphrates. In an Akkadian hymn to the goddess Nisaba, the Euphrates River was addressed as father of the gods. In the *Enūma eliš,* Marduk made the Euphrates and the Tigris emerge from the dead Ti'amat's eyes. Later commentary explained that the Euphrates came from the goddess's left eye, the Tigris from her right. The Euphrates was worshipped, with the Tigris River, at a "seat" in the temple at Babylon called "House of the Foremost Spring (?)" (George 1993: 104 no. 511). A document from the time of Shalmaneser II, king of Assyria, refers to provisions for the deified Tigris in the city of Aššur. Two Akkadian kings, Narām-Sîn and Šar-kali-šarri, record in their year names or royal inscriptions their reaching of the sources of the Tigris and Euphrates rivers. While we are not sure where they considered the rivers' source(s) to be, much later the Assyrian kings Tiglath-pileser I and Shalmaneser III (or their emissaries) travelled to the mountainous site of modern Birkleyn in Turkey, where they had carved on the walls of grottoes royal inscriptions commemorating their various triumphs. These were part of a complex network of tunnels that fed a pool apparently considered to represent the source of the Tigris and Euphrates. A depiction of king Shalmaneser III making offerings in these grottoes is found in the bronze gates excavated by Rassam at modern Balawat. In contrast, King Sennacherib left rock reliefs high up the modern Mount Judi overlooking the modern Tigris River in Iraq near the modern Iraqi-Turkish border. In a now-broken stone inscription, he claimed to have reached the sources of the Tigris and Euphrates, considered by him to be located at modern Mount Judi, the resting place of Noah's ark according to the tradition recorded in the Qur'an. The Hittite name for the Euphrates was Puratti. One Hittite text refers to an offering of a sheep made to a river whose name is written with the sign that in Babylonia designated the Tigris River. Unfortunately, we do not know how the Hittites read the sign. However, they designated part of the course of the modern Tigris river as the Aranziḫa. In contrast to the few references to the deified Tigris and Euphrates, the cult of the divine cosmic ordeal rivers Id and Ilurugu are well attested. In Babylonia Nāru was the name of the Divine River, Id the Sumerian name. See also Id. (Durand 2008: 291; Harmanşah 2007; Schachner et al. 2007; Radner 2006a; Radner 2006b; Foster 2005: 465; Woods 2005; *LAS*: 220–21; Radner and Schachner 2001; Alster, *DDDB*: 870–71; Stolz, *DDDB*: 706–9; van der Toorn, *DDDB*: 314–16; Frayne 1993: 86, 183; del Monte and Tischler 1978: 530; Grayson, *ANET*: 501–2; Speiser in Pritchard 1969a: 60–67; Heidel 1967: 18–43)

Turul, Turan, Turnat (M) Major tributary of the ancient Tigris that it joined near modern Baghdad. The probably sacred river Turul appears in the name of an Old Akkadian king Šū-Turul, but there the element Turul is not written with the prefixed divine determinative. Turul was the ancient name for the modern Diyala River. The Turul's side branch was the ancient Ṭaban. (Borger 1970: 1)

Ṭabān (M) A deified river, often mentioned with the Turul River, the modern Diyala. Most commonly attested in theophoric names, for example, in Old Akkadian and Old Babylonian personal names. An unnamed Old Babylonian period king of Ešnunna mentioned in a year-formula the construction of a silver object (statue?) of the Ṭabān. The ancient Ṭaban is probably to be identified with the modern Nahr Kan'ān (Nahr Maḥrūth), lying north east of Baghdad and flowing through ancient town of Gannanāte. The Ṭaban was a side branch of the Turul, an important tributary of the ancient Tigris. (Nashef 1982a and b; Roberts, 1972: 18)

Zuliya (Hittite), **Zuliyamma** (Hattic) Sacred river. Appears in theophoric names. (van Gessel 1998: I, 600–1; Laroche 1946/47: 41)

II. Deified Mountains

Many mountains were sacred in the Ancient Near East, a number of which were deified. Only few were actually divinized in Mesopotamia. More mountain gods are known from Elamite sources. A number are recorded as being in Syria, and many more in Hittite documents.

A handful of Mesopotamian deities such as Enlil, Inana/Ištar, and Adad occasionally bore the Sumerian epithet kur, or Akkadian *šadû*[*m*), a multi-valent term that can be translated into English as "mountain," "foreign land," or "netherworld." The Mesopotamians believed in the existence of a deified cosmic mountain, a reflection of which is found in real space in the name of an eastern precinct of the greater city of Kiš known as Ḫursag-kalama "Mountain of the Land." A religious "litany" text known in late copies from the library of Aššur-bāni-pal gives a long list of famous mountains that were to be invoked by the owner of the tablet in order to protect him from evil forces. Each mountain was identified with a particular characteristic, whether it was the trees that grew there or the stones or metals that were mined there. While none of the mountain names that appear in this literary text occurs with the prefixed divine determinative, some of them, such as Mounts Saggar and Tibar/Dibar, are attested elsewhere with the prefixed sign for divinity. According to M. Stol, only two mountain ranges from Babylonian cuneiform sources have the determinative dingir "god" before them. These are Mesopotamian Mount Ebiḫ and Syrian Mount Saggar. A third mountain, Syrian Mount Tibar/Dibar, occurs as a theophoric element in personal names and therefore was also divine.

Since much of the area of ancient Elam was mountainous, it is not surprising that deified-mountain names appear in ancient Elamite texts. While it may be that people in Susiana worshipped sacred mountains on their eastern frontier, the nature of the texts from Susa does not enable us to discern their names. The Persepolis Fortification texts from Achaemenid times yield more success. They note a handful of places where offerings to divine mountains were made. Henkelman gives a list of fully eleven such mountain names: Šaki, Akšena (the "Turquoise Mountain"), Battinaša, Irkamma, Gavarziya/Kamarziya, Ariyamma, (Ariaramnes), Širumanda, Arrimarištura, Izziran, and Ašbarpirasana. Of these, only three names, Šaki, Akšena, and one that is illegible, have the prefixed divine determinative. Many of these mountains lay in a fairly restricted area near the modern town of Kazerun, through which passed the ancient road from Susa to Persepolis. This clustering of sites may be due to the accident of discovery of the archive, which is not complete, as it is hard to imagine that mountains were worshipped only in this small area.

Several deified-mountain names appear in ancient texts from the area of what is now modern Syria and the Hatay province in Turkey. These include: Mounts Amarikku, Arduwan, Saggar, Tibar/Dibar, Šinapši, Amanus, and Ḫazzi. Mountain gods played a very important role in the religious life of the Hittites. The Hittites considered mountains to be sacred places where the gods lived, and they deified several mountains. At the national rock-cut shrine at Yazılıkaya a row of nine mountain gods is depicted, but unfortunately all their names, which were once inscribed below their depictions, have been worn away through natural erosion. A rich source of Hittite mountain names are records of various rituals. For example, the account of the festival for the gods KAL and Ala lists the following mountains: Ḫula, Tutḫaliya, Kamaliya, Taḫa, Puškurunuwa, Takurka, Uaḫarwa, Šarpa, Zaliyanu, Šariša, Kašu, and Taḫalnuna. The description of the ritual for the (Ḫ)Išuwa festival gives a long list of names of mountains where offerings were made: they include Amana (Amanus), Manuziya, Šuwarziya, Kurkutuni, Tamatara, Kalaniya, Piriš, Aninizakina, Inatarziya, Zatarziya, Irzili, Nanaparziya, A/Zara, Siniyari, Tuniyari, Kalzatapiyan, Nanni, Ḫaz(z)i, Kaizara, Zalanura, Zulita, Kurḫina, Itna, Ḫeḫe, Muliyanta, Ilиša, Zupaniu, Tišna, Upana, Ulali/Uwalalaki, Sira, Šinatila, Kurna, Tiri(ri)un, Šarašila, Šurila, Šurumiya, Ulikana, and Tutuwa. The ritual of the AN.TA.ŠUM (crocus?) festival is another rich source. While all these named mountains were probably sacred, not all were necessarily deified.

A-dar-a-an/nu (M) Deified mountain after which a village took its name. Occurs in texts from Ebla. (Archi 1997)

Akšena (E) Elamite deified mountain named in the Persepolis Fortification Tablets. Located by Koch between the ancient towns of Kaftariš and Vanta. Its neighbor was Mount Šaki. Frayne suggests a location at modern Kuh-i-Chena, 3.3 kms north of modern Wanda, ancient Vanda. (Henkelman, 2008: 536–37; Vallat 1993: 7; Koch 1987: 261)

Amanus, **Amana**, **Namni** (L, H), **Amanum** (M) Deified mountain range north of Ugarit, generally known today as the Amanus. In an Old Babylonian god list is a deity ^{d}A-ma-nu-um, presumably the Amanus mountains. The strategically located range, which reaches a maximum elevation of 2,240 m above sea level, acts as a divide between the coastal region of Cilicia beside the Gulf of Iskenderun and inland Syria. As a source of cedar the Amanus, (in a non-deified form) occurs already in royal inscriptions and year names of Narām-Sîn of Akkad and Gudea of Lagaš. Venerated by the Ugaritians, the Phoenicians, and widely throughout the Levant. Sacred also to the Hurrians and the Hittites. Occurs in Hittite sources in the form Amana. In the circle of the storm god Teššub. Mentioned in the letter salutation of an epistle of Hurrian king Tušratta to the Egyptian pharaoh Amen-hotep III. Appearing in a section of a text dealing with the major deities of the Hurrian realm, after the storm god Teššub and the goddess Ša(w)uš(k)a. Offerings to the mountain are attested in Hittite ritual texts that describe stops at various mountains. Also named Namni. (Klengel, Imparati, Haas, and van den Hout 1999: 47, 50, 138, 147, 270; Popko 1995: 97, 126; Moran 1987: 140; Edzard, Farber, and Sollberger 1977: 11; Klengel 1970: 32–35; Otten 1969: 247–60; Weidner 1924/25)

Amarikku(m) (L) Deified Syrian mountain located not far from ancient Ebla. The name appears in an Early Dynastic incantation from Ebla as Amarig, and it is attested in other sources as being a mountain. Amarig reappears in the form Amarikku(m) in much later Hurrian/Hittite contexts from Ḫattušas. Mount Ammarikku(m) can plausibly be located at the modern village of ʻAnjara, which lies a few kms northwest of modern Aleppo. (Schwemer

2001: 118; Fronzaroli 1997: 286–88; Haas 1981: 252–53)

Ammarig(u) (H, M) A deified mountain located not far to the northwest of Aleppo, possibly at modern Aanjâra. The name appears already in Early Dynastic incantations from Ebla. (Archi 1993: 77)

Arduwan (L) Deified Syrian mountain located not far from ancient Ebla. Mentioned in an incantation from Early Dynastic Ebla. Said to be a nesting place for eagles and called "Lord of the Eagle." The mountain likely lay a few kilometers from Mount Ammarikku(m). (del Olmo Lete 1999: 201, 204; Lipiński 1995: 253; Haas 1994: 462) Haas 1981: 254)

Arinna (H) In addition to being a cult center of the Sun Goddess of Arinna, the settlement was also home to the sacred mountain Arinna. A location of Arinna at modern Turkish Yerköy, south of Ḫattušas, is likely. (del Monte and Tischler 1978: 25; Güterbock 1960: 85)

Ariyaramna (E) Elamite sacred mountain mentioned in the Persepolis Fortification Tablets. Located by Koch between the ancient towns of Eyana and Vaijava (the latter, to be situated, according to Frayne, at modern Jamilah, about 38 kms southwest of modern Kazerun near Shiraz). To be associated with the modern place name Ambar. Frayne locates it 9 kms northwest of ancient Vaijava. (Henkelman, 2008: 538; Vallat 1993: 123; Koch 1987: 261)

Arnuwanta (H) Hittite sacred mountain mentioned in a text of a ritual for the gods KAL and Ala and also in a ritual concerning a monthly festival. (Lombardi 1996: 55 and note 27; del Monte and Tischler. 1978: 39; Gonnet 1968: 117–18)

Ašbarpirasana (E) Elamite sacred mountain mentioned in the Persepolis Fortification Tablets. Near ancient Visara. Located by Frayne at modern Pares Kan situated about 17 kms south of modern Kazerun near Shiraz. (Henkelman, 2008: 539; Vallat 1993: 21; Koch 1987: 261)

Aškašepa (H) Hittite sacred mountain for which a drink offering is attested. Thought to be situated in the ancient land of Pala centered on classical Blaene, modern Turkish Kargi. Frayne suggests a location for Aškašepa at modern Turkish Caybası just west of modern Turkish Kargi. (Lombardi 1996: 55; del Monte and Tischler. 1978: 47–48)

Awara (H) Hittite sacred mountain. (del Monte and Tischler 1978: 58)

Battinaša (E) Elamite sacred mountain mentioned in the Persepolis Fortification Tablets. Located between the ancient towns of Mazdaguš, Hunidata, and Vaijava. A location at the modern village of Bazin beside a 3,145 m high peak is suggested by Frayne. It lies 35 kms west of modern Kazerun near Shiraz. (Henkelman, 2008: 536–37; Vallat 1993: 39; Koch 1987: 260)

Dabar (M) Deity attested in an Early Dynastic god list from Abu Ṣalābīkh. It is possible that the god is to be associated with the deified Mount Dibar or Dabar in the Ḫabur region, especially since the deified Balīḫ River, not too far from the Ḫabur, is also in the god list from Abu Ṣalābīkh. Mander notes a possible connection with a supposed god Dabir at Ebla, but his existence there is questionable. Dabir or Deber, a demon of pestilence, is known from the Hebrew Bible and is often paired with the Canaanite god of destruction Rešep(h) (Habakkuk 3: 5). See Deber. (Mander 1986: 64–65)

Ebiḫ (M), **Jebel Ḥamrīn** Deified mountain range. In "Inana and Mount Ebiḫ," Inana vanquishes her enemy, Mount Ebiḫ. The mountain corresponds to the modern Jebel Ḥamrīn, a range that crosses the Diyala River somewhat northeast of modern Baghdad. Ebiḫ stretches from the site of Aššur into the area southeast of the city as far as the Diyala River. The literary composition bears many similarities to two ancient Sumerian hymns composed by En-ḫeduana, the daughter of Sargon of Akkad, and although she is not mentioned by name in the Ebiḫ epic, she may have been responsible for its creation. Certainly, we know that King Narām-Sîn of Akkad campaigned extensively in the region of the modern-day Jebel Ḥamrīn, and thus a dating of the creation of the epic to the reign of Narām-Sîn is a distinct possibility. The mountain is cited also in royal inscriptions that postdate the Old Akkadian period. Personal names with the theophoric element Ebiḫ occurs in tablets from the Old Akkadian period. According to Frayne, a possible depiction of Mount Ebiḫ occurs on a stone plaque found at Aššur. (*LAS*: 334–38; Leick 1999: 117–18; Frayne 1997a: 22–23; Bottéro and Kramer 1989: 219–29; Limet 1971: 11–28; Gelb 1961: 56; Gelb 1938: 67; Thureau-Dangin 1934: 84–86)

Gavaraziya, Kamaraziya (E) Elamite sacred mountain in the Persepolis Fortification Tablets. Near Mount Irkamma/Rkava. Located by Frayne at modern Iranina Kamarij, 117 kms west of modern Kazerun near Shiraz. (Henkelman, 2008: 538; Vallat 1993: 123; Koch 1987: 261)

Ḥamrīn (M) See Ebiḫ

Ḫakurma (H) Hittite sacred mountain attested in a text about a monthly festival. (Lombardi 1996: 55 and note 27; del Monte and Tischler 1978: 68; Gonnet, 1968: 121 no. 64)

Ḫaḫarwa (H) Hittite sacred mountain worshipped at the city of Nerik, the latter likely located at modern Turkish Eymir. Ḫaḫarwa was probably situated not far from Nerik. The mountain may be located at modern Turkish Karalik just southeast of Eymir. (Lombardi 1996: 55 and note 32; del Monte and Tischler 1978: 62–63; Garstang and Gurney 1959: 20)

Ḫaz(z)i (H, L) Deified mountain, the modern Jebel al-Aqra‘. It is located near the mouth of the Orontes River on the Syrian-Turkish border northeast of Ugarit. The mountain is listed in Hittite ritual texts with Mount Nanni, probably a neighboring mountain or possibly an alternate name for Ḫaz(z)i. Occurs in Hittite and Levantine sources. As Ḫaz(z)i the god was worshipped by the Hurrians and Hittites. Appears in the Hittite story of Ullikummi and occurs in Hittite treaties. At the national Hittite shrine at Yazılıkaya, in the middle section of the reliefs, an image of Teššub, the chief god of the pantheon, stands on depictions of the two chief mountain gods of the pantheon, Nanni and Ḫaz(z)i. Both Mount Ḫaz(z)i and Nanni lie in the border region of the Hittite kingdom, and so processions to the mountains to provide offerings would have involved long journeys on the part of the celebrants. Mount Ḫaz(z)i corresponds to the

Ugaritic and biblical sacred mountain Ṣaphōn and to the Mount Casius of classical sources. In the Ugaritic mythic poetry, it was the home of the storm god Ba'lu/Had-(d)ad, who held the title Ba'al-Ṣapōn. In Ugaritic god lists and cultic texts Ṣapōn was considered to be a deity in his own right. The mountain appears in Philo of Byblos' *Phoenician History* as Mount Cassios. See Ṣaphōn. (Pardee 2002: 14, 42, 43, 84, 85, 284; Wyatt 2002: 99, 142, 364; Schwemer 2001: 228–29, 233, 480; del Olmo Lete 1999: 58, 68, 127; Herrmann, *DDDB*: 132; Klengel, Imparati, Haas, and van den Hout 1999: 47, 50, 138, 147, 270; Niehr, *DDDB*: 927–29; Parker 1997a: 250; Popko 1995: 97, 112, 125, 126; Attridge and Oden 1981: 50, 51; Klengel 1970: 32–35; Otten 1969: 247–60; Goetze 1940: 32–34; Dussaud 1927: 421–22; Röllig, *RlA* IV: 241–42)

Ḫul(l)a (H) Hittite sacred mountain and minor Hittite mountain goddess. Belonging to the circle of the Sun Goddess of Arinna and her daughter Mezulla. Occurring in a Hattic hymn. The mountain is mentioned in the record of a festival for the gods KAL and Ala. In a list of gods, appears with Mount Zaliyanu, perhaps located at modern Turkish Göl Dagı. (van Gessel 1998: I, 155–57; Lombardi 1996: 55 and note 31; Haas 1994: 426, 585–86; del Monte and Tischler 1978: 114; Gonnet 1968: 123–24 Laroche 1946/47: 25; Frantz-Szabó, *RlA* IV: 490)

Ḫura (H) Hittite sacred mountain located near the ancient town of Karaḫna, the latter likely modern Turkish Akören situated just west of modern Turkish Merzifon. A location of Ḫura at modern Turkish Gürlü, 108 kms northeast of Ḫattušas, is possible. (Lombardi 1996: 55 and note 31; del Monte and Tischler 1978: 68)

Ḫurma (H) Hittite sacred mountain located by some at modern Turkish Gürün in eastern Turkey, but near ancient Kalašma, likely modern Turkish Alacahan north of Gürün. Mentioned with the ancient town of Laḫuwazanti, the latter likely modern Turkish Elbistan not far south of modern Turkish Gürün. (del Monte and Tischler 1978: 124–26)

Ḫuwaḫarma (H) Hittite sacred mountain mentioned with Mount Taḫa, the latter likely located about 65 kms south of Ḫattušas. (del Monte and Tischler 1978: 130; Gonnet 1968: 124)

Irkamma (E) Elamite sacred mountain in the Persepolis Fortification Tablets. Its neighbor was Mount Gabarzya/Kamarziya. (Henkelman, 2008: 538; Vallat 1993: 113–14; Koch 1987: 261)

Izziran (E) Elamite sacred mountain possibly located at modern Tang-i-Turkhan 17 kms west of modern Kazerun near Shiraz in modern Iran. (Henkelman, 2008: 539; Vallat 1993: 120)

Kamaliya (H) Hittite sacred mountain mentioned in a record of a festival for the gods KAL and Ala, as well as a text about a monthly festival. A location at modern Turkish Çayıralan 180 kms southeast of Ḫattušas is likely. (Lombardi 1996: 55 and note 33; del Monte and Tischler 1978: 167; Gonnet 1968: 126)

Kaššu (H) Hittite sacred mountain mentioned in a royal inscription and the record of the festival for the gods KAL and Lama. To be located at modern Turkish Gezi 21 kms northeast of modern Turkish Kayseri and just southeast of ancient Kaneš. (Lombardi 1996: 55

and note 34; del Monte and Tischler 1978: 195–96; Gonnet 1968: 127)

Lullubu(m) (M) Sacred mountain, occasionally deified. A famous landmark in the Zagros chain in eastern Iraq. The mountain gave its name to the Lullubean tribes people. It is not deified in Babylonian texts, but it does appear as a divinity in some Hittite treaties. (Laroche 1976: 166; Klengel, *RlA* VII: 166)

Manuz(z)(i) (H) Storm god and deity of Mount Manuz(z)(i). Identified with Teššub. Head of the pantheon of the ancient city of Kummanni, known in Roman times as Hieropolis. Spouse of the goddess Lilluri. Manuz(z)(i) was the central deity in a ritual celebrated for the well-being of the Hittite ruler and his family. (Popko 1995: 101, 143–44, 151)

Nišba (M) Deified mountain. Probably also known as Mount Nišpi. On an Old Babylonian period tablet copy from Nippur, the Old Akkadian inscriptions of the Gutian king Erridupizir record revolts of a certain KA-Nišba "king of Simurrum," whose name contains the theophoric element Nišba. In another inscription on the same tablet, it is recorded that KA-Nišba incited the citizens of the city of Simurrum and Lullubum to revolt and tells how Erridupizir pursued the enemy forces as far as Mount Nišba, apparently a deified mountain for the Gutian people. This Nišba likely appears in the annals of Aššur-naṣir-pal II as Mount Nišpi. A comparison of the ancient place names listed in the campaign itinerary of the Aššur-nāṣir-pal II inscription with modern place names allows a tentative identification of Mount Nišba/Nišpi with the imposing peak of Šāhā-buddin located some 34 kms northeast of Sulaimānīyah in northeastern Iraq. (Shaffer and Wasserman 2003: 1–52; Kutscher 1989: 49–60; Frayne, *RlA* XII: 508)

Pišaišapḫ(i), Pḏḏpḫ, Pišaiša, Bišašapḫi, Pišaysa (H, L) A mountain god occurring with or without the divine determinative, whose Hurrian form is Piša(i)-šapḫi. Means "He of Mount Pišaiša." He occurs in cuneiform texts from Ḫattušas, the Hittite capital city. Also on a hieroglyphic Hittite rock relief from Yazılıkaya and in a god list and alphabetic texts from Ugarit. Mount Pišaiša is to be equated to ancient Bisaisa, located in the An-Nusayriyah Mountains, a range in northwestern Syria running north-south, parallel to the coastal plain. The mountain is located between classical Apamea and Laodicea, the latter modern Latakia in Syria. In classical times the range was also known as the Bargylus Mountains. Mount Pišaiša is best known from a Hurro-Canaanite text from Ḫattušas as the deity who raped Ištar, as well as being the locale of the rape. (Schwemer 2001: 233; del Olmo Lete 1999: 85; Leick 1998: 122; van Gessel 1998: I, 359–61; Popko 1995: 127; Haas 1994: 463; Laroche 1977: 202; Laroche 1946/47: 57; Miller, *RlA* X: 576–77)

Puškurunuwa (H) Hittite sacred mountain mentioned in the record of a festival for the gods KAL and Ala and in that of the AN.TA.ŠUM festival. Perhaps located at modern Turkish Pazarören. It lies 198 kms southeast of Ḫattušas. (Lombardi 1996: 56 and note 35; del Monte and Tischler 1978: 324–25; Gonnet 1968: 133)

Saggar (L) Deified Syrian mountain. It appears in the god list An : *Anum* as the spouse of the goddess Išḫara. Mount Saggar likely corresponds the modern

Jebel Sinjar mountain range. The Sinjar mountain range lies southeast of the Ḫabur River basin, and it separates the Jezirah area of eastern Syria from the Tigris basin region of Upper Mesopotamia. (Litke 1998: 166; Stol 1979: 75–82; Dossin 1950: no. 26)

Šariša (H) Hittite sacred mountain mentioned with ancient mountains Zaliyanu and Puškurunuwa. A location at modern Turkish Sarız, 234 kms southeast of Ḫattušas, is suggested by Frayne. (Lombardi 1996: 56 and note 37; del Monte and Tischler 1978: 352; Gonnet 1968: 134–35)

Šinapši (L) Deified Syrian mountain. The mountain is recorded as a recipient of offerings in texts from Emar. It likely corresponds to the ancient Ebla place name Sanabzugum. A likely location is at modern Zanboug on the Balīḫ River north of ancient Emar. (Fleming 2000: 178; Archi, Piacentini, and Pomponio: 1993: 420–21)

Širumanda, Çiravanta (E) Elamite sacred mountain mentioned in the Persepolis Fortification Tablets. A location at modern Churum situated around 22 kms west of modern Kazerun near Shiraz is likely. (Henkelman, 2008: 538; Vallat 1993: 260; Koch 1987: 261)

Šumiyara (H) Hittite sacred mountain located near ancient Mounts Puškurunuwa and Arnuwanda. Probably located at modern Turkish Demirciören, 186 kms southeast of Ḫattušas. (del Monte and Tischler 1978: 366)

Ṣapōn, Ṣapān, Ṣapūna, Ṣaphōn, Zaphōn (L) See Ḫaz(z)i

Taḫa (H) Hittite sacred mountain located between the ancient towns of Ankuwa (likely modern Turkish Ekinciusagi) and Zippalanda (likely modern Turkish Sefaatli). May plausibly be located at the modern Turkish village of Tahiroğlu situated about 65 kms south of Ḫattušas. (van Gessel 1998: I, 35–36, 423; Haas 1994: 590; Wiggermann 1992: 153, 155; del Monte and Tischler 1978; 375–76; Gonnet 1968; 134–35)

Taḫalmuna (H) Hittite sacred mountain located near ancient Nerik and Mount Ḫaḫarwa, possibly at modern Turkish Hımiroğlu just west of Ortaköy southeast of modern Ḫattušas. (del Monte and Tischler 1978: 375; Gonnet 1975: 375)

Takurka (H) Hittite sacred mountain located near ancient Ḫanḫana, the latter likely modern Turkish Kavaklan, whereas the mountain is likely to be situated at modern Turkish Ortaköy, both 51 kms northeast of Ḫattušas. (del Monte and Tischler 1978: 387–88)

Tapala (H) Hittite sacred mountain possibly located at modern Turkish Felahiye, 126 kms southeast of modern Turkish Ḫattušas. (del Monte and Tischler 1978: 397; Güterbock 1960: 87)

Tata (H) Hittite sacred mountain located near ancient Mount Puškurunuwa. (del Monte and Tischler 1978: 413)

Tibar/Dibar (L) Deified Syrian mountain mentioned in an inscription of Narām-Sîn as the site where the king killed a wild bull. Tibar is also to be associated with the element *Tibar*, which appears in theophoric names in Old Akkadian texts. Stol suggests a connection with the modern Jebel 'Abd al 'Azīz range, which lies south of the Ḫabur river basin just west of the modern Jebel Sinjar. We suggest a location for ancient Tibar at modern Tell Bardé (the result of a mix-up of letter order), a 370 m high elevation that lies not far east of modern Tell Brak. (Stol 1979: 25–30)

Tippuwa (H) Sacred Hittite mountain located at modern Turkish Tayyıp, 27 kms southeast of modern Turkish Ḫattušas. (del Monte and Tischler 1978: 426–27; Gonnet 1976: 144; Güterbock 1960: 85)

Tuḫaliya (H) Hittite sacred mountain mentioned with Mount Tapala. Likely located at modern Turkish Eğli just northwest of modern Turkish Felahiye. Various Hittite kings adopted the mountain name as their name. (del Monte and Tischler 1978: 446; Gonnet 1976: 143)

Tutḫaliya (H) Hittite sacred mountain. Several Hittite kings were named after this god, including Tutḫaliya III, the father of conqueror Šuppiluliuma I. (Leick 1998: 122; Popko 1995: 55)

Zaliyanu (H) Mountain god, deified mountain near the northern city of Nerik and the ancient town of Kaštama. Though he could cause rain to fall, he was not a storm god. Worshipped at Kaštama near Nerik, along with his spouse Zašḫapuna and his concubine Tazzuwaši. Had an important role in the "Illuyanka Tales." Mentioned in a text concerning Nerik and the storm god of Nerik. At a festival, on the ninth day of which the (high?) priest of the cult at Kaštama processed, wooden lances of Zaliyanu were set up as part of the ceremony. (Hoffner 1998: 12, 14, 113; van Gessel 1998: I, 571–72; Popko 1995: 114; Haas 1994: 446, 462, 478. 599; del Monte and Tischler 1978: 489–90; Laroche 1946/47: 38)

Zašḫapuna, Zaḫapuna, Tašḫapuna (H) Hittite/Hattic goddess. Might have been a deified mountain. In the circle of the storm god of Nerik. Hattic *puna/pinu* means "child." Hattic name Tašḫapuna. At her cult center Kaštama, north of Ḫattušas in central Anatolia, she was spouse of the mountain god Zaliyanu and first among goddesses. She occurs in one version of the "Illuyanka Tales." Mentioned in a prayer of Muwatalli II. There was also a festival that focused on her. (Hoffner 1998: 13–14; Leick 1998: 122; van Gessel 1998: I, 566–70; Popko 1995: 114, 122, 147; Haas 1994: 310, 446–47, 463, 478, 498, 539, 597–601, 701, 705–6, 741, 777; Laroche 1946/47: 38–39)

III. Deified Rulers

A number of Mesopotamian kings were considered to be divine during their lifetime. The practice seems to have begun in the Old Akkadian period with Narām-Sîn, continued in the reign of Narām-Sîn's son and successor Šar-kali-šarrī, and was revived by Šulgi in the Ur III period. The following kings had their names written in royal inscriptions and year names with the prefixed divine determinative: Narām-Sîn and Šar-kali-šarrī of the Old Akkadian period; Šulgi, Amar-Suen, Šū-Sîn, and Ibbi-Sîn of the Ur III Dynasty; Šū-ilišu, Iddin-Dagān, Išme-Dagān, Lipit-Ištar, Ur-Ninurta, Būr-Sîn, Lipit-Enlil, Erra-imittī, Enlil-bāni, Zambīya, Iter-pûša, Ur-dukuga, Sîn-māgir, Damiq-ilīšu of the Isin Dynasty; and Rīm-Sîn I and Rīm-Sîn II of the Larsa Dynasty. Although the divine sign did not appear before their names in year names, Ḫammu-rāpi and Samsu-iluna of the First Dynasty of Babylon were treated as deified in hymns composed in their honor.

Those deified in their lifetime were worshipped with ritual and sacrifice. For instance, a temple built especially for the worship of Šū-Sîn is known from Ešnunna. It is likely that the end of the custom of considering kings as living gods came, if not before, with the last king of the First Dynasty of Babylon, Samsu-Ditānu, who died probably around 1595 BCE.

Deification of humans was not restricted to rulers. Ancestors could assume such form, as, for example, the *rephaim* at Ugarit. Others could achieve deification through their achievements, as, perhaps, with Dada-gula (see above), who may have been a famous harpist. However, among the rulers deified in their lifetime, only a few withstood the test of time; that is to say, they were still being venerated as gods long after their dynasty and its political influence had ended. The following are those who did endure as gods.

Āmmiṭtamru (L) A deified king of Ugarit, one of the Malikūma. (del Olmo Lete 1999: 139)

Āmmu-rāpī (L) A deified king of Ugarit, one of the Malikūma. (del Olmo Lete 1999: 139)

Anbu (M) Possibly a deified king of Mari. Anbu was honored in the cult at Nippur both by his appearance in the Sumerian King List and by being named in the great god list An : *Anum*. Glossed a-an-bu. (Litke 1998: 44; Vincente 1995: 241, 257)

Bazi (M) A herding god, described as a ram (*kazzu(m)*), whose home was mythical Mount Bašār, likely marked by the ancient Mount Bašār. The god is the subject of an Akkadian myth concerning his attempt to find a home for himself and his herds. Since the literary text is from Mesopotamia, it seems clear that the tradition concerning Bazi spread to the south from Syria. The human Bazi is attested as a legendary ruler of the city of Mari in the Tell Leilān recension of the Sumerian King List. The name is common in third-millennium Mesopotamia, at Mari, and elsewhere, and it is possible, albeit not certain, that Bazi was a real figure who was (later?) divinized. He appears also in the so-called "Ballad of Early Rulers," a second-millennium bilingual composition attested at Sippar, Emar, and Ugarit. (George 2009: 11; Alster 2005: 315; Vincente 1995: 258)

Danel, Danilu (L) Divinized ancestor, one of the Rephaim, and legendary king from Ugarit. In the Ugaritic story of ʻAqhat, after being childless for a long time, Danel successfully sacrificed to the god El for a son ʻAqhat. When ʻAqhat refused to give the goddess ʻAnat(u) the beautiful bow made for him by the craftsman god Koṯar, ʻAnat(u) had ʻAqhat killed. There seems little connection between Danel and the biblical Daniel other than the name. (Leeming 2005: 92–93; Wyatt 2002: 246–12; Collins, *DDDB*: 219–20; del Olmo Lete 1999: 57, 354; Parker 1997a: 49–80; Howard, *ABD* II: 17–18)

Ditānu(m), Dedān, Datān, Ditān (Akk.) (L, M) Deified ancestor of the Assyrian and Ugaritic royal line. In addition, the Didānu, Ditānu, or Tidānu was an Amorite tribe living in the westernMesopotamia. Šulgi built a wall to keep them and other foreigners out of his kingdom. Ditānu means "Bison" or "Aurochs." See Rephaim. (del Olmo Lete 1999: 311, 313; Leick 1999: 153; Spronk, *DDDB*: 232–33; Steinkeller 1992: 262)

Elissa, Dido(n) (L) Divinized, legendary Phoenician founder of Carthage. Princess of Tyre. Sister of Pygmalion, king of Tyre, and wife of Sic(h)arbas, wealthy priest of the god Melqart. According to the legend, when Pygmalion had Elissa's husband killed, she left Tyre with a group of companions taking with her Sic(h)arbas's assets and the cult objects of Melqart to ensure the god's protection. After a short stay in Cyprus, she led her group, now enhanced by a considerable number of young Cypriote women, to Libya, where she obtained land from the local king by means of a clever ruse. To avoid marriage with another local king, she committed suicide by throwing herself on a pyre. In Virgil's *Aeneid* Dido killed herself in the same way when her lover Aeneas deserted her to follow his destiny as founder of Rome. According to the legend, Elissa established a sacred wood for Juno at Carthage, but other Greco-Roman writers reported that it was Elissa herself who was venerated there. Elissa was great-niece of Jezebel, who married Ahab, king of Israel. (Hunt 2019; Quinn 2018: 115; Noël 2014: 217; Ball 2009: 20–22; Markoe 2000: 129; Moscati 1999: 114–15; Lipiński 1995: 407–11; Bonnet, *DCPP*: 150; Herm 1975: 182–84; Harden 1963: 51, 52, 58, 66; Virgil's *Aeneid* Book IV)

Enme(r)kar (M) Divinized and legendary hero-king of Uruk. Father of Lugal-banda and grand-father of Gilgameš. Appears in the Sumerian King List as having built Uruk and having ruled 420 years. (Foster 2001: 223; Jacobsen 1939: 83; Oppenheim, *ANET*: 266)

Etana (M) In the Sumerian King List, a divinized post-Flood hero-king of first dynasty of Kiš, "a shepherd who ascended to heaven" (Oppenheim, *ANET*: 265). According to a Babylonian story, when searching for a birth-giving plant, which grew only in heaven, childless Etana rescued a wounded eagle and then flew to heaven on its back. (Foster 2005: 533–54; Black and Green 2003: 78; Leick 1998: 60–61; Speiser, *ANET*: 114–18)

Gilgameš, Bilgameš (M), **Galgamiš** (H) Demigod and legendary hero. Early king (*lugal*) of Inana's city of Uruk and Lord (*en*) of Kul(l)aba, a district or town near Uruk. The Sumerian King List describes him as: "the divine Gilgameš, his father was a *lillû*, a high priest [En] of Kullab, ruled 126 years"

(Oppenheim, *ANET*: 266). After death, he became a governor and judge in the netherworld. Bilgameš is the actual form of his name, and its meaning is disputed. The usual translation, based on understanding of the "Epic of Gilgameš," is "The Old Man who Is Once Again a Young Man" but this almost certainly is not the original meaning of the name. Another possible interpretation is "The Progenitor (*pabilga*) (is as Fruitful as) the *Mes* (Hackberry) Tree/Bush."

Son of Lugalbanda or of a *lil* spirit (possibly an incubus) and the goddess Nin-sun. Later, the kings Ur-Namma and Šulgi claimed him as brother, that is, companion. In An : *Anum* he comes at the end of the gods associated with Nergal, king of the netherworld. The hymn "Šulgi O" recorded that Šulgi had a statue made of his brother Gilgameš and installed it in Nanna's E-kiš-nugal temple at Ur. In addition to "Handsome," some of his epithets were: "Offspring of Uruk," "He who Rules the Land," "Lord of Oaths," "Perfect in Strength," "Lord of the Lower Regions," and "Commander of the Anunnaki Gods."

His principal role in myth was as the hero of a cycle of short Sumerian epic compositions on tablets dating from the early second millennium BCE and also of the Babylonian "Epic of Gilgameš," which is extant in many versions from Mesopotamia, as well as from Syria, the Levant, and Turkey (Hittite). The Sumerian compositions consist of "Gilgameš and Akka," "Gilgameš and Ḫuwawa A," "Gilgameš and Ḫuwawa B," "Gilgameš and the Bull of Heaven," "The Gudam Epic," "Gilga-meš, Enkidu, and the netherworld," and "The Death of Gilgameš." The Babylonian epic is clearly based on the Sumerian compositions, but there are a number of differences. For instance, the story of the Great Flood is extant in the Babylonian epic, but not in Sumerian, though it was clearly alluded to in "The Death of Gilgameš" and also in a Sumerian fragment. Texts often refer to Gilgameš as a judge in the netherworld. Gilgameš's name occurs in the god lists from Šuruppak, which are dated to the Early Dynastic period and in similar lists of the slightly later date from Ur and Bad-tibira.

Detail depicting Gilgameš from cylinder seal. Ca. 2350–2150 BCE. Serpentine. 8.4 x 2.3 cm. British Museum no. 129479. After Collon 1982: pl. XXXI, no. 213.

Gilgameš µreceived offerings at, among other places, Lagaš in the Ur III period. During the same time he was worshipped at Ennegi, a city of the dead near Ur. He also was honored at Uruk on a regular basis. On the fourth day of the Baba Festival at Lagaš, Gilgameš was among the deities who received offerings. The latter offerings took place along the "Banks of Gilgameš," perhaps a site of the performance of rites for the dead. There might also have been a town of that name. The fifth month at Uruk was named for Gilgameš and became a time throughout Mesopotamia when sporting contests were held.

Scenes of Gilgameš and Enkidu killing Ḫuwawa and, later in the epic, the Bull of Heaven, often appear on cylinder seals. And other images of Gilgameš have now been identified. (Frayne 2010: 165–208; *LAS*: 31–40, 212–15; Black and Green 2003: 89–91; Foster 2001: 1–95; Frayne 2001: 97–155; Leick 1998: 68; Litke 1998: 220; Selz 1995: 105–6; Cohen 1993: 54, 319–20, 463; Sallaberger 1993: I, 212 note 1003; Krebernik 1986: 193, as [d]Bìl-gam-mes; Mander 1986: 64; Tallqvist 1974: 312; Falkenstein 1966: 67; Edzard 1965: 69–73; Falkenstein and Calmeyer, *RlA* III: 357–74)

Ḫadaniš (M) In the Early Dynastic period, he was a king of Ḫamazi, a city in the Zagros Mountains in what is now eastern Iraq. According to Jacobsen, Ḫadaniš's dedication of a statue to the priests in Nippur assured him a position in the Sumerian King List. Mentioned in an Old Babylonian god list and in An : *Anum*, as a protective deity of the Ekur. (Litke 1998: 42; Jacobsen 1939: 98–99; Edzard, *RlA* IV: 38)

Kirta (L) Divinized Ugaritic king. In "The Epic of Kirta," he is called "the son of [the god] Ilu." After his death, he became one of the Malikūma or Rapa'ūma. See Rephaim. (del Olmo Lete 1999: 139, 325–26, 333)

Lugalbanda (M) Deified Sumerian hero-king and warrior of early Uruk. His wife was Ninsun, the wild-cow goddess, and one of their sons was the hero Gilgameš. Lugalbanda's name, which means "Small (or Impetuous) King," was known as early as the Early Dynastic period. He appears in the Sumerian King List as "the god Lugalbanda, a shepherd, ruled 1,200 years" (Oppenheim, *ANET*: 266). In one temple list he was presented as an aspect of Ninurta, a warrior god. Lugalbanda was the protagonist of two Sumerian heroic narratives: "Lugalbanda in the Mountain Cave" and "Lugalbanda and the Anzû Bird." In the former Lugalbanda conquered mountains and wilderness despite being infected with a deathly illness, and in the latter he managed to make friends with the fierce Anzû, who declared him a hero made strong by Anzû. At the end of the composition his close relationship with Inana was evident, for she was gazing at him in the way she would look at Dumuzi. Lugalbanda was the personal god of Šulgi, and every king of the Ur III period made offerings to him at Nippur, where he had his own temple. Lugalbanda was worshipped also at, among other places, Umma and Babylon. At Uruk, he shared a temple with Nin-sun and had his own high-priestess. (*LAS*: 11–31; Black and Green 2003: 123; Leick 1999: 153; Leick 1998: 110–11; Litke 1998: 167–68; Cohen 1993: 86, 87; George 1993: 6, 93 no.

386, 110 no. 598, 138 no. 953, 166 no. 1345; Jacobsen 1976: 158; Tallqvist 1974: 351; Wilcke, *RlA* VII: 117–32)

Lugal-gešur, (M) God identified with Nergal. Probably the deified first king of Kiš. Means "King [of the] Beam(s)." (Litke 1998: 203; Tallqvist 1974: 353; Lambert, *RlA* VII: 140)

Maništusu (M) Akkadian name of a divinized king of the Sargonic period. Regnal dates 2275–2260 BCE. Attested also in two tablets from the Ur III period.

Namḫani (M) Deified governor of the state of Lagaš, attested in Šulgi's forty-second year on a tablet from Umma and in his forty-seventh on a tablet from Girsu that refers to his temple or shrine. His living son Lu-Nanna is attested from the first two years of Amar-Suena. (Sallaberger 1999: 288–90; Englund 1990: 60–63; Hussey 1915: 4)

Niqmad(du) (L) A deified king of Ugarit, one of the Malikūma. (del Olmo Lete 1999: 139, 170–73, 179)

Šarelli (L) Probably a deified queen or queenly title at Ugarit. (del Olmo Lete 1999: 197)

Ur-Zababa (M) Deified ancient king of Kiš, who, according to legend, was defeated by Sargon. The latter had been Ur-Zababa's cup-bearer. Means "Servant of Zababa." (Litke 1998: 51; Cooper and Heimpel 1983: 67–82)

Yaqaru (L) A deified king at Ugarit, the "legendary founder of the dynasty." (del Olmo Lete 1999: 179)

BIBLIOGRAPHY

Ackerman, Susan. 1989. "And the Women Knead Dough': The Worship of the Queen of Heaven in Sixth-Century Judah." Pp. 109–24 in *Gender and Difference in Ancient Israel.* Edited by Peggy L. Day. Minneapolis, Minn.: Fortress

Ackerman, Susan. 1992. *Under Every Green Tree: Popular Religion in Sixth-Century Judah.* Atlanta, Ga.: Scholars Press

Alaura, Silvia, and Marco Bonechi. 2012 "Il Carro del Rio del Sole nei Testi Cuneiformi dell'Età del Bronzo." *Studi Micenei ed Egeo-Anatolic* 54: 5–115

Alberti, A. 1985. "A Reconstruction of the Abū Salābīkh God-List." *Studi Epigrafici e Linguistici sul Vicino Oriente Antico* 2: 3–23

Albright, William F. 1935. "The Names of Shaddai and Abram." *Journal of Biblical Literature* 54: 180–93

Albright, William F. 1968. *Yahweh and the Gods of Canaan: A Historical Analysis of Two Contrasting Faiths.* Garden City, N.Y.: Doubleday

Alster, Bendt. 1972. *Dumuzi's Dream: Aspects of Oral Poetry in a Sumerian Myth.* Copenhagen: Akademisk

Alster, Bendt. 1991. "Contributions to the Sumerian Lexicon." *Revue d'Assyriologie et d'Archéologie Orientale* 85: 1–5

Alster, Bendt. 1997. *Proverbs of Ancient Sumer.* Bethesda, Md., CDL Press

Alster, Bendt. 2004. "Exit Ašimbabbar? The Reading of ^{d}Aš/dili-ím-barbar [sic]." *Journal of Cuneiform Studies* 56: 1–3

Alster, Bendt. 2005. *The Wisdom of Ancient Sumer.* Bethesda, Md.: CDL Press

Anderson, Gary A. 2001. *The Genesis of Perfection: Adam and Eve in Jewish and Christian Imagination.* Louisville, Ky.: Westminster/John Knox

Andersson, J. 2013. "58) The God ^{d}NE.DAG = 'Torch'?" *Nouvelles Assyriologiques Brèves et Utilitaires* (N.A.B.U): 99–100

Annus, Amar 2002. *The God Ninurta in the Mythology and Royal Ideology of Ancient Mesopotamia.* Helsinki: The Neo-Assyrian Text Corpus Project

(The) Apocrypha. King James Version. [No date]. New York: Harper and Brothers

Archi, Alfonso. 1990. "The Names of the Primeval Gods." *Orientalia,* new series, 59, pp. 114–29

Archi, Alfonso. 1993. "Divinités sémitiques et divinités de substrat: le cas d'Išḫara et Ištar á Ebla." Pp. 71–78 in *Mari 7: Annales de Recherches Interdisciplinaires.* Paris: Éditions Recherche sur les Civilisations

Archi, Alfonso. 1994. "Studies in the Pantheon of Ebla. II." *Orientalia,* new series, 63: 414–25

Archi, Alfonso. 1997. "Studies in the Pantheon of Ebla." *Orientalia,* new series, 66: 249–56

Archi, Alfonso, Paola Scarcia Piacentini, and Francesco Pomponio. 1993. *I nomi di luogo dei testi di Ebla: (ARET 1–IV, VII–X e altri documenti editi e inediti).*

Roma: Missione archeologica italiana in Siria

Archi, Alfonso, Francesco Pomponio, and Giovanni Bergamini. 1995. *Testi cuneiformi neo-sumerici da Umma: NN0413–0723.* Turin, Italy: Ministero per i beni culturli e ambientali, Soprintendenza al Museodella antichità egizie

Archi, Alfonso. 2004. "Translation of Gods: Kumarpi, Enlil, Dagan/NISABA, Ḫalki." *Orientalia*, new series, 73: 319–36

Arnaud, Daniel. 1986. *Recherches aux pays d'Aštata.* Emar VI/3. Paris: Éditions Recherche sur les Civilisations

Aruz, Joan, with Ronald Wallenfels. 2003. *Art of the First Cities: The Third Millennium B.C. from the Mediterranean to the Indus.* New York: Metropolitan Museum of Art and New Haven, Ct.: Yale University Press

Aruz, Joan and Michael Seymour, eds. 2016. *Assyria to Iberia: Art and Culture in the Iron Age.* New York: Metropolitan Museum of Art

Assante, Julia. 1998. "The kar.kid/*ḫarimtu*, Prostitute or Single Woman? A Reconsideration of the Evidence." *Ugarit-Forschungen* 30: 5–96

Assante, Julia. 2003. "From Whores to Hierodules: The Historiographic Invention of Mesopotamian Female Sex Professionals." Pp. 13–47 in *Ancient Art and Its Historiography.* Edited by A. A. Donahue and M. D. Fullerton. Cambridge: Cambridge University Press

Assmann, Jan. 1998. *Moses the Egyptian: The Memory of Egypt in Western Monotheism.* Cambridge. Mass.: Harvard University Press

Atallah, Wahib. 1966. *Adonis dans la literature et l'art grecs.* Paris: Klincksieck

Attinger, Pascal. 1984. "Enki et Ninhursaga." *Zeitschrift für Assyriologie* 74: 1–52

Attinger, Pascal. 1992. Review of *Le clergé d'Ur au siècle d'Hammurabi: (XIXe–XVIIe siècles av. J.-C.)*, by Dominique Charpin. *Zeitschrift für Assyriologie* 82: 125–31

Attinger, Pascal. 1995. "33) ^{d}nin-mar-ki-ga." *Nouvelles Assyriologiques Brèves et Utilitaires* (N.A.B.U): 27–29

Attridge, Harold W., and Robert A. Oden, eds./trans. 1976. *The Syrian Goddess (De Dea Syria): Attributed to Lucian.* [No place]: Scholars Press /Society of Biblical Literature

Attridge, Harold W., and Robert A. Oden, eds./trans. 1981. *Philo of Byblos. The Phoenician History: Introduction, Critical Text, Translation, Notes.* Washington, D.C.: Catholic Biblical Association of America

Aubet, Maria Eugenia. 2016. "Phoenician Politics in Colonial Context: Pyrgi Again." Pp. 147–53 in *Assyria to Iberia: Art and Culture in the Iron Age.* Edited by J. Aruz and M. Seymour. New York: Metropolitan Museum of Art

Bal, Mieke. 1988. *Murder and Difference: Gender, Genre, and Scholarship on Sisera's Death.* Bloomington, Ind.: Indiana University Press

Balkan, Kemal. 1978 (1954). *Kassiter Studien. 1. Die Sprache der Kassiter.* Millwood, N.Y.: Klaus Reprints

Ball, Warwick. 2009. *Out of Arabia: Phoenicians, Arabs and the Discovery of Europe.* London: East and West

Bartash, Vitali. 2013. *Miscellaneous Early Dynastic and Sargonic Texts in the Cornell University Collections.* CUSAS 23. Bethesda, Md.: CDL Press

Basello, Gian Pietro. 2013. "From Susa to Persepolis." Pp. 249–64 in K. De Graef and J. Tavenier, *Susa and Elam, Archaeological, Philological, Historical and Geographical Perspectives*. MDP 58. Leiden: Brill, 2012

Basile, Joseph J. 2002. "Two Visual Languages at Petra: Aniconic and Representational Sculpture of the Great Temple." *Near Eastern Archaeology* 65: 255–58

Baudisson, Wolf W. G. 1911. *Adonis und Eshmun: Eine Untersuchung zur Geschichte des Glaubens an Auferstehungsgötter und an Heilgötter*. Leipzig: Hinrichs

Baumgarten, Albert I. 1989. *The Phoenician History of Philo of Byblos: A Commentary*. Leiden, Netherlands: Brill

Beach, Eleanor F. 2005. *The Jezebel Letters: Religion and Politics in Ninth-Century Israel*. Philadelphia: Fortress

Beaulieu, Paul-Alain. 1989. "64) A Neo-Babylonian Text Mentioning Belet-duri." *Nouvelles Assyriologiques Brèves et Utilitaires* (N.A.B.U): 41–42

Beaulieu, Paul-Alain. 2003. *The Pantheon of Uruk during the Neo-Babylonian Period*. Cuneiform Monographs 23. Leiden: Brill; Groningen, Netherlands: Styx

Beckman, Gary. 1996. *Texts from the Vicinity of Emar in the Collection of Jonathan Rosen*. Padua, Italy: Sargon

Beckman, Gary. 1998. "Ishtar of Nineveh Reconsidered." *Journal of Cuneiform Studies* 50: 1–9

Bedal, Leigh-Ann. 2002. "Desert Oasis: Water Consumption and Display in the Nabataean Capital." *Near Eastern Archaeology* 65: 225–34

Belmonte Marin, Juan Antonio. 2001. *Die Orts- und Gewässernamen der Texte aus Syrien im 2. Jt. v. Chr.* Wiesbaden, Germany: Reichert

Benito, Carlos. 1969. *"Enki and Ninmaḫ" and "Enki and the World Order."* Unpublished Ph.D. dissertation, University of Pennsylvania

Bermant, C. and M. Weitzman. 1979. *Ebla: An Archaeological Enigma*. London: Weidenfeld and Nicolson

Betlyon, J. W. 1985. "The Cult of Ašerah at Sidon." *Journal of Near Eastern Studies* 44: 53–56

Betlyon, John W. 2005. "A People Transformed: Palestine in the Persian Period." *Near Eastern Archaeology* 68: 4–58

Biale, David. 1982. "God with Breasts: El Shaddai in the Bible." *History of Religions* 21: 240–56

Biblia Hebraica Stuttgartensia. . . . 1967–1977. Edited by R. Kittel. Re-edited by K. Elliger and K. Rudolph. Stuttgart, Germany: Deutsche Bibelstiftung

Bienkowski, Piotr and Alan Millard, eds. 2000. *Dictionary of the Ancient Near East*. Philadelphia: University of Pennsylvania Press

Bierling, Marilyn R., ed./trans. 2002. *The Phoenicians in Spain*. Winona Lake, Ind.: Eisenbrauns

Biggs, Robert. 1974. *Inscriptions from Abū Ṣālābīkh*. Chicago: University of Chicago Press

Binger, Tilde. 1997. *Asherah: Goddesses in Ugarit, Israel, and the Old Testament*. Sheffield, UK: Sheffield Academic

Binst, Olivier, ed. 2000. *The Levant: History and Archaeology in the Eastern Mediterranean*. Cologne: Könemann

Birchler, Anne. 2006. "Quelques réflexions sur la montagne comme lieu de culte des Hittites." *Res Antiquae* 3: 165–77

Birot, Maurice, Jean Ronbert Kupper, and Olivier Rouault. 1979. *Répertoire analytique (2e volume): Tomes I–XIV, XVIII et textes divers hors-collection. Première partie, noms propres.* Paris: Geuthner

Bittel, Kurt, Rudolf Naumann, and Heinz Otto. 1967. *Yazilikaya: Architektur, Felsbilder, Inschriften und Kleinfunde.* Osnabrück, Germany: Zeller

Black, Jeremy. 1985. "A-še-er Gi$_6$-ta, A Balag of Inanna." *Acta Sumerologica* 7: 11–87

Black, Jeremy, et al., eds. 2003. The Electronic Text Corpus of Sumerian Literature. www.etcsl.orinst.ox.ac.uk

Black, Jeremy, Graham Cunningham, Eleanor Robson, and Gábor Zólyomi, eds./trans. 2004. *The Literature of Ancient Sumer.* Oxford: Oxford University Press

Black, Jeremy, Andrew George, and Nicholas Postgate. 2000. *A Concise Dictionary of Akkadian.* Wiesbaden, Germany: Harrassowitz

Black, Jeremy and Anthony Green. 2003 (1992). *Gods, Demons, and Symbols of Ancient Mesopotamia.* Austin, Tex.: University of Texas Press

Boehmer, Rainer M. 1985. *Die Entwicklung der Glyptik während der Akkadzeit.* Berlin: de Gruyter

Bonechi, Marco. 1993a. *I nomi geografici dei testi di Ebla.* Wiesbaden, Germany: Reichert

Bonechi, Marco. 1993b. "24) A propos du sexe et de l'identification de ^{d}Kakka, á Mari." *Nouvelles Assyriologiques Brèves et Utilitaires* (N.A.B.U): 20–21

Bonechi, M. 1997. "Lexique et ideologie royale a l'epoque proto-syrienne." *MARI* 8, 477–535

Bongenaar, A. C. V. M. 1997. *The Neo-Babylonian Ebabbar Temple at Sippar: Its Administration and Its Prosopography.* Istanbul: Nederlands Historisch-Archaeologisch Instituut

Bonnet, Corinne. 1988. *Melqart: cultes et mythes de Héraclès tyrien en Méditerranée.* Leuven, Belgium: Peeters

Bonnet, Corinne. 1996. *Astarte: Dossier documentaire et perspectives historiques.* Rome: Collezione di Studi Fenici 37

Bonnet, Corinne, E. Lipiński, and P. Marchetti, eds. 1986. *Phoenicia.* Namur, Belgium: Societé Des études classiques.

Borger, Rykle. 1970. "Zwei Grenzsteinurkunden Merodachbaladans I. von Babylonien." *Archiv für Orientforschung* 23: 1–26

Bottéro, Jean. 1991. "La 'tenson' et la réflexion sur les choses en Mésopotamie." Pp. 7–22 in *Dispute Poems and Dialogues in the Ancient and Medieval Near East.* Edited by G. Reinink and Herman L. J. Vanstiphout. Orientalia Lovaniensia Analecta, 42. Leuven: Peeters

Bottéro, Jean and S. N. Kramer. 1989. *Lorsque les dieux faisaient l'homme.* Paris: Gallimard

Bowker, John, ed. 1997. *The Oxford Dictionary of World Religions.* Oxford: Oxford University Press

Bowman, Charles H. 1978. *The Goddess 'Anatu in the Ancient Near East.* Unpublished Ph.D. dissertation, Graduate Theological Union

Brinkman, J. A. 1976. *Materials and Studies for Kassite History,* volume 1, *A Catalogue of Cuneiform Sources Pertaining to Specific Monarchs of the Kassite Dynasty.* Chicago: Oriental Institute of the University of Chicago

Brody, Aaron J. 1998. *"Each Man Cried Out to His God": The Specialized Religion of Canaanite and Phoenician Sailors.* Atlanta, Ga.: Scholars Press

Brown, F., S. R. Driver, and C.A. Briggs. 1978. *A Hebrew and English Lexicon of the Old Testament*.... Oxford: Clarendon

Buchanan, Briggs. 1966. *Catalogue of Ancient Near Eastern Seals in the Ashmolean Museum,* volume 1, *Cylinder Seals.* Oxford: Clarendon

Budge, E. A. Wallis. 1969 (1904). *The Gods of the Egyptians: Studies in Egyptian Mythology.* Two volumes. N.Y.: Dover

Burkert, Walter. 1985. *Greek Religion.* Cambridge, Mass.: Harvard University Press

Burkert, Walter. 1987. *Ancient Mystery Cults.* Cambridge, Mass.: Harvard University Press

Butler, Sally A. L. 1998. *Mesopotamian Conceptions of Dreams and Dream Rituals.* Münster, Germany: Ugarit-Verlag

Buttrick, G. A., et al. 1991. *The Interpreter's Dictionary of the Bible: An Illustrated Encyclopedia.* Four volumes and supplementary volume (1992). Nashville, Tenn.: Abingdon

Caquot, André. 1960. "Le Rephaim ougaritiques." *Syria* 37: 79–90

Caquot, André. 2000. "At the Origins of the Bible." *Near Eastern Archaeology* 63: 224–27

Caquot, André and Maurice Sznycer. 1980. *Ugaritic Religion.* Leiden, Netherlands: Brill

Carter, Jane B. 1987. "The Masks of Ortheia." *American Journal of Archaeology* 91: 355–83

Castellino, G. 1959. "Urnammu/Three Religious Texts." *Zeitschrift für Assyriologie* 53: 106–32

Catagnoti, Amalia. 1992. "61) Du nouveau sur le «lance sacrée»." *Nouvelles Assyriologiques Brèves et Utilitaires* (N.A.B.U): 47

Catagnoti, Amalia. 2009. "42) A Further Attestation of ^{d}Gi$_{6}$-an at Ebla." *Nouvelles Assyriologiques Brèves et Utilitaires* (N.A.B.U): 55–56

Caubet, Annie. 2000. "Ugarit at the Louvre Museum." *Near Eastern Archaeology* 63: 216–19

Cavigneaux, Antoine. 1992. "113) Une nouvelle graphie du dieu Asgi." *Nouvelles Assyriologiques Brèves et Utilitaires* (N.A.B.U): 84

Cavigneaux, Antoine. 1996. *URUK.: Altbabylonische Texte aus dem Planquadrat Pe XVI–4/5* .... Mainz am Rhein, Germany: von Zabern

Cavigneaux, Antoine and Faruk N. H. Al-Rawi. 1993. "Gilgameš et Taureau de ciel (Šul-mè-kam) (Textes de Tell Haddad IV)." *Revue d'Assyriologie et d'archéologie orientale* 87: 97–129

Cavigneaux, Antoine and R. M. Boehmer. 1996. *Uruk.: Altbabylonische Texte aus dem Planquadrat Pe XVI–4/5 nach Kopien von Adam Falkenstein.* Mainz am Rhein, Germany: von Zabern

Charpin, Dominique. 1986. *Le clergé d'Ur au siècle d'Hammurabi: (XIXe–XVIIIe siècles av. J.-C.).* Geneva: Droz

Charpin, Dominique. 1987a. "Tablettes présargonique de Mari." Pp. 65–129 in *Mari 5: Annales de Recherches Interdisciplinaires.* Paris: Éditions Recherche sur les Civilisations

Charpin, Dominique. 1987b. "119) Le dieu Idrab." *Nouvelles Assyriologiques Brèves et Utilitaires* (N.A.B.U): 68

Charpin, Dominique. 1988. "32) Le repli des cultes sumériensen Baylonie du Nord" *Nouvelles Assyriologiques Brèves et Utilitaires* (N.A.B.U): 22

Charpin, Dominique. 1994. "39) Inanna/Estar, divinité poliade d'Uruk á l'époque paléo-babylonienne." *Nouvelles Assyriologiques Brèves et Utilitaires* (N.A.B.U): 37–38

Charpin, Dominique. 2004. "78) La dot-*nidittum* de l'*énum* du Sîn á Tutub." *Nouvelles Assyriologiques Brèves et Utilitaires* (N.A.B.U): 79

Charpin, Dominique and Jean-Marie Durand. 1985. "La prise du pouvoir par Zimri-Lim." Pp. 293–343 in *Mari* 4: *Annales de Recherches Interdisciplinaires.* Paris: Éditions Recherche sur les Civilisations

Charpin, Dominique and Nele Ziegler. 2003. *Mari et le Proche Orient à l'époque amorrite.* Paris: Société pour l'Étude du Proche-Orient Ancien

Chazan, R., et al., eds. 1999. *Ki Baruch Hu: Ancient Near Eastern, Biblical, and Judaic Studies in Honor of Baruch A. Levine.* Winona Lake, Ind.: Eisenbrauns

Choi, John H. 2004. "Resheph and YHWH SEB'ÔT." *Vetus Testamentum* 54: 17–28

Cicero. [2006]. *In Verrem II.4 (Actionis in C. Verrem Secundae Liber Quartus)*

Civil, Miguel. 1969. "The Sumerian Flood Story." Pp. 138–45 and Pp. 167–72 in *ATRA-HASIS: The Babylonian Story of the Flood.* Edited by W. G. Lambert and A. R. Millard. Oxford: Clarendon

Civil, Miguel. 1983. "Enlil and Ninlil: The Marriage of Sud." *Journal of the American Oriental Society* 103: 43–66

Civil, Miguel. 1984. "Notes on the 'Instructions of Šuruppak.'" *Journal of Near Eastern Studies* 43: 281–98

Civil, Miguel. 1987. "Feeding Dumuzi's Sheep: The Lexicon as a Source of Literary Inspiration." Pp. 37–55 in *Language, Literature, and History: Philological and Historical Studies Presented to Erica Reiner.* Edited by F. Rochberg-Halton. New Haven, Ct.: American Oriental Society

Civil, Miguel. 1993. "On Mesopotamian Jails and Their Lady Warden." Pp. 152–62 in *The Tablet and the Scroll.Near Eastern Studies in Honor of William W. Hallo.* Bethesda, Md.: CDL Press

Civil, Miguel 2002a (1991). "Modern Brewers Recreate Ancient Beer." Originally published in *The Oriental Institute News and Notes* 132

Civil, Miguel, trans. 2002b. "A Hymn to Ninkasi." The Oriental Institute, University of Chicago

Civil, Miguel. 2004. *The Series DIRI.* Materials for the Sumerian Lexicon 15. Rome. Pontificium Institutum Biblicum

Clifford, Richard J. 1972. *The Cosmic Mountain in Canaan and the Old Testament.* Cambridge, Mass.: Harvard University Press

Cohen, Mark E. 1981. *Sumerian Hymnology: The Eršemma.* Cincinnati, Ohio: Hebrew Union College

Cohen, Mark E. 1988. *The Canonical Lamentations of Ancient Mesopotamia.* Two volumes. Potomac, Md.: Capital Decisions Ltd.

Cohen, Mark E. 1993. *The Cultic Calendars of the Ancient Near East.* Potomac, Md.: CDL Press

Cohen, Mark E. 1996a. "The Gods of Suburban Umma." Pp. 27–35 in *Tablettes et images aux pays de Sumer et Akkad: mélanges offerts à Monsieur H. Limet*. Edited by Ö. Tunca and D. Deheselle. Lièges, Belgium: University of Lièges

Cohen, Mark E. 1996b. "The Sun, the Moon, and the City of Ur."Pages 7–20 in *Religion and Politics in the Ancient Near East*. Edited by A. Berlin. Bethesda, Md.: University Press of Maryland

Cohen, Mark E. 2015. *Festivals and Calendars in the Ancient Near East*. Bethesda, Md.: CDL Press

Cohen, Mark E. 2017. *New Treasures of Sumerian Literature*. Bethesda, Md.: CDL Press

Colbow, G. 1997. "More Insights into Representations of the Moon God in the Third and Second Millennium B.C." Pp. 19–31 in *Sumerian Gods and Their Representations*. Edited by Irving L. Finkel and Markham J. Geller. Groningen, Netherlands: Styx

Collins, Billie Jean 2005. "A Statue for the Deity: Cult Images in Hittite Anatolia." Pp. 13–42. in *Cult Image and Divine Representation in the Ancient Near East*. Edited by Neal H. Walls. Boston. Mass.: American Schools of Oriental Research

Collon, Dominique. 1982. *Catalogue of the Western Asiatic Seals in the British Museum. Cylinder Seals II. Akkadian - Post-Akkadian - Ur III*. London: British Museum

Comay, Joan. 1993 (1971). *Who's Who in the Old Testament Together with the Apocrypha*. London: Dent

Conti, Giovanni. 1993. "Ninirigal, Mère de Kullab." Pp. 343–47 in *Mari 7: Annales de Recherches Interdisciplinaires*. Paris: Éditions Recherche sur les Civilisations

Coogan, Michael D. 1978. *Stories from Ancient Canaan*. Philadelphia: Westminster

Cooper, Jerrold S. 1986. *Presargonic Inscriptions*. New Haven, Ct.: American Oriental Society

Cooper, Jerrold S. and W. Heimpel. 1983. "The Sumerian Sargon Legend." *Journal of the American Oriental Society* 103: 67–82

Cornelius, Izak. 1994. *The Iconography of the Canaanite Gods Reshef and Baʿl*. Fribourg, Switzerland: Fribourg University Press

Cornelius, Izak. 2004. *The Many Faces of the Goddess: The Iconography of the Syro-Palestinian Goddesses Anat, Astarte, Qedeshet, and Asherah c.1500–1000 BCE*. Fribourg, Switzerland: Fribourg University Press

Cross, Frank M. 1973. *Canaanite Myth and Hebrew Epic: Essays in the History of the Religion of Israel*. Cambridge, Mass.: Harvard University Press

Dalley, Stephanie. 2005. *Old Babylonian Texts in the Ashmolean Museum Mainly from Larsa, Sippir, Kish, and Lagaba*. Oxford: Clarendon

Dalley, Stephanie. 2009. *Babylonian Tablets from the First Sealand Dynasty in the Schøyen Collection*. CUSAS 9. Bethesda, Md.: CDL Press

Dalley, Stephanie, C. B. F. Walker, and J. D. Hawkins. 1976. *The Old Babylonian Tablets from Tell al Rimah*. London: British School of Archaeology in Iraq

Danthine, Hélène. 1937. *Le palmier-dattier et les arbres sacrés dans l'iconographie de l'Asie occidentale ancienne*. Two volumes. Paris: Guethner

Day, John. 1985. *God's Conflict with the Dragon and the Sea*. Cambridge: Cambridge University Press

Day, John. 1989. *Molech: A God of Human Sacrifice in the Old Testament.* Cambridge: Cambridge University Press

Day, John, ed. 1998. *King and Messiah in Israel and the Ancient Near East: Proceedings of the Oxford Old Testament Seminar.* Sheffield, UK: Sheffield Academic

Day, John. 2000. *Yahweh and the Gods and Goddesses of Canaan.* Sheffield, UK: Sheffield Academic

Day, Peggy L. 1991. "Why Is Anat a Warrior and Hunter?" Pp. 141–46 in *The Bible and the Politics of Exegesis.* Edited by David Jobling. Cleveland, Oh.: Pilgrim

Day, Peggy L. 1992. "Anat: Ugarit's 'Mistress of the Animals.'" *Journal of Near Eastern Studies* 51: 181–90

Delaporte, Louis, with M. Fr. Thureau-Dangin. 1920–1923. *Catalogue des cylindres, cachets et pierres gravées de style oriental.* Paris: Hachette

Deller, K. 1987a. "101) Assyrische Königsinschriften auf «Perlen»." *Nouvelles Assyriologiques Brèves et Utilitaires* (N.A.B.U): 55–56

Deller, K. 1987b. "54) *Ilabrat* und *Ilabra.*" *Nouvelles Assyriologiques Brèves et Utilitaires* (N.A.B.U): 29

Deller, K. 1991. "18) On the Names of Some Divine Doorkeepers." *Nouvelles Assyriologiques Brèves et Utilitaires* (N.A.B.U): 14–16

Del Monte, Giuseppe F. and Johann Tischler. 1978. *Die Orts- und Gewässernamen der hethitischen Texte.* Wiesbaden, Germany: L. Reichert

del Olmo Lete, Gregorio. 1999a. *Canaanite Religion According to the Liturgical Texts of Ugarit.* Bethesda, Md.: CDL Press

del Olmo Lete, Gregorio. 1999b. "The Offering Lists and the God Lists." Pp. 305–52 in W.G.E. Watson and N. Wyatt, *Handbook of Ugaritic Studies.* Brill. Leiden, 1999, pp. 305–52

de Moor, Johannes C. 1990. *The Rise of Yahwism: The Roots of Israelite Monotheism.* Louvain, Belgium: Louvain University

de Tarragon, Jean-Michel. 1980. *Le culte à Ugarit d'après les texts de la pratique en cuneiforms alphabétiques.* Paris: Gabalda

Detienne, Marcel. 1977. *The Gardens of Adonis: Spices in Greek Mythology.* London: Harvester

Dever, William G. 1982. "Recent Archaeological Confirmation of the Cult of Asherah in Israel." *Hebrew Studies* 23: 37–44

Dever, William G. 1984. "Asherah, Consort of Yahweh? New Evidence from Kuntillet 'Ajrud." *Bulletin of the American Schools of Oriental Research* 255: 21–37

Dever, William G. 2005. *Did God Have a Wife? Archaeology and Folk Religion in Ancient Israel.* Grand Rapids, Mich.: Eerdmans

Dien, Albert E. 2004. "Palmyra as a Caravan City." *Newsletter of the Silk Road Foundation* 2 #1

Dietrich, M., and O. Loretz. 1966. Review of *Amorite Personal Names in the Mari Texts,* by H. B. Huffmon. *Orientalistische Literaturzeitung* 61: 235–44

Dietrich, M., and O. Loretz. 2003. "Ḥorōn, der Herr über die Schlangen. Das Verhältnis von Mythos und Beschworung in KTU 1.100." Pp. 150–72 in *Semitic and Assyriological Studies Presented to Peio Fronzaroli.* Wiesbaden, Germany: Harrassowitz.

Donbaz, Veysel. 1991. "107) Assyrian Votive Inscription Found on Cylinder

Beads." *Nouvelles Assyriologiques Brèves et Utilitaires* (N.A.B.U): 76–77

Dossin, G. 1950. *Archives royales de Mari 1*. Paris: Impr. Nationale

Drewnowska-Rymarz, Olga. 2008. *Mesopotamian Goddess Nanāja*. Warsaw: Agade

Drijvers, H. J. W. 1997. *The Religions of Palmyra*. Leiden, Netherlands: Brill

Durand, Jean-Marie. 1985. "La situation historique des shakkanakku: Nouvelle approche." Pp. 147–72 in *Mari 4: Annales de Recherches Interdisciplinaires*. Paris: Éditions Recherche sur les Civilisations

Durand, Jean-Marie. 1987a. "14) Noms de dieux sumériens á Mari." *Nouvelles Assyriologiques Brèves et Utilitaires* (N.A.B.U): 7–8

Durand, Jean-Marie. 1987b. "97) Le dieu *Astakku." *Nouvelles Assyriologiques Brèves et Utilitaires* (N.A.B.U): 54

Durand, Jean-Marie. 1988. "8) Le nom des Bétyles á Ebla et en Anatolie." *Nouvelles Assyriologiques Brèves et Utilitaires* (N.A.B.U): 5–6

Durand, Jean-Marie. 1993a. "60) Le dieu des Enfers á Mari" *Nouvelles Assyriologiques Brèves et Utilitaires* (N.A.B.U): 49–50

Durand, Jean-Marie. 1993b. "116) Mythologèmes d'époque amorrite" *Nouvelles Assyriologiques Brèves et Utilitaires* (N.A.B.U): 96–97

Durand, Jean-Marie. 1995. "La religion en Siria durante la epoca de los reinos amorreos segun la documentacion de Mar." Pp. 127–533 in P. Mander and J.-M. Durand, *Mitología y Religion del Oriente Antiguo*, II/I. Semitas Occidentales (Ebla, Mari). Coleccion: Estudios Orientales 8. Sabadell: Editorial AUSA

Durand, Jean-Marie. 1997. "Itûr-Mêr, dieu des serments." Pp. 57–69 in *Jurer et maudire: pratiques politiques et usages juridiques du serment dans le Proche-Orient ancien Méditerranées*, Edited by S. Lafont. Paris. Revue de l'association Méditerranées, 10–11.

Durand, Jean-Marie. 2003. "110) EN-akka." *Nouvelles Assyriologiques Brèves et Utilitaires* (N.A.B.U): 121

Durand, Jean-Marie. 2005a. "60) Yakûn-Asar à Tell Brak." *Nouvelles Assyriologiques Brèves et Utilitaires* (N.A.B.U): 67

Durand, Jean-Marie. 2005b. "62) Le nom de NIN-URTA á Émar." *Nouvelles Assyriologiques Brèves et Utilitaires* (N.A.B.U): 68–69

Durand, Jean-Marie. 2008. "Les divinités, leurs temples et leurs cultes." Pp. 171–374 in *Orientalia Lovaniensia Analecta* 162. Edited by G. del Olmo Lete. Leuven, Belgium: Peeters

Durand, Jean-Marie. 2014. "Le dieu Qul(l)uḫ from Texts from Tell Sakka." *Nouvelles Assyriologiques Brèves et Utilitaires* (N.A.B.U): 133–34

Dussaud, René. 1927. *Topographie historique de la Syrie antique et médiévale*. Paris: Geuthner

Ebeling, E., et al., eds. 1920–. *Reallexikon der Assyriologie*. Berlin: de Gruyter

Edzard, Dietz O. 1965. "Mesopotamien." Pp. 37–139 in *Götter und Mythen in Vorderen Orient*. Edited by H. Haussig. Stuttgart, Germany: Klett

Edzard, Dietz O. 1997. *Gudea and His Dynasty*. Royal Inscriptions of Mesopotamia: Early Periods Volume 3/1. Toronto: University of Toronto Press

Edzard, Dietz O. and Claus Wilcke. 1976. "Die Ḫendursaga-Hymne." Pp. 139–

76 in *Kramer Anniversary Volume. Cuneiform Studies in Honor of Samuel Noah Kramer*. Edited by Barry Eichler, Jane W. Heimerdinger, and Åke Sjöberg. Kevelaer, Germany: Butzon and Bercker

Edzard, Dietz O. 2003. "Enlil, Vater der Götter." Pp. 173–84 in *Semitic and Assyriological Studies Presented to Pelio Fronzaroli by Pupils and Colleagues*. Wiesbaden: Harrassowitz

Edzard, Dietz Otto, Gertrud Farber, and Edmond Sollberger. 1977. *Die Orts- und Gewässernamen der präsargonischen und sargonischen Zeit*. Wiesbaden, Germany: Reichert

Ehrenberg, Erica. 2002. "The Rooster in Mesopotamia." Pp. 53–62 in *Leaving No Stones Unturned: Essays on the Ancient Near East and Egypt in Honor of Donald P. Hansen*. Edited by E. Ehrenberg. Winona Lake, Ind.: Eisenbrauns

Ellis, Maria de Jong. 1989. "An Old Babylonian *kusarikku*." Pp. 121–35 in *Dumu-e2-dub-ba-a: Studies in Honor of Åke W. Sjöberg*. Edited by H. Behrens, D. Loding, and M. Roth. Philadelphia: Occasional Publications of the Samuel Noah Kramer Fund

Ellis, Richard. 1977. "Mountains and Rivers." Pp. 29–34 in *Mountains and Lowlands: Essays in the Archaeology of Greater Mesopotamia*. Edited by L. Levine and T. C. Young, Jr. Malibu, Calif.: Undena

Englund, Robert K. Cuneiform Digital Library Initiative. www.cdli.ucla.edu

Englund, Robert K. 1990. *Organisation und Verwaltung der Ur III-Fischerei*. Berlin: D. Reimer

Falkenstein, Adam. 1941. *Topographie von Uruk. I. Teil Uruk zur Seleukidenzeit*. Leipzig: Harrassowitz

Falkenstein, Adam. 1964. "Sumerische Religiöse Texte." *Zeitschrift für Assyriologie* 56: 44–129

Falkenstein, Adam. 1966. *Die Inschriften Gudeas von Lagash. I. Einleitung*. Rome: Pontificium Institutum Biblicum

Farber, W. 1992. "20) Mehr Perlen für Belet-parṣe." *Nouvelles Assyriologiques Brèves et Utilitaires* (N.A.B.U): 17

Farmer, David. 2003 (1978). *The Oxford Dictionary of Saints*. Fifth Edition. Oxford: Oxford University Press

Feliu, Lluis. 1998. "44) Dagan sa *ḪAR-ri* at Terqa." *Nouvelles Assyriologiques Brèves et Utilitaires* (N.A.B.U): 45–47

Feliu, Lluis. 2003. *The God Dagan in Bronze Age Syria*. Leiden, Netherlands: Brill

Finegan, Jack. 1997 (1989). *Myth and Mystery: An Introduction to the Pagan Religions of the Biblical World*. Grand Rapids, Mich.: Baker

Finkel, Irving L. 1982. *The Series* SIG_7.ALAN = *Nabnītu*; Materials for the Sumerian Lexicon XVI. Rome: Pontificium Institutum Biblicum

Finkel, Irving L. and Markham J. Geller, eds. 1997. *Sumerian Gods and Their Representations*. Groningen, Netherlands: Styx

Flaubert, Gustave. 1962. *Salambo*. Translated by Robert Goodyear and P. J. R. Wright. London: New English Library

Fleming, Daniel E. 1992a. *The Installation of Baal's High Priestess at Emar: A Window on Ancient Syrian Religion*. Atlanta, Ga.: Scholars Press

Fleming, Daniel E. 1992b. "A Limited Kingship: Late Bronze Emar in Ancient Syria." *Ugarit-Forschungen* 24: 59–71

Fleming, Daniel E. 1993a. "Baal and Dagan in Ancient Syria." *Zeitschrift für Assyriologie* 83: 88–98

Fleming, Daniel E. 1993b. "2) Dagan and Itur-Mer at Mari." *Nouvelles Assyriologiques Brèves et Utilitaires* (N.A.B.U): 1–2

Fleming, Daniel E. 1995. "More Help from Syria: Introducing Emar to Biblical Study." *Biblical Archaeologist* 58: 139–47

Fleming, Daniel E. 1996. "The Emar Festivals: City Unity and Syrian Identity under Hittite Hegemony." Pp. 81–121 in *History, Religion, and Culture of a Syrian Town in the Late Bronze Age.* Edited by M. W. Chavalas. Bethesda, Md.: CDL Press

Fleming, Daniel E. 2000. *Time at Emar: The Cultic Calendar and the Rituals from the Diviner's Archive.* Mesopotamian Civilizations 11. Winona Lake, Ind.: Eisenbrauns

Fondation pour le lexicon iconographicum mythologiae classicae. 1981. *Lexicon iconographicum mythologiae classicae.* Zurich: Artemis

Foster, Benjamin R. 1977. "Ea and Saltu." Pp. 79–84 in *Essays on the Ancient Near East in Memory of Jacob Joel Finkelstein.* Edited by Maria de Jong Ellis. Hamden, Ct.: Archon Books

Foster, Benjamin R., trans. 1993. *Before the Muses: An Anthology of Akkadian Literature,* volume I, *Archaic, Classical, Mature;* volume II, *Mature, Late.* Bethesda, Md.: CDL Press

Foster, Benjamin R., trans. 2001. *The Epic of Gilgamesh: A Norton Critical Edition.* New York: Norton

Foster, Benjamin R., trans. 2005. *Before the Muses: An Anthology of Akkadian Literature.* Third Edition. In one volume. Bethesda, Md.: CDL Press

Frahm, Eckard. 2005. "5) Nabu-zuqup-kenu, Gilgamesh XII, and the rites of Du'uzu." *Nouvelles Assyriologiques Brèves et Utilitaires* (N.A.B.U) 4–5

Frame, Grant. 1999. "My Neighbour's God: Aššur in Babylonia and Marduk in Assyria." *Bulletin of the Canadian Society for Mesopotamian Studies* 34: 5–22

Frame, Grant. 2014. "Text Nos. 1177–178." Pp. 307–34 in *Inscriptions of the First and Second Millennia B.C.* Edited by I. Spar and M. Jursa. New York: Metropolitan Museum of Art.

Frankena, Rintje. 1954. *Tākultu: De sacrale maaltijd in het Assyrische ritueel; met een overzicht over de in Assur vereerde goden.* Leiden, Netherlands: Brill

Frankfort, Henri. 1978 (1948). *Kingship and the Gods: A Study of Ancient Near Eastern Religion as the Integration of Society and Nature.* Chicago: University of Chicago Press

Frankfort, Henri, Seton Lloyd, Thorkild Jacobsen, and Günther Martiny. 1940. *The Gimilsin Temple and the Palace of the Rulers at Tell Asmar.* Chicago: University of Chicago Press

Frayne, Douglas R. 1985. "Notes on the Sacred Marriage Rite." *Bibliotheca Orientalis* 42: 6–22

Frayne, Douglas R. 1990. *Old Babylonian Period (2003–1595 BC).* The Royal Inscriptions of Mesopotamia: Early Periods. Volume 4. Toronto: University of Toronto Press

Frayne, Douglas R. 1993. *Sargonic and Gutian Periods (2334–2113 BC).* The Royal Inscriptions of Mesopotamia: Early Periods. Volume 2. Toronto: University of Toronto Press

Frayne, Douglas R. 1997a. "23) On the Date of the 'Mountain God' Plaque from Aššur Ilušumma and Mount Ebiḫ." *Nouvelles Assyriologiques Brèves et Utilitaires* (N.A.B.U): 22–23

Frayne, Douglas R. 1997b. *Ur III Period (2112–2004 BC)*. Royal Inscriptions of Mesopotamia: Early Periods Volume 3/2. Toronto: University of Toronto Press

Frayne, Douglas R., trans. 2001. "The Sumerian Gilgamesh Poems." Pp. 99–155 in *The Epic of Gilgamesh: A Norton Critical Edition*. Edited by Benjamin R. Foster. New York: Norton

Frayne, Douglas R. 2007. "A Tentative Garšana Geography." Pp. 9–11. In *The Garšana Archives*. Edited by David I. Owen, Rudolf H. Mayr, and Alexandra Kleinerman. Bethesda, Md.: CDL Press

Frayne, Douglas R. 2009. "The Struggle for Hegemony in `Early Dynastic II' Sumer." *Journal of the Canadian Society for Mesopotamian Studies* 4: 37–75

Frayne, Douglas R. 2010. "Gilgameš in Old Akkadian Glyptic." Pp. 165–208 in *Gilgamesch: Ikonographie eines Helden. Gilgamesh: Epic and Iconography*. Edited by H. U. Steymans. Orbis Biblicus et Orientalis 245. Fribourg, Switzerland: Academic Press / Göttingen, Germany: Vandenhoeck and Ruprecht

Frayne, Douglas R. 2013. "The Fifth Day of Creation in Ancient Syrian and Neo-Hittite Art." Pp. 63–95 in *Creation and Chaos: Reconsideration of Hermann Gunkel's Chaos Kampf Hypothesis*. Edited by J. Scurlock and R. H. Beal. Winona Lake, Ind.: Eisenbrauns

Frazer, James G. 1981 (1890). *The Golden Bough: Two Volumes in One*. New York: Gramercy

Freedman, David N. 1987. "Yahweh of Samaria and his Asherah." *Biblical Archaeologist* 50: 241–49

Freedman, David N., ed. 1992–. *The Anchor Bible Dictionary*. Six volumes. New York: Doubleday

Frendo, Anthony J. and P. S. Inglott. 1991. "The Sign of Tinit: Archaeological and Philosophical Perspectives." *University of Malta Magazine* 1: 20

Fronzaroli, P. 1993. *Testi Rituali Della Regalità*. Archivi Reali di Ebla. Testi 11. Rome. Missione Archeologica Italiana in Siria.

Fronzaroli, P. 1997. "Les combats de Hadda dans les texts d'Ébla." Pp. 283–90 in *Mari 8: Annales de Recherches Interdisciplinaires*. Paris: Éditions Recherche sur les Civilisations

Frymer-Kensky, Tikva. 1977. *The Judicial Ordeal in the Ancient Near East*. Unpublished Ph.D. dissertation, Yale University

Frymer-Kensky, Tikva. 1992. *In the Wake of the Goddesses: Women, Culture, and the Biblical Transformation of Pagan Myth*. New York: Ballantine

Fuhr, I. 1977. "Der Hund als Begleittier der Göttin Gula und anderer Heilgottheiten." Pp. 135–45 in *Isin Ishan Bahriyat. I. Der Ergebnisse der Ausgrabungen 1973–1974*. Edited by B. Hrouda. Munich: Verlag der Bayerische Akademie der Wissenschaft

Fulco, W. J. 1976. *The Canaanite God Rešef*. New Haven: American Oriental Society

Gabbay, Uri. 2019. "The Mesopotamian God Dugab-šugigi." *Revue d'Assyriologie et d'archélogie orientale* 113: 123–30

Gadotti, Alhena. 2005. *"Gilgameš, Enkidu and the Netherworld" and The Sumerian Gilgameš Cycle.* Unpublished Ph.D. dissertation, Johns Hopkins University

Gadotti, Alhena. 2015. "A New Text about Nin-abul." *Nouvelles Assyriologiques Brèves et Utilitaires* (N.A.B.U): 7–11

Gadotti, Alhena and Marcel Sigrist. 2011 *Cuneiform Texts in the Carl Kroch Library, Cornell University.* CUSAS 15. Bethesda, Md.: CDL Press

Gaines, Janet H. 1999. *Music in the Old Bones: Jezebel through the Ages.* Carbondale, Ill.: Southern Illinois University Press

Galter, H. D. 1983. *Der Gott Ea/Enki in der akkadischen Uberlieferung: Eine Bestandsaufnahme des vorhandenen Materials.* Graz, Austria: Dissertationen der Karl-Franzen-Universität Graz

Garrison, Mark A. 2007. "Narunde." *Iconography of Deities and Demons: Electronic Pre-Publication*

Garstang, John and Oliver Gurney. 1959. *The Geography of the Hittite Empire.* London: British Institute of Archaeology at Ankara

Gelb, I. J. 1938. "Studies in the Topography of Western Asia." *American Journal of Semitic Languages and Literatures* 55: 61–85

Gelb, I. J. 1961. *Old Akkadian Writing and Grammar.* Chicago: University of Chicago Press

Gelb, I. J. 1992. "Mari and the Kish Civilization." Pp. 121–202 in *Mari in Retrospect: Fifty Years of Mari and Mari Studies.* Edited by Gordon D. Young. Winona Lake, Ind.: Eisenbrauns

Geller, Markham. 1985. *Forerunners to Udug-Hul: Sumerian Exorcistic Incantations.* Stuttgart: Steiner

Gentili, Paolo. 2001. "90). Nabonidus' Friends in Arabia." *Nouvelles Assyriologiques Brèves et Utilitaires* (N.A.B.U): 85–86

George, Andrew R. 1993. *House Most High: The Temples of Ancient Mesopotamia.* Winona Lake, Ind.: Eisenbrauns

George, Andrew R. 1997. *Babylonian Topographical Texts.* Leuven, Belgium: Peeters

George, Andrew R., trans. 1999. *The Babylonian Gilgamesh Epic: A New Translation.* New York: Barnes and Noble

George, Andrew R., ed./trans. 2003. *The Babylonian Gilgamesh Epic: Introduction, Critical Edition and Cuneiform Texts.* Two volumes. Oxford: Oxford University Press

George, Andrew R. 2004. "20) The Seventh Destiny-Decreeing Deity (Tintir II 24′ and K3446 + obv. 17′)." *Nouvelles Assyriologiques Brèves et Utilitaires* (N.A.B.U): 21

George, Andrew R. 2009. *Babylonian Literary Texts in the Schøyen Collection.* CUSAS 10. Bethesda, Md.: CDL Press

George, Andrew R. 2013. *Babylonian Divinatory Texts Chiefly in the Schøyen Collection.* CUSAS 18. Bethesda, Md.: CDL Press

George, Andrew R. 2015. "The Gods Išum and Ḫendursanga: Night Watchmen and Street-lighting in Babylonia." *Journal of Near Eastern Studies* 74/1: 1–8.

George, Andrew R. 2016. *Mesopotamian Incantations and Related Texts in the Schøyen Collection.* CUSAS 32. Bethesda, Md.: CDL Press

Giorgieri M., L. Murat, and A. Süel. 2013. "The Kaluti-List of the Storm-god of

Šapinuwa from Ortaköy and Its Parallels from Bogazköy." *Kaskal* 10: 169–83.

Giovino, M. 2007. *The Assyrian Sacred Tree: A History of Interpretations*. Fribourg: Academic

Glassner, J. J. 1984. "Inscriptions cuneiforms de Failaka." Pp. 30–50 in *Failaka: Fouilles franšaises 1983*. Edited by J. S. Salles. Paris: Maison de l'Orient Mediterranéen

Godwin, Joscelyn. 1981. *Mystery Religions of the Ancient World*. San Francisco: Harper and Row

Goetze, A. 1940. "The City Khalbi and the Khapiru People." *Bulletin of the American Schools of Oriental Research* 79: 32–34

Goff, Beatrice L. 1963. *Symbols of Prehistoric Mesopotamia*. New Haven, Ct.: Yale University Press

Göhde, Hildegard E. 2000. "The Rhomb, a God's Symbol." Pp. 395–415 in *Studi sul vicino oriente antico dedicati alla memoria di Luigi Cagni*. Edited by Simonetta Graziani. Naples: Istituto Universitario Orientale, Napoli

Goldenberg, David. 2003. *The Curse of Ham: Race and Slavery in Early Judaism, Christianity, and Islam*. Princeton, N.J.: Princeton University Press

Gomi, Tohru, and Susumu Sato. 1990. *Selected Neo-Sumerian Administrative Texts from the British Museum*. Abiko, Japan: The Research Institute Cho-Gaikuin University

Gonnet, H. 1968. "Les montagnes d'Asie mineur." *Revue hittite et asianique* 26: 103–70

Grayson, A. K. 1987. *Assyrian Rulers of the Third and Second Millennia BC (To 1115 BC)*. Royal Inscriptions of Mesopotamia: Assyrian Periods Volume 1. Toronto: University of Toronto Press

Grayson, A. K. 1991. *Assyrian Rulers of the Early First Millennium BC I (1114–859 BC)*. Royal Inscriptions of Mesopotamia: Assyrian Periods Volume 2. Toronto: University of Toronto Press

Green, Margaret W. 1975. *Eridu in Sumerian Literature*. Unpublished Ph.D. dissertation, University of Chicago

Green, Margaret W. 1978. "The Eridu Lament." *Journal of Cuneiform Studies* 30: 127–67

Greenfield, J. C. 1987. "Aspects of Aramean Religion" Pp. 67–78 in *Ancient Israelite Religion: Essays in Honor of Frank Moore Cross*. Edited by P. D. Miller, Jr. Philadelphia: Fortress

Greengus, Samuel. 1979. *Old Babylonian Tablets from Ishchali and Vicinity*. Leiden, Netherlands: Nederlands Historisch-Archaeologisch Instituut te Istanbul

Greenstein, Edward L., trans. 1997. "Kirta." Pp. 9–48 in *Ugaritic Narrative Poetry*. Edited by Simon B. Parker. [No place]: Society of Biblical Literature/Scholars

Griffiths, J. G. 1953. "The Egyptian Derivation of the Name Moses." *Journal of Near Eastern Studies* 12: 225–31

Groddeck, Detlev. 1997. "133) Kataḫḫa/Ḫatagga." *Nouvelles Assyriologiques Brèves et Utilitaires* (N.A.B.U): 123–24

Groddeck, Detlev. 1998. "93) À propos Maul, AoF 17 (1990), 189–90 Text Nr. 1." *Nouvelles Assyriologiques Brèves et Utilitaires* (N.A.B.U): 85–86

Groneberg, Birgitte R. M. 1997. *Lob der Ishtar: Gebt und Ritual an die Altbabylonische Venusgottin. Tanatti Ishtar*. Groningen, Netherlands: Styx

Gubel, Eric. 2016. "Crossing Continents: Phoenician Art and How to Read it." Pp. 168–79 in *Assyria to Iberia: Art and Culture in the Iron Age*. Edited by J. Aruz and M. Seymour. New York: Metropolitan Museum of Art. Guichard, Michael. 1994. "Au pays de la Dame de Nagar." Pp. 235–72 in *Florilegium Marianum I: Recueil d'études á la memoire de Maurice Birot*. Edited by D. Charpin and J.-M. Durand. Paris: Société pour l'Étude du Proche-Orient Ancien

Gurney, O. R. 1981 (1952). *The Hittites*. Revised. Harmondsworth, Mx., UK: Penguin

Güterbock, H. 1960. "An Outline of the Hittite AN.TA.ŠUM Festival." *Journal of Near Eastern Studies* 19: 80–89

Haas, Volkert. 1981. "Zwei Gottheiten aus Eblaisch-hethitischer Überlieferung." *Der Alte Orient* 20: 251–57

Haas, Volkert. 1994. *Geschichte der Hethitschen Religion*. Leiden, Netherlands: Brill

Hadley, Judith M. 2000. *The Cult of Asherah in Ancient Israel and Judah: Evidence for a Hebrew Goddess*. Cambridge: Cambridge University Press

Hall, Mark 1985. *A Study of the Sumerian Moon-God, Nanna/Suen*. Unpublished Ph.D. dissertation, University of Pennsylvania

Hallo, William W. 1976. "The Royal Correspondence of Larsa: I. A Sumerian Prototype for the Prayer of Hezekiah." Pp. 209–24 in *Kramer Anniversary Volume: Cuneiform Studies in Honor of Samuel Noah Kramer*. Edited by Barry L. Eichler, Jane W. Heimerdinger, and Åke Sjöberg. Kevelauer, Germany: Butzon and Bercker

Hammond, Ph. 1990. "The Goddess of the `Temple of the Winged Lions' at Petra (Jordan)." In *Petra and the Caravan Cities*. Edited by Fawzi Zayadine. Amman, Jordan: Department of Antiquities, Jordan

Handy, Lowell K. 1994. *Among the Host of Heaven: The Syro-Palestinian Pantheon as Bureaucracy*. Winona Lake, Ind.: Eisenbrauns

Hardin, Donald. 1963. *The Phoenicians*. N.Y.: Praeger

Harmanşah, Ömür. 2007. "Sources of the Tigris. Event, Place and Performance in the Assyrian Landscapes of the Early Iron Age." *Archaeological Dialogues* 14: 179–204

Haroutunianian, Hripsime. 2002. "Bearded or Beardless: Some Speculations on the Function of the Beard among the Hittites." Pp. 43–52 in *Recent Developments in Hittite Archaeology and History: Papers in Memory of Hans G. Güterbock*. Edited by Aslihan Yener, Harry Hoffner, and Simrit Dhesi. Winona Lake, Ind.: Eisenbrauns

Harris, Rivkah. 1975. *Ancient Sippar: A Demographic Study of an Old Babylonian City 1894–1595 B.C.* Istanbul: Nederlands Historisch-Archaeologish Instituut te Istanbul

Harris, Rivkah. 1990. "Images of Women in the Gilgamesh Epic." Pp. 219–30 in *Lingering Over Words: Studies in Ancient Near Eastern Literature in Honor of William L. Moran*. Edited by T. Abusch, J. Huehnergard, and P. Steinkeller. Atlanta, Ga.: Scholars Press

Haussig, H. W., ed. 1965. *Wörterbuch den Mythologie ... Band 1: Götter und Mythen im vorderen Orient*. Stuttgart, Germany: Klett

Heessel, Nils P. 2002. *Pazuzu: Archäologische und Philologische Studien zu Einem Altorientalischen Damon*. Leiden, Netherlands: Brill

Heidel, Alexander, ed./trans. 1967 (1942). *The Babylonian Genesis: The Story of Creation*. Second Edition. Chicago: University of Chicago Press

Heider, George C. 1985. *The Cult of Molek: A Reassessment*. Sheffield, UK: Journal for the Study of the Old Testament

Heimpel, Wolfgang. 1994. "83) ne-sag." *Nouvelles Assyriologiques Brèves et Utilitaires* (N.A.B.U): 72–73

Heimpel, Wolfgang. 1996. "The River Ordeal in Ḫit." *Revue d'Assyriologie et d'archélogie orientale* 90: 7–18

Heimpel, Wolfgang. 1997. "137) A Famous Harpist." *Nouvelles Assyriologiques Brèves et Utilitaires* (N.A.B.U): 126

Heimpel, Wolfgang. 2011. "Twenty-Eight Trees Growing in Sumer." Pp. 75–152 in *Garšana Studies*, CUSAS 6. Bethesda, Md.: CDL Press

Hendel, Ronald S. 1993. "When the Sons of God Cavorted with the Daughters of Me." Pp. 167–80 in *Understanding the Dead Sea Scrolls*. Edited by H. Shanks. New York: Vintage Books

Henkelman, Wouter. 2008. *The Other Gods Who Are: Studies in Elamite-Iranian Acculturation Based on the Persepolis Fortification Texts*. Leiden, Netherlands: Nederlands Instituut voor het Nabije Oosten

Henshaw, Richard A. 1994. *Female and Male. The Cultic Personnel: The Bible and the Rest of the Ancient Near East*. Allison Park, Pa.: Pickwick

Herodotus. 1983 (1972). *The Histories*. Translated by A. de Sélincourt. Reviser A. R. Burn. Harmondsworth, Mx., UK: Penguin

Hess, Richard S. 1993. *Amarna Personal Names*. Winona Lake, Ind.: Eisenbrauns

Hestrin, Ruth. 1991. "Understanding Asherath [sic]: Exploring Semitic Iconography." *Biblical Archaeology Review* 17: 50–59

Hinz, Walther, and Jennifer Barnes. 1973. *The Lost World of Elam: Re-creation of a Vanished Civilization*. New York: New York University Press

Hinz, Walther, Rykle Borger, and Gerd Gropp. 1969. *Altiranische Funde und Forschungen*. Berlin: de Gruyter

Hinz, Walther, and Heidemarie Koch. 1987. *Elamisches Wörterbuch in zwei Teilen*. Berlin: Reimer

Hoffner, Harry A., Jr. 1998 (1990). *Hittite Myths*. Second Edition. Atlanta, Ga.: Scholars Press

Hunt, Patrick. 2019. Entry on Carthage. *Encyclopedia Britannica*. Online.

Hurston, Zora Neale. 1991. *Moses, Man of the Mountain*. San Francisco: Harper-Perennial

Hussey, M. I. 1912. *Sumerian Tablets in the Harvard Semitic Museum*. Cambridge, Mass.: Harvard University Press

Hvidberg-Hansen, F. O. 1979. *La déesse TNT: Une étude sur la religion canaanéo punique*. Two volumes. Copenhagen: Gad

Ivantchik, Askold. 1993. "49) Corrigenda aux texts akkadiens mentionnant les Cimmériens." *Nouvelles Assyriologiques Brèves et Utilitaires* (N.A.B.U): 39–41

Jacobsen, Thorkild. 1939. *The Sumerian King List*. Chicago: University of Chicago Press

Jacobsen, Thorkild. 1953. "The Myth of Inanna and Bilulu." *Journal of Near Eastern Studies* 12: 160–88

Jacobsen, Thorkild. 1970. *Toward the Image of Tammuz and Other Essays on Mesopotamian History and Culture.* Edited by W. L. Moran. Cambridge, Mass.: Harvard University Press

Jacobsen, Thorkild. 1975. "Religious Drama." Pp. 65–97 in *Ancient Mesopotamia: Unity and Diversity.* Edited by H. Goedicke and J. J. M. Roberts. Baltimore, Md.: Johns Hopkins University Press

Jacobsen, Thorkild. 1976. *The Treasures of Darkness: A History of Mesopotamian Religion.* New Haven, Ct.: Yale University Press

Jacobsen, Thorkild. 1977 (1946). "Mesopotamia." Pp. 123–219 in *The Intellectual Adventure of Ancient Man: An Essay on Speculative Thought in the Ancient Near East.* Edited by H. and H. A. Frankfort, John A. Wilson, Thorkild Jacobsen, and William A. Irwin. Chicago: University of Chicago Press

Jacobsen, Thorkild. 1984. *The Harab Myth.* Sources and Monographs on the Ancient Near East 2/3. Malibu, Calif.: Undena

Jacobsen, Thorkild. 1987. *The Harps That Once: Sumerian Poetry in Translation.* New Haven, Ct.: Yale University Press

Joannes, Francis. 1989. "75) MUN$_x$ = ṭabtum." *Nouvelles Assyriologiques Brèves et Utilitaires* (N.A.B.U): 53

Joint Expedition of the British Museum and of the Museum of the University of Pennsylvania to Mesopotamia. 1927. *Ur Excavations,* volume 2. Oxford: Oxford University Press

Joukowsky, Martha S. 2002. "The Petra Great Temple: A Nabataean Architectural Miracle." *Near Eastern Archaeology* 65: 235–48

Jursa, Michael. 1994. "65) Zu Edubba 1, 10." *Nouvelles Assyriologiques Brèves et Utilitaires* (N.A.B.U): 56

Kaizer, Ted. 2002. *The Religious Life of Palmyra.* Stuttgart, Germany: Steiner

Kanellopoulos, Chrysanthos. 2002. "A New Plan of Petra's City Center." *Near Eastern Archaeology* 65: 251–54

Kapelrud, Arvid. 1952. *Baal in the Ras Shamra Texts.* Copenhagen: Gad

Kapelrud, Arvid. 1969. *The Violent Goddess: Anat in the Ras Shamra Texts.* Oslo: Universitetsforlaget

Katz, Dina. 2003. *The Image of the Netherworld in the Sumerian Sources.* Bethesda, Md.: CDL Press

Katz, Solomon H. and Fritz Maytag. 1991. "Brewing an Ancient Beer." *Archaeology* 44: 24–33

Keel, Othmar and Christoph Uelinger. 1998. *Gods, Goddesses, and Images of God in Ancient Israel.* Minneapolis, Minn.: Fortress

Kienast, Burkhard. 1990. "Naram-Sin *mut* Inanna." *Orientalia,* new series, 59: 196–203

King, L. 1913. "Studies of Some Rock Sculptures and Rock-Inscriptions of Western Asia." *Proceedings of the Society of Biblical Archaeology* 36: 66–94

King, L. 1968. *Cuneiform Texts from Babylonian Tablets in the British Museum,* volume 24. London: The Trustees of the British Museum

King, L. 1969. *Cuneiform Texts from Babylonian Tablets in the British Museum,* volume 25. London: The Trustees of the British Museum

Kittel, R., ed., and K. Elliger and K. Rudolph, re-eds. 1967–77. *Biblia Hebraica Stuttgartensia.* Stuttgart, Germany: Deutsche Bibelstiftung

Klein, Jacob. 1990. "Šulgi and Išme-Dagan: Originality and Dependence in Sumerian Royal Hymnology." Pp. 65–136 in *Bar Ilan Studies in Assyriology: Dedicated to Pinhas Artzi.* Edited by J. Klein and A. Skaist. Ramat Gan, Israel: Bar-Ilan University Press

Klein, Jacob. 1997. "The God Martu in Sumerian Literature." Pp. 99–116 in *Sumerian Gods and Their Representations.* Edited by I. J. Finkel and M. J. Geller. Groningen, Netherlands: Styx.

Klengel, Horst. 1970. *Geschichte Syriens im 2. Jahrtausend v.u.Z. 3. Historische Geographie und allgemeine Darstellung.* Berlin: Akademie

Klengel, Horst, Fiorella Imparati, Volkert Haas, and Theo P. J. van den Hout. 1999. *Geschichte des hethitischen Reiches.* Leiden, Netherlands: Brill

Kletter, Raz. 1996. *The Judean Pillar-Figurines and the Archaeology of Asherah.* London: Tempus Reparatum

Koch, Heidemare. 1987. "Götter und ihr Verehrung im Achämenidischen Persien." *Zeitschrift für Assyriologie* 77: 239–78

Koch, Heidemare. 1990. *Verwaltung und Wirtschaft im persischen Kernland zur Zeit der Achämeniden.* Wiesbaden, Germany: Reichert

König, Friedrich Wilhelm. 1977 (1965). *Die elamischen Königsinschriften.* Osnabrück, Germany: Biblio

Kraemer, Ross S., ed. 1988. *Maenads, Martyrs, Matrons, Monastics: A Sourcebook on Women's Religions in the Greco-Roman World.* Philadelphia: Fortress

Kraemer, Ross S. 1992. *Her Share of the Blessings: Women's Religions among Pagans, Jews, and Christians in the Greco-Roman World.* New York: Oxford University Press

Kramer, Samuel N. 1940. *Lamentation over the Destruction of Ur.* Assyriological Studies 12. Chicago: University of Chicago Press

Kramer, Samuel N. 1972 (1961). *Sumerian Mythology: A Study of Spiritual and Literary Achievement in the Third Millennium.* Revised Edition. Philadelphia: University of Pennsylvania Press

Kramer, Samuel N. 1981. *History Begins at Sumer: Thirty-Nine Firsts in Recorded History.* Philadelphia: University of Pennsylvania Press

Kramer, Samuel N. 1990. "The Marriage of Martu." Pp. 11–27 in *Bar-Ilan Studies in Assyriology: Dedicated to Pinhas Artzi.* Edited by Jacob Klein and Aaron Skaist. Ramat Gan, Israel: Bar-Ilan University Press

Kraus, F. 1955. "Provinzen des neusumerishen Reiches von Ur." *Zeitschrift für Assyriologie* 51 (17): 45–75

Krebernik, Manfred. 1986. "Die Götterlisten aus Fāra." *Zeitschrift für Assyriologie* 76: 161–204

Krebernik, Manfred. 1992. "Mesopotamian Myths at Ebla: ARET 5, 6 and ARET 5, 7." Pp. 63–149 in *Literature and Literary Language at Ebla.* Edited by P. Fronzaroli. Florence: Dipartimanto di Linguistica, Università di Firenze

Krebernik, Manfred. 2002. "Geschlachte Gottheiten und ihre Namen." Pp. 289–

98 in *Ex Mesopotamia et Syria Lux: Festschrift für Manfried Dietrich zu seinem 65. Geburtstag*. Edited by O. Lorentz, Kai A. Metzier, and Hanspeter Schaudig. AOAT 281. Münster: Ugarit-Verlag

Krebernik, Manfred. 2003. "Drachenmutter und Himmelsrebe? Zur Frügeschichte Dumuzis und seiner Familie." Pp. 151–80 in *Literatur, Politik, und Recht in Mesopotamien: Festschrift für Claus Wilcke*. Edited by W. Sallaberger, K.Volk, and A. Zgoll. Wiesbaden, Germany: Harrassowitz

Krispijn, Theo. 1990. "Beiträge zur altorientalischen Musikforschung: Section I Shulgi und Musik." *Akkadica* 70: 1–27

Kupper, Jean-Robert. 1961. *L'iconographie du dieu Amurru dans la glyptique de la Ire dynastie babylonienne*. Brussels: Palais des Académies

Kutscher, R. 1989. *Royal Inscriptions: The Brockmon Tablets at the University of Haifa*. Haifa: Haifa University Press

Kvam, Kristen E. 1999. *Eve and Adam: Jewish, Christian, and Muslim Readings on Genesis and Gender*. Bloomington, Ind.: Indiana University Press

Lafont, Bertrand. 1985. *Documents administratifs sumériens provenant du site de Tello et conservés aux Musée du Louvre*. Paris: Éditions Recherche sur les Civilisations

Lafont, Bertrand. 1992. "57) La tablette ITT II 944." *Nouvelles Assyriologiques Brèves et Utilitaires* (N.A.B.U): 43–44

Lafont, Bertrand and Fatma Yıldız. 1989. *Tablettes cuneiforms de Tello au Musée d'Istanbul: datant de l'epoque de la IIIe Dynastie d'Ur*. Istanbul: Nederlands Historisch-Archaeologisch Instituut

Lambert, W. G. 1960. *Babylonian Wisdom Literature*. Oxford: Clarendon

Lambert, W. G. 1981a. "The Reading of AMA.GAN.ŠA." *Acta Sumerologica* 3: 31–36

Lambert, W. G. 1981b. "Old Akkadian Ilaba=Ugaritic Ilib?" *Ugarit-Forschungen* 13: 299–301

Lambert, W. G. 1982. "The Hymn to the Queen of Nippur." Pp. 173–218 in *Zikir umim: Assyriological Studies Presented to F. R. Kraus on the Occasion of His Seventieth Birthday*. Edited by G. van Driel et al. Leiden, Netherlands: Brill

Lambert, W. G. 1985a. "The Pantheon of Mari." Pp. 525–39 in *Mari 4: Annales de Recherches Interdisciplinaires*. Paris: Éditions Recherche sur les Civilisations

Lambert, W. G. 1985b. "A List of God Names Found at Mari." Pp. 181–90 in *Miscellanea Babylonica: Mélanges offerts à Maurice Birot*. Edited by Jean-Marie Durand and Jean-Robert Kupper. Paris: Éditions Recherche sur les Civilisations

Lambert, W. G. 1987. "115) Šeru' in an Assyrian Treaty." *Nouvelles Assyriologiques Brèves et Utilitaires* (N.A.B.U): 66

Lambert, W. G. 1989. "Notes on a Work of the Most Ancient Semitic Literature." *Journal of Cuneiform Studies* 41: 1–32

Lambert, W. G. 2007. "An Exotic Babylonian God-List." Pp. 167–72 in *Studies Presented to Robert D. Biggs*. Chicago: Oriental Institute

Lambert, W.G. 2013. *Babylonian Creation Myths*. Winona Lake, Ind.: Eisenbrauns

Landsberger, B. 1949. "Jahreszeiten in Sumerisch-Akkadischer." *Journal of Near Eastern Studies* 8: 248–72

Landsberger, B. 1957. *The Series ḪAR-ra>>ḫubullu: Tablets I–IV. Materialien zum sumerischen Lexikon* V. Rome: Pontificium Institutum Biblicum

Langdon, Stephen H. 1931. *Mythology of All Races,* volume 5, *Semitic.* Boston: Marshall Jones

Lange, K. 2005. "Unearthing Ancient Syria's Cult of the Dead." *National Geographic Magazine* (February): 108–22

Lantos, Zsolt G. 2013. "Essai d'application de la méthode de la psychologie environnementale à travers l'exemple de la ville méso-élamite de Dûr-untaṭs (Tchoga-zanbil, Iran), site inscrit au patrimoine mondial de l'Unesco." Pp. 139–60 in *Susa and Elam, Archaeological, Philological, Historical and Geographical Perspectives.* Edited by K. De Graef and J. Tavernier. MDP 58. Leiden: Brill, 2012

Lapinkivi, Pirjo. 2004. *The Sumerian Sacred Marriage in the Light of Comparative Evidence.* State Archives of Assyria XV. Helsinki: University of Helsinki Press

Laroche, Emmanuel. 1946–1947. "Recherches sur les noms des dieux hittites." *Revue Hittite et Asianique* 7: 7–139

Laroche, Emmanuel. 1976. "Glossarie de la langue hourrite." *Revue Hittite et Asianique* 34: 7–161

Laroche, Emmanuel. 1977. "Glossarie de la langue hourrite." *Revue Hittite et Asianique* 35: 163–322

Lebrun, R. 1988. "Divinités louvites et hourrites des rituels anatoliens en langue akkadienne provenant de Meskéné." *Hethitica* 9: 147–55

Leemans, W. F. 1952. *Ishtar of Lagaba and Her Dress.* Leiden, Netherlands: Brill

Leeming, David. 2005. *The Oxford Companion to World Mythology.* New York: Oxford University Press

Leick, Gwendolyn. 1998 (1991). *A Dictionary of Ancient Near Eastern Mythology.* London/New York: Routledge

Leick, Gwendolyn. 1999. *Who's Who in the Ancient Near East.* New York: Routledge

Lemche, Niels P. 1991. *The Canaanites and their Land.* Sheffield, UK: Sheffield Academic

Lewis, Theodore J. 1989. *The Cult of the Dead in Ancient Israel and Ugarit.* Atlanta, Ga.: Scholars Press

Lewis, Theodore J., trans. 1997a. "The Birth of the Gracious Gods." Pp. 205–14 in *Ugaritic Narrative Poetry.* Edited by Simon B. Parker. [No place]: Society of Biblical Literature/Scholars

Lewis, Theodore J., trans. 1997b. "The Rapiuma." Pp. 196–205 in *Ugaritic Narrative Poetry.* Edited by Simon B. Parker. [No place]: Society of Biblical Literature/Scholars Press

Lewis, Theodore J. 2005. "Syro-Palestinian Iconography and Divine Images." Pp. 69–107 in *Cult Image and Divine Representation in the Ancient Near East.* Edited by Neal H. Walls. Boston, Mass.: American Schools of Oriental Research

L'Heureux, Conrad H. 1974. "The Ugaritic and Biblical Rephaim." *Harvard Theological Review* 67: 265–74

L'Heureux, Conrad H. 1979. *Rank among the Canaanite Gods: El, Ba'l, and the Repha'im.* Missoula, Mont.: Scholars

Limet, Henri. 1971. "Le poème épique 'Inanna et Ebih.' Une version des lignes 123 à 182." *Orientalia* 40: 11–28

Limet, Henri. 1976. *Textes sumériens de la 3e dynastie d'Ur.* Brussels: Musées royaux d'art et d'histoire

Lipiński, Edward, ed. 1992. *Dictionnaire de la civilisation phénicienne et punique.* Turnhout, Belgium: Brepols

Lipiński, Edward. 1995. *Dieux et* déesses *de l'univers phénicienne et punique.* Leuven, Belgium: Peeters

Lipiński, Edward. 2000. *The Aramaeans: Their Ancient History, Culture, Religion.* Orientalia Lovaniensa Analecta 100. Leuven, Belgium: Peeters

Lipiński, Edward. 2009. *Resheph: A Syro-Canaanite Deity.* Orientalia Lovaniensa Analecta 181. Leuven, Belgium: Peeters

Lipiński, Edward. 2012. "Dagān, the Master of Ploughing." Pp. 335–44 in *The Ancient Near East, a Life!* Edited by T. Boiy et al. Leuven, Belgium: Peeters

Litke, Richard L. 1998 (1958). *A Reconstruction of the Assyro-Babylonian God-Lists, AN : dA-nu-um and AN: ANU ŠÁ AMELI.* New Haven: Yale University

Livingstone, Alasdair. 1986. *Mystical and Mythological Explanatory Works of Assyrian and Babylonian Scholars.* Oxford: Clarendon

Livingstone, Alasdair. 1989. *Court Poetry and Literary Miscellanea.* State Archives of Assyria III. Helsinki: University of Helsinki Press

Lloyd, Seton. 1967. *Early Highland Peoples of Anatolia.* London: Thames and Hudson

Loding, Darlene. 1976. *Economic Texts from the Third Dynasty.* Philadelphia: Published for the Trustees of the Two Museums by the Babylonian Fund

Lombardi, A. 1996. "Ideologia della regalità nella tradizione antico-ittità." *Mesopotamia* 31: 49–80

Lombardi, A. 1997. "Il culto della montagne all'epoca di Tudaliya IV: continuità e innovazione." *Studi Micenei ed Egeo-Anatolici* 39: 85–110

Lombardi, A. 1998. "Note su Šarpa e Šarlaimmi, montagne sacre di Ḫupišna." Pp. 65–84 in *Studi e testi.* Edited by S. de Martino and F. Imparati. Florence: Eothen 9

Longacre, Robert E. 2003. *Joseph: A Story of Divine Providence: A Text Theoretical and Textlinguistic Analysis of Genesis 37 and 39–48.* Winona Lake, Ind.: Eisenbrauns

López-Ruiz, Carolina. 2016. "Greek Literature and the Lost Legacy of Canaan." Pp. 316–31 in *Assyria to Iberia: Art and Culture in the Iron Age.* Edited by J. Aruz and M. Seymour. New York: Metropolitan Museum of Art.

Lucian. 1976. See Attridge and Oden. 1976

Maier, Walter A., III. 1986. *'Asherah: Extrabiblical Evidence.* Atlanta, Ga.: Scholars Press

Maiocchi, Massimo. 2009. *Classical Sargonic Tablets Chiefly from Adab in the Cornell University Collections.* CUSAS 13. Bethesda, Md.: CDL Press

Mallowan, Max E. L. 1978. *The Nimrud Ivories.* London: British Museum, Colonnade Books

Mallowan, Max E. L. and Georgina Herrmann [1974]. *Furniture from SW.7 Fort Shalmaneser: Commentary, Catalogue, and Plates.* London: British School of Archaeology in Iraq

Mander, Pietro. 1986. *Il Pantheon di Abū Ṣalābīḫ: Contributo allo studio del panthe-*

on sumerico arcaico. Series Minor XXVI. Naples: Istituto Universitario Orientale, Dipartimento di Studi Asiatici

Marcus, David, trans. 1997. "The Betrothal of Yarikh and Nikkal-Ib." Pp. 215–18 in *Ugaritic Narrative Poetry*. Edited by Simon B. Parker. [No place]: Society of Biblical Literature/Scholars

Margalith, O. 1987. "The Legends of Samson/Heracles." *Vetus Testamentum* 37: 63–70

Margueron, Jean-Claude. 1995. "Emar, Capital of Aštata in the Fourteenth Century BCE." *Biblical Archaeologist* 58: 126–38

Markoe, Glenn E. 2000. *Phoenicians*. Berkeley, Calif.: University of California Press

Martin, Harriet P., Francesco Pomponio, Guiseppe Visicato, and Aage Westenholz. 2001. *The Fara Tablets in the University of Pennsylvania Museum of Archaeology and Anthropology*. Bethesda, Md.: CDL Press

Matouš, L., ed. 1962. *Inscriptions cuneiforms du Kultépé*. Prague: Éditions de l'Académie Tchéchoslovaque des Sciences

Matsushima, Eiko. 1987. "Le rituel hiérogamique de Nabu." *Acta Sumerologica* 9: 131–75

Matthiae, Paolo. 1981. *Ebla: An Empire Rediscovered*. Garden City, N.Y.: Doubleday

Maul, Stefan. 1988. *"Herzberuhigungsklagen": Die sumerisch-akkadischen Eršaḫunge-Gebete*. Wiesbaden, Germany: Harrassowitz

Mazar, Amihai. 1990. *Archaeology and the Land of the Bible 10,000–586 B.C.E.* New York: Doubleday

Meador, Betty de Shong. 2000. *Inanna, Lady of Largest Heart: Poems of the Sumerian High Priestess Enheduanna*. Austin, Tex.: University of Texas Press

Meier, Gerhard. 1937–1939. "Kommentar aus dem Archiv der Tempelschule in Assur." *Archiv für Orientforschung* 12: 237–46

Mellaart, James. 1967. *Çatal Hüyük: A Neolithic Town in Anatolia*. London: Thames and Hudson

Menen, Aubrey. 1973. *Cities in the Sand*. New York: Dial

Menzel, Brigitte. 1981. *Assyrische Tempel*. Rome: Biblical Institute

Mettinger, Tryggve N. D. 2001. *The Riddle of Resurrection: "Dying and Rising Gods" in the Ancient Near East*. Stockholm: Almqvist and Wiksell

Meyer, Marvin W., ed. 1987. *The Ancient Mysteries. A Sourcebook: Sacred Texts of the Mystery Religions of the Ancient Mediterranean World*. San Francisco: Harper and Row

Michalowski, Piotr. 1986. "An Early Old Babylonian Loan Document." *Journal of Cuneiform Studies* 38: 167–71

Michalowski, Piotr. 1988. "Sîn-iddinam and Iškur." Pp. 265–75 in *A Scientific Humanist: Studies in Memory of Abraham Sachs*. Edited by E. Leichty and M. de Jong Ellis. Philadelphia: Distributed by the Samuel Noah Kramer Fund, The University Museum

Michalowski, Piotr. 1993. "The Torch and the Censer." Pp. 152–62 in *The Tablet and the Scroll: Near Eastern Studies in Honor of William W. Hallo*. Bethesda, Md. CDL Press

Michaud, Ewan. 2000. "11) Le culte du dieu Kamul en Elam; une nouvelle brique de Sutruk Nahhunte (1190–1155)." *Nouvelles Assyriologiques Brèves et Utilitaires* (N.A.B.U): 14–15

Milano, Lucio, and Aage Westenholz. 2015. *The "Šu-ilišu Archive" and Other Sargonic Texts in Akkadian*. CUSAS 27. Bethesda, Md.: CDL Press

Miller, Naomi, and Alhena Gadotti. 2009. "The KHALUB-tree in Mesopotamia: Myth or Reality?" Pp. 239–43 in *From Foragers to Farmers, Papers in Honour of Gordon C. Hillman*. Edited by A.S. Fairbairn and E. Weiss. Oxford: Oxbow Books

Milton, John. 1975. *Paradise Lost: An Authoritative Text, Backgrounds and Sources, Criticism*. Edited by Scott Elledge. New York: Norton

Mirelman, Sam. 2010. "33) The gala musician Dada and the si-im instrument." *Nouvelles Assyriologiques Brèves et Utilitaires* (N.A.B.U): 40–41

Molina, M., ed. Database of Neo-Sumerian Texts. www.bdts.filol.csic.es

Monaco, Salvatore F. 2011. *Early Dynastic mu-iti Cereal Texts in the Cornell University Collections*. CUSAS 14. Bethesda, Md.: CDL Press

Moran, William L. 1987. *Les lettres d'El-Amarna: Correspondance diplomatique du pharaon*. Paris: Éditions du Cerf

Moran, W. L. 1992. *The Amarna Letters*. Baltimore, Md.: Johns Hopkins University Press

Moscati, Sabatino. 1999 (1965). *The World of the Phoenicians*. London: Orion Phoenix

Mouterde, René. 1939. "Le dieu syrien Op." Pp. 1:391–97 in *Mélanges syriens offerts á Monsieur René Dussaud*. Two volumes. Paris: Guethner

Mullen, E. Theodore, Jr. 1980. *The Divine Council in Canaanite and Early Hebrew Literature*. Chico, Calif.: Scholars

Nakata, I. 2011. "The God Itūr-Mēr in the Middle Euphrates Region During the Old Babylonian Period." *Revue d'Assyriologie* 105: 129–36

Nashef, Khaled. 1982a. *Die Orts- und Gewässernamen der mittelbabylonischen und mittelassyrischen Zeit*. Wiesbaden, Germany: Reichert

Nashef, Khaled. 1982b. "Der Taban-Fleuss." *Baghdader Mitteilungen* 13: 117–41

Nashef, Khaled. 1986. "The Deities of Dilmun." Pp. 340–66 in *Bahrain through the Ages: the Archaeology*. Edited by Shaikha al Khalifa and Michael Rice. London: KPI

Nashef, Khaled. 1991. "97) A Further Note on the Name of the Doorkeeper of the Netherworld." *Nouvelles Assyriologiques Brèves et Utilitaires* (N.A.B.U): 67–68

Negbi, Ora. 1976. *Canaanite Gods in Metal: An Archaeological Study of Ancient Syro-Palestinian Figures*. Tel Aviv: Tel Aviv University Press

Nehmé, Laïla. 2000. "The World of the Nabataeans: A Kingdom between Syria and Arabia. 312 B.C.–106 A.D." Pp. 140–85 in *The Levant: History and Archaeology in the Eastern Mediterranean*. Edited by Olivier Binst. Cologne: Könemann

Nemet-Nejat, Karen. 1993. "A Mirror Belonging to the Lady-of-Uruk." Pp. 163–69 in *The Tablet and the Scroll: Near Eastern Studies in Honor of William W. Hallo*. Bethesda, Md. CDL Press

Neumann, Erich. 1970 (1955). *The Great Mother: An Analysis of an Archetype*.

Princeton, N.J.: Princeton University Press

Niditch, Susan. 1992. "Genesis." Pp. 10–25 in *The Women's Bible Commentary*. Edited by Carol A. Newsom and Sharon H. Ringe. Louisville, Ky.: Westminster/John Knox

Nissinen, Martin and Risto Uro, eds. 2008. *Sacred Marriages: The Divine-Human Sexual Metaphor from Sumer to Early Christianity*. Winona Lake, Ind.: Eisenbrauns

Nöel, Marie-Pierre. 2014. *Elissa la Didon grecque, dans la mythologie et dans l'histoire*. Montpellier, France: Université de Montpellier

Novotny, Jamie R. 1999. "11) The Pronunciation of Ištarān." *Nouvelles Assyriologiques Brèves et Utilitaires* (N.A.B.U): 14–15

Oden, R. A., Jr. 1976. "The Persistence of Canaanite Religion." *Biblical Archaeologist* 93: 31–36

Oldenburg, Ulf. 1969. *The Conflict between El and Ba'l in Canaanite Religion*. Leiden, Netherlands: Brill

Oliva, Juan. 1993a. "42) Aštar *ṣarbat* in Ebla." *Nouvelles Assyriologiques Brèves et Utilitaires* (N.A.B.U): 32–34

Oliva, Juan. 1993b. "94) Ashtarte (*ša*) *abi* of Emar: A Basic Approach." *Nouvelles Assyriologiques Brèves et Utilitaires* (N.A.B.U): 78–80

Oliva, Juan. 1993c. "98) Akk. *Pilakku* und Emar. *Pirikka*." *Nouvelles Assyriologiques Brèves et Utilitaires* (N.A.B.U): 82

Oliva, Juan. 1994. "15) Seeking an Identity for Diritum." *Nouvelles Assyriologiques Brèves et Utilitaires* (N.A.B.U): 16–77

Olyan, Saul M. 1987. "Some Observations Concerning the Identity of the Queen of Heaven." *Ugarit-Forschungen* 19: 161–74

Olyan, Saul M. 1988. *Asherah and the Cult of Yahweh in Israel*. Atlanta, Ga.: Scholars Press

Orthmann, Winnfried. 1975. *Der alte Orient*. Berlin: Propyläen

Oshima, Takayoshi. 2011. *Babylonian Prayers to Marduk*. Orientalische Religionen in der Antike 7. Tübingen, Germany: Mohr Siebeck.

Otten, H. 1969. "Die Berg- and Fluss-listen im Ḫišuwa-Festritual." *Zeitschrift für Assyriologie* 59: 247–60

Otto, Adelheid. 2000. *Die Entstehung und Entwicklung der klassisch-syrischen Glyptik*. Berlin: de Gruyter

Ovid. 1967 (1955). *Metamorphoses*. Translated by Rolfe Humphries. Bloomington, Ind.: Indiana University Press

Owen, David I. 2013. *Cuneiform Texts Primarily from Iri-Sagrig / Al-Šarrāki and the History of the Ur iii Period*. Nisaba 15. Bethesda, Md.: CDL Press

Owen, David I. and Alexandra Kleineman. 2009. *Analytical Concordance to the Garšana Archives*. CUSAS 4. Bethesda, Md.: CDL Press

Owen, David I. and Rudolf Mayr. 2007. *The Garšana Archives*. CUSAS 3. Bethesda, Md.: CDL Press

Ozaki, Tohru, Marcel Sigrist, and L. Verderame. 2006. *Ur III Administrative Tablets from the British Museum*. Madrid: Consejo Superior de Investigaciones Cientificas

Pagels, Elaine. 1981. *The Gnostic Gospels*. New York: Random House/Vintage

Pardee, Dennis. 2000. "Ugaritic Studies at the End of the 20th Century." *Bulletin of the American Schools of Oriental Research* 320: 49–86

Pardee, Dennis. 2002. *Ritual and Cult at Ugarit.* Edited by T. J. Lewis. Atlanta, Ga.: Society of Biblical Literature

Parker, Simon B., ed. 1997a. *Ugaritic Narrative Poetry.* [No place]: Society of Biblical Literature/Scholars

Parker, Simon B., trans. 1997b. "Aqhat." Pp. 49–80 in *Ugaritic Narrative Poetry.* Edited by Simon B. Parker. [No place]: Society of Biblical Literature/Scholars

Parker, Simon B., trans. 1997c. "The Betrothal of Yarikh and Nikkal-Ib." Pp. 215–18 in *Ugaritic Narrative Poetry.* Edited by Simon B. Parker. [No place]: Society of Biblical Literature/Scholars

Parker Simon B. 2000. "Ugaritic Literature and the Bible." *Near Eastern Archaeology* 63: 228–31

Parpola, Simon. 1993."The Assyrian Tree of Life: Tracing the Origins of Jewish Monotheism and Greek Philosophy." *Journal of Near Eastern Studies* 52: 161–99

Pasquali, Jacopo. 1998. "1) Su ^{d}*ga-na-na* e ^{d}BAD-*ga-na-na-im.*" *Nouvelles Assyriologiques Brèves et Utilitaires* (N.A.B.U): 1–3

Pasquali, Jacopo. 2006. "64) Eblaita ^{d}*gú-ša-ra-tum* = ugaritico *kṯrt.*" *Nouvelles Assyriologiques Brèves et Utilitaires* (N.A.B.U): 61–63

Pasquali, Jacopo. 2007. "44) Ancora sul teonimo eblaito ^{d}*Ga-na-na*: Alcune osservazioni comparative." *Nouvelles Assyriologiques Brèves et Utilitaires* (N.A.B.U): 48–49

Pasquali, Jacopo. 2008. "50) Une hypothèse à propos du role de ^{d}KU-ra dans la ritual royal éblaïte." *Nouvelles Assyriologiques Brèves et Utilitaires* (N.A.B.U): 67–69

Patai, Raphael. 1990. *The Hebrew Goddess.* Third Enlarged Edition. Detroit, Mich.: Wayne State University Press

Paulus, Susanne. 2013. "Elam und Babylonien in der 2. Hälfte des 2. Jt. v. Chr." Pp. 429–50 in *Susa and Elam, Archaeological, Philological, Historical and Geographical Perspectives.* Edited by K. De Graef and J. Tavernier. MDP 58. Leiden: Brill

Peckham, J. Brian. 2014. *Phoenicia: Episodes and Anecdotes from the Ancient Mediterranean.* Winona Lake, Ind.: Eisenbrauns

Peterson, J. 2009a. "33) ^{d}Al-gar-sur$_{9}$-ra, son of Lugalbanda and Ninsun." *Nouvelles Assyriologiques Brèves et Utilitaires* (N.A.B.U): 43

Peterson, J. 2009b. "39) A Sumerian Literary Fragment Involving the God Irḫan." *Nouvelles Assyriologiques Brèves et Utilitaires* (N.A.B.U): 52

Pettey, Richard J. 1990. *Asherah, Goddess of Israel.* New York: Lang

Pettinato, G. 1980. "Pre-Ugaritic Documentation of Ba'l." Pp. 203–9 in *The Bible World: Essays in Honor of Cyrus H. Gordon.* Edited by G. Rendsburg. New York: KTAV

Pettinato, Giovanni and Helmut Waetzoldt. 1985. "Dagan in Ebla und Mesopotamien nach den Texten aus dem 3. Jahrtausend." *Orientalia* 54: 234–56

Phillips, J.A. 1984. *Eve: The History of an Idea.* San Francisco: Harper and Row

Philo of Byblos. 1981. See Attridge and Oden. 1981

Podany, Amanda. 2002. *The Land of Ḫana. Kings, Chronology, and Scribal Tradition*. Bethesda, Md. CDL Press

Polvani, A.M. 2010. "Identification of the Goddess Ḫuwaššinna with the Goddess Ga.Z.BA.YA." *Orientalia*, new series, 79: 232–41

Pomponio, Francesco and Giuseppe Visicato. 1994. *Early Dynastic Administrative Tablets of Šuruppak.* Napoli: Istituto Universitario Orientale di Napoli

Pomponio, Francesco and Giuseppe Visicato. 2015. *Middle Sargonic Tablets Chiefly from Adab in the Cornell University Collections.* CUSAS 20. Bethesda: CDL Press

Pomponio, Francesco and Paolo Xella. 1997. *Les dieux d'Ebla: Étude analytique des divinités éblaïtes à l'epoque des archives royals du IIIe millénaire.* Münster, Germany: Ugarit-Verlag

Pope, Marvin. 1955. *El in the Ugaritic Texts.* Leiden, Netherlands: Brill

Pope, Marvin. 1981. "The Cult of the Dead at Ugarit." Pp. 159–79 in *Ugarit in Respective: Fifty Years of Ugarit and Ugaritic.* Edited by Gordon D.Young. Winona Lake, Ind.: Eisenbrauns

Popko, Maciej. 1995. *Religions of Asia Minor.* Warsaw: Academic Publications Dialog

Porada, Edith. 1948. *Corpus of Ancient Near Eastern Seals in North American Collections: The Collection of the Pierpont Morgan Library.* Two volumes. New York: Pantheon, Bollingen Series XIV

Porada, Edith. 1993. "Seals and Related Objects from Early Mesopotamia and Iran." Pp. 44–53 in *Early Mesopotamia and Iran: Contact and Conflict, 3500–1600 BC.* Plates 79–95. London: British Museum

Porten, Bezalel. 1969. "The Religion of the Jews at Elephantine." *Journal of Near Eastern Studies* 28: 116–20

Porter, Barbara N., ed. 2009. *What Is a God? Anthropomorphic and Non-Anthropomorphic Aspects of Deity in Ancient Mesopotamia.* Casco Bay, Me.: Casco Bay Assyriological Institute

Porten, Bezalel. 1968. *Archives from Elephantine: The Life of an Ancient Jewish Military Colony.* Berkeley, Calif.: University of California Press

Porten, Bezalel. 1969. "The Religion of the Jews at Elphantine." *Journal of Near Eastern Studies* 28: 116–20

Postgate, N. 1987. "BM 18796: A Dedication Text on an 'Amulet.'" *State Archives of Assyria Bulletin* 1: 57–63

Potts, Daniel. 2013. "In the Shadow Kurangun." Pp. 129–38 in *Susa and Elam, Archaeological, Philological, Historical and Geographical Perspectives.* Edited by K. De Graef and J. Tavernier. MDP 58. Leiden: Brill, 2012

Powell, Marvin. 1976. "Evidence for Local Cults at Presargonic Zabala." *Orientalia*, new series, 45: 100–4

Powell, Marvin. 1987. "The Tree Section of Ḫur-ra = ḫubullu." *Bulletin of Sumerian Agriculture* III: 145–51

Powell, Marvin. 1989. "Aia ≈ Eos." Pp. 447–55 in *Dumu-e2-dub-ba-a: Studies in Honor of Åke W. Sjöberg.* Edited by H. Beh-rens, D. Loding, and M. Roth. Philadelphia: Occasional Publications of the Samuel Noah Kramer Fund

Prechel, Doris. 1996. *Die Göttin Ishhara: ein Beitrag zur altorientalischen Religion-*

sgeschichte. Münster, Germany: Ugarit-Verlag

Pritchard, James B., ed. 1969a. *Ancient Near Eastern Texts Relating to the Old Testament*: Third Edition with Supplement. Princeton, N.J.: Princeton University Press

Pritchard, James B., ed. 1969b. *The Ancient Near East in Pictures Relating to the Old Testament*: Second Edition with Supplement. Princeton, N.J.: Princeton University Press

Pritchard, James B. 1978. *Recovering Sarepta, A Phoenician City: Excavations at Sarafand, Lebanon, 1969–1974, by the University Museum of the University of Pennsylvania.* Princeton, N.J.: Princeton University Press

Pruzsinsky, Regine. 2003. *Die Personennamen der Texte aus Emar.* Studies on the Civilization and Culture of Nuzi and the Hurrians 13. Bethesda, Md.: CDL Press

Quinn, Josephine C. 2018. *In Search of the Phoenicians.* Princeton, N.J.: Princeton University Press

Radner, Karen. 1998. "Den Gott Salmānu (Šulmānu) und seine Beziehung zur Stadt Dūr-Katlimmu." *Welt des Orients* 29: 33–51

Radner, Karen. 1999. *Ein NeuAssyrische Privatarchiv der Tempelgoldschmiede von Assur.* Saarbrücken, Germany: In kommission bei SDV Saarbrücken Druckeri und Verlag

Radner, Karen. 2006a. "How to Reach The Upper Tigris: The Route through the Tur Abdin." *State Archives of Assyrian Bulletin* 15: 273–305

Radner, Karen. 2006b. "An den Ursprung des Tigris schrieb ich meinen Namen – Archaologische Forschungen am Tigris-Tunnel." *Antike Welt* 37: 77–83

Radner, Karen and Andreas Schachner. 2001. "From Tushan to Amedi: Topographical Questions Concerning the Upper Tigris Region in the Assyrian Period." Pp. 749–776 (pp. 749–752 figures) in *Salvage Project of the Archaeological Heritage of the Ilisu and Carchemish Dam Reservoirs: Activities in 1999.* Edited by Tuna Numan, Jean Öztürk, and Jâle Velibeyoğlu. Ankara: no publisher

Rahner, Hugo. 1955. "The Christian Mystery and the Pagan Mysteries." Pp. 146–210 in *Pagan and Christian Mysteries: Papers from the Eranos Yearbooks.* Edited by Joseph Campbell. New York: Harper and Row

Redford, Donald B. 1992. *Egypt, Canaan, and Israel in Ancient Times.* Princeton, N.J.: Princeton University Press

Reed, W. L. 1949. *The Asherah in the Old Testament.* Fort Worth, Tex.: Christian University Press. Originally Yale University dissertation

Reiner, Erica. 1956. "Lipšur Litanies." *Journal of Near Eastern Studies* 15: 129–49

Reiner, Erica. 1970 (1958). *Šurpu: A Collection of Sumerian and Akkadian Incantations.* Osnabrück, Germany: Biblio

Reiter, Karin. 1992a. "73) Eine Aussergewöhnliche Schreibung für Nergal?" *Nouvelles Assyriologiques Brèves et Utilitaires* (N.A.B.U): 55–56

Reiter, Karin. 1992b. "74) Errakal und Istar-Errakal." *Nouvelles Assyriologiques Brèves et Utilitaires* (N.A.B.U): 56

Renger, Johannes. 1967. "Götternamen in der altbabylonischen Zeit." Pp. 137–

71 in *Heidelberger Studien zum Alten Orient*. Edited by D. Edzard. Wiesbaden, Germany: Harrassowitz

Ribichini, Sergio. 1981. *Adonis: Aspetti `orientali' di un mito greco*. Rome: Consiglio nazionale delle ricerche

Richter, Thomas. 1992. "25) Ergänzungen zu Lugal-gudua." *Nouvelles Assyriologiques Brèves et Utilitaires* (N.A.B.U): 21

Richter, Thomas. 1999. *Untersuchung zu den lokalen Panthea Süd- und Mittelbabyloniens in altbabylonischer Zeit*. Münster, Germany: Ugarit-Verlag

Richter, Thomas. 2004. *Untersuchung zu den lokalen Panthea Süd- und Mittelbabyloniens in altbabylonischer Zeit (2. verbesserte und erweiterte Auflage)*. Münster, Germany: Ugarit-Verlag

Roaf, Michael, Bahija Isma'il, and Jeremy Black. 1988. "History of Ana." Pp. 1–5 in *Excavations at Ana: Qal'a Island*. Edited by A. Northedge, A. Bamber, and M. Roaf. Warminster, UK: Aris and Phillips

Roberts, J. J. M. 1972. *The Earliest Semitic Pantheon: A Study of the Semitic Deities Attested in Mesopotamia before Ur III*. Baltimore, Md.: Johns Hopkins University Press

Robertson, J. M. 1993 (1903). *Pagan Christs*. New York: Barnes and Noble

Robertson, Noel. 1982. "The Ritual Background of the Dying God in Cyprus and Syro-Palestine." *Harvard Theological Review* 75: 313–59

Römer W. H. Ph. 1965. *Sumerische 'Königshymnen' in der Isin-Zeit*. Leiden, Netherlands: Brill

Römer W. H. Ph. 1967. "Studien zu altbabylonischen hymnisch-epischen Texten." Pp. 185–99 in *Heidelberger Studien zum Alten Orient*. Edited by D. Edzard. Wiesbaden, Germany: Harrassowitz

Römer W. H. Ph. 1991. "Miscellanea Sumerologica II. Zum sog. Gudam-Text." *Bibliotheca Orientalis* 48: 363–78

Rosenberg, David. 2006. *Abraham: The First Historical Biography*. New York: Basic Books

Rostovtzeff, M. 1933. "Hadad and Atargatis at Palmyra." *American Journal of Archaeology* 37: 58–63

Roth, Martha T., et al., eds. 1956–. *The Assyrian Dictionary of the Oriental Institute of the University of Chicago*. Twenty volumes. Chicago: The Oriental Institute

Rowe, A. 1930–1940. *The Four Canaanite Temples of Beth-Shan*. Two volumes. Philadelphia: University of Pennsylvania Press

Rubio, Gonzalo. 2010. "Reading Sumerian Names, I: Ensuḫkešdanna and Baba." *Journal of Cuneiform Studies* 62: 29–43

Saggs, H. W. F. 1959–1960. "Pazuzu." *Archiv für Orientforschung* 19: 123–27

Sallaberger, Walther. 1993. *Der kultische Kalender der Ur III-Zeit*. Two volumes. Berlin: de Gruyter

Sallaberger, Walther, Aage Westenholz, Pascal Attinger, and Markus Wäfler. 1999. *Mesopotamien: Akkade-Zeit und Ur III-Zeit*. Freiburg, Switzerland: Universitätsverlag Freiburg

Salonen, A. 1939. *Wasserfahrzeuge in Babylonien, nach sumerisch-akkadischen Quellen: (mit besonderer Berücksichigung der 4. Tafel der serie ḪAR-ra ḫubullu): Eine lexikalische und kulturgeschichtliche Untersuchung*. Helsinki: Universität Helsinki

Salonen, A. 1942. *Nautica Babyloniaca: Eine lexikalische und kulturgeschichtliche Untersuchung*. Helsinki: Societas Orientalis Fennica

Sasson, Jack M. 1981. "Literary Criticism, Folklore Scholarship, and Ugaritic Literature." Pp. 81–98 in *Ugarit in Retrospective: Fifty Years of Ugarit and Ugaritic*. Edited by Gordon D. Young. Winona Lake, Ind.: Eisenbrauns

Sasson, Jack M., ed. 1995. *Civilizations of the Ancient Near East*. New York: Scribner's

Sasson, Jack M. 2001. "Ancestors Divine?" Pp. 413–28 in *Veenhof Anniversary Volume: Studies Presented to Klaas Veenhof*. Edited by W. van Soldt. Leiden, Netherlands: Brill

Schmidt, Brian B. 1996. *Israel's Beneficent Dead: Ancestor Cult and Necromancy in Ancient Israelite Religion and Tradition*. Winona Lake, Ind.: Eisenbrauns

Schmidt, Brian B. 2000. "Afterlife Beliefs: Memory as Immortality." *Near Eastern Archaeology* 63: 236–39

Schrakamp, Ingo. 2015. "The Value sig_x of SAR in Third Millennium Sources." AfO, 42: 196–98

Schroeder, O. 1920. *Keilschrifttexte aus Assur verschiedenen Inhalts*. Leipzig: Hinrichs

Schwartz, J. H. 1993. *What the Bones Tell Us*. New York: Holt

Schwemer, Daniel. 2001. *Die Wettergottgestalten Mesopotamiens und Nordsyriens im Zeitalter der Keilschriftkulturen: Materialien und Studien nach den schriftlichen Quellen*. Wiesbaden, Germany: Harrassowitz

Sefati, Yitschak, ed./trans. 1998. *Love Songs in Sumerian Literature: Critical Edition of the Dumuzi-Inanna Songs*. Ramat Gan, Israel: Bar-Ilan University Press

Seidl, Ursula. 1989. *Die babylonischen Kudurru-Reliefs: Symbole mesopotamischer Gottheiten*. Freiburg, Switzerland: Universitätsverlag; Gottingen, Germany: Vandenhoeck and Ruprecht

Selz, Gebhard. 1989. "Nissaba(k) `Die Herrin der Getreidezuteilungen.'" Pp. 491–97 in *Dumu-e2-dub-ba-a: Studies in Honor of Åke W. Sjöberg*. Edited by H. Beh-rens, D. Loding, and M. Roth. Philadelphia: Occasional Publications of the Samuel Noah Kramer Fund

Selz, Gebhard. 1992. "Enlil und Nippur nach präsargonischen Quellen." Pp. 189–225 in *Nippur at the Centennial: Papers Read at the 35e Rencontre Assyriologique Internationale, Philadelphia 1988*. Edited by M. de Jong Ellis. Occasional Publications of the Samuel N. Kramer Fund 14. Philadelphia: The University Museum

Selz, Gebhard. 1995. *Untersuchung zur Götterwelt des altsumerischen Stadtstaates von Lagaš*. Occasional Publications of the Samuel N. Kramer Fund 13. Philadelphia: The University Museum

Selz, Gebhard. 1997a. "`The Holy Drum, the Spear, and the Harp.' Towards an Understanding of the Problems of Deification in Third Millennium Mesopotamia." Pp. 149–94 in *Sumerian Gods and Their Representations*. Edited by M. Geller and I. Finkel. Groningen, Netherlands: Styx

Selz, Gebhard. 1997b. "36) TÙN = tùn bei Gudea." *Nouvelles Assyriologiques Brèves et Utilitaires* (N.A.B.U): 32–34

Shaffer, A. and N. Wasserman. 2003. "Idd(i)-Sîn, king of Simurrum: A New Rock-Relief Inscription and a Reverential Seal." *Zeitschrift für Assyriologie* 93: 1–52

Sharlach, Tonia. 2002. "Foreign Influence on the Religion of the Ur III

Court." Pp. 91–114 in *General Studies and Excavations at Nuzi.* 10/3. Studies on the Civilization and Culture of Nuzi and the Hurrians 12. Edited by D. I. Owen and G. Wilhelm. Winona Lake, Ind.: Eisenbrauns

Shepsut, Asia. 1993. *Journey of the Priestess: The Priestess Traditions of the Ancient World* .... London: Harper Collins, Aquarian

Sigrist, Marcel. 1972. "Offrandes dans le temple de Nusku à Nippur." *Journal of Cuneiform Studies* 29: 169–83

Sigrist, Marcel. 1983. *Textes économiques Néo-Sumériens de l'université de Syracuse.* Paris: Éditions Recherche sur les Civilisations

Sigrist, Marcel. 1984. *Neo-Sumerian Account Texts in the Horn Archaeological Museum.* Institute of Archaeology Publications, Assyriological Series 4. Berrien Springs, Mich.: Andrews University Press

Sigrist, Marcel. 1988. *Neo-Sumerian Account Texts in the Horn Archaeological Museum.* Institute of Archaeology Publications, Assyriological Series 5. Berrien Springs, Mich.: Andrews University Press

Sigrist, Marcel. 1989. "Le deuil pour Šu-Sîn." Pp. 499–505 in *Dumu-e$_2$-dub-ba-a: Studies in Honor of Åke W. Sjöberg.* Edited by H. Behrens, D. Loding, and M. T. Roth. Occasional Publications of the Samuel Noah Kramer Fund 11. Philadelphia: The University Museum

Sigrist, Marcel. 1990. *Tablettes du Princeton Theological Seminary époque d'Ur III.* Occasional Publications of the Samuel Noah Kramer Fund. Philadelphia: The University Museum

Sigrist, Marcel, Carney E. S. Gavin, Diana L. Stein, and Constance Menard. 1988. *Neo-Sumerian Account Texts in the Horn Archaeological Museum.* Institute of Archaeology Publications, Assyriological Series 6. Berrien Springs, Mich.: Andrews University Press

Sigrist, Marcel and Tohru Ozaki. 2009a. *Neo-Sumerian Administrative Tablets from the Yale Babylonian Collection,* part I. Madrid: Consejo Superior de Investigaciones Cientificas

Sigrist, Marcel and Tohru Ozaki. 2009b. *Neo-Sumerian Administrative Tablets from the Yale Babylonian Collection,* part II. Madrid: Consejo Superior de Investigaciones Cientificas

Simons, Frank. 2019. "The Goddess Kusu." *Revue d'Assyriologie.* 112:123–48

Sjöberg, Åke W. 1960. *Der Mondgott Nanna-Suen in der sumerischen Überlieferung.* Stockholm: Almqvist and Wiksell

Sjöberg, Åke W. 1967. "Zu einigen Verwandtschaftsbezeichnungen in sumerischen." Pp. 201–31 in *Heidelberger Studien zum Alten Orient. Adam Falkenstein zum (60.Geburtstag) 17. Sept. 1966.* Edited by D. O. Edzard. Wiesbaden, Germany: Harrassowitz

Sjöberg, Åke W. 1973. "A Hymn to the Goddess Sadarnuna." *Journal of the American Oriental Society* 93: 352–53

Sjöberg, Åke W., ed. 1992–. *The Sumerian Dictionary of the University Museum of the University of Pennsylvania.* Two volumes. Philadelphia: The University Museum

Sjöberg, Åke W. and Hermann Behrens. 1984. *The Sumerian Dictionary,* volume B. Philadelphia: The University Museum

Sjöberg, Åke W., E. Bergmann, Gene B. Cragg, and Enheduanna. 1969. *The Collection of the Sumerian Temple Hymns.* Locust Valley, N.Y.: Augustin

Smith, Mark S. 1985. *Kothar wa-Hasis, The Ugaritic Craftsman God*. Unpublished Ph.D. dissertation, Yale University

Smith, Mark S. 1990. *The Early History of God: Yahweh and the Other Deities in Ancient Israel*. [San Francisco]: HarperSanFrancisco

Smith, Mark S. 1995. "The God Athtar in the Ancient Near East and His Place in KTU 1.1 I." Pp. 627–640 in *Solving Riddles and Untying Knots. Biblical, Epigraphic, and Semitic Studies in Honor of Jonas C. Greenfield*. Winona Lake, Ind.: Eisenbrauns.

Smith, Mark S., trans. 1997. "The Baal Cycle." Pp. 80–180 in *Ugaritic Narrative Poetry*. Edited by Simon B. Parker. [No place]: Society of Biblical Literature/ Scholars

Smith, Mark S. 2001. *The Origins of Biblical Monotheism: Israel's Polytheistic Background and the Ugaritic Texts*. New York: Oxford University Press

Sommerfeld, W. 2002. "Der Stadtgott von Ešnunna." Pp. 701–7 in *Ex Mesopotamia et Syria Lux: Festschrift für Manfried Dietrich zu seinem 65. Geburtstag*. Edited by O. Lorentz, Kai A. Metzier, and Hanspeter Schaudig. AOAT 281. Münster: Ugarit-Verlag

AOAT 281: 701–6

Soyez, Brigitte. 1977. *Byblos et la fête des Adonies*. Leiden, Netherlands: Brill

Soysal, Oguz. 2002. "7) Eine hattische 'Notzeit' Beschreibung." *Nouvelles Assyriologiques Brèves et Utilitaires* (N.A.B.U): 8–9

Spar, Ira and Eva von Dassow. 1988. *Private Archive Texts from the First Millennium B.C.* Turnhout, Belgium: Brepols

Spronk, Klaas. 1986. *Beatific Afterlife in Ancient Israel and the Ancient Near East*. Neukirchen-Vluyn: Neukirchener Verlag

Steible, Horst. 1967. *Ein Lied an den Gott Haya*. Unpublished Ph.D. dissertation, Freiburg University

Steible, Horst. 1975. *Rimsin, mein König: drei kultische Texte aus Ur mit der Schlussdoxologie ^{d}ri-im ^{d}sin lugal-mu*. Wiesbaden, Germany: Steiner

Steible, Horst. 1989. "Die Beziehungen zwischen Gatumdu und Inanna im Spiegel der Bauinschriften der Lagaš-I und -II-Zeit." Pp. 507–13 in *Dumu-e2-dub-ba-a: Studies in Honor of Åke W. Sjöberg*. Edited by H. Behrens, D. Loding, and M. Roth. Philadelphia: Occasional Publications of the Samuel Noah Kramer Fund

Steinkeller, Piotr. 1981. "Studies in Third Millennium Paleography 2. Signs ŠEN and ALAL." *Oriens Antiquus* 20: 243–49

Steinkeller, Piotr. 1982. "The Mesopotamian God Kakka." *Journal of Near Eastern Studies* 41: 289–94

Steinkeller, Piotr. 1989. *Sale Documents of the Ur-III-Period*. Stuttgart, Germany: Steiner

Steinkeller, Piotr. 1990. "14) The Reber Statue." *Nouvelles Assyriologiques Brèves et Utilitaires* (N.A.B.U): 11

Steinkeller, Piotr. 1992. "Early Semitic Literature and Third Millennium Seals with Mythological Motifs." Pp. 243–75, with plates, in *Literature and Literary Language at Ebla*. Edited by Pelio Fronza-roli. Florence: Dipartimento di Linguistica, Università di Firenze

Steinkeller, Piotr. 1997. "On Rulers, Priests and Sacred Marriage: Tracing the Evolution of Early Sumerian Kingship." Pp. 103–37 in *Priests and Officials in the Ancient Near East: Papers of the Second Colloquium on the Ancient Near East, The Middle Eastern Culture Center in Japan.* Edited by K. Watanabe. Heidelberg: Winter

Steinkeller, Piotr. 2005. "Of Stars and Men: The Conceptual and Mythological Setup of Babylonian Extispicy." Pp. 11–47 in *Biblical and Oriental Essays in Memory of William L. Moran.* Edited by A. Gianto. Rome: Editrice Pontifico Istituto Biblico

Steinkeller, Piotr. 2013a. "How Did Šulgi and Išbi-Erra Ascend to Heaven?" Pp. 459–78 in *Literature as Politics, Politics as Literature: Essays on the Ancient Near East in Honor of Peter Machinist.* Edited by D. S. Vanderhooft and A. Winitzer. Winona Lake, Ind.: Eisenbrauns

Steinkeller, Piotr. 2013b. "More on the Nature and History of the Goddess Nanaya." *Nouvelles Assyriologiques Brèves et Utilitaires* (N.A.B.U): 107–10

Steinkeller, Piotr. 2016. "Nanna/Suen, the Shining Bowl." Pp. 615–25 in *Libiamo ne' lieti calici. Ancient Near Eastern Studies Presented to Lucio Milano on the Occasion of his 65th Birthday by Pupils, Colleagues and Friends.* Edited by Paola Corò, Elena Devecchi, Nicla De Zorzi and Massimo Maiocchi. AOAT 436. Münster: Ugarit-Verlag

Stol, Marten. 1979. *On Trees, Mountains, and Millstones in the Ancient Near East.* Leiden, Netherlands: Ex Oriente Lux

Stol, M. 2000. *Birth in Babylonia and the Bible: Its Mediterranean Setting.* Groningen, Netherlands: Styx

Stone, M. E. 1992. *A History of the Literature of Adam and Eve.* Atlanta, Ga.: Society for Biblical Literature

Streck, M. and N. Wasserman 2012 "More Light on Nanaya." *Zeitschrift für Assyriologie* 102: 183–201

Strong, Anthony. 2002. *The Phoenicians in History and Legend.* [No place]: 1st Books Library

Stuckey, Johanna H. 2001. "'Inanna and the *Huluppu* Tree'; An Ancient Mesopotamian Narrative of Goddess Demotion." Pp. 91–105 in *Feminist Poetics of the Sacred: Creative Suspicions.* Edited by Frances Devlin-Glass and Lyn McCredden. Oxford: Oxford University Press

Stuckey, Johanna H. 2002. "The Great Goddesses of the Levant." *Bulletin of the Canadian Society for Mesopotamian Studies* 37: 27–48

Stuckey, Johanna H. 2011. "Queen of Heaven and Earth: Inanna-Ištar of Mesopotamia."Pp. 19–38 in *Goddesses in World Culture,* volume 2, *Eastern Mediterranean and Europe.* Edited by Patricia Monaghan. Santa Barbara, Calif.: ABC-CLIO/Praeger

Such-Gutiérrez, M. 2003. *Beiträge zum Pantheon von Nippur im 3. Jahrtausend.* Rome: Università degli studi di Roma "La Sapienza"

Such-Gutiérrez, M. 2005/6. "Untersuchungen zum Pantheon von Adab im 3. Jt." *Archiv für Orientforschung* 51: 1–49

Szarzynaka, Krystyna. 1993. "Offerings for the Goddess Inanna in Archaic Uruk." *Revue d'Assyriologie* 87: 7–29

Tallqvist, Knut L. 1974 (1938). *Akkadische Götterepitheta.* Hildesheim, Germany: Olms

Talon, P. 2005. *Enuma Elish.* State Archives of Assyria Texts 4. Helsinki: University of Helsinki Press

Tavernier, Jan. 2007. "19) LÍL and ḪÉ.GÁL in Elamite?" *Nouvelles Assyriologiques Brèves et Utilitaires* (N.A.B.U): 19–20

Tavernier, Jan. 2013. "Elamite and Old Iranian Afterlife Concepts." Pp. 471–89 in K. De Graef and J. Tavernier, *Susa and Elam, Archaeological, Philological, Historical and Geographical Perspectives*. MDP 58. Leiden: Brill, 2012

Teixidor, Javier. 1979. *The Pantheon of Palmyra*. Leiden, Netherlands: Brill

Teubal, Savina J. 1984. *Sarah the Priestess: The First Matriarch of Genesis*. Athens, Ohio: Ohio University Press

Teubal, Savina J. 1990. *Hagar the Egyptian: The Lost Tradition of the Matriarchs*. San Francisco: Harper and Row

Thompson, T. L. 1974. *The Historicity of the Patriarchal Narratives: The Quest for the Historical Abraham*. Beihefte zur Zeitschrift für die alttestamentliche Wissenschaft 133. Berlin: de Gruyter

Thureau-Dangin, François. 1903. *Recueil de tablettes Chaldéens*. Paris: Leroux

Thureau-Dangin, François. 1934. "Notes assyriologiques." *Revue d'Assyriologie* 31: 83–96

Thureau-Dangin, François. 1975 (1921). *Rituels Accadiens*. Osnabrück, Germany: Zeller

Tinney, S. 1989. "3) ᵈen-gi₆-du-du: *muttarrû rube* A Note on Erra I 21." *Nouvelles Assyriologiques Brèves et Utilitaires* (N.A.B.U): 2–4

Trémouille, M.-Cl. 1999. "La religion des Hourrites." Pp. 277–91 in *Nuzi at Seventy-five*. Studies on the Civilization and Culture of Nuzi and the Hurrians. 10. Bethesda, Md.: CDL Press

Trible, Phyllis. 2006. *Hagar, Sarah, and Their Children: Jewish, Christian, and Muslim Perspectives*. Louisville, Ky.: Westminster/John Knox

Tsukimoto, A. 1985. *Untersuchungen zur Totenpflege (Kispum) im alten Mesopotamien*. Neukirchen-Vluyn, Germany: Butzon and Berker

Tubb, Jonathan N. 1998. *Canaanites*. Norman, Ok.: University of Oklahoma Press

Tubb, Jonathan N. 2003. "Phoenician Dance." *Near Eastern Archaeology* 66: 122–25

Tubb, Jonathan N. 2016. "A New Millennium – A New Order: Philistines, Phoenicians, Aramaeans, and the Kingdom of Israel." Pp. 88–103 in *Assyria to Iberia: Art and Culture in the Iron Age*. Edited by J. Aruz and M. Seymour. New York: Metropolitan Museum of Art

Turcan, R. 1989. *Les cultes orientaux dans le monde romain*. Paris: Les Belles Lettres

Tuzet, Hélène. 1987. *Mort et resurrection d'Adonis: Étude de l'évolution d'un mythe*. [Paris]: Corti

Vallat, François. 1987. "89) *ᵈU = élamite usan/iššan*." *Nouvelles Assyriologiques Brèves et Utilitaires* (N.A.B.U): 48

Vallat, François. 1988. "14) ᵈUmu à l'époque néo-élamite." *Nouvelles Assyriologiques Brèves et Utilitaires* (N.A.B.U): 9

Vallat, François. 1993. *Les noms géographiques des sources suso-élamites*. Wiesbaden, Germany: Reichert

Vallat, François. 1998. "Elamite Religion." Pp. 335–42 in *Encyclopaedia Iranica VIII*. Edited by Ehsan Yarshater. Costa Mesa, Calif.: Mazra. Also available online

van der Toorn, Karel. 1998. "Goddesses in Early Israelite Religion." Pp. 83–97 in *Ancient Goddesses: The Myths and the Evidence*. Edited by L. Goodison and C. Morris. Madison, Wisc.: University of Wisconsin Press

van der Toorn, Karel, Bob Becking, and Pieter W. van der Horst, eds. 1999. *Dictionary of Deities and Demons in the Bible*. Second Extensively Revised Edition. Leiden, Netherlands: Brill/ Grand Rapids, Mich.: Eerdmans

van Dijk, Johannes. 1962. "Die Inschriftenfunde." Pp. 39–62 in *XVIII. Vorläufiger Bericht über die von der Deutschen Archäologischen Institut und der Deutschen Orient-Gesellschaft aus Mitteln der Deutschen Forschungsgemeinschaft unternommenen Ausgrabungen in Uruk-Warka, Winter 1959/60*. Edited by Heinrich J. Lenzen et al. Berlin: Mann

van Dijk, Johannes, ed./trans. 1983. *Lugal ud me-lám-bi Nir-Gál: French and Sumerian*. Leiden, Netherlands: Brill

van Gessel, B. H. L. 1998. *Onomasticon of the Hittite Pantheon*. Three volumes. Leiden, Netherlands: Brill

van Seters, John. 1975. *Abraham in History and Tradition*. New Haven: Yale University Press

van Seters, John. 1994. *The Life of Moses: The Yahwist as Historian in Exodus-Numbers*. Louisville, Ky.: Westminster/John Knox

Vanstiphout, Herman L. J. 1990a. "The Mesopotamian Debate Poems: A General Presentation (Part I)." *Acta Sumerologica* 12: 271–318

Vanstiphout, Herman L. J. 1990b. "57) A double entendre Concerning Uttu." *Nouvelles Assyriologiques Brèves et Utilitaires* (N.A.B.U): 40–44

Vanstiphout, Herman L. J. 1991. "Lore, Learning and Levity in the Sumerian Disputations: A Matter of Form, or Substance?" Pp. 23–46 in *Dispute Poems and Dialogues in the Ancient and Medieval Near East*. Edited by G. Reinink and H. L. J. Vanstiphout. Orientalia Lovaniensia Analecta 42. Leuven, Belgium: Peeters

Vanstiphout, Herman L. J. 1992. "The Mesopotamian Debate Poems. A General Presentation (Part II): The Subject." *Acta Sumerologica* 14: 339–67

Veldhuis, Niek. 1997. *Elementary Education at Nippur: The Lists of Trees and Wooden Objects*. Uunpublished Ph.D. dissertation, University of Groningen

Veldhuis, Niek. 2002. "Studies in Sumerian Vocabulary." *Journal of Cuneiform Studies* 54: 67–77

Veldhuis, Niek. 2004. *Religion, Literature, and Scholarship: The Sumerian Composition Nanše and the Birds, with a Catalogue of Sumerian Bird Names*. Leiden, Netherlands: Brill/Styx

Viaggio, Salvatore. 2008. "40) Sîn of Kamanim." *Nouvelles Assyriologiques Brèves et Utilitaires* (N.A.B.U): 52–53

Vincente, Claudine-Adrienne. 1995. "The Tell Leilan Recension of the Sumerian King List." *Zeitschrift für Assyriologie* 85: 234–70

Visicato, Giuseppe and Aage Westenholz. 2010. *Early Dynastic and Early Sargonic Tablets from Adab in the Cornell University Collections*. CUSAS 11. Bethesda, Md.: CDL Press

Volk, Konrad. 1995. *Inanna und Šukaletuda: zur historisch-politischen Deutung eines sumerischen Literaturwerkes*. Wiesbaden, Germany: Harrassowitz

Von Soden, Wolfram. 1992. "53) Ein ungewöhnliches Fragment aus Hattusas." *Nouvelles Assyriologiques Brèves et Utilitaires* (N.A.B.U): 41–42

Waetzoldt, Hartmut 1972. *Untersuchungen zur Neusumerischen Textilindustrie.* Rome. Centro per le Antichità e la Storia dell'Arte del Vicino Oriente

Waetzoldt, Hartmut 1997. "96) Die Berufsbe-zeichnung Tibira." *Nouvelles Assyriologiques Brèves et Utilitaires* (N.A.B.U): 90–91

Waetzoldt, Hartmut. 2001. *Wirtschafts- und Verwaltungstexte aus Ebla.* Materiali epigrafici di Ebla 12. Rome: Università degli studi di Roma "La Sapienza."

Wang, Xianhua. 2011. *Metamorphosis of Enlil in Early Mesopotamia.* AOAT 385. Münster, Germany: Ugarit-Verlag

Ward, William H. 1902–1903. "The Asherah." *American Journal of Semitic Languages and Literatures* 19: 33–44

Warmington, B. H. 1993 (1969). *Carthage.* Revised Edition. New York: Barnes and Noble

Watanabe, K. 1990. "94) [d]Abbutanitu «(göttliche) Fürsprecherin»." *Nouvelles Assyriologiques Brèves et Utilitaires* (N.A.B.U): 72–73

Watson, P. J. and W. B. Horowitz. 1993. *Catalogue of Cuneiform Tablets in Birmingham City Museum.* Warminster, UK: Aris and Phillips

Wegner, Ilse. 1981. *Gestalt und Cult der Ishtar-Shawushka in Kleinasien.* Kevelaer, Germany: Butzon and Bercker

Weidner, Ernst F. 1924/25. "Altbabylonische Götterlisten." *Archiv für Keilschriftforschung:* 1:1ff.

Weinfeld, M. 1972. "The Worship of Moloch and the Queen of Heaven and its Background." *Ugarit-Forschungen* 4: 133–54

Weisberg, David B. 1991. *The Late Babylonian Texts of the Oriental Institute Collection.* Malibu, Calif.: Undena

Weiss, Harvey. 1985. *Ebla to Damascus, Art and Archaeology of Ancient Syria: An Exhibition from the Directorate-General of Antiquities and Museums Syrian Arab Republic.* Washington, D.C.: Smithsonian Institute

Wenning, Robert. 2001. "The Betyls of Petra." *Bulletin of the American Schools of Oriental Research* 324: 79–95

West, Martin. 1997. *The East Face of Helicon: West Asiatic Elements in Greek Poetry and Myth.* Oxford: Clarendon

Westenholz, Aage. 1975a. *Old Sumerian and Old Akkadian Texts in Philadelphia Chiefly from Nippur,* part 1, *Literary and Lexical Texts and the Earliest Administrative Documents from Ur.* Malibu, Calif.: Undena

Westenholz, Aage. 1975b. *Early Cuneiform Texts in Jena: Pre-Sargonic and Sargonic Documents from Nippur and Fara in the Hilprecht-Sammlung vorderasiatischer Altertümer, Institut fur Altertumswissenschaften der Friedrich-Schiller-Universität, Jena.* Copenhagen: Munksgaard

Westenholz, Aage. 1987. *Old Sumerian and Old Akkadian Texts in Philadelphia,* part 2. Copenhagen: Museum Tusculanum, University of Copenhagen

Westenholz, Aage. 2014. *A Third-Millennium Miscellany of Cuneiform Texts.* CUSAS 26. Bethesda, Md.: CDL Press

Westenholz, Joan G. 1997. "Nanaya: Lady of Mystery." Pp. 57–84 in *Sumerian Gods and Their Representations.* Edited by I. J. Finkel and M. J. Geller. Groningen, Netherlands: Styx.

Westenholz, Joan G. 1998. "Goddesses of the Ancient Near East 3000–1000 BC." Pp. 62–82 in *Ancient Goddesses: The Myths and the Evidence*. Edited by L. Goodison and C. Morris. Madison, Wisc.: University of Wisconsin Press

Westenholz, Joan G. 2000. *Cuneiform Inscriptions in the Collection of the Bible Lands Museum Jerusalem: The Emar Tablets*. Cuneiform Monographs 13. Groningen, Netherlands: Styx

Westenholz, Joan G., ed. 2004. *Dragons, Monsters and Fabulous Beasts*. Jerusalem: Biblelands Museum

Whitney, K. William, Jr. 2006. *Two Strange Beasts: Leviathan and Behemoth in Second Temple and Early Rabbinic Judaism*. Winona Lake, Ind.: Eisenbrauns

Wiggermann, F. A. M. 1983 (1981–1982). "Exit *talim*. Studies in Babylonian Demonology, I." *Jaarbericht van het vooraziatisch-egyptisch Genootschap ex oriente lux* 27: 90–105

Wiggermann, F. A. M. 1986. *Babylonian Prophylactic Figures: The Ritual Texts*. Amsterdam: Free University Press

Wiggermann, F. A. M. 1992. *Mesopotamian Protective Spirits: The Ritual Texts*. Groningen, Netherlands: Styx

Wiggermann, F. A. M. 1997. "Transtigridian Snake Gods." Pp. 33–49 in *Sumerian Gods and Their Representations*. Edited by I. L. Finkel and M. J. Geller. Groningen, Netherlands: Styx

Wilcke, Claus. 1989. "Die Emar-Version von 'Dattelpalme und Tamariske'—ein Rekonstruktionsversuch." *Zeitschrift für Assyriologie* 79: 161–90

Wilhelm, Gernot. 1989. *The Hurrians*. Warminster, UK: Aris and Phillips

Wilhelm Gernot. 2010. "Eine Anrufung mit Bezug auf die Verwandtschaftsbeziehungen hethitischer Götter" *Orientalia*, new series, 79: 268–72

Will, E. 1996. "Adonis chez les Grecs avant Alexandre." *Transeuphratène* 12: 65–72

Winter, Irene J. 2016. "The 'Woman at the Window': Iconography and Inferences of a Motif in First-Millennium B.C. Levantine Ivory Carving." Pp. 180-193 in Assyria to Iberia: Art and Culture in the Iron Age. Edited by J. Aruz and M. Seymour. New York: Metropolitan Museum of Art

Wolkstein, Diane and Samuel N. Kramer, eds./trans. 1983. *Inanna, Queen of Heaven and Earth: Her Stories and Hymns from Sumer*. New York: Harper and Row

Woods, Christopher. 2005. "On the Euphrates." *Zeitschrift für Assyriologie und Vorderasiatische Archäologie* 95: 7–45

Woolmer, Mark. 2017. *A Short History of the Phoenicians*. London: Tauris

Wyatt, Nicolas. 1985. "The `Anat Stela' from Ugarit and Its Ramifications." *Ugarit-Forschungen* 16: 327–37

Wyatt, Nicolas. 1999. "The Religion of Ugarit." Pp. 305–52 in *Handbook of Ugaritic Studies*. Edited by W. G. E. Watson and N. Wyatt. Leiden, Netherlands: Brill

Wyatt, Nicolas. 2002. *Religious Texts from Ugarit*. Second Edition. London: Sheffield insert after Wyatt 2002

Xella, Pablo. 1991. *Baal Hammon: Recerches sur l'identite et de l'historire d'un dieu phenico-punique*. Rome: Consiglio nazionale delle recherche

Xella, Paolo, ed. 2001. *Quando un dio muore: morti e assenze divine nelle antiche tradizioni mediterranee.* Verona, Italy: Essedue Edizioni

Xella, Pablo, ed. 2012–2013. *The Tophet in the Phoenician Mediterranean.* Verona: Essedue Edizioni

Yamashita, Tadamori. 1963. *The Goddess Asherah.* Unpublished Ph.D. dissertation, Yale University

Yıldız, Fatma and Tohru Gomi. 1988. *Die Puzriš-Dagan-Texte der Istanbuler archäologischer Museen.* Stuttgart, Germany: Steiner

Yıldız, Fatma and Tohru Ozaki. 2000. *Die Umma-Texte aus den Archäologischen Museen zu Istanbul,* volume 5, *Nr. 3001–3500.* Bethesda, Md.: CDL Press

Yon, Marguerite. 2006. *La citê d'Ougarit sur le tell de Ras Shamra.* Winona Lake, Ind.: Eisenbrauns

Younger, K. Lawson, Jr. 2009. "The Deity Kur(r)a in the First Millennium Sources." *Journal of Ancient Near Eastern Religions* 9: 2–23

Zatelli, Ida. 1998. "The Origin of the Biblical Scapegoat Ritual: The Evidence of Two Eblaite Texts." *Vetus Testamentum* 48: 254–63

Zawadzki, Stefan. 2005. "8) A Neo-Babylonian Text Concerning the Work in the Ninmaḫ Temple." *Nouvelles Assyriologiques Brèves et Utilitaires* (N.A.B.U): 7–8

Zawadzki, Stefan. 2006. "39) Cake Offerings for the Gods of the Ebabbar Temple in Sippar." *Nouvelles Assyriologiques Brèves et Utilitaires* (N.A.B.U): 36–38

Zettler, Richard L. 1992. *The Ur III Temple of Inanna at Nippur: The Operation and Organization of Urban Religious Institutions in Mesopotamia in the Late Third Millennium B.C.* Berlin: Reimer

Zettler, Richard L. and Walther Sallaberger. 2011. "Inana's Festival at Nippur under the Third Dynasty of Ur." *Zeitschrift für Assyriologie* 101: 1–71

Zevit, Ziony. 2000. *The Religions of Ancient Israel. A Synthesis of Parallactic Approaches.* London: Continuum

Zgoll, Annette.1997. "Inana als nugig." *Zeitschrift für Assyriologie* 87: 181–95

Zimmern, Heinrich. 1918–1919. "Der Schenkenliebeszauber Berl. VAT 9728 (Assur) – Lond. K. 3464+Par. N. 3554 (Nineve)." *Zeitschrift für Assyriologie* 32: 164–84

Zimmern, Heinrich. 1928. "Die babylonische Göttin im Fenster." *Orientalische Literaturzeitung* 31(1): 1–2

Chronological Chart of Rulers Referenced

(many dates approximate)

Pre-Dynastic Uruk		ca. 3100
Early Dynastic period		2900–2334
Sargonic period		
	Sargon	2334–2279
	Rimuš	2278–2270
	Maništusu	2269–2255
	Narām-Sin	2254–2218
	Šar-kali-šarri	2217–2193
	Dudu	2189–2169
	Šu-Turul	2168–2154
Lagash		
	E-anatum	ca. 2400
	Ur-Nanše	ca. 2250
	Gudea	22nd century
Gutian period		
	Erridupizir	ca. 2200
Ur III period		
	Ur-Namma	2112–2095
	Šulgi	2094–2047
	Amar-Suen	2046–2038
	Šū-Sîn	2037–2029
	Ibbi-Sîn	2028–2004
Old Babylonian period		
	Iddin-Dagān	1974–1954
	Išme-Dagān	1953–1935
	Ibni-šadū'ī	ca. 1940
	Lipit-Ištar	1934–1924
	Ur-Ninurta	1923–1896
	Sumu-el	1894–1866
	Lipit-Enlil	1873–1869
	Sîn-iddinam	1849–1843
	Warad-Sîn	1834–1823
	Ur-Du-kuga	1830–1828
	Sîn-māgir	1827–1817
	Rīm-Sîn I	1822–1763
	Iaḫdun-Līm	1811–1795

Anam	ca. 1800
Irdanene	ca. 1780
Ḫammu-rāpi	1792–1750
Zimrī-Līm	1775–1762
Samsu-iluna	1749–1712
Ammi-ṣaduqa	1646–1647
Abi-ešuḫ	1711–1684
Samsu-Ditānu	1625–1595
Old Assyrian period	
Šamšī-Adad I	1808–1776
Hittite Old Kingdom	
Ḫattušili I	1650–1620
Telipinu	1525–1500
Kassite period	
Kadašman-Ḫarbe I	early 14th c.
Burnaburiaš II	1359–1333
Kurigalzu II	1332–1308
Hittite New Kingdom	
Ḫattušili II	1420–1400
Šuppiluliuma I	1344–1322
Muršili II	1321–1295
Muwatalli II	1295–1272
Ḫattušili III	1267-1237
Tutḫaliya IV	1237–1209
New Kingdom Egypt	
Amenhotep III	1387–1350
Akhenaten	1350–1334
Rameses II	1290–1224
Middle Elamite	
Ḫumban-numena	1350–1340
Untaš-Napiriša	1340–1300
Šūtruk-Naḫūnte I	1185–1155
Šilḫak-Inšušinak I	1150–1130
Ḫuldelutuš-Inšušinak	ca. 1110
Mittani	
Tušratta	ca. 1360
Šattiwaza	ca. 1340
Neo-Assyrian	
Tiglath-pileser I	1114–1076
Shalmaneser II	1030–1019
Adad-Nirari	911–891
Aššur-nāṣir-pal II	883–859
Shalmaneser III	858–824

Sennacherib704–681
Esarhaddon 680–669
Aššur-bāni-pal 668–627

Israel, Judea
Davidca. 1000–960
Solomonca. 960–920
Ahab874–853
Josiah641–609

Neo-Elamite
Šutruk-Naḫḫunte717–699
Šilḫak-Inšušinak IIca. 600–575
Attaḫaniti-Inšušinakca. 520

Neo-Babylonian
Nabonidus555–539